The Legacy of Israel in Judah's Bible

History, Politics, and the Reinscribing of Tradition

The Legacy of Israel in Judah's Bible undertakes a comprehensive reevaluation of the Bible's primary narrative in Genesis through Kings as it relates to history. It divides the core textual traditions along political lines that reveal deeply contrasting assumptions, an approach that places biblical controversies in dialogue with anthropologically informed archaeology. Starting from close study of selected biblical texts, the work moves toward historical issues that may be illuminated by both this material and a larger range of textual evidence. The result is a synthesis that breaks away from conventional lines of debate in matters relating to ancient Israel and the Bible, setting an agenda for future engagement of these fields with wider study of antiquity.

Daniel E. Fleming has taught and served in the Skirball Department of Hebrew and Judaic Studies at New York University since 1990, when he received his doctorate in Near Eastern Languages and Civilizations from Harvard University. He currently serves as Chair of the Advisory Committee for NYU's Institute for the Study of the Ancient World. The current volume was launched with financial support from a Guggenheim Fellowship (2004). Fleming was also a senior Fulbright Fellow to France (1997–8) and recipient of a one-year research fellowship from the American Council of Learned Societies (2004–5). He is the author of three books and co-author of a fourth: *The Installation of Baal's High Priestess at Emar* (1992); *Time at Emar* (2000); *Democracy's Ancient Ancestors* (Cambridge, 2004); and, with Sara J. Milstein, *The Buried Foundation of the Gilgamesh Epic* (2010). Fleming has contributed many articles on topics related to the ancient Near East to a range of professional journals and collected works.

Advance Praise for *The Legacy of Israel in Judah's Bible*

"For decades the field of biblical studies has been engaged in a series of literary and historical debates regarding the Hebrew Bible and ancient Israel, yet there has been little consensus about these subjects. Fleming breaks through this impasse with a remarkably fresh insight into Israel as an association of groups engaged in collective and collaborative politics differing considerably from Judah's more centralized political life. Fleming also explores several important cross-cultural analogies for Israel's tradition of collaborative politics from the ancient Near East and traditional societies from Mesoamerica, the American Southwest, and pre-Viking Denmark. For this aspect of his research, Fleming draws heavily on recent theory on power and political organization. This book is a superb piece of scholarship; every chapter marked by deep erudition and engaging insights. No professor or graduate student interested in the Hebrew Bible or ancient Israel can do without it."

> – Mark S. Smith, Skirball Professor of Bible and Ancient Near Eastern
> Studies, New York University

"Scholarly debate about the early history of Israel has run into the sand. Extreme conservatives and radical revisionists shout across each other with little solid gain. The combination of a thoroughly critical analysis of the written sources together with an informed use of archaeological and other sources has been lacking until now. With his major proposal that we should disentangle the account of Israel from the Bible that has come to us from Judah, Fleming has broken this stalemate. While his analysis will no doubt provoke debate, nobody can deny the authority of the scholarship that he displays."

> – H. G. M. Williamson, Regius Professor of Hebrew,
> University of Oxford

The Legacy of Israel in Judah's Bible

History, Politics, and the Reinscribing of Tradition

DANIEL E. FLEMING
New York University

CAMBRIDGE
UNIVERSITY PRESS

CAMBRIDGE UNIVERSITY PRESS
Cambridge, New York, Melbourne, Madrid, Cape Town,
Singapore, São Paulo, Delhi, Mexico City

Cambridge University Press
32 Avenue of the Americas, New York, NY 10013-2473, USA

www.cambridge.org
Information on this title: www.cambridge.org/9781107669994

First published 2012

Printed in the United States of America

A catalog record for this publication is available from the British Library.

Library of Congress Cataloging in Publication Data

Fleming, Daniel. E.
The legacy of Israel in Judah's Bible : history, politics, and the reinscribing of tradition /
Daniel E. Fleming.
    p. cm.
Includes bibliographical references and index.
ISBN 978-1-107-02431-1 (hardback) – ISBN 978-1-107-66999-4 (pbk.)
1. Narration in the Bible.   2. Bible. O.T. – Criticism, Narrative.   I. Title.
BS1182.3.F54   2012
221.6'7–dc22   2011045919

ISBN 978-1-107-02431-1 Hardback
ISBN 978-1-107-66999-4 Paperback

To my students,
with whom I have learned what is in this book

Contents

Preface

As we read the Bible, no matter how self-consciously careful we may be, it is natural to let it set our expectations, to provide the framework for understanding its contents. The narrative center of the Bible is a meandering account of the origins and experiences of a people named Israel. In a form that has been connected by various seams, this narrative begins with creation and Israel's ancestry in Genesis; continues through Moses' leadership in Exodus, Leviticus, Numbers, and Deuteronomy; and then addresses the life of this people in its own land, through Joshua, Judges, Samuel, and Kings. These nine books have been called the Primary History, or the Enneateuch, and no matter the specific process by which they reached their finished form, their guiding story suffuses our sense of what the Bible offers for historical evaluation.[1] Even the isolation of a "biblical Israel" from whatever existed in history defers to this overarching vision (Davies 1992).

One central idea in this biblical narrative has repeatedly drawn the critical attention of biblical scholars and historians: it has to do with a single people from beginning to end. The two kingdoms of Israel and Judah that are described in the books of Kings ultimately belong to one people of Yahweh, called Israel. Historians in particular have labored to use the Bible cautiously in their reconstructions, and nonbiblical evidence has played a greater role in recent years, especially as archaeology yields more material and drives historical analysis. A handful of nonbiblical texts present two kingdoms that are first visible in the mid-ninth century, first identified as Israel and the House of David and later treated by the Assyrians as Samaria and Judah. From these texts and the findings of archaeology alone, it is not clear how the two kingdoms were related. At this point, the Bible warrants a second look, because its story of a

---

[1] For the first term, see Freedman and Mandell (1993); cf. Freedman and Kelly (2004). The latter word has gained interest especially in Germany, as reflected in the recent book by Erik Aurelius (2003), the overview by Konrad Schmid (2006), and the wider discussion in Thomas Römer and Konrad Schmid (2007).

single people ends with an unexpected twist. When we reach 1 and 2 Kings, the last books in what I will call the Bible's primary narrative, the text describes a division into two polities, most often called Israel and Judah. The story begins with one people and takes for granted throughout the ultimate reality of a single people of the god Yahweh, but it ends with the same two kingdoms known from nonbiblical writing. It is clear, then, that two distinct peoples, identified with two separate kingdoms, stand as a historical backdrop to the unified portrait of the Bible's narrative.

Here, we confront an underappreciated oddity. Historically, the Bible is Judah's book, the collected lore of Judah's survivors after defeat by Babylon in the early sixth century. The primacy of Judah in formation of the Bible is transparent in its remaining books, where the words of prophets and the assorted "Writings" (Psalms, Proverbs, etc.) display overwhelming preoccupation with Judah and Jerusalem. In the long narrative from Genesis through Kings, Judah becomes the southern of two kingdoms in the last book, and it appears occasionally before this as one tribe in the Bible's occasional scheme of one people Israel divided into kin-based segments. Nevertheless, the story of origins and early life, including the founding of monarchy, is the story of Israel, the other kingdom. Israel is the family established in Genesis; Israel goes into Egypt and escapes in an exodus under Moses; Israel conquers a land for itself under Moses and Joshua; Israel lives in this land without kings until Saul and David bring a change of political regime. To explain its past, the people of Judah tell the story of Israel, only making sure that we know Judah was one part of a larger group.

To locate the biblical narrative in history, we must decide how to read the Bible's representation of Judah as part of Israel. The question is not so much whether some connection existed but whether the people of Judah would have shared the same stories as Israel, with the same ideas about identity and the past. If the kingdoms of Israel and Judah reflect distinct peoples with deeply different notions of who they were and how they became so, it is essential to disentangle Israel's and Judah's stories. Judah's stories about early Israel cannot be assumed to be the common property of both peoples. By the logic of Israel's centrality to many of these traditions, it would make sense for the core conceptions to come from Israel without reference to its southern neighbor, despite Judah's eventual possession of the collection. Whatever elements of the biblical narrative originate in Israel would reflect different assumptions from the texts once they entered Judah's sphere. Perspectives on early Israel from Israel itself would likewise offer different possibilities for historical continuity with the peoples portrayed. At its root, such material would be grounded in societies with the same shape as those that carry its transmission. "Biblical Israel" as found in Israel's own traditions, excavated from beneath an overlay of Judah uses, presents a different proposition both biblically and for historical consideration.

These basic observations drive all that follows. Naturally, there are a multitude of complications, including the reality that the actual written contributions of both Israel and Judah involve settings both during the lives of each kingdom and among communities after the demise of each at the hands of Assyria and Babylon. It is clear that the two peoples were culturally close to one another, and there were numerous contacts in various periods. The Bible finally offers only a finished text, with nothing left untouched by scribes from the people of Judah, so that we have no direct access to Israel's stories unfiltered. Reconstruction of history during the monarchies of Israel and Judah, and all the more for earlier epochs, must still begin with archaeological evidence and analysis. Establishing a basis for dialogue between biblical text and history is rarely straightforward, given the complex transmission of the texts and the various scribal agendas that motivate them.

The book is divided into four parts in pursuit of the various dimensions of this problem. Above all, my distinction of Israel from Judah is not ultimately geographical, as north from south, though geography does help identify Israelite content in the Bible. The purely geographical division assumes a homogeneity of social and political culture that must be challenged. Archaeologists have long observed that the kingdoms of Israel and Judah present vastly different profiles, with Israel far larger and more diverse (Finkelstein 1999). Biblical portrayals of Israel and Judah, when calibrated according to their awareness of early patterns, complement the conclusions from archaeology. The Bible suggests a profound contrast between Israel and Judah at the macro level of social organization, the large scale of political decision-making. Israel's geographical decentralization contributed to forms of collaborative political life that contrasted with custom at home in the kingdom of Judah, where Jerusalem came to play a role unparalleled in the north. In their reception of traditional tales about early times, writers from Judah had no political heritage by which to comprehend the structures of Israel, which were foreign to them in ways not true for scribes working from an Israelite background.

After this basic argument is introduced in Part I, Part II undertakes to establish the reality of this contrast in specific texts that preserve narrative content from Israel. Rather than attempt a systematic list and discussion that addresses every possible text, I define categories and consider at least one text of interest for each main type and phase in the biblical narrative about Israel. Some of these are widely understood to have ancient antecedents and to originate in Israel, while others display possibilities inherent in the logic of my Israel/Judah distinction. To get at Israel's own literary lore, unencumbered by Judah's reading and revision, it is necessary to disentangle Israelite content from the constant company of additions and alterations. This is a task that belongs to technical "literary history" in biblical scholarship, and I engage in conversation with this discipline as a nonspecialist. Because my objective is ultimately historical, I do not intend to reconstruct the full transmission process of each text, and, for historical application, such reconstructions can be so precise as to be unconvincing, especially when set beside a host of competing renditions. With each case examined in this section, I emphasize the isolation of persuasively Israelite, non-Judahite narrative material.

I have chosen to discuss the Bible before providing a broader context for the political phenomena that are essential to my analysis. Part III elaborates what I call the "collaborative" politics that play a more prominent role in Israel than in Judah. Alternatives to centralized decision-making by kings and their administrations have been the topic of wider discussion among anthropologically oriented archaeologists. Certain early peoples display similar traits and offer a way to see the practices of Israel and Judah as part of a universal set of political choices. Beyond these comparisons that lack any historical relationship to the peoples of the Bible, however, two groups from the second-millennium Near East present a backdrop and framework for thinking about such structures in the Iron Age Levant: the Amorites and the Arameans. This contextualizing of Israel's political heritage serves as a transition to Part IV, which finally addresses questions of history more specifically.

The Bible's relationship to history has been the recurrent concern of scholars even before the dawn of modern archaeology. In recent years, archaeologists have won the right and responsibility to lead the formulation of history for the Iron Age Levant, and yet such history is difficult to situate in relation to Israel and Judah without some reference to the Bible, if only to repudiate its schemes. Among biblical scholars, there is more uncertainty than ever about dates and settings for composition and revision – or, individual certainty cannot overcome the depths of disagreement that leave onlookers to choose between wildly diverging options. I will not contribute to resolving this state of affairs by adding one more voice to the clamor, but my hope is to introduce new questions to the debate and to open up new possibilities for relating the Bible to ancient history. The Bible not only confronts us with an unavoidable narrative for the background of Israel and Judah; it also offers views of ancient society that are rarely available to modern audiences. These were not the great powers of the ancient world, and the texts are not the official documents of ruling courts, however much their scribes may belong to a professional class that served the ruling institutions of various times and places. In the Bible, we hear voices from the other side, whether as echoes from the Iron Age or in the work of writers from after the two kingdoms came to an end, and their populations struggled to preserve some sense of shared identity in the aftermath.

I myself am most interested in the difficult early periods, where the biblical texts stand impossibly distant from the past they attempt to explain. For these questions, as for conundrums like the origins of the Arameans, all conclusions are bound to rely on conceptions of ancient society more generally. It matters tremendously, therefore, to reconsider the basic political character of Israel and the possibility that biblical stories from Israel could contribute to understanding its place in the early Levant. In the concluding section, I take up major historical problems that do not necessarily depend on biblical evidence – especially because this writing is far later than the settings in question. These problems are affected powerfully, however, by social conceptions that pertain very much to Israel as recalled at the foundations of certain biblical texts: the populations of the southern Levant in the Late Bronze Age, before Israel; the relationship of Canaan to Israel in the early Iron Age; and the shape of the Israelite monarchy. I address these in chronological order, without intending systematic coverage. That, I leave to the historians.

This book ultimately attempts a bridge between the worlds of biblical scholarship and archaeologically based history, with my contribution working from my own specialization in written evidence. It addresses the structure and character of the Bible's primary narrative through my vision of a particular relationship between a hodgepodge of lore about early Israel that has been taken over and recast radically by generations of scribes from Judah. This Israelite lore, when considered on its own, presents a picture of ancient Israel that contrasts sufficiently with standard "biblical" schemes as to provoke a reevaluation of what the Bible may offer historical investigation. It is my hope that by taking ever more seriously the biblical division between what comes from the distinct peoples of Israel and Judah, the character of each will come into sharper relief.

Daniel E. Fleming

Acknowledgments

More than one fairy tale begins with a party to which all important people are meant to be invited, and yet one crucial person is fatally omitted from the list. With hope that any who are left out are more forgiving than these characters tend to be in literature, I attempt here an unavoidably abbreviated account of those who have helped with this project. I am grateful to all nonetheless.

In 2004, I received a Guggenheim Fellowship for the opening phase of research on this book, a vote of interest in the combination of my career's work in both biblical and cuneiform studies. My goal was to draw on everything I had encountered through years of exposure to a range of Near Eastern literature and society, to put all of my own assumptions about the Bible and Israel's history to the test. The finished volume should be considered my return on the confidence loaned me in this grant, with appreciation for the support that it represented. Also in 2004, Cambridge University Press published a previous book, and I have returned with satisfaction to obtain their help with this one. Lewis Bateman shepherded the book through the process, and he has my particular thanks for his patience and efficiency at every stage. We even managed to agree on a title. Likewise, I managed to obtain again the sure hand of Stephanie Sakson as copy editor. Among the several people at Cambridge University Press who worked to bring this volume to press, Anne Lovering Rounds played the role of coordinator.

I have dedicated this volume to my students, with whom I have learned and grown through all my years of teaching. I arrived at New York University in 1990, and since then I have taught both undergraduates and graduates. Among the latter, it has been a particular privilege to work with doctoral students, shared first with Baruch Levine and now with Mark Smith. An even smaller group consists of the doctoral students for whom I served as advisor, and my dedication applies above all to them: Marjorie Gursky (2000), Esther Grushkin (2000), Dalia Finkelstein (2000), Hwan Jin Yi (2002), David Santis (2004), Esther Hamori (2004), Lauren Shedletsky Monroe (2004),

xvii

Deena Grant (2008), Sara Milstein (2010); Brendon Benz (2012), Cory Peacock (2012), Daniel Oden (2012); Mahri Leonard-Fleckman and Sari Slater (current dissertations); and Diego Barreyra, Elizabeth Knott, and Rachel Angel (current doctoral advisees). I would like to think that I could have developed the ideas in this book in a different environment, without the opportunity to work with students at an advanced level over years of contact, often continuing after graduation. It is unlikely. You all have my lasting gratitude and profound respect.

Many have contributed directly to the production of this book, some by reading the manuscript in one or more phases, others by specific discussions related to the project. Three of my graduate seminars read some or all of the manuscript at different stages. Among my current and former students, I received particular help from several. Perhaps the first to respond to two drafts was Stephen Russell, who was working on the early biblical traditions relating to Egypt, and whose early reactions contributed to my sense of direction. Brendon Benz has been great company generally; he has been a frequent partner in conversation about historical implications, and his Amarna discoveries have been eye-opening. At every stage of this effort, Lauren Monroe has read the drafts and weighed with me the ideas as they emerged, contributing her artist's eye for what works or is not quite right, along with constant encouragement and friendship. I have learned how to read for different voices in one text, especially with Sara Milstein, my coauthor, with whom new ideas always explode out of talk; there will always be more wood to chop. In the last phase of work, Mahri Leonard-Fleckman gave the perfect writer's gift, reading every chapter as I produced it, spotting sections that needed one more level of polish and expressing enthusiasm that helped me through the trek. At relevant points in the book, I have cited the research produced by each of these scholars, the ultimate demonstration of the quality of their minds and a proper acknowledgment of my debt.

Through my years at NYU, I have enjoyed the best of all possible working situations in the Skirball Department of Hebrew and Judaic Studies. Mark Smith has shared responsibility for biblical and Near Eastern fields since 2000, and I could not imagine a more ideal colleague for every aspect of our work, for which Mark sets the highest standards. In his responses to this project, Mark has given me a reality check, a sense of where I stand on matters large and small, drawing on his enormous experience and insight. In New York, I have also benefited from the presence of David Carr, especially as a sounding board regarding the transmission and revision of biblical texts. Both David and Mark read two drafts of this project. Other colleagues who read and responded to all or part of the manuscript include Ted Lewis, Adam Miglio, and Jacob Wright. All have my lasting appreciation for contributions beyond what I can detail here.

This project involved interaction with theoretical models developed by archaeologists from a range of fields. Both Richard Blanton and Gary Feinman kindly provided suggestions for reading material relevant to collaborative politics. While Anne Porter's ongoing research on early Near Eastern society has only just come to fruition in a forthcoming book, her ideas have represented a constant challenge to my preconceptions, and my overall interpretation of Israel's collaborative political life reflects a continuing dialogue. In every aspect of this study, my own thinking has evolved in dialogue, especially with those listed above. Where I have gone astray, I have most likely been warned already and chose to persist in my ways. The scope of the project is ambitious, and I have risked transgression into fields not my own, particularly in history and archaeology. I hope that my readers will find the effort worthwhile even where they must correct or dispute elements of my treatment.

Some thirty years ago, when my wife Nancy first supported my quest to become a teacher and scholar, my goal was to study the Bible. Through the intervening years, I have persisted in my biblical interest, though I have written books only based on cuneiform texts. This at last is the book that I have intended to write since the beginning, not from any preconceived path but as an effort to rethink my own understanding of the basics. Nancy has walked with me through what seems like the various ages of this journey, beyond the initial trial of a dissertation and the insecurities of job-hunting and tenure evaluation. With this renewed appreciation, I celebrate with her the fruit of a long labor completed in tandem. For all that this is my work, the result is equally hers.

D.E.F.

Abbreviations

A.	Louvre Museum siglum
AHw	W. von Soden. *Akkadisches Handwörterbuch*. 3 vols. (Wiesbaden: Harrassowitz, 1965–81)
ARAM	*ARAM* Periodical, ARAM Society for Syro-Mesopotamian Studies (London)
ARM(T)	Archives Royales de Mari (Textes)
ASOR	American Schools of Oriental Research
BA	*Biblical Archaeologist*
BaM	*Baghdader Mitteilungen*
BARev	*Biblical Archaeology Review*
BASOR	*Bulletin of the American Schools of Oriental Research*
Bib	*Biblica*
BN	*Biblische Notizen*
CAD	I. J. Gelb et al. (eds.), *The Assyrian Dictionary of the Oriental Institute of the University of Chicago* (Chicago: Oriental Institute, 1956–)
CANE	J. M. Sasson (ed.), *Civilizations of the Ancient Near East*, 4 vols. (New York: Scribners, 1995)
CBA	Catholic Biblical Association
CBQ	*Catholic Biblical Quarterly*
CRRAI	Compte rendu de la Rencontre Assyriologique Internationale
EA	J. A. Knudtzon, *Die El-Amarna-Tafeln*, 2 vols. (1915; reprint, Aalen: Otto Zeller, 1964)
FM	*Florilegium Marianum*
IEJ	*Israel Exploration Journal*
JAR	*Journal of Archaeological Research*
JARCE	*Journal of the American Research Center in Egypt*
JBL	*Journal of Biblical Literature*
JCS	*Journal of Cuneiform Studies*
JESHO	*Journal of the Economic and Social History of the Orient*

JNES	*Journal of Near Eastern Studies*
JSOT	*Journal for the Study of the Old Testament*
JSS	*Journal of Semitic Studies*
LAPO	Littératures Anciennes du Proche-Orient
M.	Siglum for tablets from Mari
M.A.R.I.	*Mari: Annales de recherches interdisciplinaires*
NEA	*Near Eastern Archaeology*
OEANE	E. M. Meyers (ed.), *The Oxford Encyclopedia of Archaeology in the Near East* (Oxford: Oxford University Press, 1997)
Or	*Orientalia*
PEQ	*Palestine Exploration Quarterly*
RA	*Revue d'assyriologie et d'archéologie orientale*
RHPR	*Revue d'Histoire et de Philosophie Religieuses*
RIMA	Royal Inscriptions of Mesopotamia Assyrian Periods
RIMB	Royal Inscriptions of Mesopotamia Babylonian Periods
RIME	Royal Inscriptions of Mesopotamia Early Periods
RlA	E. Ebeling et al. (eds.), *Realexikon der Assyriologie* (Berlin: de Gruyter, 1928–)
RSO	Ras Shamra – Ougarit
SEPOA	Société pour l'Étude ddu Proche-Orient Ancien
SJOT	*Scandinavian Journal of the Old Testament*
Syria	*Syria: Revue d'art oriental et d'archéologie*
TA	*Tel Aviv*
TLZ	*Theologische Literaturzeitung*
UF	*Ugarit-Forschungen*
VT	*Vetus Testamentum*
WO	*Die Welt des Orients*
WZKM	*Wiener Zeitschrift für die Kunde des Morgenlandes*
ZA	*Zeitschrift für Assyriologie und Vorderasiatische Archäologie*
ZABR	*Zeitschrift für Altorientalische und Biblische Rechtsgeschichte*
ZAW	*Zeitschrift für die alttestamentliche Wissenschaft*
ZDPV	*Zeitschrift des Deutschen Palästina-Vereins*
ZTK	*Zeitschrift für Theologie und Kirche*

PART I

INTRODUCTION
Israel and Judah

I

Why Israel?

The Bible would make a fascinating historical source, if only we could figure out how to use it as such. It is unique as a written corpus from the ancient world, not because it is religiously sacred, though perhaps its uniqueness is a result of the process that made it so. The Bible regales us with tales from the world of Egypt, Assyria, and Babylonia, offered from the perspective of the runaways and the defeated. It reports the reigns of kings not in the voice of royal propaganda but with distance and capacity for critique. It presents what are cast as the ruminations of men who spoke for God against both the people and the powers that led them. All this writing may date to settings long after the occasions portrayed, yet the literature is patently a patchwork of reused materials, not always well understood, certainly not a straightforward work of unified fiction.[1]

Often, current discussion of the Bible's relationship to history revolves around the notion of "historicity."[2] Did it happen, or happen the way the story says? Did the individual characters exist? More broadly, does the story preserve some memory or knowledge of the time portrayed? If the answer is "no" or there is significant doubt about the matter, it can be difficult to make a case for historical investigation before the date of the latest editor's hand, and this will in no way illuminate the object portrayed. Since the nineteenth century, the task of tracing the process of a text's formation carried with it the hope of access to earlier historical settings, especially at the oldest core. Julius Wellhausen's famous analysis of sources in the Pentateuch (1885) was defined as *Prolegomena to the History of Israel*. The question is what historical knowledge can be sifted from narrative that has been constructed through

---

[1] This thought recalls Erhard Blum's statement that the Bible is neither "history" nor "literature" in the modern senses, especially literature as fiction, with no claim to depict the real world (2010, 61).

[2] This vocabulary is now ubiquitous, but it became prevalent in biblical study through challenges to particular historical reconstructions, especially in the early work of Thomas Thompson (1974).

layers of revision and combination. Literary-historical analysis such as that of Wellhausen will continue unabated, in spite of its frustrations. As historical settings are proposed and explored for earlier phases of biblical writing, the primary division may be between content from the people of Israel and content from the people of Judah. In the obscure process of its creation, the Bible joined the stories and the experiences of these two peoples into one, explaining Judah as part of Israel and Israel as belonging to the proper authority of Judah's royal house of David. Historically, Israel and Judah were distinct, and it is the voice of Israel in particular that can be lost in Judah's choir. If we are to gain ground in reassessing the historical utility of the Bible for study of ancient Israel, or the southern Levant in the context of broader antiquity, the isolation of Israelite content in the Bible offers an essential point of departure.

A. Judah's Bible

The Bible, as I will call the Tanakh or Christian Old Testament, belongs to and was created by the people of Judah, whose identity may be rendered in English as "Judahite," "Judean," or "Jewish" for the same Hebrew designation as *yĕhûdî*. Although Jews have taken and been given a variety of names throughout their history, this one derives from their direct origin in the kingdom of Judah, as distinct from its immediate neighbor to the north, which the books of Kings designate Israel.[3] When I define the primary division of biblical material as coming from Judah or Israel, I refer to those who would have understood themselves as belonging to the people identified by one kingdom or the other, both during their existence and afterward. Insofar as people from Judah laid claim to the name Israel, I consider this a Judah perspective, whatever the merits of the claim. Although it is not certain how the kingdom of Judah was named before the eighth century, the inheritance of Israelite material takes place after the realm was definitely called Judah and may be considered literally Judahite. It is possible that people from Israel still identified themselves with that kingdom and its heritage both after the Assyrian conquest of the late eighth century and after Babylon's replication of the Assyrian empire in the early sixth century. While the kingdoms of Israel and Judah are habitually paired as "northern" and "southern," I have worked to avoid this terminology. In spite of the geographical juxtaposition, which does offer convenient points of reference, the two are not mirror images in political or historical terms. This is essential to the whole interpretation offered here.

For focus on the people directly related to the kingdom that was dismantled by the Babylonians in 586 B.C.E., I will use the form "Judahite," for its parallel with the complementary form "Israelite." The importance of the Bible's Jewish or Judahite character can be underestimated. When the peoples called Israel and Judah are treated as a single entity, differentiated only by minor matters

---

[3] For a thoughtful review of the early use of "Judah" terminology in the postmonarchic transition, see Blenkinsopp (2009), "Judeans or Jews?" 19–27.

of degree in the biblical account of their past, the particularly Judahite matrix for all biblical writing may be missed. It is finally Judah's idea that the two kingdoms shared a much older identity, with Judah part of the larger entity named Israel. We do not have clear access to Israelite views of the relationship. In simple historical terms, the Bible was created by the people of Judah, with its key stages of formation taking place just before the fall of Judah's kingdom and then in the generations afterward, as a Judahite or Jewish people struggled to maintain an identity against various forces of dispersion and assimilation.

The Judahite nature of the Bible can be seen first of all in its traditional structure as Tanakh: Torah (Teaching), Nevi'im (Prophets), and Ketuvim (Writings). It appears that the Torah was fixed in Jewish sacred tradition before the Nevi'im and the Ketuvim, which were collected according to different lines of reasoning and perhaps closed at roughly the same time (van der Toorn 2007, chapter 9). The Judah character of the whole collection is most explicit in these latter two sections, which directly address the period of the kingdoms, the fall of Judah, and what followed. Without the sweeping historical and communal preoccupations that dominate the Nevi'im, the Ketuvim most clearly derive from Judah's world. They are gathered around the long and venerable books of Psalms and Proverbs, associated with David and Solomon, respectively. These were the founding kings of Judah, as recalled in biblical tradition, and they were honored for song and wisdom. Although David and Solomon are celebrated as rulers of an inclusive Israel, the books are evidently the heirloom of Judah, with the main point of reference Jerusalem, city of palace and temple.[4] Every other book in the Writings is arguably of the same Judahite world, either associated with Jerusalem or composed in settings after the kingdom's end.

Working forward, the Nevi'im are likewise dominated by Judahite content and concerns, though this section incorporates material focused on Israel, aside from Jerusalem and the house of David. The second part of the Nevi'im, or Latter Prophets, consists of fifteen books of writing and lore defined by named prophets: Isaiah, Jeremiah, and Ezekiel; then twelve shorter works. Of these, only the oldest writing may reflect the world of Israel, in Hosea and Amos; the three long opening books all belong to Judah. The first part, traditionally called the Former Prophets, constitute a history of the people from their entry

---

[4] Although the Psalms are widely agreed to represent a collection shaped in the "Second Temple period," a category defined by the temple to Yahweh in Jerusalem, the particular location and range for that process need not have occurred in Jerusalem itself. In one exchange, Gillingham (2010, 120–1) sets her interpretation of the dominant transmittors against that of Zenger (1999), as "levitical singers" in Jerusalem instead of refugees in the diaspora longing for their sacred point of reference. Both approaches are Judah- and Jerusalem-centered. Whether early or later, the book of Proverbs is defined by kings from the house of David: Solomon (1:1 and 10:1) and Hezekiah (25:1). In an unusual approach to texts from the intellectual life of scribes, David Carr argues that Proverbs comes from the earliest stratum of biblical composition, probably in the early monarchy, measured by the Solomonic association (2011, chapter 14, "Proverbs and Israel's Early Oral-Written Curriculum"). This treatment of the setting was once more standard (e.g., McKane 1970, 8–9).

into the land they long possessed to the fall of each kingdom, first Israel in 720 B.C.E., and then Judah.[5] These books will form an important part this study: Joshua, Judges, 1 and 2 Samuel, and 1 and 2 Kings. Through the reigns of David and Solomon, this sequence is defined first of all by Israel as the principal category, so that Judah takes center stage only with the division into two kingdoms, which is recounted in 1 Kings 12. In spite of Israel's dominant position as the people in view through this narrative history, Judah's pervasive interest is still visible. Through the books of Kings, Judah is ultimately the guardian of Yahweh's temple and of his chosen royal house at Jerusalem. Israel is brought down by the "sin of Jeroboam," the founding king of the northern realm at the time of the split, and no Israelite ruler can shake this indictment. The destination of these books is the collapse of Judah and the survival of its people in Babylonian exile. Before Kings, the books of Samuel are occupied with David, who makes Jerusalem his capital. A time before kings is recalled in the book of Judges, which has little interest in Judah except in the opening that frames it in chapter 1, signaling the ultimately Judahite audience for the whole. Finally, Joshua takes for granted the priority of Judah in conquering this Promised Land and in defining tribal allotments for Israel's peoples (Josh. 10, 15). A case can be made for larger literary connections that can come only from later, Judahite hands, but Judah's ultimate interest can be seen from the content alone.[6]

This leaves the Torah, a tangle of teaching and story bound together under the authority of Moses. Both story and teaching are framed above all by writing that is broadly considered "priestly," a type that displays various affinities with ritual, sacred occasions and personnel, and the institutions of religion.[7] The book of Leviticus and large parts of Exodus and Numbers reflect this type, which seems to have Jerusalem's sacred structures as a norm.[8] The same

---

[5] The chronology of Samaria's final defeat as the capital of Israel is complicated, in that the last king Hoshea appears to have been deposed in 722 by Shalmaneser V, who then died that year, so that Sargon II had to consolidate Assyria's control of the region in 720 (Rainey 2006a, 232–35).

[6] Richard Nelson (1997, 8) considers that even what he identifies as the predeuteronomistic (before Josiah and the exile) level of Joshua has a "distinctly Judahite" outlook, with particular reference to the southern campaign of chapter 10.

[7] This broad characterization is not affected significantly by any number of nuances, including the debate over whether there was once a freestanding priestly document, one point on which Blum (1984) and Carr (1996) disagree, and current interest in defining "post-priestly" material (e.g., Kratz 2002; Otto 2002).

[8] This is even the interpretation of the priestly (P) writing in the circle of scholars that date it within the period of monarchy. Menahem Haran (1978, 146–7) associated the whole priestly program with the vision of Hezekiah's reform (2 Kings 18), though the cultic traditions would have had earlier antecedents. Working in dialogue with Israel Knohl's hypothesis (1995) of a Holiness (H) school revision of P, Jacob Milgrom (1991, 34) attributes the work of H to the time of Hezekiah and places the roots of P in eleventh-century Shiloh, before the monarchy, but as the direct source for Jerusalem temple and Judah religious traditions. It has been proposed that priestly (P) writing came instead from Bethel, in the period just after the fall of Judah and destruction of the Jerusalem temple (Fritz 1977, 154–7). One direct response to this minority view comes from

Jerusalem temple appears to be the point of reference for the priestly author of the creation story in Genesis 1 (Smith 2010, 70). Unlike the rest of the Bible, however, Judah's role in the Torah is largely submerged beneath the rubric of Israel, evidently as part of an emphasis on Israel as a unity before entry into the land. In Exodus through Deuteronomy, Judah is only named in tribal lists. Beyond the large quantity of priestly writing, the degree of Judahite scribal responsibility for the Torah is a matter of debate. The dominance of the priestly, evidently Jerusalem-based voice, however, places the finished version of this biblical section in a Judahite setting as well, evidently to serve a community that defined itself in part by religious practice after its political distinctness was lost.[9]

What remains to consider is the narrative that spans the books of Genesis through Kings, in the Torah and the Former Prophets. Through most of its length, this extended narrative is occupied with Israel, until Solomon's departure at the end of 1 Kings 11. This strange fact is one of the most important features of the Bible's basic structure. Based on the larger character of the Bible as the literary trove of Judah's survivors, its grand narrative should recount the origins, history, and identity of the people of Judah. Instead, Judah's story of origins turns to the history of a people called Israel to explain how events led to the appearance of David, the founder of Judah's royal house. This other people of Israel in fact represented the chief rival of Judah to the north, a sometime oppressor of the smaller realm to the south. Somehow, the eventual survivors of Judah, long after the kingdom of Israel had failed, considered that their own history was best told in terms of this neighbor, with whom they understood themselves to be deeply connected.

Could writers from Judah have created this Israelite background without any reference to Israel's own lore? It is possible, but such material should betray an ultimate ignorance of Israel's land and society. As we will find in the texts reviewed in Part II, this is far from true. Considerable material from this primary narrative assumes an Israelite geography and Israelite social and political structures. Judahite scribes constructed their grand narrative from the remains of Israel's own heritage, often obscuring the distinct tones of the Israelite tales that they had taken on. Before any questions of date, such as writing from before or after the fall of Judah, the first crucial distinction among the contents of the Bible must be between the mass of finished Judahite composition and the bits of material from Israel. This Israelite material may be sparse and difficult to extract with confidence, but it was so powerful that it gave form to the primary biblical narrative as we have it.

Klaus Koenen (2003, 75), who finds it unexpected that the Jerusalem priesthood would build its authority on Bethel practice and priestly lore. Because Zadok was a priest associated specifically with David, an editor had to find an older authority linked to the Sinai tradition and went to Aaron – not because of a link of priestly tradition to Bethel.

[9] Lester Grabbe (2003, 222–3) characterizes the primary purpose of Leviticus as "theological," casting a religious vision for Persian-period Jews. Similar views are widespread.

B. The Problematic Place of Israel

Over the course of the twentieth century, the Bible gained a substantial historical context from the results of archaeology in the lands occupied by Israel and
Judah, as well as from a growing mass of textual evidence from the wider Near
East, especially in cuneiform. As work continued on how the Bible took form,
the historical dimension of "literary history" could increasingly be evaluated
in terms that reached beyond the biblical storyline on its own. As embodied
especially in the work of William F. Albright and his students, the prospects
for grounding the biblical narrative in early history seemed impressive.[10] In
his *History of Israel*, John Bright observed that earlier hesitation to find any
more than "reminiscences" in the ancestor narratives of Genesis could now
be considered too cautious. Rather, "it has become increasingly evident that
a new and more sympathetic evaluation of the traditions is called for," based
mainly on "archaeological research" (1981, 68–9).

Meanwhile, European biblical scholars responded to the new evidence with
equal interest but with a reservoir of caution regarding how the texts must
then have been created and transmitted. Even where their interests tended
more toward reconstructing Israelite society and religion in a Near Eastern
context, Americans relied heavily on the work of German specialists such as
Albrecht Alt, Martin Noth, and Gerhard von Rad.[11] In spite of considerable
differences in perspective, this generation shared one crucial conception: that
a "United Monarchy" under kings David and Solomon was central to the
preservation and transmission of traditions about Israel's past. From this starting point, interpreters could disagree about how much the biblical narrative
from Genesis through Judges remembered of life before monarchy, but the two
later kingdoms could only be viewed as fractions of the whole called Israel.

In recent decades, the relationship of the Bible to history has been transformed once again. Naturally, there is enormous variety in approaches, so the
change is most visible in what is taken by most as common ground and what
must be defended. The United Monarchy of David and Solomon is no longer
a standard point of reference in discussion of settings for composition of substantial biblical documents. Focus has drifted into later periods, beginning with
the world of Israel and Judah as separate kingdoms. David and Solomon still
dominate the later part of the primary biblical narrative, and they must be
accounted for, but if the writing itself derives from the separate kingdoms and
their descendants, the political framework for these figures must also be evaluated in terms of advocacy and memory. The literary foundation for a unified
Israel that included Judah can no longer be located confidently in the reign of
Solomon. Instead, the first biblical efforts at combining longer narratives into

---

[10] Albright's influence is difficult to overestimate; see, for a statement of his broad perspective,
    From the Stone Age to Christianity (1957).
[11] For a sampling of their work translated into English, see Alt (1968), Noth (1966a, 1972, 1981),
    and von Rad (1962 and 1965).

collections with inclusive, perhaps "national," interest may come from the time of the two kingdoms. The unity in question must then be either Judah or Israel, and the perspectives expressed may not be shared by both communities. In the current environment, "Israel" must be defined afresh, in relation to kings, as an entity that preceded kings, and in relation to Judah.

While I do not intend to review at length the scholarship that has brought us to the current interpretive situation, certain basics are essential. As I see it, the most significant shift in the past generation has been the abandonment of the notion that key biblical collections were created in the tenth century, under the united Israel of David and Solomon. This idea now has little support, and it is necessary to grasp the extent to which its credence has been lost. With writing from a United Monarchy no longer defining early Israel by a unity that included Judah, the early stages of biblical composition must be located in two separate kingdoms of uncertain relationship. Some have already grappled with this need, and their work represents my point of departure.

1. Israel and Judah United

While the mid-twentieth century was peopled with numerous great figures who contributed an enormous variety of innovative and sometimes enduring ideas to the study of ancient Israel and the Bible, the most important was perhaps Martin Noth (1902–1968). Noth's syntheses represented a point of departure for both historians and biblical scholars, even when individual elements were challenged. Although he favored Albrecht Alt's hypothesis of a more peaceful process of original Israelite settlement rather than a military conquest, Noth took seriously the Bible's portrait of a time of judges, when the Israel of David and Solomon already existed without need of kings. He accounted for Israel's premonarchic unity by a tribal league that shared worship of a single god Yahweh (1966b). For the Bible itself, Noth envisioned a strong continuity between the first written texts and oral lore that lay behind these. Furthermore, the golden age of David and Solomon, as depicted in the books of 2 Samuel and 1 Kings, could provide a setting for considerable early writing in the Bible. In his *History of Israel* (1960), Noth devotes a section to "Israel's Intellectual and Cultural Life under David and Solomon" (pp. 216ff.). With the influx of new wealth, and the framework of a royal administration, writing became more widespread. The Bible's "wisdom tradition" goes back to this time, and with laudable caution, Noth suggests that most of the narrative for a united Israel first took some written form in Solomon's age:

Difficult though it is to compile a real history of Israelite literature, since most of the writings incorporated in the Old Testament are anonymous and impossible to date precisely, and on the whole not extant in their original separate forms, it is, nevertheless, possible to make one or two fairly certain statements in the present context.... Writing which it is possible to describe as literature, in the sense of having been the deliberate and considered work of a professional writer, has come down to us first from the age of David and Solomon. (p. 219)

"Legendary material" as found in the books of Moses, the occupation of the land in Joshua, and in the Judges tales, is older than the monarchy and went through a complicated process of recording, before the form of "historical chronicle" appeared during the period of David and Solomon, to replace popular legends (p. 219). The first incentive for creating such chronicles was the figure of David himself (p. 220), who inspired the account of his rise in 1 Sam 16:14–2 Sam. 5:10, composed during David's own life, and then a tale built around who would succeed him, written some time before Solomon's death (2 Sam. 7–20; 1 Kings 1–2). Although the dates for other compositions are less secure, "it is probable that the oldest large-scale literary recapitulation and formulation of the extensive and originally oral material of the Pentateuchal tradition, the work of the so-called Yahwist, may be attributed to this period" (p. 222). The combination of invasion accounts in Joshua 1–12 could come from the period just after Solomon's death (p. 222).

According to this approach, which Noth shared with most others from his period and which remains influential in some circles today, all the main elements of the Bible's narrative for early Israel already existed in a retrievable biblical form before the separation into two kingdoms that we encounter in 1 Kings 12. Israel is described as a unity that included Judah, and the texts can be trusted historically because they were created when this unity had not yet been broken. After all, the David narratives themselves present Judah as David's first domain (2 Sam. 2–4), and Judah is the first to welcome David's rule after Absalom's revolt (2 Sam. 19). The Bible's people could look back to Israel as their original name because the two kingdoms shared the same narrative heritage. In the Torah, two parallel renditions of Israel's beginnings were preserved in separate settings and later combined into one. The older Yahwistic (J) version, which freely invoked God as Yahweh from the first chapters of Genesis, was first put in writing during the united monarchy and remained the property of David's house at Jerusalem after the political split.[12] An Elohistic (E) version, which reserved the name "Yahweh" for revelation at Sinai and preferred the generic "God" (Elohim) in the book of Genesis, took distinct form in the northern kingdom that took the name Israel after its separation from Judah, whether in the ninth or eighth centuries (Jaroš 1982, 26–30). Already in the united monarchy, then, an account of Israel's origins included a sequence of ancestors named Abraham, Isaac, and Jacob, who were promised some part of Canaan as a future land for their descendants. This burgeoning family moved to Egypt, from which it had to be rescued through breathtaking divine intervention under the leadership of Moses. The relationship of the Torah to the book of Joshua was disputed, but the account of invasion by a single Israelite people was widely

---

[12] One particularly influential portrait of the J source was sketched by Gerhard von Rad, who cast its author as a major intellectual force, the one who gave theological shape to much of the Bible's account of Israel's origins, specifically as part of a Solomonic "enlightenment" ("The Form-Critical Problem of the Hexateuch," in von Rad 1966, 1–78). For a succinct account of key stages in the development of research on J, see Römer (2006a).

dated to roughly the same period.[13] For Israel before the divided monarchy, this left the book of Judges and the narratives of Saul, David, and Solomon. The united monarchy, celebrated as David's glory yet dependent on the previous achievement of Saul, was widely considered an early inspiration for historical interest and grounded in composition very closely to the events portrayed. Judges had to be left a special case, because the absence of Judah and Jerusalem required a northern setting. The whole picture, which contrasts so sharply with biblical portrayals of Israel and Judah as kingdoms, was understood to derive from premonarchic times. When Wolfgang Richter (1966, 339) proposed his still-influential hypothesis of a Book of Saviors in Judges 3–9, he dated the connected composition to the reign of Jehu in the mid-ninth century, based on sources from before the monarchy.[14]

2. The Breakdown of Consensus

Although there remain advocates of this older system in updated versions, the past generation has brought wave after wave of challenges, with repeated proposals that the larger compositions were much later than once thought, along with doubt that much survives of the building blocks from which these were created.[15] In the United States, the most prominent early critic was John Van Seters, who argued the main outline of his analysis in two early books before working out the details of his pentateuchal interpretation in two more.[16] After a key early initiative by Lothar Perlitt (1969), the tide of European opinion began to turn with H. H. Schmid's argument (1976) that the Yahwist (J, in the books of Moses) must date to the same general time as the Deuteronomist, so the late seventh or sixth century.[17] At close to the same time, Rolf Rendtorff (1990 [1977]) proposed an alternative to the extended J and E sources of the old system that would still allow the possibility of shorter early compositions, in

[13] Noth defined a "Deuteronomistic History" that followed Deuteronomy and incorporated the rest of the Bible's primary historical narrative, including Joshua, Judges, 1 and 2 Samuel, and 1 and 2 Kings. This left the frame for the Bible's earliest Torah in Genesis, Exodus, Leviticus, and Numbers, effectively a "Tetrateuch" (Noth 1972). The alternative was that the conquest recounted in Joshua must have been linked to the exodus escape story at an early stage, thus creating an effective "Hexateuch" (von Rad 1966, "The Form-Critical Problem of the Hexateuch").

[14] In his recent study of how the book of Judges took form, Philippe Guillaume (2004, 13) maintains the hypothesis of a Book of Saviors, which he dates to the late eighth century, after the end of Israel as a kingdom.

[15] In his contribution to the Anchor Bible commentary series, William Propp (1999, 49) analyzes the book of Exodus in terms of the classic sources, attributing E to the northern kingdom and J to the south, without committing himself to more specific dates of origin. Ronald Hendel, who is responsible for a new Anchor Bible commentary on Genesis, likewise retains the J and E sources of the Documentary Hypothesis, though it is not clear to which dates he attributes their composition (2005, 37, etc.). Richard E. Friedman has offered a systematic defense of the old system with early dates (2005; cf. 1987).

[16] The crucial arguments are found in Van Seters (1975; 1983), followed by Van Seters (1992; 1994).

[17] Schmid's initiative was then developed by his student Martin Rose (1981).

particular separating the ancestor stories of Genesis from the Moses narrative of Exodus and Numbers.[18] Different expressions of widely held and mainstream European approaches to the nine books of the Bible's primary narrative are found in works translated into English by Reinhard Kratz (*The Composition of the Narrative Books of the Old Testament*, 2005), Thomas Römer (*The So-Called Deuteronomist*, 2005), and Konrad Schmid (*Genesis and the Moses Story: Israel's Dual Origins in the Hebrew Bible*, 2010). In general, these begin with the Persian-period labors of the defining authorial hands and then working back cautiously to their sources, which are most likely "preexilic" (before Judah's end in 586) but which probably cannot be traced back before the eighth century, whatever their ultimate origins. The scribes of Solomon's court have largely disappeared from view.[19]

All this is not to say that writing from the time of David and Solomon is impossible to imagine for any part of the Bible's primary narrative. At the end of his *Formation of the Hebrew Bible* (2011), David Carr delicately explores the possibility of compositions that he would call "early monarchal" – without specific reference to Solomon. These include an archaic primeval history within Genesis 2–4 and 6–8, and the Covenant Code in Exodus 20–3.[20] Aside from the materials relating to the reign of David and his succession, which represent a special case to be discussed in Chapter 6, the earliest parts of the primary narrative in the books of Genesis through Judges most likely come to us through the (northern) kingdom of Israel in the ninth to eighth centuries. Carr's list of such texts includes early versions of the Jacob and Joseph stories in Genesis, the Moses-exodus story in the book of Exodus, a core prose Balaam narrative in Numbers 22–4, and individual accounts from the book of Judges.

In the current climate of biblical studies as defined against the backdrop of ancient history, the unified character of an early Israel that included Judah cannot be maintained by texts convincingly dated to a United Monarchy. Instead, even our earliest biblical material appears to come to us through the social boundaries of two separate kingdoms: Israel and Judah. The relationship between these two kingdoms, along with their individual histories, must be considered matters for investigation. No matter one's general inclinations regarding the capacity of the Bible to preserve early lore, or the dates and settings for the first written renditions of such lore, it is urgent to understand better the separate characters of Israel and Judah. Although these may intersect at diverse points in history, they cannot be treated as a single entity, two flavors of the same cultural or ethnic product. Too much of the Bible's primary

---

[18] This initiative was likewise extended by a student, when Erhard Blum (1984) developed a more detailed account of Genesis without recourse to the J and E sources.

[19] There remain some in continental Europe who reserve a role for tenth-century writing in the composition of the David-Solomon traditions themselves; see Dietrich (2007) and Vermeylen (2000). Dietrich sees a process of oral and written transmission that occupied centuries but that began in short texts and narratives with origins quite close to the reigns of the figures portrayed.

[20] Carr rejects the argument for a seventh-century adaptation from the Code of Hammurabi, as developed in detail by David Wright (2009).

narrative is defined by Israel and its concerns, and too much of the finished work clearly serves the needs of people identified with Judah, to leave the contrast unaddressed.

3. The Implications of Writing under Two Kingdoms

Even within the framework of the mid-twentieth century and its near consensus regarding the existence of large biblical compositions from the "united monarchy," there was some interest in "northern" writing. Given the inclusion of Judah in a larger and earlier Israel, the two kingdoms that followed the reigns of David and Solomon have commonly been termed "northern" and "southern," to reflect the greater whole. Origin in northern settings could be recognized by geography alone, as with Jacob's visits to Bethel (Gen. 28:17, 19; 35:7), Mahanaim and Penuel (32:3, 31), and Shechem (33:18); and the book of Judges is littered with references to peoples and places outside Judah's horizon. In Genesis, this geography could be attributed to premonarchic tradition, taken up in a tenth-century J document, but the E source, which would become prominent in the Jacob cycle, was generally considered the possession of the northern kingdom.[21] In a set of studies aimed to trace the impact of northern kingdom settings on later biblical texts, especially Deuteronomy, H. L. Ginsburg (1982, 1) coined the form "Israelian" to distinguish material from the "northern kingdom," as opposed to "Israelite" for the usage that included Judah.[22]

The recent impetus toward later compositional dates, however, has brought new urgency and clarity to the questions of how Israel and Judah were related, and how Judah came to inherit written material from its neighbor. Different targets of concern have led to different analyses. One immediate conclusion may follow the removal of the united monarchy as a compositional setting: Judah was never part of Israel, and the very notion of a unified Israel incorporating the populations of both kingdoms is possible only once the northern kingdom ceased to exist. Reinhard Kratz (2000, 2006; cf. Levin 2000) addresses two main obstacles to this result: the reference to "the two houses of Israel" in Isa. 8:14 (cf. Ephraim and Judah in 7:17); and the combination of Judah with Israel in David's domain (esp. 2 Sam. 2 and 19). For Kratz (2005, 170–82), Judah's first claim on David in 2 Samuel 19 is part of the earliest narrative, but this must date from the late Judah monarchy, between 720 and 586, so that it represents a literary attempt to take over the identity of the dominant northern state. Nadav Na'aman (2010) endorses Kratz's findings without reservation and adds the analogy of Babylon's desire to step into the shoes of its once-dominant

---

[21] For full-length treatments, see Coote (1991), Graupner (2002), Jaroš (1982), and Jenks (1977). The existence of an E source has been oft doubted, even without Rendtorff's decisive separation of the patriarchs from the Moses story; see, for example, Westermann (1985, 31–5).

[22] Ginsberg gave particular attention to the book of Deuteronomy (chapter 2) and then discussed Micah 6–7 and certain Psalms (47, 77, 80–81). The conceptual framework of this book does not differ greatly from standard approaches to northern and southern branches of a larger Israel, and his terminology did not gain general acceptance.

neighbor, Assyria, at the end of the seventh century.[23] Kratz's analysis of 2 Samuel forces a late date based on the inclusion of Judah, a topic to which we will return in Chapter 6. Meanwhile, H.G.M. Williamson (2011, 94) has now challenged Kratz's interpretation of Isaiah's two houses of Israel: "In my opinion, the essence of the case for retaining an early date for 8:11–15 ... is that the paragraph does not ... allude to Isaiah 7 (which was added to the first-person account), but that it does ... show close literary affinity with the whole of 6:1–11." Although I am attracted to Williamson's literary argument, the historical background for the "two houses" in Isa. 8:14 remains to be explained.

Two other recent works take on a problem that aligns still more closely with the one that defines this book: How can we account for such attention to Israel in Judah's Bible? Ernst Axel Knauf (2006, 293) poses the question in terms of the classic division, though not necessarily against the backdrop of a previously unified Israel: When and how did northern traditions such as the exodus from Egypt and leadership by saviors before the time of kings finally arrive in Judah? In general, northern material in the Bible is thought to have come to Judah with refugees from the northern kingdom after its defeat in 722/720. Knauf argues that the connection is later and that the first evidence for Judah's claim on the identity of Israel does not appear until the sixth century. The link would be Bethel, which he understands to have superseded Jerusalem as the predominant scribal center of Judah during the period of Babylonian rule. Bethel's trove of Israelite writing, which included the Jacob story in Genesis 25–33, the Book of Saviors in Judges 3–9, and the core of Hosea 4–11, would have first reached Judah in the final years of that kingdom, when Bethel and Benjamin were subsumed into it (ca. 650–586 B.C.E.). The following centuries of Persian domination were marked by competition and conflict between Bethel and a resurgent Jerusalem, and although Jerusalem won out, the Bethel traditions became part of Judah's Torah and sacred writing. The crucial question here is whether a clear Israelite identity and literature would have to have survived somewhere in that region for more than one hundred years, until it could be incorporated into Judah. If so, this Israelite literature would have to have maintained a substantial memory of Israel's distinct political character long after Assyria's takeover, and Bethel would have to have kept a stable scribal culture and canon for generations after Israel's demise. Regardless of how one interprets the history of Bethel, Knauf's proposal confronts the same oddity that lies at the center of my project.

Independently, but in a similar vein, Philip Davies (2007b) has suggested another seventh/sixth-century solution to the Israel conundrum, this time from the Bible's historical narrative without reference to Genesis and the Torah.[24] For Davies, the long historical narrative of Israel and Judah takes its Israelite framework from a first "history of Israel" that came from Benjamin (pp. 104–8). The original setting for this history is revealed by the dominance of

---

[23] Na'aman (2010, 14–15) emphasizes the vast superiority of Israel through the ninth and early eighth centuries, until Judah emerges as a state just at the moment of Israel's demise.

[24] Davies promises a monograph on Benjamin, to develop this thesis in greater depth.

leadership from Benjamin in the core material of Joshua, Judges, and 1 Samuel. As observed long ago by Martin Noth, the named targets of Israel's opening assault in Joshua are concentrated in the region of Benjamin: Gilgal, Jericho, and Ai, followed by the inadvertent treaty with Gibeon. The hero stories in Judges 3–9, which are widely considered the core of the current book, lead off with Ehud, the left-handed Benjaminite. Finally, Israel's first king is Saul of Benjamin, even though the text now casts him as Yahweh's first try, before the scepter is handed to David. As with that of Knauf, Davies' solution focuses on the geographical centrality of Benjamin, at the southern end of Israel yet just north of Jerusalem. The geography is indeed tantalizing, though Davies overplays Benjamin's role. One might say that this material is focused on the hill country north of Judah, including the territories of both Benjamin and Ephraim.[25]

Davies does bring attention to one unique historical feature of Benjamin: it is the one region and people that appear to have belonged to both kingdoms. This part of his argument has provoked Na'aman (2009b, 215–17) to articulate the alternative, that the Bible rightly ascribes Benjamin to the kingdom based at Jerusalem from the first moment of division, recorded in 1 Kings 12:21. King Asa's fortification of Ramah in 1 Kings 15:17–22 is historically plausible, and archaeological evidence for settlement patterns and material culture indicate a longstanding orientation of the Benjamin region toward the south. Nevertheless, the biblical claims come from Judah texts that may be calculated to explain the situation that clearly pertained after Israel was incorporated into the Assyrian empire. It appears that the Mesopotamian power allowed Judah's domain to encroach slightly to the north, as reflected in the account of Josiah's religious reforms, in which the king is said to have interfered with the shrine at Bethel (2 Kings 23:15); also, Jer. 17:26 includes "the Land of Benjamin" in a list of Judah constituents.[26] Josiah may never have undertaken a massive campaign to incorporate the old Israel into his kingdom, but this less ambitious achievement could have brought with it a rich written legacy.[27] In the Bible, Israelite material seems to claim Benjamin as part of its community, without reference to Judah.[28] For Davies' argument to work, Benjamin must have been part of Israel before 720, so that it can serve as the conduit for literature that

---

[25] One significant factor could be the particular date of the Ehud narrative and the manner of its incorporation into a larger composition. If it were added to an existing Deborah/Barak/Gideon/Abimelech collection, it would perhaps give a Benjaminite spin to this portrait of an Israel before kings. (This question arose in conversation with Sara Milstein, based on her work with the book of Judges.)

[26] See Chapter 3 for discussion of Jeremiah 17, which appears to reflect the late Judahite monarchy. In her detailed study of 2 Kings 23, Lauren Monroe (2011, 78–83) attributes the basic reference to Bethel in verse 15 to the core text, which is a nondeuteronomistic ritual declaration of independent origin.

[27] On the limited scope of Josiah's northern expansion, see Na'aman (1991).

[28] Benjamin is included with Ephraim in the Song of Deborah (Judg. 5:14), and Ehud's position in Judges 3 yields a string of savior stories that makes Benjamin keep company with the peoples of Deborah, Barak, and Gideon, who are linked to Ephraim, Naphtali, and Manasseh. Saul of Benjamin is Israel's first king (1 Sam. 9–10).

would find its way into Judah's Bible. Even if he is right about Benjamin's shifting affiliations, the question once again is how much of the biblical lore about Israel really took form in Benjamin, whether or not Benjamin could have played a key role in its transmission to Judah. Regardless of the answer, Davies has likewise perceived the centrality of this problem to the entire character of the Bible, which we expect to define its history by Judah alone.

Into this debate I intend to insert a line of inquiry that has not played an adequate role in biblical interpretation: how do the contrasting social and political characters of Israel and Judah help distinguish material from each domain, and then help judge the implications of such distinctions? This contrast is the focus of one more introductory chapter.

2

Israel without Judah

This investigation has the aim of probing more deeply the two separate identities that framed the early formation of biblical writing, the kingdoms of Israel and Judah. These two names were not the only ones by which the two kingdoms were known, and they could be used to identify people without reference to kingdoms, certainly after and probably before those monarchies. Nevertheless, these labels offer a point of entry into the social and political structures that shaped early biblical writing. The names Israel and Judah do not offer a universal key to fixed identities through time, and they belong to a complex geography of shifting identities.[1]

Understanding the limitations of names, it is necessary to acknowledge exactly what we have: in this application to the two kingdoms, Israel and Judah are political identities. As such, they apply to large-scale social structures, with large populations that incorporate multiple regions, numerous settlements, and countless households. Their differences and eccentricities will have to do with how each one operates as a polity, regardless of how homogeneous each may be internally or how similar or different their local communities may be across this political divide. In the Bible, where whole peoples are often in view, contrasts between the political cultures of Israel and Judah can help us understand the perspectives from which stories were created or revised. However village life in Israel may have resembled the same in Judah or Moab, certain patterns accompanied the constitution of each as politically united. Such patterns were bound up with politics, but they had implications for religion, for economics, and for any other aspects of society that were affected by political lines of organization and authority. In this second introductory chapter, I will outline a specific hypothesis of political contrast and its implications for the construction of the Bible's primary narrative in Genesis through Kings.

---

[1] One thinks of Randall Garr's "dialect geography" (1985), where language use has a life of its own, even as language identities, so far as names exist, are tied to social identities and are socially constructed.

Both Israel and Judah are attested to in writing outside the Bible – Israel as an enemy of Egypt, difficult to categorize, in the Late Bronze Age Merenptah Stela; and both Israel and Judah as kingdoms of the ninth to sixth centuries in cuneiform and alphabetic sources (see Chapter 15).[2] Archaeologists and historians may discuss Israel and Judah as distinct entities, yet the Bible draws them together in ways that are difficult to escape. Israel and Judah are studied as one, where Israel and Moab would not be.[3] I do not mean to change this biblically inspired habit; rather, I hope to understand it better, to pull Israel and Judah apart more effectively, so as to apply the biblical account of Israel in new ways to historical questions about the region and its peoples. If we search the Bible for contrasting perspectives that align with the kingdoms of Israel and Judah as separate settings, the political differences between the two are striking. Judah is presented as far more centralized than Israel.[4] Likewise, the various dimensions of Israel's relatively reduced centralization both help to pinpoint biblical texts with Israelite roots and to suggest fresh historical interpretations. This political contrast lies at the heart of both the biblical analysis in Part II of this book and the historical discussion in Part IV.

A. A Polity, Not an Ethnicity

For all its familiarity, the name "Israel" remains elusive. Early studies focused on the biblical range of use, which is considerable.[5] As part of his larger account of the Bible's literary history, Martin Noth (1966b) looked for an analogy to Israel in the Greek amphictyony, thus taking seriously the tribal organization

---

[2] Even Egyptologists vary in their usage for this name, between the older reading as Merenptah, for clarity, and this correction to Merenptah. With my choice, I follow the *Oxford Encyclopedia of Ancient Egypt* (Sourouzian 2001).

[3] Here also, I invoke "Moab" not as a fixed and universal identity but as the name of what Mesha claimed to rule as king in his much-studied royal inscription. Bruce Routledge (2004) even proposes that this text reflects Mesha's political formulation of Moab as a state. In fact, the study of cultural common ground between Israel and Moab can be fruitful, and there is much to understand in the specific relationship between the Moabite polity and eastern Israelite peoples such as Gad, which is mentioned in the Mesha text (see Finkelstein and Lipschits 2010; Monroe 2007).

[4] Beyond the life of the kingdoms themselves, later writers from the survivors of Judah divide their conception of Israel in various ways. Idealized in the past, Israel in transition from Egypt to the Promised Land is cast in collective terms as an association of tribes with equal standing, as with encampment around the tabernacle in Numbers 2. This is a classic priestly text (Levine 1993, 64–5), with a vision that probably postdates Judah's monarchy, however late this may be. The arrangement serves a congregation assembled for worship with no political intent, however, and even this portrait envisions Moses as something like a ruler in a theocratic mode, not entirely different from the messianic expectation that future restoration will come with a king from David's line. Postmonarchic writing from Judah should be influenced by contemporary political circumstances, but the ideals of Judah's monarchy linger.

[5] The most extensive early study of the name, in two volumes, is that of Eduard Sachsse (1910; 1922). Another important early work is that of Carl Steuernagel (1901), who distinguished between a Leah group and a Rachel group of tribes, with reference to Genesis 29–30.

attributed to Israel in the books about its formative past. This comparison drew careful criticism as inadequate at several levels, especially in the work of Mayes and de Geus.[6] Nevertheless, the biblical portrayal of a tribal association long remained a powerful point of reference for understanding the nature of earliest Israel, until more recent evaluation of the whole body of Torah narrative. It is obvious from texts such as the priestly and otherwise late canonical lists in the Torah, the vision of restored Israel in Ezekiel 48, and the genealogies that introduce the Chronicles of the House of David (1 Chron. 1–8) that writers from after Judah's fall thought of Israel both in its beginnings and in its future as an affiliation of tribes.[7] The question is how far back this notion really goes. Certain texts remain particularly difficult to attribute to such postmonarchic perspectives, especially the poems that incorporate variable groupings: the Song of Deborah (Judg. 5), the blessings of Jacob (Gen. 49), and the blessings of Moses (Deut. 33).[8] The strongest reason to take seriously a tribal aspect to early Israel is still the Bible itself, with its "tribal" terminology.[9] Outside the Bible, there is no surviving reference to any division of Israel into component members. Israel is an enemy to face, recognized only as a single unit.[10]

In recent years, archaeologists have struggled with how to name the peoples who left material remains in the southern Levant during the Late Bronze and early Iron Ages. As will be discussed further in Part IV, nonbiblical writing offers a framework for the mid-ninth century and afterward, but this leaves a massive gap for the preceding centuries. The late thirteenth-century Egyptian reference to Israel in the Merenptah Stela offers too little detail to identify populations with specific regions and sites. For the Iron Age I in particular,

---

[6] Mayes 1974; de Geus 1976, esp. chapter 2, on "The System of Twelve Tribes."

[7] For the Torah, see, e.g., Gen. 35:23–6; Exod. 1:2–4; and Numbers 1–2. The various lists of twelve tribes are discussed carefully by Ulrike Schorn (1997), especially chapter 1.

[8] Along with an extensive bibliography, there are fairly recent monographs focused on all three of these texts: Neef (2002) on Judges 5; Macchi (1999) on Genesis 49; and Beyerle (1997) on Deuteronomy 33.

[9] In mid-twentieth-century discussion of evolutionary schemes for social development, the "tribe" applied to relatively simple societies, without permanent political institutions. The classic formulation of this definition is that of Service (1975), with a hierarchy of four stages of social complexity: band, tribe, chiefdom, and state. Rather than accept the restrictions of such a limited definition, some have adopted a pragmatic usage, based especially on relationship by kinship (see Khoury and Kostiner 1990). The Bible applies the term *šēbeṭ* to the grouped peoples who make up the primary constituents of Israel, even in the Israelite context of Gen. 49:16 (see Part II for the analysis of this text by Macchi, 1999), and the ancestral system of Genesis renders these peoples literal brothers by the birth narrative in chapters 29–30. It is simplest to translate the Hebrew term as "tribe," with common usage, and to accept the challenges of interpreting this "tribal" category on the large social scale envisioned by the term in biblical references to early Israel.

[10] The closest case would be the Mesha inscription from Moab, which isolates individual settlements as targets for attack: Ataroth (lines 10–13), Nebo (lines 14–18), and Jahaz (lines 18–21). "The land of Ataroth" is said to have been the home of "the men of Gad" within memory (*m'lm*, line 10), which seems to indicate time before Omri's arrival, but they are confronted as part of Israel.

it is not clear how to name the populations of settlement in the central hill country. In a monograph that reflected his early reflections on new survey evidence, Israel Finkelstein (1988, 27) called these people "proto-Israelites" based on the likelihood that their descendants took the name of Israel. As Finkelstein himself has argued more recently, however, it is not clear who did call themselves "Israel" before the kingdom of the ninth century (see Part IV).

While the excavated and surveyed evidence from archaeology remains central to any historical discussion of the Iron Age I, and texts may offer only occasional help with specific historical problems, the issue of naming must begin with writing. It is one thing to ask what named peoples may have occupied the high country of the southern Levant in the Late Bronze and early Iron Ages. To a great extent, we do not know. It is another thing to ask who and what was earliest Israel, by name. Working from the texts that provide the direct evidence for names, I prefer to treat Israel as a social group, not an ethnic group, and most likely the name of a body that acted politically, especially in the sense of a unified social body in conduct of war and peace under coherent leadership. That is, early Israel is best pursued as a polity, not as an ethnicity (see Chapter 15).[11]

At the same time, my entire analysis of the biblical evidence for Israel rests particularly on a political distinction between Israel and Judah. Historical Israel, to borrow Philip Davies' turn of phrase, appears to have been characterized by a political framework that was strikingly different from that of historical Judah. The very preservation of this contrast in the biblical accounts of Israel and Judah demonstrates some continuity between the Bible and history, though the relationship must be evaluated case by case for individual texts and issues. Where the biblical writers worked with older material, this could be preserved and reworked by scribes no longer familiar with key aspects of that earlier society. In particular, the actual political life and landscapes of Israel and Judah were recalled only indirectly after each kingdom came to an end. Politics rarely interests the biblical writers for its own sake, and political information is preserved only as part of a matrix for stories about divine acts and the people caught up in them. The affairs of God and his contacts are remembered, while the world they inhabited is transformed to fit the writer's own time, like Renaissance paintings of biblical and classical narrative. Certain elements of such older material, however, survive the transmission into later settings, because they are essential to the narrative, and the jarring contrast can point

---

[11] In this approach, I am in considerable sympathy with Philip Davies, who offered a similar declaration in controversial mode roughly twenty years ago (1992). Dissatisfied with vague applications of details from "biblical Israel" to historical issues, Davies proposed to separate "biblical" from "historical" Israel for analytical purposes. "In fact," he says, "the historian must in the end be driven back to the only workable definition, namely the political: a *political* entity in the strict sense, a kingdom occupying the northern Palestinian highlands" (p. 54). Davies' definition of political Israel by the kingdom of the ninth and eighth centuries alone is unnecessarily and even implausibly restrictive, and I will explore in Part IV the background of the kingdom. Nevertheless, the political focus is realistic and clearly defined.

to older historical assumptions embedded in the texts. For example, the entire notion of an eastern conquest, after which a part of Israel takes up residence in the Transjordan, reflects the geographical diversity of Israel and contradicts the dominant theme of a Promised Land west of the Jordan River. The vision of a restored Israel in Ezekiel 48, represented by the old conquest system of twelve tribes, locates the whole people in bands that recreate this western Promised Land, ignoring the east. All of the Bible's accounts of land taken from Sihon and Og, therefore, no matter how late, reflect the political character of Israel, which the people of Judah did not share and did not understand.

This intersection of polity and geography in the case of Israel, west and east, evokes the language of "political landscape" adopted by Adam Smith (2003) in his study of "early complex polities." In an archaeological approach to history, Smith chooses to focus on the interplay of political entities across space rather than on the pursuit of ethnicity. Although his work is defined by centralized authority, without reference to collaborative expressions of political life, Smith's basic categories are directly relevant to my own political focus in approaching ancient Israel and its biblical legacy. Smith begins with the idea of the "landscape," which reflects a fabric of human conceptions about the spaces they inhabit, developed in particular historical circumstances according to relationships between groups:

Landscape . . . refers to the broad canvas of space and place constituted within histories of society and cultural life. Landscape arises in the historically rooted production of ties that bind together spaces (as forms delimiting physical experience), places (as geographic or built aesthetics that attach meanings to locations), and representations (as imagined cartographies of possible worlds). (p. 11)

One major expression of shared space is effectively "political," in that it depends on social relationships rooted in power and legitimacy (p. 69). Smith's interest in politics revolves around "sovereign authority," including especially the relationships central to its "production, maintenance, and overthrow" (pp. 11–12). He tends to assume a strong political center, as he considers the ways in which people interact with the driving authority. The attraction of his terminology lies in the combination of two terms in the phrase "political landscape," a way of acknowledging the mutability of identities and power across time and types of exchange. As we address the kingdoms called Israel and Judah, defined as such in the books of Kings and bearing these names at different stages of their political existence, and having uncertain relationship to each other through time, the idea of a political landscape is adequate to the complexity of the problem.

Smith's framework is less illuminating for the decentralized aspects of ancient Israel, as indicated in several biblical traditions, including that of the associated tribes. For this problem, Anne Porter's analysis of the "early polity" offers a broader perspective (2010). Like Smith, Porter sets aside the category of the "state," in part so as to avoid the common dichotomy of tribe and state.[12] Porter observes that in early polities, kinship remains a key mode of interaction, and she outlines four ways to think about "constituent relationships" in these settings. First, "polity morphology and spatial organization" can vary in ways not acknowledged by Smith. That is, polities may involve control of contiguous territory, but they may also involve links over distance, with kinship as one way to explain such ties. Second, "social configuration" addresses the role of kinship in politics, as opposed to class. For themselves, people in early polities tended to identify their social location by kinship, while categories of class were usually applied by others. Third and fourth, Porter considers "political ethos" and "political practice," the ways in which groups conceive of themselves and what groups actually do, in the short term.

Porter's first two categories of investigation are most useful for Israel as an early polity. By her attention to kinship and alternative spatial possibilities, her approach provides a caution against the standard assumption that all polities, Israel included, occupied a connected territory. Israel's eastern affiliates, as suggested in the Bible and mentioned in the ninth-century Mesha inscription from Moab, need not have been related to Israel in direct territorial terms. Likewise, the picture of associated peoples in the Song of Deborah (esp. Judg. 5:14–18) does not require territorial connection. A precedent for such political identity across distance would be the peoples of the Binu Yamina confederation as found in the early second-millennium archives from Mari. These groups considered themselves to be ruled by kings, the accepted leadership title for standing as a full-fledged polity, yet their actual populations straddled more than one large kingdom. The five Binu Yamina peoples (or tribes) were counted in the Mari military census, yet Yaminite populations were also located in the domains of three more western powers, Yamhad (Aleppo), Qatna, and Amurrum.[13] This intrinsically unexpected situation could apply to the people of Gad who are named in the Mesha inscription (above), if they had a longstanding association with Israel that applied even when another eastern polity – Moab – developed a regional dominance. Meanwhile, the Bible envisions early Israel to have been made up of affiliated groups in different regions. This picture should be taken seriously in historical terms for the very contrast it offers to anything in the experience of people from Judah, even as it may be hampered by a lack of direct experience with this kind of nonterritorial political affiliation. Failure to comprehend this structure would be a sign of later composition by scribes who understood the "tribes" to be real political actors even as they could not envision a world before the (later?) kingdom's more territorial order.

---

[12] Smith explains at length his various reasons for abandoning the "state" as a category useful to analysis of early societies (pp. 94–101). Above all, he objects to the "denotational insecurity of the term," as an entity impossible to define consistently. The problem then with letting the word mean different things in different situations is that analytical types tend to be regarded as "enduring spatial forms with their own historical inevitability" (p. 96).

[13] For extended discussion of the political situation at Mari, see my *Democracy's Ancient Ancestors* (2004a).

With this biblically defined project, I undertake to examine ancient Israel in political terms. A political framework allows historical investigation that acknowledges the centrality of archaeological evidence at the same time as it provides a fruitful line of inquiry into the biblical traditions. Moreover, such political focus suits well the character of the nonbiblical written evidence for early Israel. Both Israel and Judah appear as kingdoms in royal inscriptions from other peoples that encountered them as potential antagonists: Assyria, Babylon, Aram, and Moab. As stated already, "Israel" and "Judah" are not fixed identities by which we can always expect these kingdoms to be named. The rulers of opposing powers tended to see Israel and Judah in the image of their own domains, defined especially by their kings and capitals. For the emerging empire of Assyria, Israel is most often "Samaria" or the "House of Omri," from the royal city and the ruler who established it (see Part IV). Early Judah is the "House of David," not clearly named as "Judah" until the late eighth century.[14] For the moment, the point is that these names represent specific political identities with specific periods of use. Israel and Judah may have origins in social identities different from the kingdoms we know from the early first millennium, but these would have been no more permanent and broadly "ethnic" than this definition by the kingdoms they became. Also, the inscriptional evidence provides no basis for viewing Judah as part of Israel, as in the Bible's tribal scheme. The eventual affiliation of the two in biblical perspective calls for explanation, but outside evidence offers no reason to consider this an early phenomenon. The nature of each identity is understood better by treating them as separate until the period when their combination can first be demonstrated. When the possibility of their distinct characters is given serious consideration, the biblical portrayals of Israel and Judah also can be seen to contrast beyond what is commonly observed.

B. The Political Contrast between Israel and Judah

By the eighth century, Israel and Judah shared dialects of Hebrew and the god Yahweh, and they appear to have shared similar patterns of social organization and settlement at the local level,[15] taking into account local conditions and

---

[14] The first nonbiblical reference to Judah by name seems to be in Tiglath-pileser III's tribute lists, for "Jehoahaz of Judah," in 734. See Text no. 11:11', in Cogan (2008, 56). This evidence will be addressed further in Chapter 6, with treatment of David, and in Chapter 18, with discussion of the historical kingdoms. It is odd that the name "Judah" first appears in securely dated nonbiblical evidence after the name "Israel" ceases to be part of Assyrian usage in the royal annals.

[15] The continuity of local social organization between Israel and Judah is reflected in the discussion of Avraham Faust (2000). Food processing in villages was concentrated in a particular zone, and smaller sites often had just one installation for everyone's crop. Storehouses appear to have been communal, and Faust envisions something like a local council of elders as a basis for group decision-making at the village level. Nothing indicates that such patterns were different in Israel and Judah.

individual choice.[16] The resemblance between the languages does not demonstrate a common identity, in that linguistic variation may have a strong geographical component, especially before the eighth century. As attested in the
ninth-century Mesha inscription, the language of Moab is much like Hebrew,
more so than the Deir 'Alla text of the late eighth or early seventh century,
which was found in territory that could once have belonged to eastern Israel.[17]
The god Yahweh is more telling, if only we could tell how early this deity was
associated with Judah, not just regionally but specifically. The southern desert
texts of Kuntillet 'Ajrud come from a region south of Judah, perhaps at the
start of the eighth century, yet their references to Yahweh seem more attuned to
Israel than to Judah.[18] This connection between Israel and Judah is important
and calls for a historical explanation, even if it does not establish a generally
shared identity between the peoples of each kingdom. However we define the
common cultural ground of Israel and Judah, the Bible presents contrasting
political traditions and landscapes. As political, these differences pertain to the
larger social scale, beyond the local village. The differences have to do with
leadership in relation to the people and with the constituent parts of each polity
in relation to the whole.

I propose that biblical content originating in Israel can be distinguished
from the dominant content from Judah in part by these contrasting political
assumptions, along with the more obvious criteria of geography and the absence
of Judah-oriented or late integrative themes.[19] The following lists summarize
how the Bible presents the differing political frameworks for Judah and Israel.
For Judah, this applies only to the kingdom identified with rule by the house
of David. In the case of Israel, the portrayal envisions an extended period
in the land before monarchy, with traits appropriate to that setting. These
features will be documented in Part II, with discussion of selected biblical
texts. By assembling these contrasting political visions of Judah and Israel, I do
not mean to give them straightforward historical validity. Nevertheless, these
details are not generally direct or even conscious portrayals of the two realms

---

[16] I do not want to create the impression either of absolute regional uniformity or of environmen-
tally determined variation. By "choice," I thus refer to the role of human "agency" in history
and social construction, a category of increasing interest in study of social change in antiquity.
For a recent review of the category in archaeological research, emphasizing the integration of
agency and structure in the work of Anthony Giddens and Pierre Bourdieu, see Andrew Gardner
(2008). An edited volume with specific interest in the Near East has just appeared (Steadman
and Ross 2010).

[17] On the whole question of defining individual Northwest Semitic languages in the Levant,
including the role of emergent polities, see Sanders (2009).

[18] "Yahweh of Samaria" is defined by Israel's royal capital. The bibliography is enormous; for a
recent study and a start with the literature, see Mastin (2009). On the religious implications
generally, see Mayes (1997) and Müller (1992).

[19] The last category of "integrative" themes is unavoidably malleable, and major disagreements
arise over how to define what constitutes an example and how to date them. It is clear, however,
that the final stages of biblical arrangement belong to the postmonarchic period, among the
survivors of Judah.

by the biblical writers. They represent both a basis for separating Israelite material from a Judahite matrix and a body of noteworthy traits for historical consideration.

1. Judah
   a. The king and the sacred center were both located at Jerusalem. Yahweh's temple in Jerusalem is often portrayed as the dominant sacred site, even before efforts at further centralization. Moreover, the palace and the temple precinct are physically contiguous in the same part of the Jerusalem citadel. Both structures are linked to the origin of the monarchy in the era of David and Solomon, so that they are identified by and rooted in the establishment of a single royal line. In the Bible's rendition, the temple is built as a royal sanctuary.
   b. Any rejection of old leadership or advocacy for someone new had to be understood in continuity with the house of David. It is often observed that the house of David survives the entire duration of Judah's kingdom, so that Judah is considered more politically stable than the "northern kingdom." In fact, Judah endured major disruptions in its succession of rulers, but no one could establish legitimacy without a claim to kinship with the line of David, as envisioned for the accession of Joash under Jehoiada the priest (2 Kings 11).
   c. The constituent parts of Judah had no apparent social or political definition as peoples with their own decision-making capacity. For the seventh century, several regional entities within Judah are assumed in Jeremiah 17, where they include Benjamin as one possible exception. Before the arrival of the Assyrian power, it is possible that only town centers represented such subdivisions, with sites such as Lachish, Libnah, Beersheba, and Hebron. No biblical tradition exists for "tribes" of Judah.
   d. There is mention of collective leadership in Judah, including the *'am hā'āreṣ* ("people of the land") as a broad assembly and "elders" as a more limited representation, but such terminology is defined only with reference to Jerusalem as the political center. Collective leadership is never said or implied to involve representatives of groups that inhabit different regions or centers or kinship bodies within Judah.[20]

[20] The issue of a collective political voice in Judah is linked to a fascinating and somewhat obscure pattern in attested names. As mentioned earlier, nonbiblical reference to Judah begins only in the second half of the eighth century, just after the emergence of the kingdom as a large-scale polity, in contrast to identification as the House of David in the ninth-century inscription from Tel Dan, to be discussed in Chapter 15. Although evidence is too limited for more than a sketch of possibilities, this pattern raises the question of whether the name "Judah" itself suggested a political mode no longer defined as by the House of David. Likewise, the *'am hā'āreṣ* only appear as part of this large-scale polity. The name "Judah" may refer to some place and perhaps people before the eighth century, but it is not clearly the name of what is ruled by the house of David in the ninth century.

2. Israel

    a. Royal capitals are never identified with Israel's principal sacred centers: Gibeah, Shechem, Tirzah, and Samaria as capitals; versus the sacred centers of Bethel in particular, as well as Dan, Gilgal, Mizpah, and Mount Carmel. In this context, it is striking that the Mount Ebal site (Deut. 27:4, 13; Josh. 8:30, 33) is near Shechem but not part of the town, and its use is attributed to the time before kings. The isolation from the town itself is striking, because Late Bronze and early Iron Age Shechem had a prominent temple that seems clearly to have been built before Israelite occupation of the city.[21]

    b. Individual rulers could be deposed without recourse to the departing royal house, unlike the house of David in Judah. Through the house of Jehu, the first person to be granted kingship in a new royal line was never deposed, according to the biblical portrayal: Saul, David, Jeroboam I, Baasha, Omri, and Jehu.[22] This pattern testifies to the settled nature of the right to rule, once affirmed, even as the treatment of successors indicates the power of other constituents in Israel.[23] The notion of anointing may be linked to this agreement not to depose, and a literary elaboration may be found in the theme of David's refusal to take Saul's life (1 Sam. 24, 26). The sons of these founding rulers must then prove themselves, with uneven results: Solomon (of David), Ahab (of Omri), and Jehoahaz (of Jehu) survive evaluation by their constituents, while Eshbaal/Ishbosheth (of Saul), Nadab (of Jeroboam I), and Elah (of Baasha) are all murdered in their second year, evidently a stereotyped term of office for the weak and unworthy.[24] The insecure status of royal successors in Israel suggests a protracted period of struggle between the concentrated power of kings and some kind of collaborative counterbalance, whatever its political basis. Clearly, each new king wished to hand off power to a successor, and no

---

[21] On this structure, see Stager (1999); cf. Campbell (1991); Jaroš (1977); Milson (1987); and Wächter (1987).

[22] The one exception would be Zimri, who is said to become king (1 Kings 16:10), seated on his throne (v. 11), yet never acclaimed so by any embodiment of Israel. His reign is said to last only seven days (v. 15), in a description that launches the tale of Omri's rise (vv. 15–18, 21–2). We may doubt that the symbolic figure of seven days reflects a chronicle of kings and the lengths of their reigns, except perhaps in his role as assassin.

[23] This characterization is distinct from, yet must be made with acknowledgment of, Albrecht Alt's groundbreaking distinction of a more "charismatic" tradition of leadership and monarchy in the north, as opposed to the fixed dynastic tradition of the south. These issues will be discussed further in Part IV.

[24] For the three instances of two-year reigns, see 2 Sam. 2:10; 1 Kings 15:25; and 1 Kings 16:8; cf. Ahaziah son of Ahab (1 Kings 22:41). Although interpreters consistently regard the two-year reign of Saul in 1 Sam. 13:1 as a scribal error, the number recalls the pattern of early rejection (Sara Milstein, personal communication). Whenever this duration was assigned, it seems to treat Saul as a failed king, perhaps in contradiction to the tradition of his anointing, which renders him untouchable.

biblical tradition envisions any attempt to thwart the coronation of royal sons. As a historical portrait, the books of Samuel and Kings suggest a gradual progress in rulers' capacity to hold power based on the authority of their lineage, in that the families of Omri and Jehu last three and four generations, respectively.[25]

c. There was a tradition in Israel of constitution as an association of tribes (*šēbeṭ*), which once represented viable decision-making units, as portrayed variously in the book of Judges. The Song of Deborah offers the fullest portrait of collaboration in going to war.[26] In the schema of Samuel and Kings, which were composed and transmitted under the shadow of David's royal line, any political role for a collective body distinct from royal service was rendered simply in terms of "Israel," without reference to (or recollection of?) individual tribes.[27] After the end of both kingdoms, probably under late Persian or early Hellenistic rule, Chronicles reflects a revived notion of tribal identities, conflating the vision of primal categories going back to the ancestors from Genesis, the wilderness wandering, and Joshua's territorial division with the long period of organization as two kingdoms. It is possible that the silence regarding tribes reflects the language of Israelite kingship itself, as it addressed a collected association of constituent peoples. The language of simple "Israel" in relation to its kings, as seen in the Omri narrative, compares with standard language for kings and the people who must respond to them in evidence from early second-millennium Mari in Syria.[28]

These contrasts between the biblical portrayals of Israel and Judah are substantial, even as they must be qualified by various nuances of text and history. As a finished product, the primary narrative is not intended to present two radically different political frameworks that operated contemporaneously. Israel's most striking expression of decentralized political life, its tribes, is accounted for by the premonarchic age, without early content for Judah. Both Israel and Judah are ruled by kings, the clear manifestation of individual authority. The distinctions between these two entities must be explained as the result of separate processes of political development in settings where both individual and collaborative power came to different equilibria.

---

[25] Ahab's son Azariah dies after two years, as if by divine judgment, followed by Joram, another son of Ahab, who rules twelve years before Jehu kills him (2 Kings 3:1; 9:24). Jehu is followed by Jehoahaz (2 Kings 13:1), Jehoash (13:10), and Jeroboam II (14:23), until Jeroboam's son Zechariah is murdered after six months (15:8). No other royal line had the chance to establish itself securely before the onslaught of the Assyrian empire.

[26] Judges 5:14–18; see also Deborah and Barak in 4:10; Gideon in Judg. 6:33–5 and 7:23–4.

[27] The clearest reference to the political reality of individual tribes in Israel on their own terms may be the old core of Genesis 49, which includes at least the six tribes found in verses 13–21 (see Chapter 5).

[28] In the Akkadian terminology of the Mari archives, the population ruled by the king as a body is called the *mātum*, or "land"; see Fleming (2004a, 119–21).

C. The Contributions of Israel and Judah to Biblical Narrative

In the end, the Bible belongs to Judah, and writers from Judah and its heirs contribute to and shape the current form of every biblical book. This renders all the more striking the fact that Judah's origins are subordinated to those of Israel as the larger entity and that very little is said about Judah's particular role before the monarchy. This pattern appears to reflect the adoption by Judah of Israel's distinct traditions about origins, which did not include Judah when they were created.

These features may be explained by the following hypothesis:

> *Only in Israel was there a perceived need to explain this people's existence before and apart from kings.*

That is, writers from Judah came to share this interest in ancestral identity and life as a people before kings, but they derived the interest from Israel and developed it around Israelite lore. In the biblical narrative about the formative past, the first episode that is constructed around a character of primary interest to Judah revolves around David and the establishment of his royal house. In vivid contrast to Israel, therefore, Judah's identity is bound up from the beginning with kingship, like the account of Babylon in the Enuma elish, where Marduk places his own royal rule at the center of the whole creation.[29] Judah as a name may be much older than its identification with the kingdom ruled from Jerusalem; that kingdom, however, was defined from the start by its royal house of David, and all references to Judah as a political actor before kings are later and depend on the framework of tribes already developed for Israel. Finally, while the narratives accumulated around David must ultimately have been preserved in Jerusalem for what became the kingdom of Judah, even these originally defined his rule entirely in terms of Israel, without reference to a separate people of Judah.[30]

This hypothesis regarding the biblical portrayal of the distant past has a corollary:

> *All primary phases of the Bible's account of the past before David originate in Israel and reflect Israel's political perspective.*

---

[29] The Enuma elish explains in one system the creation, or perhaps reordering, of the world, as an expression of the sovereignty of Marduk as king of the gods, after his defeat of the sea-goddess Tiamat and her army of lesser deities and monsters. After Marduk has arranged the celestial bodies to mark the basic structures of time, and he has taken advantage of Tiamat's carcass to organize the waters that provide for the earth, he is honored as king and proceeds to build Babylon as his own residence, along with a temple there as his palace (Tablet VI).

[30] Thus, in recognizing the unexpected role for a competing people of Judah in the tale of Absalom's revolt, Kratz resolves the problem by concluding that the entire narrative must derive from a time after Israel's fall, pushing the core David story to an implausibly late date. I will propose in Chapter 6 that a more workable solution is to reserve an earlier date for the David story and to explain Judah's role as a later addition.

These phases would include:

- explanation of identity by genealogy, especially as sons of one father, Jacob;
- escape from Egypt under the leadership of Moses;
- Joshua's leadership in establishing initial hegemony in the land;
- extended life in the land under decentralized political conditions, without kings; and
- Saul as the first successful king of Israel.

I have rendered these phases in terms that already reflect some development, as with Joshua and "hegemony" and Saul as king, a title that may come to us only as part of a package designed to defend David's right to the office. All of them, however, are derived directly from Israelite stories. In the process of adaptation to new schemes, the Israelite narrative starting points were transformed in various ways, in part to suit the schematization required for creation of a connected story. My corollary is intended to be adaptable, with room for the possibility of other Israelite components. It nevertheless requires at least this essential set in order to have significant explanatory value.

Beyond this list, a wide range of associated material has less certain Israelite origin, to my eye. Most likely, the prelude to the ancestors in Genesis 1–11 comes into the Bible by way of Judah and Jerusalem, as suggested by the similarity of sacrificial language in the non-priestly flood text of Gen. 8:20–1 to standard terminology from Leviticus and Ezekiel. This narrative combination, if it is old, does not address "this people's existence before and apart from kings" and is rather concerned with beginnings – again, like the Enuma elish.[31] The larger genealogical relationships defined with Abraham and Lot, and with Isaac and Esau, are often treated as from Judah, because Abraham and Isaac have southern geographical associations with Hebron and Beersheba. Various solutions could account for these figures, including old southern lore not originally defined to account for peoples of either Israel or Judah; later stories created to imitate the Jacob ancestor type; or even that these stories are also Israelite, and the southern sites have no particular association with Judah or the southern kingdom as a separate entity after Solomon. The mountain of God may appear first in Israelite tradition in connection with the escape from Egypt, but no part of the law is clearly associated with Israel rather than Judah.[32] Most of the "conquest" vision in Joshua is driven by a Judah-centered perspective, though its object is defined as Israel and encompasses the most ambitious Israelite territorial claims, including a large region east of the Jordan River. Every sentence in this paragraph should raise enormous

---

[31] As mentioned earlier, David Carr (2011, 456–69) makes a case for the very early origin of a combination that included the stories of Eden, Cain and Abel, and the Flood.

[32] This material represents a huge realm for exploration in these terms. Much depends on the origins of the instructional core of Deuteronomy, as well as its relationship to Exodus 20–3. On the basic problem, see Levinson (1997).

questions and challenges, yet none of these questions should undermine the hypothesis proposed here. As I see it, all of the Judahite contributions to the Torah, Joshua, and Judges work from a framework that derives ultimately from Israel. In the individual chapters of Part II, I explore individual texts that provide a test for both the hypothesis and its corollary, although their viability will finally depend on work far beyond my own.

D. Israel without Judah in History

This study of Israel's "legacy" in Judah's Bible involves literary history in a way that contrasts somewhat with what often comes to be its standard practice. My goal is not to account for the finished forms of each biblical text in question by tracing a full process of transformation through specific stages of redaction that lead to the existing text. It is not even clear that the transmission process can be treated as if each stage took place through the copying and alteration of individual manuscripts. Especially in the earlier phases of transmission, texts may have existed in considerable variation, and production of new manuscripts may generally have depended on writing from memory, without conscious reproduction of the previous text word by word, even when the text was known well enough to do so if desired.[33] Rather, while acknowledging the reality that most biblical texts changed significantly through time, I seek to probe the historical contexts for the earlier phases of their transmission in order to sharpen our reading of the Bible's primary narrative in light of historical questions. Unavoidably, therefore, my search to isolate Israel from Judah in the settings for creation and transmission of biblical texts involves historical concerns at every point.

The historical dimension of this literary-historical study must be part of a dialogue, not a one-way interrogation. We need to know more than just where to put biblical content in history; it is equally important to consider how that content contributes to the historical record, the basis for reconstructing history. This question of the Bible's historical utility is more pressing than ever in current discussion, when archaeological finds have taken center stage in historical reconstruction, even as the biblical narrative cannot quite be forgotten. When archaeologists oversimplify the biblical material as deriving from the seventh century or as postexilic, they give up the opportunity to interact with the Bible

---

[33] The premise of David Carr's *Writing on the Tablet of the Heart* (2005) is the probability of copying by memory rather than by sight. Carr argues that this method continued beyond the biblical period into late antiquity, even as expectations of copying shifted toward an ideal of word-for-word or letter-for-letter reproduction. In earlier periods, however, the relative fluidity of textual reproduction seems to be related to a distinct idea of what memorization demanded, with specific words less important than a firm grasp of content. Carr's approach is based to a significant degree on recent work on cuneiform literature, especially from the richly documented Old Babylonian period (early second millennium). For an argument in favor of learning and reproduction of literary texts by memorization, see Paul Delnero (2010). In her New York University Ph.D. dissertation, Sara Milstein (2010) seeks a more fully developed method for applying the insights of Mesopotamian cuneiform literature to the problem of textual revision in the Bible.

in more nuanced terms. While such nuanced interaction has always been available through detailed literary-historical analysis of the Bible, the relationship of the Bible to history has most often been cast in terms of "historicity," the ratification or repudiation of stories as such. By focus on Israel and Judah as the primary division among settings for biblical writing, I mean to shift the direction of historical inquiry back toward history itself. Instead of beginning with the question of whether a given biblical narrative or picture is accurate and therefore useful for history, we can follow the archaeologists and let the historical questions come first. The following offer just a sampling.

What was going on in southern Palestine at the end of the Late Bronze Age, and how does the entity called Israel in Egypt's Merenptah Stela fit in? The transitional period of the Iron Age I has been thoroughly excavated yet is little documented in written sources. We know that Egypt withdrew from the region during the middle of the twelfth century and that the Philistines arrived some time during this period. By the start of the first millennium, the great Phoenician cities of Tyre and Sidon had established themselves as centers of influence. Inland, the situation is harder to follow. In the ninth century, we find kingdoms of some scope, including the Aramean polity based at Damascus, Israel of Omri and Ahab, the House of David, and Mesha's Moab, along with other groups encountered by the Assyrians. Even this list is prejudiced by interest in the Bible's world. By the ninth century, both Israel and the House of David are kingdoms, but there is no reason to assume the same for Egypt's earlier encounter with Israel. How did Israel become a kingdom, and what is the relationship between the kingdom and an older entity by the same name? The House of David is a separate case: When did it come to be called Judah, and what was its early relationship to Israel? Was there an entity called Judah before the House of David came to be identified with this name?

These questions focus on the earlier periods of Israel's and Judah's existence, in parallel with the Bible's primary narrative, which attends above all to the origins and early life of Israel, including the founding of its monarchy and its supposed division into two kingdoms. I have asked little about religion or culture or the movement of population or a host of social and economic issues, in favor of attention to basic political layout, the broad limbs of a landscape, partly to emphasize how little we know securely. Also, I have chosen questions for which the Bible does offer several concrete answers, within a well-known framework. Israel began as outsiders who had a tradition of moving their flocks and herds in a region that the Bible sometimes calls Canaan. They established a permanent presence by displacing the various indigenous populations of Canaan, who were either killed or subjugated. The primary identity of this new people is considered to be Israel, although various named groups belonged to the larger entity, including a group called Judah. Israel existed for some time without kings, so that identification as a monarchy is presented as a novelty, not something intrinsic to Israelite identity. David and his house originally ruled Israel, and the isolation of David's royal line in a southern realm called Judah only follows the failure of one descendant, Rehoboam, to maintain support from Israel as a whole.

If we begin with the historical questions, rather than simply asking whether the biblical narrative is "historical" or has a high "historicity" quotient, it remains to be considered whether the Bible provides usable historical evidence in any terms. I conclude that biblical narrative can be useful for historical reconstruction in fresh ways if we focus on the settings for the production and transmission of texts, and on how these settings allow older traditions to remain in continuous circulation. Because the Bible ultimately served the people of Judah as they grappled with the dissolution of their kingdom and the possibility of maintaining an identity on other terms, all of its contents have been filtered through Judahite assumptions. Yet this Jewish Bible gives pride of place to a long account of the past that revolves around the origins and early life of Israel, an anomaly that immediately raises the possibility that Judah took over a heritage that came from an entity called Israel. If so, everything in the narrative from Genesis through Kings is liable to include two types of material: content that derives from settings in Israel that relate directly to Israel as the object of interest, and content that reflects the adaptation of Israelite lore so as to account for Judah's connection to this past. None of this material need be simplistically "historical," as if it were a report of circumstances to take at face value, and the historical implications of each biblical text will vary individually.

When we ask historical questions about Israel, however – the Bible's own narrative preoccupation – content from settings in Israel puts us one step closer to its subject. Without Judah's effort to explain Israel as part of its own past, the Israelite content is more directly indigenous, an internal effort to account for a people's own character. For historical questions about early Israel, the Israelite content in the Bible at least offers an insider's view. Its assumptions about Israel's political landscape may be rooted in the experience of those structures, or at least in the direct memory of them. Israelite material in the Bible may still stand at great distance in time from the events and settings that it portrays. Just as writing about the kingdom of Judah comes both from the monarchy itself and from generations after its demise, we may have to take into account a postmonarchic Israelite community, whether still in its old territory or as fugitives in Judah. The historical significance of such writing lies not in its absolute date but in its continuity with Israelite society and culture. Embedded in Israel's own lore may be perspectives on its identity and past that contrast with what we receive through Judah's points of view.

When archaeologists and historians speak of the Bible's seventh-century perspective, they refer in fact to the perspective of Judahite scribes after the fall of the Israelite kingdom. The seventh century is indeed far removed in time from events described for David and earlier, but a deeper and unrecognized obstacle may be that scribes from Judah are explaining the heritage of Israel, a separate polity and distinct people. Where it is possible to isolate Israelite content from its Judah-based revision, this material can offer concepts for historical evaluation that are quite different from what is often called the biblical view. For example, the standard scheme of a united monarchy, followed by the secession of the north from David's royal house, ignores the simple continuity of the people governed by Saul, David, and Solomon with the Israel ruled by

Jeroboam, Omri, and Jehu. Judah is the outlier, requiring special explanation. Such an Israel began as an association of peoples not organized as a kingdom, and its monarchy represents a transition, built onto a political tradition that did not require the fixed institution of kingship. Kings had to deal with the prior structures, to win their support, to undermine their power, or to put them out of business – but nevertheless to acknowledge them. Set against the modern chronologies of archaeology, this picture of Israel would reach back into the Iron Age I, into the period without written evidence, without independent reference to the reigns of David or Solomon. We cannot read it directly as history; yet the picture contrasts with Judah's claim to represent Israel itself, as the fraction of this people still devoted to David's royal house. It is in large part the notion of a united monarchy that invites us to regard Israel and Judah as one people, a single cultural unit even for archaeological interpretation, a single ethnicity for the question of origins. If we let the Israelite voices of the Bible speak for themselves, so far as we can isolate them, we confront a distinct and sometimes novel biblical perspective for historical evaluation. The result can be historically relevant in ways not previously anticipated.

With his provocative book, *In Search of "Ancient Israel"* (1992), Philip Davies introduced a compelling contrast between "biblical Israel" and "historical Israel," where little connection could be found between the two. If "ancient Israel" is the objective, Davies is correct that one will reach entirely different destinations if one lets the Bible itself define the terms, as opposed to making history as such the framework. This dualism, however, is unsatisfying for both biblical and historical interpretation. A search for early Israel in history is impoverished by the outright exclusion of the Bible as potential evidence. Even if not one of the Bible's accounts of early events and characters had any basis in fact, its texts could still offer important historical information through the writing that expresses Israelite notions of who these people were. The key would be to determine what in the Bible belongs to Israel, as opposed to Judah, and then to define the historical questions that could be illuminated by this Israelite content. At the same time, readers of the Bible who mean to understand its rendition of the past will not want to bypass any hope of historical context for this literature. Even the contrasting political frameworks still visible for Judah and Israel in the biblical narrative suggest some historical connection, a basis in the structures of the two kingdoms themselves. When we isolate Israel's legacy within Judah's Bible – the larger work arranged for us by people from the sphere of Judah – we improve the prospects for fruitful conversation between biblical and historical investigations. On both counts, we gain by trying to understand what Israelites themselves thought of their past, as it is embedded in biblical writing.

E. Texts for Closer Study

In choosing a structure for the reasoning advanced in this book, I have given priority to a review of certain biblical texts. My starting point for investigating this "legacy of Israel" is the Bible's portrayal of early Israel as a collected body, an active political entity that preceded kings and that could negotiate with them. I then intend to reflect on Israel's place in the history of the southern Levant, working from categories and ideas that belong to the Israelite content in the Bible. The historical discussion and wider concern for patterns in ancient politics depend directly on the notion that the Bible offers this resource, and I want readers to grapple with some specific textual evidence before moving to questions of history and society.

To begin a case for this approach, I have chosen a relatively small number of biblical texts from different sections of the primary narrative, each of which represents a different aspect of Israelite material. In some cases, my conclusion that a text has an Israelite foundation will be uncontroversial, as with examples from the book of Judges; in at least the case of the eastern conquest in Deuteronomy 2–3, I advance an unconventional proposal, and my choice of this text reflects that novelty, even as it serves a need to explore the Moses material. Before beginning my selection of Israelite samples, I devote brief attention to Judah (Chapter 3). My goal in that chapter is mainly to develop the contrast between how Israel is understood in Israelite and Judahite settings, as well as to show how Judah's political heritage, with Jerusalem as a powerful center for royal authority and prestige, could influence perceptions of an Israelite past.

Once I move to texts based on Israelite material, I organize these by type rather than in narrative sequence. I begin with texts from Judges and Genesis that reflect a tradition of Israel as an association of distinct peoples, sometimes defined as tribes. These represent an aspect of the narrative that can be evaluated in political terms, not just by geography. It is rooted in an understanding about the nature of Israel as it inhabited the land, unrelated to what are gathered as origins stories in Genesis through Joshua. The Judges stories are thus central to the whole project and a point of departure, not because they are the best or clearest examples of Israelite content, but because they represent a combination of a uniquely Israelite political order and a vision of Israel before monarchy. Judah has no counterpart to this. Then, in the Jacob story of Genesis, one major purpose is to account for the relationship between the various peoples of Israel in terms of kinship, as sons of one father. Where the Judges stories generally take the plurality of Israelite peoples for granted, without effort to explain the basis for their affiliation, this tribal scheme takes on the explanatory task and even offers a particular hierarchy of status by factors of birth order and mother. Together, the accounts of collaboration and conflict between Israelite peoples and the kinship system of Jacob's family display a decentralized political life in which no one group, location, or elite can dominate a larger Israelite whole. This political composition of multiple peers has no counterpart in Judah and presents the most striking contrast between Israel and Judah in political terms.

Even when Israel is treated as a single unit, however, the collective power of that unit as distinct from individual leaders is sometimes vividly portrayed. For this material, I begin once again with texts that involve life in the land, where the political picture derives most directly from experience, without narrative extrapolation to a time of origins. For reasons that appear to reflect a later, though perhaps still Israelite, sense of history, the editors have gathered the stories of Israel's separate peoples into what is now the book of Judges, the repository of tales from before monarchy. Likewise, the institution of kingship is defined against a coherent population that must agree to be ruled, and the political life of this population is generally rendered in terms of Israel, even when loyalties are divided, as in the war between Omri and Tibni (1 Kings 16:21–2).[34] As a body that interacts with its kings, Israel as a political collective is most clearly visible in the narratives of Omri and David. The former is short, though striking in its portrayal of the collective. The latter is much longer and attracts much more scholarly attention. It is not Israelite in the sense that I have defined this, but in the probable antiquity of its core, it is likewise not Judahite, and it preserves striking renditions of Israel as political body.

Only after I treat these biblical accounts of collective Israel under kings do I turn to what are now origins stories in the books of Exodus through Joshua. Among these, I have chosen to delve more deeply into two tales that may not have begun as origins stories, or at least not in terms of Israel's first existence. Both Moses and Joshua are presented as military leaders under whom Yahweh allows his people to establish themselves in a specific land, in one case east of the Jordan River, and in the other case in the territory of Ai. I reserve the case of Benjamin for last, with its strange juxtaposition of all-out war between this people and Israel, followed by the emergence of Saul as Israel's first king from the group that had just been brought to the verge of annihilation. This unique literary combination, which may once have belonged to a single narrative, is now divided between the books of Judges and Samuel.[35]

I understand all of these texts to have originated in Israelite settings before they were combined with other stories to serve various new visions of the past, some from Israel itself and some from Judah, with varying degrees of certainty. What is crucial is that each one preserves aspects of a political experience that appears to have been foreign to Judah, and these political images are of substantial historical interest. My sampling of texts is incomplete, but it will illustrate the analysis that undergirds my hypothesis of Israel's core contribution to the Bible's primary narrative. From this foundation we will be able to turn to larger questions of politics and history.

---

[34] The one narrative exception to this pattern is the statement that Ishbosheth son of Saul was king over Gilead, the Ashurites, Jezreel, Ephraim, and Benjamin (2 Sam. 2:9).

[35] This is proposed by Milstein (2010), chapter 4.

PART II

ISRAELITE CONTENT IN THE BIBLE

3

Writing from Judah

It is common in modern technical parlance to divide biblical writing by the exile, the devastating blow that brought an end to the institutions of Jerusalem status and authority: the ruling house of David and the temple of Yahweh. Relatively early texts are "preexilic," often revised for "postexilic" needs, with the relative balance between these categories a matter of debate. Although there is increasing attention paid to the activity of scribes from the kingdom of Israel and its survivors, references to preexilic writing often have in mind Judah of the seventh century, during the reigns of Hezekiah, Manasseh, and Josiah. Indeed, these were the glory days of the kingdom of Judah, as reflected in the massive growth of Jerusalem during the eighth century (e.g., Na'aman 2007b), and the situation in this period may have influenced greatly both the production of texts and their political assumptions.[1] At this point, it is clear that the kingdom was called Judah, and our biblical portrait of Judah's monarchic politics appears to derive mainly from this later stage of the monarchy.

According to 2 Samuel 5, Jerusalem first became a capital city for the royal house of David with David himself, when he made it the base from which he ruled Israel. After having established this political center, David is said to have brought the ark of God to Jerusalem, thus combining political with sacred status (2 Samuel 6). Solomon is then envisioned to have consolidated this powerful pairing by constructing a monumental-scale palace and temple (1 Kings 6–7). Nothing in the remaining text of Kings hints that this combination of authorities entered Jerusalem at a later date, such as with the city's success in the eighth century, when the kingdom became a large-scale polity

---

[1] William Schniedewind (2004) may overstate the argument for the production of significant writing only in what he defines as mature "state" societies, but there is certainly a strong connection between these phenomena. "Writing was not unknown in early Israel, but the level and sophistication of early Israelite literature was necessarily tied to the development of the state" (p. 49). The moment when an otherwise oral lore was cast in writing came with urbanization in the eighth century (p. 63, and chapters 5 and 6).

that some would call a "state." We must therefore beware of attributing this centralization only to Judah's growth. We will return to the question of the early kingdom and Jerusalem; our biblical evidence is concentrated in texts occupied with David, Solomon, and Rehoboam's establishment of a new kingdom in 1 Kings 12. Recognizing this limitation, my objective here is to give a sense of Judahite political perspectives as displayed in a range of texts both during and after the monarchy.

A. Judah in Kings: The Primary Narrative

Judah appears in the Bible's primary narrative as a fully operational polity only in 1 Kings 12, when Rehoboam retreats to Jerusalem and begins rule of a small southern realm.[2] In the refrains that structure the remaining account of the two kingdoms, Rehoboam's domain is called "Judah" (1 Kings 14:21, 29), though this convention clearly belongs to a collection from a much later date. Throughout, we are dealing with some combination of later collecting and sources of uncertain character. Nevertheless, notable patterns emerge that suggest a contrast with Israel.

1. Jerusalem as Capital and Sacred Center

Jerusalem's position as both royal seat and location of Yahweh's primary temple is repeated often through the books of Kings, as well as in the prophetic books. The entire scheme of royal critique in the books of Kings, however it relates to deuteronomistic writing, may assume the geographical collocation of palace and temple.[3] Throughout the books of Kings, rulers are held responsible for the religious choices of the people as a whole. For Judah itself, the standard is David; after the people have introduced all sorts of religious abominations under Rehoboam (1 Kings 14:22–4), Asa is credited with their removal. "Asa did what was right in the eyes of Yahweh, like his father David" (15:11).[4] The same religious leadership is assumed for Israel, however, evidently in imitation of the Jerusalem norm. Jeroboam I consolidates his power after the removal

---

[2] Judah's role in the David narrative will be addressed with that king in Chapter 6.

[3] The scheme of evaluating kings as good or bad is essential to the narrative structure in the books of Kings and does not involve directly the larger storyline from Joshua, Judges, and 1 and 2 Samuel. If it is "deuteronomistic," then it is limited to this block of time and the limited period of the two kingdoms, not applied to Saul, David, and Solomon. Some have attributed it to a Judah writer either in the time of Hezekiah or inspired by that king: see Weippert (1972), Weippert (1973), Barrick (1974), Mayes (1983), Lemaire (1986), and Provan (1988). For review of the more recent literature from a perspective open to a predeuteronomistic composition in the books of Kings, see Hutton (2009, 102–12).

[4] See also 2 Kings 14:3 (Amaziah); 16:2 (Ahaz); 18:3 (Hezekiah); 22:2 (Josiah). When kings of Judah go astray, they are likewise considered to follow some prior model. In some cases, this is not even a king from David's line but is rather Ahab, the notorious husband of Jezebel, son of Omri: Joram son of Jehoshaphat, who married a daughter of Ahab (2 Kings 8:18); Ahaziah son of Joram, from the same tie by marriage (8:27); and more surprisingly, Manasseh son of Hezekiah (21:3).

of Rehoboam by initiating changes in religious practices (1 Kings 12:25–33), and the prophet Ahijah condemns him for failing to imitate David's example (14:8). The calf images of Jeroboam then become the basis for condemnation of all Israelite rulers on religious grounds.[5]

Although comparison to David and Jeroboam serves an editorial framework that can sometimes stand in stark tension with the contents of individual royal narratives, the assumption that all kings serve as the ultimate religious leaders may reflect the political perspective of Judah. The most striking case is that of Jehu, who seizes power in a bloodbath and then turns his violence against all who support the worship of Baal (2 Kings 9–10). In the account of Jehu's religious purge in Israel (chapter 10), the temple of Baal is placed in Samaria, and Baal's sacred personnel are killed by gathering them to this temple in the capital. Such centralization may reflect a Judahite framework and perspective, although this part of the Jehu text is separate from the scheme of faithful and unfaithful kings.[6] For comparison, the books of Hosea and Amos show what criticism of Israel could look like, and they spread political responsibility more broadly.[7]

Individual stories in the books of Kings include repeated allusions to rulers who stave off foreign threats with payments from temple wealth. Shishak carries away loot from both temple and palace, and Rehoboam has to replace Solomon's golden shields with bronze, which are used every time he enters the temple (1 Kings 14:26–8). The same liberty with temple wealth is exercised by Asa, who offers silver and gold from both temple and palace to Ben-Hadad of Damascus in return for a treaty (1 Kings 15:18). Amaziah loses similar treasure from both domains to Jehoash of Israel (2 Kings 14:14), and Hezekiah's tribute to Sennacherib of Assyria likewise includes gold and silver from the temple, along with precious metals from the palace (2 Kings 18:15–16). Regardless of which valuables actually changed hands in which periods, the combination is a theme of the Kings collection, always with reference to Judah and Jerusalem, in writing that must originate in Judah.

The close association of king and temple is also taken for granted in accounts of specific events. One instance that is recounted in detail is the accession to the throne of Joash as a child, under the sponsorship of the priest Jehoiada, in

---

[5] See 1 Kings 15:26 (Nadab); 15:34 (Baasha); 16:7 (the house of Baasha/Elah); 16:19 (Zimri, though he only reigns seven days!); 16:26 (Omri); 16:31 (Ahab, adding the evil of Jezebel); 22:53 (Ahaziah); 2 Kings 3:3 (Jehoram); 10:29 (Jehu, in spite of his campaign against Baal); 13:2, 6 (Jehoahaz); 13:11 (Jehoash); 14:24 (Jeroboam II); 15:9 (Zechariah); 15:18 (Menahem); 15:24 (Pekahiah); and 15:28 (Pekah).

[6] I am aware of no excavated evidence for a temple of Baal at Samaria, although we cannot count on such an argument from silence. One possibility is that Judahite writers assume one there, without direct knowledge.

[7] Peter Machinist (2005, 162–3) observes that in Hosea, prophetic blame is put on the people as a whole, rather than just on the king and his circle (8:4; 10:1–4; 13:10–11). Israel is pictured as installing kings and their officials in the face of Yahweh's anger (8:4; 13:9–11). Altogether, the prophet is troubled by more than problems with any individual king, and this suggests a difficulty with monarchic power as a whole (p. 174).

2 Kings 11–12. Joash is hidden from his murderous grandmother Athaliah in the temple (11:3), which becomes both a potential rival to the palace in political power and a natural support for any royal claim. Although a priest, Jehoiada commands guards who serve the monarchy and recruits them to back the young claimant to the throne (11:4–11). Joash is revealed at the temple, then crowned there, and so far as there is collective acclamation, it consists purely of congregants at the temple (11:12). The palace is so close to the temple that Athaliah hears the noise and can see the young king standing by the temple pillar according to standard practice (11:13–14). Joash is then portrayed as supporting temple renovation by authorizing a special fund-raising program (12:4–5). Whatever the date of this text, the description of temple and palace in proximity reflects the plan of Jerusalem's acropolis.[8] The same concentration of sacred and royal power at the center of Jerusalem is assumed in other biblical writing about the monarchic period.[9]

Jerusalem offers a unique tension between biblical content and the possibility of evidence from archaeology. The city often stands at the very center of the Bible's view, yet the Temple Mount is inaccessible to excavation, and much of the early city is covered by the contemporary Old City. There is little doubt that by the middle of the eighth century, Jerusalem had expanded into a major residential city. The Bible's accounts of David and Solomon have inspired a constant stream of debate over Jerusalem in the tenth century, which at least

---

[8] Although Christoph Levin (1982) proposed the isolation of a core narrative that reduces the attention to Jehoiada and the temple, the combination of priests and military personnel in a geography that juxtaposes temple and palace seems essential to the narrative, whatever its date. The question of whether Athaliah's execution was originally joined to Joash's accession is not crucial, though the combination assumes the proximity of palace to temple (see Long 1991, 146–7). Both parts of the narrative depend on familiarity with the configuration of Jerusalem during the monarchy, as is widely supposed. See the readings of Volkmar Fritz (2003, 296–300), who follows Levin yet accepts the cluster of temple and palace, priest and king, as basic; and Marvin A. Sweeney (2007, 342–3), who emphasizes the story's contribution to a Hezekian version of the whole royal history, emphasizing the instability of Judah after Jehu's coup, with the constant presence of David's house as the unspoken alternative. In an early article, Mario Liverani (1974) proposed an underlying ninth-century piece of propaganda for the legitimacy of the regime, based on comparison with the Idrimi inscription from Alalakh and the apology of Hattushili III; and see the extended study of the text as (Judahite) "political rhetoric" by Patricia Dutcher-Walls (1996). Other accounts of individual rulers combine the interests of king and temple. Hezekiah prays in the temple for deliverance from the Assyrian siege (2 Kings 19:1–2). Manasseh makes additions to temple worship, although the writer does not approve (2 Kings 21). Josiah's reforms begin with temple renovation (2 Kings 22:4–5), and his cult purification starts by removing items from the temple (2 Kings 23:4–7).

[9] For example, Isaiah receives his calling at the temple and can meet the king face-to-face in Jerusalem (Isa. 6–7); for an eighth-century setting, see Roberts (2005). According to Psalm 78, Yahweh's choice of Judah over Joseph and Ephraim includes Mount Zion, where he "built his sanctuary" (vv. 67–9), and David as shepherd (vv. 70–2). Frank-Lothar Hossfeld (in Hossfeld and Zenger 2005, 290–2) concludes that the primary text of Psalm 78, including this closing section, must reflect Jerusalem and Judah under active monarchy, because there is reference neither to demise nor to doing wrong, in contrast to the other kingdom.

seems to have been much smaller than the eighth-century center.[10] Regardless of how Solomon's capital fares in ongoing debate and research, there is a possibility that Jerusalem began to expand into a commercial hub with some residential base during the ninth century (Na'aman 2007b; Reich et al. 2008).[11] If Jerusalem had a prominent urban role during the period before this, both in the tenth century and back to the Late Bronze Age, it would have been as an administrative center without significant residential population.[12] Whether or not such a city could have sustained a substantial scribal culture, the Bible shows little sign of having been shaped by the perspective of Jerusalem from this early period.

2. The House of David

The most obvious contrast between the kingdoms of Israel and Judah is the maintenance of one royal house through all the centuries of Judah's monarchy. This consistency can give the false impression that succession was straightforward in a stable framework. The tale of David's immediate succession sets a norm for the whole account of Judah through the books of Kings: there is plenty of room for competition and bloodshed, but the successful nominee must have a claim to descent from David (1 Kings 1–2). Jehoiada's advocacy for the boy Joash suggests the same pattern. Although he commanded a force adequate to stage a coup against the queen Athaliah, without a personal basis for claiming descent from David, he had to work through a plausible heir. In simple terms, a powerful priest produces a boy who appears to be just older than the length of Athaliah's reign and who declares that she is a usurper. Whether or not the boy's identity must be accepted, the queen's overthrow was possible only with the link to David's house. Jehoiada himself is understood to have no imaginable basis for setting himself up as king.[13]

The persistence of David's house in Judah's monarchy must not be equated with political stability. Rather, it expresses a particular configuration of power, based on a particular royal ideology. Another illustration of the power in this

---

[10] A useful starting place is the collection of articles in Vaughn and Killebrew (2003), including those by Cahill, Finkelstein, Killebrew, Lehmann, Reich and Shukron, Schniedewind, Steiner, and Ussishkin.

[11] This is a matter of dispute between Na'aman (2009a) and Finkelstein (2008), the latter of whom doubts that Jerusalem had developed any significant population before the first impact of the Assyrian empire. The question is historically important but not crucial for the interpretations advanced here.

[12] This is the interpretation advocated by Uriel and Shai (2007); Jerusalem was "a royal-cultic center, purposely separated from a large population of residents" (p. 162). One basis for pushing the notion of a Jerusalem-based kingdom back to the late tenth century is the detailed chronological framework provided for the kings of Israel and Judah, which provides exact dates that go back to Jeroboam I and Rehoboam (1 Kings 14).

[13] Joash is often found to be a less than credible candidate for kingship, and other historical explanations for the story have been proposed, even with acceptance of its relative antiquity. Liverani (1974) suggested that Joash may have been the son of Jehoiada, who was the husband of king Ahaziah's sister; cf. Ahlström (1993, 600).

idea is found in the descent from Joash. Amaziah becomes king after his father Joash is assassinated by two of his officials (2 Kings 12:20–1). After a reign of 29 years, Amaziah is killed in his turn, this time based on what seems to be widespread opposition to his rule. Some unnamed group plots against him in Jerusalem, and the king's support is so reduced that he flees to Lachish, where he is killed by men sent from Jerusalem (14:19). "All the people of Judah" then make his sixteen-year-old son Azariah king in his place, with no further reference to those responsible for his father's demise. This seems to have been a coup with considerable support, or at least ineffectual opposition, yet the future must lie with the dead king's own son, and no claim to found a new royal house is conceivable.

The accounts of Joash, Amaziah, and Azariah treat the period before Tiglath-pileser III appears on the scene in the mid-eighth century, before transformation into the large-scale entity that the Assyrians knew as Judah. It is not certain how the kingdom was named before the eighth century, and the books of Kings preserve only glimpses of its political life, still under the stock terminology of Judah. Whatever the kingdom's identity in the ninth century, when the Arameans referred to it only by its ruling House of David (Chapter 15), this royal ideology of a single dynastic line seems to have survived all the external threats and internal changes from the tenth century through the end of the monarchy. David's right to rule was somehow intrinsic to the very existence of the realm, and any political novelty had to be accommodated to this starting point.

3. No Union of Political Constituents

Israel's tradition of tribes has no counterpart in Judah, according to Judahite writing in the Bible. The only view of Judah as a kingdom before the Assyrian conquest comes from 1 and 2 Kings, and in this material it is difficult to be sure what reflects earlier or later perspectives. Details from this material focus more on towns than on bodies defined by region or kinship. During the early ninth century, Asa fortifies Ramah, north of Jerusalem, as an extension of Jerusalem authority (1 Kings 15:17). Later in that century, Libnah rebels against Judah during the reign of Jehoram (2 Kings 8:22).[14] Libnah is mentioned again as Sennacherib's target in 701, after Lachish, which becomes his base of operations (2 Kings 19:8; cf. 18:14). In the late ninth century, Lachish is Amaziah's destination when he flees Jerusalem (2 Kings 14:19), and Amaziah is on the losing end of a battle with Israel that takes place at Beth Shemesh (vv. 11, 13). Libnah, Lachish, and Beth Shemesh are all in the western foothills, which represent a distinct region that could be ruled by the house of David, without being part of the "Judah highlands" (*har yĕhûdâ*). Finally, Judah has access to the sea through Elath (2 Kings 14:22; Azariah, late ninth century), which

---

[14] Libnah is in the Shephelah between Lachish and Gath, a border town at the edge of Philistine dominion. Ron Tappy, the excavator of Tel Zayit, considers Libnah a possible identification for his site, which has significant Late Bronze occupation (2008, 11).

is lost to Edom in the eighth century (2 Kings 16:6; Ahaz).[15] In all of 1 and 2 Kings, Libnah's revolt is the only act of distinct political will depicted for any entity within the realm of Judah, and it is set before the arrival of the Assyrians and the accompanying transformation of Judah. No biblical text envisions a town giving up affiliation with Judah during the period of Assyrian hegemony, so the political assumptions inherent to the Libnah crisis could reflect earlier conditions.

4. Collective Participation Defined by the Jerusalem Center

Collective political activity is not restricted to Israel. In Judah, however, group participation in leadership and decision-making is always defined by location at Jerusalem, especially through service at the palace or assembly at the temple, the two dominant institutions of Judah's centralizing structure. Therefore, collective activity as such does not distinguish Israel from Judah; rather, it is the dependence of the collective on the political center that sets Judah apart.[16] As with the preceding features of Judah's political character, it is difficult to isolate evidence for Judah before the Assyrian intrusion. There are striking continuities in the ruling house of David and the collocation of palace and temple in Jerusalem, yet the city grew remarkably in the eighth century, before the arrival of the Assyrians, which then contributed to changes already under way.[17] Almost all the evidence for collective involvement by the populace belongs to the late monarchy, which raises the possibility that these biblical references reflect real political innovation accompanying the growth of Jerusalem as center of Judah's emergent large-scale polity in the eighth and seventh centuries.[18]

[15] Mothers of royal offspring are often identified by their place of origin. Excluding Jerusalem, these include Zibiah from Beersheba (Joash, 2 Kings 12:1), Jedidah from Bozkath in the Shephelah (Josiah, 2 Kings 22:1), and Hamutal from Libnah (Jehoahaz and Zedekiah, 2 Kings 23:31; 24:18).

[16] One expression of collective authority in biblical writing deserves mention here, although its definition at the town level excludes it from any contribution to the larger governance of Israel or Judah as a whole. In his detailed study of the town elders in Deuteronomy, Timothy M. Willis (2001, 308–12) observes that most of the texts involving elders have been expanded to make them more "national," which he understands to reflect a late monarchic setting in Judah. Willis considers the original versions of these laws in Deuteronomy to have a more local interest, which he (tentatively) suggests may reflect their origin in the kingdom of Israel. One could equally envision a local tradition in late monarchic Judah that was revised to suit developing concerns within that realm or even after its demise.

[17] Baruch Halpern (1991) develops the profound impact of Assyrian presence on the social and economic structures of Judah in the seventh century.

[18] In contrast, portrayals of dominating centralization driven by the palace are entirely set in the pre-Assyrian era. After David's census (2 Sam. 24; 1 Chron. 21) and Solomon's administration and forced labor (1 Kings 4 and 9), there are few references to the separate kingdom of Judah. Asa fortifies Ramah, Geba, and Mizpah against Israel by the labor of "all Judah – no one was exempt" (1 Kings 15:22; tenth/ninth century). Two texts from Chronicles address royal acts of administration: Jehoshaphat keeps a standing army in Jerusalem and stations further troops in

In the books of Kings, accounts of group-oriented action are clustered almost entirely in the last generation of Judah's monarchy.[19] After the murder of his brother Amon, Josiah is placed on the throne by "the people of the land" (*'am hā'āreṣ*, 2 Kings 21:24). The same group is given responsibility for the accession of Jehoahaz as his successor (23:30). His brother Jehoiakim is set up by the Egyptians in his place, and has to raise tribute from the *'am hā'āreṣ* in order to meet Egypt's demands (23:35). Picking up Talmon's observation that the group's actions are always concentrated in Jerusalem, Christopher Seitz proposes that this is the refugee population of the larger kingdom, which flooded the city after Sennacherib's campaign in 701.[20] Such a model would also work with Na'aman's argument that refugees came from Judah, not Israel.[21] From the Jerusalemite perspective of the authors of Kings, according to Seitz, these were to be distinguished from the longstanding populace. While Seitz's interpretation may be untenably precise, the inclusive language as the "land" and use at Jerusalem suggests an application of the phrase to just that combination of the gathered populace in the presence of Jerusalem authority.[22] Before the collapse of Israel and Sennacherib's devastation of Judah, king Ahaz of Judah is said to have been inspired to commission an altar like the one he saw in Damascus while meeting Tiglath-pileser (III) of Assyria (2 Kings 16:10–16). This altar would receive both the burnt offering of the king and those of "the people of the land" (*'am hā'āreṣ*, v. 15). None of this evidence offers a compelling basis for locating this phenomenon before the growth of Jerusalem in the eighth century. In this late monarchic setting, "the people of the land" present a novel and striking collective in Judah's political life, even as they remain defined strictly by the centrality of Jerusalem as the political and religious capital of the realm.

In light of the above discussion, it is possible therefore that the kingdom based at Jerusalem developed new roles for collaborative political life in the eighth century, roles that were based on the presence of large numbers in the city proper. Such a vision of Jerusalem as not merely open to visitors but home to an enduring constituency would have been conceivable only with the new urban landscape of the later monarchy. This collective political expression presents

---

fortified towns through all of Judah (1 Chron. 17:13–19; late ninth century), and he is said to have placed judges in these towns (19:5).

[19] The one pre-Assyrian exception is found in the Joash tale, in the lines that describe the boy king's acclamation by "the people of the land" and the religious cleansing that follows by destruction of a temple for Baal (2 Kings 11:14, 18). While the Joash narrative seems to preserve a monarchic-period account of a ninth-century event, these two references derive from added sections that wrap up loose ends, including the execution of Athaliah and the undoing of her religious crimes.

[20] Talmon (1967); Seitz (1989), "Excursus: The 'People of the Land,'" 42–71.

[21] Na'aman (2007b, 36–8) argues that the largest component of Jerusalem's new population after the Assyrian military campaigns would have come from Judah itself, especially from the Shephelah, rather than from the fallen kingdom of Israel. See also Guillaume (2008).

[22] Citing Ernest Nicholson's earlier study (1965), John Thames (2011) argues that the phrase is contextual, without technical meaning. To my mind, the application of the language is too limited to Judah and Jerusalem to support interpretation as a purely ad hoc usage.

a completely different history and social configuration from the decentralized tradition of Israel. One notable feature of the name "Judah" in contrast to the House of David is the fact that it is not defined by king or capital, and this identification by a land could coincide with the fresh sense that a "people of the land" could wield power as a group. In contrast to Hosea and Amos, who are not treated as having access to king and court, the political activity of Isaiah, Micah, and Jeremiah at Jerusalem could reflect the same shift.[23]

B. Judah's Appropriation of Israelite Identity

It is clear from the massive literature of early Judaism that the people of Judah came to understand themselves as heirs to the identity of Israel. It is not so clear when and how this occurred. Given the ownership of the name by the kingdom north of Judah, it would be logical to conclude that the appropriation by Judah could have taken place only after 720.[24] Yet this solution is still not entirely satisfying, because someone from Judah must have perceived a basis for the connection. Would it be enough simply to covet the reputation of the more powerful northern polity? Perhaps so, but the answer is uncertain. Whenever people from Judah began to call themselves "Israel," the use of the name takes on very different associations in its new context, and these reflect the distinct political traditions of the two kingdoms. The radically different conception of Israel among the survivors of Judah during the Persian period is nicely illustrated in the books of Chronicles, which recast the history told in the books of Samuel and Kings. Before exploring this material, we will consider a set of older texts that reflect earlier stages of the appropriation process.

1. *Early Expressions in the Prophets*

In the past decade and more, a debate has risen around the question of whether the name Israel could have been applied to both kingdoms before the end of the northern one. One potential source of evidence is writing cast as prophetic and associated with events from the eighth century, before the final Assyrian defeat of Samaria. Against various interpreters who place all such identification of Judah with Israel either after 720 or after the final collapse of Judah in 586, H. G. M. Williamson (2011) defends possible examples from the eighth century

---

[23] Jeremiah's prophetic calling is to be "a fortified town" against "all the land," enumerated as "the kings of Judah, its leaders (*śārîm*), its priests, and the people of the land" (1:18). Later in the book, we hear of two extended confrontations between the prophet and Judah authorities, both times involving people gathered at the Jerusalem temple and leaders associated with the palace (26:9–12, 16; 36:8–15, 19–23). Interpretation varies on whether Jeremiah 26 and 36 come from the prophet, his scribe Baruch, and his immediate circle. Holladay (1989, 22–3, 102–3, 253–4) and Lundbom (2004, 283–4, 301, 583–4) take these as close to the setting portrayed; unlike Carroll (1986, 509–15). Whether or not the events described took place in some form, the detail of urban geography and political landscape for the court and its vicinity suggests knowledge of this monarchic world.

[24] See the discussion of Kratz and Na'aman in Chapter 1.

in Mic. 3:9–10, Ps. 78:41, and Isa. 8:14.[25] Among these, Isa. 8:14 offers a particularly provocative case for a Judahite view of a larger Israel while the northern kingdom by that name still existed. If one concludes that such a view is a priori impossible, then the text may be considered later, yet the language and ideas are unique to this context, which explicitly addresses the reality of two kingdoms. If the text is later than the eighth century, it is through the eyes of someone looking back at Israel and Judah when they existed side by side.

Isaiah 8:14 is embedded in a speech that begins in verse 11 with reference to the writer in first person: "Indeed Yahweh spoke to me as follows, when he held fast (my) hand and warned me not to walk in the way of this people" (v. 11). The speaker must not buy into claims of conspiracy, must not share the people's objects of awe. Only Yahweh should strike awe. "He will become a sacred place and a stone to strike and a rock to make stumble for the two houses of Israel; a trap and a snare for the one who lives in (or is enthroned in) Jerusalem" (v. 14). Williamson argues for a date before 720 based mainly on comparison with the account in chapter 6 of the writer's visionary experience that compelled him to take the role of messenger. "In my opinion, the essence of the case for retaining an early date for 8:11–15 . . . is that the paragraph does not . . . allude to Isaiah 7 (which was added to the first-person account), but that it does . . . show close literary affinity with the whole of 6:1–11" (p. 94).[26] The name would have been preserved in the liturgy of the Jerusalem temple, where Yahweh would have been invoked as "God of Israel."

Whether before or after the kingdom of Israel fell to Assyria, Isa. 8:14 expresses a view from Judah that both realms constituted a single larger reality named for the larger, northern kingdom. This could be seen as a kind of "me too" attempt to hitch Judah to the dominant northern power, based on nothing more than a current desire to share that prestige. Such a claim, however, requires some basis for imagining the association. Judah may have been subordinate to Israel in the past (cf. Jehoshaphat in 1 Kings 22:45), but Isa. 8:14 indicates parity. Both Israel and Judah maintained traditions for the worship of Yahweh, and Yahweh is the focus of the Isaiah text. Yet this in itself does not define a political bond. While the worship of Yahweh may be a

---

[25] Williamson responds to the notion that this is a postmonarchic idea from the sixth century (Becker 1997; Davies 2007). For a somewhat earlier date, between 720 and 586, see Kratz (2006) and Na'aman (2010).

[26] Before the latest reevaluation of the whole "united monarchy" tradition of David and Solomon in 2 Samuel and 1 Kings, most interpreters found no reason to date Isaiah 8 after the fall of Israel. Referring to Isa. 6:1–13; 7:1–17; and 8:1–22, Blenkinsopp (2000) comments, "Except for obvious glosses (e.g. 6:13b; 7:8b) and 'on that day' additions (7:18–25; 10:20–23), these accounts give the appearance of having been composed close to the events described. While this is not impossible, it was inevitable that the earlier event would be interpreted and construed in the light of what happened about three decades later and that the interpretation and construction would become part of the text." That is, these events from before the final Assyrian devastation would be recalled in part for their very connection to that disaster. See also Kaiser (1972, 97, 104) and Wildberger (1981, 288, 360).

factor, a more direct political solution is to be found in the tradition that David ruled Israel. At least some blocks of the David narrative appear to be quite old, completely unaware of political conditions from the later environment of the two kingdoms, and strangely combining familiarity with Israelite politics with David as protagonist (see Chapter 6). Although I am not persuaded that the early David material includes Judah, the notion that David's fame derived from rule of Israel forges an ancient bond between the founder of the southern kingdom and the northern realm. By speaking of "the two houses of Israel," the writer of Isa. 8:14 appears to echo a claim that the house of David never gave up its heritage as onetime rulers over Israel. Such a claim would lie at the root of Judah's eventual appropriation of the Israel name, never fully abandoned by the house of David. It is possible, as Williamson suggests, that while any identification with Israel was lost to everyday use, a link between Yahweh and Israel could have survived in the Jerusalem temple.

Once the kingdom of Israel was removed from the scene, it is very likely that its own survivors strove to preserve a sense of identity, and this effort may have contributed to bodies of Israelite material that found their way into the Bible. At the same time, however, seventh-century Judah offered a functioning kingdom, and if the royal house of David maintained a claim to an ancient connection with Israel, there could be much to gain from the prestige of this name and the larger realm it had long identified. Parts of Jeremiah and the books of Micah and Zephaniah offer a sense of how Judah could begin to take over the name Israel for itself during a time when memory of the fallen kingdom was still fresh. The book of Jeremiah does recall "Israel" as a category distinct from Judah,[27] yet a larger unity between Israel and Judah as one people is striking, and this unity seems to include a shared narrative of origins. Jeremiah 2 is cast entirely as a prophetic message delivered in Jerusalem (v. 1). The opening words, however, address Israel as a bride who first knew Yahweh in the wilderness but then was overtaken by harm, echoing the images of Hosea 2 (Jer. 2:2–3). If this refers to the Assyrian defeat of Israel as a kingdom, then the writer is still using the old separate identity. Still, the story of this fallen people recalls an exodus from Egypt and a journey through the wilderness to a beautiful land (vv. 6–7), a story not recounted as if it were the special possession of Israel, to the exclusion of Judah. The accusation of dependence on the human powers of Egypt and Assyria (v. 18) is leveled as a standing rebuke, a call to repent. With one breath, the writer reproves "the house (or Greek, 'sons') of Israel" for treating wood and stone as gods (vv. 26–7), while with the next, he declares, "Indeed your gods, Judah, have come to match the number of your towns" (v. 28). Even if the writer remains fully aware of Israel as a distinct kingdom, it seems that Judah and the inhabitants of Jerusalem are deeply identified with Israel as one people who share one origin with Yahweh

---

[27] For Israel and Judah as separate "houses," see Jer. 3:18; 5:11, 15; 11:10; 13:11; 31:27; cf. Israel and Judah in 30:3–4; 32:30; 33:14; and 50:33.

out of Egypt. If we are still to avoid understanding Judah as one with Israel, it is a short step from Jeremiah 2 to that later conception.[28]

The book of Micah can likewise distinguish Israel and Judah as two kingdoms (1:5), but more often, "Israel" refers to the audience at hand, which is Judahite.[29] In chapter 3, for example, the prophet speaks to "the heads of Jacob and the rulers of the house of Israel" (v. 1; cf. vv. 8–9), with threats of ruin that finally reach the door of Zion and Jerusalem (vv. 10–12). This section may offer one of the more plausible preexilic Judahite adoptions of Israel's name and heritage.[30] Zephaniah is ostensibly somewhat later, based on the reign of Josiah, though its contents are less firmly rooted in monarchic Judah. Ehud Ben-Zvi (1991, 347–58) has argued that the whole book is "postmonarchic."[31] Zephaniah focuses on Judah and Jerusalem (1:4; etc.), before turning against various neighbors (chapter 2). Israel appears as a remnant only after the sky has fallen (3:13–14), and this text cannot be dated with confidence to the time before the Babylonian takeover.

Writing in the prophetic mode flourished in the period immediately after the end of Judah's kingdom. Isaiah takes form as a book in this later period, so that much of its contents is beyond confident dating. After chapter 40, where the end of the kingdom is assumed, the name "Israel" is appropriated for the Judahites without hesitation.[32] Ezekiel's entire vision for a future hope is cast as a restoration of "the land of Israel" for "the house of Israel" (40:2, 4), and it finally hearkens back to the ancient idea of Israel as a collection of tribes in chapter 48. Unlike the territorial lists of Joshua, however, the tribal scheme is purely literary, with no connection to land occupied in any known time by any

[28] Jeremiah 2 is a difficult chapter that may be taken as a blend of oracles from one voice (Lundbom 1999, 258) or the overlay of a later revision onto an earlier recension (Holladay 1986, 62, etc.). Both Lundbom and Holladay understand this material to belong to the prophet Jeremiah, from before the Babylonian victory. If the section is considered to be postexilic (e.g., Carroll 1986, 115–16), the association of Judah with Israel is unsurprising and barely worth comment. A similar issue arises in Jer. 31:1–6, which closes with a call to the people of Samaria and Ephraim to go meet Yahweh at Zion. The separate people of the defunct kingdom may be in view, but they are invited into full unity with Judah.

[29] The heading imagines the prophecies of Micah to have occurred during the reigns of Jotham, Ahaz, and Hezekiah, contemporary with Isaiah, and likewise defined by Judah. Judah still exists as a kingdom, at least for some part of the book (e.g., 1:8–15; 3:1–12). David Carr (2011, 329–31) treats Micah 1–3 in his chapter on writing from the Neo-Assyrian period.

[30] Hans Walter Wolff (1990, 95–7) associates Mic. 3:1–12 with the named prophet, as reflected in the first-person voice, and he understands Micah to apply the name Israel to Judah and Jerusalem without hesitation in 3:1. According to Delbert Hillers (1984, 43), by calling the people of Judah "Jacob" or the "House of Israel," Micah follows an old religious tradition; cf. Andersen and Freedman (2000, 388).

[31] Adele Berlin (1994, 33–5, 136–7) cites Ben Zvi cautiously, without commitment to one setting, while observing that the reference to a "remnant of Israel" in 3:13 continues into the postexilic period and offers no help with dating. Carr (2011, 333) observes that Zephaniah 1 is the chapter most widely agreed to have pre-exilic material.

[32] Yahweh's commitment to his people through time is tied to the name "Israel" and is invoked as Judah's hope (e.g., Isa. 40:27; 41:8; etc.; 45:25; 46:3).

known evidence. The tribes have nothing at all to do with politics, and their geographical distribution is artificially planned in stripes north and south of Jerusalem.

2. *The Books of Chronicles*

By the latter part of the sixth century, writers who took the prophetic mantle identified the people of Judah with Israel, for the sake of both its narrative and its religious heritage. The Bible also preserves literature from the long Achaemenid ("Persian") rule that followed, although the exact quantity is difficult to determine, given the roles of compilation and revision in the formation of a finished Bible. Nevertheless, the books of Chronicles provide a major literary work that offers an ideal crucible for testing Persian-period conceptions of Israel among the descendants of Judah. Although Chronicles covers almost the same chronology as the books of Samuel and Kings, and it uses earlier sources that overlap with Samuel and Kings, there is widespread agreement that it was created in the late Persian or early Hellenistic period, probably in the fourth or early third centuries.[33] This date deep into the postmonarchic world of Judah's descendants is then particularly useful when combined with Chronicles' focus on the history of David's royal line, in the very period that gives us the two kingdoms of the Israel/Judah division. Moreover, large blocks of the Chronicles text match material from Samuel and Kings and do not come from the later writer's milieu, whatever their origin.[34] Older perspectives that stand closer to the time of the monarchies are then directly juxtaposed with contributions from a world where the kingdoms are a distant memory, known only from ancient texts such as the ones incorporated into the Chronicles project.[35]

Where Chronicles differs from Samuel and Kings, its contents are liable to date to this much later period, and where its usage of the name "Israel" is different, this use generally reflects settings long after both kingdoms existed. The genealogies and other lists of 1 Chronicles 1–9 treat Israel as the defining unit for the people in question, even though the Chronicles narrative will focus almost exclusively on David's royal line and so finally on the kingdom of Judah. Israel has become an ethnicity without reference to a polity. The narrative of Chronicles begins with David, reusing materials that have parallel versions in

[33] For further discussion and bibliography, see Knoppers (2003a, 116); Carr (2011, 196–201, chapter on pre-Hasmonean Hellenistic parts of the Bible). Knoppers (2003b) compares the genealogies of 1 Chronicles 1–9 to Greek examples but emphasizes that the affinity does not require a date before Alexander in 332 B.C.E., but may reflect a fifth/fourth-century setting.

[34] Most have imagined that at these points Chronicles must rely on the text of Samuel and Kings, but Graeme Auld (1999) has proposed an alternative, that this joint material existed on its own, separate from either biblical context.

[35] Because the books of Chronicles incorporate material that is so clearly added in a late period, apparently long after the books of Samuel and Kings were complete, there has been much discussion of how to characterize this work. Isaac Kalimi (2005; 2009) has defended vigorously the notion that the Chronicler should be regarded as a historian, writing with "sacred-didactic" purpose. Another solution has been to consider the books more as a work of theological reflection (e.g., Ackroyd 1991).

Samuel and Kings, supplemented by other odds and ends, culminating with a long section that credits David rather than Solomon with the major role in temple-building preparations.[36] Where Chronicles tracks Samuel, we do find the same references to collective Israel as a political force, reflecting the much earlier perspective of some David material. The most obvious example is perhaps Israel's acceptance of David as its king in 1 Chron. 11:3a (cf. 2 Sam. 5:3).[37]

The David narratives in Chronicles display interesting hints of new assumptions about Israelite identity. In 2 Sam. 5:6, David sets out to take Jerusalem from the Jebusites, with the assault launched by "the king and his men." According to 1 Chron. 11:4, "David and all Israel" attack the citadel. The Samuel text treats this feat as the work of David and a force that is personally loyal to him. Israel is not mentioned, and there is no reason to read it into the text. The writer recognizes that Israel does not automatically join David in battle but must be mustered for war. 1 Chronicles 11 completely loses the political nuances of the archaic Israelite kingdom. If David conquers, it must be with the Israel he rules.

Like the priestly tribal lists in Numbers, Chronicles does portray Israel as consisting of tribes that offer identities for fighting units, especially before the division into two kingdoms. David is said to attract fighters from all twelve of Israel's tribes, expanding on the idea that "Israel" came to Hebron to make him their king. The listing of twelve is a composite that leaves too many participants and forces all the eastern tribes to be counted together in the twelfth position (1 Chron. 12:37 with Reuben, Gad, and the half-tribe of Manasseh).[38] Levi is counted as a fighting group (vv. 26–8), and Joseph is divided into Manasseh and Ephraim, with Manasseh counted twice for western and eastern components.[39] The core ideas of Israel choosing David as king and of Israel's tribal composition are inherited from earlier tradition. The actual list, however, is a literary construction that includes every tribal participant known from the Torah and then provides a census in priestly fashion. David's

---

[36] Sara Japhet (2006) observes that Chronicles subtly attempts the same shift of credit with regard to the wall of Jerusalem.

[37] See also 1 Chron. 14:2 (cf. 2 Sam. 5:12), with David established as king over Israel, and 14:8 (cf. 2 Sam. 5:17); 19:10, 16–17 (cf. 2 Sam. 10:9, 15–17), for Israel mustered for war with Aram. Note that in its presentation of David, Chronicles begins in chapter 11 with his coronation and conquest of Jerusalem. His rule is established once and for all over Israel, without reference to Judah. At the same time, Judah, Jerusalem, and the temple stand at the center of the narrative (see Dietrich 2007, 7–8).

[38] Schorn (1997, 19–20) places Chronicles last in her chronology of development for the biblical twelve-tribe system. She observes that although an echo of the tribal-geographical scheme survives in Chronicles, this aspect has become subordinated to genealogical concerns. The primacy of Judah in chapter 12 matches the same position in chapters 4–8.

[39] Japhet (1989, 280–1) considers the genealogies to cover fourteen tribes, as they address all the possible tribal categories from their sources. She concludes that Samuel and Kings, in contrast, "deliberately avoid the tribal framework" (p. 307), a reading that appears to treat the tribal scheme as universally known and available for application.

story in the books of Samuel never attempts such a list, and the tribal accounts in the poetry of Genesis 49, Deuteronomy 33, and Judges 5 show the composite nature of the list in 1 Chronicles 12.[40] Moreover, the list in Chronicles adds nothing to the tradition from 2 Sam. 5:1–3 (cf. 1 Chron. 11:1–3) that "Israel" asked David to be their king. Many Chronicles texts take their cue for Israelite identity from their sources shared by, if not directly from, Samuel and Kings, and these may preserve a memory of Israel's collective political character.

Chronicles tends to universalize Israelite identity in a way that loses touch with the political realities suggested in the versions of Samuel and Kings. The pair of texts describing David's census of Israel is best known for the contrasting renditions of who instigated the idea: Yahweh in 2 Sam. 24:1, but Satan in 1 Chron. 21:1, removing Yahweh himself from blame. Chronicles also seems to have lost the political vision of Samuel. In 2 Sam. 24:1, David is led to take a census of "Israel and Judah," maintaining the division that was introduced with David's initial rule over Judah from Hebron and subsequent selection by Israel (2 Sam. 2:1–4 and 5:1–3). Whereas Samuel treats Israel and Judah as distinct, a political situation that certainly characterized the ninth and eighth centuries, Chronicles identifies Israel with what the Jews had become, the whole people of God. Judah needs no separation.

Through the book of 2 Chronicles, the notion of a separate kingdom called Israel is shared with the books of Kings. The particular vision of Chronicles is most striking after the fall of Israel. Israel is understood to be the whole people, from both kingdoms, and with the Israelite kingdom now defunct, all who worship Yahweh by Judahite norms are called Israel. Hezekiah invites all Israel, north and south, to celebrate the Passover in Jerusalem (2 Chron. 30:1). Even though most northerners scorn his messengers, a few do come (vv. 10–11), and those who celebrate the feast can be called "Israelites" (v. 21).[41]

As a whole, the books of Chronicles maintain a persistent vision of a unified Israel, a vision rooted especially in the tradition of David, more than Moses, and a world before the two separate kingdoms.[42] In a setting long after the demise of both Israel and Judah as independent polities, the Chronicler aggressively celebrates this tradition of unity under David and minimizes any isolation of

[40] For full discussion, see Schorn (1997, 8–20).

[41] Although the books of Chronicles do not follow the reigns of Israel's kings as found in the books of Kings, they acknowledge the existence of this realm and consider it part of the larger Israel once ruled by David. Japhet (1989, 318) concludes that the writer displays an ambivalent attitude: the other kingdom is based on a sin, yet its establishment fulfills the words of the prophet Ahijah. Ralph Klein (2006, 46) finds that "while the Northern Kingdom is considered politically and religiously illegitimate by the Chronicler, the residents of that territory are considered part of Israel."

[42] Williamson (1977, part II); cf. Knoppers (2003a, 81–2). The whole story of Israel in Chronicles begins with David and Solomon, so as to account for the key institutions of Judah, the dynasty of David, and the temple in Jerusalem (Dyck 1998, 134). On the centrality of David, see also Ben Zvi (2007).

Israelites from the people of Judah.[43] While the tradition of David as ruler over all Israel reflects old notions of the priority of Israel to Judah, its expression in Chronicles betrays a perspective disconnected from the world of two kingdoms. After the separation, Chronicles recognizes the northern kingdom in a way that is consistent with the books of Kings. By the end of this narrative, Judah lays claim to the name "Israel," not excluding northerners but only welcoming them as part of the true Israel insofar as they join Judahite worship of Yahweh under Judahite kings.[44]

Fairly often, Chronicles slips into using the name "Israel" where only Judah can be intended, an extreme expression of the core vision.[45] When 1 Chronicles 9 describes the people who returned to Jerusalem in a text shared with Nehemiah 11, they are divided into "Israel, the priests, the Levites, and the devoted ones (*nĕtînîm*)" (1 Chron. 9:2).[46] Rehoboam is said to have abandoned the instruction of Yahweh, "and all Israel with him" (2 Chron. 12:1, cf. v. 6). Jehoshaphat appoints officials to address just this need, defined as Levites, priests, and kin-group heads for Israel (2 Chron. 19:8; cf. 2 Chron. 23:2 with Jehoiada as leader). The idea of "Israel" as the gathered people at worship appears in 2 Chron. 32:5 for giving offerings and tithes under Hezekiah. Josiah's Passover is celebrated by "the Israelites" in 2 Chron. 35:17 (contrast 2 Kings 23:21–3).

Along with this creeping appropriation of Israelite identity by later Judahites, and in spite of the many continuities between Chronicles and Samuel–Kings, Chronicles also tells a tale by its omissions. If we look below the surface, the elements of the Samuel–Kings texts that most directly display a separate collective called Israel are among the missing material in Chronicles. This is not surprising for accounts of Israel-centered events after the split, but it is striking

---

[43] Williamson (1977, 25–6) observes that in 1 Chronicles 10 to 2 Chronicles 9, with the kingdom of David and Solomon, Israel is presented as a fully united kingdom, without serious tensions – unlike the portrayal in 2 Samuel.

[44] Dyck (1998, 131) emphasizes the centrality of Jerusalem in Chronicles, which presents a spatial scheme that moves from the world to Israel to Jerusalem to its temple, in a "Judahite-Levitical-Jerusalemite" vision of Israel. Even in its treatment of the two kingdoms, Chronicles emphasizes a unity in Jerusalem-based terms: the point is that "Israel is made up of all tribes united under David and around the Jerusalem temple" (p. 158). Steven Schweitzer (2007, 47–52) finds that Chronicles represents less a propaganda for current Persian or Hellenistic period conditions than a utopian ideal, with Israel always a greater entity than the list of tribes that returned from Mesopotamia. For Ben Zvi (2005, 195), the result of the Chronicler's handling of tradition is to divide God's people into Yehud and non-Yehud, the latter as peripheral to the central attributes of Jerusalem, temple, and the scribes themselves.

[45] Japhet (1989, 323) considers this usage to be fairly rare and confined to standard phrases, including "princes of Israel" (2 Chron. 12:6; 21:4), "heads of families of Israel" (2 Chron. 19:8; 23:2), "king of Israel" (2 Chron. 21:2; 28:19, 27), "enemies of Israel" (2 Chron. 20:29), and simple equation with Judah (2 Chron. 15:17; 17:1; 24:16). Just the option of substituting the name "Israel" for "Judah," however, reflects the passage of time.

[46] For this kind of division, compare the worshiping community of Psalms 115:9 and 118:2, where Israel is parallel to "the house of Aaron" and "those who fear Yahweh."

for David's reign. Chronicles leaves out most of the stories of intrigue and revolt that could be painful to partisans of David. These include the conflicts involving Abner, Absalom, and Sheba, all of which emphasize a separate Israel that could turn against the iconic king. It is the positive account of Israel choosing David that survives.

C. Judah and Its Land

After Israel no longer existed as a kingdom, its name seems to have become more accessible to those in Judah who already identified with its heritage. In a process that appears to have taken considerable time and that remains largely obscure, the name "Israel" was applied to the descendants of Judah. Judah could claim to be part of a larger Israel from high antiquity, but non-Judahites from that larger Israel could participate in the life of Israel only after the monarchies if they came to Jerusalem – at least figuratively – and worshiped on Judah's terms.

Judah itself, however, remains almost more of a mystery than Israel. By the time the kingdom based at Jerusalem was clearly called "Judah," the capital had grown into a major population center, surely bringing political change, perhaps including a new role for the Jerusalem populace. The Bible reveals little of what Judah may have been before the flourishing eighth century. The name itself may have been attached to the southern highlands, as reflected in phrases including "the highlands of Judah" (Josh. 11:21), "the wilderness of Judah" (Judg. 1:16), and "the southern steppe (*negeb*) of Judah" (1 Sam. 27:10).[47] There may have been an early southern people of Judah, though our ability to recognize it in biblical writing is obscured by the shadow of the eighth/seventh-century kingdom. The evidence for a tribal association of Israel now reflects careful attempts to include Judah, but these either derive from whole texts with clear dependence on later schemes and Judah points of view or display hints of having been added to Israelite material in order to make sure Judah was not left out (see the following chapters).

The political landscape of the south is therefore little known. Archaeology indicates that the southern highlands remained relatively empty of settlement through the Iron Age I, while regions farther north began to grow in population.[48] It is likely that pastoralism played a significant role in the regional economy, and it would be surprising not to find tribally organized groups in such a setting. Nevertheless, the Bible preserves no tradition that the kingdom of Judah was built from tribal components. In stories about times before the rule of kings, southern mobile and pastoralist peoples such as the

---

[47] See the discussion of Blenkinsopp (2009, 20–1). Edward Lipiński (1973) proposed that the word may have an Arabian background, associated with Arabic *whd/wahda*, "terre raviné."

[48] This was central to the synthesis of Israel Finkelstein (1988, 326), and it is now commonly observed (e.g., Killebrew (2005, 165).

Midianites, the Kenites, and the Ishmaelites are excluded from Israel, even if some may be envisioned to enjoy friendly relations.[49] The land allotments of Joshua 13–19 locate a people named Simeon in the south near Beersheba, but there is no narrative tradition to help evaluate this assignment, and Simeon is missing from Deuteronomy 33 and Judges 5, which include two relatively early tribal lists. Nothing suggests that Judah itself was a tribal association like Israel, and without such a tradition, it appears that the basis for unity within the Jerusalem-centered kingdom was the royal house of David. Various populations may have been incorporated into the kingdom on various terms; as observed earlier, only certain urban centers are mentioned in the books of Kings.

For the last phase of the kingdom, during the seventh century, the book of Jeremiah offers some detail for Judah's territorial composition. Jeremiah 17:26 lists the origins of people from all through the kingdom who will gather to keep the Sabbath at Jerusalem:

- the towns of Judah;
- the outskirts (dependent villages?) of Jerusalem;
- the land of Benjamin;
- the Shephelah (western foothills);
- the highlands ("mountain");
- the Negev (southern desert).

These seem to be understood as regional divisions. Only Benjamin is singled out by different terminology that could imply a political entity, as a "land," although nothing in the book ever envisions "Benjamin" acting as a body.[50] Nowhere in the Bible do the terms "Shephelah," the "Negev," or the "highlands" name political or social groups that act as such or that define individual identity. The book of Jeremiah represents a Jerusalem-centered point of view, which may limit our ability to perceive social structures that could have contributed to the Judah population. This perspective, however, does seem to reflect the assumptions or objectives of the political center at Jerusalem. From this view, Judah consists of no association of discrete constituent bodies, and there is not even a second city of political significance.

Throughout the Bible's primary narrative, the south comes up repeatedly and sometimes unexpectedly, as with Absalom's retreat to Hebron to win the support of Israel against David (2 Sam. 15). This region clearly had a significant impact on biblical lore and on the peoples who contributed to the Bible, even if not necessarily through the particular vehicle of a people called Judah.

---

[49] Moses is said to have married a Midianite after he fled Egypt (Exod. 2:16, 21; 3:1; cf. 18:1; Num. 10:29); the heroine Jael, wife of a Kenite, plays a key role in the defeat of Israel's enemies by killing Sisera (Judg. 4:17; 5:24); less positively, an Ishmaelite caravan sells Joseph to the Egyptians (Gen. 37:25–8; 39:1).

[50] This detail is nevertheless striking, and it suggests a heritage of independent identity that contrasts with the more geographical categories in this list.

The history of this southern territory demands continued investigation, without the assumption that we know the names and affiliations of its inhabitants even through much of the Iron Age. It was only as a kingdom, however, that the south became the driving force behind the collection of biblical writing, and the survivors of this kingdom, with its distinct political and religious assumptions, became the first community to define itself around a Bible as sacred text.

4

An Association of Peoples in the Land (The Book of Judges)

In the Bible's primary narrative, the first six books – Genesis through Joshua – are set in a time of origins, all cast as a prelude to actual life in the land of Israel. The long books of Samuel and Kings introduce the rule of kings as a new thing, with the initial success of David and Solomon followed by a confusing division into two, with David's line restricted to the smaller southern realm and the name "Israel" kept by the dominant northern one. Only the book of Judges, twenty-one chapters long, treats a period when Israel occupied a land of its own yet without kings and without a decisive unity. The book assembles a variety of unrelated stories, featuring people and places that are utterly distinct as we move from setting to setting. There is evident editorial effort to create from these a coherent narrative, especially by the formulation of a cycle of wrongdoing, divine wrath, and eventual rescue in Judg. 2:11–19, though this scheme is layered with other attempts.[1]

As we try to disentangle the threads of editorial thought and to imagine what points of view they represent, one feature of the book stands out: the almost complete absence of content based in Judah. This is all the more impressive in light of the Judahite interest applied to the collection at two peripheral levels. The core set of heroic leaders is introduced by a brief, spare account of Othniel the Kenizzite (Judg. 3:7–11). As Caleb's younger brother, Othniel responds to the generic need of Israel by entering into generic combat with an enemy named Cushan-rishathaim. Victory results in forty years of peace. Nothing except the names offers any specifics; there is really no story. Caleb is linked to Judah, so that Othniel provides an indirect connection with this people before the

---

[1] For discussion of this introductory section, see, among many others, Brettler (2002, 22–8); Guillaume (2004, 114–28); Lindars (1995, 91–129); Richter (1966, 319–43). All of my investigation of Judges has been carried out in conversation with Sara J. Milstein, whose work on the book in chapters 3 and 4 of her dissertation (2010), along with subsequent thought, has influenced my approach in numerous ways.

proper narrative string begins with Ehud (3:12–30).[2] At an even larger level, the book as such is introduced by explicit reference to Judah in chapter 1. In an independent account of Israel's first possession of the land, Judges 1 takes a tack different from that of Joshua by dwelling on the people's failures instead of on victory. This list of failures at the end of the chapter, however, is preceded by a celebration of Judah as the first to engage the enemy and the most successful among its brethren (1:1–20). The interest of Judah writers in the final framing of the book is transparent.

Beyond these, however, the tales of Judges revolve around people without Judah connections: Ehud of Benjamin; Deborah from the vicinity of Ramah and Bethel; Barak of Naphtali; Gideon the Abiezrite, associated with Manasseh; Abimelech, ruler of Shechem; Jephthah of Gilead, in the east; Samson the southern Danite, man of the Philistine margins; Micah and the northward-moving Danites; and finally, Benjamin at war with Israel.[3] The entire amalgam of Judges stories seems to be drawn from Israelite lore, or built around it, at least. This means that the notion of a period of life in the land without kings – or at least without a fixed institution for all of Israel – likewise derives from Israel. Judah adopted it and incorporated it into the larger narrative that now spans Genesis through Kings, but Judah's contribution to such a portrait is secondary, relatively shallow, and late.

When we turn our attention to the abundant Israelite material in the book of Judges, we should be struck above all by its lack of centralization – in both political and literary terms. Faced with a medley of heroes, villains, and victims, all defined differently, later editors eventually settled on a system without any institution. Yahweh would provide leaders when needed, in whatever location a crisis arose, without need of all Israel. In what became an appendix to the book, chapters 17–21 included a refrain that could be read as a judgment on the whole premonarchic age: "In those days there was no king in Israel; everyone did what was right in his own eyes" (17:6; 21:25; cf. 18:1; 19:1). In fact, the tales from the time without kings generally assume no larger unity and appear to have been preserved at first for their local interest. This diversity and modest scale in itself indicates a vision of a decentralized political landscape.

All the old stories in Judges appear to come from various settings in Israel, with Judah having no hero to contribute before David. Certain texts seem to begin with very limited horizons, not accommodated to the notion of a larger Israel. I have chosen the juxtaposed but originally distinct stories of

---

[2] Martin Noth (1943, 50, etc.) assigned Othniel to the deuteronomistic production of the cycle in Judges 2–16; also Brettler (2002, 27); Richter (1964); and Soggin (1981, 47).

[3] Samson's father Manoah is identified as coming from Dan in Judg. 13:2 (cf. v. 25). Much of the Samson story plays out on Philistine turf: Timnah in chapters 14–15; Gaza in chapter 16. One episode has the Philistines come into Judah in order to capture Samson at a place called Lehi (15:9–10), the location of which is unknown (Rainey 2006a, 141). This geographically based reference suggests no partisan Judah interest and appears more deeply rooted in the Samson collection, which has a southern and coastal orientation without concern for any Israelite or Judahite polity.

Gideon and Abimelech in Judges 8 and 9 to represent this type. Other texts are occupied at base with a dramatic event that involves either the cooperation of or conflict between more than one people who are known at least by later audiences to belong to Israel. The Song of Deborah (in Judges 5) and the war between Ephraim and Gilead (Judg. 12:1–6) display the alternatives. Finally, early revisions that recast texts as having to do with Israel as such may have arisen in Israelite circles, without reference to Judah. Each of these phenomena warrants a closer look, although discussion will necessarily be brief. Through all the stages of this literary process, the material assumes a landscape of distinct groups that had to negotiate their relationships as need arose. This decentralization remained the backdrop of Israelite politics under kings.

A. Local Tales: Gideon and Abimelech

In the finished book of Judges, an extended account of Gideon (chapters 6–8) is linked to the story of Abimelech (chapter 9) by the notion that the two were father and son. This combination is widely viewed as secondary, and when considered on its own, Abimelech's confrontation with Gaal and Shechem has nothing to do with Gideon and his affairs or even with Israel (de Castelbajac 2001; Jans 2001; Schöpflin 2004). Christoph Levin (2000) judges it perhaps the oldest material in the Bible, in that it lacks any normative biblical interest and could be read against the setting of competing local powers in the Late Bronze Age.[4] This primary tale, which appears in Judg. 9:26–54, is fronted by an explanation of how Abimelech became king of Shechem and a prophetic parable against this choice (in 9:1–25). The foregrounding elements clearly postdate the narrative that follows, in part because Abimelech is not presented as the king of Shechem in his conflict with that town. Rather, Shechem is one component of a larger realm, so that Abimelech must be represented there by a local governor (*śar hā'îr*) named Zebul (v. 30).[5]

   While the construction of the Gideon complex is more difficult to unravel, a case can be made that the earliest and most independent material stands at the end, in the Transjordan pursuit of Zebah and Zalmunna (8:4–21).[6] This story

---

[4] In his recent commentary, Walter Gross (2009, 87) considers that the account of Abimelech could go back to the late twelfth century, though the core text as we have it must date to the early monarchy. Earlier, it was possible for Soggin (1981, 164) to speak of its "basic historicity."

[5] The difficult line in verse 28 identifies Zebul as Abimelech's administrative representative (*pāqîd*); see below. In his current doctoral dissertation at New York University, Brendon Benz (2012) proposes that the political situation in Judges 9 resembles what is found in the fourteenth-century letters from el-Amarna, where Lab'ayu also rules a domain that includes Shechem without designating it as his capital. Contrast the common conclusion that Lab'ayu ruled a territorial kingdom defined by Shechem as capital, as in Finkelstein (2005b).

[6] Milstein (2010, 204–7) proposes that the current Gideon complex was built mainly by stages of new introduction, beginning from combination of the Gideon and Abimelech war stories in chapters 8 and 9. Gross (2009, 83) identifies a core story of pursuit (8:5–9, 12c, 13–21), which he considers to date no earlier than the end of the tenth century; he likewise considers chapter 7 to be based on what follows.

never mentions Israel, and the 300 men in 8:4 are simply identified as Gideon's, like David's 400 in 1 Sam. 22:2 and Abram's 318 in Gen. 14:14. Gideon's arguments with Succoth and Penuel involve no larger groups, such as the tribes mustered in Judg. 6:34–5 and 7:23–4. The engaging account of how a massive Israelite army was winnowed down to 300 (7:1–8) would have been composed to explain Gideon's modest personal force. The Midianite conflict in Judg. 8:4–21 has nothing to do with either the divinely empowered rout of the enemy camp in 7:8–22 or the campaign against Oreb and Zeeb in 7:23–5 and 8:1–3. Instead, kings named Zebah and Zalmunna seem to have fought successfully at Tabor, where they killed Gideon's kin (8:18–19), and, in turn, Gideon pursued them to seek vengeance. Like the encounter between Abimelech, Gaal, and Shechem, Gideon's Transjordan adventure offers a story with local interest, lacking any reference to constituent groups in Israel and without any concern for Israel itself.[7] These two texts therefore provide an ideal starting point for an examination of the political landscape of the Israelite Judges material.

1. Abimelech

I begin with Abimelech in Judges 9, as the clearest case of an old local tale outside the Israel framework. In 9:26–54 alone, Abimelech is a given; any introduction has been replaced by the scheme that treats him as the king of Shechem.[8] He is provided identifying detail only in verse 28, where he is "the son of Jerubbaal" and is said to have served Hamor the father of Shechem.[9] The city of Shechem is subordinate to his rule, at the same time as it is susceptible to the advances of an outsider who offers a better arrangement. The presence of a "governor" suggests that Abimelech ruled a domain with more than one such official, so with several urban centers. At the end of the story, Abimelech is killed in the siege of a town called Thebez that is portrayed in terms similar to Shechem, with a fortress (*migdāl*) inside the town ('*îr*, v 51; cf. v. 46 for Shechem). After Gaal insinuates himself into leadership at Shechem, Zebul sends messengers to Abimelech at Tormah, which is his current base of operations (v. 31; cf. Arumah in v. 41).

Abimelech moves to attack Shechem by means of "the people (*'ām*) who were with him" (vv. 33–4, 48).[10] This category may be applied to named

---

[7] The archaic character of Judg. 8:4–21 allows Malamat's (2004, 70–1) identification of resonance with Hittite vassal treaties. Soggin (1981, 152) emphasizes the initiative of Gideon, with minimal theological interest, as a basis for affirming "the probable authenticity and antiquity of the section."

[8] Verse 55 provides a link to the next section of the book, along with the Kings-like critique in vv. 56–7 (e.g., Becker 1990; Jans 2001; Schöpflin 2004). The exact bounds of the early narrative are difficult to establish, given its current placement in a larger context. Gross (2009, 87) works within the framework of 9:22–56.

[9] The latter description parallels the characters of Genesis 34 and may be added, so that the Jerubbaal connection is likewise difficult to locate with confidence in the original narrative. In any case, Abimelech is best identified by his relationships in the story.

[10] The word *'ām* is used consistently to describe Abimelech's fighting force: 9:35–38, 43, and 49.

communities gathered for battle, as with Zebulun in the Song of Deborah (Judg. 5:18), and it refers to the forces joined with Omri on behalf of Israel against the Philistines (1 Kings 16:16). Neither Gideon's 300 men nor David's 400 are called a "people," though both are likewise "with him" (Judg. 8:4; 1 Sam. 22:2). It is likely that the word *'am* was used first of all with named bodies of people and that the application to any body of fighters is secondary.[11] In Judges 9, however, it would at most reflect the assumption that Abimelech rules some polity that is represented by the "people" with him; the text has no interest in the name of such a polity, which certainly must not be understood as Israel.

Throughout the Abimelech narrative, political actors are identified only as individuals or as towns, never as any larger entity. Abimelech and Gaal compete for influence at Shechem, and Zebul defends the prerogatives of Abimelech. Gaal is never said to gain leadership at Shechem; Zebul reports only that "Gaal and his brothers have entered Shechem" to turn the city against Abimelech (v. 31). The city always functions as a collective, most often with the phrase *ba'ălê šĕkem*, "the owners/citizens of Shechem," perhaps referring to heads of household (vv. 26, 39, 46, 47).[12] The same epithet applies to Thebez, where this category is distinguished from "all the men and women" as the whole population takes refuge in its *migdāl* fortress (v. 51). Two other categories define the people of Shechem. When the fortress of Shechem is torched, all the inhabitants ("men," *'ănāšîm*) perish (v 49); and the population as a whole may be called the "people" (*'am*, vv. 29, 42–43). In contrast to Abimelech's "people," the city of Shechem never attempts to fight their antagonist. They only retreat into their defenses and hope for the best – as in the case of Thebez.

2. Gideon

After reading the long account of Israel's struggle with the Midianites in Judges 6 and 7, we may expect the concluding episode in chapter 8 to fit comfortably into the social structures and identities already introduced for Gideon, in contrast to the foreignness of Abimelech, whose rule is not even tied to Israel. On its own, however, the tale of Gideon in the Transjordan in Judg. 8:4–21 has much in common with that of Abimelech and Shechem. Again, Israel is never mentioned, and there are no group identities beyond the towns of Succoth and Penuel. Zebah and Zalmunna are the two "kings of Midian" (vv. 5, 12), a place or a population, not clearly a polity. Once, the fighters are called Easterners

---

[11] Mark Smith (2009, 53–4, with literature on the term in n. 46) interprets the use of *'am* in the Song of Deborah alone in similar terms: the application to Zebulun in 5:18 is older, and then it is applied to the people as a whole in verses 2, 9, 11, and 13, which he considers part of a hymnic revision. In that context, I am not sure that "the people of Yahweh" in verse 13 must be considered extraneous to the battle poem; without it, the alliance has no common identity.

[12] The interpretive problem recalls the difficulty with ranges of meaning for the Akkadian words *awīlum* ("gentleman") and *qaqqadātum* ("heads") in early second-millennium diplomatic correspondence (Fleming 2004a, 142–3, 200–1). The first may sometimes refer to a higher class within a town's population, a group with a deciding voice in collective action; and the latter refers to leadership in uncertain terms, which I propose may reflect individual households.

(*bĕnê qedem*, v. 10), which likewise seems more a type than a political entity. These kings have evidently crossed into the highlands west of the Jordan River, where they fought and seem to have defeated kinsmen of Gideon at Tabor (v. 18). They have returned homeward, while Gideon pursues them with a mass of "men" (*'îš*) who are identified only by commitment to their leader (v. 4; cf. v. 15). Elsewhere, they are Gideon's "host" (*ṣābā'*, v. 6) and "the people who are at my feet" (*'ām*, v. 5), equally defined in personal terms. The fighting force of Zebah and Zalmunna is called a "camp" (*maḥăne*, vv. 10–12), which is caught by surprise and slaughtered. Only Zebah and Zalmunna have any interest for Gideon, however, and it is their lives he wants in exchange for those of his family.

As in the story of Abimelech, the polities that bear names are towns – this time, Succoth and Penuel, just east of the Jordan along the Jabbok River (vv. 5–9, 13–17). In every case, Gideon deals with the towns as collective bodies, although the terminology varies. Most generically, "the men (*'ănāšîm*)" of Succoth and Penuel speak and are spoken to, disciplined, and killed (vv. 8–9, 14, 16–17). Succoth's governing assembly attracts special notice because of how Gideon brings retribution on them: he gets a written list of the seventy-seven "leaders" (*śārîm*) and elders of the town so that he can torture them with thorns (vv. 14–16). These towns respond to Gideon very much as do Shechem and Thebez in the tale of Abimelech. When confronted, they do not fight: they take refuge in their strongholds. In his threat to punish the town for its inhospitality, Gideon identifies Penuel by its fortress (*migdāl*), and this is what he tears down upon his return (vv. 9, 17).

Both the Abimelech and the Gideon stories place at center stage well-known towns in Israel: Shechem, Succoth, and Penuel. The reason why both stories found their way into the Bible must be that these towns were prominent in Israel, and the tales of their trials kept a place in local lore. It is intriguing that Abimelech arrives in the later collection as a villain, while Gideon finds a more positive role, perhaps because his bold revenge on the Midianites offers a fearsome yet admirable figure. In the two stories themselves, all three towns suffer at the hands of a demanding military leader who expects such settlements to cooperate in spite of the leader's general absence. Comparison with the Abimelech scenario suggests that Gideon's claim on Succoth and Penuel rests on a similarly elastic threat: Do these towns dare risk independence, balancing their fixed fortifications against the mobile fighting force of a strongman who requires ad hoc subordination? The ambiguity of the political situation displays a world where individual authority had to be negotiated constantly and sometimes violently with local communities. Perhaps the violence was rarer than the Judges tales imply, and these were the more memorable for their failures.

B. Collaboration and Competition: The Song of Deborah and the Shibboleth

Not all of the core material in the book of Judges is focused on local crises that destroyed well-known towns. Other early content is built around a different political framework for narrative drama. Instead of the focus on individual leaders and their conflicts with enemies and constituents, these stories set the stage with peoples that played a part in Israelite life. As with Shechem, Succoth, and Penuel, Ephraim, Gilead, and others must have entered biblical narrative as part of Israel, at least as defined at the time of the kingdom. Yet there was no sense that such texts and tales had to be about Israel per se. There was nothing programmatic about these texts, placing them into some larger scheme. I use the delicate category of "text" in this case, rather than the generally serviceable "narrative," because one of my examples is the list of those who did and did not join in battle against the Canaanites in the Song of Deborah (Judg. 5:14–18). This poetic account sets up a tension between what at first appears predictable praise for various named allies in a successful military campaign and then a surprising lament over supposed allies who preferred to stay at home. Collaboration is the ideal, both celebrated and invited. In the case of the confrontation between Gilead and Ephraim in Judg. 12:1–6, it is the breakdown of cooperation that attracts attention. Again, military collaboration was expected, but its failure results in two supposed allies turning against each other in all-out war. Because both of these texts are preoccupied with the phenomenon of alliance in itself, they allow us to see another dimension of Israelite society as it was imagined to have played out in a landscape without kingship and its impulse toward unity.

1. The Song of Deborah

The Song of Deborah has attracted intense attention in recent generations of biblical scholarship because of its potential antiquity and therefore its useful-ness to historical reconstruction of early Israel. This poem exults in the victory of Israel over "the kings of Canaan" (Judg. 5:19), along with the assassina-tion of a leader named Sisera by a woman from whom he expected sanctuary. The groups involved do not follow categories anticipated from other biblical writing, and there is no explicit awareness of the monarchy to come. Judah is omitted from both the groups praised and those chided, and the list of peo-ples only partially aligns with the tribes in Genesis 29–30: Machir and Gilead (vv. 14, 17) are not among Jacob's sons.

Although the whole Song of Deborah appears to be Israelite, the text appears to have undergone some process of revision, and there are a multitude of reconstructions.[13] For my focus on political categories and perspective, it is most important to recognize that the name "Israel" is restricted entirely to the opening section, in verses 2–11.[14] Given the absence of this unifying identity from the body of the poem, after the introductory hymn, it is easiest to explain these verses as an addition or part of one. In European interpretation, some

---

[13] For a sense of the entire literature, see Neef (2002). Among the more recent studies, note especially Fritz (2006) and Smith (2009). Jacob Wright offers two new evaluations of the poem and the prose narrative in Judges 4 and 5 together (2011 and forthcoming).

[14] The name Israel occurs eight times in this section and never after that: see verses 2–3, 5, 7 (twice), 8–9, and 11.

kind of revision has long been considered likely.[15] Rather than approach the Song of Deborah as a single narrative that underwent expansion, I consider the main composition to have occurred by combination of two prior poems, which are both introduced and bound together by the opening hymn and setting of the scene.[16] The Jael section of the Song (vv. 24–30) includes no reference at all to Israel or any of its peoples, which both suggests its separate origin and removes it from relevance for this study. Verses 14–18, as long observed, present a detailed portrait of a military alliance involving many groups elsewhere identified with Israel, and this section warrants examination of its social categories.

Ten groups are named in these short lines, some without further definition. Ephraim, Benjamin, Machir, Zebulun, and Issachar join in the campaign (vv. 14–15a). The first three all appear to be governed by the same verb, "to come down" (*yrd*), with the subject *mĕḥōqĕqîm* seeming to define some type of leadership. Zebulun is likewise qualified with a unique phrase that has to do with wielding the "staff" (*šēbeṭ*, also the word for "tribe"). Issachar's "leaders" (*śāray*) are "with" Deborah, like the forces of Abimelech and Gideon. It is surely significant that each description offers a different way to qualify the participation of these groups in the military alliance. All are plural and emphasize collective action, yet the variety of terminology communicates individuality, as opposed to a standard representation demanded by some central authority or institution. Following these five contributors to the alliance we are introduced to four nonparticipants: Reuben, whose absence occupies three poetic lines (vv. 15b–16), Gilead, Dan, and Asher. Among these, only Reuben is identified as consisting of plural "divisions" (*pĕlāggôt*), another unique term in the list. Finally, the text returns to two who did join the fray: Zebulun again, this time as a "people" (*'ām*) that scorned its life for death" (v. 18), and Naphtali. This use of *'ām* seems to indicate the entire "people" by the name of Zebulun.

---

[15] Most often, the Song is divided into an old core with later additions, the earlier material beginning with "the days of Shamgar" and Deborah as mother (vv. 6–8), and the main body combining the list of peoples who fight the "kings of Canaan" (vv. 14–22) and the report of Sisera's death at Jael's hand (vv. 24–30). See the detailed discussion of mostly German literature in Neef (2002, 54–9), chapter 3 on the Song as a literary unity. Note also the recent monograph by Charles Echols (2008). Wright (forthcoming) proposes a different scheme, whereby a core hymn in Judges 5 was expanded with reference to the prose in chapter 4. To my eye, the poetry in 5:14–23 in particular lacks the continuity with ideas and identities from the prose that would sustain the hypothesis that it depends on chapter 4.

[16] There is a profound contrast between the battle against the kings of Canaan in verses 14 (or 12) to 23 and Jael's exploit in verses 24–30. Without the prose texts that assure us of a Kenite link to Israel, including the note in Judg. 4:11 that Heber was related to Moses by marriage, the Song by itself provides no basis for connecting Jael to Israel. While the Jael section is related to the battle only by the figure of Sisera, the opening sequence with Israel offers references to the material that follows in both narratives. The time of the conflict is placed in the days of Shamgar son of Anath, a figure mentioned in passing in Judg. 3:31, and in the days of Jael (5:6). Leadership is then attributed to Deborah, Barak's female counterpart in the call to war (5:7 and 15; cf. v. 12).

As a whole, Judg. 5:14–18 is all the more striking for the absence of the name "Israel." The text by itself displays a tradition of collaboration, without either the authority of a shared name or a single leader. Even Deborah and Barak are double-billed. Based on this one text, we cannot assume that the association served any occasion but war, in this case as defense against attack by an immediate neighbor. Intriguingly, the coalition is not defined simply by its participants, as in texts such as the Assyrian royal annals, when these cite various alliances united in opposition.[17] According to the Song, the four nonparticipants were under some obligation to come to the aid of their allies, and their failure to appear was no basis for a permanent breach of relations. The mildness of the rebuke promises the possibility of future connection. In verse 23, the curse called down on the mysterious Meroz allows no hope of relationship, perhaps explaining the absence of the name from any other biblical text. From the vantage of this poem, this sort of military alliance was the affair of peoples not defined by cities or settlements. In this respect, we are shown a mode of political association that contrasts completely with the focus in Judges 8 and 9 on towns as the units to be dominated by individual authorities such as Abimelech and Gideon. Behind the contrasting interests of these vastly different writings, the reality of the political scene in this region before or apart from kings remains difficult to assess. The texts in Judges suggest that both perspectives be taken into consideration.

2. Shibboleth

Among the texts that deal with peoples in contact, conflict could also provoke interest. A short yet vivid example recalls the failure of relations between Ephraim in the west and Gilead in the east, as defined by the Jordan River (Judg. 12:1–6). The story begins with the assumption that an individual leader named Jephthah has led a campaign against the Ammonites, who lived north of Gilead in modern Jordan. The collective "men (*'îš*) of Ephraim" cross the Jordan River to confront Jephthah with the accusation that he failed to include them in his call to battle, accompanied by a threat to burn his house down upon him. Jephthah retorts, "I and my people (*'ām*)" – military language familiar from the tales of Gideon and Abimelech – had a dispute with the Ammonites. Ephraim was called but did not come, so Jephthah engaged the enemy without them. Now, he understands Ephraim to have come to fight against him, and he proceeds to assemble "all the men (*'ănāšîm*) of Gilead" to fight Ephraim. Once battle is engaged, Jephthah disappears from the tale, which seems to incorporate a separate snippet of lore regarding Ephraim's slaughter at the hands of Gilead. After Ephraim is defeated in the east, those who attempt to cross the Jordan are found out by their western pronunciation of the word "shibboleth."

---

[17] For example, Israel contributes to a coalition against the Assyrians led by Damascus against Shalmaneser III, in the oldest Assyrian reference to the kingdom (see Chapter 15).

Unlike the colorful poetry of Judges 5, where the diversity of participants is highlighted by the unique language associated with each, this short narrative is not concerned with the character of Ephraim and Gilead. The two antagonists can be defined simply, with nothing in their composition to distinguish them. Their differences will be clear enough in the closing lines, with the linguistic snare. The shibboleth text is divided between the first part with Jephthah, who fights both the Ammonites and Ephraim as if by his own divinely granted power (vv. 1–3), and the second part where Ephraim and Gilead settle their differences with reference to neither Jephthah nor Yahweh (vv. 4b–6, after Jephthah's strange muster in v. 4a).[18] While the section with Jephthah clarifies his innocence against an unjust accusation, linked to a battle recounted in chapter 11, the second part of the text envisions a conflict that has nothing to do with Jephthah and the Ammonites, provoked by an obscure insult against Gilead. Ephraim claims that the Gileadites are "fugitives (*pĕlîṭîm*) of Ephraim," and so the actual "fugitives of Ephraim" who straggle back toward their homeland after defeat are caught by their inability to blend in with the derided Gileadites.

Each antagonist is identified collectively, and the political act of war is an expression of deep animosity rooted in regional prejudice. At the same time, the insult that launches the bloodbath is based on some possibility of shared origin. Israel is never mentioned, and the shibboleth story of verses 4–6 is played out as if it were a family feud gone bad. Both parties are insiders, and the eventual Israelite framework for collecting such material resonates easily with the players. Both of these texts reflect the assumption that early Israel consisted of diverse and sometimes rival peoples. The material itself did not name Israel because the stories did not exist to celebrate this unity. Eventually, such stories became the raw material for writers who did have Israel's very identity in view, and the combinations that resulted may represent the latest stage of Israelite composition in the book of Judges, before this passed into the possession of Judah.

C. The Association of Israel

In broad terms of transmission history, the book of Judges suggests some sort of compositional effort between the sweeping Judah-based framework and the fairly short units with interest in specific crises in the background of Israelite peoples. My goal is not to offer one more literary-historical system for the book as a whole, but rather to explore the Israelite character of many of its contents. Even among those who agree that much of Judges originated in Israelite settings, there will be substantial debate regarding the date and

---

[18] The previous lines give the impression that Jephthah and his fighters are already present, having already joined to defeat the Ammonites. It is widely held that this chapter combines an old independent statement of east/west conflict (in vv. 4b–6) with a fresh introduction that links this to Jephthah (in vv. 1–4a); Soggin (1981, 221; from Richter 1966); Gross (2009, 612–13).

location of various phases of combination and more extended composition. One prominent example is Wolfgang Richter's (1964, 1966) hypothesis of a "Book of Saviors" that would be preserved in large swaths of Judges 3–9. Richter dated this Israelite collection to the reign of Jehu, based on its supposed antimonarchic attitude; following his teacher, Ernst Axel Knauf, Guillaume (2004, 13) endorses the idea and puts it just after the kingdom's fall, with a similar sense that the composition offers a heroic alternative to monarchy.[19] Others have doubted whether any extensive collection existed before the exilic/postexilic work of a deuteronomistic author or someone like him (Becker 1990; Lindars 1995). Such debates must be settled on a case-by-case basis, yet I find some signs of transmission and combination within Israel, before the material passed into Judah's sphere. In particular, many of the core components of Judges do not mention Israel by name, and when these are revised under the aegis of Israelite unity, the interests in some instances still exclude Judah and suggest a perspective from Israel – the name that is invoked. What follows is a sampling, not intended to be exhaustive.

1. The Song of Deborah

In my treatment of Judg. 5:14–18, I observed that the name "Israel" only appears in the hymnic introduction to the Song (vv. 2–11), where it occurs eight times. Yahweh is vaunted as "the God of Israel" (vv. 3, 5); Deborah leads as "a mother in Israel" (v. 7); and Israel defines the crisis of battle – those who suffer, who come to fight, and whom Yahweh delivers. This section of the Song names no subunit and attends only to the overarching unity. Without geographical clues, one could attempt a much later setting, perhaps even in Judah. Nevertheless, the language remains archaic, lacking turns of phrase from Jerusalem/Judah poetry, as known by Psalms, prophets, and elsewhere. Above all, the hymn begins with an evocation of Israel mustered for battle as a "people" (*ʿām*, v. 2), a theme that recurs with the same terminology after the introduction of Deborah (v. 9). Also, it is hard to imagine that a writer from Judah would have accepted the list of peoples in verses 14–18 untouched, without finding a way to insert his own countrymen into the event. The Song of Deborah is therefore most likely a piece of Israelite writing at every level.

If the Song was composed from preexisting materials, as I envision, only the final author found it necessary to place the whole event under the banner of Israel by name. While there is no way to date this choice, it is not necessary to avoid the period of the monarchy.[20] The tradition of constituent peoples within Israel, defined tribally or otherwise, would have coexisted with the rule

---

[19] Gross (2009) avoids the "Retterbuch" terminology but speaks of a predeuteronomistic hero narrative that probably dates to the late seventh century.

[20] Many Americans still date the poem to the premonarchic era (e.g., Schloen 1993; Stager 1988). This approach is joined to interpretation as a finished text that was not revised, and the signs of composition from existing material would suit a somewhat later date. E. A. Knauf (2005b) suggests the tenth or early ninth century; as does Gross (2008, 82–3).

of kings, as suggested by Jean-Daniel Macchi for the tribal sayings of Gen. 49:13–21 (see Chapter 5). It may even be that the clear unity provided by the monarchy would offer a natural framework for casting the victory against the Canaanites as belonging to Israel.[21]

2. *Gideon's Three Hundred (Judges 7)*

The complete Gideon complex of Judges 6–8 revolves around a conflict with the Midianites, an inland group that the Bible never presents as occupying a fixed territory, in contrast to Edom, Moab, and Ammon. It appears that two different Midianite engagements have been combined: against Oreb and Zeeb in 7:23–8:3, and against Zebah and Zalmunna in 8:4–21. These episodes are handled without reference to each other, and only the first involves the collaboration of peoples: Naphtali, Asher, and Manasseh in 7:23, with Ephraim as a separate body in 7:24 and 8:1–3. As the text now stands, both engagements have been set up by a memorable sequence in 7:1–22, in which Gideon must reduce a muster of 32,000 men to the 300 who will chase Zebah and Zalmunna across the Transjordan in chapter 8. Although 7:23–5 has a coalition fight the Midianites near the Jordan River, the earlier part of the chapter treats this battle as superfluous, because Yahweh himself has already defeated the Midianite camp with Gideon's 300 men, who terrorize them with torches and trumpets.

According to Sara Milstein's reconstruction of the early stages of revision in creating the Gideon complex, the process began by combination of the city-centered tales of chapters 8 and 9 (2010, 189–207). The narrative now found in Judg. 7:1–22 was added as a "revision through introduction" in order to adapt Gideon to the "savior" type, as found with Ehud and Deborah in chapters 3–4 (pp. 209–10). Two new ingredients become central to 7:1–22, just as in the opening hymn for the Song of Deborah: Yahweh as deliverer, and Israel as the people saved. Yahweh is the dominant actor throughout. He gives Gideon repeated instructions on how to select the right 300 men from all those who are willing to fight; these are the ones who throw themselves down to drink water like dogs (v. 6). Once the 300 men are set apart, Yahweh has Gideon visit the enemy camp so he can hear the report of a dream that foretells Midian's defeat (vv. 9–14). With this divinely granted certainty of victory, Gideon is ready to attack immediately, with a plan that features shouts of Yahweh's name at the moment of attack (vv. 18, 20). Yahweh himself wins the battle by having the Midianites slay each other in the dark (v. 22).

Throughout the story, we find reference neither to named Midianite leaders nor to named peoples collaborating to fight them. The mass of fighters is first a "people" (*ʿām*, vv. 2–3, etc.), and then Yahweh expresses a concern that

---

[21] Under kings, all those who respond to and interact with the royal administration would be defined together as the people "Israel," like the use of the Akkadian word *mātum* ("land") to name a kingdom as well as to identify the realm by the mass of all who are ruled (Fleming 2004a, 119–21).

"Israel" could take credit that belongs to their god, if they defeat Midian by strength of numbers (v. 2). With the 300 needed soldiers in hand, Gideon dismisses "all the men of Israel" to go home (v. 8) – so that Israel can act solely as the beneficiary of Yahweh's deliverance. When someone interprets the Midianite dream, he recognizes only Gideon, "man of Israel," as the threat, and defeat is promised as God himself has handed Midian over to this human agent (v. 14). Gideon finally launches his plan from "the camp of Israel" (v. 15), still identified by the point of muster.

Judges 7:1–22 does not include the notion that Yahweh raised up a "deliverer" (*môšiaʿ*) for Israel, as with Ehud in 3:15. Instead, Yahweh promises that he himself will "deliver" (verb *yšʿ*) the people, and he tells Gideon, "I will give Midian into your hand" (v. 7). The same promise is made to Barak through Deborah, through whom Yahweh declares, "I will give him (Sisera) into your hand" (Judg. 4:7). In deciding how the Gideon story was eventually combined with other hero narratives set in a time without kings, composition in Israel need not be tied to Richter's hypothesis of a Book of Saviors.[22] Other possibilities are feasible, including a gradual expansion of the text, with Deborah material joined earlier than the Ehud story. One indication of such a process could be the similarity between the divine guarantees given to Barak and Gideon, which contrast with Ehud's own promise to Israel that "Yahweh has given your enemies into your hand" (3:28).

A combined Deborah/Barak and Gideon/Abimelech narrative would reflect geographical interests touching various core regions of Israel: the towns of Shechem, Succoth, and Penuel, on either side of the Jordan River; a Midianite war that involves Naphtali, Asher, Manasseh, and Ephraim; and Barak's muster of Zebulun and Naphtali (4:10), whatever the date of Deborah's identification with Ephraim (4:5). Such material, joined under the auspices of Israel as the people of Yahweh, fits naturally into an Israelite scribal setting, and it is unnecessary to consider these religious ideals the exclusive domain of Judah and later periods. Moreover, the addition of the Ehud tale in front of these, whenever it was accomplished, would create a collection that is introduced by a Benjaminite hero. Such a narrative work would still stand outside the sphere of Judah, even as it could finally offer the kind of transitional setting proposed by Philip Davies (2007b) for the transfer of Israelite lore to Judah.

One other detail suggests an Israelite context for the early collection of this material: each hero is the communal property of a different Israelite group, so that the assemblage as a whole offers a model for Israelite collaboration under Yahweh's power. No single region or city center is permitted to dominate the picture of this period. Ehud is from Benjamin; Deborah from Ephraim; Barak from Naphtali; Gideon from Abiezer and Manasseh (6:11, 15); Abimelech

---

[22] In thinking through this issue, I have benefited from conversation with Sara Milstein and Lauren Monroe, both of whom doubt the necessity of a single compositional act for the first combination of hero stories in Judges. This line of thought was provoked in part by Jack Sasson's hesitation to accept Richter's *Retterbuch* (personal communication).

rules Shechem. Further, Jephthah comes from Gilead in the east (11:1), and Samson represents the southern foothills, next to the Philistines (13:2, 25; 14:1; etc.). These locations probably date from different stages in the development of Judges as a book, yet their variety suggests a pattern that emphasizes Israelite collaboration and decentralization. When Judah is eventually included through Othniel (3:7–11), it follows the introductory model of Ehud and Benjamin, framing the whole by leading it (Milstein 2010).[23] This pattern shows how an Israelite mindset dominated the formation of Judges in a way that allowed it to maintain a deeply Israel-oriented cast even when it was taken into Judah's sphere. Such an orientation need not be attributed to a single moment or reconstructed composition. The process by which Judges took shape appears to have stayed in the circle of Israel for a considerable period, so that multiple phases of its transmission and revision took place there. At some point, the people of Judah gained access to this collection of stories without kings and made it a prelude to their narrative of David and the two kingdoms. Even with this objective, they did not strip Judges of its Israelite character, a character that makes it the starting point for my analysis of Israelite content in the Bible's primary narrative.

[23] In the last stages of Judges' growth, a new introduction was added that bridges the conquest under Joshua and this period of early life in the land. Judah completely dominates Judges 1, as its success contrasts with the serial failure of Israel's other tribes. Oddly, the report of Israel's failure to defeat the Canaanites incorporates the unexpected success of Joseph, which makes Bethel its home (1:22–6). Milstein (2010, 146–61) makes a case for the "revision through introduction" of this chapter on its own, with a Bethel tradition recast in service of Judah's preeminence. Gross (2009, 145–54) considers the list of failures to be the work of a postexilic author using Joshua and other prior materials, looking at the rest of Israel from the vantage of Yehud.

5

The Family of Jacob

The books of Judges and Genesis are ultimately founded on similar visions of Israel's political character as an association of distinct peoples. In Judges, the assumption of such an arrangement is visible especially in the core tales that involve collaboration or confrontation between groups, as in the Song of Deborah (Judg. 5:14–18) and the Ephraim/Gilead conflict (12:1–6). While the Judges tales take for granted the decentralized association, and none of them offers a formal explanation for their relationship, the Jacob story in Genesis accounts for Israel's unity through the bond of brotherhood. For the ancient Near East, this explicit account of a tribal association as sons of one ancestral father is rare, perhaps even unique. Neither the well-documented peoples of the second-millennium Mari archives nor the variety of first-millennium references to Arameans and Chaldeans are characterized by clear relations of brotherhood, as supplied by the Genesis genealogy.

The most detailed indigenous writing that relates to these social structures is found in the royal correspondence of the Mari archives from early second-millennium Mesopotamia.[1] In this material, large-scale groups that act as politically independent players are not always defined by cities or "lands" (Akkadian *mātum*), and their membership may transcend the boundaries of entities defined by settlements. It is useful to call such groups "tribes" (see Chapter 13 on Amorites). At Mari, the best-documented division is unified in a spatial scheme, as Sons of the Right Hand (Binu Yamina) and Sons of the Left Hand (Binu Sim'al).[2] At Mari and beyond, one may occasionally speak

---

[1] The best general introduction to the letters from the Mari archives, with numerous translated texts organized by theme, is that of Jean-Marie Durand (1997, 1998, 2000). Crucial early interpretation of the social landscape is found in Charpin and Durand (1986) and Durand (1992), extended in the lengthy study by Durand (2004). See also Fleming (2004a).

[2] For a general discussion of these confederations in the Mari evidence, see Fleming (2004a), chapter 2. This material will be addressed further in Chapter 13, on the Amorites. Kinship relationships in the social landscape attested at Mari are also explored carefully by Adam Miglio (2010).

of "brotherhood" (*aḫḫūtum/atḫūtum*), but this is applied to any political relationship that could be set in the metaphor of the nuclear family, with allied kings or peoples thus rendered "brothers."[3] I am not aware of cuneiform evidence for any allied peoples who understood themselves to be literal brothers in a genealogical system such as that of Genesis.

A considerable literature has developed on the ethnology and anthropological investigation of tribal societies, hearkening back especially to the proposals of E. E. Evans-Pritchard (1940).[4] One essential element of anthropological interpretation was "segmentary lineage," or tribal relationships among peers, ideally defined by brotherhood descended from a common ancestor (Sahlins 1968, 50–2; Caton 1990, 90–9). Such tribal organization naturally calls to mind the family scheme of Jacob in Genesis, and it can be too easy to make the connection with Genesis without recognizing the impressive novelty of the biblical phenomenon. Above all, the evidence for actual genealogical systems linked to tribal social organization is overwhelmingly oral. In a provocative reflection on the primacy of orality among the tribal Balga of modern Jordan, Andrew Shryock (1997) addresses the tensions between oral and written modes of discourse for both modern tribal groups and the anthropologists who study them. Among the Jordanian Bedouin, the orality of tribal genealogy is essential to its use in constructing history. "This mode of history making is not only textless, it is avowedly *antitextual* as well" (p. 34). Local efforts to produce written renditions of oral lore can inspire angry antagonism. "It would seem that tribal history, in its spoken forms, simply refuses to become historiography. It cannot be made textual and, at the same time, retain its peculiar genius: its malleability, its capacity to include and exclude with a word – its deft ability, if need be, to disappear entirely" (p. 34).

Against the backdrop of oral genealogy, the Genesis account of Jacob comes as a surprise for its very textuality. It appears to be a written expression of just the material that Shryock finds to be steadfastly oral in modern settings. By its biblical form, the Jacob family scheme would seem to give up the "malleability" that made it supremely useful for negotiating contemporary relationships. Shryock (p. 33) concludes that the Jordanian Balga could not imagine discussing genealogical history in the abstract, outside the context of current issues. Viewed in terms of modern textuality, written genealogy steps outside current usefulness. Yet Shryock's model could also highlight the role of textual malleability in ancient writing. It may be that we should no more expect the Genesis genealogy to reflect a single authorial moment than we would imagine such for oral lore. Fluidity is essential to the application of genealogical

---

3 For the general usage, see the *CAD* s.v. *aḫḫūtu* 3 "brotherhood (referring to a political relationship)," most often applied to rulers; and *atḫūtu*, "relationship between brothers and sisters, friendly political relations (between allies of equal standing), partnership relation," especially (b) "in political contexts," with examples from Mari and el-Amarna, all involving kings. Dustin Nash is currently working on a doctoral dissertation devoted to the language of brotherhood in the Bible and ancient Near Eastern texts (Cornell University).

4 The classic biblical application of this literature is that of Robert Wilson (1977).

history to the present situations, and this suits the nature of ancient textual transmission.

One more dimension of Shryock's study relates directly to Jacob in Genesis. Shryock (p. 21) decries segmentary analyses that result in the definition of "timeless social relationships," as if genealogy had nothing to do with history. To the contrary, this lore belonged to a long and stable tradition: "their genealogical knowledge was not simply a model of social topography; it was a way of articulating past and present, a way of transmitting and talking about history" (p. 22). Moreover, stories told to Shryock in 1989/90 were told in very similar form to European travelers throughout the nineteenth century. "The long genealogies of 'Adwani shaykhs, which I was prepared to dismiss as fiction, could be traced, using textual and epigraphic evidence, well into the eighteenth century" (p. 23). As a whole, therefore, "tribal history was a *received* tradition, a rich canon of memorized stories and poems, most of them demonstrably old." If we combine this line of argument with the aspect of malleability, we should expect in the Jacob lore an intersection between traditions with ancient roots and concerns from a later date of composition.[5] The Jacob genealogy should be about Israel's past, as relevant to Israelites who still have a stake in the identities of the separate peoples recalled. This biblical tradition is most at home in an Israelite setting, not in Judah. Equally, it reflects an inclusive impulse, as do the revisions in Judges that emphasize Israel by name.

A. The Birth Narrative (Genesis 29:31–30:24) and the Twelve Tribes of Israel

As a story, the Jacob material in Genesis is more coherent than the Abraham texts that precede it. Jacob provokes his brother Esau to blood lust by stealing his father's blessing (ch. 27); he runs away to his family in Syria, where he marries the sisters Leah and Rachel (chs. 28–9); after having many sons, he sneaks away from Laban, his father-in-law, who pursues him and forces a formal treaty (chs. 30–1); and he is finally reconciled to Esau, after wrestling a divine figure for a blessing (chs. 32–3). In this plot, with its memorable scenes of human wants in conflict, the list of births in Gen. 29:31–30:24 slows the action drastically and can strike us as a sideshow. Nevertheless, Jacob's first purpose is to beget the sons who will represent Israel, and the text lingers because the relationships between these sons are relevant to later communities. While the whole Jacob cycle may preserve important elements of Israelite, non-Judahite conceptions of the past, the heart of the text's political sensibility is found in the account of the family itself.

---

[5] Shryock's analysis of Jordan's Balga offers an alternative to the more stark limitations placed on traditional memory in the work of Harald-Martin Wahl in his study of the Jacob traditions (1997, 271–3, etc.). By recognizing continuity of tradition, we do not arrive at "historicity"; rather, we reach toward earlier conceptions of identity and its application to Israel through time.

1. The Jacob Story as Israelite

Geography alone has long connected Jacob with the north: his outward journey leads him through Bethel (28:10–22), and he returns to Shechem (33:18–20); on the way home, he stops in Mahanaim and Penuel, east of the Jordan (32:2–3, 23–33) – all sites in Israel.[6] This landscape does not seem to have originated in Judah. Confirmation that the Jacob story was known in Israel by the eighth century may be found in Hosea 12, as part of a book occupied with the situation of this realm before it fell to Assyria (de Pury 2001).[7] In this chapter of Hosea, a few laconic references suggest whole episodes that are familiar as Genesis narratives: birth as Esau's twin (v. 4a); wrestling with God (vv. 4b–5a); encounter with God at Bethel (v. 5b); and flight to Syria to get a wife, where he had to work as a shepherd to obtain her (v. 13).[8]

There is a geographical obstacle to the alignment of Hosea's Jacob references and the full narrative found in Genesis. Only two geographical details are offered in Hosea, if nothing is assumed from Genesis: Jacob used to meet and speak with Yahweh at Bethel (12:5), and he fled to Syria (Aram, v. 13). Although verses 4–5 know of Jacob's struggle with God, otherwise called an "angel," this episode is not located in the east at Penuel, nor is it associated with naming as "Israel." Flight to and return from Aram do not require reference to sites east of the Jordan River, which appear only with Jacob's return in Genesis 31–3. The book of Hosea as a whole appears to be oriented toward the west, where Israel had its capital; the land is frequently called Ephraim for its western highlands (4:17; 5:4; etc.).[9] In contrast, the return portion of the Jacob

---

[6] Other sites include the Aramean boundary established at Galeed/Mizpah (31:47–8) and Succoth as an initial camp, before settlement at Shechem (33:17). Albert de Pury's long investigation into the Jacob cycle (1975) works within the framework of Israelite geography. Then, the related volumes of Erhard Blum (1984) and David Carr (1996) develop the notion of an independent Jacob cycle that was expanded in stages to include Joseph and then the other ancestral narratives.

[7] As understood by de Pury, the Hosea text assumes knowledge of an established story that has much in common with Genesis 25–35. More recently, Blum (2009) places similar emphasis on the evidence of Hosea. A full version of the Jacob cycle in Genesis 25*, 27–33 would already have existed by the first half of the eighth century. Jean-Daniel Macchi (2001, 150–2) argues carefully that Hosea 12 may have much in common with the Jacob cycle of Genesis, but it knows nothing of the theological justification of the binding "composition-stratum" of that text, which must therefore be later than Hosea. To my mind, this valuable observation does not prove the binding compositional layer of Genesis 31 later than Hosea 12; it means only that the Hosea writer is working with a version of some theological independence.

[8] Cf. Gen. 25:21–6a for the birth of twins; 32:23–33 for wrestling with God; 28:10–22 (cf. 31:13; 35:1–7) for meeting God at Bethel; 27:41–5 for the flight to Syria; and 29:15–30 (cf. 30:25–43; chapter 31) for working as a shepherd to get a wife. The competition with Esau is implied by both the birth and the Syrian flight (verb *brḥ*; also Gen. 27:43).

[9] Various other details display the western vantage, whether the interest lies more to the north or to the south: note that the prophet's first son is named Jezreel, the royal stronghold (1:4–5); and religious offenses are assailed in relation to Gilgal (4:15; 9:15); Beth-aven/Bethel (4:15; 5:8; 10:5, 8); Gibeah (5:8); Ramah (5:8); and Samaria (8:5–6). Murder is committed on the way to Shechem (6:9). In the east, Gilead is once condemned as a "city" of wrongdoers (6:8); the east is not excluded, but the composition and transmission of Hosea appear to have taken place in the west.

cycle – and only the return – lingers in the east, with multiple episodes and bits of tradition naming known eastern Israelite sites: Mizpah, Mahanaim, Penuel, and Succoth. The wrestling episode represents the most striking contrast, claimed for Penuel in Gen. 32:23–33, along with the very identification of Jacob as Israel. Yet in Hosea 12, it is left without a specific location and could be assumed to occur in the west. It appears that when the current Jacob cycle of Genesis was put together, it combined versions or variants from west and east.[10] Neither Hosea nor Genesis, however, suggests an origin in Judah.

Beyond geography, the birth narrative in 29:31–30:24 reflects the political configuration of Israel, not Judah: the people of Israel are defined by kinship, as a tribal family, brothers who are the sons of one father. Each people named as a brother shares standing in the family as a son of Jacob, while the scheme of four different mothers allows nuances of status. This differentiated status draws attention to one more observation from Shryock's study of "oral history" among the tribal people of Jordan: the historical dimension of their oral and genealogical traditions provides a basis for explaining higher and lower rank.

When 'Abbadis challenge the 'Adwan, they assert an equality of honor that 'Adwanis fail to discern. The language in which the two tribes confront each other is intrinsically unbalanced, and the rhetorical tools needed to build historical truth – namely, poetry and genealogy – have accumulated, over time, in the hands of dominant shaykhs. Thus, in the Balga today, colloquial memory is composed of speech acts that reimpose power differentials located in a real, historical past. *There is nothing in orthodox segmentary theory, which takes either the moral or the political equality of tribes for granted, that can explain why asymmetries of this sort should ever arise* [emphasis added]. Yet Haj Ahmad Yusif explains the origins of 'Adwani dominance with perfect clarity: it is the handiwork of his ancestors, who made history in epic, spectacular ways. (1997, 211)

In the birth narrative of Genesis 29–30, the determination to explain differences of tribal importance would also belong to a mode of discourse that interprets a present social landscape by inequities recalled from a real past. The Jordanian tribal analogy leads us to expect that the Genesis scheme would have been created to explain the experiences of existing groups. Even with Judah included, the portrait of a family that incorporates all the peoples of Israel derives from Israel, the society that produced the Judges traditions.

Within the Jacob cycle of Genesis, the account of all Israel's people by its differentiated tribes is tied to the western, Bethel-linked component of the Jacob collection. The eastern interest emerges only with the return to meet Esau in chapter 31, and the role of the children in that encounter is dependent on the birth narrative of chapters 29–30. Jacob separates his eleven sons according to their mothers (32:23; 33:1–7). Joseph and Rachel come last, in the place of honor, and this son evokes Bethel directly, as reflected in the conquest of this

---

[10] Uwe Becker (2009) proposes that Bethel was inserted into the Jacob narrative only after the fall of Jerusalem in 587, following Knauf's (2006) interpretation of Bethel's prominence under Neo-Babylonian hegemony. Bethel is the one site recalled in Hosea 12, however, and this shifting of the tradition to a later period is unwarranted. Walter Dietrich (2001, 201) considers the eastern material in the Jacob story to be older than the rest, potentially as early as the reign of David.

town in Judg. 1:22–6, in which Joseph is a people of its own, separate from the failures of Ephraim and Manasseh (vv. 27–9). Like the book of Judges, the Jacob text in Genesis appears to have circulated in Israel, evidently in different locations with varied forms and contributions, before it reached Judah. The birth narrative may come from a relatively later and systematizing hand.

2. Evaluating the Twelve-Tribe Tradition in the Jacob Cycle

The first feature of the family scheme in the Genesis Jacob cycle is the fact that it is divided into two parts: the main birth narrative linked directly to the account of Leah and Rachel in chapters 29–30 (29:31–30:24) and the separate birth of Benjamin in Ephrathah/Bethlehem after return from Syria (35:16–20). In both narrative and geographical terms, these stories are totally separate: Benjamin has his own location of birth, the only son who is homegrown in the future land; and his birth is tied to Rachel's death, which is marked by a shrine in Bethlehem. The claim on Rachel's grave is somehow separate from Benjamin, because Bethlehem is south of Jerusalem, solidly in the region associated otherwise with Judah.[11] It seems therefore that the tale of Benjamin's birth was built onto the existing tradition of Rachel's tomb, at a time when someone could identify Benjamin with Judah and the south. There is no reason to imagine that any birth story for Benjamin had a separate existence apart from Rachel and Bethlehem, so it appears that the account of Benjamin's birth was composed to complement the larger birth narrative now in chapters 29–30.

Equally, the birth narrative of Gen. 29:31–30:24 culminates in Joseph, the long-awaited son for Rachel. This role for Joseph also survives in the account of his treatment as Jacob's favorite in the sequence of Genesis 37, which shows no awareness of Benjamin as a second son from Rachel. So far as Joseph supplies the anticipated fulfillment of Rachel's desire in the birth narrative of Genesis 30, we are faced with a counting problem: only eleven sons are born, and the Bible's later counts lead us to expect twelve – including Benjamin. The evident solution is that the birth narrative must incorporate at least one level of revision, so that the eleven sons in chapters 29–30 already anticipate Benjamin, whose birth was not part of the original tale. Awareness of the coming Benjamin birth is displayed first of all in the duplicate etymology provided for him in 30:24: after having declared in verse 23 that God has removed (verb *'sp*) her disgrace, "she named him Joseph, saying, 'May Yahweh add (verb *ysp*) another son for me.'" The question then is whether this is the only addition that assumes a count of twelve.[12]

---

[11] See esp. Judg. 17:7, where the Levite of the Dan narrative is introduced as a man "from Bethlehem of Judah" (also vv. 8–9). In the Goliath story, David is identified as "the son of a certain Ephrathite from Bethlehem of Judah" (1 Sam. 17:12). Interestingly, Bethlehem is not included in the list of Judah towns in the highlands for the initial conquest according to Josh. 15:48–60, though it is part of the Judah genealogy in 1 Chronicles 2, in the line of Caleb through Hur (v. 51).

[12] The notion of twelve Israelite tribes clearly represents an attempt to incorporate the widest possible range of groups, and Judah in particular. In spite of Noth's interpretation as part of the earliest definition of Israel as an amphictyony (1966b), it is natural to expect the number twelve

It is possible that the eleven remaining sons were part of an original count that excluded Benjamin, but this seems unlikely, if only based on the unprecedented number. As argued carefully by Erhard Blum (1984, 106–7), the birth sequence does not sustain successful division by the J and E sources of the Documentary Hypothesis. The story is certainly preoccupied with the competition between Leah and Rachel, with Leah the unloved first wife introduced in 29:1–30. The larger purpose, however, is to account for Jacob's family as a unit, and even the earliest version should present what could be considered a full set of tribal sons.[13] Further, the distinction of status by four distinct mothers appears to be intrinsic to the description of a tribal family. This means that Bilhah and Zilpah, the servants of Rachel and Leah in 30:4–13, are original to the birth narrative, and the first notices of their service, attached to each marriage in 29:24 and 29, probably represent additions in anticipation of this position as mothers.[14] The four sons of the servants are Dan, Naphtali, Gad, and Asher, all of which are named in the core list of tribal sayings in Genesis 49, to be discussed below. All but Gad appear in the Song of Deborah, with Dan and Asher paired as coastal groups who fail to join, and Naphtali the one participating people praised at the end of the sequence (Judg. 5:17–18). These groups are less celebrated in the finished biblical collection, but they were clearly central to early Israel.

The substitution of the two servants for Jacob's two wives in Gen. 30:4–13 is framed by a competition between sisters that begins with Leah's success: "Rachel saw that she had not borne a child for Jacob, and Rachel was jealous of her sister" (30:1). Leah must have at least one son already. In the episode that follows the two sons born to the servant Zilpah, Leah's son Reuben brings his mother mandrakes (v. 14). Leah then trades these for a night with her husband, whom Rachel monopolizes, with Issachar resulting. The text recalls Leah's status as unloved wife (v. 15), introduced in the earlier part of chapter 29. Reuben and Issachar are thus assigned to Leah, linked by the elder brother's gift that leads to the younger. Issachar and Zebulun represent a consistent pair

---

to reflect an all-inclusive and therefore later perspective. In his landmark study, de Geus (1976, 112–15) considered the twelve-tribe system to be a secondary but still monarchic development, adapted to the incorporation of Judah. More recently, some have considered the picture of twelve to be a postmonarchic idealization (e.g., Levin 1995).

[13] In this respect, Westermann's hypothesis of an expanded story of sisterly competition is unconvincing (1985, 471–7). His core narrative would include only Reuben from 29:31–2, the exchanges of 30:1–6 that produce Dan from Rachel's servant Bilhah, the birth of Zebulun after Reuben brings his mother mandrakes (30:14–18), and the concluding birth of Joseph in 30:22–4.

[14] In its tale of Jacob's departure and Laban's pursuit, chapter 31 proceeds as if only Leah, Rachel, and their own children were in view, with reference to the servants only tacked onto the search of tents in verse 33. Rachel and Leah speak of "our children" (v. 16); Jacob puts "his children and his wives" on camels (v. 17); Laban complains about not saying goodbye to his "sons" and "daughters" (v. 28, cf. 32:1); he claims ownership of both daughters and sons but says, "my daughters, now, what shall I do about these today? Or about their children that they have borne?" (v. 43). Their own childbirth is all that is mentioned.

in the independent tribal lists of early poetry, and the combination is expected here as well.[15]

As an explanation of Israel's unity in family terms, the birth narrative would then have included at least eight tribes: Reuben, Dan, Naphtali, Gad, Asher, Issachar, Zebulun, and Joseph. Geographically, this collection would account for regions north and south of the Jezreel Valley, east and west of the Jordan River:

> North of the Jezreel Valley, in the west: Dan, Naphtali, Asher, Issachar, Zebulun;
> South of the Jezreel Valley, in the west: Joseph;
> East of the Jordan River: Reuben, Gad.

Although the collection of eight is weighted to the north and east, Joseph represents the entire central highlands as the long-awaited son of Rachel, Jacob's beloved. This may already envision the genealogical interpretation of Ephraim and Manasseh, the two peoples that dominated the region, as the sons of Joseph (so, Genesis 48).[16] Benjamin would be the expected neighbor to the south of Joseph, but he is omitted from the core birth tradition, only tacked on as a second favorite son by the Bethlehem birth story of 35:16–20.

Every biblical tradition for the geography of the central highlands regards this as the domain of Ephraim and Manasseh, with Joseph only linked to land with the conquest of Bethel (Judg. 1:22–6). To give Joseph a prominent position as a people in early Israel, he must be made the father of the two major groups in the region – evidently, in the interest of some specific constituency, most easily identified with the scribal and religious center of Bethel. In geographical terms, therefore, the omission of Ephraim and Manasseh (or Machir) from the birth narrative is perhaps its most arresting feature. Then with the removal of Benjamin, the Joseph-oriented account lays claim to the entire political heartland of the Israelite kingdom. As evidence for setting, this suggests the framework of Israel, yet at a relatively later date – perhaps no earlier than the eighth century, when Bethel is so visible in the books of Hosea and Amos (e.g., Hos. 12:5; Amos 4:4; 5:5).[17]

---

[15] In Gen. 49:13–15, Deut. 33:18–19, and Judg. 5:14–15, the pair is always rendered as Zebulun and Issachar, rather than the reverse in the birth narrative of Gen. 30:18–20.

[16] One indication of the antiquity of Ephraim as dominant group in the central highlands is its leading position in the Song of Deborah (Judg. 5:14). There, Manasseh is missing, in favor of Machir, with no reference to Joseph. The tribal lists of Genesis 49 and Deuteronomy 33 give priority to Joseph as a category (Gen. 49:22–6; Deut. 33:13–17); only the latter makes the explicit connection between Joseph and the two other names (v. 17).

[17] It is difficult to determine whether such a conceptual innovation could have occurred any earlier than this, and decisions regarding dates will depend on systematic choices about the combination of biblical stories into larger narratives. The chronology for such combination has tended to shift later over the past generation, but it remains unstable. For me, the key considerations are the secondary character of Joseph's replacement of Ephraim and the Israelite framework for the discussion of how to name and explain the central highlands.

This leaves three more groups for evaluation: Simeon, Levi, and Judah, the other early sons of Leah in Gen. 29:33–5. Judah is a special case: it clearly represents a known people and polity, embodied in the monarchy by that name. It is less certain, however, when that kingdom was first called Judah (see Chapter 3), and the old poetic tribal lists do not settle its ancient inclusion in Israel. Judah is missing from the Song of Deborah (Judg. 5:14–18), and its incorporation in Gen. 49:8–10 and Deut. 33:7 is debated.[18] If we are to take Judah as part of the original birth narrative, yielding nine tribes, the absence of Benjamin is troubling. Geography would place Benjamin at the south end of the central highlands, as a longstanding and essential bridge – or barrier – between Judah and Israel. Incorporation of Judah without Benjamin would create an awkward gap in the tribal map. Simeon and Levi are then difficult because they have no clear place in the geography of Israel at all. Although the Joshua land allotments define a territory around Beersheba in the deep south of Judah (Josh. 19:1–9), Simeon has no place in the Judges tales, and its mention in Gen. 49:5 only reflects the Dinah text of Genesis 34. Any inclusion of Simeon would have to be brought with Judah, as part of a local southern tradition. Finally, Levi never represents a political entity or territory.[19]

It is impossible to separate the original list from additions with certainty, but the set of eight presented above is most plausible.[20] Although I imagine that the name of "Judah" was very likely linked to some part of the southern highlands at an early date, perhaps even before David and Solomon, I see little solid biblical evidence for Judah's early incorporation into Israel as one of its "tribes." Simeon and Levi likewise have no geographical basis for a connection with the association defined by Jacob's family in Genesis 29–30. Among the first four sons of Leah, only Reuben is found in the Song of Deborah (Judg. 5:15–16), where this people is located east of the Jordan River. The tradition of an eastern location is confirmed by the land allotments of Josh. 13:15–23, along with the tradition of two and a half tribes occupying the territory taken from Sihon and Og (Numbers 32). The complex of biblical reference to Reuben is substantial, and the role as Leah's firstborn and provider in Gen. 29:32 and 30:14 suggests a traditional respect for a real constituent of

---

[18] For a review of the ideas advanced in monographs by Beyerle (1997), de Hoop (1999), Macchi (1999), and Schorn (1997), see Sparks (2003). Against the notion that Judah was added to the roster of Israel only in the sixth century, Sparks concludes that Judah is original to Deut. 33:7, and its tribal saying was expanded in Gen. 49:8, 10–12. These two poems probably date from the eighth century, in contrast to the ninth-century list from the Song of Deborah, which omits Judah.

[19] Schorn (1997, 63–79) omits the whole set of Leah's first four sons from the original text, in part based on difficulties such as these. In spite of Reuben's incorporation in the Song of Deborah (Judg. 5:15–16), Schorn's entire project revolves around the proposition that this people was never part of Israel and only appears in the Bible as part of Judah's post-Israelite reimagining of the distant past.

[20] I would like to thank Aron Freidenreich for his contribution to the process by which I reasoned through these problems.

Israel.[21] With its count of Leah's "three sons" after Levi (29:34) and the "six sons" after Zebulun (30:20; cf. 17 and 19), our finished text underscores that all of Leah's offspring are essential and looks forward to the addition of Benjamin to yield the perfect twelve (so, 30:24).

By this analysis of Gen. 29:31–30:24, no narrative ingredient is lost by the removal of Simeon, Levi, and Judah from the older birth story. Both wives and both servants retain their roles in delineating nuances of social status. Rachel remains in competition with Leah, with all the same episodes. Joseph is still the destination, so that Rachel is finally satisfied, and Jacob's beloved gives birth to his favorite son. All of this is central to the genealogical purpose of the story. The crucial contribution of this text to Israelite lore is its explanation of Israel as a tribal family. Like the Song of Deborah and the Ephraim/Gilead conflict in Judges, the Genesis birth narrative pictures Israel as an association of distinct peoples that must somehow cooperate. Only here, however, do we find the classic notion of a tribal society with current relationships defined by ancestral kinship. This picture forms a key part of the Bible's constellation of Israelite traditions about identity.[22]

B. An Extended Genealogy in the Jacob Story

The essential genealogy of the Jacob story combines two generations to define the peoples of Israel as a family of brothers, sons of one father. Genesis in its current form introduces Jacob by two earlier generations, as the son of

---

[21] For the basic argument that Reuben was part of an early Israelite association, the foundational reference remains Cross (1988).

[22] The development of Joseph as ancestral favorite among the family of Jacob was then applied to a separate story for this figure, inspired directly by the account of sons in Gen. 29:31–30:24 in the context of the Jacob cycle. In a sense, both the birth narrative of chapters 29–30 and the account of the dreams in chapter 37 are "Joseph stories," staking the same claim to leadership in Israel, with priority over Ephraim and Manasseh. Whatever the date of the oldest Joseph narrative and the process of its transmission into what is now Genesis 37 and 39–47, the same Israelite, probably Bethel-based perspective appears to launch it. The named characters of the Joseph narrative are the precise group that follows the birth sequence of chapters 29–30 plus 35, only lacking Levi: Reuben, Simeon, Judah, Joseph, and Benjamin. These suggest a later setting, probably in Judah, as reflected in Judah's leading role as sympathetic son, after the initial debacle of Joseph's sale into slavery, especially when he becomes the brothers' spokesman in the later stages of their negotiations with both Jacob and Joseph (Gen. 43–4). The whole Joseph story is frequently placed in postmonarchic Judah contexts in recent interpretation. Emphasizing its points of contact with material from Exodus, Deuteronomy, and other narrative outside Genesis, Georg Fischer (2001) dates the whole Joseph story to the Persian period. Macchi (1999, 123–7) also regards the whole story as a "novella of the diaspora." Nevertheless, this more complete narrative must depend on a tale linked more directly to the Genesis birth narrative alone and likewise inspired by advocacy for Joseph in Israel. Such would work for the very limited original story envisioned by Peter Weimar (2006) in verses 5a, 6–7, 8a, 9, 11a, 12, 17, 18, 22a, 23, 24, and 29–30. If we imagine an early version of the Joseph story that names Reuben as the sympathetic brother, this could confirm the original place of Reuben in the birth narrative and suit the same late Israelite setting. The possibility of an older "Reuben" level of the Joseph story was first suggested by Redford (1970).

Isaac and the grandson of Abraham. We could treat any reference to Abraham and Isaac in the Jacob story as secondary, inspired by combination with other narrative material, except that two parts of the Jacob cycle mention these ancestors in nonstereotyped ways. Isaac and his wife Rebekah are crucial to the introduction of Jacob and Esau, as both parents are central to the birth account, after which they divide in their preferences, and Rebekah instigates Jacob's flight (Gen. 25:21–34; 27:1–45). Then the tale of Jacob's return is cast as a flight from Laban (Genesis 31), who was introduced in 27:43 as Rebekah's brother, and the constant tension between Jacob and Laban is finally resolved by a treaty and boundary marker set up on oath to the god or gods of Abraham and Nahor as "their fathers" (31:53).[23] These references to Isaac and Rebekah, and Abraham and Nahor, are not superficial adjustments to fit separate stories, and they suggest that the genealogical framework of the Israelite Jacob story could encompass more than just the two generations of Jacob and sons.

Although the birth narrative in Genesis 30 revolves around Jacob and his sons in two generations, the competition between Rachel and Leah takes for granted their marriage to Jacob in a previous episode. This situation is set up in the main part of chapter 29, where Jacob arrives in the land of the Bene Qedem (Sons of the East) and inquires after "Laban son of Nahor" (vv. 1, 5). Jacob loves Rachel, yet is tricked into marrying Leah first, so that the sisters are doomed to competition from the start. Genesis 29–30 are thus deeply intertwined, with the first chapter preparing the ground for the birth narrative in the second. Taken by itself, the birth narrative in Genesis 30 would not require a setting outside the future land of Israel. Laban is never mentioned, and there is no reference to Jacob's work as a herdsman. The whole family lives together in proximity, and both Reuben and Jacob come in daily from the "field" (śāde, vv. 14, 16). Chapter 29 places the birth account in the context of Jacob's sojourn in the east, and that story presumes a reason for flight to a new country, which is provided by the exchange with Isaac and Esau in chapter 27. This whole exchange introduces another dimension to the genealogy of Jacob and its purposes, a dimension that has nothing to do with the goal of explaining the unity of Israel as a family under one father.

The story of the two brothers in Genesis 25, 27, and 32–33 now frames the birth of Jacob's family and his encounter with God east of the Jordan River. In itself, however, it explains the relationship between Jacob and Esau, who represent two peoples from the same father. Although the peoples of Jacob and Esau are separated by Jacob's ambition, they are nevertheless twins by the same mother, with the closest possible family connection. None of Jacob's individual sons shares such a bond. With its play on the older twin's ruddiness (ʾādōm/ʾĕdōm), even without the explicit note at the end of 27:30, Esau is

---

[23] In Genesis 24, which was once considered a J narrative but is now widely dated late and to a Judahite writer, Laban is still Rebekah's brother (v. 29), but another generation is added to the simple statement of 31:53, so that Nahor is Laban's grandfather rather than father (24:15, 24). Already, Blum (1984, 158–61) located the chapter in his deuteronomistic compositional layer.

equated with the kingdom of Edom, south of Moab on the east side of the Jordan Rift Valley. The connection between Jacob/Israel and Esau/Edom is the special preoccupation of Genesis 27, when each son comes to Isaac for his paternal blessing, and once again, the explanation is given a genealogical framework, adding a third generation to the Jacob clan. This relationship between Jacob and Esau has nothing to do with Laban and his eastern or Syrian people, so that the two interests appear to have been combined in order to organize both sets of diplomatic concerns on the basis of family conflicts and resolution. The question is how Edom could have been of particular interest to Israel, as opposed to Judah, which offers an easier southern proximity. Within the collection from Genesis 27–33, the entire geography indicates an Israelite compositional setting, yet the Esau thread, firmly interwoven as it is, is geographically unexpected and calls for investigation.

The whole Jacob/Esau plot depends on the notion that Jacob was the younger twin and supplanted his brother by trickery. The most egregious episode is recounted in Genesis 27, where Rebekah incites her favored son to subvert Isaac's intent by an elaborate hoax, cooked up in camp while Esau is out hunting for game to supply the ritual meal for his blessing. When Isaac inadvertently gives Jacob the older son's blessing, he promises both wealth and superiority. The latter is defined in sweeping terms: "May peoples serve you, and may clans bow to you. Be master of your brothers, and may your mother's sons bow to you" (27:29). This blessing does not appear to derive from the Jacob/Esau story itself, in that it plants the recipient in a whole family of brothers, all with the same mother, which likewise has no counterpart in the scheme of Jacob's sons.[24] At any rate, it cannot provide a setting for composition in an imagined period of domination over Edom.

Isaac's belated blessing on Esau could attempt a more direct commentary on political relations with Edom. This text anticipates a time when whoever is represented by Jacob will dominate the people represented by Esau: "By your sword you shall live, and your brother shall you serve; yet when you turn restive, you shall tear off his yoke from your neck" (Gen. 27:40). Based especially on these lines, along with Edom's southern location, some understand Genesis 27 as a Judahite text, in which the issue of relations with Esau must address tensions between Edom and Judah, not Israel.[25] Certainly, Edom became a major preoccupation for Judah after the withdrawal of Assyrian power, when Edomites began to move into Judah's eastern low country.[26] When joined to

---

[24] In this respect, it is not clear that the independent blessing texts are later additions based on combination with the birth of Jacob's sons in chapters 29–30 (so Westermann 1985, 436).

[25] See, e.g., Vorländer (1978, 299) and Wahl (1997, 250). Wahl declares that only two possible settings can explain the superiority of Jacob in the brother scheme of Genesis 27: the early monarchy and the seventh to fifth centuries. Only the latter is possible in terms of the general character of the text and its larger context.

[26] For a review of basic background, see Bartlett (1989). There is a stream of sixth-century prophecy against Edom in the Bible, including Jer. 49:7–22; Obadiah; Ezek 25:12–14; and cf. Isa. 21:11–12.

the resolution of this conflict in Genesis 33, however, the picture in chapter 27 envisions positive relations between Jacob and Esau as neighbors and peers, without subordination on either side.[27] Even with the humiliation depicted in chapter 27, Esau is drawn in sympathetic terms. Laban, who finally represents Aram in Genesis 31, is shown in a more negative light than Esau, who behaves honorably throughout every stage of his exchanges with Jacob. Further, the primary identity of Jacob's twin is Esau, not Edom, and "the sons of Esau" constitute the immediate company of Israel as a backcountry herding people, as portrayed in the eastern conquest account of Deuteronomy 2–3 (see 2:4). Esau and Jacob are at peace, and Esau has committed no offense.

Given the larger prominence of Israelite material in this part of the Jacob story, and the integration of the Esau conflict into the sweep of migration to and return from Laban's land, we must consider the possibility that Esau's relationship to Jacob in Genesis derives ultimately from Israel, not Judah. The great peculiarity of the Genesis portrayal is the definition of this link in terms of twins, indicating the closest imaginable proximity between brothers. It is not necessary that such a relationship be proposed for direct neighbors, and in fact, political alliances can leap-frog adjacent peoples.[28] With Yahweh's southern affinity, Israel may have understood itself to share even a religious heritage with its kin from the family of Esau.[29]

Abraham plays a much smaller role in the Jacob cycle than Isaac, yet he does appear in one reference that cannot be dismissed out of hand as editorial adaptation.[30] At the conclusion of Jacob's truce with Laban, Isaac and Abraham are invoked as ancestral witnesses, without reference to the promises.[31]

---

[27] Cf. the analyses of Blum (1984, 185) and J. A. Emerton (2004, 114–16). Because the idea of subordination derives solely from Gen. 27:40, in Esau's blessing, it is tempting to consider this a Judahite revision, especially if it requires the Judah perspective. Esau's original response to Isaac would conclude with the complaint, "now he has taken my blessing" (v. 36), and the section from that point through verse 40 would piggyback a second-class blessing for Esau onto the blessing for Jacob that is required by the primary plot.

[28] This could be true in the Mari evidence, where Yasmah-Addu's Mari kept close ties with Qatna, so as to stave off any threat from Yamhad, which lay between them. In the so-called Syro-Ephraimite war of the late eighth century, Judah looked for help beyond Israel and Damascus to the looming power of Assyria (Isaiah 7).

[29] The classic texts come from old hymns to Yahweh's going out to battle: from Sinai, Seir, and Mount Paran in Deut. 33:2; from Seir and Edom in Judg. 5:4 (cf. Sinai in v. 5); from Teman and Mount Paran in Hab. 3:3. Among these, the Song of Deborah is certainly Israelite, and Deuteronomy 33 appears so; for a detailed study within a fairly traditional framework, see Beyerle (1997). Habakkuk 3 is attached to later Judahite prophetic writing, though nothing in its contents points directly to Jerusalem or Judah; for the basic general investigation, see Hiebert (1986). On Yahweh's southern origin, see the pertinent sections of Lang (2002), Smith (2001), and van der Toorn (1996), which represent only a small sample of an enormous literature.

[30] Given the occurrence of Abraham in a Jacob text, it may be natural to conclude that Gen. 31:53 must be aware of the biblical Abraham narrative in some form (so Carr 1996, 257 n. 74). As discussed here, the narrative connection is not straightforward.

[31] Yahweh appears to Jacob at Bethel as "the god of your father Abraham and the god of Isaac" (Gen. 28:13), before promising land and descendants. This sequence is extended to include

After he has been vindicated from Laban's accusation of theft, innocently unaware of Rachel's deceit, Jacob declares that all his wealth during the time with Laban came from the fact that "[he] had the god of [his] father – the god of Abraham and the fear of Isaac" (v. 42). Laban does not want battle, however, and instead offers to make peace. To this end, he calls on the god of Abraham and the god of Nahor, evidently their two ancestral deities, to adjudicate any future dispute between their peoples. In his turn, Jacob swears the treaty oath itself by a deity defined by "the fear" (*pahad*) of his father Isaac (31:53). From this text alone, we could not tell that Isaac was the son of Abraham. Laban is a descendant ("son") of Nahor, according to Genesis 29:5, but otherwise, Abraham and Nahor are simply more distant ancestors.[32] According to Genesis 31, therefore, Abraham is not the name of a people and should be understood instead as an ancestral authority, with power to link distant relatives by his name.

Together, the roles of Isaac and Abraham in the Jacob cycle need not be removed automatically as reflections of the combined Abraham–Isaac–Jacob narrative in something close to our current book of Genesis, from a Judahite and postmonarchic setting. It is possible that Abraham and Isaac are first of all Jacob's antecedents, and their interest lies in how they relate Jacob to the peoples of Aram and Edom. If these had a place in Israelite thought, they would indicate that the genealogical approach to identity could explain relationships beyond the immediate family of associated tribal peoples. The multigenerational scheme of Israel's ancestry may therefore be more than a literary construct designed to piece together characters and stories from completely isolated origins.[33]

C. Genesis 49: The Sayings of Jacob

I have begun my investigation of Israelite writing in the Bible with a combination of Judges and Genesis because these two books share traditions that

---

Jacob in the possibly deuteronomistic introduction to Yahweh at Sinai (Exod. 3:6, 15–16; cf. 4:5) and appears in various other forms as shorthand for the ancestral contacts with God during the Genesis era.

[32] If we take Laban as Nahor's literal "son" in Gen. 29:5, then the generational relationship between Laban and Nahor on the one hand and between Jacob and Abraham on the other is asymmetrical, which is perhaps unexpected, with Nahor and Abraham in comparable religious roles.

[33] Within the framework considered here, the southern associations of Abraham and Isaac do not automatically demonstrate origins of their story traditions in Judah. Hebron and Beersheba, the two principal southern towns linked to these figures, have no clear political connection to the kingdom centered at Jerusalem and the house of David. Hebron's role in the rise of David (see Chapter 6) may even suggest the possibility of a relationship to Israel rather than to Judah, insofar as the David story is defined by Israel. Beersheba is not even firmly located in Judah, according to the tradition of tribal allotments that considers it part of a separate Simeon region (Josh. 19:2). The origins and literary histories of these biblical narratives must be worked out individually, with the possibility of some Israelite contribution to the process.

perceive Israel as an association of distinct peoples, rather than as a single unit acting collectively. Genesis offers an explanation of this association that does not appear in Judges: by hearkening back to an ancestral age, it presents Israel as kin, a family of brothers who share the same father, Jacob. The Jacob narrative then extends this genealogical account of Israel by casting back to generations before Jacob that explain relations between Israel and its inland neighbors, the Sons of Esau (or Edom) and the Damascus-based realm of Aram. At the center of the interpretation of Israel as a family stands the birth narrative of Genesis 30, in which the sons of Jacob are defined by four different mothers. In its final form, which most likely comes from Judah, Gen. 29:31–30:24 becomes the fountainhead of tribal lists in the Bible. The book of Genesis includes a second tribal list, however, that is not simply dependent on 29:31–30:24, although it stands in some relation to it: chapter 49 is a poem that collects Jacob's last words to his sons. This text offers a second key point of reference for the tradition of a tribal association in Genesis.

Genesis 49 consists of a series of statements about twelve tribes, naming all twelve sons of Jacob from chapters 29–30, without mention of Ephraim and Manasseh. Only the first four statements to Reuben, Simeon and Levi, and Judah include direct address to the sons in the voice of a father, plus the statement to Joseph in the last part of the text.[34] This contrast offers one immediate division in the collection. Moreover, the contrasting voices reflect a deeper difference of perspective in Genesis 49: where we find simple declarations about the various peoples of Israel, there would be no reason to read these as part of a family system without the wider Jacob narrative. In particular, the central series of six tribes in verses 13–21 involve brief statements without hint of relationship to Jacob as sons or to each other as brothers. Elements of the sections for Judah and Joseph share this perspective, as does the short Benjamin statement that closes the poem (v. 27). These direct statements are not genealogical, and they need have no connection to Jacob, his family, and his story. In effect, the address to Reuben and the others in a father's voice provide a genealogical framework for Genesis 49 that is not intrinsic to all of its contents.

This translation to the genealogical world of the Jacob story also aligns with one more critical detail from Genesis 49: only the first four and the last two tribes match the narrative order of Genesis 29–30, plus Benjamin in chapter 35. The same block of short sayings in 49:13–21 follows a sequence unrelated to the family pattern of chapter 30. Genesis 49 thus breaks down into two

---

[34] The declaration to Reuben begins, "you are my firstborn" (v. 3) and maintains the use of first-person perspective for the speaker and second-person for the addressee. Next, Simeon and Levi are treated as a pair, without address to them but with first-person statements in verses 6–7. Judah is addressed as "you" and "my son" (vv. 8–9). Joseph is addressed as "you" in verses 25–6, without clear allusion to Jacob as speaker. Also note verse 18, a brief prayer that has nothing to do with the framework of tribal statements: "I have waited for your deliverance, O Yahweh."

groups of material, with an independent block picked up in a framework that follows the Jacob story:

Genesis 49	Genesis 29:31–30:24; 35:16–20
Reuben	Reuben
Simeon	Simeon
Levi	Levi
Judah	Judah
Zebulun	Dan
Issachar	Naphtali
Dan	Gad
Gad	Asher
Asher	Issachar
Naphtali	Zebulun
Joseph	Joseph
Benjamin	Benjamin

Based in part on observations such as these, Jean-Daniel Macchi (1999) argues persuasively that Gen. 49:13–21 must be treated as a distinct collection with a compositional setting separate from the final poem. Based on the inclusion of Gad, which is known in the late ninth-century Mesha inscription, and the general political setting that would allow such focus on northern and eastern peoples within Israel, Macchi dates this prior collection to the ninth-century period of Omride expansion. The block of six groups would therefore be Israelite. For Macchi, the rest of the poem, with the narrative connections to the birth stories and to the misdeeds of Reuben, Simeon, and Levi (Gen. 34:25–31; 35:22), must belong to the postmonarchic period, after 586.

In terms of the tribal tradition, it is significant that Genesis 30 and 49 share the same set of six at the center of each text. The match of six names suggests a stable association of northern and eastern groups that stood – perhaps as a unit – in relation to the groups of the so-called central highlands, which came to dominate the kingdom of Israel from Benjamin in the house of Saul and from Ephraim in a series of royal houses and capitals that ended up with Samaria. In the birth narrative, the dominant peoples were assigned to Rachel, Jacob's preferred wife, yet the geographical contrast remains in Genesis 49, without the scheme of mothers. In spite of Macchi's conclusions regarding Gen. 49:13–21, the consistent character of this block of six tribes does not settle the extent of the literary core in each composition. In Genesis 29–30, the set of six leads inexorably to Joseph as the long-awaited son of Rachel, and Reuben is assigned a special role in helping his mother Leah bear more sons. It is possible, therefore, that the collection of tribal statements in Genesis 49 included other groups as a literary composition on its own. Based on the contrast of sequence and independent content, the account of the six peoples by itself appears not to be based on Genesis 30. This set is framed by two longer statements, both of which describe dominant peoples: Judah in verses

8–12 and Joseph in verses 22–6. In its current form, however, the promise that Judah will always be home to kings does not suit a writer from Israel (v. 10).

The closing line of the Joseph statement presents a special problem in that it speaks of blessings to be "on the head of Joseph, on the brow of the consecrated one among his brothers" (v. 26), language that could suggest Jacob's family. Yet the terminology of "brothers" has wide use in the ancient Near East for defining political relationships without need of a genealogical framework, and dependence on the Jacob cycle is not certain. Moreover, this line represents the one part of the Joseph statement in Genesis 49 that matches exactly the Joseph section of Deuteronomy 33, the one other poem built around the tribal scheme (Deut. 33:16). In both contexts, the shared line refers to blessings on Joseph's head, though the specific gifts differ. As a whole, Deuteronomy 33 is dominated much more by the notion of blessing, with the divine involvement that accompanies it,[35] though the figure of Joseph seems to inspire separate expressions of blessing in both texts.[36] If the Joseph statement in Gen. 49:22–6 has been revised in transmission, it is difficult to determine its layering with confidence.

The extent of the tribal list in the original composition of Genesis 49 remains out of reach. Comparison with Gen. 29:31–30:24 indicates the feasibility of incorporating the block of six into a longer collection, but the match of sequence for the others between the birth narrative and the poem point to a dependence of structure.[37] Reuben, Simeon, and Levi are too much defined by outside narrative to make sense as part of the original composition, especially when combined with the strong voice of father to son. Judah could be included only without the promise of kingship (Sparks 2003, 332), most likely with the lion statement stripped of the line with second-person address: "Judah is a lion's cub – *from the prey, my son, you went up*; he bent and lay down like a lion, and like a great cat, who shall rouse him?" (v. 9).[38] If the previous three tribes

---

[35] Several of the sayings involve literal "blessings": Joseph (v. 13), Gad (v. 20), Naphtali (v. 23), and Asher (v. 24).

[36] Deuteronomy 33 adopts a sequence totally unrelated to the Genesis narrative, though it maintains the ideal of twelve, in a scheme of ten units: Reuben, Judah, Levi, Benjamin, Joseph (Ephraim/Manasseh), Zebulun/Issachar, Gad, Dan, Naphtali, and Asher. While this poem may likewise preserve a body of Israelite sayings, its contents reveal much less of Israel's political world. For example, Dan is a lion's cub – an image of power without political detail. The date of Deuteronomy 33 is impossible to establish with confidence. Beyerle works within a more traditional historical schema than Macchi or Schorn, and he concludes that the text is premonarchic based on the lack of reference to king or state (pp. 278–9). This feature may reflect a greater distance from the royal interest and administration than the set found in Gen. 49:13–21, but there is no special basis for placing it before the ninth to eighth centuries. The list makes most sense as Israelite in origin, though its transmission into Judah could have shaped it in uncertain ways. With the brief reference to Judah in verse 7, we face the same set of historical choices and challenges as with Judah in Genesis 49.

[37] Sparks (2003) argues that Genesis 49 worked originally from a set of ten, with only Simeon and Levi added. The statements for Reuben and Judah would have been modified.

[38] Carr (1996, 250–1) likewise envisions a revised Judah statement, as part of a general recasting of 49:3–12 by a Judahite writer who intends to set up Judah's right to lead. He allows for the

are additions, however, Judah's place at the head of the list would be surprising for an Israelite author. Such a position would seem to compete with Joseph's priority as the favorite, as in the birth narrative, and so from a Judahite point of view. If Judah were part of a more inclusive Israelite list, this would require both interpretation within the framework of Israel's political dominance and the possibility of a relatively late date, in the eighth century. It remains to be proven that a people named Judah were incorporated into an association called Israel in any period, and it remains uncertain whether the kingdom ruled by the house of David was named Judah before the eighth century. New external evidence could lead to more secure conclusions.

Although Joseph and Benjamin offer a natural geographical pair, it is hard to avoid recalling the combination as Rachel's two sons in the preceding Jacob story. If these two belonged in the list, it would have to be by a geographical association that likewise invited the shared link to Rachel. The metaphor for Benjamin as a wolf resembles the image of Issachar as a donkey, beginning with the animal and shifting to human activity without directly abandoning the image: the donkey accepts forced labor (v. 15), and the wolf divides plunder (v. 27). As the final figures in the tribal list, Joseph and Benjamin would represent together the central highlands west of the Jordan, joined as a pair like Ephraim and Benjamin in the Song of Deborah (Judg. 5:14). Recalling the historical problem with Joseph as stand-in for both Ephraim and any other people from the central highlands, the listing of Joseph by name is the most serious difficulty with envisioning his incorporation in any significantly early roster of Israelite peoples. Without mention of Ephraim and Manasseh, Joseph's solitary place assumes not only his priority in the birth narrative but also the combination of the two highland groups in Genesis 48. As argued for 29:31–30:24, this is an Israelite perspective, but not an early one, and probably associated with Bethel.

The initial composition of Genesis 49 could have included more than the core list of six, but this poem cannot be used as biblical proof for schemes of ten or twelve tribes for early Israel. Lacking certainty regarding the roles of Judah, Joseph, and Benjamin in Genesis 49, the most important result of this analysis is the probability of an old group of six peoples, which Macchi dates to the ninth century. Genesis 49:13–21, at least, would have an explicit setting in the kingdom of Israel, and the set shows that decentralized regional identities could be celebrated as part of a larger unifying order, without necessarily threatening the royal administration. If Genesis 49 can attend to the individual peoples of Israel for their own sake, even during the monarchy, then so can various phases of writing in the book of Judges and the family framework of Jacob. Tribal identities, perhaps along with political activity, can coexist with the centralizing authority of kings. It is therefore unnecessary to require that Israelite traditions of the tribes must either come to us in forms that postdate the kingdom,

possibility of earlier and irretrievable versions of the statements for the first three groups, so that Judah need not have been the first tribe in the older composition.

after 720, or derive implausibly from a premonarchic age, before the tenth
century.

The most explicit acknowledgment of a monarchic framework in Gen.
49:13–21 is found in the statement for Asher: "Asher – his bread is rich,
and he is the one who provides delicacies for the king" (v. 20). Macchi understands the saying for Issachar to assume subordination to royal administration
as well: "When he saw that the refuge was good and the land was pleasant, he
set his shoulder to the load and accepted forced labor" (v. 15). The term for
"forced labor" (*mas*) implies either servitude to another people, as of Israel in
Egypt (Exod. 1:11), or the central authority of royal administration, as under
Solomon (1 Kings 5:27; etc.). Unlike the Song of Deborah, where the sole act of
each regional people is the decision whether or not to join combat, the peoples
of Gen. 49:13–21 act as units for their individual interests. Issachar chooses
obedience to the royal administration for its own benefit. Likewise, Dan is
assumed to govern itself within the framework of the polity explicitly named
Israel: "Dan shall judge his people as one of the tribes of Israel" (v. 16). Other
peoples offer less direct evidence yet may be read as decision-making bodies:
Gad wards off raiders as a unit, calling on neither the king nor a larger muster
(v. 19), and Asher's service to the palace appears to be supplied by this group
under this name (v. 20).

These groups act as distinct units, but the saying for Dan regards them as
equivalent parts of a whole, "the tribes (*šēbeṭ*) of Israel." While this terminology may be so familiar to readers of the Bible that it passes us by without a
second thought, it cannot be taken for granted and suggests a unifying system
not mentioned in the Song of Deborah. Given that this evidence derives from
a poem that directly acknowledges the authority of a royal administration, it
is possible that the standardization of all groups as "tribes" of Israel appears
only at the time of the monarchy. Again, we find ourselves dealing with a text
that affirms both the supremacy of kings and the abiding significance of Israel's
individual peoples, who still act – politically – according to these regional
identities. In this core set of tribal statements, there is no role for the genealogical system of Jacob's family, and Gen. 49:13–21 reminds us that the kinship
framework is only one interpretation of the bonds that join the Israelite association of peoples. Genesis 49 shares this lack of kinship language with the book
of Judges generally, and it highlights the rarity of its expression in Jacob's
family.

6

Collective Israel and Its Kings

In my investigation of Israelite content in the Bible's primary narrative from Genesis through Kings, I have chosen not to begin with Genesis and proceed through the Bible's own sequence. Instead, I have organized the discussion according to the two primary political expressions of Israel as portrayed in the Bible: an association of peoples capable of cooperation or conflict; and a collective body that interacts with individual leaders on this unified basis. The framework of associated peoples allows a clearer view of the decentralized political foundation on which the kingdom of Israel was built, and this aspect makes it a good place to begin. The decentralized association is rooted in the portrayal of Israel in the land, without necessary reference to origins stories, and the book of Judges thus offers the best starting point for grasping this political essence. The genealogical explanation of Genesis is conceptually secondary, though we encounter it first as we read the Bible.

Israel's messy decentralization is only rarely on display, more often concealed behind presentation as an active collective body – a political reality that is itself concealed in many texts behind the assumed power of individual leaders. Here also, the political conception belongs to concrete practice, and we have the best opportunity to see its relationship to real structures when we read accounts of life in the land. I therefore begin with two kings of Israel, Omri and David, treating Omri first because he is more obviously defined as a king of Israel, without any connection to Judah. The oldest versions of origins stories about Israel in action, especially under Moses and Joshua, emphasize the unity of the people as they relate to these ruling figures and thus resemble more closely the tales about kings. Early editors then seem to have excluded these from the collected accounts of time in the land without kings; they regarded texts with conquered cities or land to represent a different type, with the conquest of Gibeah and Benjamin a special case (Chapter 9). As with Jacob in Genesis, it is best to deal with Moses, Joshua, and Benjamin after establishing the political type with Omri and David.

This early classification could already have taken place among Israelites, in tentative steps toward combining stories to relate as part of time before kings. What eventually became a "premonarchic" age in the land, as now defined in the book of Judges, would have been first imagined in Israel. It seems that the premonarchic idea was created specifically from stories about subgroups, peoples within Israel that did not represent the whole. At first, the interest was simply the fact that the groups were part of Israel, having experienced these conflicts outside the framework of the kingdom. It may even be that the very identity of these peoples without reference to Israel was what suggested to early editors the logic of location in a time without kings. By contrast, stories of Israel as a whole could imply a different setting, which came to be the time of origins.

There is little direct attention to the "northern" kingdom of Israel in the Bible outside the books of Kings, where Israel is the setting for the religious concerns associated with collections for the prophets Elijah and Elisha (1 Kings 17–2 Kings 9) and the seizure of power by Jehu (2 Kings 9–10). The prophetic books of Hosea and Amos are devoted mainly to the affairs of Israel but offer little detail regarding its political character. The book of Amos shows little if any interest in Israel's kings and spreads the prophetic blame liberally among the people at large.[1] Hosea 8:1–4 refers to the selection of kings, which is attributed to Israel in collective terms.[2] We must rely mainly on Kings for the character of the Israelite kingdom – as distinct from any "united monarchy" that supposedly preceded it. Generally, the affairs of Israel are reported from Judah with a jaundiced eye, perhaps preserving some historical detail, but with little sense of Israelite political custom.[3] The one significant exception is the

---

[1] The reference to Jeroboam II in Amos 7 may be a later addition, along with the notion that Bethel is a royal sanctuary; the very notion of such centralized cult may suggest a monarchic setting in Judah of the seventh century. Jeremias (1998, 7) attributes 7:9–17 to revision from the period of Jeremiah, in the early sixth century, when Hosea and Amos were read together.

[2] After complaining that both covenant (*bĕrît*) and instruction (*tôrâ*) have been ignored, the writer is appalled that Israel still approaches Yahweh as if their fidelity is uncompromised. He continues: "Israel has spurned what is good; let an enemy pursue him. They have made (someone) king, but not from me. They made (someone) leader, but I did not know" (8:3–4). Hosea is said to marry during the reign of "the house of Jehu" (1:4), which could refer only to Jeroboam II (785–45). Jeroboam came to the throne as the son of Jehoash, without any need to ratify the rule of a new royal house. There is no reason to connect Hos. 8:4 to this period and king, however, even if the contents suggest an eighth-century setting. Wolff (1974, 137) reads Hos. 8:1–14 as derived from the same historical setting as 5:8–7:16, which he dates to 733, after Hoshea ben Elah's revolt, at the time of Tiglath-pileser III's invasion. Andersen and Freedman (1980, 33) comment, "While the oracles against the house of Jehu must precede the end of the dynasty, subsequent references to a sequence of illegitimate kings (Hos. 8:4) and to what is probably the assassination of one of them (Hos. 7:3–7) point to the chaotic period following the decease of the powerful and long-lived Jeroboam." While eighth-century settings cannot be taken for granted in the transmitted text of Hosea, the origin of these sections in actual Israelite circumstances is plausible.

[3] The repeated references to "Chronicles of the kings of Israel" (1 Kings 14:19 for Jeroboam I; and for each Israelite ruler thereafter) do not indicate any direct Israelite composition in the Bible, though such annals may have provided information about dates and synchronisms for

brief account of Omri, who founded Israel's capital at Samaria and launched an era of expansion and success (1 Kings 16:15–28). The description of Omri's reign is marked by repeated recognition of collective "Israel" as a distinct political force that functions as a counterweight to the individual authority of the king. This very feature may be regarded by some as late and out of place, but it is in fact unusual and striking, a plausible expression of the same noncentralizing political tradition that produced the tribal scheme.[4] Of all the texts in 1 and 2 Kings, this may be the closest to an Israelite portrayal of the Israelite kingdom, once the deuteronomistic elaborations are set apart.[5]

Having defined the political character of collective Israel in material wholly unrelated to Judah, we may turn to David and Solomon. Although these two kings are the icons of Judah's royal line, especially through the enduring "house of David," they are defined in Samuel and Kings above all by rule over Israel. In the David narrative especially we find references to collective Israel as a decision-making body, much as it appears in the Omri text. This feature is prominent in the accounts of political tensions in David's kingdom and suggests a historically useful memory of Israelite ways, as distinct from Judah's political tradition. This political recollection resurfaces in 1 Kings 12, which depicts the first emergence of two parallel kingdoms as the secession of a large northern group from the house of David. Again, the theme of united opposition to royal leadership is attached to Israel – not to Judah – though the text considers the house of David to deserve permanent authority to rule. Together, the texts for Omri and David and the division into two kingdoms preserve a striking picture of monarchy in balance with a powerful collective voice outside itself.[6]

---

the reigns of Israelite kings. Na'aman (1999) concludes that the Kings writer (as if one!) had better sources for Judah than for Israel; the writer knows more than just names and dates, but the stories available were not annalistic and have limited historical use. In any case, the voice of narrative about Israelite kings does not generally reflect their own interests. For instance, the prosperous reign of Jeroboam II is recorded in standard terms of religious critique, even as he is credited with extending Israel's borders far to the north and south (2 Kings 14:23–9). This short text treats the king as accomplishing all by his individual authority, without reference even to an army.

[4] Stefan Timm (1982, 280) interprets the war between Omri and Tibni as historical, with Tibni actually ruling a separate rival kingdom, but the role of "all Israel" in the biblical account reflects a later and deuteronomistic view of the situation.

[5] The Omri material is strikingly different from other narratives for the separate kingdom of Israel, yet it is not usually given special attention as a rarity. When Omri is the direct focus, the text's literary character and its political assumptions are not generally in view (e.g., Kuan 1993; Schneider 2004).

[6] The tradition of a strong counterbalance to royal authority raises the question of whether any part of the Bible's portrait of prophecy relates to this dynamic. Texts such as the account of Micaiah in the presence of Ahab and Jeshoshaphat (1 Kings 22) present kings as having a stable of full-time prophets to guarantee their safe standing with God (or the gods), at the same time as an occasional outlier could stand against the trend and oppose the king publicly. As part of the larger divinatory endeavor, prophecy must have been a part of life at every royal court, but it is more difficult to judge to what degree prophets could side against royal inclinations. So far as they did, one possible base of power, or source of safety, could have been the collective influence

A. Omri

The report on Omri's rise and reign in 1 Kings 16 has a literary flair in its description of Zimri's role, and it would be imprudent to presume that this was a court chronicle, an official record from the king's scribal service.[7] Nevertheless, the contents do follow the structure of royal public inscriptions. The text begins with the military successes that secure the king's throne and then concludes with the building project that remains the greatest visible expression of his magnificence.[8] When the large structuring elements are removed, whether these are deuteronomistic or part of an editing scheme peculiar to the books of Kings, the report of Omri's reign consists of three parts:

- Omri's leadership in the defeat of Zimri (vv. 15–18);
- Omri's success against his rival Tibni (vv. 21–2);
- the building of Samaria as royal capital (v. 24).[9]

of the body politic and the individuals who could sway it. In this project, I do not take on the enormous challenge of interpreting either the tradition of a prophetic institution in Israel and Judah or the separate tradition of writing in prophetic voice, so as to invoke this kind of divine authority. There was probably a significant role for public and politically independent prophecy in Israel, as reflected in the gathered lore surrounding Elijah and Elisha in 1 Kings 17–2 Kings 9. For an overview of the interplay between politics and prophecy, see Zevit (2001, 495–503). The traditions of Elijah and Elisha address Israel without reference to Judah and appear to originate in Israelite circles. For one approach to the material with focus on the legitimation of Jehu, see White (1997).

[7] The Zimri story should be read as part of an original Omri narrative, and it is only the Kings editor who has broken this into a separate "regnal account" – a scheme picked up without question by Sweeney (2007, 201–4).

[8] Compare the Mesha inscription, which intermingles the same two elements of military achievement (lines 5–21a) and construction (lines 21b–27), with a similar combination in the broken final section of the text; and the Aramaic inscription for Zakkur, king of Hamath, with survival of siege (lines A 1–17) followed by construction (lines B 1–15). For translations and bibliography, see COS 2.137–8, 155. The biblical text for Omri does not follow the self-aggrandizing mode of royal inscriptions; it is rather the structure of the contents that appears to be inspired by such royal literature.

[9] Verse 19 explains Zimri's death as the result of his sins, by which he followed in Jeroboam's footsteps, and verses 25–6 place Omri in the same tradition. This is a regular critique of Israelite rulers that characterizes the specific narrative of the two kingdoms, from 1 Kings 12 to 2 Kings 17. It begins with Ahijah's prophecy: 1 Kings 14:16 (Ahijah on Jeroboam himself); 15:26, 30 (Nadab); 16:2–3 (prophet Jehu on Baasha), 19 (Zimri), 26 (Omri), 31 (Ahab); 22:52 (Ahaziah); 2 Kings 3:3 (Joram); 10:29 (Jehu); 13:2 (Jehoahaz), 11 (Jehoash); 14:24 (Jeroboam II); 15:9 (Zechariah), 18 (Menahem), 24 (Pekahiah), 28 (Pekah). Only Shallum, who reigned just one month, and Hoshea, the last king of Israel, are spared this line, which is even inserted into the midst of praise for Jehu's suppression of Baal worship. Back in 1 Kings 16, verses 20 and 27 provide the refrain that refers readers to the chronicles of the kings of Israel for Zimri and Omri, a separation that gives the false impression that we have two different sources for the received material. The length of Omri's reign, which probably derives from a received list, is reported in verse 23. Omri's death and the succession to Ahab are found in verse 28. Timm (1982, 41–2) regards 1 Kings 16:24 as a predeuteronomistic source for the building of Samaria, a status that he does not accord to the reports of war with Zimri and Tibni.

In terms of sheer space, the establishment of Omri's rule receives much more attention than his construction of Samaria, but the significance of that project could not have been missed.

The royal source for the Omri report is evident in how the Samaria project is described as the sole responsibility of the king, who bought the land himself and built his capital as if a personal residence.[10] We can therefore expect that the accounts of how Zimri and Tibni were defeated will also reflect a palace perspective. In these earlier sections of the Omri report, Israel appears several times as a decision-making body that is distinct from kings. From the royal view, Israel's prominent role is included because the king celebrated his selection by this collaborative group, just as the David narratives consider his wooing and winning of Israel's support to be a constant source of pride, even when rebellion threatens all the king's achievements. It is assumed that an Israelite king must have the support of this body in order to rule – the people are not an obstacle to overcome.

Given the royal perspective, the collective decision-making group may be acknowledged, but it is still viewed from outside itself. The king and his court see the people as a whole body, under the name of Israel, rather than by its constituents, be they tribes or towns or other entities. The particular power recognized for the collective Israel is the ability to select and depose kings. We first hear of Omri for his role in the removal of Zimri, which reads coherently without knowing the prior statement about Zimri's murder of Elah, his predecessor (1 Kings 16:9–10).[11] As the report opens, "the people" (*hāʿām*) are first of all a fighting body, in this case encamped against the Philistines at Gibbethon (v. 15b).[12] After Omri becomes king, "the people Israel" are said to divide between support for him and for a rival named Tibni (v. 21), and the ensuing conflict is described in terms of "the people" who follow one or the other (v. 22). Evidently, this is a military struggle, in that it results in the defeat of the Tibni faction and the death of its leader.[13] Alternatively, the collective is

---

[10] Simon Parker (2006) proposes that the process of revision imagined for the books of Kings has a precedent in the longer royal inscriptions from Judah's neighbors, including texts from Hadad-Yisʿi (KAI 309), Mesha (KAI 181), Zakkur (KAI 202), and Eshmunazor (KAI 14). Each of the first two texts incorporated and extended an earlier inscription of the same genre to take account of historical developments since the first version was composed, and this would offer some hard evidence for the process commonly understood to take place in the compilation of Kings.

[11] The core account of Zimri's removal of Elah is found in 1 Kings 16:9–10, where Zimri is identified as a military officer who assassinates the king on his own initiative and without stated motive. Because Zimri appears in the Omri account only in order to rule seven days and be deposed, it is conceivable that the explanation of his own accession to the throne is secondary to the Omri narrative, required by the creation of a framework of reigns in sequence.

[12] Gibbethon is north of Ekron and west of Benjamin, outside what need be considered the Judah sphere.

[13] Along with the introduction of the "people" as a fighting force in 1 Kings 16:15, the verb *ḥzq* is used for military superiority in Deut. 11:8, over those who populate the promised land; and in 1 Kings 20:23 and 25, with the question of whether Israel or Aram can defeat the other.

called "all Israel" when it makes Omri king (v. 16) and again when it returns
with Omri to besiege Zimri at Tirzah (v. 17). In his original role, before attacking Zimri, Omri is identified as military commander "over Israel" (v. 16), an
identity that equates the whole people with muster for battle. Those who vote
are those who fight. We find the same pattern in Mari references to assemblies
of king Zimri-Lim's Hana people.[14]

In this Israelite royal account, the collective people are identified by the name
"Israel" and have two functions: they muster to fight an external enemy, the
Philistines; and they choose a preferred ruler. The detail in the latter function is
important. The short reign of Zimri indicates that his coup was never accepted
by the body of Israel or that his removal of Elah may have been accepted, but
not his own rule in Elah's stead.[15] Israel initiates his rejection by choosing their
military commander as successor and returning immediately from the field of
battle to depose Zimri.[16] Then, the struggle for power between Omri and Tibni
is defined by the supporting halves of Israel on each side, so that one part of
Israel overcomes the other, rather than one leader defeating the other.

Finally, it is significant that Omri's choice of Samaria and its renovation
are treated as the king's own project, not the domain of collective Israel. The
construction of Samaria as a new royal capital follows a pattern in the establishment of new royal houses for Israel that stands at odds with the Judahite
ideal of a Davidic dynasty. The pattern is not a feature of any one narrative or compilation, and it may best be explained as the actual way in which
kingship functioned in relation to Israel as a political body. Up to and including Omri, each royal house that ruled Israel was associated with a new base
of power (see Chapter 18). Jehu's decision to keep Samaria as his capital
shows that the institutions of monarchy had come to carry more weight than
any particular king. In Judah, both kingship and royal seat were inherited in

---

[14] On "meeting" (*puḫrum*) and "talks" (*riḫṣum*), both of which can have this military dimension,
see Fleming (2004a, 206–7 and 208–10). The *puḫrum* simply derives from the verb "to gather,"
and when it refers to the men who muster for battle, it combines a military and a political aspect,
in that the fighters have to agree to take part before they become an army ready for battle. The
term *riḫṣum* has to do only with the political dimension of the muster, when participation and
its conditions must be negotiated among the groups involved.

[15] This reading would follow the combination of Zimri and Omri accounts, which cannot be
assumed to be part of a single original narrative. It is also possible that the Zimri/Elah statement
in 1 Kings 16:9–10 belonged to the Omri narrative and was understood as necessary to explain
the brief reign of Omri's predecessor.

[16] Omri was the "military commander" (*śar ḥaṣṣābā'*) "over Israel," a role that is not defined by
royal service, though a king would naturally have the highest authority, or at least prestige.
In verse 9, Zimri is also given a military role as "commander of half the chariotry." If 16:9–
10 include what was once the introduction to the Omri narrative, the contrast is interesting.
"Israel" seems to be identified with the "fighting force" (*ṣābā'*) that "encamps" (verb *ḥnh*) as
"the people" (*hā'ām*). Zimri's leadership of the chariotry may associate him more narrowly with
the king. Solomon sets up bases for the royal chariotry (1 Kings 9:19), called "his chariotry" in
9:22 (cf. 10:26). If the contrast goes back to the old Israelite narrative, Omri is more a man of
the people, a natural leader for Israel.

dynastic mode. In Israel, neither legacy was weighty enough to demand inheritance until Samaria became the capital. Excavations there show the extent of what the house of Omri built as the physical plant for new royal power.[17] Samaria joined Jerusalem as a permanent capital, and Israelite writers also came to identify monarchy with a single place, in contrast to what is portrayed for earlier times. This pattern of new royal families choosing new centers from which to rule thus appears to be based in actual practice through the early ninth century, which survived in texts that were compiled and revised into later periods.

The Omri account presents Israel's collective political capacity as commensurate with its military function. This expectation parallels the account in a Mari letter about negotiations over leadership, in which a general attempts to instigate a coup by making his case to the entire mustered military force:[18]

On the 5th of Lilliatum, (as the day) was getting on, the Numhâ army began to assemble in the midst of Qaṭṭarâ. [When] the army had assembled, Kukkutanum (the general [*rab amurri*]) [left] his town of Nunasaru, showed up at the assembly of the army, and laid his complaint [before] the army as follows....
(The rebellion is not my fault.)
Kukkutanum said [this and] many other things to the assembly of the army, and he both put the army in a craze and moved the consensus of the commoners to revolt against Haqba-hammu[19] their [lord]. [So Haqba]-hammu unknowingly sent Kakiya to the assembly of the army [at] Qaṭṭarâ [in order to] carry out deliberations and to launch a military expedition(?). They killed [that man], while the commoners went over to the side of Kukkutanum, and they (all) began to make an assault on Qaṭṭarâ.

In the context of gathering to prepare for war, the body of fighters, who are described here as "commoners" (*muškēnum*), have a collective voice and can determine a political choice, in this case to depose a king – or attempt to do so.[20] Such assembly without identification of allegiance by people of origin resembles the simple "Israel" of the Omri and David accounts. This alternative view of collective action is also part of a decentralized political structure that appears to be characteristic of Israelite tradition in the Bible.

---

[17] Ron Tappy (1992, 214–15) emphasizes the continuity between the finds from periods that probably overlap the houses of Omri and of Jehu, which would confirm the interpretation suggested by the very retention of the site as capital. No great transformation of the site under Jehu need be expected.

[18] The translation is taken from Fleming (2004a, 207), with text in n. 177 (ARM XXVI 412:6–10, 16–22).

[19] Haqba-ḫammu was the second-ranking leader and brother-in-law of king Asqur-Addu of the paired cities of Qaṭṭarâ/Karanâ during the reign of Mari's king Zimri-Lim.

[20] ARM XXVI 412 was sent to king Zimri-Lim of Mari by Yasim-el, a man in his royal service. It seems that those in the circle of the Mari court took for granted the possibility of such a collective response to leadership. If anything, the portrayal of such unified action may reflect the perspective of kings and their courts, for whom the action of full units was the ultimate concern.

B. David

In the finished books of Samuel and Kings, David is treated by writers from Judah as the founder of a kingdom based at Jerusalem that would continue through the last gasp of independence for God's people, as Judah was dismantled by Babylon in the early sixth century (2 Kings 24–5). Through the prophet Nathan, Yahweh promises that he will never remove his commitment (*ḥesed*) from the house of David as he had done with Saul (2 Sam. 7:15). Solomon's success in building a temple in Jerusalem is recalled as fulfillment of a promise to David (1 Kings 8:15–20), and David's son reminds Yahweh that this royal house should never end, if its scions keep faith with their god (vv. 24–6). When the kingdom divides, and Solomon's son Rehoboam refuses to relinquish his southern power base at Jerusalem, the prophet Ahijah ratifies the arrangement in advance by allowing Jeroboam ten tribes, while keeping one unnamed tribe for David as heir to the promise of a "guaranteed house" (*bayit ne'ĕmān*; 1 Kings 11:38). Henceforth, the Jerusalem stronghold is "the City of David" (1 Kings 14:31; 15:8; etc.), and Judah's kings are measured by their imitation of David, as recounted elaborately for Abijam son of Rehoboam in 1 Kings 15:3–5.

With such wholehearted embrace of David by the Judahite writers who gave us the finished history, it is difficult to read the long account of David himself without taking for granted a perspective from Judah. Nevertheless, the accumulated stories of David in the books of Samuel define him above all by his rule over Israel, and these texts sometimes display Israel as a political body in terms very like what we find with Omri. We must therefore reevaluate the David narrative to consider how its eventual reception in Judah could have reshaped older political assumptions. I conclude that the David lore in 2 Samuel preserves plausible memories of Israelite collective politics because these memories inhere in material that knows David only as king of Israel. In terms of transmission history, David's particular relationship to Judah appears to be secondary, as later writers reassured Judahite audiences that their royal founder kept a special place for Judah. If correct, this means that Judah's claim on the legacy of Israel was based in one large part on the house of David's real origin as early kings over Israel. Equally, it leaves unanswered a host of historical questions about the first existence of Judah as a definable place or people and the process by which it became identified with the kingdom ruled by the descendants of David.[21]

1. The Transmission of Early David Material
After decades of consideration as some of the earliest writing in the Bible, the David narrative in the books of Samuel is currently undergoing profound

---

[21] My discussion of David and Judah reflects ongoing conversation with Mahri Leonard-Fleckman, who has worked extensively on this issue in development of a doctoral dissertation at New York University. Her initial insight was the strange appearance of Judah in the Absalom story only in 2 Samuel 19.

reevaluation. In the early twentieth century, Leonhard Rost proposed that a tenth-century "Succession Narrative" could be isolated from the larger David account (roughly 2 Samuel 9–20; 1 Kings 1–2), and this came to be accompanied by a similarly ancient "History of David's Rise" (roughly 1 Samuel 16–2 Samuel 5).[22] One reason for the relative durability of interpretations that envision early material is the fact that the David narrative displays fairly little deuteronomistic editing.[23] Nevertheless, the Saul story in 1 Samuel has been integrated substantially into the account of David's emergence as legitimate king, and this combination must be explained and located in time and place. Before deuteronomistic incorporation into a larger scheme, a Saul–David narrative seems to have begun in 1 Samuel 9 with the appearance of Saul and then to have taken up the main mass of old David material.[24] This text would be decidedly Judahite, "prophetic" or otherwise, and the question is then how to define its sources.

In his influential volume on the Bible's primary narrative, Reinhard Kratz (2005, 174–82) gives such weight to this predeuteronomistic Saul–David assemblage that he minimizes the amount of material that could have belonged to any earlier and independent David traditions.[25] There are two somewhat older collections: an "Absalom cycle" in 2 Samuel 13–14 (with Amnon), and 15–20 (with revolts by Absalom and Sheba); and Solomon narratives in 2 Samuel 11–12 and 1 Kings 1–2, into which the Absalom cycle has been integrated. These may have underlying sources, but in their existing form, they depend on the preceding accounts of Saul and David. At the center of the

---

[22] Rost first proposed the existence of a Succession Narrative almost a century ago (1926, esp. 119–253). Stefan Seiler (1998, esp. 314–21) still maintains the existence of this text in close to its originally proposed form and dated to the time of Solomon. On the History of David's Rise in Solomonic guise, see Grønbaek (1971). During the 1970s, the work of Tryggve Mettinger (1976) on early Israelite kingship could depend entirely on the hypothesis of these tenth-century sources. In a carefully argued volume that takes account of trends toward later dates, Walter Dietrich (2007, 21–2, 235–40) still advocates a large core of very early material in the David narrative. For a useful chart that chronicles the various definitions proposed by numerous recent scholars for the David material, see Johannes Klein (2002, 137–8). The Succession Narrative is reevaluated in the context of later possible settings in Römer and de Pury (2000b). See also the broad critique of the History of David's Rise as literary concept in J. Randall Short (2010).

[23] Here, the careful analysis in the Samuel commentaries by P. Kyle McCarter is still viable (1980 and 1984).

[24] The work of Klein (2002) is useful especially for its identification of various comparisons and allusions that involve these two characters through the two books of Samuel. Although neither discusses such a work as a "Saul–David" composition, both McCarter and Dietrich (above) envision a composition with such scope: a late eighth-century prophetic redactor for McCarter and a predeuteronomistic "Erzählwerk" for Dietrich (see Klein's chart for Saul-oriented narrative definitions). Note also the recent analysis of Wolfgang Oswald (2009, 13–14, 29–30), who lays out a development for the David material that begins with a David–Saul narrative in 1 Samuel 9–2 Samuel 8, originally separate from a Court History (cf. Succession Narrative) based in 2 Samuel 9–20 without 2 Samuel 11–12 and 1 Kings 1–2, both of which involve the prophet Nathan.

[25] Kratz's basic approach is taken up by Aurelius (2003).

Absalom story is a brief tale that would have focused only on Israel and its opposition to Judah under David (in 2 Sam. 15:1–6, 13; 18:1–19:9a). For Kratz, the claim that David ruled both Israel and Judah can have been feasible only after the demise of the larger kingdom, so between 720 and 597. Thomas Römer (2005, 91–6) likewise removes the Solomon stories of 2 Samuel 11–12 from the earlier David material, along with what he calls the "scandalous chapters" 15–17 and 19 to produce a shorter and entirely positive court history that he considers may have circulated in the seventh century.[26] In this analysis, David's flight eastward across the Jordan River is imagined to have been inspired by the exile, which then dates 2 Sam. 15:7–17:29 and 19:9b–20:13 no earlier than the sixth century.

These seventh-century and later dates do not account for the portrayal of collective Israel as a political actor in the revolts launched by Absalom and Sheba in 2 Samuel 15–20.[27] It is difficult to see how Judahite tales of the earliest house of David could avoid assuming a political framework familiar to Judah, with its Jerusalem hub. Instead, the stories of revolt assume a framework much like the one envisioned in the Omri texts of 1 Kings 16. The references to the collective people in opposition, however, relate to David's rule over Israel only, without mention of Judah, and it is not clear that Judah represents part of this political portrait. At least, Judah's involvement must be proven, and we will return to this question below.

2. Israel in the David Narrative

As portrayed in the books of Samuel, David comes to power as an outsider to both Judah and Israel. Jesse's family is located at Bethlehem in the story of David's anointing (1 Sam. 16:1, 4), but this town plays no role in his development of an independent power base during the reign of Saul.[28] After Saul's death, David consolidates his power in the south by taking up residence in Hebron (2 Sam. 2:1–4). For an extended period, David operates as a free agent in southern and eastern regions on the margins of Philistine and Israelite power. His constituency includes his immediate kin, defined as his "father's

---

[26] See also the more detailed analysis in this vein by Rudnig (2006).

[27] Jeremy Hutton (2009) offers a thoughtful alternative to these European interpretations, with direct engagement of their methods and conclusions. He proposes first of all that the motif of journey across the Jordan and return belongs to an Israelite (my terminology – and western) conception much older than the Mesopotamian assaults by Assyria and Babylon. His transmission history retains notions of composition and date not far from those expressed in McCarter's Samuel commentaries. The rebellion tales would belong to a very early source for the Transjordan exile of David included in 2 Sam. 15:1–37* + 16:15 – 19:16*; (20*) (pp. 221–4). Jacques Vermeylen (2010), who has steadfastly pursued the possibility of Solomonic-period writing in the Bible, likewise offers a carefully constructed opposing view. His core David narrative is found in 2 Sam. 13:1–2, 6–23*, 28–9, 37–9*; 14:23–4, 29–33; 15:1–18*, 27–8, 30–7*; 16:16–20; 17:1–4, 15–16, 21–6*; 18:1, 6–9, 15–17, 21, 31–2; 19:1–4*, 9–16*, 41–3.

[28] David's connection to Bethlehem is recalled in the Goliath story (1 Sam. 17:12, 15), and when he determines to leave Saul's court permanently, his excuse is a family sacrifice at Bethlehem (20:6, 28). The town is firmly linked to his family yet has nothing to do with his political life.

house" (*bêt 'ab*), along with men who had left their own communities because of difficulties, financial or otherwise (1 Sam. 22:1–2). At one point, Saul declares that he will ransack the clans (*'elep*) of Judah for David, though David himself is never said to seek support among these peoples (1 Sam. 23:23).

The text for David's accession to rule over Israel, 2 Samuel 5:1–3, is of uncertain date and provenance.[29] In any case, both here and in the preceding chapters, Judah is ignored to a remarkable degree.[30] The principal action revolves around a continuing war between "the house of Saul" and "the house of David" (2 Sam. 3:1, 6) – not between Israel and Judah. When Joab kills Abner, David insists on mourning and burying his enemy with pomp and ceremony, so that "all Israel" would know that David was innocent in the affair. From the start, David is in competition for rule over Israel, and Judah is only a footnote. Eshbaal (Ishbosheth), the son of Saul, is murdered by his own people after Abner's death (2 Samuel 4), and this leaves the way clear to the enthronement of David.[31] Israel's choice of David is confirmed by a treaty (*běrît*) with "all the elders of Israel" (5:3), who apparently represent "all the tribes of Israel" (v. 1) – again, for alliance with David, not with Judah.[32] Unlike the prophetic anointing envisioned in 1 Samuel 16, the assembled representatives of Israel anoint David as king (5:3). With its celebration of David's triumph over Saul, this portrayal combines the sensibilities of monarchal memory with the unavoidable necessity to win the support of the body politic – much as in the account of Omri. A royal perspective is preserved in the image of Israel's leaders groveling before David at Hebron, rather than inviting him to meet them in familiar Israelite territory.

Throughout the David narratives, the king remains a free agent, having to win the support of people with whom he has no intrinsic bond. David fights his wars as he did during the reign of Saul, with a military force that is defined by service to its leader. After becoming king of Israel, "the king and his men" set out to capture Jerusalem (2 Sam. 5:6), which is understood to belong to a people called the Jebusites, who belong to neither Israel nor Judah. He then turns the tables on the Philistines, and in the aftermath, "David and his men"

---

[29] One essential part of Leonard-Fleckman's preliminary analysis (2011) is the priority of this brief text to 2 Sam. 2:1–4, which imitates it. The reference to Yahweh's promise in 5:2 links this event to 1 Samuel 16, where Samuel selects David to be future king, even as the duplicated anointing in 5:3 suggests a lack of connection with the earlier text. Logically, 2 Samuel 5:3 would be prior, not dependent on the other text, which gives David a divine calling parallel and finally superior to that of Saul.

[30] See 2 Sam. 2:7, 10; 3:10.

[31] The book of Chronicles omits the messy account of how David took Israel from the son of Saul, but it preserves the original name of this son as Eshbaal in a genealogical list (1 Chron. 9:39), where the offensive Baal-name is not changed to "Shame" (Bosheth).

[32] As found in verse 3, with a meeting at Hebron, the account of David's accession looks back only to the conflict between the houses of Saul and David, as recorded in 2 Sam. 2:8–4:12. Verse 2 represents an effort to incorporate this into a larger Saul–David complex. Some version of the opening verse 1 could have contributed to the older statement; the "tribes of Israel" appear in the old saying for the people of Dan in Gen. 49:16.

loot their idols (5:21). The list of David's military achievements in 2 Samuel
8 chants the refrain, "David struck...; David captured...; David took...."
Israel is not mentioned, because for the writer, these are not the first of all
Israel's wars.[33]

Collective Israel comes back to the center of the David story only in order to
turn against him in revolt, reminding us that David and his core supporters are
politically separate from the people they rule. The distinct character of Israel
is especially visible in the rambling tale of Absalom's attempt to supplant his
father (2 Samuel 15–19).[34] Absalom's conspiracy targets directly the Israelite
association, with unusual acknowledgment of their tribal identifications.[35] As
people come to David's court with a legal problem, Absalom asks, "What
town do you come from?" and the answer is, "Your servant is from one of
the tribes of Israel" (2 Sam. 15:2).[36] Israel is the consistent focus throughout
the Absalom section, with Judah only an afterthought, once the rebellion is
quelled.[37] David's son begins his revolt as David had launched his own reign,
at the southern center of Hebron. Like his father, Absalom then woos the larger
body of Israel, this time by messengers sent secretly "among all the tribes of
Israel" (v. 10).

As Absalom's revolt unfolds, Israel participates as a collective that must
be won or lost. Although David's son launches his coup from Hebron, Judah
is never a target. At first, Absalom seems to have achieved victory, not by
military superiority but by the support of collective Israel. "The messenger
came to David, saying, 'The heart of the men of Israel has been after Absalom'"

[33] A separate account of a war with the Ammonites and the Arameans does finally present something like an Israelite conflict. In a final push, David gathers "all Israel" to move eastward
across the Jordan River, where they are victorious (10:17; cf. v. 9). This idealization gives the
section the feel of later revision.

[34] Focus on the Absalom sections of 2 Samuel provided Conroy (1978, 101–4) with an independent
basis for challenging the then-dominant definition of a Succession Narrative that included 1
Kings 1–2 and that was defined by Solomon's ultimate interests. Conroy considered this unit to
have nothing to do with Solomon, whose future existence is never in view (unlike the Bathsheba
material of chapters 11–12), and he refutes individually the claims for supposed allusions to
succession. The Absalom–David story comes to full resolution without need of 1 Kings 1–2.

[35] Through the history of the two kingdoms, the term "tribe" is rare. Solomon's kingdom is not
generally defined by Israel's tribes, just as his narrative in 1 Kings 1–11 has little if any interest
in the political life of collective Israel. In Solomon's dedication of the Jerusalem temple, Yahweh
is said to have chosen Jerusalem out of "all the tribes of Israel" to build a house (1 Kings 8:16;
cf. 2 Kings 21:7, of the temple desecrated during the reign of Manasseh). Ahijah prophesies that
ten tribes of Israel will be taken from the house of David, leaving one of "the tribes of Israel"
that includes Jerusalem (1 Kings 11:32; cf. 14:21, of Rehoboam's establishment there). In a text
from a distinct source, Elijah is said to build an altar with twelve stones for the twelve "tribes
of the sons of Jacob" (1 Kings 18:31).

[36] Again, note the phrase "tribes of Israel," familiar from the old core statement for the people of
Dan in Gen. 49:16.

[37] David is said to invite the elders of Judah to lead the tribes of Israel in escorting the king back
to Jerusalem (2 Sam. 19:10–16). The remaining Israelites then rush to take part, but it is too
late (19:40–4). Judah prevails, as suits the later bearers of the David tradition.

(15:13).[38] Only the "land" immediately surrounding Jerusalem is portrayed as regretting David's departure – and that not in terms of Judah (15:23).[39] With Israel back in play, Jonathan's son Mephibosheth (Meribbaal) is accused by his own servant of staying in Jerusalem with the hope that "today the house of Israel will restore to me the kingdom of my father" (16:3).[40] This is unrealistic, whether or not the accusation is fair. While David is making his getaway, "Absalom and all the people, the men ('îš) of Israel, entered Jerusalem" (16:15). Hushai pretends to choose Absalom over David by the logic that "Yahweh, this people and all the men ('îš) of Israel" have chosen the son (v. 18).[41] The true traitor Ahithophel then advises Absalom to demonstrate the finality of his accession by publicly taking over his father's harem in full view of "all Israel" (vv. 21–2). Absalom is now no mere pretender. He has assumed the prerogatives of kingship, with all its accoutrements.

With Absalom firmly ensconced in Jerusalem, the problem is not how to maintain Israel's support but rather how to defeat David decisively and so prevent him from taking back Israel by force. Collective Israel is represented as a key part of the decision-making process as the new king struggles to choose a strategy. When Ahithophel proposes immediate pursuit, "the advice was deemed right (verb *yšr*) in the eyes of Absalom and in the eyes of all the elders of Israel" (17:4; cf. v. 15). Hushai undermines this prudent position by emphasizing David's fearsome military competence, well known among "all Israel" (17:10). Instead, the false counselor advocates a traditional muster of all Israel, from Dan to Beersheba (17:11, 13). It is possible that this passage pokes fun at the cumbersome old tradition, portrayed in the books of Samuel as far less effective under Saul than David's fighting force, which is based on personal loyalty. "Absalom and all the men of Israel" prefer this advice to the better idea of a rapid response. Perhaps the representatives of the collective Israel are portrayed as naturally inclined to choose the course of action that acknowledges a long-established avenue for their power. The narrator is not impressed and does not intend his readers to be. Even as he scoffs at the muster of all Israel, however, he assumes its reality.

---

[38] The "men" of Israel (collective "man") are not the same as the "Israelites" ("sons of Israel"). In Mari evidence from the early second millennium, "the sons of (a place)" are simply its inhabitants, all who live there and are identified by the place. "The men of (a place)" represent the collective body with the capacity to make decisions, such as whether to go to war. Where we encounter '*îš yiśrā'ēl* in the Bible, we must consider whether this old decision-making mode is emphasized. Here, Israel has decided to accept Absalom as king, perhaps even to fight for him (cf. the "men of Judah" who come to make David their king in 2 Sam. 2:4). For the Mari evidence, see Fleming (2004a, 180–90), chapter 4C, "The Collective Face of Towns or Lands."

[39] 2 Sam. 15:23 suggests a more limited application for the '*ereṣ*, perhaps just describing the circle of villages that are dependent on the central town in a direct economic sense.

[40] As with Eshbaal for Ishbosheth, 1 Chron. 9:40 preserves the name "Meribbaal" as Jonathan's only son.

[41] This statement makes me wonder whether "the people" are a smaller unit of leadership than "the men (man) of Israel" in 16:15.

The battle develops as a confrontation between "Absalom and all the men of Israel with him" in pursuit (17:24) and "David and all the people" (v. 22), who take refuge in Ishbosheth's former eastern base of Mahanaim (v. 24).[42] David's "people" end up being more than a match for the force gathered from the muster of "all Israel," proving the military advantages of a standing army that answers directly to its one lord. It is worth noting that all the language of David's "people," including his "servants" and his "house," reflects the structures of classic Near Eastern monarchy. Collective organization was messier and less predictable, with more nebulous lines of authority.[43]

The story of Absalom's revolt is followed quickly by another event of the same type, which may be a literary echo of the prior event. Sheba's revolt follows the same broad political pattern as Absalom's, with "all the men of Israel" abandoning David for an alternative (20:1–2).[44] The contents of the calls to revolt by Sheba against David and then Israel itself against Rehoboam in 1 Kings 12:16 share wording so precisely that they suggest a literary relationship. Because the Sheba episode provides a conclusion to the conflict between Israel and Judah in 2 Sam. 19:41–4, we will return to this text with discussion of Judah in the David stories. The text appears to draw on ideas from Israel's revolts against both David through Absalom and Rehoboam through Jeroboam.

One more David tale is tacked onto the end of the books of Samuel, as if from a separate collection. The king takes a census and thus offends Yahweh, and then he restores himself to his god's favor by building a new altar to

---

[42] The use of *hā'ām* is difficult to parse. It is neither tribal nor in any sense "national," defined by Israel or Judah. It does not seem to be defined by Jerusalem, which largely remains in place, or even by its dependent towns or "land" (*'ereṣ*), which lament his departure (15:23). The best comparison with Akkadian terminology may be the word *nišū*, which is often translated "people," but which derives from the idea of "dependents" on a household head (see Fleming 2004a, 139–41). Mesopotamian kings may call their subjects their "people," as if an extended household. In 2 Samuel 15, the text perhaps defines David's *'ām* for us by setting out each group that joins him. First, "the servants of the king," those in direct service, promise to follow their master's lead (vv. 14–15). When David leaves Jerusalem, he brings "his house," except for ten concubines from his harem (v. 16). Together, the "servants" and the "house" are then called "all the people" (v. 17). Ittai from Gath and all his retainers join this core and seem thus to be added to the *'ām* (vv. 22–3). The language of "servants" and "house" surely includes whatever fighting force was bound to David by personal bonds. We know that for David, this had always been the center of his power, and Hushai's misleading advice is persuasive by its reputation (17:8–10). Once they are rested and prepared, David's personal force overwhelms whatever the muster of "all Israel" could produce (18:1–8).

[43] See 2 Sam. 17:26; 18:6–7. In 18:7, "the people (*'ām*) of Israel" are struck down (verb *ngp*) "before the servants of David," contrasting the two political and military structures. When describing both sides in the same breath, the writer bypasses the term *'ām* for David's supporters.

[44] Sheba says, "We have no share (*ḥēleq*) in David," and Israel begins its revolt against Rehoboam, "What share do we have in David?" (1 Kings 12:16). Then, "We have no hereditary portion (*naḥălâ*) in the son of Jesse," continuing the negative *'ên* in 2 Sam. 20:1, or "What hereditary portion do we have in the son of Jesse?" from *mâ* in 1 Kings 12:16. Sheba calls, "Each one (*'îš*) to his tents, Israel," while Israel itself concludes, "To your tents, Israel. Now tend your (own) house, David." For the last verb, I follow the versions and replace *r'h* with *r'h*.

Yahweh next door to Jerusalem (2 Samuel 24). Although Joab blames David for a strategic misstep, the census is introduced as the result of Yahweh's anger against Israel (v. 1), and Israel is the victim of the plague that he sends as punishment (v. 5). The king orders Joab and his officers to "roam through all the tribes of Israel" from Dan to Beersheba to register "the people" for military draft (v. 2; cf. v. 4). In spite of the focus on "Israel" together, by its old tribal composition, the Judahite origin of the text is reflected in the division of the people into Israel and Judah (vv. 1, 9). Of course, it is also still a David narrative.

3. David and Judah

Although history is essential to evaluating the composition and transmission of biblical texts, disentangling text from history can be particularly difficult in the case of David in the books of Samuel. Through the early phases of my research, I took for granted that the David narrative was Judahite at every level, though perhaps very old at the core. David was ultimately the property of Judah, the kingdom with a political tradition that measured royal legitimacy by ability to establish descent from this founder. The Tel Dan inscription even identifies the realm south of Israel as the House of David. These stories of David thus represent the ultimate validation of Judah's monarchy as central to the larger narrative about Israel's beginnings. Given this function, it is no wonder that some scholars place the whole David collection after 720, when Judah could first lay claim to the heritage of the fallen kingdom of Israel (e.g., Kratz 2005).

The problem is that the David narrative appears very old, with little sign of deuteronomistic handling, layers of earlier combination and revision, and a political landscape unfamiliar to seventh-century Judah. As a result, many would still date the early strata of the David narrative to a time closer to his reign (e.g., Vermeylen 2010). Such a scenario, however, would require transmission at Jerusalem across centuries of separate southern rule, even if initial composition could have occurred during a "united monarchy" of Israel and Judah together. In consideration of this early David narrative, the historical problem becomes pressing. The material itself is overwhelmingly preoccupied with David's reign over Israel, yet nothing suggests a historical connection between David and Israel except the Bible's own account of David and Solomon. Working back from the careful chronology of two kingdoms that begins with Jeroboam and Rehoboam, David and Solomon would have to have reigned sometime in the tenth century. This early period provides the only possible setting to explain the association of David with Israel before the fall of Israel allows Judah to lay claim to its neighbor's name and heritage. Is an early date even possible?

The best way to resolve this conundrum is to begin with the narrative as such, which has clearly undergone stages of compilation and revision. We must begin with the fact that provokes the interpretive problem: Israel's centrality to the composition at every level. In current discussion, the "History of David's Rise" and the "Succession Narrative" are no longer taken for granted as two long documents from close to the reigns of David and Solomon, and smaller blocks of text provide the starting point for piecing together the transmission and revision of the David material. In dialogue with Kratz, Hutton accepts the notion that a "Solomonic Apology" in 2 Samuel 11–12 and 1 Kings 1–2 was made the framework for a prior account of David that focused on Absalom. Whereas Kratz envisions an "Absalom cycle" in 2 Samuel 13–14 (with Amnon), 15–19 (his revolt), and 20 (Sheba's revolt), Hutton defines what he calls the Transjordanian exile of David in chapters 15–20 only.[45] The revolts of Absalom and Sheba treat Israel as an active political body, as in the core Omri text, and yet they likewise do mention Judah. This material is therefore the best place to begin an evaluation of Judah in the David narrative.

Judah first appears in the Absalom story after Absalom himself has died, and David has mourned him. With Israel in turmoil and David still east of the Jordan River, the king sends messengers to "the elders of Judah" to ask their leadership in returning him to the west (2 Sam. 19:12). Judah agrees and David crosses the Jordan in their company, with a thousand men from Benjamin for good measure (vv. 15–18). After the journey is complete, the Israelites complain that they have been shamed by their exclusion, but the Judahites maintain their right, and this leads to a second rejection of David in favor of Sheba, from Benjamin (19:41–20:2).[46] This time, Judah appears to support David (20:4–5), though a delay in Amasa's muster of the people leads to his assassination by Joab (vv. 6–13).

Although Judah plays a significant part in the transition between the revolts, its role has the specific purpose of bridging two stories that appear to have had separate origins. The entire Absalom tale is recounted from complex motivations to tragic outcome without reference to Judah (2 Sam. 13:1–19:9a). An account of Sheba's death at Abel of Beth-maacah likewise lacks Judah (20:14–22), as well as any character or location from the Absalom narrative except the ubiquitous Joab as military commander. This independent tale has been joined to the much longer story of Absalom by an elaborate bridge that gives Judah a special role. Emerging from confrontation with Joab over Absalom's execution, David both approaches Judah to back his return from the east (19:12) and offers Amasa the place of Joab (v. 14).[47] Sheba's revolt is thus a response

---

[45] Hutton (2009, 222) limits the text to 2 Sam. 15:1–37*; 16:15–19:16*; and (20*); Kratz (2005, 174–5) argues that very little in the account of David's reign does not assume combination with the story of his rise to power, and this is his basis for isolating an Absalom cycle as one prior building block for the larger narrative.

[46] McCarter (1984, 414–15) translates so as to bridge the two directly: "The men of Judah were more stubborn in the things they said than the men of Israel, and a scoundrel named Sheba son of Bichri the Benjaminite, who happened to be there, blew the shofar and said, 'We have no share in David and no estate in the son of Jesse! Every man to his tent, Israel!' So all Israel left David to follow Sheba son of Bichri, while the men of Judah accompanied their king from the Jordan to Jerusalem" (2 Sam. 19:44–20:2).

[47] Amasa is introduced as the man appointed by Absalom as commander of the army (2 Sam. 17:25).

to David's preference for Judah, which is cast in terms that anticipate 1 Kings 12. Meanwhile, Amasa must be removed for Joab to make sense as commander when Sheba is killed, and Amasa becomes expendable by his failure to muster Judah. With this excuse provided for Joab's assault, Judah disappears from the scene, and their muster is superfluous. The separate origin of the final episode is reflected also in Joab's identification of Sheba as "a man from the Ephraim highlands" (v. 21), not as the Benjaminite introduced in verse 1.[48]

Judah's place in 2 Samuel 19–20 can thus be understood as one element of a compositional bridge that allowed Sheba's death to be appended to the Absalom story, cast as a second revolt.[49] The isolation of Judah as one against ten (19:44) implies the tribal scheme also found in Ahijah's prophecy to Jeroboam (1 Kings 11:31, 35), and this elaborates the theme of tribes in the Absalom narrative (2 Sam. 15:2, 10), where no numbers are given. The count of ten, combined with the incorporation of Judah, displays a secondary hand, consciously locating Judah in Israel's tribal framework.

Once we recognize that Judah was added to the Absalom narrative in order to connect it to the confrontation with Sheba, we must reconsider the character of Hebron in 2 Samuel 15. On its own in this context, Hebron has no connection to Judah, and we would not know from the Absalom tale that David had ruled a separate kingdom of Judah from that capital, as stated in 2 Sam. 2:1–4.[50] Through the rest of chapters 2–4, David operates as an independent ruler, in competition with Eshbaal (Ishbosheth) through Joab and Abner as military proxies.[51] Hebron is essential to the narrative as his base of power, though Judah has no active role in the drama.[52] The whole conflict is described as "the battle between the house of Saul and the house of David" (3:6), and the episode recounted in 2:17–32 pits Benjamin and the men of Abner against "the servants

---

[48] This Benjamin connection may be related to the statement in 19:18 that a thousand men from Benjamin joined Judah in escorting David from the east, and together. Likewise, the identification with Benjamin evokes a potential rivalry with the house of Saul, a theme also pursued in chapter 21 with stories about the Gibeonites and Mephibosheth son of Jonathan.

[49] In 2 Sam. 20:21, Joab declares that Sheba son of Bichri "has lifted up his hand" against David the king. This notion of Sheba's opposition to David is then given a context by the dispute between Israel and Judah and Sheba's call to separate in verses 1–2. The writer of the bridge works from an aspect in the material available to him, elaborates on it, and links it to another story in his possession.

[50] David asks Yahweh whether he should go up to "one of the towns of Judah," and he is instructed to choose Hebron (v. 1). He and his men then take up residence in "the towns of Hebron" (v. 3), so that "the men of Judah" respond by coming there to anoint David king over the House of Judah (v. 4). David rules over the House of Judah at Hebron for seven years and six months (v. 11; cf. 5:5).

[51] The conflict between David and the house of Saul is played out by Joab and Abner as proxies. See esp. 2 Sam. 2:32, Joab and his men return to Hebron; 3:2–5, David has sons in Hebron, including Absalom; 3:19–20, 22, Abner negotiates with David at Hebron; 3:27, 32; 4:1, Joab murders Abner at Hebron, where he is buried; 4:8, 12, Ishbosheth's head is brought to David at Hebron, where it is buried with Abner.

[52] See the framing references in 2 Sam. 2:7, 10; 3:10.

of David" (v. 31).[53] David is clearly a king (e.g., 3:31, etc.), with a capital in the southern highlands, but only the opening defines his realm as Judah. Finally, "all the tribes of Israel" come to Hebron to make David their king. Although it remains unclear how the Hebron tradition developed over time, the Absalom story must be treated as the point of reference, with 2 Samuel 2–4 more likely adapted to suit Absalom than the reverse. Chapters 2–4 envision that David once ruled a rival domain from the south, based at Hebron; the Absalom narrative appears to share the tradition of a prior southern base for David, which becomes a credible place for his son to establish himself as successor. The limitation of Judah's active role to 2:1–4 suggests that the further definition of a seven-year reign may be an attempt to clarify the connection between David and the later kingdom by this name. David rules Israel for 40 years, like Solomon (2 Sam. 5:5; 1 Kings 2:11; 11:42), and the seven years over Judah appear to be subtracted from 40, rather than added with 33 to yield this ideal sum.[54] An initial reign from Hebron therefore is rooted more deeply in the text than the interpretation of that reign in terms of Judah, creating a division that anticipates the situation during the period of two kingdoms.[55]

I have argued so far that all the references to Judah in 2 Samuel are influenced by later consciousness of the separate kingdom by that name.[56] If Judah is to be the domain ruled by David's house, it must have been present at the creation, a distinct part of David's own kingdom, even as the oldest traditions for his reign celebrate him only as king of Israel.[57] In contrast, the book of

---

[53] Only in verse 17 is Abner's force identified with Israel, again facing the servants of David.

[54] In 1 Kings 2:11, we have the simple sum of seven plus 33, while in 2 Sam. 2:11 and 5:5, David's reign lasts seven years and six months.

[55] Leonard-Fleckman (2011) concludes that the introductory passage in 2 Sam. 2:1–4 has been shaped to reflect the text for David's selection as king of Israel in 2 Sam. 5:1–3, and there is no independent account of David's accession to the throne of Judah.

[56] Several texts define the kingdom by Israel and Judah together, reflecting the later identification of the two realms by these names, as in the books of Kings. Uriah says the ark is at Succoth with Israel and Judah (2 Sam. 11:11); the prophet Nathan recalls that Yahweh gave David the House of Israel and the House of Judah (2 Sam. 12:8); Saul's zeal for the sons of Israel and Judah explains why he wiped out the Gibeonites (2 Sam. 21:2); David's census is for Israel and Judah (2 Sam. 24:1); separate counts for Israel and Judah (v. 9) treat Judah as a kingdom of comparable size to the rest of Israel put together (500,000 vs. 800,000). These numbers contrast with Saul's muster of Israel and Judah in 1 Sam. 11:8, where Judah is counted by the tribal idea of ten versus one (30,000 vs. 300,000); cf. 10,000 from Judah among 200,000 from Israel in 1 Sam. 15:4. Note also the heading for David's lament over Saul and Jonathan, which names "the sons of Judah" as audience (2 Sam. 1:18); and Abner as a "dog's head from Judah" in 2 Sam. 3:8, where "from Judah is not in the Greek text and most likely a later gloss (so, McCarter 1984). This combination of Israel and Judah also appears in 1 Samuel, though less frequently: men of Israel and Judah attack the Philistines after Goliath is dispatched (1 Sam. 17:52); and Israel and Judah are said to love David as a leader under Saul (1 Sam. 18:16).

[57] David's southern activity is also associated with Judah in the Philistines' first encounter that brings him into the fray (Sucoh, 1 Sam. 17:1). After David has fled Saul, Gad tells him to go to the "land of Judah" (22:5; cf. 23:3); and Saul searches for David among "the clans of Judah" (23:23).

1 Samuel may preserve references to Judah that do not assume the kingdom and regard it instead as a regional term, evidently for the southern highlands. In this material, which introduces David as a rival to Saul during that king's reign, David is said to come from another southern town: Bethlehem, close to Jerusalem, and identified as "of Judah" only in 1 Sam. 17:12.[58]

Once Saul and David are separated as enemies, David is envisioned to have established himself as an independent political player in the south, with an ambiguous relationship to the Philistines, the mortal enemies of Saul and Israel (esp. 1 Samuel 27, 29–30). In 1 Sam. 30:14, a captured slave explains that his master was part of a group raiding "the *negev* of the Cherethites, and against the one of Judah, and against the *negev* of Caleb," where each region has a part in the southern wilderness. When David and his men attack the slave's former masters, these people are feasting with the spoil seized "from the land of the Philistines and from the land of Judah" (v. 16). Later, David offers a share of his own spoils to a variety of southern towns that represent the range of his interest: Bethel (not the northern site), Ramoth-negev, Jattir, Aroer, Siphmoth, Eshtemoa, Racal, "the villages of the Jerahmeelites," "the villages of the Kenites," Hormah, Bor-ashan, Athach, and Hebron (30:27–31). These are defined in the preceding verse (26) as represented by "the elders of Judah," perhaps anticipating the move to make David king at Hebron in 2 Sam. 2:1–4.

Behind these references to a southern inland region may be preserved a geographical definition of Judah that does not anticipate the later kingdom and that need not be primarily political, as a people. If the name "Judah" indeed derives from the region, this would be the origin of the kingdom's identity in the eighth and seventh centuries. This early background to Judah remains nearly opaque with the current evidence. The most important conclusion is that the narrative for David's reign in 2 Samuel recalls him above all as king of Israel, and this persistent fact reflects the nature of the oldest sources for this narrative. After David's house took refuge in a separate southern realm, its partisans remained heirs to a tradition of the founder that was oblivious of the later division and did not share its political terminology and assumptions. Collective Israel is preserved in the David narrative as a reflection of this early political landscape.

C. 1 Kings 12: The Secession of David's House

In contrast to the long collection of David lore in 1 and 2 Samuel, the Solomon narrative in 1 Kings 1–11 offers little sense of Israel as a distinct political entity, a people to be wooed and won. Solomon's text is heavily colored by types from the literature of Judah: the king as wise (chapter 3), as dominating

---

[58] Most often, David and his father Jesse are simply said to come from Bethlehem (1 Sam. 16:1, 4, 18; 17:15, 58; 20:6, 28; 2 Sam. 2:32 for Asahel as one of the family; 23:14–16). The specification as part of Judah in 1 Sam. 17:12 appears to be for clarification, not necessary or assumed in the general narrative use with David.

or domineering (chapter 9), as perverted by foreign influence (chapter 11).[59] Whatever the dates of the details, the Solomon texts have little interest in Israel as a polity and show little awareness of its distinct character. Even the administrative district list in 1 Kings 4 offers only indirect reflections of Israelite divisions, without acknowledging them to have any decision-making powers or social identities of their own, though the list may be quite old and seems to preserve a memory of such political reality.[60] Solomon is not remembered for his rule of Israel; it is simply taken for granted.

The distinct character of Israel is picked up again only in 1 Kings 12, a text that includes a declaration of independence parallel to the account of Sheba's revolt in 2 Sam. 20:1–2. As the two texts now stand, Sheba's rebellion anticipates the coming reality of separate kingdoms, and David is portrayed as holding together a combined realm that the reader knows will not be sustained. The shared language in the two texts confirms the impression given by 1 Kings 12 on its own, that the separation of Judah from Israel is told from Judah's point of view. Though Solomon's son Rehoboam is ridiculed, his stupidity is mourned as responsible for the loss of what should have been – a single kingdom of Israel under a permanent Davidic head.

Based on nonbiblical evidence alone, there would be no reason to conclude that the kingdoms of Israel and Judah were ever joined under one ruler or that the house of David once led the kingdom of Israel. By the ninth century, there are two kingdoms, and archaeological evidence alone cannot answer the question of how they were related in their earliest days. I have already argued that the elaborate tradition of David's successful domination over Israel, in spite of frequent opposition, probably indicates that Israel once accepted the rule of his house. The eventual rejection of that house, after Solomon, fits the pattern of turnover that characterizes Israel through the earlier monarchy, when the collaborative, noncentralizing political tradition still maintained considerable influence (see Chapter 18). The account in 1 Kings 12 offers an explanation for how there came to be two kingdoms that shared the same language and devotion to the god Yahweh. Although the Judahite preference of the text is obvious, and the occasion for the crucial split is described with literary flair that betrays reliance on known formulae, the reality of such a crisis remains

---

[59] These features are developed in the work of Knauf (1991, 1997, 2005a); see also Niemann (1997).

[60] Although the work is quite old now and literary-historical study has shifted considerably since its publication, Tryggve Mettinger's full-length study of Solomon's officials remains a useful point of reference for 1 Kings 4 (1971, esp. 111–23). The list of districts has twelve entries, which by itself suggests the likelihood of adaptation to a later editorial vision rather than an ancient Jerusalem-based scheme of twelve tribes. The districts are defined in diverse terms. The first regions are identified mainly by lists of towns. Only at the end do we find the sequence Naphtali, Asher and Zebulun, Issachar, and Benjamin – a combination that overlaps somewhat with the northern Israelite lists from Genesis 30 and 49, with the addition of Benjamin. Judah is missing from the districts, a fact that was easily understood to reflect Solomon's preference for his own tribe. If we do not assume the existence of Judah at this time, however, the silence suggests that Judah was not named because it was not there.

plausible. As with the David narrative, the occasion of division between the two peoples brings with it a focus on the decision-making process on both sides, including aspects of a collective or collaborative leadership that would align with the pervasive tradition observed as central to Israel in various biblical writings. The essential negotiation is between Rehoboam and the people of Israel, not between Rehoboam and Jeroboam as individual leaders.

Israel is treated as an entity capable of making decisions that are distinct from any one leader's will. Rehoboam, the son of Solomon, does not automatically inherit the right to rule Israel but has to leave Jerusalem to visit the gathered representatives of Israel on their own turf at Shechem. "All Israel had come to Shechem to make him king" (v. 1). When Jeroboam gets involved, "he and all the assembly of Israel" confront Rehoboam with a demand to reduce obligations to the king (vv. 3–4). Israel does not reappear as such until the entertaining story of Rehoboam's folly is complete (vv. 5–15).[61] Then, "all Israel" is said to reject rule by the house of David (v. 16). Their response is quoted as a collective, and it offers no direct acknowledgment of Judah as a separate state. Rehoboam has to escape the encounter in his chariot, and his spokesman is stoned by the crowd. This is not yet outright war, but the conflict is quite similar to the struggles recorded between Zimri, Omri, and Tibni in 1 Kings 16. The only state in view is Israel, and its body politic is simply deciding whom it prefers as king. "All Israel" summons Jeroboam back to their assembly and "makes him king over all Israel" (v. 20), the same action carried out by collective Israel in the Omri material. Judah's perspective is maintained as part of the narrative comment, but even this treats Israel as a distinct collective, evidently following the logic of the core story. "Israel" has rebelled against David (v. 19), and only the Israelites of Judah still serve David's house (v. 17).[62] As in the David narrative of 2 Samuel, it is possible that the specific references to Judah in verses 17 and 20 are secondary clarifications of a narrative that assumed the reality of a southern kingdom without naming it except by its ruling "house of David" (vv. 16, 20).[63]

---

[61] If this Judahite text has been composed from a narrative that was based on something more like a (still Judahite) report of the political separation, the concentration of "Israel" references outside the nice literary creation could indicate that 12:1–3 and 16–20 have more direct knowledge of Israelite political tradition. Note that the talk of "elders" (or older generation) and "young men" in the account of Rehoboam's decision follows a trope also found in the early second-millennium Sumerian story of Gilgamesh and Aga. In both literary works, the two groups do not represent separate councils. The assumption is that kings surround themselves with advisors and associates of various kinds, without constitution as formal bodies. In 1 Kings 12, the focus on decision-making in the royal circle may derive from the court at Jerusalem and so reflect the Judah setting (cf. Katz 1987).

[62] This terminology appears to indicate non-Judahites who are living in the south and who decide to accept rule by Rehoboam. Whatever the circumstances of the tenth century, this phrase by itself suggests that such a distinction applied to the population of later Judah, perhaps during the last phases of the monarchy.

[63] Uwe Becker (2000, 219) reads the main story as 12:1, 3b–19*, with the core in verses 1, 3b–14, 16, and 18. In his view, the story was never independent before integration into the Deuteronomistic History, though it may reflect an older version from the north (p. 215).

Tribal language appears only once in the tale of Rehoboam's rejection, to describe Benjamin's siding with Judah (v. 21). Benjamin's association with Judah persists into the Persian period, where it represents the only tribal group included by name with the Judahites who returned from Babylonia.[64] In 1 Kings 12:21, the concern to account for Benjamin as the one "tribe" that aligns itself with Rehoboam and the "House of Judah" appears to reflect conditions after Israel's end in 720. The detail of Benjamin exhibits the principal tension embedded in this chapter: an image of Israelite political structure is preserved in an explicitly Judahite text, probably from after the fall of Israel's kingdom. Wherever we imagine the roots of this story, it should be considered separate from the preceding Solomon collection. The bridge between Solomon and the narrative of two kingdoms is accomplished with the prophecy of Ahijah in 1 Kings 11 and 14. Chapter 12 is focused on Rehoboam, and even the references to his father do not imply a compositional connection to the Bible's Solomon section. The account of Rehoboam's failure to rule Israel introduces the long account of two kingdoms that continues at least through 2 Kings 17, and the focus on Jeroboam's religious activities at the end of the chapter serves that larger literary creation.

As a whole, the books of Samuel and Kings are dominated by the interests of Judah, and this interest shapes every aspect of the account of monarchic leadership that traverses this long narrative. Because of the ancient association of David with Israel, this material retains viable recollections of Israelite political tradition even as these are preserved for the separate southern kingdom. There is some other Israelite content in these books. We will return to the traditions about Saul, which suggest a body of lore preserved among the people of Benjamin.[65] The Elijah and Elisha blocks in 1 Kings 17–2 Kings 9 appear to have roots in Israel, but the material in them that treats king Ahab is less securely Israelite and displays little of its political situation.[66] Israel's king Jehu, who launches a new royal house in a spray of blood and with passionate opposition to Baal, is given considerable and generally positive attention (2 Kings 9–10), but the religious perspective may suggest observers from Judah, however close to the events.[67] The conflicts between Israel and the house of

---

[64] See Ezra 1:5; 4:1; 10:9; Neh. 11:4, 7–9. On Benjamin in the sixth and fifth centuries, see Blenkinsopp (2006); Edelman (2001).

[65] Although Saul may in fact have come from Ephraim, if 1 Samuel 1 originally anticipated the king's birth, the capital at Gibeah offered a basis for Benjamin to claim him and to preserve Saul lore (see Milstein 2010, 225–31).

[66] Walter Dietrich (2000) considers that the biblical Omrides, perhaps for polemical purposes better called "Ahabides," were made the Judahite code for the kingdom of Manasseh (696–41). On the historical problems, see Na'aman (1997c).

[67] The Jehu story may represent some of the best evidence for a predeuteronomistic collection about prophets and kings. Anthony Campbell's (1986) proposal of a ninth-century work is generally considered to attribute too much to an Israelite writer. For attribution of the combination of prophetic oracles and royal houses to deuteronomistic writing, based on earlier material, see McKenzie (1991, 79). Na'aman (1997c, 1999) finds the deuteronomists' sources for Judah to be better than for Israel, with Israelite history filled in from prophetic stories. In an attempt to

David that are recounted in 2 Samuel and 1 Kings 12 appear to preserve features of Israelite political life under kings, though these are filtered through the eyes of writers from Judah. Only the short Omri text appears to come from Israel itself, with a vivid description of Israel as a decision-making body that stands distinct from its kings, who can rule only by its consent. The language of Israel as a collective political body is thus firmly embedded in the framework of monarchy. Israel is the people ruled, and the people who must accept rule. Set against its kings, Israel is a unity by its very need to negotiate with individual power.

outline the process by which the monarchic histories were created, Auld (2000) proposes that a Judahite account of David's line was augmented by longer accounts of David and Solomon, a king list for Israel, the Elijah–Elisha "cycle," and a "peroration" on the fall of Israel. This system includes no place for the Omri material. Würthwein (2008) distinguishes an older Jehu narrative, which portrays him as a brutal usurper, from the religious interest that he attributes to deuteronomistic revision.

7

Moses and the Conquest of Eastern Israel

In my review of Israelite material in the Bible, I began with texts from Judges and Genesis. These texts grapple with a tradition in which Israel consisted of separate peoples that cooperated or competed on the basis of a larger affiliation. This tradition became crystallized into the Bible's persistent scheme of Israel's twelve tribes – counted differently depending on the occasion. Most often, however, Israelite narrative presents Israel as a single body, and its collective political character is expressed only in its function as a group that is distinct from its leaders. This collective character is the norm throughout the older Moses material in Exodus and Numbers; it marks the core accounts of conquest under Joshua; and it defines what Saul rules as the first king of Israel. Each of these clusters calls for attention and will be addressed in a separate chapter.

The most difficult of these Israelite narrative traditions is the cluster involving Moses, because it is particularly complex. In final form, the affairs of Moses fill the books of Exodus, Leviticus, Numbers, and Deuteronomy, a large portion of which are devoted to various collections of his religious instruction, or *tôrâ*. This teaching comes to play a central role in defining the postmonarchic community of Judah's survivors, and the question of whether it has roots in Israel is important but secondary to the task of evaluating the Bible's primary narrative.[1] The Moses narrative itself is found mainly in Exodus and Numbers.

---

[1] For this issue, the key text is the Covenant Code found in Exodus 21–3. David Wright (2009) has argued for a direct literary relationship between this biblical text and the Code of Hammurabi from Babylon, a legal collection first composed in the early second millennium B.C.E but copied by scribes as part of first-millennium curriculum. For Wright, the only feasible date for such a scribal exchange would be the seventh century, after Assyrian conquest of Israel and Judah but before what appears to be the late monarchic production of the core law in Deuteronomy. In his *Formation of the Hebrew Bible* (2011), David Carr acknowledges Wright's evidence for the Mesopotamian connection yet finds the seventh-century date unlikely, especially because there is little interest in the monarchy in the Covenant Code. Carr suggests that such Mesopotamian scribal contacts could have occurred in "the early Israelite monarchies" – not specifying united, northern, or southern. The outcome of this discussion is essential for

In the first, Moses brings Israel out of Egypt to a mountain in the wilderness to the east; in the second, he leads them from the mountain into the land of Moab east of the Jordan River, after the people refuse a direct assault on the land of Canaan (Numbers 13–14). The book of Deuteronomy begins in chapters 1–3 with a brief history of how the people found themselves east of the Jordan, a section constructed from story elements that overlap with material found in Exodus and Numbers.

The tradition of exodus from Egypt appears to be associated especially with Israel west of the Jordan River, as reflected in the perspectives of Hosea and Amos.[2] These prophetic references show no awareness of a journey east of the Jordan, an assault on Sihon and Og in the east, or a crossing of the Jordan River that linked the eastern conflict with a western conquest. As a narrative in Exodus, the drama is intensified by delay, and rather than a single crisis, Israel suffers a lingering resistance from Egypt's king. They finally depart in the middle of the night, at Pharaoh's own command, without raising a weapon in battle (Exod. 12:29–36). Egypt's attempt to keep Israel in service is combatted by their god Yahweh in a series of plagues, without an active role for the people (in Exodus 7–11). The defeat of an Egyptian army by drowning at the Reed Sea fits the same pattern of divine victory unsullied by any need for human combat (Exodus 14).

Moses' leadership in the exodus story contrasts with what we find in the eastern conquest. There, Moses is like Joshua – a military leader who could be compared to characters like Gideon or even Saul. In the account of departure from Egypt, however, Moses makes only a religious demand, to bring the people out of Egypt to celebrate a feast for Yahweh (Exod. 5:1, 3; etc.). With Aaron in tow, Moses confronts Pharaoh with messages of Yahweh's power and a promise to intervene on behalf of his people. He is not a general but a prophet, as evidently envisioned in Hos. 12:14: "By a prophet Yahweh brought up Israel out of Egypt."[3] Moreover, Moses' prophetic character is defined in the story of escape by his individual confrontation with the Egyptian king, rather

---

determining the origins of biblical "law" (*tôrâ*), and the Israel/Judah distinction must be taken more seriously in isolating the background of the Covenant Code/Deuteronomy connection (cf. Levinson 1997). I do not undertake this major project here.

[2] See Knauf (2006, 292); Russell (2009, 55–63). As with all Israelite writing in the Bible, the prophecy in Hosea and Amos became part of Judah's scripture only by a process of transmission that at some point brought it into Judahite hands. Russell identifies the following references to Egypt as part of the eighth-century and therefore Israelite tradition: Hos. 2:16–17; 7:11, 16; 8:13; 9:3, 6; 11:1, 5, 11; 12:2, 10, 14; 13:4; Amos 3:9; 9:7. Along with the commentaries, note especially Hoffman (1989).

[3] In light of this distinction, Moses' role in Exod. 24:3–8 suggests a separate origin for that mountain tradition. There, he is more like a priest, or at least his religious leadership does not have the prophetic cast of the escape story. The mountain role, where Moses leads in a covenant-making ceremony, perhaps matches best the stream of thought that makes him the mediator of divine instruction, as expressed in Deut. 33:8–11. Beyerle (1997, 125–6) follows many in attributing the references to covenant and teaching to a later revision, which would be Judahite.

than by any message for the people of Yahweh. In this respect, he resembles figures such as Samuel, Nathan, and Elijah, whose roles are defined above all by their relationships to monarchs. With this focus, Israel's political nature is not brought into the narrative. Perhaps the most striking aspect is the very fact that the people are led by a prophetic figure rather than by a military leader or ruler. Moses attracts a range of roles in the Torah narrative, but the exodus itself casts him first of all as Yahweh's emissary.

The second large movement in the Moses stories brings Israel out of the southern wilderness and into the land east of the Jordan River. By this observation, I set apart all the traditions of the mountain of God and the wandering in the wilderness. The first represents a destination that gives Israel a religious identity as the people of Yahweh, without defining them by where they come from or where they end up.[4] The second is a journey without destination, a narrative innovation developed from the Israelite tradition of the wilderness as an antecedent to life in a flourishing land (esp. Hos. 13:4–5).[5] In contrast to both these and the exodus story, the movement from the wilderness into Jordan has a direct geographical connection to Israel in that this invasion accounts for its entire eastern territory. For my treatment of the Moses traditions in relation to Israel, I choose for extended study one of the texts that bears this tradition of an eastern conquest: Deuteronomy 2–3, rather than Numbers 20–1, which are usually given priority. The version of the campaigns against Sihon and Og in Deuteronomy 2–3 is not clearly dependent on the Numbers rendition, and I propose that it offers an independent view of a narrative that must have origins

---

[4] It is possible that the tradition of the mountain of God has Israelite roots. Analysis of Exodus 19–34 has tended in recent years toward later dates and Judah-based settings, and the antiquity and location of its components remain questions of sharp dispute. A simpler line of reasoning may follow the link between Elijah and the mountain of God in 1 Kings 19. After a confrontation at Mount Carmel, the prophet Elijah heads south in his flight from Jezebel, queen of Israel. Forty days after he leaves Beersheba, Elijah reaches "the mountain of God, Horeb" (v. 8), a combination of names found otherwise only with Moses' meeting in Exod. 3:1. Elijah is the only prophet identified directly with Moses, and the account of Elijah's experience of Yahweh's presence in verses 11–13 has no biblical counterpart. Whenever it found its way here, and whether or not it is composite, the whole mountain episode does not seem a deuteronomistic creation and appears to originate in Israel, not Judah (see, e.g., McKenzie 1991, 83–7). In documentary theory for the book of Exodus, the mountain is identified with Sinai in the J and P sources, and with Horeb in E and D. For a thoughtful presentation of the evidence and possible implications, see Booij (1984). Some still maintain a date before the late Judahite monarchy for core elements of the mountain narrative in Exodus 19–34, such as Erich Zenger (1996, 273). Especially since Lothar Perlitt's foundational work (1969), many have found little to isolate as definitively early in this section. Blenkinsopp (1997, 115) considers the whole a deuteronomistic composition, based in part on correspondences with Deuteronomy 4–5 and 9–10; Ska (2006, 213–14) considers that the text may have earlier roots, but it has been revised constantly to suit the communities that used its ideas through time.

[5] On the interpretation of this text in the larger book, see Dozeman (2000); Russell (2009, 61–2). For one approach to the function of the wilderness in the book of Numbers, as it relates to the theme of Israel's rebellious nature, see Römer (2007).

in Transjordan Israel.[6] The Israelite interest of this tradition and of these texts does not lie in the detail of its political character, about which little is revealed. Rather, the eastern focus by itself speaks to the geographical diversity of Israel and challenges our own propensity to let the finished Bible lead us toward the western "Promised Land," as if this represented the perspective of all Israel. As already observed, the eastern conquest displays Moses as a leader in more familiar guise, unlike the spokesman for Yahweh that dominates our consciousness. In the end, the eastern conquest also warrants extended attention because my interpretation highlights its independence from western-oriented accounts of early Israel. In a decentralized society, we should expect diverse ideas about national origins, and the east is too easily subsumed in the perspective of the west.

A. The Eastern Invasion

The exodus story by itself would be excruciatingly unsatisfying. Israel escapes from Egypt and finds itself in the wilderness. Surely, they must have another destination. In its full form, the Bible offers two: the Mountain of God, where Israel will meet Yahweh and receive a template from Yahweh for life as his people in their own land; and the land itself, where Israel will begin at last the life promised to their ancestors. The second of these destinations is given full account in the book of Joshua, which celebrates Israel's possession of its Promised Land, defined by invasion of the western highlands by way of Jericho and Ai, at the eastern threshold of Benjamin. This invasion under Joshua is based on a turn of events from the Torah narrative that might otherwise be unexpected: the prior conquest of a considerable chunk of land east of the Jordan River, which the finished Judahite version of Numbers 32 treats as something of an embarrassment.[7] The tribes of Reuben and Gad, along with the awkwardly labeled "half-tribe" of Manasseh, request permission to settle the conquered region and are granted this with the proviso that they join their fellow Israelites in an attack on the actual Promised Land across the Jordan. After exodus from Egypt and wandering in the southern wilderness, it is odd to find Israel entering Canaan directly from the east.

---

[6] On the importance of the Transjordan in biblical narrative, see David Santis (2004), with focus on religious aspects.

[7] Numbers 32 appears to have a complex origin, and eastern Israelite sources are possible, as with the description of Machir/Manasseh settlement in verses 39–42 (see the treatments of Numbers 32 in Gray 1903 and Levine 2000). The language of two and a half tribes and the overall notion that these peoples had to ask permission to settle outside the Promised Land, however, assume a late adaptation to the scheme of twelve tribes and a western perspective. Levine (p. 479) considers the identification of Manasseh as a "half tribe" to derive from Deut. 3:11–12, as deuteronomistic, but one could equally argue that the Deuteronomy text reflects later editing under the influence of Numbers 32. In either case, this is an artificial accommodation based on the division of Joseph into the two groups of Ephraim and Manasseh.

Immediately, the unexpected interest in the east suggests a community there that demanded inclusion, if we are not to take this as a purely intellectual exercise in explaining the old reality of Israelite population in Jordan. One could seek such a community in Persian period peoples linked to Judah, though I am not aware of any secure evidence for eastern groups of this date finding a voice in the Bible. Another possibility is that the scheme in Joshua results from addressing an immovable narrative object, a received story that places Moses and Israel in Jordan. This object would be the account of an eastern conquest under Moses' leadership, consisting of an assault on the dominions of Sihon and Og, rulers over Heshbon and Bashan. Interpreters have adopted so readily the western focus of the finished Bible that they have generally underestimated the most basic feature of this tradition: it explains how Israel came to occupy a large region east of the Jordan River. Various biblical traditions confirm the importance of this eastern part of Israel. Gilead is listed in the Song of Deborah (Judg. 5:17) and is the homeland of the hero Jephthah (Judges 10–11). Saul's son Eshbaal/Ishbosheth makes Mahanaim of Gilead the base of his rule (2 Sam. 2:8–9), and then David makes Mahanaim his refuge and camp for counterattack against Absalom (2 Sam. 17:24). Elijah is a Gileadite (1 Kings 17:1), as is Jehu, founder of Israel's most enduring royal house (2 Kings 9:1, 4). No great sacred site is remembered to be in the east, and the activities of these kings and leaders are recounted with an eye to the west. Almost always, eastern Israel appears in the Bible casually, carried along with each narrative stream. The tradition for a conquest of land in Jordan logically derives from an eastern population, but biblical accounts of this eastern conquest have no clean association with lore from the kingdom of Israel.[8] My question is whether the eastern interest of this tradition could nevertheless have originated in the kingdom called Israel, which included a substantial Jordan population, before it was adapted to the frameworks of later, Judah-oriented compositions.

1. Defining an Israelite Tradition

In Numbers 20–1, Moses sends messengers from Kadesh to the king of Edom asking to pass through his land, and the Israelites are warned off (20:14–21). After interludes with Aaron's death, the defeat of Arad, and the plague of poisonous snakes, the Israelites move on to Moab, where we are offered bits of songs about the land but no tale of conflict or negotiation (21:10–20). Ammon is never mentioned. In this format, the narrative sets up the Balaam series, which

---

[8] In making this assertion, I reason against common approaches that treat the eastern conquest as no more than a practice run for the assault on the western Promised Land. Thomas Römer (2005, 125) observes that in Deuteronomy 1–3, the story of spying out the land is a prologue to conquest of the Transjordan, as opposed to the centrality of Numbers 13–14 in the rebellion cycle of Numbers 11–20, which he considers a later collection. He nevertheless considers that as part of the Moses introduction in Deuteronomy, this provides the paradigm for the themes of conquest and loss of the land that extend from Joshua to Kings. Sihon and Og are mythical figures who inhabit an undefined land, so that their defeat can serve as an idealized paradigm for successful conquest (n. 33).

is based on Moab's fear of Israelite attack *after* the defeats of Sihon and Og (22:2–4). Before those crucial battles, and having arrived in the neighborhood of Moab, Israel offers Sihon the Amorite the same peaceful passage that had been offered to Edom, and like the Edomites, Sihon brings an army against Israel (21:21–3). This time, however, Israel takes them on and defeats them (21:24–5), after which they are said to dispatch Og of Bashan (21:33–5). In Numbers 20–1, the notion that Israel wants only to pass through both Edom and the territory of the Amorites assumes a western Promised Land as the destination. Israel has no business in the east, and they only end up controlling land there because of Sihon's folly. Such a perspective is at odds with the reality of the geography of the Israelite kingdom, which included significant populations east of the Jordan throughout its existence. It probably displays a Judahite hand.

In the majority of scholarship, recent and otherwise, Deuteronomy 1–3 is understood to be based on the related texts in Exodus 18 and Numbers 13–14 and 20–1.[9] Dozeman (2002, 177) describes this as "free adaptation," Gertz (2006, 104–5) as "relecture."[10] Various reasons are given, including the fact that every episode in Deuteronomy 1–3 has a counterpart in the other two books, so that the Deuteronomy collection as a whole seems derivative rather than original (Perlitt 1985, 158).[11] The coherence of the Deuteronomy text is likewise interpreted as a reflection of the reworking process rather than as evidence of independence from the fragmented Numbers text.[12] Mayes (1979, 133–4) observes the construction of the narrative in Deut. 2:1–3:11 as five repeating episodes with repeating elements, including the movement of Israel to a new location, Yahweh's instruction on how to proceed, some history of past settlement, the issue of obtaining food, and the outcome as departure or occupation.[13]

---

[9] Gertz (2006, 103–4) observes that in his Deuteronomy commentary, Preuss (1982, 77) could take for granted the notion that Deuteronomy 1–3 introduced the history that extended through 2 Kings 25, but "times have changed" – so that the text relates to more specific (and later) narrative developments. Rendtorff (1995) has advocated a similar approach for Sihon and Og in particular.

[10] Nelson (2002, 25) says that Deut. 1:19–46 "condenses" Numbers 13–14, which is an earlier narrative about sending spies into the land. By his approach, the motif of buying food is more at home in Num. 20:19 than in Deut. 2:6 (p. 36 n.3); and the lack of deuteronomistic language in the Sihon account of Num. 21:21–31 proves that it must be older than Deuteronomy 2:26–36 (p. 44).

[11] Perlitt also objects that Deuteronomy 1–3 provides no geographical information that is not paralleled in Joshua and Judges 1, though this may reflect an editorial leveling of these texts in the latest periods of their combination.

[12] Perlitt (1985, 161) considers the author of Deuteronomy 1–3 a forceful shaper of the traditions, as evident in the speech form itself, as second-person in the mouth of Moses. Yahweh's role is prominent.

[13] Mayes concludes that "there is little to show that this pattern belonged to any pre-deuteronomistic stage of the tradition; rather, it is due to deuteronomistic and post-deuteronomistic systematizing of varied material."

Perhaps the most compelling of these arguments is Deuteronomy's lack of any episode not found in Exodus and Numbers, with material matching three different sections of what those books present as a wilderness trek. Somehow, the original author of Deuteronomy 1–3 was working from a version of the wilderness narrative that was at least a variant of what underlies Exodus and Numbers. The problem is that the renditions of these stories in Deuteronomy diverge so significantly from the parallel texts that they are difficult to see as derived from the other books. In an interpretive world with early J and E documents, it was almost automatic to assume that Exodus 18 and Numbers 13–14 and 20–1 were older than Deuteronomy 1–3, which so clearly represent the latest introductory addition to a book that was already understood to be later than J and E. The first challenges to the standard direction of dependence came with early questions about the traditional Documentary Hypothesis. In a reevaluation of the Numbers 21 parallels, John Van Seters finds that there were relatively few matches with the wording of Deuteronomy 2–3, and he argues that the direction of dependence should be reversed, so that deuteronomistic writing must be earlier than the non-priestly writing in the Torah.[14] Martin Rose (1989, 133) follows a similar approach, also considering the main non-priestly narrative in Exodus and Numbers to serve as part of a new introduction to the Deuteronomistic History in Deuteronomy through Kings.

Since the early challenges of Van Seters and others, analyses of composition and revision in the books of Moses have varied widely, with increasing attraction to postexilic editing for collections even later than the sixth- or fifth-century deuteronomistic and priestly writing. In this interpretive environment, opinions on the dependence of Deuteronomy 1–3 remain divided, and some have maintained with Van Seters that this text preserves evidence of an independent tradition for the wilderness and eastern conquest. Römer (2005, 125 and n. 32) concludes that Deuteronomy 1–3 must contain older accounts on which the authors of Numbers relied; these accounts in turn reflect older traditions that are impossible to reconstruct.[15] If the Deuteronomy texts were taken from Exodus and Numbers, why is there so little evidence of direct citation? In the parallel between the spy stories in Numbers 13–14 and Deuteronomy 1, the latter lacks crucial scenes, such as Moses' successful intercession for the people, which contrasts with Yahweh punishing Moses in Deut. 1:37. While the episodes in Deuteronomy 1–3 indeed parallel texts found in Exodus and

---

[14] Van Seters (1972; 1980) laid out his original analysis with useful charts comparing the contents of Numbers 21, Deuteronomy 2–3, and Judges 11. The only points of closely matched wording occur in the following phrases: sending messengers (Num. 21:21; Deut. 2:26); "let me pass through your land" (Num. 21:22; Deut. 2:27); going by the highway (Num. 21:22; Deut. 2:27); going out against Israel at Jahaz (Num. 21:23b; Deut. 2:32); and capturing all the towns (Num. 21:25; Deut. 2:34). As shared points of reference, this list shows considerable similarity. For a literary dependence, however, the divergence is substantial. Van Seters developed this interpretation as part of a larger system in *The Life of Moses* (1994, 363–403).

[15] As observed above, he considers these to be ahistorical and lacking any anchor in real geography.

Numbers, the historical review lacks most of the conflict stories that dominate Numbers 11–25: the quail of chapter 11; Miriam and Aaron against Moses in chapter 12; Korah, Dathan, and Abiram in chapter 16; the serpent in chapter 21; and Baal-peor in chapter 25 (Römer 2006b). Only the spying episode is included, and it serves as the direct preparation for conquest of the land – eastern though it is – as opposed to its situation long before arrival in Numbers 13–14. For Römer, this whole view of the wilderness period in negative terms is postdeuteronomistic (so postexilic), in contrast with the attitudes found in Hosea, Jeremiah, and even Deuteronomy 8. Deuteronomy 1–3 does not seem to be based on this non-priestly Numbers collection, and it is more likely that both sets of stories share a common ancestor, so that they are effectively variants.[16] The speech form in Deuteronomy is itself "deuteronomistic," shared with the classic examples of Joshua (Joshua 23), Samuel (1 Samuel 12), and Solomon (1 Kings 8), a type not found in the rest of the Torah.

My analysis of Deuteronomy 2–3 begins where Römer's leaves off; namely, that this account of an eastern conquest represents an independent variant of the tradition also reflected in Numbers 20–1, adapted to the format and perspective of Moses' speech to the people in Jordan. Eventually, as the two divergent versions were embedded in works that came to share the same audience, accommodations were made to reconcile them, such as the evident addition of the Og narrative to Num. 21:33–5.[17] Unlike Numbers, Deuteronomy 2–3 present the eastern lands of Sihon and Og as the gift of Yahweh, which they undertake to conquer by his direct command (2:24; 3:2). This land is the true inheritance of Israel, unlike the lands belonging to the sons of Esau (2:4, 8) and the sons of Lot (2:9, 19). Here, geography provides an obvious point of reference for identifying the origin of the tale: this is an etiology for the presence of Israel in this eastern territory and is most naturally understood to come from these people themselves. The treatment of this land as a grant from Yahweh in Deuteronomy shows this aspect of the rendition to be closer to an Israelite form of the tradition.[18]

Although Deuteronomy 1–3 now serve as an introduction to the book of Deuteronomy that looks forward to the contents of Joshua as the ultimate entry into the Promised Land, the conquest account retains features that do not clearly belong to that Deuteronomy–Joshua combination. Read on its own, without assuming the reference to Kadesh in 1:46, Deut. 2:1 describes an itinerary that might be taken to begin in the vicinity of Egypt, soon after departure: "Then we turned to set out into the wilderness by way of the

---

[16] For this view, see also Achenbach (2003); Otto (2000, 12–109).

[17] The notion that the Sihon–Heshbon conflict once stood alone in the Numbers account is confirmed by Judges 11, where Og is never mentioned.

[18] In the full rendition of the conquest in Deut. 2:24–3:7, the command to take possession of the land stands in tension with the specific request to Sihon in 2:29, where Moses speaks of crossing the Jordan into the land that Yahweh is giving to Israel. This line reflects the adaptation of the eastern conquest tale to the larger scheme of combination with Joshua, as would suit the role of Deuteronomy 1–3 as introduction to such a combined narrative.

Reed Sea, just as Yahweh had said to me, and we went around in the Seir highlands for a long time." Alternatively, this bridge between the scouting tale and the eastern conquest may attach the latter to Egypt in a way not envisioned by the core narrative, where the people begin their approach to this land from the southeastern land of Seir, a country associated with Yahweh's presence in the old hymnic poetry of Deut. 33:2 and Judg. 5:4. Yahweh's command in Deut. 2:3 then represents a release from the period of wilderness life, which has taken place in Seir: "You have been going around in these highlands long enough; turn yourselves toward the north." The following verse then launches the sequence of movements through lands that are already committed to other groups, until the people reach the lands of Sihon and Og. The primary material of this narrative appears in the following verses:

- 2:1–6, the command to leave Seir and bypass the territory of the sons of Esau;[19]
- 2:8–9, movement forward toward "the wilderness of Moab," where Ar is already assigned to "the sons of Lot";[20]
- 2:17–19, approach to the territory of Moab and Ar, which brings the people near Ammon, likewise assigned to "the sons of Lot";[21]
- 2:24, 32–6, conquest of Sihon the Amorite, king of Heshbon;[22]
- 3:1–7, conquest of Og, king of Bashan.

With this list, I have not intended to strip away all elements of secondary material, as if such could be done with a text that has experienced more than one phase of revision. These verses represent only the part of the text that best preserves whatever remains of an older Israelite narrative tradition. What remains has the shape of a coherent account to serve the introductory function in Deuteronomy. If we consider the reference to a western conquest in 2:29 an addition, however, it is not clear that the narrative anticipates the book of Joshua, and so the story in itself need not reflect the later role of Deuteronomy 1–3 as large-scale literary introduction. Likewise, the lead line in 2:1 may not be based on the entire Exodus–Numbers scenario for conflict at the Reed Sea, followed by meeting with Yahweh at his mountain, and then forty years waiting for the rebellious exodus generation to die. Rather, it seems to picture a wilderness experience more like the one in Hosea (cf. 13:4–5), before Yahweh is ready to turn the people loose on the land prepared for them.

---

[19] Deut. 2:7 refers to forty years in the wilderness, a tradition familiar from other biblical renditions of the period after the exodus (Num. 14:33–4; etc.), and not assumed in the "many days" of 2:1.

[20] Verses 10–16 combine geographical notes with a reminder of the forty-year motif, in that it took thirty-eight years to reach the wadi Zered (v. 14). The Kadesh point of departure is only part of the larger framework, here and in 1:2, 19, and 46.

[21] Verses 20–3 continue the pattern of added explanations of local peoples, in travelogue fashion.

[22] Verses 25 and 29 seem particularly conscious of the larger narrative that leads to a western conquest. The Sihon narrative is discussed further below.

The perspective of the core narrative revolves around Yahweh's assignment (verb *ntn*) of land (*'ereṣ*) to each people as an inherited portion (*yĕrûšâ*) (2:5, 9, 19). This picture of each people given its own land by God who is sovereign over all recalls the scheme of Deut. 32:8–9, which may come from Judah in the ninth or eighth centuries.[23] It is not Deuteronomy's own notion of inherited land, which is based on the word *naḥălâ* (Deut. 4:21, 38; 15:4; 19:10; etc.).

The most striking feature of the opening section for the eastern invasion in Deuteronomy 2–3 is the characterization of the Transjordan peoples by names that recall the genealogical scheme of Genesis: "the sons of Esau" and "the sons of Lot." While such cross-reference may in some settings indicate a revising writer's sense of a wider scribal collection, these texts offer no direct link to the Genesis narratives beyond the names themselves, which are almost unique as designations of these eastern groups. In contrast to the Jacob story in Genesis, where Isaac tells Esau that he will serve Jacob and then have to throw off this yoke, Deuteronomy 2 has the sons of Esau receive their land as a simple gift, with no question of conflict between brothers. This amicable spirit contrasts with the exclusion of Ammonites and Moabites from worship based on their support of Balaam in Deut. 23:3–6, in the main body of instruction. Further, the lands of Esau and Moab are named Seir and Ar, a tradition lacking in Genesis (Deut. 2:1, 4, 9, 18).[24]

The source for Deut. 2:1–23 must be at least non-D, and in some sense pre-D. Deuteronomy 2 thus attests the strongest link between Genesis and the four books of Moses outside priestly and deuteronomistic writing. Although the sons

[23] Deuteronomy 32 is frustratingly difficult to date and locate. The text offers no sense of political or social organization, and Yahweh's people are simply called Jacob (v. 9) and Jeshurun (v. 15). "The sons of Israel" in verse 8 reflect a famous correction from "the sons of El," preserved in the Greek and Qumran texts. The divine name Elyon (v. 8) is strongly if not uniquely associated with Jerusalem: see Gen. 14:18–20; and frequently in the Psalms (e.g., 9:3; 18:14). Elyon appears in the fourth Balaam oracle (Num. 24:16) and in Isa. 14:14, which Levine considers eastern, but which is most easily taken as Judahite in the book of Isaiah (see Levine 2000, 230–4). In a long and frankly cautious study, Paul Sanders (1996, 431–5) finds that the poem is pre-exilic and independent, possibly but not definitely "northern" (my "Israelite"). Andreas Reichert (1986) suggests a seventh-century date from protodeuteronomic circles that merged Israelite and Judahite traditions. He considers the "rock" of verses 4, 15, 18, 30, and 37 to be closely related to the Zion tradition (esp. 1 Sam. 2:2; Ps. 18 (=2 Sam. 22):3, 32, 47; Isa 30:29; Pss. 78:35; 89:26; 95:1; 144:1). "Jacob" in verse 9 would be Israelite. With focus on the role of Elyon in distributing peoples to gods, Mark Smith (2004, 110) also considers the possibility of Israelite ideas preserved in a poem that is finally from Judah.

[24] Elsewhere in the Bible, only Psalm 83:9 speaks of the sons of Lot, in a sequence that suggests an Israelite perspective. This last of the psalms of Asaph has the people's enemies say, "Come, let us wipe them out from being a nation (*gōy*), so that the name of Israel is remembered no more" (v. 5). The alliance of enemies includes the tents of Edom, the Ishmaelites, Moab, the Hagrites (cf. Hagar), Byblos, Ammon, Amalek, Philistia, the inhabitants of Tyre, and Assyria (vv. 7–9). Then, the psalm recalls two victory traditions known to us from Judges and mixed together: the defeat of Sisera and Jabin under Deborah and Barak (Judges 4–5) and the defeat of Midian and its rulers under Gideon (Judges 6–8). Geographically, these conflicts were Israelite, and the whole mix of opponents is far from any Judahite standard. The reference to Endor as part of the Sisera tradition (v. 10) is obscure but evidently Israelite.

of Lot are assigned no specific relationship to Israel, the identification suggests familiarity with a Lot tradition that would define an ancestral kinship with Moab and Ammon. Perhaps it would be natural for the Bible's core explanation of these eastern peoples to come from the part of Israel that inhabited the same region. Deuteronomy 2 appears to share with Genesis some version of the Jacob–Isaac and Abraham–Lot stories that lay out the principal family tree for Israel and its inland neighbors. Such a shared tradition between Genesis and Deuteronomy 2 requires no literary or even direct narrative connection. These texts may assume the same genealogical framework without assuming the same stories behind that genealogy. We cannot tell. The likelihood of an eastern interest or even source for some part of the Genesis ancestor lore is indicated by Jacob's involvement with eastern sites in chapters 31–3 and perhaps by the very concern to incorporate the northeastern peoples of Moab and Ammon in the Abraham–Lot story.

2. Sihon and Og

Both Numbers 21 and Deuteronomy 2 identify the first target for an eastern attack with three names: Sihon as king, the Amorites as general population, and Heshbon as the principal settlement. Sihon is called "king of the Amorites" in Numbers (21:21, 26, 34) and "king of Heshbon" in Deuteronomy (2:24, 26, 30; 3:6), where he is also "the Amorite" (2:24) and "king of the Amorites" (3:2). The interpretation of Heshbon raises problems that are entangled in larger systems with later compositional dates and implied Judahite origins for the entire tradition of an eastern invasion.[25] Knauf (1990, 135) considers that the idea itself is driven by the fiction that Israel came from outside Palestine, and without archaeological confirmation of an early site, ahistorical explanations may be suggested, with Heshbon first a Moabite city after the fall of Israel.[26] The idea that Heshbon was the city of Sihon can then be considered secondary, and the Amorites may be regarded as a deuteronomistic and late Judahite designation for the supposed conquered populations in both eastern and western regions. Og and Bashan offer even fewer points of reference and little basis for decisive argument.[27]

---

[25] Excavations have made it difficult to place the origins of Heshbon before Iron Age I (ca. 1200–1000), and no substantial town existed at Tell Hesban until some time between the tenth and ninth centuries. Geraty (1997) dates "Stratum 17," with its large reservoir, to the ninth and eighth centuries, while James Sauer (1994) raises the date of construction to the tenth century. The difference is not crucial for this analysis.

[26] Hans-Christoph Schmitt (1988, 29–30, 38) identifies the earliest Heshbon tradition in the poems of Num. 21:27–30 and Jer. 48:45–6, with origin in the eighth to seventh centuries; cf. Knauf (1990, 136). In Jeremiah 48 and Isaiah 15–16, Heshbon is associated not with early Amorites but with Moab (Miller 1989, 578); Rose (1981, 155–6).

[27] Knauf (1990, 135–6) suggests that Og appears on a sixth/fifth-century sarcophagus from Byblos, which would confirm his fictional character in the Bible. I find the equation of the two names with one person to represent a considerable stretch. Rose (1981, 157) cites Noth's conclusion that no Israelite occupation of Bashan is known before David. It is not clear how such a statement can be controlled beyond biblical references.

Isaiah 15–16 and Jeremiah 48 suggest that by the seventh century, Heshbon was solidly Moabite, and nothing indicates any Judahite affiliation after that date. In the late ninth century, Mesha describes his consolidation of power without reference to Heshbon, which would not yet have been a defining regional center. The point of the Heshbon story is that Israel held rights to a territory that was pre-Moabite and pre-Israelite, available because it was held by "Amorites" who were kin to neither Israelites nor Moabites.[28] Although the term "Amorite" is sometimes considered universally late and Judahite, the word itself is ancient and deeply embedded in the identities of Syrian tribal peoples of the second millennium.[29] Genesis 48:21-2 may preserve a use of the word that is separate from the stereotyped connection with Canaan and that portrays a people in competition with Israel for the highlands of Shechem: "I myself hereby give you Shechem, (as) one over your brothers, which I took from the hand of the Amorites by my sword and by my bow."[30]

Both Numbers 21 and Deuteronomy 2–3 present Israel's eastern invasion as the fruit of two victories, first over Sihon king of the Amorites at Heshbon, and then over Og king of Bashan. Together, these territories fill all of the land available when Edom, Moab, and Ammon are considered off-limits. This regional vision is only part of the primary narrative in Deuteronomy, however, because the short Og segment in Numbers 21:33-5 takes over both the wording and the focus of Deuteronomy.[31] In Numbers, the essential invasion narrative

---

[28] The Mesha inscription and the biblical identification of Heshbon with Moab provide chronological bounds for the early Sihon tradition. As suggested by Levine (2000, 131-3), Heshbon defined the southern part of east Israel because it was a major center at the time when the story was conceived. Levine suggests a date for the original "ballad" (Num. 21:27-30) in the mid-ninth century, when the Omrides held the region. Heshbon may not have been large enough to qualify as the dominant town of the region until after Mesha, however, and the lack of any characterization of Heshbon as Israelite suggests that the narrator chose a site that was no longer held by his people.

[29] For the term Amorite in late context, see the discussion of Genesis 14 in Loretz (1984). Wolff (1977, 168) considers the oldest conceptions of Amorites in the Bible to identify them with the mountains, as opposed to the Canaanites of the coastal plain, regardless of the actual dates of the texts in question: Num. 13:29; Deut. 1:7; Josh. 11:3.

[30] Blum (1984, 219 n. 39) concludes that Gen. 48:22 is a Shechem tradition independent of Genesis 34. He finds three principal contrasts between the two texts: chapter 34 envisions Hivite inhabitants, as opposed to the Amorite in 48:22; chapter 34 requires taking the city, whereas 48:22 envisions the residents to be gone already; and while chapter 34 provides an etiology for the curse on Simeon and Levi, 48:22 is an etiology for Shechem as residence for Joseph. This last characterization of the Dinah story may apply only to its revised form. Noth (1981, 27) considered Gen. 15:16 and 48:22 to be Elohistic (E). Genesis 15 is now seen as a later text, but I see no basis for treating Gen. 48:22 as anything but a precompositional fragment – except the word "Amorite," by itself. Wolff (1977, 168-9) regards the Amorites in Amos 2:9 (vs. the deuteronomistic addition in v. 10) as eighth-century and similar to Elohistic usage in Noth's two texts, along with Num. 21:21, 25-6, 31; 22:2. Carr (1996, 211 n. 69) observes that while 48:21-2 are secondary and linked to the promise theme, verse 22 is probably an older tradition of Jacob conquering Shechem.

[31] The language of "giving" the people to Israel is found in both conquests of Deuteronomy (2:31, 33; 3:2, 3), as is the slaughter of the opposing army (2:33; 3:3), and the *ḥērem* extermination

combines the tense standoff with Edom and the defeat of Sihon. Moab is absent from this pair of parlay accounts but is inserted into the conquest sequence in fragments gathered before and after the victory over Sihon. I will discuss the Sihon narrative in Numbers before addressing the double story in Deuteronomy.

The Sihon tradition in Numbers comes to us in two main segments, a prose rendition of the defeat and occupation of Sihon's land (21:21–5), and a poem about Sihon, Heshbon, and Moab that now explains how northern Moab came to be Amorite (21:27b–30, cf. 26–7a). Neither segment derives from the other, although the poem has perhaps been adapted to complement the preceding prose. Levine (2000, 123–5) considers the original poem to have celebrated Israel's capture of northern Moab by defeating Sihon, who ruled the region from Heshbon.[32] If the Heshbon poem of Numbers 21:27–30 did originally celebrate victory over Moab, then it takes for granted a prior Moabite presence there. The tradition that Heshbon was once Amorite insists that Israel's right to and occupation of the area preceded Moab. The primary prose of 21:21–5 would not require that Moab had any interest in Heshbon before the Amorites *or* the Israelites, a view shared by Deuteronomy 2. Sihon held land under his own auspices and was no Moabite king.

Editors appear to have labored to harmonize Numbers 21 and Deuteronomy 2–3, so that the Sihon narrative in Deuteronomy is now a blended product.[33] Analysis of the transmission history must be tentative, but much of Deuteronomy 2:24–37 may constitute expansions. As I read the passage, the core account is found in 2:24 (or v. 31) and 32–6.[34] This is where Yahweh informs Moses that Israel has been given possession of Sihon's land, and the victory follows immediately. Sihon, his sons, and his army are slain first, and the population is then slaughtered by the sacred *ḥērem* to Yahweh. In the finished text, Yahweh speaks in verses 24–5 as if there had been no interruption from verse 19. Throughout the prelude, each instruction begins, "Yahweh said to me" (Deut. 2:2, 9, 13, 17). The omission here is awkward, although the "crossing" command resembles the instruction for the Zered valley in Deuteronomy 2:13, which itself is isolated awkwardly. Some identification of Sihon's constituency is expected from the Og story (3:2), and verse 24 would provide it. The text

---

(2:34–5; 3:6–7). These must be original to the Deuteronomy texts and then copied from Deut. 3:1–3 into Num. 21:33–5. Rose (1981, 306–7) follows Noth in this solution.

[32] This requires that the title "king of the Amorite(s)" (21:29) be removed as an editorial manipulation. Levine suggests a ninth-century date, when Israel seized the region under Omri and Ahab (p. 132).

[33] Rose (1981, 309) chides Van Seters with reason for treating Deut. 2:26–37 as a homogeneous unit.

[34] Verse 37 uses very late language when it refers to "everything that Yahweh commanded." This is common in both priestly (e.g., Exod. 25:22; 29:35) and deuteronomistic (e.g., Deut. 1:3) writing.

is redundant with verse 31, however, and this gives the impression of compositional fiddling. Verses 26–30 then provide a rationale for the attack. Moses sent an offer of peaceful passage, and Sihon refused it. Yahweh hardened his "spirit," an extrapolation from the heart that is found only here.[35] The details of the parlay share bits of the messages to Edom and Sihon in Numbers 20–1 without matching any section exactly, and the entire motif treats the eastern invasion as an accident.

Without the awkward interpolation, Deuteronomy 2–3 becomes more conceptually coherent. The tradition of a second eastern conquest in Deuteronomy 3 constitutes a full complement to the Sihon narrative, paired with it, and by no means an artificial copy from the Sihon account.[36] Deuteronomy 3 also consists of diverse elements, and only verses 1–7 contain the primary story of how Israel defeated Og king of Bashan.[37] The primary narrative develops along lines much like the Sihon story, without wooden repetition. A fresh movement begins the sequence, toward Bashan, whose king and people come out to defend themselves (v. 1). Yahweh declares to Moses that Og has already been given to Israel (v. 2), and Israel annihilates the whole military force (v. 3). They capture all his towns (v. 4a) and put them to *ḥērem* destruction (v. 6), keeping only livestock and authorized spoils of war (v. 7).[38]

Beyond the broad likeness between the two story lines, the two invasion accounts share crucial conceptions. These eastern lands are the gift of Yahweh, requiring no rationale but that they are part of what this god has deeded to his people. As a divine grant, the land is to be purged of all inhabitants. Every "town" is put to the *ḥērem* (2:34 and 3:6), an act that is defined by population,

---

[35] Viewed concretely, it is difficult to understand how "wind" may be hardened, and this idiom seems to be constructed without any sense of its parts.

[36] My interpretation therefore reverses completely the analysis of Manfred Weippert (1979, 24), who considers the Numbers version of Sihon's defeat (21:21–6) to be the original text for the prose account of an eastern invasion. Before the radical challenge of Van Seters, in particular, who led a broad reevaluation of the relationship between Deuteronomy 1–3 and its parallels, it was too easy to overlook the degree of independence in Deuteronomy. I conclude that the overlapping material in Deut. 2:26–30 is the one main block that is inspired by the Numbers narrative and so inserted into an account governed by very different logic.

[37] Deut. 3:8–11 assembles miscellaneous Og and Bashan lore that has no intrinsic connection to the primary story. The introductory phrase "across the Jordan" (v. 8) is deuteronomistic and assumes in any case a western perspective; see Deut. 1:1, 5; 3:20, 25; 4:41, 46, 47, 49; 11:30; Josh 1:14; 12:1; 13:18. Deut. 3:12–20 moves on to treat division of the land, based on a variety of material. The notion of two and a half tribes (vv. 12–13) is not native to eastern or Israelite tradition.

[38] Verses 4b–5 provide details about the captured land, incorporating a tradition of sixty towns in the Argob region. This tradition appears three times in Judahite texts, always referring to eastern territory, however. Joshua places this in the territory of Manasseh, as settlements of Jair, once belonging to Og of Bashan (13:30). Solomon's list of district supervisors locates them in Ramoth Gilead, associated with Jair of Manasseh (1 Kings 4:13). The late Judahite genealogy of Judah in Chronicles borrows Jair for the preferred patriarch, though there remains a connection to Gilead (1 Chron. 2:22–3).

"men, women, and children." Nothing is burned. This is the old Israelite *ḥērem* tradition described by Lauren Monroe, preserved in its classic form in the Ai *ḥērem* of Joshua 8:26–7.[39] That text even concludes with the same exclusion for livestock (*bĕhēmâ*) and spoils (*šālāl*). The *ḥērem* commanded in Deuteronomy 20 sets a different standard, with women and children fair plunder for towns outside the land (vv. 14–15), and no living thing to be saved in the deeded land (vv. 16–17). Israel's *ḥērem* against the people of Sihon and Og clears the land for the people of Yahweh. The point of the two campaigns is not magnification by duplication. Together, the domains of Sihon and Og constitute the lands that will have an Israelite population. Heshbon represents the south, and Bashan represents the north.[40] The invasion narrative of Deuteronomy 2–3 requires both because its goal is to carve out a claim for Israelite settlement east of the Jordan River. Even the lands set off-limits for the sons of Esau and the sons of Lot contribute to a full account of eastern territory. As such, the invasion narratives of Deuteronomy 2–3 are borrowed from no other part of the Bible, and they do not derive from deuteronomistic schemes. They are unique in the Bible and difficult to explain except as the traditions of the region celebrated, the east country of Israel.

B. The Eastern Tradition of Balaam

In our review of the Torah's account of Israel in the east, the Balaam traditions deserve notice. The contents of Numbers 22–4 are explicitly located in the land east of the Jordan River, and this setting for the prose framework then suggests that the embedded poems, or at least some of them, also come from the east.[41] Balaam is named in the poems themselves as the oracle who speaks them (24:3, 15), and the surrounding narrative likewise revolves around Balaam and his exchanges with Balak king of Moab. Israel appears only as a threat, and Moses is never mentioned. This material thus offers little regarding the character of Israel or even regarding its presence in the east, and its interest for this project lies in the very fact of its presence in the Bible.

---

[39] Monroe identifies four shared elements in the *ḥērem* tradition found in the Moabite Mesha inscription, in newly applied Sabaean evidence, and in the foundational biblical idea: (1) destruction on a massive scale and conflagration, (2) local rather than regional execution, performed on "towns," (3) some segment of the town killed and consecrated to the attackers' god, and (4) erection of a cult installation, consecrated to that god (2007; 2011, chapter 3). Monroe considers the *ḥērem* of Joshua 8 to represent the most direct expression of this tradition in the Bible, where these elements align most closely with the Moabite and Sabaean practices. By comparison with those texts, she includes the building of an altar at the end of her primary narrative, which is thus defined as Josh. 8:1–30. On the biblical *ḥērem* generally, see Stern (1991); and on Deuteronomy in particular, Hoffman (1999).

[40] See the geographical sketch in Santis (2004, 168–77). The systematic claim on eastern territory is found not in the primary narrative but in separate fragments of geographical tradition (Deut. 3:8–11; 4:47–9).

[41] See the discussion in Levine (2000, 230–4). Russell (2009, 78–119) makes the Balaam poems the point of departure for his treatment of the Egypt tradition in eastern Israel.

One striking omission from the narrative introduction to Deuteronomy is any mention of Balaam, who appears only in the restrictions against Moabites later in the book (23:5–6). In the book of Numbers, Balaam plays a prominent role through three chapters (Numbers 22–4) that are presented as if inspired by the conquest of eastern Israel. The opening line provides a seam that binds what follows to the account of Sihon and Og by reference to Israel's treatment of the Amorites (22:2). After this, the narrative mentions only Israel's successful escape from Egypt and its sheer mass (22:5, 11), two indications of divine favor that imply no history of military victory. Nothing is said of Sihon and Og, and Israel's presence in the east is only to be inferred by Balak's anxiety for Moab. No contact has yet been suggested between Israel and Moab, in contrast to the negotiation between Moses and Edom (20:14–21), and unlike the Deuteronomy narrative, there has been no divine warning against molesting Moab.

While the isolated addition of a seemingly secondary plot could suggest a very late text, the Balaam narrative has long been considered to include potentially old and eastern Israelite material.[42] The story forms a long and coherent whole, built around a sequence of poetic pronouncements that occupy much of the second part (23:7–10, 18–24; 24:3–9, and 15–19; along with poetic appendices in vv. 20–4). Unlike the prose that surrounds it, these poems display no dependence on the larger Torah narrative, and they have long been listed among the archaic poetry first endorsed by Albright.[43] The prose is a separate case. In some respects, it is quite independent of the preceding Numbers narrative, as with Moses' absence and definition of Israel's threat by simple divine favor rather than by success at war. After the opening lines, we lose any sense of this people's past; they are only the king's "enemies" (23:11; 24:10). The people are called "Israel" only in 24:1–2, where the group is also said to be encamped "according to its tribes," a picture of its composite nature that otherwise has no place in the story and suggests the tribal arrangement in the late lists that begin the book of Numbers. If a late and Judahite form of the narrative was dependent on the larger Numbers collection, this may have constituted the revision of a prose account that was older, independent, and already perhaps from eastern Israel.[44] This prose, in turn, would have been constructed from even older poems. The combination of poetry in the name of a god named El ("The God") and a visionary named Balaam is now known outside the Bible in a set of inscriptions from Deir 'Alla in modern Jordan, and

---

[42] Ulrike Sals (2008) places the "origin of the final text" in Persian times.

[43] A brief scholarly genealogy could be constructed by way of Albright (1922), Cross (1950; cf. Cross and Freedman 1975), and Robertson (1972).

[44] Levine (2000, 143 and 149) considers the prose story proper to begin in 22:3 and regards the references to Egypt as basic. The one significant addition involves the talking donkey (22:22–35), as widely understood (for bibliography, see Russell 2009, 83 n. 31). Recent arguments for a late date throughout include Schüle (2001, 50–85) and Witte (2002). For Witte, both messenger cycles of 22:1–20 already belong to his *Grundschicht*.

these confirm in rough terms the eastern geography of the Balaam narratives in Numbers.[45]

In a way, the Balaam oracles are commonly identified as Israelite more by context than by content. So far as Deir 'Alla provides context by sharing the Balaam tradition, it suggests an eastern setting. The narrative of Numbers 22–4 moves Balaam through similar territory, somewhat to the south. By themselves, the poems never locate Israel, which is repeatedly paired with "Jacob" (23:7, 10, 21, 23; 24:5, 17, 18–19). Balak king of Moab (23:7, cf. 18) brings the speaker from Aram (23:7). The fourth oracle envisions a future king who will defeat eastern rivals, Moab (linked to "the sons of Seth") and Edom/Seir (24:17–18). Israel itself never names a political actor. Indirectly, the third oracle speaks of the people at war, devouring their enemies (24:8). To some extent, the poems look Israelite because they lack any clear Judahite content. To my eye, the fourth poem suggests possible associations with Judah, in spite of the continued use of "El" (24:16).[46]

Levine locates the setting for the Balaam poems by comparison of this fourth oracle with the "Heshbon Ballad" of Numbers 21:27–30. Both describe the defeat of Moab, with focus on Ar (21:28 and 24:19, by Levine's reading) in its northern region. Levine (2000, 231–2) takes the reference to Agag in 24:7 as east-oriented, and the first two poems proclaim that Moab cannot evict Israel from the east. Based on the Balaam poems, Levine proposes a "Transjordanian" biblical repertoire, which could also have included the "Sheol oracle" of Isaiah 14 (pp. 208–9). Because western Israel also endured sporadic conflicts with these same eastern neighbors, it would be equally possible to interpret the Balaam oracles as coming from west of the Jordan, if their narrative content were different.[47] The geographical setting of Deir 'Alla is suggestive but cannot prove that Balaam belonged only to the poets of eastern regions.

In the end, I concur with Levine's inclination toward an east Israelite origin for the Balaam material in the Bible, but the strongest evidence for this must come from the narrative that surrounds the poems. If we recall that the Egypt references in the opening messenger sequence stand out from the remaining tale, it is possible to imagine a version of the prose that was based only on Balak's demand that Balaam curse at his royal client's will. Setting aside the donkey distraction, Balaam's activity is limited to his preparations for each

---

[45] Levine includes a lengthy discussion of these inscriptions in the second volume of his commentary (2000, 241–75). See also Caquot and Lemaire (1977); Hackett (1980); Hoftijzer and van der Kooij (1991).

[46] The introduction is taken almost word for word from the third poem (24:3–4 and 15–16). Only an epithet with the Jerusalem title "Elyon" is added (v. 16). A ruling "staff" (*šēbeṭ*) will arise out of Israel (v. 17); this is the same word as the ruling staff out of Judah in Jacob's blessings (Gen. 49:10). The victories over Moab and Edom at least contrast with the prose traditions of both Numbers and Deuteronomy, especially for Edom.

[47] For example, Saul's reign begins with battles against the Ammonites (1 Samuel 11) and the Amalekites, led by Agag of the third Balaam poem (1 Samuel 15).

poetic oracle and his exchanges with Balak afterward. Balaam makes a sacrifice before each approach to Yahweh: seven bulls and seven rams on seven altars for three occasions: at Bamoth-baal (22:41–23:2), on top of Pisgah (23:14), and at the summit of Peor looking out over the Jeshimon (23:28–30). None of these exchanges is dependent on the Numbers narrative generally. Moses, and even Israel, are effectively absent as actors. Israel's interest lies in the fact that their god will bless only them, even through the oracular mediation of a celebrated seer with no clear political loyalties.

Meindert Dijkstra (1995) proposes a specific setting for the prose narrative based on the geography of the three offerings and oracles. The three locations ring the sacred center of Nebo, which Dijkstra identifies as the compositional setting for a unified narrative, during the ninth century. Nebo is never mentioned in the text, and I find this specific setting to be speculative. Nevertheless, Balaam's itinerary indicates an east Israelite tradition for the central scheme of multiple oracles. Only three sites are named, before the first three poems, and the lack of a fourth setting adds to my suspicion that the fourth poem does not belong to the original collection. It appears that the three oracles and the three locations for pronouncing them together comprise an Israelite narrative from east of the Jordan River, without reference to Egypt or Israel's movement through the land.

The most striking political detail in the poems could point to a western connection if not western authorship: Israel is assumed to have a king. This impressive monarch is celebrated repeatedly and directly, not as a distant hope. "Yahweh their god is with them, and the shout of the king is among them" (23:21); "Their king will be exalted more than Agag, and his kingdom will be raised up" (24:7); and in the fourth oracle, "a staff will stand up out of Israel" to conquer Moab, the sons of Seth, Edom, and Seir (24:17–19). We may interpret the ruler as Yahweh himself, but the comparison with Agag and the identification of a "staff" suggest a human monarch.[48] Such royal power recalls Mesha's complaint that Omri and Ahab oppressed Moab until his own fight to liberate them. Reference to Omride power would suggest a western connection for the poetry, yet Israel's activities are focused solely in Jordan, according to this vision. These details would place the poems in the ninth century. The Balaam material offers little sense of Israel as a whole, but it does add evidence to the reality of Israel's presence in the east.

As a whole, the biblical narrative for Israel coming out of Egypt and ending on the verge of entry into a Promised Land in Canaan offers no geographical clues to its origin until the people reach the territory east of the Jordan River. The exodus itself can be identified as Israelite by statements in the books of Hosea and Amos, but many other important story elements are more difficult to locate. Rather than probe this material in depth, I have turned instead to the

---

[48] Levine takes the reference to a king in 23:21 as divine (2000, 184), the king with Agag as human (p. 197), and the staff as a "meteor," nevertheless applied to a human ruler (p. 200).

one set of texts that offers a geographical basis for identification as Israelite, an underexploited eastern orientation. These tales were originally the possession of people who lived in the east, and we must not assume that they belonged to larger schemes that could be integrated with the narrative of a western Promised Land. This knowledge in itself shapes our sense of Israel in the Bible's primary narrative.

8

Joshua and Ai

Conceptually, the tradition of escape from Egypt requires a place to go, a happy ending. Numbers 21 and Deuteronomy 2–3 provide this in the east, in a tradition that does not of itself assume combination with a western campaign. The Bible as we now have it provides the book of Joshua, with its crossing of the Jordan River from the east (chapters 3–4), the assault on Jericho (chapter 6), followed by eventual victory at Ai (chapters 7–8), forced compromise with the Gibeonites (chapter 9), and at last a sweeping success against the assembled forces of first the south, then the north (chapters 10–11). The rest of the book is built around detailed territorial definitions for all the tribes, both east and west of the Jordan (chapters 13–19), with special consideration for the Levites (chapter 21). All this is framed by speeches from Joshua himself in chapters 1 and 23, which have long been understood as classic examples of deuteronomistic work, in making this collection part of a larger history.[1]

Although the western conquest led by Joshua depends in its full expression on the old Israelite tradition of exodus from Egypt, the book gives it a limited and finally Judahite perspective. Like the later revisions of the Moses traditions, which integrate the tribal scheme of Genesis into the old tales of departure and invasion, the book of Joshua pictures a conquest by twelve tribes. Perhaps this tribal focus allows Judah to be given a special role; in any case, the establishment of all Israel, far beyond the borders of Judah, is essential. Moreover, the geographical ambitions of the book are considerable, reaching beyond the proven accomplishment of Israel in any period. Joshua mixes an Israelite ideal with an overwhelmingly Judahite realization. For all the narrative located in the territory of Israel, it is extremely difficult to isolate plausibly Israelite material. In the end, the one most convincing text is the account of Joshua's victory at Ai in chapter 8. This alone provides a starting point for understanding the construction of a western conquest from the tradition of Joshua as ancient

---

[1] See, e.g., Nelson (1997, 6), who identifies the principal deuteronomistic structuring passages as 1:1–18; 8:30–5; 12:1–6; 21:43–22:6; and 23:1–16.

warrior leader. Joshua 8 belongs to the family of biblical texts that presents Israel as a collective unit, especially for going to war, and as such, the text belongs with the various Moses materials.

A. Joshua the Book

As I have read the biblical tradition of an eastern invasion, it began with a truly eastern perspective, by which the defeats of Sihon and Og provided the basis for possession of a whole territory under the initial leadership of Moses. This conquest is no second thought, an accident on the way to the Promised Land across the Jordan. Moreover, it requires no continuation into the west at all. No biblical tradition places Moses in western Israel or Judah, an oddity that inspires considerable authorial effort to explain not just this absence but his substantial presence in another part of Israel, east of the Jordan. A whole book of biblical instruction places Moses in Israelite territory, in land just taken from Sihon and Og (Deut. 4:44–9), where he dies and is buried (Deut. 34:5–6).[2]

By this approach to the eastern invasion, I adopt the same strategy as for the escape from Egypt, treating the two traditions as originally separate and of interest to different Israelite peoples, east and west of the Jordan River. In narrative terms, neither the escape from Egypt nor the conquest of the east requires a conquest of the central highlands of Israel. Both stories imagine that the Israelite peoples did not originally control the land that came to be theirs. They entered from the south, in one case from Egypt into the western highlands, in the other from the southern backcountry across Edom and Moab to the land on the east side of the Jordan running north of the Dead Sea. It is therefore the escape from Egypt, not the stories of Israel in the east, that suggests an invasion of the western highlands that are generally understood as the heartland of Israel. That tale, however, only brings the people out of Pharaoh's power, without explaining how they established themselves in a new land, or even if they did so as a unit. By the time we reach the book of Judges,

---

[2] The overwhelming tradition that Moses ended his life in eastern Israel had to be explained by writers from the west. The priestly version of the people's rebellion at Massah and Meribah makes this the reason for Moses' early retirement (Num. 20:12; vs. Exod. 17:2–7). Deut. 3:21–9 embraces an option that is more generous toward Moses: Yahweh refused to let Moses enter the western land, in that the leader would bear the blame of his people's unnamed wrong. Together, Deuteronomy 3 and 34 preserve a core tradition of Moses' death that is not colored by the deuteronomistic duty to explain his failure to move west with the others. Efforts to find a precise textual survival of such a core lead to the visit to the top of Pisgah (Deut. 3:27; 34:1), seeing the land (3:25; cf. 27; 34:1) and the valley opposite Peor (3:29; 34:6), along with Moses' death and burial in 34:5–6 (see Garcia Lopez 1994, 61; Stoellger 1993). The account in Deut. 3:26–8, even defined this way, renders the west central in a way that the burial itself does not. Ultimately, this strange tradition of Moses being prevented from entering the Promised Land is most simply explained as received lore that had to be accounted for. Its logical origin is eastern Israel itself. Moses led the conquest of what became eastern Israel, and he dies not on foreign soil but in the eastern homeland. Frank Cross (1988, 52 n. 20) suggests that the note in Deut. 34:6b about the location of his burial being forgotten is polemical, minimizing the importance of a place still sacred to people in the east.

the peoples of Israel are simply present, with only the late addition of chapter 1 to acknowledge the issue of how they overcame the local populations. This leaves the book of Joshua to fill this significant narrative need.

The problem is that the book of Joshua, like Judges 1, was shaped by strong Judahite interests and seems to have attracted wave upon wave of uplifting commentary – perhaps a natural inclination in later writers for whom these events were the highlight of God's dealings with his people. The Judahite framework is so intrusive that it is difficult to isolate the foundation for an Israelite account of entry into the land. At the same time, the book is full of lore about Israel in larger terms, so that it is hard to imagine composition in Judah without Israelite sources.[3] The military conflicts that establish Israel's supremacy over the western highlands are described in the first part of the book, from chapters 6–12. These in turn are divided into two encounters at the individual sites of Jericho and Ai, on one hand, and two open-field battles, on the other hand, with the assembled kings of first southern, then northern cities, as if the land were already divided into Judah and Israel. Before Jericho, chapters 3–5 bring the Israelites across the Jordan River into the western Promised Land, an endeavor that assumes the narrative need to combine a western conquest with the eastern tradition in Numbers and Deuteronomy.[4] If there is an Israelite center to the western victories in Joshua, it will only be somewhere in chapters 6–12, not the larger unit from chapters 2–12.[5]

---

[3] This is particularly true of the descriptions of tribal territories in Joshua 13–19. Even if these have been idealized to fit a maximal vision of what Israel once inhabited, they do not appear to represent baseless inventions from late Judahite imagination. The question is where such descriptions could have been reproduced so as to end up available to scribes from Judah who treasured the notion that Yahweh had once carved out a space for his people in this land, space that included the peoples of both Israel and Judah. Josiah's supposed ambition to restore a greater Israel was never more than minimally achieved and is difficult to prove in biblical texts securely dated to his reign (originally in Alt 1953, "Das System der Stammesgrenzen im Buch Josua," I.193–202). It is more certain that after the fall of Judah, its people took refuge in the recollection of God's first establishment of a people for himself under the name of Israel, and the whole package of tribes and land would have been reproduced as part of that inheritance. Given the many elements that could not originate in a completely Judahite setting, such a vision must have had sources.

[4] Although Gilgal is in the territory of Benjamin, this choice of a landing point probably reflects the need to bridge east Israel with Jericho, the first battle site in received material. Graeme Auld (2000, 353–4) observes several similarities between the accounts of Joshua 3–5 and 1 Kings 8–9, all of which are best explained by a Jerusalem setting for the editorial combinations. He resists the idea that these similarities require a single integrated history, but his combinations do require composition from diverse materials, and once beyond the ark itself, some of the parallels are less persuasive.

[5] Based on the earlier proposals of Alt, Martin Noth worked more from Joshua 2–12 as a whole in his reconstruction of a Benjamin-focused literary block. For Noth (1971, 12), a Benjaminite conquest tradition was maintained at Gilgal, with the earliest core in chapters 2–8. Whereas Noth placed this collection in the ninth century, Martin Rose (1981, 163–5) attributes it to conditions in Benjamin just after the fall of Israel in 720. Römer and de Pury (2000a, 113–14) comment that debate as of the late 1990s reflected uncertainty about whether the collection was composed for Josiah's expansion or for a demoralized audience after the exile.

In the second part of this battle sequence, the two open-field engagements are currently set up to favor Judah, in that the first opposition comes from the south, led by the king of Jerusalem (chapter 10).[6] After the first miraculous victory, on a day when the sun stands still and Yahweh rains down huge hailstones from the sky, Joshua leads separate attacks against the participating towns. Only after Judah is taken do the people turn to the land of Israel, which should have been the logical endpoint for the tradition of escape from Egypt (chapter 11). Where the south is represented by Jerusalem, the obvious political center of Judah, the north is represented by Hazor, on the distant fringe of what became Israel. Moreover, the northern war is recounted without naming any kings besides Jabin of Hazor, and no named towns are taken. It seems that the writer knows the south much better than the north. Therefore, while it is possible that a tradition of battle with Hazor may go back to Israelite sources, even Joshua 11 is told as if by an outsider.[7] Knauf (2008, 17) observes that according to Josh. 10:40–2, the conquered south is identical to Judah's borders between 597 and 586 B.C.E., including the highlands, the Negev, the western foothills (Shephelah), and as far north as Gibeon.[8] Specifically, Gibeon would make Benjamin part of this Judahite Promised Land, though the list of kings and battle sites mentions nothing from this transitional territory. Although I do not find the specific scenario for transmission history compelling, Knauf's reconstruction shows how deeply Judahite is the essential structure of the conquest in Joshua.

If Joshua 10–11 do not provide an Israelite account of a full conquest of the western highlands, then the book lacks any such story, as does the entire Bible.[9] The idea of a systematic conquest of the western highlands and so the land as a whole appears to be the product of Judahite writers from an unknown date.[10] Whatever was imagined to follow escape from Egypt in the Israelite circles that transmitted this story, it was not unified, full-scale war. The

---

[6] The other leaders come from Hebron, Jarmuth, Lachish, and Eglon, a combination that would cover the highlands south of Jerusalem and the western foothills, together with the heartland of the kingdom of Judah.

[7] Jabin of Hazor appears in both Joshua 11 and Judges 4, where he is joined artificially with Sisera, who is the real focus of the battle led by Deborah and Barak. In the Song of Deborah, Sisera has no affiliation with Hazor, which seems to derive from the Joshua tradition.

[8] The southern conquest would belong to the earliest stage of composition, as part of an early exodus–conquest combination, the basis for a hexateuchal idea if not such a six-book set (so, Konrad Schmid 2010).

[9] Joshua 12 is constructed from a combination of the conquest accounts in the two preceding chapters and the stories of Sihon and Og, thus reflecting awareness of the eastern tradition and the attempt to join them into one itinerary.

[10] The division of the land into components comparable to Judah and Israel indicates at least awareness of the two kingdoms. My analysis does not exclude the possibility that the Judah-oriented conquest tale came from before the exile. It has been proposed that Joshua and Josiah are linked by their names, offering a plausible setting for the Joshua tradition (Nelson 1981; Monroe 2011, 56–64, with "Agents of Renewal: Joshua, Josiah and Ezra"). This could account for chapters 10–11, if linked to the motif in Isaiah 7–8 of Judah's claim to rule all Israel through the heritage of David.

book of Hosea mentions repeatedly the notion that Israel came up from Egypt, and this is associated with a life in the steppe (*midbār*) before settlement in a land with vineyards (2:16–17; 13:4–5).[11] There is no hint of military conflict or displacement of the previous residents of the land.

This leaves Joshua 6–9, which include the engagements at Jericho and Ai, followed by the clever deception of the Gibeonites, who make a treaty with Israel by pretending to travel from a great distance. Both the miraculous breaching of Jericho and the successful ambush at Ai are provided with introductions that lay the groundwork for the divinely granted victories: Joshua sends spies who are sheltered by Rahab the prostitute (chapter 2) before the town is ritually besieged (chapter 6);[12] and Achan's illicit plunder after Jericho leads to initial defeat at Ai (chapter 7) before the town's destruction by *ḥērem* to Yahweh (chapter 8). In both cases, the actual defeats of Jericho and Ai are recounted directly, without reference to a larger campaign or stories outside their own horizons.[13] The links to the surrounding context are provided by the preparatory material. Joshua sends the spies to scout out "the land," not just Jericho (2:1, 3), and Rahab's support is based on knowledge that follows the larger biblical narrative: drying up the Reed Sea, and defeat of Sihon and Og (v. 10). At stake is the promise that Yahweh has given his people "all the land" (v. 24; cf. v. 9). After Jericho, a first defeat at Ai is explained by Achan's wrongdoing at Jericho. Even if Joshua 7 has been expanded in more than one phase, it serves above all to link the Jericho and Ai stories and is thus secondary to both of them.[14] The central accounts of victory at both Jericho and Ai therefore appear to stand on their own, free of connections to the more fully edited biblical narrative, with its later and Judahite character.[15]

---

[11] Hos. 2:16–17; 12:14 (verb *'lh*); 11:1 ("I summoned my son from Egypt"); 12:10; 13:4 ("I am Yahweh your god, from the land of Egypt"); cf. return to Egypt in 8:13; 9:3; 11:5.

[12] On the Jericho siege tradition, see Fleming (1999). While the narrative motif may be ancient, nothing about its application to Joshua 6 offers either a date or a geographical origin, which depends only on Jericho itself.

[13] Knauf (2008, 73) remarks on the distinct character of the Ai account in Joshua 7–8, which he considers inserted from a separate source, later than the primary collection built around Jericho and the southern conquest.

[14] Friedrich Fechter (1998, 34–74) concludes that Josh. 7:14–21, the essentially distinct part of the Achan narrative, in which the man is identified as the cause of Israel's defeat, depends on the Jericho tale. In effect, the whole story of Achan's crime serves as a literary bridge between chapters 6 and 8. The hierarchical system of tribe, clan, and family is therefore idealized and cannot be taken as evidence for such a tiered scheme in early Israel. The Achan story is commonly considered secondary to the larger Ai narrative: e.g., Nelson (1997, 98–9); Knauf (2008, 73). In social historical terms, the hierarchy of Josh. 7:14–18 suggests a centralizing administrative mindset that is not otherwise characteristic of Israelite material in the Bible.

[15] This is also the conclusion of Kratz (2005, 206). Daniel Hawk (2008, 152) offers an attractive explanation of the editorial work that recasts what he sees as the "paradigmatic battle accounts" of Jericho, Ai, and Gibeon. Each of these battle accounts has been provided with a second narrative pattern by introducing them with dramatic stories of Rahab, Achan, and the leaders of Gibeon, which have the collective effect of humanizing the local inhabitants. While some interpreters include Gibeon among the core stories of Joshua, to do so is questionable. In its full

B. Jericho and Ai

In spite of contrasting plots, each memorable in its own way, the tales of Jericho and Ai have significant features in common. Joshua is essential to both, where he functions as both military leader and intermediary with Yahweh, much like Moses in the eastern invasion.[16] Geographically, Jericho and Ai lie at the eastern and northern fringes of what becomes the land of Benjamin, though neither story mentions any group but united Israel, like the escape from Egypt. Finally, both tales revolve around the necessity to perform *ḥērem* on the cities involved, killing every inhabitant, male and female (6:21; 8:24–5).[17] Along with these narrative details, it may also be significant that neither Jericho nor Ai were old Israelite towns with longstanding populations.[18] Both sites appear to have been known for being empty, and this adds to the logic of explaining them in combination.[19]

Although the two stories share these features, they do not appear to have been composed together originally and rather appear to have been combined

form, the account assumes a command not to enter into treaties with the local people, along the lines of the command in Deut. 7:1–5, and this would indicate a deuteronomistic combination. The initial story is vivid and individual, as contained in Josh. 9:3–15, and Römer (2005, 86–9) includes it in his original conquest narrative, which he dates to the time of Josiah and builds from the conquests of Jericho and Ai, the establishment of a vassal relationship with Gibeon, and the general defeat of the south in Joshua 10. By this interpretation, the Gibeonites would undertake their subterfuge purely to avoid a slaughter like those at Jericho and Ai, and Israel loses nothing except the opportunity to gain more territory – with no special divine command at stake. Like the Achan narrative, however, the Gibeonite deception makes sense only in light of the previous *ḥērem*, whether at Jericho or Ai or both, and it is therefore secondary. I therefore hesitate to treat it as part of demonstrably Israelite tradition. If anything, the subordination of people from the region of Benjamin could make sense as part of seventh-century Judahite perspective, in this case, even from the time of Josiah. Hawk (p. 152) isolates only Josh. 10:6–15, the battle at Gibeon against massed southern kings, as the original Gibeon victory account.

[16] Knauf (2008, 70) considers that Joshua is characterized differently in Joshua 8 and is one basis for distinguishing separate sources. The conquest of Jericho in chapter 6 legitimates Joshua as Moses' successor in an Exodus–Joshua combination. In chapter 8, he is given a more heroic stature that contrasts with chapters 6 and 10. While there are other reasons for attributing chapter 8 to a different source, the nuances of Joshua's leadership cannot provide a basis for dating one narrative later than the other.

[17] It is possible to exclude the *ḥērem* from the original Jericho account (so, Knauf 2008, 70), but this is unnecessarily forced, as the total destruction of the city is a natural outcome of the divine victory; contrast Römer (2005, 87). While the slaughter of Jericho's residents form an early part of the narrative, Rahab's plea for exclusion reflects a separate story piggybacked onto the Jericho account.

[18] In spite of relative proximity, Ai should not be identified entirely with Bethel, a conclusion that too easily adopts the perspective of Gen. 12:8 and Abraham. Knauf (2008, 83) places the Ai narrative of Joshua 8 in sixth-century Bethel, as part of the larger competition that he envisions between the Bethel and Jerusalem scribal circles in that period (cf. Knauf 2006).

[19] I could draw the conclusion about the occupation of Jericho and Ai from the Bible itself, in contrast to Shechem, Bethel, or even Jerusalem. These two sites have long been known to archaeologists for the obstacle they offer to a simple conquest at the end of the Bronze Age, as confirmation of the biblical accounts. In fact, the emptiness of both sites during the Iron Age I helps to explain their combination, whether in Israelite or in monarchic Judahite terms.

secondarily, unlike the invasion accounts for Sihon and Og in Deuteronomy 2–3. Aside from the totally different plots and developments, this is visible in contrasting notions of *ḥērem* practice: at Jericho, every person and animal is to be killed, while at Ai, only the humans are slain, and the people are permitted to take livestock as plunder. The instruction for Jericho is more like the total slaughter commanded in Deut. 20:16–18 than what is done at Ai, but the language of the instruction in Joshua 6:21 shares nothing with Deuteronomy and is therefore hard to regard as directly deuteronomistic. Ai's *ḥērem* in Josh. 8:2, 26–7, directly contradicts the Deuteronomy law and corresponds exactly with what is done to the towns of Sihon and Og in Deuteronomy 2–3.

The *ḥērem* is a regional religious and military tradition with particular affinities to inland peoples in the Levant and Arabia (Monroe 2007). Along with a well-known reference in the ninth-century Moabite Mesha inscription, the word appears in slightly later Sabaean texts with similar intent. Consistently, the *ḥērem* involves destruction of towns and their consecration to the primary deity of the attacking people, so that possession of the larger domain is effectively transferred to a new population.[20] This is by no means the universal ancient practice in war, where imperial conquest is more likely to preserve the local populace and structures intact in order to harvest the wealth they produce. War by *ḥērem* is more an affair of competition between smaller groups on a local scale, where the people themselves are understood to represent only a threat to the newcomers. Monroe finds no evidence for this approach in the great first-millennium Mesopotamian empires and considers the practice more at home in highland or backcountry domains, associated with a distinct strategic conception in early polity formation. By their culmination in *ḥērem* destruction, the battle traditions in Joshua 6 and 8 for Jericho and Ai align with inland customs that are deeply ingrained in the early first millennium. This practice is not in itself Israelite rather than Judahite, but it is not a late and theologically driven creation.

The specific continuity between the language and procedure with Sihon and Og in Deuteronomy 2–3 and with Ai in Joshua 8 adds to the viability of seeing at least the Ai narrative as originally Israelite.[21] Here, the substantial parallels

---

[20] Monroe (2011, 48) observes that in the Moabite and Sabaean contexts, *ḥērem* "served as an affirmation of the exclusive relationship between a people on its land, and the patron deity from whom that land was granted."

[21] I do not attempt to reconstruct the exact form of an original Ai conquest narrative. Nelson (1997, 111) removes first of all a deuteronomistic element in verses 1–2, 22b, 27, and 29; while Römer (2005, 88) proposes a version that omits the ambush scenario that is shared with Judges 20, along with the *ḥērem*, which he also excluded from the Jericho narrative. Kratz (2005, 201) does almost exactly the reverse, with an equally abbreviated result, building his core text around the bare bones of the ambush (8:1–2a, 10a, 11a, 14, 19). The Moabite and Sabaean evidence discussed in this paragraph indicates that texts are not necessarily understood better by stripping away every interpretive motif as secondary. In an intriguing effort to apply textual critical evidence to problems of transmission history in earlier stages, Michael van der Meer (2004, 416) argues that significant sections missing from the Greek text (Josh. 8:11b–13, 26) reflect an attempt to harmonize tensions and doublets in the Hebrew text. Van der Meer's older,

of custom and narrative in the Moabite and Sabaean texts are crucial. Römer (2005, 84–5) proposes that the core conquest narrative in Joshua, which he defines to include both the Jericho and the Ai episodes, were influenced by Assyrian warfare accounts that would have been accessible to the people of Judah in the seventh century.[22] The combined evidence of Mesha and the Sabaean texts, however, shows that the narrative for the defeat of Ai is decidedly non-Mesopotamian and belongs to an indigenous tradition for claiming right to a new land. Whatever the origin of these victory tales, their format shows no sign of adoption from foreign models.

Joshua is portrayed as the military leader for Israel by name. After he has laid out his plan of attack, the day begins with a muster of "the people," who are led by Joshua himself and "the elders of Israel" (8:10). As a fighting force, Joshua's people are called "Israel" when they face the men of Ai.[23] Joshua himself has no title, in contrast to the "king" of Ai (vv. 14, 23, 29), and his authority as individual commander seems to derive from the idea that Yahweh himself will guide his military judgment. At the key moment when victory is to be decided, Yahweh tells Joshua to signal for the ambush by brandishing his spear toward Ai (v. 18), and Joshua promises the people victory based on assurance that their god will give them the town (v. 7). Moses leads his people in attack on Sihon and Og with the same divine assurance of victory (Deut. 2:31; 3:2).[24]

Joshua 8 shares its scheme of deception and ambush with the final victory of Israel over Benjamin in Judges 20, which lies at the center of an account of all-out war against Benjamin in chapters 19–21 (Milstein 2010, chapter 4). Although Benjamin suffers a terrible loss and is almost wiped out entirely, the tale is told in terms that are strikingly sympathetic toward the victims, and the most obvious setting for its composition is Benjamin itself, most likely when this land still belonged to Israel.[25] Milstein proposes that in combination with 1 Samuel 1 and 11, the Benjamin war seems to have been made into a prelude to Saul's rise as Israel's first king, with Benjamin as his own people and base of power. In any case, the geographical foci of the two

----

predeuteronomistic text is not quite as lean, with the full ambush account and destruction of the city by *ḥērem* (8:10–14, 16, 18–20, 26).

[22] Römer cites the work of Younger (1990), who does not use these comparisons to date the Joshua narratives to the Neo-Assyrian period. Römer considers the Neo-Assyrian parallels closer than the Mesha text; if this is true at some level, it does not apply to the deeper structure described by Monroe (see above) and thus to the basic narrative for conquest by *ḥērem*.

[23] See Joshua 8:14–15, 17, 21–22, 24, 27; the form is always "Israel," never "the sons of Israel."

[24] Römer deletes these texts as adding a secondary religious scheme, but again, the essential contribution of the divine role to Moabite and Sabaean *ḥērem* texts favors inclusion of this component in an early version of the narrative – both here and in Deuteronomy 2–3. In my own reconstruction, either Deut. 2:24 or 2:31 belongs to the core narrative, but probably not both, as they repeat the same divine command.

[25] We will return to this material in the next section. Benjamin is a formidable foe to Israel, defeated in the end only by divine favor and the same ambush technique.

ambush stories are remarkably close, at Ai and Gibeah, both in the highlands of Benjamin.[26]

This proximity could work in two ways. On one hand, both could belong to the lore of Benjamin itself, so that Joshua the leader originally belonged to Benjamin, not Ephraim, in spite of the later list of scouts in Num. 13:8. Such would strengthen Benjamin's identification with Israel, and if no battle tradition was linked to the escape from Egypt, then Benjamin's heritage of early conflict could be borrowed to help create one. Yahweh's central role, with Joshua bearing the name "Yahweh is deliverance," would intensify the identification with Israel. By this scenario, Ai would have no larger identity or association; it is never called Canaanite or the like. It is territory to be taken by Israel.

On the other hand, both stories could reflect Israel's conflict with Benjaminite peoples in the early days, when Benjamin could have been no different from other "Amorites" who were associated with the western highlands. In this case, Joshua's Ephraim identity would be appropriate to competition for this region, and Ai stands with Bethel in what could have been disputed territory.[27] By this scenario, Ai was a Benjaminite town, as later geography would indicate, and Benjamin was once part of neither Israel nor Judah. The similar ambush story in Judges 20, where Benjamin is the explicit enemy at Gibeah, could inadvertently preserve evidence that early military conflicts in what became Israel took place between groups that competed for the same land. Neither of the competing groups need have been totally destroyed, so that both were incorporated into Israel, the association that eventually dominated. We would have only a sympathetic rendition of the battle between Israel and Benjamin because this was taken over and probably rewritten for use in Benjamin in support of an alignment with Israel under Saul. In either case, Joshua 8 would be Israelite, not Judahite, in that its Benjamin interest would predate its incorporation into the southern kingdom that was left standing after the Assyrian conquest.

The Jericho story is more difficult. Joshua plays an equally central role, and *ḥērem* is still the ultimate result, but the encounter is played out in ritual rather than military terms. Moreover, the ark is central to the event, and the overall narrative occurrence of this artifact in the Bible must ultimately be explained

---

[26] It does not appear to me that one ambush story derives directly from the other. The main commonality is the ambush itself, which involves drawing the defenders outside the city with a false impression of easy victory and then turning on the open town. In Judges 20, the initial battle account in verses 29–37 mentions no burning of the city nor smoke as a signal, as is basic to the plan in Josh. 8:8, 19–21. The ambush of Gibeah is then retold in Judg. 20:38–41, introducing the fire and smoke as signal, and repeating the count of thirty Israelites slain in the initial exchange (vv. 31 and 39). This detail seems to have been leveled between the two accounts, apparently from Joshua 8 into Judges 20.

[27] See the boundary description for Ephraim in Josh. 16:1–2, which makes Bethel part of Ephraim's southern frontier, and the description for Benjamin in 18:13, for that tribe's northern edge. Bethel is called a town of Benjamin in 18:22, while no town list is provided for Ephraim. This detail could reflect a setting in Judah after the fall of Israel, when Benjamin began to be incorporated into the kingdom of Judah.

by its arrival in Jerusalem.[28] The ark is active during only two phases of Israel's history: with arrival in the western land and with the establishment of David's dynasty in its capital, both of which seem to be traditions preserved at Jerusalem in Judah (Fleming, forthcoming a). The notion that Israel entered the Promised Land with Yahweh present in the ark appears above all with the Jordan River crossing of Joshua 3–4, so as to extend the tradition of an eastern invasion into the west. So far as the Jericho account partakes of this image, with the priests carrying the ark around the city walls seven times, it makes the victory over Jericho into Yahweh's processional arrival in the land that will now be his, universalizing the effect of one set of fallen walls. The question is whether this is a ritualized revision of a simpler narrative that also included the *ḥērem* command.[29] It is possible that the Jericho story was added to the Ai account as a prelude, and its original Israelite character is tenuous. Throughout the main narrative, the participants are "the people," with references to Israel limited to sections that link to the wider motifs of Rahab and Achan.[30]

In the end, the one secure Israelite contribution to the massive conquest of the western highlands portrayed in the book of Joshua may be the victory over Ai in chapter 8. Joshua himself is indispensible to that account, and this position as heroic leader would lie at the root of the extended biblical effort to link his stature to that of Moses. Israelite tradition included separate stories of leadership under Moses and under Joshua. In the west, Moses was a prophet who led Israel out of Egypt, while in the east he was a divinely ordained military commander more like Joshua. Without connection to Egypt and exodus, Joshua was known for a great victory in the same region that celebrated Moses for nonmilitary leadership, the central highlands of Ephraim. There is no sign in the Bible that Israelite tradition ever combined Moses and Joshua or created a single story out of the Egypt escape and military victories at Ai or elsewhere.[31] The expansion of Joshua's role into the conquest that opens the book by his name appears to have been accomplished in Judah as part of a relatively late project to explain how Yahweh gave to his people a unified land that included all the regions of Israel and Judah. In this vision, Yahweh promised Israel a

---

[28] Like Yahweh's role in Joshua 8, the ark is frequently removed as secondary to the core Jericho narrative: e.g., Coats (1987, 28); Römer (2005, 87); Schwienhorst (1986, 40–3). The ritual aspect of the narrative is more essential to its form than these analyses assume, however, and I hesitate to remove the ark as a basis for finding a non-Judahite base.

[29] Most commentators envision some such process. Schwienhorst (1986) proposes a scheme of command and fulfillment for a silent siege followed by a battle cry that brings down the city walls.

[30] In Josh. 6:1, Jericho is locked against "the Israelites" (*běnê yiśrā'ēl*), a form that contrasts with the other uses and may reflect the larger combination. In verse 18, "the camp of Israel" will bring the *ḥērem* on itself if anyone takes plunder for himself, anticipating Achan's crime. The same phrase occurs in verse 23, with Rahab's rescue, and her family is said to live "in Israel's midst" until the present day (v. 25).

[31] This would hold true whether or not Konrad Schmid is correct in his hypothesis of an early Exodus–Joshua combination, which he attributes to late monarchic Judah.

large territory that lay entirely west of the Jordan River, and Israel's population in the east came about by the accident of early victories against Sihon and Og.

This ancient scribal project was perhaps inspired by the theme in Joshua 8 of sacred slaughter to Yahweh, which then infuses the whole sequence of interwoven stories in chapters 2–9, before the systematic conquest portrayed in chapters 10–12. Rahab protects Israel's spies, and this will release her from the *ḥērem* against Jericho. Because he disobeys the Jericho command, Achan then ruins Israel's chances at Ai. With eminent good sense, the people of Gibeon then wrangle a treaty out of their enemies by pretending to come from outside the territory doomed to the same demolition.[32] Through the sweeping victories that follow, Joshua and Israel lay claim to the land by performing the *ḥērem* slaughter against every defeated town, first south, then north.[33] In the scheme of the book as a whole, this devotion of the existing population to sacred destruction provides the basis for division of the land into tribal allotments. From the perspective of a later people, the Canaanites and their associates were easy enough to wipe out. They had been dead already for centuries.

---

[32] Joshua 9 offers connections to the preceding combined narrative with references to Jericho and Ai together (v. 3), the camp at Gilgal (v. 6), miracles in Egypt (v. 9), and Sihon and Og (v. 10).

[33] For the word itself, see Joshua 10:28, 35, 37, 39, 40; 11:11, 12, 20, 21.

9

Benjamin

As the distinct identities of Israel and Judah become increasingly significant in biblical and historical investigation, the importance of Benjamin likewise increases.[1] This one people occupied the land where the kingdoms of Israel and Judah met, in the highlands just north of Jerusalem, which the land allotments of Joshua attribute to both Judah and Benjamin.[2] Benjamin is associated with Ephraim in the Song of Deborah (Judg. 5:14), but the books of Kings claim it for Judah from the first division between Rehoboam and Jeroboam.[3] Dispute over Benjamin's alignment has been renewed between Nadav Na'aman (2009b), who maintains the view of Kings, and Philip Davies, who concludes that Benjamin belonged to Israel until its end in 720.[4] In the Bible, Benjamin is isolated from the other Israelite peoples in key respects, including

---

[1] The pivotal role of Benjamin in the development of biblical traditions about Israel and Judah is to be the focus of a forthcoming book with Lauren Monroe as coauthor. Philip Davies (2007b) signals that he intends a full-scale study of the same people, also still in progress. The substantial work of Schunck (1963) is still valuable, but it depends on a framework that is now dated.

[2] Joshua 15:8 makes Jerusalem part of the northern boundary of Judah, and verse 63 laments the failure of Judah to take possession of Jerusalem, while 18:27 includes Jerusalem (Jebus) among the towns of Benjamin. Judges 1 reflects the same ambiguity, with Judah given credit for taking Jerusalem (v. 8) and then Benjamin blamed for failure to do so (v. 21), in terms very like the complaint about Judah in Josh. 15:63.

[3] 1 Kings 12:21, 23; in early conflict between the two kingdoms, Asa of Judah is said to have built (fortifications) at "Geba of Benjamin and Mizpah" (15:22), to prevent the advance of Israelite influence from the north.

[4] In Na'aman's view, archaeological evidence shows that Benjamin was an integral part of Judah through the eighth and seventh centuries, and the account of Asa in 1 Kings 15 pushes the affiliation back through the ninth century (part 1, 216–17). Davies (2007b) doubts that Judah's actual incorporation of Benjamin can be sustained by these two Judahite texts in 1 Kings 12 and 15, and he considers the Bible's accounts of early Israel in Joshua, Judges, and 1 Samuel to reflect a particularly central role for Benjamin. This centrality is the clue that explains how Judah inherited Israel's stories, brought with Benjamin in the seventh century when it switched affiliations and became part of Judah under Assyrian sovereignty.

the separation of its ancestral birth narrative from all the others (Gen. 35:16–20) and the tale of war between Benjamin and all Israel in Judges 20.

The most effective way to understand Benjamin may therefore be to take more seriously this distinct character, to let this people take its own place in the history reflected in biblical writing, as more than simply territory to be won or lost in competition between Israel and Judah – though won and lost it must have been. According to the Bible, Benjamin was somehow a people apart. Other Israelite peoples may likewise merit consideration in separate terms, not essentially different from Benjamin within Israel. At the least, Benjamin's distinctness played out in a unique way because of its location in crucial territory between Jerusalem and the Ephraim highlands, the nexus of conflict between Israel and the house of David. Nevertheless, the very name suggests something more unusual, and the full weight of Benjamin's strange character may be appreciated best by beginning with the fact that its name is shared with a major tribal group from early second-millennium Syria. From this material, we will move to the biblical texts.

A. Benjamin and the Binu Yamina

As a whole, the peoples who came to be associated with Israel bear names that can only be taken as local and limited phenomena. Israel itself is named only once in an Egyptian document, a declaration of its relative obscurity. Dan perhaps suggests the Danuna or Danaioi of Egyptian and Greek sources, though the linguistic identification is inexact, and only the mention of Dan with ships in the Song of Deborah allows a geographical connection with the coast.[5] The most striking linguistic match between an Israelite people and a group known from other Near Eastern evidence has always been between Benjamin (Bin-yamin) and Mari's Binu Yamina. In this case, the early second-millennium date and distant north Syrian location of the Binu Yamina have inspired natural caution, although their tribal character offered a tantalizing possibility of association. Although the connection was tried and discarded years ago, the negative conclusion was based on an inadequate understanding of the Mari evidence, which has since been transformed by a new generation of study. I have proposed elsewhere that the link be resurrected, and the main argument warrants review here (Fleming 1998; 2004b). The Bin-yamin category is not so far removed from that of the Amorites, another term that originates in Mesopotamia, with a genealogical line to the first-millennium Levant that is no clearer than that for Bin-yamin.[6] It would appear, then, that the people who

---

[5] The city of Dan, which becomes the logical center for a Danite population in Israel, is north of the Kinneret lake, inland from Tyre. On a possible connection with the Sea Peoples, see Stager (1988, 228–32), associated with "clients" (cf. Hebrew *gēr*).

[6] The word "Amorite" (Akkadian *amurrûm* and Sumerian *mar-tu*) may have originally referred to "pastoralists" within many parts of Syria and Mesopotamia (Porter 2007; Sallaberger 2007), rather than to "western" outsiders from an eastern Mesopotamian point of view, as commonly held. The term then gave its name "Amurru(m)" to a specific people identified as a decentralized

could fight and best Israel in Judges 20 and who gained early prominence as part of Israel under Saul got their name from a broad tribal association once established in Syria.

After the Mari archives were discovered in the 1930s, one of the first items of public interest was the existence of a name that seemed to match the biblical Benjamin (Dossin 1939, 983; Parrot 1950, 6). The Mari group is consistently rendered with the logogram DUMU(mes) for "sons" and the syllabic *ia-mi-na* for the second part of the name, to be read *Binū Yamina*, "Sons of the Right Hand."[7] Early interpreters of the evidence suggested that the Bible's Bin-yamin could have been a southern offshoot of the older Syrian group (Schmökel 1950; von Soden 1948), but it was objected that Yaminite settlement in the Mari evidence was not specially southern (Schunck 1963, 7; Thompson 1974, 64; Weippert 1971, 112). In his influential critique of attempts to link Genesis to history, Thompson (1974, 62–6) concluded that the Binu Yamina were not even a proper name but only a geographical reference to "Southerners" and that the eventual use of such directional terms for proper geographical names is so common that one can expect more than one group of "Sons of the South," without any genetic relationship between them. As examples of the latter phenomenon, he cites Yemen in southern Arabia, a Transjordanian Arabic tribe of Benjamin, Teman of Edom, and for a "Northern" alternative, the Aramean city of Sam'al (Zinjirli).

Countless texts show the impossibility of treating Mari's Binu Yamina as anything other than a proper name.[8] The Binu Sim'al and the Binu Yamina formed a complementary pair of coalitions among a tribal population that represented their larger identity in terms of this left/right division. As a dual terminology, the "left" was meaningless without the corresponding "right," and this grand split was understood to reflect not a narrow concentration of settlement but an ancient allotment of pastoral grazing ranges. The crucial text describes the long-accepted pasturage of the Sim'alite "Sons of the Left Hand" as the upper Habur River basin, while that of the Yaminite "Sons of the Right Hand" encompassed the territories of Yamhad (Aleppo), Qatna, and Amurru:

While the land of Yamhad, the land of Qatna, and the land of Amurru are the range(?) of the Yaminites – and in each of those lands the Yaminites have their fill of

---

polity in the mountains between the Orontes River and the Mediterranean, which was already established by the early second millennium. It is not clear whether the biblical category arrived through descendants of the specific western polity or by the meandering passage of the broader term through irrecoverable usage across time. For further discussion, see Chapter 13.

[7] Thompson (1974, 66) objected that the necessary reading of the cuneiform as *mārū yamina* reduced the direct verbal similarity. Hayim Tadmor (1958, 130 n. 12) argued that the logogram cannot represent West Semitic *binu(m)*. However professional scribes read this spelling, we now have at least one personal name that shows the western form, *Bi-ni-ia-mi-na* (ARM XXII 328 iii:16), suggesting that native West Semitic speakers would have used the expected noun *bin-* (Durand 1998, 418).

[8] See the discussion of tribal categories in Charpin and Durand (1986); Fleming (2004a, chapter 2, "The Tribal World of Zimri-Lim"); Durand (1998, 417–511, "Les Bédouins"); Durand (2004).

barley and pasture their flocks – from the start(?), the range(?) of the Hana has been Ida-Maraṣ.[9]

Yamhad and Qatna represent the major western kingdoms of the early second millennium, and the latter governed territories that reached south into what is now southern Syria and Lebanon. The name "Amurru" represents the polity that is better attested for the later second millennium in evidence from Amarna and Hattusha, in the mountains north of Lebanon and southeast of Ugarit.[10]

It is evident that the "right hand" (*yamina*) was associated with the south, as in Biblical Hebrew, so that the Mari coalitions are indeed divided as "Northerners" (Binu Sim'al) and "Southerners" (Binu Yamina), in broad terms that span modern Syria. Furthermore, while directional references may be common in names of people and places, the forms of such names are far from generic and identical. The Syrian Binu Sim'al and Binu Yamina offer a conceptual pair, based on the metaphor of the human body, which is lacking in Israel's solitary "Son of the Right Hand." The names of the two Amorite coalitions are evidently self-assigned, self-referential, ideologically symmetrical, and therefore neutral. There is no junior partner, one defined from the centrality of the other.[11]

Biblical scholars have long explained Israel's tribe of Benjamin as "southern" with reference to Ephraim, the dominant region and tribe in the highlands between Jerusalem and the Jezreel Valley.[12] If Benjamin is really "southern" in local terms, however, it is from an Ephraimite point of view, not that of Benjamin itself. Our two "Benjamins" would be based on two wholly different conceptions. This interpretation of Israel's Benjamin in purely local terms was more viable when the earlier Binu Yamina could also be understood as a local northern Mesopotamian phenomenon of modest scale.[13] Now that we know the Binu Yamina as a far-flung association whose pastures were oriented toward southwestern Syria, Israel's tribe is surely easier to explain as a secondary application of the old name. So far as the name "Benjamin" was actually

---

[9] *ki-ma ma-at Ia-am-ha-ad*[ki] *ma-at Qa-ṭá-nim*[ki] *ù ma-at A-mu-ri-im*[ki] *ni-iK-hu-um ša* DUMU[meš] *Ia-mi-na ù i-na ma-tim še-ti* DUMU[meš] *Ia-mi-na še-em i-ša-bi ù na-wa-šu-nu i-re-i-em ù iš-tu da-ar-ka-tim ni-iK-hu-um ša Ha-na*[meš] *I-da-Ma-ra-aṣ*; see Fleming (1998, 61 n. 91), reproduced there with the generous permission of Jean-Marie Durand. Since the time of my citation, the full letter (A.2730) has been published by Durand (2004, 120–1; with the first part of the letter in ARM XXVI/2, p. 33 n. 24). For extensive comment on the text and its context, see Miglio (2010, 75–6, 182–4). In Zimri-Lim's Binu Sim'al circle, those affiliated with the king's own tribe were most often called just "Hana," or "tent-dwellers."

[10] A location south of Qatna should be ruled out by the frequent juxtaposition of Qatna and Hazor; see Bonechi (1992, 10 n. 7). For Amurru in the Late Bronze Age, see Singer (1991).

[11] From Thompson's list, only the Arabic Benjamin would offer an exact match, and the name may derive directly from the biblical tradition or even, though it is less likely, from the same Syrian tribal split.

[12] See, e.g., Mayes (1974, 82); Schunck (1963, 15); Thompson (1974, 59–60); Zobel (1965, 111–12). Most recently, Na'aman (2009b, 337) concludes that the name must refer to the southernmost of the clans settled in the central highlands during the Iron Age I.

[13] See Weippert (1971, 112); Schunck (1963, 7); Thompson (1974, 64).

understood to originate by reference to Ephraim, this would have been an effort to interpret an existing term against local geography.

The combination of evidence for a sweeping Syrian Binu Yamina people in the early second millennium and the Bible's isolation of a people apart should inspire a reevaluation of the historical framework for Benjamin in Israel. Somehow, the biblical name probably derives ultimately from the earlier Binu Yamina, elements of which may have contributed to the populations of southern pastoralists. Their descendants would not have been limited to Israelites, but would also have contributed to other peoples of the Iron Age, especially inland, such as the Ammonites and the Moabites. The Mesopotamian name "Amorite" would also have entered the southern palette of people-names through Syria, probably also by way of groups moving inland, so that biblical usage still occasionally preserves this association, as opposed to the lowland Canaanites. In purely Mesopotamian terms, as measured by the early second-millennium evidence from Mari, the Binu Yamina would have been a subset of people associated with the Amorite language. Although centuries stand between the Mari usage and the biblical evidence, the Mesopotamian names of the Bible's Bin-yamin and Amorites suggest that some relationship could have persisted. The point of this observation is not to speculate about the possible connection but rather to consider why one name was attached to a people that became part of Israel, while the other came to embody one class of irreconcilable outsiders. Benjamin's war with Israel indicates that this people did not join the people of Yahweh easily. It is possible that identification by this distant category reflected association with highland peoples who were somehow aligned differently from others who joined Israel, perhaps because they kept names that linked them to old northern ancestry.

Proper evaluation of the problem would require an archaeological dimension. I mention only brief details here. Some of the earliest Iron Age I fortifications in the highlands occurred in this region, as well as some of the earliest new settlements of this period.[14] If "Israel" already existed in some form by this time, as indicated by the Merenptah stele (see Chapter 15), then this twelfth-century phenomenon would represent something distinct from and contemporaneous with early Israel. One could even imagine a movement of Benjamin/Yaminite peoples from inland into this territory in the early Iron Age I. Avraham Faust (2006, 131) considers that "the land of Benjamin appears to have had the most elaborate and complex social structure in the highland during the eleventh century B.C.E., particularly its latter part." By this focus on the land of Israel before kings, I do not mean to locate the biblical texts to this period. If we seek a powerful Benjamin of modest population but considerable resources and power, however, this may be the appropriate time.

---

[14] In his early review of early settlement, Finkelstein (1988, 322–3) listed Mount Ebal, Giloh, Izbet-ṣartah, Beth-zur, el-Ful, en-Naṣbeh, and Bethel. He observes that in the Iron Age I, there are fewer early settlements than for the highlands to the north (Ephraim/Manasseh), but they are larger – especially Tell el-Ful (Gibeah) and Tell en-Naṣbeh (Mizpah).

The Bible's genealogy in Genesis, its muster list in Judges 5, and the other evidence for an association of peoples as Israel do not indicate an intrinsic relationship and equivalent origins. Benjamin seems to have been part of Israel's political landscape early, but it did not assimilate easily.

B. Benjamin and Saul

In the tribal schemes reflected in the books of Genesis and Judges, the position of Benjamin is oddly ambiguous. Benjamin is arguably missing from several of the early collections:

- the birth narrative in Genesis 29–30, even in its final form; Benjamin's birth is separated to Gen. 35:16–18, when Rachel dies;
- Jacob's poetic sayings in Genesis 49, where it is tacked on after Joseph at the end, keeping to the birth narrative sequence (v. 27);[15]
- the Joseph-focused collection of Israelite failures against their Canaanite neighbors in Judges 1, where it is tucked in after Judah, before Joseph (v. 21).

Clearly, Benjamin was added to all of these texts by writers who found its presence essential, usually in combination with Judah, most likely at a time when Benjamin had been joined to Judah. The question is why Benjamin was not part of the core Israelite lists in the first place. If Benjamin had always been attached to Judah – a doubtful proposition in any case because of uncertainty about how old the Judah political name may be – then it is difficult to explain Benjamin's presence in two other key collections:

- the muster of peoples to fight the kings of Canaan in the Song of Deborah, where it is attached to Ephraim with an awkward second person, "after you, Benjamin, among your peoples ('*ămāmêka*)" (Judg. 5:14);
- the collection of Israelite hero stories found at least in Judges 3–9, where Benjamin is the people of Ehud, the first of the set, who killed the king of Moab (3:15).

Overall, both of the Joseph collections (Genesis 30 and Judges 1) omit Benjamin. These are most likely preserved at Bethel, which the Joshua territorial account even attributes to Benjamin, though at its border with Joseph (Josh. 18:22; cf. 16:1–2; 18:13). One explanation for this would be that Benjamin was subsumed into Joseph from a Bethel point of view, before Judah's dominance. Both Joseph and Benjamin seem not to have been included in the core list of Jacob's sayings, which do not appear to have represented an attempt to list all of Israel's peoples, in that they omit the likely seat of the ninth-century kings, in Ephraim. Of the two sets that do include Benjamin, one considers Benjamin to be an adjunct to Ephraim (Judg. 5:14). Only the Ehud story gives Benjamin a

---

[15] Benjamin appears between Levi and Joseph in Deut. 33:12, with a bland blessing that is hard to evaluate.

completely separate identity, and this occurs with wordplay for a "left-handed" hero, to complement the name Benjamin as "Son of the Right Hand" (Judg. 3:15, 21). The same combination applies to the 700 deadly warriors of Gibeah in the account of Israel's war with Benjamin (Judg. 20:15–16). Together, these Israelite lists present Benjamin as ancient yet somehow marginal – associated with Ephraim and perhaps Joseph, yet distinct, and distinct especially in their dangerous left-handedness.

In the long narrative of Israel's life in the land that now spans the books of Judges, Samuel, and Kings, Benjamin plays one other major role – yet also a role that expresses a strange historical marginality. Benjamin is claimed to have produced the first king of Israel, Saul son of Kish, who ruled from Gibeah, just north of Jerusalem. The plausibility of a link to Benjamin is augmented by the fact that the early material in the David narrative understands Saul to have been Benjaminite. When David is based at Hebron, his proxy Joab fights a war with the house of Saul, represented by the men of Benjamin even though Eshbaal (Ishbosheth) son of Saul remains east of the Jordan at Mahanaim (2 Sam. 2:15, 25–31). A later, more expanded David collection takes for granted that his legitimacy cannot be explained without reference to Saul, who must have lost favor with Yahweh, the god of Israel. In this David narrative, which may even have begun with Saul's divine selection in 1 Samuel 9, this prior Israelite king is called first of all "a man from Benjamin" (9:1). Yet this is an odd tradition, distanced from the Benjamin communities of the later monarchies, whether in Israel or in Judah. The house of David had unassailable authority to rule later Judah, and no other royal house of Israel is recalled to have been Benjaminite. Saul's rule over Israel seems always to have been something ancient, an argument for Benjamin's significance or legitimacy. The question is, for whom.

In its current setting in 1 Samuel, the long story of Saul as the first king of Israel is fully integrated into a narrative about David's legitimacy (e.g., Edelman 1996b, 148). By joining the selection of each king and Saul's rejection under the figure of Samuel as prophet, Saul's entire reign is given a framework that leads to David. From the other side, David is introduced as a faithful servant of Saul, an insecure ruler who then drives David away out of fear that this upstart will supplant him. Given every chance to dispose of Saul, David acknowledges the king's divine appointment and waits until Saul dies in battle with the Philistines before pursuing the throne himself. All this is necessary because David is to rule over all Israel, not simply over Judah, and Saul's claim as the first accepted king of Israel seems to have been undeniable and unavoidable. There was no way to establish David's legitimate rule of Israel without accounting for the transition from the house of Saul.

In order to create this account of David's right to be king of Israel, the writer or writers drew on and elaborated a body of existing Saul lore, at least some of which may have constituted a single narrative. The material devoted solely to Saul is found in 1 Samuel 9–15, which takes us from his selection as king to rejection by Samuel, followed by David's anointing in chapter 16.[16] Although the poem in 2 Sam. 1:19–27 is framed as David's lament, and it expresses a personal love for Jonathan, David himself is nonetheless absent from the text, which could be read as a celebration of Saul from his own circle.[17] A large part of 1 Samuel 9–15 is preoccupied with the establishment of Saul as king, an interest that suits his portrayal as the first king of Israel even as it expresses the immovable tradition of his legitimacy on every front. He is designated and anointed by the prophet Samuel (9:1–10:16), identified through divination in Yahweh's presence (10:17–27), and ratified by popular acclamation after military success (11:1–15). Saul's rejection holds equal interest for the final narrative, as the necessary counterbalance to his divine election. Through Samuel, Yahweh declares an end to Saul's kingship not once but twice, each time for straying from Yahweh's ritual demands (13:7–15; chapter 15).[18]

Given such preoccupation with Saul's selection and rejection, little room remains for his actual reign. Even his victory in chapter 15 over Agag and Amalek is made a defeat. Nevertheless, Saul is depicted above all as a military commander who builds an Israelite kingdom by a series of successes. Under his leadership, Israel defeats the Ammonites at Jabesh Gilead, east of the Jordan (11:1–11); the Philistines at Micmash in Benjamin, initiated by Jonathan's raid (13:1–7, 16–22; 14:15–23); and Amalek in the south (15:1–9). No building is associated with Saul, and he is responsible for no administrative institutions.

At the center of the Saul tradition in 1 Samuel there must be writing from those who venerate his memory without commitment to David, and these partisans are most simply identified with Benjamin. Such writing may lie behind the accounts of Saul's tainted victories in 1 Samuel 13–15, but the one clear case is found in 1 Sam. 11:1–11, which celebrates Saul's leadership without hint of criticism or anticipation of David.[19] Messengers from Jabesh Gilead

---

[16] The story of the witch of Endor in 1 Samuel 28 does not involve David directly, but it has as its goal to get word from Samuel, the prophet who oversaw the rejection of Saul, and Samuel promises Saul's death, which will lead to David's accession to the throne.

[17] See Edelman (1996b, 151); the poem does not call Saul "king," though he is portrayed on a royal scale. Mark Smith (personal communication) points out that the first-person voice of David appears only at the end of the poem in verses 26–7, which would appear to be added to a poem from the circle of Saul partisans in verses 19–25.

[18] Walter Dietrich (2007, 274) regards the essence of the entire Samuel-Saul combination in 1 Samuel 15 to originate in Israel, without any reference to the house of David. Every passage that relates Samuel to Saul, however, anticipates Saul's failure and replacement by David.

[19] Many interpreters have seen an earlier account of Saul's first selection underneath the full text of 1 Sam. 9:1–10:16. This story would have culminated in Saul's receipt of special signs, without reference to kingship or any specific calling. See McKenzie (2000, 293–6), who considers the authoritative proof to remain that of Schmidt (1970, 63–80). The geography of this earlier rendition has Saul roam Israelite territory, including both "the Ephraim highlands" (*har 'eprayim*) and "the land of the Yaminite" (*'ereṣ yĕmînî*) in search of his lost donkeys (9:3–4). Without the larger roles for Samuel and his anointing Saul for kingship, the earlier narrative could be considered Israelite, and in fact Benjaminite, based on the opening genealogy. If this introduces a larger Saul–David complex, however (see Chapter 6), then we may not be able to attribute

come to Gibeah to ask for help, so that Jabesh will not be subjugated to the Ammonites. Saul musters an army for war by sending segments of two slaughtered cattle to "all the regions of Israel" (vv. 6–7), a definition that avoids both the standardized "tribal" terminology and the count of twelve.[20] They respond in fear of Yahweh, which inspires them to go out "as one man." Saul has no troops of his own and no office from which to command, even as a chosen spokesman for Israel's god. The spirit of Yahweh overwhelms him, and the people perceive this with his message of butchered meat. It is not necessary to take this sequence as the one standard procedure for Israelite muster, but the account is immersed in a culture of decentralized and collaborative action. In the main text, Saul is treated as an established leader, even as he is not named a king.[21] This narrative would be at home among the Israelite hero stories of Judges 3–9. There is nothing about the text to connect it to Judah, unless one approaches it with the prior assumption that any geographical association with Benjamin must reflect the time when it was considered part of Judah.

On its own, 1 Sam. 11:1–11 does not identify Saul as a Benjaminite; it does, however, locate him at "Gibeah of Saul" (v. 4), which the messengers from Jabesh Gilead treat as the logical objective for their plea to Israel. Gibeah is strongly associated with Benjamin, especially in narratives about the early period. It is specifically called "Gibeah of Benjamin" only in texts before the appearance of David.[22] 1 Sam. 11:1–11 offers no background for Saul, a lacuna that may originally have been filled by the birth narrative now attached to Samuel in chapter 1 (see below). In the Saul story as a whole, he is associated

the Benjamin name to the original story. With such uncertainty, I have given this material little weight in my analysis of the Israelite Saul.

[20] The specification of 300,000 Israelites and 30,000 Judahites in verse 8 introduces a concern for Judah and a sense of tribal scale (ten to one) that is not indicated by the muster itself. This detail appears to be added for Judahite consumption. Likewise, the addition of Samuel to Saul in verse 7 is out of place.

[21] Both the representatives from Jabesh and the recipients of the call to muster understand Saul to have authority already, not needing a victory to prove his right to rule. After the battle account, the reference to men who had opposed Saul's reign picks up a motif from the end of the Mizpah enthronement and attempts to explain Saul's leadership in terms of the larger narrative about selection of the first king over Israel (10:27; 11:12–13). This is therefore not part of the primary Jabesh Gilead story. Samuel's call for a confirmation of Saul's kingship at Gilgal is also superfluous and serves larger structural interests (11:14–15). Miller (1974, 165–7) suggests that the complaint and response can be included in the original story, which would then be defined as 10:26–7; 11:1–13, 15. It is not clear, however, that the original story in either 9:1–10:16 or in chapter 11 cast Saul as "king." Without the focus on kings in the early traditions, Edelman's (1984) historical objections to 1 Samuel 11 as a foundation narrative for Israel's monarchy become less pressing.

[22] 1 Sam. 13:2, 15; 14:16. This phrase defines Gibeah as the principal settlement of the Benjamin people, a status assumed in the Benjamin war story of Judges 20 (see below). The kingship of Saul gives rise to a second identification of the town as "Gibeah of Saul" (1 Sam. 11:4; 15:34; 2 Sam. 21:6; Isa. 10:29). In the biblical narrative, Saul is first introduced to the site when he joins a band of prophets there after Samuel anointed him (1 Sam. 10:5, 10).

with Gibeah and Benjamin through his leadership there rather than as a place of origin. Perhaps like Jerusalem for David, or even Hebron, Gibeah was significant for its prestige as a base of power, and it was assumed that such centers could be taken by those from outside.

The other biblical narrative that associates Saul with Benjamin in an Israelite context comes from the core David material, during the period before he supplanted Eshbaal (Ishbosheth) son of Saul as king of Israel. As discussed in Chapter 6, David was originally remembered especially for his rule over Israel, without apparent reference to Judah, and this old David material thus provides a view of Israel preserved in a Jerusalem setting. According to 2 Samuel 2, Abner, the commander of Saul's army, brings the heir to Mahanaim in Jordan, where he can have some distance from David and his forces. Abner is said to make Ish-Bosheth king over "Gilead, the Ashurite, Jezreel, Ephraim, Benjamin, and all Israel" (v. 9).[23] In the whole Bible, this is the only description of Israel as a kingdom that consists explicitly of associated peoples. They are not called tribes, and the list is nonstandard.[24] Although the picture is rare, it reminds us that the collaborative political structure of Israel probably remained active under kings, even when our meager textual resources focus only on the unified polity. This vision of an Israelite kingdom of allied peoples defines a swath that straddles the Jordan across the midsection of the larger biblical territory. David holds the south from Hebron, and Jezreel appears to mark the northernmost component. The central highlands are represented by Ephraim and Benjamin together.

In spite of this picture of the house of Saul ruling a larger Israel that included regions to the north and east, the David narrative treats Benjamin as Saul's particular people. Although Mahanaim is east of the Jordan River, Abner brings troops to Gibeon in the west in order to confront David's forces under Joab.[25] When the two groups meet, they agree to a ritual combat that is defined as twelve "for Benjamin and for Ishbosheth son of Saul" and twelve "from the servants of David" (2 Sam. 2:15). All twenty-four warriors kill each other, and Abner's men get the worst of the combat that ensues. In the aftermath, Abner gathers local support to stave off Joab's pursuit (vv. 25–8), and this fighting force is defined as two units, "from Benjamin" and "the men of Abner" (v. 31). Ish-Bosheth's refuge east of the Jordan represents no real shift in regional support for Saul's royal house, which is still associated with Benjamin.

[23] The first three objects are introduced with the preposition *'el*, and the other three with *'al*, yielding two clusters. Ephraim, Benjamin, and all Israel seem to represent a group identified with the central highlands, so that the others may be eastern and northern, with "the Ashurite" a striking anomaly. Rather than equate this with the tribe of Asher, it may be better to accept this as an unknown and probably early participant in Israel.

[24] It is intriguing that David's own rule over Israel is never defined in terms of such an Israelite association, so that this text seems rooted in an Israelite idea that never inspired a claim by the house of David.

[25] This meeting in Gibeon is a key part of Edelman's argument that the actual Saul may have launched his career as a local leader there, rather than at Gibeah (1996b, 156–7).

In the end, Saul's significance for the tradition of David's legitimacy may obscure an equally weighty purpose for the Saul tradition: the interest of Benjamin itself. The abiding reverence for this hero among the people of Benjamin would have provided the setting for preservation of Saul stories and composition of Saul texts through the generations after his royal house ceased to compete for rule over Israel. The possibility of Benjamin partisanship need not have been submerged entirely beneath the mass of David's narrative, even if in the Bible this had the last word.[26]

C. Benjamin Apart: War with Israel

With the biblical treatment of Saul so firmly embedded in the account of how David could be the legitimate king of Israel, it is difficult to get a clear view of Saul outside that framework. I have already discussed 1 Sam. 11:1–11 as the one text with a logic untouched by David's interests, and this text leads us into an alternative configuration of biblical material that may shed further light on both Saul and Benjamin. Sara Milstein (2010) has reconstructed a previously unrecognized "Saul complex" that would have combined the story of the Benjamin war in Judges 20–1 with an account of Saul's birth now reflected in 1 Samuel 1 and finally with his victory in 1 Sam. 11:1–11. This reading combines the two most striking biblical recollections of Benjamin as a people in action: to the positive contribution of Israel's first king is joined an account of how Benjamin found itself at war with the very people Saul came to rule. In Milstein's reading, the combination is not a coincidence.

The story of Benjamin's war with Israel now includes a prologue and denouement that span Judges 19–21, tacked onto the end of the book of Judges after the tale of Micah and the people of Dan (chapters 17–18). Late features in parts of the Benjamin narrative lead some to date the entire block to the postmonarchic period.[27] Other interpreters consider that an older story has undergone a process of expansion.[28] The content itself suggests origin in an independent

---

[26] One other question is whether the core Saul narrative could be considered to have interest for the kingdom of Israel as a whole, without David and beyond the particular partisanship of Benjamin. If the concern to explain the first king of Israel belongs to the combination with the David narrative, then the (northern) realm of Israel would have had no stake in Saul on that ground. It is possible that the account of Saul's muster in 1 Samuel 11 affirms the tradition of alliance, but if so, the story itself still offers no alternative setting for preservation than Benjamin itself.

[27] See, e.g., Amit (2006, 647–8); Blenkinsopp (2006, 638–43); Guillaume (2004, 204–6).

[28] This approach includes the nuanced reflections on the problem by Georg Hentschel and Christina Niessen (2008), who understand the main narrative of war between Benjamin and Israel to be woven together from two variant threads, both independent of the explanations for how the war began and what happened afterward. They define these threads by the distinct references to "the sons of Israel" and "the man of Israel," which Becker (1990) had considered evidence for later revision by a hand using the latter. For Hentschel and Niessen, the sections with "the man of Israel" reflect the older of the two versions, based on the simple notion of an ambush.

story, not spun off from familiar biblical schemes. Benjamin itself is old, as seen in the Song of Deborah, and the notion of all-out war between Benjamin and Israel, ending in the systematic slaughter of the smaller people, treats them like foreigners. Israel acts as a body, whether strategically as the collective "man of Israel" (vv. 17, 20, 22, 33, 36–42) or in approach to Yahweh as "the sons of Israel" (esp. vv. 19, 23–7). Finally, beneath the surface of the finished story with its bizarre tale of communal crime in chapter 19, the people of Benjamin are respected as tough and nearly indomitable. There is unexpected sympathy that raises the possibility of a Benjamin setting at some stage of composition.

In Milstein's analysis, a Benjaminite complex that had combined the war account with Saul's birth and heroic debut was recast in cunningly ugly terms. The horrific concubine tale of Judges 19 was added by a Judahite writer who was ready to keep the Saul complex as a separate composition but to twist its intent (in Judges 19–21; 1 Samuel 1; 11:1–11). This text was broken up only at a very late stage so that the explicit Saul material of 1 Samuel 11 could be incorporated into the Saul–David narrative, leaving 1 Samuel 1 to be transferred to the prophet and Judges 19–21 to be added eventually to the one book that addressed life before kings, along with chapters 17–18. Milstein's focus is the scribal technique that she calls "revision through introduction," and she does not intend a complete literary history of these texts. Only the major phases of transformation are relevant to her study, and for my purposes, only the first phase involves non-Judahite writing: the creation of the Saul complex by combining the two Saul narratives with a previously unrelated tale of Benjamin at war with all Israel.

Milstein begins by affirming the old idea that 1 Samuel 1 was originally a story of Saul's birth, as suggested by the repeated wordplays on Saul's name rather than Samuel's, especially in the matching form *šā'ûl* when Hannah says, "All the days that he lives, he is *loaned* to Yahweh" (v. 28).[29] This association of 1 Samuel 1 with Saul would identify him with Yahweh's sanctuary at Shiloh, as opposed to Benjamin or Gibeah – a distinct tradition that would have made easier the transfer of names to Samuel. The combination of Saul and Shiloh suggested by 1 Samuel 1 then drew Milstein's attention to the role of Shiloh in Judg. 21:15–24. There, the people of Israel address the near-annihilation of Benjamin by finding wives for the remaining warriors at a Shiloh festival rather like the one envisioned for Hannah's family in 1 Samuel 1. No numbers are mentioned, and Milstein understands the first attempt to get wives for Benjamin in Judg. 21:1–14 to represent a later revision of what originally served as a simple solution to the survival of Benjamin after the defeat recounted in Judges 20.[30] This tale of war and survival would have been told in Benjamin circles,

---

[29] The root "to ask" or "to loan" (*š'l*) occurs seven times in connection with the child. For this frequently argued position, see Hylander (1932); Dus (1968); McCarter (1980, 62–6); Römer (2005, 94); and Davies (2007b, 107).

[30] The 400 women obtained in Judg. 21:12 recall the note in 20:47 that 600 Benjaminites escaped to the Rock of Rimmon. This shortfall leaves room for the Shiloh story, which in itself has

without the sense of grievance and retribution created by the abuses of Gibeah in chapter 19, itself part of a later revision.

This argument is crucial to Milstein's reconstruction, which proposes a provocative combination of material now distributed across Judges and 1 Samuel. First, as read without 1 Samuel, Judges 20–1 identifies all the people of Benjamin after the war with Israel as part-Shilonite. Meanwhile, the Shiloh focus of Saul's birth account in 1 Samuel 1 represented a problem for Benjaminite claims to the heritage of Saul, as reflected in his Gibeah base in chapter 11. By setting the story of war and its aftermath in front of the Saul material of 1 Samuel 1 and 11, both the Shiloh and the Benjamin associations could be reconciled by emphasizing the roots of all Benjamin in Shiloh and Ephraim. As Milstein sees it, the attraction of the combination lay in the Shiloh restoration of Benjamin, not in the war as such, and the account of war between Israel and Benjamin became part of the Saul complex through a unit now expressed in Judg. 20:14–48 and 21:15–24. Originally, the Benjamin war in Judg. 20:14–48, the birth of Saul preserved in 1 Samuel 1, and Saul's victory over the Ammonites in 1 Sam. 11:1–11 were composed in different settings for different purposes. The first and the third were Benjaminite, as became the Saul complex created by linking them.[31]

If Milstein is correct in connecting material from Judges to the Saul tradition, then the two principal Benjamin traditions in the Bible entered it together and were separated only at a later stage. Benjamin appears as an individual in Genesis and sporadically through the rest of the Bible as a tribe, a region, or an identifier. As a people, however, Benjamin has two roles: they fight an all-out war against Israel, as if the two were foreign to each other; and they revere Saul as a great ancient leader of Israel and are shown to fight on behalf of his son against the forces of David. Nothing in the Saul complex proposed by Milstein presents him as "king," and it is not clear that the early Benjamin material, which precedes the incorporation of the region into Judah, linked Saul to the title claimed for David. This fact in itself would confirm the pre-Judahite character of the early Saul traditions in the Bible. Only in the David narrative must Saul be the first king so that his successor may lay claim to his role and his reputation. Certainly, the David narrative envisions a house of Saul that produced an heir, and this heir attempts to maintain an established dominion,

---

no concern for numbers. Also, the geography of the Shiloh solution is natural to a war in the Benjamin region, as opposed to the trek to Jabesh Gilead, east of the Jordan River.

[31] The Benjamin composition of the underlying war story in Judges 20 is still reflected in the sympathy with which the battle itself is recounted. Benjamin twice defeats Israel in spite of what the current text presents as an overwhelming numerical disadvantage. Even at a third try, Israel cannot overcome Benjamin head-on, so they resort to cunning. In the reading of Hentschel and Niessen, this sympathy would be associated with the "sons of Israel" variant of the war narrative, which is not as old but still independent. Without commitment to this approach, it is worth noting that this variant would have a particular association with Bethel, where Israel gathers to consult Yahweh (vv. 18, 26), a town located at the northern edge of Benjamin territory in Josh. 18:13.

unlike the saviors whose memories depend only on individual victories against outside enemies.

Of the two Benjamin traditions, that of Saul is potentially important for questions about both the early monarchy and the later situation of the Benjamin people. The other tradition of war between Israel and Benjamin, in what it presents of the relationship between the two peoples, is shocking. Unlike the conflict between Ephraim and Gilead in Judg. 12:1–6, during which the men of Ephraim are distinguished only by their different pronunciation of the word "shibboleth," Benjamin and Israel are presented as foreigners to each other. Stripped of the concubine prelude and its portrayal of the conflict as a disciplinary matter between tribes, the war story has more the feel of a conquest narrative like that of Joshua at Ai. As in Joshua 8, the Israelites are treated as a block throughout the actual battle narrative; we hear about "tribes" of Israel only in the transition (20:2, 10, 12). Judah is specified as the first to suffer defeat against Benjamin (v. 18), in a line that probably fits some stage of Judahite retelling.[32] As against Sihon, Og, and Ai, Israel acts as a collected unit for battle, though in this case there is no heroic leader, and decisions are portrayed as corporate. Whereas divine guidance can be had directly through Moses and Joshua, no matter the location, Israel without an inspired commander must seek Yahweh at Bethel. Against Benjamin, Israel must organize for battle as a collective entity. At Bethel, the mustered forces of Israel mourn their defeats before Yahweh and ask his guidance, and in the field, they plan and execute their strategy as a group.[33]

In spite of their defeat, Benjamin is presented as Israel's equal in military capacity, a formidable presence on Israel's southern flank. Throughout the narrative, Benjamin is portrayed as separate from Israel, called "brothers" only in the transitional (and later Judahite) explanation for the war (v. 13). Taken on its own, the people of Benjamin are little different from those of Ai in Joshua 8, according to this parallel tale of ambush and slaughter. Benjamin has no king, and there is no explicit *ḥērem* command, though the slaughter is extensive and likewise defined by towns (Judg. 20:48). From the vantage of Judges 20, the chief town in Benjamin is Gibeah, which will become Saul's capital as first king of Israel. Gibeah is the precise counterpart of Ai, as the fortified center of resistance to Israelite dominance. Counts of fighters and casualties litter the text, so that we understand both the odds against Benjamin

---

[32] Milstein observes that Judah likewise goes first in Judg. 1:1, in the Judahite revision of the Joseph scheme of undefeated Canaanites. It is not necessary to reconstruct a purely Benjaminite version of the war story, which has now clearly been built into a later text that is finally critical of both Benjamin and Saul. Evidence for the conscious reference to Saul in Judges 19 is the gruesome butchering of the Levite's concubine to send throughout Israel as a muster for war, in imitation of Saul's muster by ox parts (1 Sam. 11:7). The Benjamin war was then passed on through Judahite hands until it reached its eventual home at the end of Judges.

[33] Blenkinsopp (2006, 642–3) compares the pattern of weeping, fasting, and inquiring of Yahweh in Judg. 20:22–4 and 26–8 with the Book of Maccabees. It is not clear to me that such a ritual portrayal of military defeat and response offers a viable chronological measure.

and the extremity of their decimation at the end. Benjamin has nearly been wiped out of existence, like the enemies of Israel in the conquest stories. If we did not already assume that Benjamin belonged to Israel, Judges 20 could be read as another such conquest tale from Joshua.[34]

The portrayal of Benjamin as a people set apart from Israel has an echo in the account of Jacob's sons in Genesis. At least, he is not part of the original Joseph scheme in either the birth narrative of Genesis 30, where Joseph is Rachel's long-awaited child, or the basic notion of Joseph as favorite son in the Egypt story, "because he was a son of his older years" (Gen. 37:3). Benjamin seems not even to exist until the brothers set out for Egypt, and Jacob keeps his youngest at home (42:4). All the brothers until Joseph are born in Syria, and when Jacob meets Esau on his return, Rachel and Joseph take pride of place as the last to be introduced (33:7). Benjamin arrives only with Rachel's death, the one son born in the land, linked to Bethlehem in what appears to be a Judahite effort to account for his birth, when the Israelite Jacob narrative simply omitted it.[35]

Myriad explanations have been proposed to account for the formation of Judges 19–21, with varying chronological frameworks.[36] While the terrible tale of the Levite and his concubine in chapter 19 is so strikingly revolting that it may be taken as relatively early, it offers an apparent allusion to the similar Sodom scene, and the twelve body parts assume the Judahite formulation that is never otherwise associated with a battle account. The language of the deliberations in 20:1–13 and 21:1–14 includes the term *'ēdâ* ("assembly"), which is consistently late. If we allow the motifs of the left-handed Benjaminite, the feint and ambush against a fortified foe, and the massacre in battles of conquest to belong to broader types with early exemplars, the war narrative itself generally lacks such features.[37] Far from being Judah's rant against Persian-period competition from Benjamin, the narrative displays a mainly Benjaminite perspective, itself set against the framework of an Israelite battle of conquest. With the focus on survival and reconciliation with the Israelite enemy, the war account of

---

[34] One further point of comparison is the ambush motif itself, which is constructed differently in each narrative and should not be explained by simple allusion. For Hentschel and Niessen (2008, 34–5), the lack of any divine role in the older "man of Israel" variant of Judges 20 shows that the ambush framework belongs to the deepest level, which does not share basic elements of the ambush in Joshua 8. Gregory Wong's reading of Judges 20 as allusion to Joshua 8 too quickly makes this part of a larger hypothesis of allusion in Judges 17–21, according to which all of this material makes regular references back to the stories of the "major judges" (2006, 57–9, 79–83).

[35] Blum (1984, 110–11) regards the brief account of Benjamin's birth in Gen. 35:16–18 as based on a tradition separate from the narrative of Genesis 29–30, even if its addition was made to round out the full number of twelve Israelite tribes. If so, it would seem that Benjamin is the one tribe that insists on birth in the land because it must defend itself against the charge of being foreigners. The odd fact that Benjamin is the only one born in Israel would then confirm his separate and slightly suspect status as alien to the others and to the land.

[36] For bibliography, see Milstein (2010, chapter 4).

[37] Contrast the reading of Blenkinsopp (2006, 638–42).

Judges 20–1 offers a glimpse of *ḥērem* slaughter from the victims' vantage. This presentation of an Israelite people as having once been assaulted like the Canaanites or Amorites of early occupation is unique in the Bible and raises the question of how Benjamin came to be the one people remembered this way. Somehow, this may be related to the unique status of the name Benjamin itself, which is the only people associated with Israel that is also known from the cuneiform writing of earlier Syria and Mesopotamia.

D. Benjamin, Israel, and Judah

If we are to imagine the existence of an independent Benjaminite story of Saul and his restoration of this people to respect after their decimation at the hands of Israel, how would it have survived to be taken up into the Bible? In her review of the biblical rivalry between the houses of Saul and David, Diana Edelman (2001, 72) identifies only two plausible settings for such competition: the tenth century, after the death of Eshbaal son of Saul, and the last third of the sixth century, after Sheshbazzar or Zerubbabel and Yeshua claim leadership over Yehud. Nothing in the intervening period accounts for partisans of Benjamin at the center of a conflict over who could rule an entity called Israel. Edelman prefers the later setting, and her conclusion keeps company with a wave of new attention to Benjamin in the sixth century, as evidenced in archaeology and reflected in the Bible.[38] The problem with Edelman's approach is that it leaves no room for interest in Benjamin before the fall of Judah, no natural period for the maintenance of old traditions, as seems common to much biblical writing that displays a tension between systematic schemes and simpler underlying narratives. Is there no home for "preexilic" Benjamin lore – especially when it exhibits a tone that is so like other Israelite material?

The land of Benjamin does indeed appear to have had special importance at the time of the Judah's fall. The key archaeological observation is that the region defined as Benjamin in the Bible survived the Babylonian takeover of the early sixth century with remarkably little damage.[39] The biblical starting point has been the story of Gedaliah's abortive governorship at Mizpah just after the fall of Judah (Jeremiah 40–1). Mizpah of Benjamin is then understood as the political center of the region through the time when Jerusalem had been destroyed and had not yet rebounded (Blenkinsopp 2006; Knauf 2006).[40]

Perhaps the starting point should be the seventh century, when the Benjamin region increased in population as part of the same growth exhibited for Judah and the area around Jerusalem (Magen 2004, 1–2).[41] This growth is reflected

---

[38] An important historical context for this set of problems is now provided in Lipschits (2005).

[39] See Blenkinsopp (2006, 644); Magen (2004, 2–3).

[40] This historical reading has a counterpart in recent evaluation of Mizpah in Saul's selection as king according to 1 Sam. 10:17–27, which may also be linked to the sixth century (McKenzie 1998).

[41] For the situation leading up to this time, see Broshi and Finkelstein (1992).

in the territorial description of the kingdom in the book of Jeremiah, where Benjamin is the only constituent that is called a "land" ('*ereṣ*).[42] While the word '*ereṣ* can be applied to regions not defined by action as a polity, it does not to my knowledge indicate a region or people within the kingdom of Judah, except for Benjamin.[43] By this phrase, "the land of Benjamin" appears to be accorded a special status in the kingdom of Judah, evidently as preserving a form of identity that did not apply to other territories within the realm: the foothills or Shephelah, the highlands, the southern wilderness or Negev. When the kingdom of Judah was first defeated and then dismantled by the Babylonians at the start of the sixth century, Benjamin's separate identity may have surfaced in a refusal to follow the party of resistance in Judah's last years. Long before the current period of interest, Abraham Malamat (1950) proposed that Benjamin surrendered separately to Babylon and therefore survived in better condition than other parts of the kingdom.[44] Excavations of individual towns in Benjamin corroborate some version of this picture.[45]

While the evidence for Benjamin in the sixth century may support the notion of competition between Benjamin and Jerusalem under early Achaemenid (Persian) rule, it does not necessarily explain the prominence of Saul in the books of Samuel. This complex material is interwoven with the David narrative at a deep level, almost certainly during the time of the monarchies, and the notion that David legitimately succeeded Saul to rule over Israel must likewise predate the Persians (e.g., Klein 2002). The question then becomes why such a rivalry would have been preserved on either side, not only in Judah but also among the people of Benjamin. Whether or not the conflict between the House of David and the House of Saul originated in actual events when Israel was first ruled by kings, the stories about it must have retained their audiences through the ninth and eighth centuries.

Here, the independence of Benjamin may offer a solution. If the people of Benjamin maintained a vigorously separate identity throughout the early first millennium, no matter the political dominance of the kingdoms to the north and south, the tradition of Saul could have kept an audience throughout. Just as

[42] Jer. 17:26; 32:44; 33:13; for Benjamin as "land," see also Jer. 1:1; 32:8; 37:12.

[43] The word is standard with Israel and frequent for Judah. Other "lands" associated with peoples linked to Israel include Ephraim (Judg. 12:15, burial); Ephraim and Manasseh (Deut. 34:2; 2 Chron. 30:10); Gad and Gilead (1 Sam. 13:7); Gilead alone (Num. 32:1, 29; Josh. 17:5, 6; 22:9, 13, 15, 32; Judg. 10:4; 20:1; 2 Sam. 17:26; 1 Kings 4:19; 2 Kings 10:33; Zech. 10:10; 1 Chron. 2:22; 5:9); Naphtali (1 Kings 15:20; 2 Kings 15:29); and Zebulun (Judg. 12:12, burial). The combination is lacking for Asher, Dan, Issachar, Joseph, Machir, Manasseh individually, Reuben, and Simeon. I include the last two in part to point out that the Joshua land allotments do not call the tribes "lands," even as "the land of Gilead" is included in the portion for Manasseh (Josh. 17:6).

[44] Malamat is cited by Magen (2004, 3); and note Lipschits (2005).

[45] At Gibeon (el-Jib), there is little evidence to distinguish the sixth century clearly, and no destruction marks the end of the Iron Age (Edelman 2003). Jeffrey Zorn (2003) describes a flourishing city at Mizpah (Tell en-Naṣbeh) in the sixth century, which continues through the late fifth century.

the house of David came to be inseparably linked to the southern realm, Saul as founder would have supplied a constant point of reference and pride for those who intended to call themselves the people of Benjamin. This tradition could become a rallying cry for Benjamin in the sixth century, but it would have carried weight because it was already venerable. The viability of such an interpretation depends in part on a fresh examination of the biblical texts for Benjamin and Saul. These suggest that Benjamin was distinct from Israel and Judah to a degree not matched by other peoples that were understood to belong within the Israelite sphere. Saul would therefore have been remembered in Benjamin throughout the period of the two kingdoms, not as a rival to David but as a hero of this people, like Jephthah for Gilead. Benjamin itself most likely remained part of Israel as long as that kingdom endured (so, Davies), and its recognition as a "land" in Jeremiah 17 may reflect its special status as a people who could be taken into Judah only with an unusual degree of regional identity – if not autonomy. This then became the basis for Benjamin's distinct policy toward Babylon in the sixth century.

10

Israelite Writers on Early Israel

With Benjamin, we have finished a review of the evidence for a range of
Israelite voices preserved in the primary biblical narrative that runs from Genesis through Kings. While the discussion has required a level of detail that
may be a burden to those without particular interest or training in the field,
specialists will see immediately the extent to which each treatment represents
an overview. My hypothesis throughout has been that Israelite material in the
Bible is characterized by more than just distinct geography; it also displays
a social organization that resulted in different political traditions. The path
that led to monarchy in Israel did not produce the consistent combination of
political and sacred centers as at Jerusalem, and Samaria seems not to have
become a dominant population center as was Jerusalem in the eighth and seventh centuries. The contrast that is rooted in different historical developments
is sharpened by the likelihood that the Bible's earlier Judahite writing derives
mainly from this later monarchy, with its massive Jerusalem hub. Another biblical expression of Israelite society is the sheer variety of perspectives, which
reflect a wide range of place, with accompanying local interests.

Based on all the lines of evidence that allow isolation of Israelite content,
including geography, politics, and topical interest, it is possible to piece together
a biblical view of ancient Israel that does not partake of some common gener-
alizations about what pertains to "Israel" or "the Bible." Taken together, these
texts may allow a fresh dialogue between the disciplines of history, archaeology,
and biblical studies, with new possibilities for how the Bible relates to historical
questions. One somewhat surprising pattern in the Israelite material is a vivid
recollection of how a distinct herding tradition shaped Israel's origins. A major
role for pastoralism in the early southern region is clear from archaeological finds, but texts from Judah preserve little of this, and the Bible's account
of ancestral shepherds seems to originate in Israelite narrative. Other offerings for historical study result simply from stripping away certain assumptions
from the later and Judahite combination of biblical texts. With this concluding
review, we set the stage for further examination of the "collaborative" political

tradition so strongly displayed in the Bible's Israelite material (Part III), and for reflection on selected historical questions that relate to broad issues of social and political organization.

A. The Herding Tradition

Israelite stories about life before establishment as a people consistently envision a mobility that is linked to pastoralist subsistence – an economic reliance on herding more than agriculture. This is true both of Jacob's family and of Israel under Moses. The self-conscious contrast between how people kept sheep in the land and how the ancestors did so is evident in roles ascribed to Joseph in Genesis 37 and to David in 1 Samuel 16. As the youngest of many brothers, Joseph is kept in camp while his elders take responsibility for the principal economic base of the family: the flocks, which graze at a distance that requires days of travel. David's older brothers also take responsibility for the family's financial priority: the farm. As the youngest, David is sent out with flocks that are kept close enough to the farm to allow easy recall on the same day.[1] The notion of pastoralism with long-distance movement appears to be linked to the idea that Israel and Judah were foreign to the land they now inhabited, so that normal agriculture would have been impossible, as understood by the audience for these narratives. The historical question of whether this distinction was a complete fiction is important but not our focus here. Rather, our immediate consideration is the contribution of this perspective to the narrative baseline for Israel's conception of a past age.

1. *Genesis*

Jacob and his family stand at the center of the portrait of an ancestral age in Genesis. Read on its own, the Jacob cycle has a more limited purpose, to define the ties that bound Israel in terms of kinship in a single nuclear – if somewhat extended – family. Although Jacob is understood to have come from the land that became Israel, he cannot marry and bear children there and must go far away to Syria, the land of his kinsman Laban. Movement with sheep dominates every level of the Jacob story. He encounters Laban as a herdsman sheikh. Their financial dealings are defined entirely by the distribution of wealth in the form of livestock. Jacob's flocks and Laban's flocks move at such distances from each other that contact is only occasional. Although Laban is somehow associated with Haran, no actual town is ever in view through all the exchanges between the two men. By the time Jacob suggests a scheme for building his own wealth, the two men have developed large camps that remain separate, even including women and children.

This social landscape suffuses every part of the Genesis ancestor narratives, with later contributors picking up the Israelite theme. Core elements of the

---

[1] For a more extended discussion of this contrast between the portrayals of Joseph's and David's families, including citation of various specific texts from Mari, see Fleming (2008).

stories for other generations also preserve striking images of pastoralist life that may also come from Israel, not Judah. As already observed, Joseph's family is imagined to live as long-distance herdsmen. When Joseph is sent to check on his brothers, he travels from the Hebron Valley (Gen. 37:10) to Dothan (v. 17), not far from Taanach and Megiddo.[2] When the family arrives in Egypt, they settle in Goshen because they are herdsmen (Gen. 46:32–4; 47:3–4). Modern readers automatically assume a framework of local herding where all livestock remains close at hand, as in the plague of Exod. 9:1–7. Ancient readers who had lost familiarity with long-distance herding may likewise have envisioned flocks that were kept near settlements, as in their own setting, yet the Egypt narrative at least carries with it the possibility of movement into the backcountry. As in the Jacob story, the account of Joseph going into Egypt has no interest in the towns of Canaan.

For the period before Jacob, the family of Abraham is considered to consist entirely of herdsmen. In the core narrative of Abraham and Lot, the separation between the two clans follows the inability of their herdsmen to share the same grazing lands (Gen. 13:8–9). Although Abraham comes to be associated with the southern sites of Hebron/Mamre (Gen. 13:18) and Beersheba (21:31), this narrative assumes Bethel and Ai as the last point of reference (13:4), and the southern locations need not prove origin in Judah. Abram's proposed solution to a conflict between herding groups evokes the world of Syrian pastoralists that gave rise to the definition of Binu Sim'al and Binu Yamina by their grazing ranges:[3] "Is not the whole land before you? Suppose you split off from me. If (you choose) the left (*haśśĕmô'l*), I will go to the right, and if (you choose) the right (*hayyāmîn*), I will go to the left." The terms for "left" and "right" are directly cognate with the Amorite names, though in Genesis they do not refer to north and south. In spite of the historical distance, the Genesis division and the Amorite pair share a remarkably similar set of assumptions. Both traditions use the language of right and left hands, a pair defined by the human body, for pastoralists who are allotting pasturelands. In both, the original corporeal sense is preserved, not dependent on the application of these to south and north. It is significant that in both cases it is grazing land that is in question and that this is distributed according to such a duality. We are not dealing with political domains or even with settlement. Finally, both uses of the left/right framework are large-scale, defining regions that reach beyond local terrain. In effect, Abram takes the hill country of the western Promised Land, and Lot takes the rift valley of the Jordan River. For both the Genesis and the Amorite

---

[2] If the reference to the Valley of Hebron in Gen. 37:14 is read as late, then 46:1 and 5 place Jacob even further south at Beersheba. Some also read Gen. 46:1–5 as late. As I understand the introduction to the Joseph story in Genesis 37, where Joseph is the favorite son and Benjamin is not in view, the image of travel over distance is essential to the account of his sale into slavery. The geographical markers are not to be removed easily as editorial flourishes, and the core story of Genesis 37, with Joseph as Jacob's favorite youngest son, must originate in Israel.

[3] This biblical comparison was originally observed by Jean-Marie Durand, in his advanced seminar at the École Pratique des Hautes Études in April 1998.

pastoralists, the division of pasture does not imply political control. Abram does not rule the Canaanite highland towns any more than Lot rules Sodom and Gomorrah. The same is true for the Binu Yamina pasturage in the lands of Yamhad, Qatna, and Amurru.

2. Out of Egypt and Beyond

Genesis clearly portrays the ancestors as living by their flocks and herds; the four books of Moses are less often read this way. Israelite tradition in the books of Moses nevertheless supposes a pastoralist way of life at several points. The story of Moses and the escape from Egypt repeatedly presents Israel as pastoralist, with primary subsistence from its flocks. In larger terms, even without any connected narrative, this is the social and economic framework that allows the emergence of Israel in a new land by movement from outside.[4]

To a considerable degree, the distinct portrait of herding life in the Joseph story reflects a deep continuity with the account of Israel's escape under Moses in the book of Exodus.[5] One explanation for the similarities between the two narratives may lie in the possibility that they were known in the same scribal circles before they were joined to form one text.[6] As seen in Stephen Russell's recent work (2009) on the early Egypt tradition, the conception of this as an actual escape from the land of Egypt into the people's own land is characteristic

---

[4] The sacred wilderness mountain is in Midianite grazing range, and the Midianite priest joins in worship of Yahweh, as natural common ground (Exod. 18:1–12). Some version of this tradition is picked up in a fragment now located at the end of the Sinai collection. When Israel is ready to move on, Moses expects his Midianite in-laws to move with them (Num. 10:29–30). In the stories of avoiding the eastern neighbors on the way to fight Sihon and Og, Israel is told to pay for what the people and their livestock drink (Deut. 2:6; cf. Num. 20:19). Water is the crucial need for herding peoples, as seen in the conflict at the well shared by the Midianites in Exodus 2.

[5] This continuity is due in part to the current literary connection between the books of Genesis and Exodus, a link that can no longer be assumed to be the work of J and E documents that cross the Torah books. It is clear that the priestly narrative (P) envisions a sequence, but non-priestly possibilities are in dispute, especially Gen. 46:1–5, which reports Jacob's move to Egypt. Whether or not this text is earlier than the priestly narrative, potential links between the books appear to have been composed at a fairly late date, and Israelite perspectives preserved in each may be rooted in each block of material rather than in the act of their combination. Propp (1999, 50–1) defends an early set of links between Genesis and Exodus as part of the Elohistic (E) source, to which he attributes Gen. 50:24–5. His source analysis is derived carefully and independently from his close reading of Exodus, yet he works entirely within the literary-historical framework of J and E documents from early settings, an approach that faces considerable difficulties both in historical terms and in its notion that Genesis and Exodus were joined at such an early date (Schmid 2010).

[6] This appears to be what is envisioned by Konrad Schmid (2010), who understands the first direct literary connection to be that of P, with Gen. 12:10–20 a literary bridge that anticipates the exodus story. Schmid suggests that the typological links between this text and the Moses story reflect knowledge of the exodus narrative without attempt to join them directly. For discussion of the same problem, with argument for pre-priestly (but still not Israelite?) literary links between Genesis and Exodus, see Carr (2001).

of western Israel, and it would not be difficult to imagine both narratives circulating at Bethel.[7]

With this possibility of a shared scribal setting in mind, it is worth noting further expressions of conceptual continuity between the Joseph and exodus narratives. The Joseph story envisions a full-scale sojourn in Egypt for the whole Jacob family, whether or not this sets up the long stay that will result in the exodus with Moses. More specifically, the Joseph and the exodus stories share the notion that the Israelites supported themselves primarily as herdsmen and that this added to their outsider status in Egypt. Joseph's journey to his brothers defines the family in terms of long-distance herding (Gen. 37:12–18). When he makes plans to bring them all to Egypt, Joseph sends a message to his father Jacob: "You will live in the land of Goshen, so you will be close to me – you, and your children, and your children's children, and your flocks, and your herds, and all that you have" (45:10). On Jacob's arrival, Joseph explains how he will smooth the way for Pharaoh's approval: "My brothers and my father's house, who were in the land of Canaan, have come to me. The men are herdsmen of flocks (*ṣō'n*); indeed, they have been men of livestock (*miqneh*). They brought along their flocks, and their herds, and all that they have" (46:31–2). Pharaoh will then ask how they make a living, and they should answer the same way: "Your servants have been men of livestock from our youth until now, us just like our fathers." Based on this, Pharaoh will have them live in the land of Goshen, "because every herdsman of flocks is repugnant to Egypt" (v. 34).

The exodus from Egypt is framed by a similar characterization of Israel.[8] From the beginning, there is never a question of the Israelites sneaking away. Moses and Aaron go to Pharaoh and make the request outright, not for permission to leave permanently but only to travel for three days into the wilderness (*midbār*) to offer sacrifices to Yahweh (Exod. 5:3; cf. v. 1). The god of Israel is not known to Egypt because he has no sanctuary there. People who by custom gather in the wilderness to worship their god must identify themselves and their sustenance by that terrain. The Israelites are primarily herdsmen who have natural affinity with the backcountry east of Egypt. This impression is confirmed by one detail in the unfolding argument between Moses and Pharaoh. When Pharaoh offers his first compromise, that the people could have their feast "in the land" (8:21), Moses counters that "what is sacrificed to Yahweh our god is

---

[7] Russell (2009), chapter 2. Setting aside Exodus itself as of uncertain provenance, Russell begins with the account of the golden calves in 1 Kings 12:25–33 and references to the exodus in Hosea and Amos, prophetic collections with strong connections to Bethel.

[8] David Carr considers the portrayals of pastoralism in the Joseph and the Moses stories to represent a disjunction between the two (2001, 284). Whereas the pastoralist life of Jacob's people is portrayed positively in Gen. 46:31–47:6, the same people are slaves in the Moses story. Instead, I consider the slavery of the exodus tradition to be an overlay, taking for granted the prior tradition of a pastoralist past, which the story does in fact share with the Joseph narrative. Indeed, the slavery theme has nothing to do with the deeper assumption about how Israel lived, and it comes out of the account of escape, without even recognizing the logical tension.

repugnant to Egypt" (v. 22). According to the two narratives that place Israel in Egypt, the stories of Joseph and of Moses, three things can be described, literally, as "the repugnance of Egypt" (*tô'ēbat miṣrayim*). Along with sacrifice to Yahweh in the exodus account, the Joseph story observes that "eating bread with the Hebrew" and "every herdsman of flocks" are repugnant (*tô'ēbâ*) to Egypt (Gen. 43:32; 46:34).[9]

In light of what the Egyptians find "repugnant" in the Joseph story, the repugnance of Yahweh's sacrifices in the Moses tale fits well with a pastoralist way of life. Pharaoh may propose to have Israel celebrate its feast in Egypt, but the only festival in view is one to be held in the wilderness. As told in the combined narrative that survives, the feast actually celebrated by Israel is at the mountain of God (Exod. 18:5, 12), with the priest of a pastoralist people taking a leadership role. Jethro's Midianites are defined by their herding life, as seen in Moses' rescue of his daughters and by the work that brings Moses to the mountain (Exod. 2:16–22; 3:1). With Egypt's "repugnance" as the link between Hebrews and herding, it is perhaps not by accident that "the god of the Hebrews" is the deity who demands worship in the wilderness. Moreover, the pastoralist economic base for the ancestors coming out of Egypt is essential to this Israelite tradition. Certain Torah writing is out of touch with this herding way of life and has lost this thread of Israelite social identity. An idea that was foreign to settled life in the first millennium is preserved unconsciously as part of a tale of older times.

Aside from the language of "repugnance" and its association with herdsmen in the Joseph story, Israel is assumed to live by pastoralism in the exodus/plague narrative on its own. Moses insists that his people must observe their festival for Yahweh with all their livestock; Pharaoh knows that if Israel leaves these behind, Egypt will have them as hostages (Exod. 10:24–6). Once the people leave with their herds and flocks, nothing of value keeps them in Egypt. When Israel finally departs, they take the livestock with them (Exod. 12:31–2). In the distinct tradition of Moses' flight to Midian (chapter 2), we encounter the same social context: he goes to live with herding peoples. It is generally supposed, if anyone thinks twice about it, that escape offered no choice but the wilderness. Egypt's tale of Sinuhe recounts the adventures of a palace official who flees in the face of political instability at home. He makes his way toward Asia,

---

[9] This cluster of objectionable people and practices casts Hebrew identity into association with pastoralism in a way that is not generally assumed. It is possible that the origin of the word "Hebrew" itself derives from the pastoralist way of life associated with the contrast between Egyptians and the people of Jacob that survives in both of these stories (see Fleming, forthcoming b). There is no hint that in the time of biblical writing, the pastoralist associations of the word "Hebrew" were remembered. They are preserved only indirectly through a story that depends on the identity of Israel's ancestors as both herdsmen and, in Egyptian eyes, outsider Hebrews. Redford (1970, 235) considers such "racial exclusion" to date from the Saite and Persian periods, when racial tensions in Egypt were strong – as opposed to the New Kingdom. It is not necessary, however, to envision a writer who has been in Egypt, especially during a time when Jews were there. The whole idea of being "Hebrew" puts them in a larger class, not limited to Israel.

like Moses, but chooses first of all the major centers, including Byblos. Sinuhe ends up with the king of "Upper Retenu," some part of Palestine, a place of great agricultural wealth: figs, grapes, barley, and emmer (lines 80–5).[10] Moses chooses otherwise, reflecting a different perception of the early alternative to settled Egypt. In the Israelite tradition of Moses, he goes to live with people like his own. Jacob does the same thing when he flees Esau to live with Laban among herdsmen, as if this choice was automatic.

It seems that both the Joseph and the exodus stories envision an abiding dependence on herding and a capacity for mobility before Israel's settlement in its own land. Both narratives are framed by movement of a whole people across considerable distance, from the southern Levant to Egypt and then the reverse. It is not even clear that the scale of the two movements should be considered to be massively different. Jacob's family arrives in Egypt as a community of households built around many brothers, easily a group in the hundreds.[11] Without the priestly preoccupation with counting, the exodus numbers are not obviously on a larger scale.[12] Two midwives are sufficient to help all Israel with its births (Exod. 1:15). No distinction of tribes or brothers is declared, and the people are always simply "Israel." In the perspective of first-millennium Israel, the ancestors who preceded establishment in the land as independent peoples had to be mobile and live as herdsmen because they did not yet control the land they occupied.[13] The herding tradition is maintained as an explanation for how to live without land of one's own, not because the storytellers kept any direct awareness of such pastoralist life.

3. The Wilderness in Judahite Perspective

It is possible that Israelite tradition preserves the notion of a pastoralist heritage with a sense of its viability that is diminished in later Judahite perspective,

[10] On Sinuhe's flight and the portrayal of the Levant in this Egyptian story, see Morenz (1997); Morschauser (2000); Obsomer (1999); Rainey (2006b).

[11] This vision does not require the specific number twelve, which is only found in Joseph's second dream (Gen. 37:9–10) and not in the long set of exchanges between Joseph and his brothers in chapters 42–5. Benjamin's presence may assume the full number, but the failure to mention it is notable.

[12] At the start of the book of Exodus, Israel is said to have multiplied tremendously (1:7), so that a "new king" (not called "Pharaoh") complains that they have become too numerous and may join Egypt's enemies (1:9–10). This theme never reappears in the actual exodus account, with its plagues, and it should be attributed to a revision. Even when Pharaoh accuses Israel of evil intent, because Moses insists that the whole population must go, including women and children, there is no question of numbers or supporting Egypt's enemies (10:8–11). For the enormous numbers, see 600,000 in Exod. 12:37.

[13] On the *ḥērem*, see Monroe (2007; 2011, chapter 3). The idea that a people must destroy entirely the resident populations of settlements in territory to be taken over is not standard to ancient Near Eastern warfare, and it seems to be associated particularly with groups that have traditions of prior mobility. In the context of Israel, it may then be that this way of thinking belongs to the same wider notion that associated taking over a new land from outside with pastoralism. Before occupying Israel, the people had to have been mobile – even if any specific memory of such a time is remote and beyond reach.

even if ways of life had changed among both peoples. In later texts that appear to be Judahite, it was a miracle that the ancestors survived the deadly desert. I begin with Deuteronomy 8, at the center of the book's programmatic speech and definitive D voice, whether it dates to the seventh or the sixth century.[14] Moses contrasts Israel's coming wealth and luxury with the hardship of the wilderness. Without the miraculous provision of manna (v. 3), the people would have gone hungry. After they settle in this land of plenty, there is a danger that the people will forget Yahweh, who supplies their every need. Yahweh's qualities are defined by action: "the one who caused you to travel in the great and fearsome desert, (with) venomous snake and scorpion, a place of thirst, without water" (v. 15). For the writer of Deuteronomy 8, the *midbār* is truly a "desert," not merely the open country away from settlement, a neutral "wilderness." Because of the utter barrenness of this wasteland, Yahweh had to provide water from the rock and, again, manna as food.[15]

Modern readers of the finished text will rarely flinch at this bleak description. Prepared by familiarity with the manna story of Exodus 16, we assume that this portrait of desolation is universal. It is not obvious, however, that any Israelite tradition shares the idea that the wilderness was barren and required divine intervention for survival. According to the Israelite perspective underlying Deuteronomy 2–3, the wilderness is certainly large, but the issue of deprivation does not come up.[16] Israel spends a long period in or near the Seir

---

[14] On recent approaches to dating different material in Deuteronomy, see Römer (2005, 73–81). Römer distinguishes a first edition that reflects the influence of Assyrian literature, especially the loyalty oaths of Esarhaddon (seventh century). This collection emphasized centralization and loyalty: Deut. 6:4–5 as the opening, and chapter 28 as the conclusion; with legal material including chapters 12–13; 14:21–9 (taxes); 15 (social prescriptions); 16:1–17 (festivals); 16:18 and 17:8–13 (judges and officers, without reference to a king); 18:1–8 (priestly income); chapter 19 (cities of refuge); parts of chapters 21–5 (social and cultic laws); and closing with 26:2, 3a, and 10–11, before the curses in chapter 28. The literary fiction of the book as Moses' departing speech reflects the situation after the fall of Judah to Babylon at the end of the sixth century (p. 124). "The theme of the land becomes dominant in 8:7–20*; 9:1, 4–6*: in Deuteronomy 8 it is opposed to the wilderness, which is described as a space of death and danger where Israel could only survive with Yahweh's help" (p. 130). There is no allusion to rebellion, the later theme that dominates the book of Numbers, and so this material stands closer to Jer. 2:4–9, which is from the sixth century. Not all would now agree that Deuteronomy is based at all on a perspective during Judah's monarchy (so Pakkala 2009).

[15] The theme of miraculous provision also appears in Ps. 78:15–41, in a pattern that may be charted as water–rebellion–manna–birds–rebellion–wonders – deeply dependent on the full Torah narrative; Ps. 105:40–41, with reference to quail, bread of heaven, and water; Ps. 106:13–15, on craving, rebellion, and Yahweh's provision; and Neh. 9:19–21, mentioning manna and water. The stories of complaint have been understood as an old and persistent element of the Torah narrative, reflecting the traditional earlier dates for J and E documents (so, Frakel 2002, 314–17). Based on comparison with references in the prophetic writings and the Psalms, however, Römer (2007) now proposes that the entire theme of complaint is a later development from after the exile.

[16] The reference to Yahweh's provision in Deut. 2:7 is attached to the idea that the people spent forty years there, which appears to be part of a separate, non-Israelite tradition of a rebellious generation that needed to die before the land could be taken.

hills, habitable land shared by their brothers, the sons of Esau (2:1–4). The same "great and fearsome desert" introduces the scouting story in Deut. 1:19, but this opening section is probably a later contribution to the book's vision (vv. 19–21).

It is possible that the stories of how Yahweh provides manna and quail as food (Exodus 16 and Numbers 11) have no Israelite component. Both chapters are composed with a dominant priestly perspective that may depend on prior tradition. No part of the manna or quail narratives, however, suggests either identifiable Israelite content or any connection with other Israelite narrative. The statement of the manna's disappearance in Josh. 5:12 is associated with the Passover and probably depends on priestly influence.[17] Manna is mentioned also in the recapitulation of the origins stories in Psalm 78:12–31, a text that combines many of the major ingredients of the finished Torah. Yahweh splits the sea for Israel to pass through (v. 13), and he provides both manna (v. 24) and birds (v. 27) for food. Similarly, Psalm 105 recounts how Yahweh supplied quail and "the bread of heaven," along with water from the rock (vv. 40–1). It seems that Judahite writing, generally later than Israelite tradition and reinterpreting the Israelite narrative that it inherited, subtly redirected the wilderness element.[18] When they emphasize the barrenness of the "desert," Judahite writers only display the assumptions of their own interpretation. They take for granted that Israel had come through a wasteland that was truly uninhabitable.[19]

It is odd that Judah would not have preserved a comparable view of Israel's wilderness heritage. The explanation must not lie in contrasting ways of life during the later monarchic period and afterward, in spite of local variety in subsistence practices across both realms. It appears instead that the perspective of Judahite writing reflects the recycling of a tradition original to Israel and reinterpreted by those with new objectives. The contrast has to do above all with continuity of tradition, and its lack. Israelite narrative does not consciously portray the early people as pastoralists so much as leave intact the elements that assume this life. It is less clear whether the tone of the recasting reflects any current dimension of the social and intellectual world of the Judah scribes. Writing from Judah seems to derive mainly from Jerusalem circles, and it may be that these distanced themselves in a new way from the wilderness of a pastoralist age, perhaps reflecting the impact of the large Jerusalem center, and its enduring reputation even after 586. This trend would reflect not so much a later date than those of various Israelite traditions as the particular attitudes among the educated class at the Jerusalem capital in the last two centuries

---

[17] See the discussion in Rose (1981, 52, etc.).

[18] Brettler (2007) considers that while Psalm 105 shows familiarity with both J and P versions of the Exodus plague stories, the primary source is J. My point is that the psalm combines sources and relies on Judah perspectives when it reaches the tales of God's provision in the wilderness.

[19] This perspective is missing from the wilderness as perceived in Hosea; see the discussion in Dozeman (2000); Römer (2007, 430); Russell (2009, 55–63).

before its destruction at the hands of Babylon. The region of Judah itself was more sparsely populated in the Late Bronze Age and settled later in the Iron Age than places further north (Finkelstein 1988).

B. Israelite Biblical Narrative

At the center of this long section on Israelite content in the Bible stands the notion that recognizing this material is essential to understanding the shape of the narrative that extends from Genesis and the Torah through Kings at the end of the Former Prophets. I have expressed this notion by the hypothesis that every major framing idea about Israel before the monarchy originates in Israelite writing. While such a sweeping statement begs to be contradicted, it is in fact intended to be flexible, open to adaptation as the evidence develops. Equally, it is intended as a generalization, qualified by what I consider subsidiary categories of Judahite expansion. At every level, the hypothesis of Israelite inspiration for the story of early Israel offers a foundation for understanding the existing form of a Bible created as the sacred writings for the Jewish people, the people of Judah. Book by book, the Bible takes its shape from the needs and scribal habits of people from Judah through centuries after Israel the kingdom had been dismantled, and its people no longer maintained recognizably distinct communities.

Now that we have reviewed a cross-section of the biblical history, with emphasis on the periods before the monarchy, it may be useful to consider what this history looks like in purely Israelite terms. One general point is crucial: the Israelite material gathered in the preceding review does not represent a single Israelite history and is certainly not a single Israelite document or source. We cannot say that the scribes of Israel had no sense of a connected past; we have too little evidence to know this. The limited evidence of the Bible, however, suggests that Israelite scribes never attempted to create a connected text or set of texts that would treat the past or some large segment of it as a whole. Israelite stories about the past were conceived on a more limited basis. Many of them suggest a background in tales that may have been rendered independently, without incorporation into any collection. One expression of this lack of connection is the idiosyncratic Benjaminite combination of war with Israel and Saul's heroic leadership. At the same time, much of the Israelite material in the Bible appears to have undergone an early phase of combination with other narrative so as to produce a modest complex with some wider object, still to serve readers or hearers from Israel, either before its political end or soon enough afterward to preserve a definable Israelite identity.[20] Of course, how and how long such could have continued remain pressing questions. These Israelite collections offer an important alternate view of the past, without the

---

[20] Significantly, the Benjamin material was not incorporated into any Israel combination or collection, but must have been preserved in Benjamin for its own sake. It was brought into larger biblical narrative only by connection with the existing Saul–David text.

assumptions of Judah's world. For the following summary of Israel's contribution, we follow the chronology of the current Bible.

1. *The Ancestors*

Israel's ideas about the remote past begin less with a sense of chronological distance than with the logical starting point for explaining identity in family terms, by kinship. Even in its finished form, the book of Genesis is still governed by this idea, and at least in this broad sense, Israel contributed this entire category to the biblical narrative. Israel as a people may be understood as a large and thriving family, numerous sons from one father and different mothers. The very number of sons proves success, as divine approval and provision. This family of Jacob, which was not based on a specific count of offspring, such as twelve or ten, is the focus of the ancestral framework. Israel's decentralized nature is the very point: it is a coalition, an association forged from discrete units that must find some basis for unity. As a family, the bonds are resilient, even where they do not prevent conflict. The cycle of Jacob's flight to Syria and return to his homeland in Genesis 27–33 was constructed from diverse materials with different origins, with the result still reflecting an Israelite setting, more likely in the west – perhaps at Bethel – than in the east. This cycle adds one generation before Jacob in his father Isaac, through whom a relationship with Esau or Edom as twin brother is defined. A further genealogical step back may be found in Abraham as ancestral participant in the treaty with Laban, who is represented by Nahor in a comparable role.

These more distant figures function under the same logic as Jacob's family: paternity accounts for relationships between offspring. It is therefore not necessary to seek separate Abraham and Isaac peoples; the role of these patriarchs was to explain how their offspring were associated. Outside the Jacob cycle, Abraham and Isaac have developed further narrative roles, not evidently derived from their Jacob appearances, and both display links to lands south of Israel's kingdom. One key part of the Abraham–Isaac narrative is the sequence that introduces Lot as Abraham's kin, from whom will stem the peoples of Moab and Ammon. It is not clear from the Genesis texts whether the Abraham–Lot narrative came into the Bible through Israel or through Judah, but an Israelite setting cannot be ruled out. The eastern conquest narrative of Deuteronomy 2–3, which treats this part of Israel as a divine grant rather than as an accident, seems to have Israelite roots and identifies Moab and Ammon as "the sons of Lot."

At the end of Genesis, the Joseph story reveals its heritage in Israel by the name of its protagonist, who would naturally be identified with Bethel. In its extant form, this story could provide evidence for the survival of some Israelite lore in scribal circles that remained separate from Judah custom, whether at old Israelite sites such as Bethel or in refugee communities that survived in Jerusalem or other towns of Judah. The one part of Genesis that seems to take even its basic form from a Judahite setting is the prologue assembled at the front of the book, with creation and flood at center. None of this material shows an

Israelite interest, and Jerusalem would supply the most obvious location for its composition and transmission.

2. Establishment in the Land

Israelite content in the Bible offers no general account of how Israel was established in its own land. The longest story that addresses the question is most occupied with Moses' stubborn negotiation with Egypt's pharaoh, who is willing to let his people endure one disaster after another rather than let the people of Yahweh go out into the wilderness to worship him. This is a tale of how Israel got out of Egypt, not an explanation of settlement and political control. It assumes a striking distance from the land and some kind of transition, undefined. Moses is a prophet, a spokesman for Yahweh, not a military leader. If there is a destination, it is only the wilderness, where the people are to worship Yahweh.

Isolated Israelite traditions provide the basis for the biblical scheme of conquest, without envisioning a systematic invasion. One group accompanies Moses from the southern wilderness of Seir, their home for an unspecified time, past the peoples of Esau, Moab, and Ammon to the eastern kingdoms of Sihon and Og, which Yahweh has handed over to them. In an unrelated tale, Joshua leads Israel to victory over Ai, in the western highlands not far from Bethel. No point of origin is specified. The story of all-out war against Benjamin may originate in a similar concept, taken up by the people of Benjamin themselves as background to resuscitation under Saul. These stories have in common the notion that occupation of new land requires the defeat of its controlling towns and the total extermination of their populations, under the oversight of Yahweh as god of the people established thereby. This *ḥērem* practice was not a general approach to warfare; rather, it applied specifically to the first creation of a new polity in a new place, based on the assumption of one population replacing another.

The finished Torah brings Israel from Egypt to Mount Sinai and from there into the wilderness, where they must waste forty years waiting for a rebellious generation to die, so that their more innocent children can inherit the Promised Land. The route toward that land finally moves from south to north through Jordan, constrained by the inherited tale of Sihon and Og. This leaves the Promised Land to the west, and Israel must cross the river in order to invade, with Jericho the first target. The combination of eastern and western conflicts into one campaign is a later and Judahite project. Nevertheless, each main element of the present exodus–conquest scheme appears to originate in Israel. The people lived under Egyptian power, which became oppressive, perhaps by preventing them from circulating into the eastern backcountry as was their custom. They took over the urban centers of a land that had not been under their own control, and this shift was associated with a previous life in the wilderness. This new land was not to be had without a fight. Even the idea that Yahweh met the people at his sacred mountain seems to have Israelite seeds, though the tradition of instruction passed on through Moses is so laden with

Judah's religious commitments that it is difficult to penetrate to a demonstrably Israelite background.

Unlike the ancestral family of Genesis, the various accounts of how Israel came to be established in their own land do not delineate separate peoples. In each story, the unity of one people against its enemies is emphasized, though this need not assume an emphasis on the unity of Israel's actual constituent groups, as if all were present in every tale. Joshua's defeat of Ai pits "Israel" against an enemy to be annihilated and supplanted, but this may be understood as a local manifestation of the biblical people, not identical to the eastern groups that took the lands of Sihon and Og. It does not perhaps matter which representatives of Israel shared Moses' experience in Egypt, so long as the later people by that name partake of the victory. This attitude toward participation by representation contrasts with the birth narrative of Genesis 30 and the hero stories in Judges, which address directly the need for different Israelite peoples to see themselves as a whole, beneath their individual identities. In the books of Exodus through Joshua, only later Judahite writers merged these approaches into one. They created from these isolated episodes a single journey from Egypt to the Promised Land, with stops at Mount Sinai and Mount Pisgah, east of the Jordan River. They explained the awkward route and evident delay by the people's own unwillingness to accept the gift granted by their god. And they made sure that everyone was accounted for at every stage of the journey, so that all the tribes moved together in a grand parade. Naturally, then, the invasion of the land demanded the participation of every group, including those who had just found their own new homes to the east in Jordan. The book of Joshua is a very Judahite product, built from this desire to systematize, yet it was likewise created from the skeleton of Israelite ideas about how the people began.

3. Life before and after David

The book of Judges is a biblical marvel, by itself a vivid signal that Judah grappled awkwardly sometimes with a tradition that was not finally its own. Whereas a book such as Joshua integrates Judah into the history of Israel by giving it proud priority in the conquest and apportionment of land, Judges offers little conceptual space for Judah, which seems to have preserved no old stories of its own as a contribution. Israel's actual existence as a people in a particular land, a people who could leave remains capable of historical study through excavation, begins in the Bible with the book of Judges. This is the one biblical book that treats such a period before kings, and every bit of lore that reflected life and leadership on other terms found its way into Judges, however late the addition. There is abundant evidence for editing and further elaboration of Judges in Judahite hands, and yet with each new version, only stories about non-Judahite groups were put forward. Judah simply did not have tales about its own people before kings.[21] This contrast between Israel

---

[21] One could regard the story of Judah and Tamar in Genesis 38 as a counterexample. This tale works from the received notion of an ancestral family, and it offers an account of Judah's basic

and Judah has enormous political ramifications: Judah did not define itself outside the house of David and its kingdom; Israel existed without kings and regarded monarchy as an appendage.

In the material gathered for this period before kings, no durable government is suggested. Individual heroes arose to meet individual crises, and with the collection headed by Ehud, the unity of Israel is expressed in the participation of different groups. The Song of Deborah alone celebrates the benefits of coalition, with the impression from the mustered peoples confirmed by identification of all as "Israel" in the prologue. At the same time, Israel may be embodied by representatives from a more limited region, as in the prose rendition of Barak's battle, with only Zebulun and Naphtali at his back.

Judah's first major contribution to the Bible's history is David and his royal house, and this narrative was based on old material that recalled the founder purely as king of Israel. David's appearance is recalled in the longest early narrative of the whole sequence, which now fills the two books of Samuel and which was framed as a combined account of Saul and David. By casting David's kingship as a replacement for Saul's, the Saul–David complex serves to introduce the entire transition to the monarchic government known to the early biblical writers from Israel and Judah. It is not clear that the Israelite material for Saul even identified him as a "king," so that the Bible may preserve no Israelite account of how its own monarchy arose as an institution. The independent Saul material that may once have been attached to the Benjamin war at the end of Judges treated this leader more in the mode of Israel's heroes, as found in Judges 3–9 and the account of Jephthah. With the arrival of David, kingship is established through rule of Israel alone, not as a "united monarchy." Although the books of Samuel recognize Israel's political integrity as a body capable of decision without kings, the unity of this body is always the issue in question: what will Israel do? Will it accept a given leadership? This focus on Israel as a single unit is the natural extension of the monarchic interest that guides the remaining history, the last books of which are appropriately named "Kings."

Once the division into two kingdoms is acknowledged in 1 Kings 12, the narrative bounces between Israel and Judah with conscious effort to align their individual progress. In the section occupied with the two kingdoms, from 1 Kings 12 to 2 Kings 17, Israel is colored throughout by "the sin of Jeroboam," its first ruler after separation. No Israelite ruler can come away innocent, even when the material suggests or attracts sympathetic themes, as with Jehu's assault on Baal. In spite of repeated references to the Annals of the Kings of Israel, and of Judah, nothing in these books indicates citation from any such chronicles. The one account that most plausibly derives from Israel directly is that of Omri, which at least reflects the structure of a royal inscription in its reports on how he came to power and then how he built Samaria as a new

division into clans, all with a moralizing tone that both allows ancestral failure and emphasizes willingness to provide justice in the end. It does not have to do with Judah as a people.

capital. With the establishment of Samaria, Israelite monarchy became a more effective centralizing force, even if regional identities remained important. The capital did not move again until the Assyrian conquest, and Jehu's royal house lasted longer than any other before his. Although the books of Kings provided a home for one more block of writing with Israelite roots, the collections surrounding the prophets Elijah and Elisha, Judah became the ultimate focus, and its defeat by Babylon the ultimate destination. The organizing principal was the fidelity of kings, with history determined by royal character, an interpretation that reflects the centralizing assumptions of Judah, Jerusalem, and the house of David.

The Bible's history from Genesis through Kings thus concludes according to a structure from Judah, in fact from its great contribution to this rendition of the past. Kingship dominates the long latter part of the historical narrative, as assembled in 1 and 2 Samuel and 1 and 2 Kings. From the moment when the monarchy is launched through the struggle between Saul and David, the future of Yahweh's people is understood to be driven above all by the choices of kings. This perspective is very much native to Judah, even though none of this writing can be interpreted plausibly as the direct product of royal scribes in the production of official court documents. Israel's kings would also have attempted to gather power to themselves, as is clear from the very pattern suggested in the construction of Samaria by Omri and the maintenance of a longstanding royal house by Jehu. The Bible's heritage of Israelite lore, however, has little interest in kings. In Judah's Bible, with David the royal prototype, there was probably little room for a competing literature of northern kings, and it was the portrait by collage for a time before monarchy that attracted a Judahite audience – a time that defined Israel as a people. The absence of Israelite royal narrative is not hard to understand in this Judahite product. What is more striking, and is the driving interest of this book, is the absence of an original narrative framework for the beginnings and early life of Judah before David.

PART III

COLLABORATIVE POLITICS

II

Collaborative Politics

As I have envisioned Israel and Judah, these two kingdoms do not represent two segments of a single people with a seamless shared culture. Their differences reflect more than geographical variety, and the political contrasts embodied in the two kingdoms represent more than local developments constructed on the same historical foundation. Indeed, there were local differences that had a geographical component, and each kingdom developed along distinct lines. More deeply, however, Israel formed a political identity without need of kings, and monarchy was added to this identity. Israel was an association of peoples from different environments in the southern Levant, both west and east of the Jordan River, both north and south of the Jezreel Valley. The political character of decentralized alliance then persisted under kings, in spite of natural royal efforts to augment individual power, and the Bible preserves a number of different expressions of this decentralized and noncentralizing inclination. In contrast, the realm finally called Judah in the books of Kings came into existence only because the ruler from David's line refused to be deposed and took refuge in Jerusalem, where he could hold power over a reduced southern domain. This southern kingdom came to be called Judah, probably an old name linked to the highlands south of Jerusalem. With Jerusalem as sacred and political center, as well as the original power base for defining such a southern polity as a single unit, this kingdom was shaped by a different logic, and the interplay of individual authority with alternative influences would never have been the same as in Israel. I have chosen to call the strong tradition of decentralized power in Israel "collaborative politics."

In constructing a train of thought for this project as a whole, my priority has been to define the contrast between Israel and Judah and then to gather a set of texts that demonstrate the phenomenon of a separate Israelite perspective in the Bible. Having outlined the biblical situation, it is now essential to probe further the phenomenon of collaborative politics in itself. In the Near East, Israel did not exist in a vacuum, and the particular combination of monarchy with associated peoples or tribes appears not to have been rare, though the sources for ancient writing rarely describe it from personal experience. The one body of literature in which such an insider view is expressed in rich variety is the royal correspondence of the palace at Mari in early second-millennium Syria. Many of the peoples attested in the Mari archives belong to the heritage known as Amorite, and this material offers an important historical point of reference. Later, at the end of the second millennium and during the early part of the first, the Arameans display similar social structures, though the written evidence for them is more limited. Together, the Amorites and the Arameans provide a context for the appearance and social character of Israel in the Iron Age southern Levant.

Beyond the ancient Near East, the coexistence of individual political power with alternatives rooted in the larger populace has been a historical commonplace, as has been the difficulty in getting a clear view of the identities that shape these alternatives. Archaeology can suggest their existence, though there can be a tendency to resort to collaborative forms only in the absence of highly developed central authority. In other ancient settings, as in the Near East, extensive writing tends to be produced under the auspices of the center. The last generation of archaeology has generated some dissatisfaction with the limits of past analytical frameworks for the collaborative or collective dimension of political life. Two theoretical initiatives, using the language of "heterarchy" and "corporate" political strategy, contribute to a systematic reevaluation of the structures by which we interpret evidence for early Israel and the Near East. The same effort to acknowledge a greater variety of social and political configurations has led to fresh study of individual regions and peoples, which likewise can illuminate the character of Israel.

A. Kingdoms, States, and Tribes

To locate Israel in a larger conversation about the nature of ancient society, it is necessary to make conscious choices regarding terminology as this relates to interpretive frameworks. Much of the archaeologically based discussion of early Israel has revolved around the category of ethnicity, which will be addressed in Chapter 15, and the emergence of the state.[1] For my focus on the contrasting political characters of Israel and Judah, the latter discussion is directly relevant, yet the terminology of the "state" and its implications are problematic. In the evolutionary framework of Elman Service (1975), the state and the tribe are mutually exclusive categories, manifestations of radically different stages in social development. Tribal organization reflects relatively simple social structure and is associated with smaller groups, while the state

---

[1] For one recent example, see the "Forum" of comments by several archaeologists and historians in *NEA* 70 (2007), in response to Avraham Faust on "Rural Settlements, State Formation, and 'Biblical Archaeology'" (4–9).

represents the culmination of a process that produces complex structures for large-scale entities. In ancient social landscapes of the sort that included Israel, as well as the contemporary Arameans and the Amorite peoples before them, tribal organization is one dimension of complex social systems that included substantial kingdoms. While growth and change certainly took place among each of these groups, the standard approach to "state formation" is not the most effective vehicle for exploring the relationships between centralizing and distributed, collaborative decision-making in Israel and similar polities.

1. The Kingdom

Although the biblical narrative of early Israel is intensely interested in how this people began, including a period without kings, the first period of significant biblical composition was almost certainly monarchic. The Bible was constructed for the survivors of Judah, and some uncertain but very large portion of its contents was created in this postexilic Judahite environment. Other large portions of the Bible, such as the collection of writings in the prophetic voice, were inspired by life under kings, especially those of Judah. The primary narrative of the Bible from Genesis through the books of Kings, however, is occupied with even earlier periods, and it is difficult to judge the antiquity of its origins. Whatever written and oral background these older elements may have had, the older directly retrievable narrative or compositional strands often date most plausibly to the time of the two kingdoms, Israel and Judah. One example is the sayings of Jacob, cited just previously, which are attributed to the ancestor of high antiquity and yet which acknowledge openly the reality of monarchy.

If we set aside for the moment the concept of the state, from which historians demand a certain level of complexity, scale, and institutionalized order, what we find in the biblical account is kingship. Among various leadership titles, the one that demands the respect of institutional continuity is the *melek*, usually translated "king." In the finished primary narrative, this is the type of leader requested by the elders of Israel from Samuel when they judge his sons inadequate to inherit his role (1 Sam. 8:5). The earlier materials for the life of Saul do not appear to identify him by this title, but the texts that are concerned to account for Saul as David's predecessor work explicitly with this category.[2] At the crucial moment when divine favor is transferred from Saul to David, Samuel tells Saul that Yahweh has "torn the kingship (*mamlĕkût*) of Israel" from him like the corner of Samuel's robe that has just torn away in Saul's hands (1 Sam. 15:28). Samuel grieves at this loss, and Yahweh comforts him with the declaration that one of Jesse's sons will replace Saul as *melek*

---

[2] The old tale of Saul's victory over the Ammonites in 1 Sam. 11:1–11 does not call him *melek*, a term only introduced with the framing narrative around this (10:19, 24; cf. the cognate verb in 11:12, 15). When Saul is introduced in the story of the lost donkeys in 1 Sam. 9:1–10:16, Samuel anoints him as *nāgîd*, a title for leadership that appears preparatory to monarchy (9:16; 10:1).

(1 Sam. 16:1). In the full books of Samuel and Kings, the institution of king-ship appears to be identified especially with David, and Saul must be identified as a king because the keepers of David's lore understood him to have competed with a prior power in the house of Saul.

With the overlap of writing transmitted in Judah and contents defined by Israel, this account of David replacing Saul is difficult to parse for its concept of kingship. It appears that kings are expected to pass the title on to a son, as played out in the competition for David's role that finally leaves Solomon in power (1 Kings 1). Yet Samuel's sons are assumed to take over his leadership until the elders refuse this (1 Sam. 8:5). Saul establishes no new capital and builds no palace, in contrast to David, whose first act is to take Jerusalem from the Jebusites to make it a royal capital. David is not said to build a palace, an endeavor attributed only to Solomon (1 Kings 7:1). His role as "king" may be expressed instead in the lines that follow a list of his military achievements:

David ruled as king (*yimlōk*) over all Israel, and David ensured justice and fairness for all his people. Joab son of Zeruiah was over the army; Jehoshaphat son of Ahilud was record-keeper;[3] Zadok son of Ahitub and Ahimelech son of Abiathar were priests; Seraiah was scribe; Benaiah son of Jehoiada was (over) the Cherethite and the Pelethite; the sons of David were priests. (2 Sam. 8:15–18)

The focus of these lines is institutional, with roles defined that have precedence over the people assigned to them. In what is probably a Judah-based frame-work, the royal administration incorporates sacred roles as priests – not only for specialists outside the king's family but also for the king's own sons. There is a fixed military leader over an "army" (*ṣābā'*), not defined as "the people" (*'ām*), and two different administrative roles are named, at least one of which requires writing.

For my purposes here, it is unnecessary to undertake a full definition of kingship from this or other biblical material. The point is that biblical writers had something formal in mind when they applied the term *melek*, and they themselves struggle to explain its essential features at the time of its origins. In spite of the limits inherent in a Judahite point of view, David's kingship does not appear to be equated with the full apparatus of the late Jerusalem-based monarchy. We have no counterpart for the kingdom of Israel after Jeroboam I, though the Bible suggests noticeable differences between the two domains, with both structures associated with the *melek* terminology (see Chapter 18). In each case, the king embodies an impulse to draw decision-making toward a single center with a durable institutional structure, the physical manifestation of which comes to be a palace and its administration. This does not mean that as head of "state," the king or his elite circle held all power in the form of coercive force.

---

[3] The word *mazkîr* refers to "one who calls to mind," which McCarter (1984) renders as a "remembrancer."

Biblical writers made an effort to schematize the political traditions of Israel, so that stories of constituent peoples or tribes acting as independent players are gathered into the book of Judges. It is nevertheless unlikely that tribal structures were confined to a period before kings, particularly when the Judges stories must have been transmitted through the monarchic age. The clearest example of tribes coexisting with kingship is found in the core of the Jacob sayings in Genesis 49, where Asher is said to provide "delicacies for the king" (v. 20). In the book of Judges, the groups that hold such standing as members of an Israelite political community are often simply identified by name, without an overarching category. Genesis 49:17, however, applies the word *šēbeṭ*, which is sensibly rendered "tribe," as it becomes the Bible's dominant rubric for Israel's composition from the tradition of Jacob's family. Any historical account of the Israelite monarchy must build in a place for these tribes and the centrifugal counterbalance to individual power that they represent.[4]

2. Tribe and State

I have chosen to avoid the term "state" in the context of this investigation. The category is widely used in discussion of ancient societies, applied to the polities of most institutionalized governance, often of largest scale and complexity.[5] While I do not insist that the term must be abandoned for application to antiquity, I find that its use tends to be prejudiced toward individualized and centralized authority, and it is often embedded in a problematic scheme that makes it the evolutionary successor of tribes and chiefdoms.[6] Because the Bible, along with other writing from the ancient Near East, offers its own terminology for isolating institutional political power with an individual head, I will speak of kings and kingship where specifically relevant and leadership where the categories are less precise or clearly defined. I embrace the term "tribe" as translating efficiently a mode of social and political organization that provides the possibility of association as peers, sometimes under the ideal of kinship.

The challenge, then, is to establish a conceptual system capable of integrating tribes and monarchy in what Adam Smith would call a political landscape.

---

[4] For study of a decentralized political landscape, power is better understood as multidirectional. In this respect, I am sympathetic to Michael Mann's formulation of social power composed of "networks" defined by various relationships between people and groups (1986, 1–2). Daniel Miller and Christopher Tilley (1984, 5) undertake to define power in a way that avoids polarized oppositions: individual versus collective, intentional (by agents) or structural, repressive or productive. As they define it, "power to" is "a positive social force intimately involved in the production, reproduction and transformation of the social order" (7).

[5] See, e.g., Liu and Chen (2003); Feinman and Marcus (1998); Yoffee (2005).

[6] Adam Smith (2003, 94–102) seems to have reached a similar conclusion in his study of the political landscape. Aside from his systematic critique of the category, it obscures rather than illuminates the object of study. Smith's approach focuses especially on a "relational" definition of space, and he finds that space and place have little role in common theoretical discussion of the state. "[T]he State is built on both an absolute ontology of space and an absolute ontology of politics. . . . But, like space, politics arises in relationships between groups and individuals, not full grown from a repertoire of types" (101–2).

To this end, the new work of Anne Porter (2012) offers one of the most sweeping efforts to start afresh in understanding ancient society, particularly as this includes tribal or kin-based dimensions. For Porter, all of the recent and laudable attempts to reconfigure our interpretive models and terminology have foundered on the isolation of power into a world of "haves," in opposition to all "have-nots": "The end result of all this is ultimately still a problem of agency: only the elite have it."[7] The best reason to continue the theoretical investigation of the ancient state is that it provides unlooked-for ways to think about alternative and substate powers, "many of which are understood to be based in traditional if not archaic ways of being."

This cautious openness to the ancient state as an analytical category brings Porter to the "tribe." Echoing Adam Smith, who discards the term "state" as impossible to define for all its supposed instances, Porter concludes that the "tribe" was set aside by anthropologists because there is "no one set of common features derivable from multiple ethnographic examples that can give rise to a core meaning to this label."[8] The problem is that tribe and state are not categories of the same kind, to be set against one another as alternative formations. Tribal identifications are expressions of kinship as definition of belonging and not, and the important question is, "What is going on that prompts the tribe to behave in an exclusionary – or inclusionary – way?" The tribe itself, if we keep the term, is not in itself a political category, though it has a political aspect that is contingent on the individual features of each one's character and situation. Instead, it "should be defined as a set of *social* relationships based on idioms and/or practices of kinship and descent as the means through which people understand their place in society and the nature of their relationships with others," recognizing that "each group can define both the rules which create their social relationships and the various ways they practice them as they may." Porter thus considers that whereas the state is intrinsically a political category, the tribe is a social category that may be adapted to a variety of political settings and forms. Tribe and state cannot define a dichotomy of mutually exclusive societal types.

In her provocative reevaluation of analytical categories, Porter is ambivalent about the continued use of "tribe," at least as I read her. Although the term may have failed in its academic application, however, it will not go away.[9] In modern settings, this is because so many groups identify themselves as tribes, and it is difficult to find a more effective rubric to describe the cluster of features usually envisioned for such groups. Porter acknowledges that the tribe

---

[7] Chapter 3: "North/South, Tribe/State: False Dichotomies and Third Millennium Polities." Throughout, I cite with appreciation to the author a draft of the manuscript that does not represent its final form.

[8] Also, the notion of "tribal" society has often carried a pejorative association, especially for Africa.

[9] For the reappearance of the tribe in recent archaeological research, see Parkinson (2002).

is here to stay, "[b]ut if in the modern world the tribe cannot be denied, in the ancient world it most certainly can." She would prefer to cull from the tribal category the aspects of group definition and kinship framework, if I may simplify, that remain pertinent to discussions of ancient society. Without attempting to retrace Porter's own exploration of how the elements conventionally attributed to tribe and state mingle in early Near Eastern situations, which she illustrates by taking apart and reordering the usual interpretation of the mid-third-millennium Ebla archives, I return to her observation about modern tribes.

The use of *šēbeṭ* in the Bible does not define a social or political type that is universally applicable to the ancient region or even to Israel narrowly. Nevertheless, it serves an idea of unity among otherwise distinct peoples, a unity that is given in one literary tradition the most explicit kinship framework imaginable, as the family of Jacob. In my discussion of biblical texts, I tried to reserve use of the "tribal" category to this self-identification as a collection of *šēbāṭîm* ("tribes") and otherwise to speak of "peoples" or "groups." Accepting Porter's argument that such kinship-based identity is social, without a particular political formulation associated with it, the indigenous construction of Israelite tribes as a set represented one conceptual solution to the political problem of coordinated action among distinct peoples. Eventually, the system of twelve tribes became part of an idealized past, with no political relevance to the survivors of Judah. In its creation, however, "the tribes of Israel" represented one dimension of Israel's decentralized political landscape, and this aspect makes them significant for historical study.

B. Approaches to Collaborative Politics

I have described the political landscape of early first-millennium Israel as decentralized, even when it was ruled by kings. This terminology is practical and simply descriptive, but it is also negative, defined by alternatives to the center. Also, this decentralization stands in tension with the obvious political center represented by the monarchy, along with the newly stable administrative center established by Omri at Samaria.[10] Nevertheless, I have proposed to apply the biblical material from Israel to historical questions about Israel, beginning with the Bible's evidence for a nonroyal political tradition of separate regional actors and a collective capacity separate from kings. In the study of premodern societies, the past generation has brought increasing interest in such alternatives to centralized political power, and my own work benefits from the conversation that has surrounded various expressions of this phenomenon.

---

[10] Judah represents a separate case, with the southern kingdom defined first of all by the retreat of Rehoboam to his Jerusalem capital when deposed by Israel (see Chapter 18). The collective structures that the Bible associates with Judah's kingdom, such as the *'am hā'āreṣ* ("people of the land") may not arise until the growth of the capital in the eighth century.

As a positive definition of decentralization, I speak of "collaborative politics." Where the "collective" implies a process and results that serve some unity, "collaboration" identifies the only way to achieve results when neither individual authority nor the unifying imperative of tradition can be assumed. This terminology does nevertheless characterize the phenomenon by the possibility of concerted action by otherwise distinct political entities. In describing social units in action I may use the generic term "polity," with the "political" referring to joint action or organization by groups beyond the familial level. The term "politics" is fraught with questions of scale, and I prefer to apply it more rather than less broadly. Certainly, "political" activity and organization need not be restricted to states or kingdoms. The entire analysis of "factions" in premodern settings is based on the identifications of subsidiary actors in larger polities, groups "whose single function appears to be gaining access to limited physical and social resources."[11] In ancient Israel, such factions could in theory include elites with shared access to power by means other than longstanding organization by town or "tribe," but it appears that both regional centers and regional peoples were basic constituents of the whole. So far as the activities of peoples such as Gad or Gilead and settlements such as Shechem or Shiloh impinge on the actions and identity of Israel as a unit, I consider these activities "political."

As a whole, the analysis of factions assumes that more "complex" societies are dominated by individual leaders and that "factional competition" plays out in reference to a well-defined center.[12] In the following discussion, I focus instead on two almost concurrent initiatives: Carole Crumley's "heterarchy" (1995) and the "corporate political strategy" of Richard Blanton and Gary Feinman (Blanton et al. 1996). Both of these approaches have attracted attention among archaeologists working with politically diverse settings, and location of ancient Israel in a general conversation about premodern politics brings them into consideration. It must be kept in mind that this is not a literature on democratic politics, and I do not characterize these phenomena as democracy, although the background to Greek democracy may be studied profitably in light of such traditions. I have found this anthropologically oriented archaeology the most relevant theoretical literature for the problem of collaborative politics in Israel and the Near East.

As we consider theoretical models for understanding ancient political systems, it is essential to keep in mind the specific need that we face both in the biblical literature and in the history of the southern Levant. In its Judah guise, the Bible organizes the past according to its own schema, with tribal action

---

[11] Brumfiel (1994); the edited volume represents the point of departure for this analytical approach.

[12] This pattern characterizes the individual articles in Brumfiel and Fox. For example, the piece by Stephen Kowalewski (1994), who contributed to the theoretical work of Blanton and Feinman to be discussed below, envisions an entirely "centralized" community at Monte Albán in the Valley of Oaxaca, based on the huge Main Plaza.

gathered mainly to time before kings, and monarchy assigned primary responsibility – by Yahweh – for the people's choices. If we are to allow Israelite material a chance to speak for itself, and if we intend to make a critical application of Israelite content to historical questions, we must be aware of our own conceptual frameworks. Furthermore, my characterization of Israel and Judah by contrasting political traditions risks oversimplification and the false impression of complete dissimilarity. The theoretical approaches reviewed in the rest of this chapter emphasize the interplay of separate social impulses: one that augments individual influence and power, and the other that tends to distribute power through groups. These coexist in all settings; the political dissimilarity between Israel and Judah is defined by different balances between these impulses.

1. Heterarchy
One recent approach to alternative political configurations is neatly expressed in Carole Crumley's hypothesis of "heterarchy," a direct contrast to the drumbeat of "hierarchy" in typical analyses of state-based power. By this line of thought, Crumley does not intend the simple "band" and "tribal" societies of an evolutionary system, but rather more elaborate situations that may occur in the "stratified societies" of Service's chiefdoms and states. In a 2003 collection of studies that apply the concept to the early Maya, Crumley develops at some length the idea she helped to define some years earlier (1995).

The term "heterarchy" comes from an early study of brain function, as "self-organizing systems in which the elements stand counterpoised to one another" (McCulloch 1945). As a political phenomenon, "[h]eterarchies of power – coalitions, federations, leagues, associations, communities – are just as important to the functioning of many states as they are to more egalitarian groups (bands and tribes)." Heterarchical polities are characterized by administrators with reliable information from many sources, decisions that reflect consensus, decision-makers who hear a variety of possible solutions to problems, and greater value for the contributions of disparate members of the community, so that society is better integrated and the work force proud and energized. The advantages of heterarchy are offset by the fact that consensus is slow and difficult, and with such slow decision time, solutions are delayed.

Clearly, Crumley approves of the pattern, and she approaches political society as if heterarchy would develop frequently based on its merits. Consideration of social advantage is a valuable starting point for explaining actual systems, and this makes particular sense with systems that are defined by diversity and collaboration. At the same time, this discussion pays less attention to the ambitions and objectives of individuals seeking to draw power to themselves and the social advantages of cooperation with such individuals. In the case of the Late Classic Maya, however, she reflects on the possibility of two modes in tension, as perhaps would have been found in monarchic Israel. "One might imagine a struggle between very different value systems, one cherishing the collectivity and community and the other honoring status, individual and lineage, ascribed and achieved" (p. 143). Picking up Joyce Marcus' "dynamic model" for Mayan politics, with the coexistence of single-ruler and councilor forms of organization across time and space, Crumley characterizes the above struggle as between the forces of decentralization, seen as kinship, and of centralization, seen as kingship (Marcus 1986; McAnany 1995). For her own work on the European Iron Age (ca. 800–52 B.C.E), however, she finds that the framework for decentralized politics is not kinship but political parties based on patron–client relations. This alternative raises the questions of how communities may be organized and motivated through means other than kinship, and how centralization may occur without kings. While the Israelite setting almost certainly involves a kinship framework, it is worth noting the challenge not to assume uniformity for all noncentralizing political situations.

One substantial benefit to Crumley's proposal is surely the word "heterarchy" itself. Numerous specialists working with a wide range of premodern societies are seeking ways to talk about more complicated and nuanced political systems, in which power evidently operates along multiple axes and directions, and decisions are made with the participation of varied groups beyond a small ruling circle. In a word, "heterarchy" defines an alternative to hierarchy, a framework for power transmitted in parallel units rather than in series from top to bottom. In its simplicity, there is room for the concept to be refined and nuanced, with or without the sense of idealism expressed by Crumley herself. One may find heterarchies of decentralized elites or discuss the heterarchical nature of factions that vie for power in a centralized state. In application, it seems that some archaeologists have adopted the term with a pragmatic attitude, not committed to a specific interpretive paradigm but appreciating the label for a category of phenomena to be examined.

Scarborough and Valdez (2003) focus on the "interdependency" of Maya communities that were formed from widely dispersed populations, so that the large centers had to work cooperatively with smaller sites so as to take full advantage of far-flung resources. Others treat heterarchy and hierarchy as primary axes for the definition of social order in any given setting. Tourtellot et al. (2003, 37) prefer to pursue this combined approach, considering that heterarchy can contribute to the analysis of various ranks, levels, and systems within a larger structure, taking into account multiple hierarchies or less ranking than might first be assumed.[13] While such adaptation of heterarchy to more standard hierarchical analyses avoids the reduction of the concept into another social typology, it can also tame its implications. Most of the specific applications lack reference to politics, where large-scale and high-level decision-making could be shaped by collaborative action.[14] As observed previously, Crumley herself

---

[13] Compare Houk (2003, 52), who argues that relationships between elites and nonelites were hierarchical, while the subsistence economy and distribution of utilitarian goods were organized heterarchically.

[14] One interesting example outside the edited volume is the review of recent work on sub-Saharan Africa by Ann Brower Stahl (2004). In her treatment of western Africa, she refers to "heterarchy"

speaks directly of "heterarchical polities," and this political scope envisions a more all-encompassing application for nonhierarchical patterns in social life, not to be relegated to cooperative economic arrangements among the peasantry. In my study of early Israel in biblical tradition, I confront evidence for collaboration that reaches the level of political structure, and so far as heterarchy is a useful concept, it is in Crumley's more ambitious sense. At the same time, the reality that heterarchy may coexist with hierarchy matches the situation in monarchic Israel, and it will be most useful to think in terms that acknowledge both. To this end, we turn to the alternative theoretical framework of Blanton, Feinman, and company.

2. Corporate and Network Strategies

At almost the same time as the concept of heterarchy was first advanced, Richard Blanton and Gary Feinman published with two others another approach to the same range of phenomena (1996). Whereas heterarchy was offered as a social type, in conscious contrast to hierarchy, Blanton et al. proposed a continuum of interaction between two "strategies." This approach is expressly political, which adds to its usefulness. In their original publication (Blanton et al. 1996), the authors characterized the collaborative strategy as "corporate" and the centralizing strategy as "network" (cf. Feinman 2000, 211). Feinman directly compares the corporate/network approach to heterarchy, which was not under discussion when the initial article appeared: "Although I concur that a more multidimensional or heterarchical perspective is necessary to compare societal organization and decision-making (see Crumley 1995), it also is useful to consider and build on prior studies that already have highlighted either different modes of leadership or distinct socioeconomic strategies." The corporate/network dimension of analysis is then intended to be applied in conjunction with analysis of hierarchical complexity.[15] Choice of the term "strategy" reflects an interest in the aims and practices of social actors, rather than types that describe whole societies (Feinman 2001, 221).

According to this interpretive system, exclusionary power strategy can exist on either a large or a small scale, and it is built around efforts to monopolize control of the sources of power. With corporate strategy, power is shared across different sectors of society in a way that inhibits exclusionary strategies. Corporate political power is not confined to societies with minimal hierarchy, and in ancient settings, corporate behavior tends to be overlooked or

in the Middle Niger, as explored in the work of the McIntoshes, who envision "a long-standing resistance to monopolized power" and "the durability of heterarchical arrangements" (p. 150); see Roderick J. McIntosh (1998) and Susan Keech McIntosh (1999). Without contradicting the conclusions of the excavators, Stahl expresses caution and does not endorse their political interpretation.

[15] Feinman is specifically concerned that the corporate/network analysis neither be advanced as a new typology nor be supposed to replace focus on hierarchy (p. 213).

underestimated (Blanton et al. 1996, 2).[16] Above all, this framework envisions both strategies functioning simultaneously in every social system, even as one or the other tends to dominate. According to Blanton, Feinman, and company, political action is "inherently conflictive."

Because this spectrum can be applied to societies of varying scale and degree of hierarchy, it can be useful to the study of Israel and Judah without having to settle boundary disputes over what constitutes a chiefdom or a state, either in general or in the history of these two peoples. Feinman speaks of "orthogonal dimensions" along which this analysis can be applied, with one axis defining variation from egalitarian to hierarchical social organization and the other indicating "network" (so, "exclusionary") or corporate power strategies. None of these is determined by scale alone, although larger populations tend to be associated with more hierarchical organization. In Feinman's scheme, ancient Rome was extremely hierarchical throughout its period of influence, but the republic functioned with a predominance of the corporate strategy until the empire brought individual power and network power to the fore. Old Kingdom Egypt was hierarchical with network strategy, while Uruk-period Mesopotamia and the third-millennium Harappan polities of the Indus Valley were marked more by corporate power. In the material more directly relevant to the specialties of Feinman and Blanton, the Classic period Teotihuacan of Central America was like the Roman republic, both hierarchical and yet corporate, even as the Classic Mayan polities were characterized by a generally network-type strategy. In the American Southwest, the earlier period of Pueblos was both egalitarian and corporate, developing into a later period that became more hierarchical within the same corporate tradition.[17]

I have adapted Feinman's graphic portrait of this scheme, as shown in the following figure.[18]

---

[16] In the corporate strategy, economic resources are more dispersed, leadership is less personalized, and ostentatious displays with individual aggrandizement are less common. One encounters communal ritual, public construction, large cooperative labor tasks, and suppressed economic differentiation. All of these traits can be found at levels of substantial social scale. Corporate hierarchies may be characterized by power-sharing and dampened economic differentiation, yet they are still characterized by hierarchical decision-making and nonconsensual politics (Feinman et al. 2000).

[17] For my work, the follow-up by Feinman is more productive than the recent development by Blanton and another colleague of an attempt to generalize this approach across premodern societies by a combination of description and "collective action theory" (Blanton and Fargher 2008). Collective action theory explains how self-interest can lead to group-based rather than just individualized action, especially with regard to economic choices. This can lead to language that is historically out of place in ancient Near Eastern settings, such as the common citizen being viewed as "taxpayer," and the economic focus is difficult to apply to the biblical renditions of Israel and Judah.

[18] This figure follows the general schema of Feinman's figure 12.2, "Selected historic examples compared along two orthogonal dimensions" (2000, 215). I have placed Israel and Judah on the chart in order to give a rough sense of where they could fit, without knowing how Feinman would treat them.

Network and Corporate Strategies on a Hierarchical-Egalitarian Spectrum

Roman empire	**most hierarchical**
	Roman republic
	Classic Teotihuacan
Old Kingdom Egypt	Classical Athens
8ᵗʰ-century Judah? *8ᵗʰ-century Israel?*	
Classic Maya	Period I Monte Alban
early monarchic Israel?	
	later Southwest U.S. pueblos
	Iron Age I Israelite highlands?
	early Southwest U.S. pueblos
	most egalitarian
network strategy predominates	corporate strategy predominates

Along these dimensions of relative hierarchy and predominant political strategy, I understand Israel to have roots in a social landscape less marked by hierarchy, though not "egalitarian." With the appearance of kings and palace-based administrations, Israel is drawn toward both greater hierarchy and a better-established network political strategy. In Judah, which would have displayed comparable hierarchy generally, the network political strategy with its greater reliance on the Jerusalem center gained greater dominance than in Israel of the same period, where traditional corporate political strategy retarded the expansion of network power. I adopt this terminology specifically in order to explain my sense of where Israel and Judah belong, without intending to apply it globally to my discussion of history.

Throughout the application of this analytical approach, it is assumed that network or centralizing activity is always at work. It is unnecessary to decide whether a given polity is a "corporate state" or an "exclusionary state." When Israel comes to have what the local language calls "kings," this need not represent an absolute transition from one political type to another. The Bible's identification of tribes is associated primarily with the time before kings, and as a system, it is thought to derive from a time before Israel existed as a united entity in the land. Nevertheless, Saul's son Eshbaal (Ishbosheth) takes up leadership with the support of separate peoples (2 Sam. 2:9), and the core list proposed by Macchi for Genesis 49 acknowledges a monarchic framework, most directly with Asher in verse 20. Aside from the limitations imposed by the evidence, the theoretical framework of corporate and network or exclusionary strategies for power allows the consideration of both centralizing and persistent multicentered political forces at work. Even in Judah, where the centralizing phenomenon is marked, and where the contrast with Israel becomes a useful tool for distinguishing biblical voices and settings, it is not necessary to exclude the corporate dimension to political life.

For Israel and Judah themselves, in the context of Near Eastern systems that I studied in relation to the early second-millennium archives from Mari (Chapter 13), the corporate category is not entirely adequate to the range of political configurations presented in the evidence. At a single site, decision-making may devolve from a ruler and an elite that answers to the ruler in a manner that recalls the network strategy, or it may be spread among a wider base, whether elite and representative or more inclusive. In my Mari study (2004a), I called this "collective governance," with special interest in polities defined by cities or towns. As reflected in the biblical narrative, Israel and Judah both show some expression of collective decision-making at a central site, though Judah's cluster of symbolic authority for king and god at Jerusalem has no counterpart in Israel. What really distinguishes Israel from Judah, however, seems to be its literal decentralization, the grounding of political power in groups with their own regional identities and structures. The collaboration of these regional groups is less easily defined as "collective," in that its execution may take different forms in different periods or with different purposes. Certainly, the Mesoamerican examples (Chapter 12) that inspired the corporate terminology are centralized in a way unimaginable for early Israel, with enormous public plazas constructed for ritual gatherings at sites with overwhelming symbolic dominance. I do not want my interpretation of Israel to become entangled in this expression of group-based politics.

Having reviewed the concepts of heterarchy and corporate political strategy, I return to my own category of collaborative politics. My goal in contemplating these interpretive approaches is not to choose one or to create my own system for general application. Rather, early Israel belongs to historical discussion of these worldwide phenomena, and I want to place my study into a theoretical landscape that reflects struggle with similar problems. In spite of the obstacles inherent in a traditional text of enduring religious value to communities through modern time, the fact that the Bible was more than the product of royal or even temple administrations, along with Israel's decentralized and collaborative heritage, allowed it to preserve written evidence of rare antiquity for politics in this mode.

12

Outside the Near East

I have said that the Bible preserves rare early written evidence for collaborative political assumptions in the Near East. There is other such evidence, and the rarity of the biblical material has more to do with its literary character than with writing as such. To provide a more immediate context for the biblical tradition of decentralized and associated "tribal" peoples, I will turn to the Amorites and the Arameans, who offer first an essential background and second a contemporary comparison for Israel. Outside the Near East, collective or corporate political forms are classically associated with Greece and Rome, and there is a massive literature on these peoples and their political cultures. These histories are so distinct, however, and the eventual dominance of each political center so overwhelming, that Athenian democracy and republican Rome are not generally part of the broader discussion of collaborative politics. Moreover, the comparative discussion of political forms tends to be the domain of anthropologists, and when early societies are involved, of archaeologists in conversation with anthropology. In the case of ancient Mesoamerica, therefore, while the scale is also impressive, the work has still fallen mainly to the archaeological disciplines.

To locate early Israel in a theoretical landscape of other polities with notable collaborative aspects, and to provide some more concrete notion of the phenomena that inspired analyses by heterarchy or corporate strategy, I review in this chapter a few of the settings in question. Three regions have attracted attention in relation to these questions. Above all, Mesoamerican civilization has been central to the discussion, whether in corporate/network terms, as hierarchy and heterarchy, or otherwise. The scale of the polities involved is massive, as with Teotihuacan, which Blanton et al. present as their ideal case. Explanations for noncentralizing practices and ideas cannot be based here on primitive evolutionary types, as related to bands and tribes. Feinman is invested in the study of the pre-Hispanic American Southwest, where pueblos represent a public interest not evidently driven by rulers or exclusionary power. Crumley works first of all with early European societies, and one study of pre-Viking Denmark offers a thought-provoking comparison for the interaction of monarchy with existing collaborative traditions in early Israel.

A. Mesoamerican Antiquity and Massive Scale

Blanton, Feinman, Kowalewski, and Peregrine (1996) propose their model as an analytical path forward in the much-debated interpretation of Mesoamerican politics, and they offer Mesoamerican history as their primary test case. For the task at hand, rather than highlight the clearest examples of corporate strategy, they undertake a review of two millennia and more against the grid of network and corporate politics, a model of the systemic approach they envision for any application. The evidence for each strategy is especially the presence or absence of the sovereign at the center of the physical remains left by a given people: massive public burial for the ruler, the size and centrality of the palace, and ritual dominance of the king as expressed in religious iconography. Alternatives show public construction without the ruler at center and festival representations or other religious artifacts that suggest symbolic systems with no special role for kings.

In particular, Teotihuacan, in the Basin of Mexico (ca. 300–750 C.E.) provides the "foremost manifestation of the corporate strategy in ancient Mesoamerica" (p. 9). Although the site is notable for its massive buildings and constructed public spaces, these display no concern to glorify any ruling group. In contrast to earlier periods of dominant network power, texts include neither named rulers nor patrimonial rhetoric. Public buildings abound, but no definite palace has been identified. Public religion emphasized a cosmology of rain, earth, sun, moon, and other elements of nature without need of a monarch. Network power revived after the decline of Teotihuacan, which was large enough to control a much larger region. In a scheme reminiscent of the marauding nomads so often attributed to the Orient, Blanton and company observe a loose association of corporate structure with regions that sustain intensive agriculture, so that network power tends to emerge out of the margins. After a period of network dominance, the Aztecs of Late Post-Classic Mexico display a return to corporate patterns. All gods were incorporated into the one Aztec cosmos, and history was to be rewritten so as to include all peoples in one genealogy of origins. This analysis downplays what strikes an outsider as symbolic imperialism, an assault on factional rivalries that could undermine the individual power of the ruler. Such unification is not clearly inclusive in its real political scope.

A useful comparison for the analysis by Blanton, Feinman, and company is the collected volume on heterarchy and the ancient Maya by Scarborough et al. (2003). Whereas the corporate/network application emphasizes again the variable history of Maya political life, with focus on the presence or absence of a dominant role for a sovereign, Scarborough and Valdez (2003, 3) begin with what they consider the enduring patterns of Maya settlement.[1] From the start, Maya settlement was widely dispersed, so that resource acquisition and use began as relatively decentralized. During the Late Classic period of their focus (ca. 600–900 C.E.), the large Maya centers served as distribution hubs that linked the scattered communities of the agricultural landscape. The plazas of such centers constituted the physical expression of Mayan interdependency during a period that Blanton et al. identify broadly with network strategy. If this period is indeed to be associated with a strong central power, it is no wonder that the efforts to interpret its various individual bodies of excavated and settlement data in heterarchical terms end up limited to social relations outside the political domain.[2]

More than the textual and archaeological evidence for early Israel, the Mesoamerican discussion reminds me immediately of Late Bronze Emar in northern Syria.[3] The most striking feature of the rituals described in one archive of religious administrative documents is the absence of an essential role for the king. Even rites that explicitly involve the city as a whole do not make the ruler a central player – in one case, even a festival underwritten primarily from palace funds (Fleming 1992a). In my consideration of arguably Israelite content in the biblical narrative, I did not attempt a case for any of the ritual and legal material in the Torah. Indeed, the core tradition of three annual festivals in Exodus 23 and 34, Leviticus 23, Numbers 28–9, and Deuteronomy 16 never envisions a role for a king or ruler, but this is more generally characteristic of biblical ritual and has been taken to reflect its postexilic settings. The narrative itself may reflect a selection that excludes stories from the circles of Israelite kings, except for David, whose royal house was the legacy of Judah. It is certainly impressive that Israel's narrative lore in the Bible includes so much from life without kings, and this may display an alternative public focus similar to what Blanton and Feinman identify in the corporate situations of Mesoamerica. The Mesoamerican landscape in itself is less immediately useful to investigation of early Israel than this question of the presence or absence of sovereigns in the symbolic system of a society.

---

[1] In a somewhat hasty critique, Yoffee (2005, 178) objects that the corporate/network model inappropriately characterizes states entirely by their form of leadership. The observation is astute, yet Yoffee too quickly dismisses the entire effort to understand better the workings of noncentralizing political patterns.

[2] Two contributions reflect on the relationship between settlements in a larger landscape, with the heterarchical model providing a basis for resisting interpretation by settlement hierarchies: Houk (2003) and King and Shaw (2003). King and Shaw then ask whether the bigger sites in the Petén must be assumed to dictate policy to the smaller sites found in the Three Rivers region (pp. 75–6).

[3] The essential recent work is the collection of d'Alfonso, Cohen, and Sürenhagen (2008). My own work on the religious life of Emar as seen in the written evidence is gathered especially in Fleming (1992b, 2000).

B. The American Southwest: Cooperation in More Modest Settings

The American Southwest is the basis for Gary Feinman's interest in corporate political strategies, and although the societies in question are of modest scale, they display striking evidence for group activity that cannot be explained by lack of hierarchy in primitive and egalitarian conditions. This evidence inspired a volume of collected essays that approach the problem from different vantages, including that of Feinman himself, edited by Mills (2000). Each contributor works from the particular material that is most familiar to her or him, within different theoretical frameworks, yet the trend of the evidence is consistent. I cite two examples.

1. The Communal Sites of the Hohokam in Premodern Arizona

Suzanne Fish (2000) and Paul Fish begin their discussion by observing that the archaeological record for Southwest societies does not generally permit much view of leaders and elites. There are no special signs of wealth or coercion for personal ends, no exclusive insignia or prominence in art or iconography (p. 155). Ethnography allows a view of the same society from a later period, with emphasis on kinship relations that is complemented by the archaeological finds. Early Hohokam villages, starting from about 500 C.E., are constructed with two to six houses opening onto a single courtyard or shared work area, and these in turn tend to be grouped in clusters, all generally interpreted in kinship terms (p. 157).

Along with these residential patterns, however, there are signs of communal activity that need not be explained by family relationship. What Fish and Fish call "communities" are defined by groups of interrelated settlements, visible first of all by their spatial clustering, and then confirmed by special construction at central sites. In earlier periods (ca. 600 C.E.), these are caliche-capped mounds, which then give way to earthen-banked ball courts (ca. 750–950), followed finally by platform mounds at the center of such sites. These public structures show no connection with the architecture or symbols of the village residential pattern. They serve the needs only of the larger associated communities. In the final "Classic" period, ritual is focused on the central mounds of the leading sites, and the earlier ball courts likewise belong to communal life with no rationale in the kinship ties of villages (pp. 161–3).

Over the course of several hundred years, there is a trend toward greater exclusivity in communal events, with direct participation limited to fewer members with more specialized roles. This trend is not, however, accompanied by what may be expected as hallmarks of centralizing power. Trade in exotic raw materials and finished crafts is widely dispersed among settlements and residents. There is some evidence for inequality of wealth, especially at the central sites, but wealth is not accompanied by unique consumption of specialty items by a few households or individuals. No extremely wealthy burials or elaborate residences were found, nor was there evidence of a system of prestige goods shared only by elites (pp. 166–7).

The Hohokam are particularly intriguing for the evidence of a community-based centralization based on neither kinship nor kingship. Interpreted on their own terms, the ball courts and platform mounds require no family-based structure and no imagined "clans" as the organizing principle for building and gathering. At the same time, the ethnographies for the same people show a reverence for the collaborative tradition that is interpreted in a kinship framework both inspired by actual past practice and not grasping its logic. We may think of the Bible's tribal framework for Israel, which also falls back on kinship as a way to remember and explain the collective practices. Without resorting to Martin Noth's amphictyony and the notion of a central shrine, local centers in ancient Israel may have served communal uses without the involvement of a dominant individual authority. In the Bible, the communal center is evoked in images such as the muster of Israel at Shiloh in 1 Samuel 1–4 and the assembly of the people to consider Rehoboam at Shechem (1 Kings 12).[4]

2. Casas Grandes (Chihuahua): The Great Pueblo

Casas Grandes, just south of the New Mexico border and dating to between 1200 and 1450 C.E., is one of the largest known prehistoric pueblos. To set the stage for their evaluation, Michael Whalen and Paul Minnis (2000, 168) cite Gregory Johnson, a Near Eastern archaeologist, who said, "Casas looks elite – even to me" (1989, 386). The site is considered to be the center of one of the major regional systems of the American Southwest and northern Mexico. Early interpretation envisioned a centralized polity with hereditary rulers of foreign descent. The platform mounds and ball courts were taken to be in Mesoamerican style, and there were many exotic imports. Surrounding towns and villages were considered to be dependent on the central pueblo (pp. 169–70).

In their reevaluation, Whalen and Minnis conclude that there is much less evidence for centralization than first proposed. Generally, there is no evidence for military incursions that would have led to foreign rule, and there is little more evidence for sustained trade between Casas Grandes and regions to its north and south. The exotic finds seem to reflect individual hoards for the elite, not storage reflecting local production and the basis for large-scale regional exchange. Eighteen platform mounds have varied form and are not necessarily public, and the water control systems of the surrounding area show no evidence of construction under authority from this central site (pp. 170–1).

---

[4] I have chosen examples that probably originate in early Judah, although they may recall patterns from Israel. The Shiloh texts in 1 Samuel have been gathered around the ark, which is taken by the Philistines in the narrative of chapters 4–6, settled in Kiriath Jearim of what became Judah (6:21–7:1), and finally brought to Jerusalem by David (2 Samuel 6). This movement of the ark into Yahweh's eventual residence at Jerusalem suggests a ritual procession that would have pertained to the city of David, preserved in Judah (see Fleming forthcoming a). The Shechem tradition is linked to the notion that Jeroboam I made this his first capital, in what appears to reflect actual Israelite conditions, although the account of Rehoboam's rejection is told with retrospective disappointment on Judah's side.

According to the authors, the picture of a central site and large-scale trade envisions communal craft guilds in the style of Blanton and company's "corporate" political interpretation. This application of Blanton and Feinman reflects the large-scale centralization of Mesoamerican public life, whether for network or corporate politics, in enormous shared spaces. Whalen and Minnis resist the analogy to the Mesoamerican central sites, and propose instead a "noncorporate" approach, defined by competitive leaders and factions. The settlement pattern for the region surrounding Casas Grandes does not suggest centralization at the major site, and there are many ball courts within a day's walk, which suggest to the authors multiple competing centers of power (pp. 175–6). They prefer the interpretive model of "heterarchy" to that of Blanton and Feinman.

This discussion of a major Southwest American site shows how the details of a social system can be reevaluated once overall confidence in an interpretive model has been shaken. Wealth and its display need not indicate the centralization of power, and even if the Casas Grandes pueblo was occupied by a leader with some claim to larger authority, the distribution of settlements and ritual ball courts, among other finds, suggests that actual power was negotiated among a wider circle, even in purely geographical terms. What can seem at first to be evidence for elite domination from a single center may require explanation by a more distributed political structure. In Israel, Samaria has all the physical hallmarks of elite power with a hierarchical base, and textual evidence may confirm that Omri and Ahab functioned as heads of successful kingdoms. Nevertheless, the Israelite polity must be interpreted as a system with more than one center, and perhaps with organization at the center that reflected integration with forces outside the palace and outside Samaria. The particular character of the noncentralized political system at Casas Grandes remains unclear. In the heterarchical approach of Whalen and Minnis, it is not clear how a center of a scale far beyond all other sites in the region could have resulted from competition among factions.[5]

C. Viking and Pre-Viking Denmark: Transition to Monarchy

During the first decisive period of biblical composition, Israel and Judah existed as adjacent kingdoms with seemingly similar political structures. Both archaeological investigation and the biblical narrative suggest that these kingdoms were relative newcomers to the scene, especially when compared with the older polities of Egypt or Mesopotamia. I am proposing that the arrival of monarchy took different shapes in Israel and Judah and that while Israel remained the larger and more influential power, its kingdom experienced a much slower ascent of royal authority, and strong collaborative and distributive traditions of decision-making persisted until its fall. A similar process has recently been

---

[5] Whalen and Minnis conclude with the same question, proposing that the burst of growth must have occurred at the very end of the period in question (p. 179). Casas Grande was eight to ten times the size of the next largest community in the region.

traced for the Danish political landscape before the medieval kingdom by Tina Thurston (2001) in a study that is hampered somewhat by the evolutionary framework of chiefdoms and states. Thurston's work is constructed around the problem of "state formation," and her main conclusion is that the Danish state emerged gradually through three centuries of Viking rule, rather than rising full-blown in 1075. There may be no reason to object to such a result, but for comparison with Israel, the most interesting part of her analysis lies in the details of the path by which the kingdom of Denmark arose from its Viking antecedents.

The period from 700 to 1075 C.E. is considered the Viking Age, which had been seen to be populated by warlike, fragmented groups that were finally supplanted by the Danish state. Between 1000 and 1050, fortresses, storehouses, palaces, and temples appeared "suddenly" (p. 5), though the centralizing power that produced them had been considerable for some time. Thurston proposes that "[t]he key to this uneven development is in the antagonistic resistance of traditional, horizontally organized institutions to centralization processes" (p. 6), a statement that could be applied word for word to Iron Age II Israel. Before the Viking Age, what Thurston calls "chiefdoms" were constituted with bonds of mutual obligation, and rulers were chosen with the approval of an assembly that could depose or assassinate those who had lost credibility. In case of war, an overlord would be elected among the "chieftains," only holding authority until the threat dissipated (p. 7; cf. chapter 3). All this recalls common portrayals of Israel before kings, although both may be stereotyped.

However these distributed centers of power took actual form, the Viking Age itself offers an analogy for the interaction of emergent centralizing forces with the substratum of traditional collaborative decision-making. Thurston considers that early "state-building rulers" did not attempt conquest, but rather accepted a voluntary union under their leadership that she calls hegemony, as opposed to domination (p. 12).[6] In this framework, resistance to central power came from the majority, not a small group. For a hundred years, the most prominent expression of this was the independence of Scania, a region and polity that is now mostly part of Sweden and at considerable distance from the Viking centers in modern Denmark. Scania was won to Viking rule without warfare, deportation, or depopulation. Instead, the outsiders avoided direct conflict and reached for greater power in stages, first in the framework of alliance, then as hegemony. Dramatic changes were made in the location and function of central places, so as to create new landscapes of power. Where possible, traditional places were made redundant (pp. 36–7). During the early

---

[6] Routledge (2004, chapter 2) endorses the same terminology in his discussion of the emergence of the Moabite state, with a careful and original application. Working from the theoretical foundation of Antonio Gramsci, Routledge identifies "hegemony" as the combination of domination and consent (p. 29). The state is the effect of a process embedded in a specific historical matrix that unites an ensemble of social forces and positions, so that hegemony is the result of force and consent operating together (p. 37).

Israelite monarchy, the establishment of Samaria by Omri would have reflected a similar strategy, as perhaps would have Jerusalem under David.

The distance of Scania from the centers of Viking power to the west brings to mind the principal geographical divisions in the Israelite landscape. We could consider what became the kingdom of Judah to be separate in such terms, although this southern region appears to have belonged to an Israelite polity only under David and Solomon. Otherwise, the rift valley of the Jordan River and the Jezreel–Esdraelon plains divided the highlands of Ephraim, Benjamin, and Manasseh from the northern and eastern peoples of Israel. Based on biblical writing, at least, we cannot tell to what extent the centralizing programs of the royal houses of Omri and Jehu succeeded in displacing traditional places of meeting and symbolic heft. When Tiglath-pileser III conquered Israel for the Assyrians, he defined provinces by the names Samaria, Megiddo, and Gilead, a division that may suggest how little the north and east were integrated with the Ephraim highlands even by 732 B.C.E. (Miller and Hayes 1986, 333; Rainey 2006a, 236).

Throughout the Viking Age, the interplay of centralizing, or what Blanton and company would call "network," power and "corporate" traditions of assembly and collaboration are particularly striking in the development of kingship, which Thurston considers not to be well understood (p. 82). There is little written evidence, and material evidence is difficult to read directly as expressions of monarchy. Thurston identifies strategies for integration in the encouragement of urbanization, the construction of canals and fortifications for military advantage, and the transformation of law (pp. 86–90). In all of Scandinavia, the authority of assembly was time-honored, on both local and regional terms. The regional assemblies were identified with particular settlements, most of which had pre-Christian religious associations. Kings had to overcome the political and legal prerogatives of the assemblies in order to establish a centralized royal authority. In general, Viking Age kings had to travel to the regional assembly at Viborg to be crowned. Even in 1074, the assembly insisted on the eldest son of the departed king, who had favored the next in line, and it had its way. Early Swedish law, recorded in 1020, stated that the assembly could elect or reject a king (p. 85). The kingdom of Israel appears to have experienced a similar long struggle between an ambitious monarchy and entrenched expectations that decisions would be shared more broadly.

As a whole, the Viking situation is illuminated by a combination of archaeological and written evidence that permits examination of increasing but contained monarchic centralization. Viking Denmark should prevent us from assuming that once kingship is in place all regions either quickly fall into line or rebel and exclude themselves from the newly centered polity. On the contrary, this setting shows a long process more like what seems to take place over centuries in Israel, before Jehu's royal house achieves the greatest degree of centralized power, at least for the western highlands.[7] In Judah, the house of David

---

[7] Ron Tappy (2001, 575–7) considers that because Jehu comes from east of the Jordan, his royal house would have maintained an ongoing connection to this region, at the same time as its kings

would have struggled for the same kind of increased centralization, with a symbolic role for Jerusalem and its temple that is never matched by Samaria. There may also have been independent entities in the south that resisted Jerusalem's authority, such as the town centers of the Shephelah foothills in the ninth century. If so, however, the Bible recalls no tradition of collaborative decision-making that gave such centers a voice of their own in a larger association, like that of Israel.

ruled from Samaria in Ephraim. Although the house of Jeroboam I came from the Ephraim highlands in the central west, Baasha was associated with Issachar, to the north, as was Omri. Although Tappy emphasizes the animosity between regions, and indeed the division may have run deep, the long survival of a royal family with ties to the east may have represented one important factor in keeping east and west together.

13

The Amorite Backdrop to Ancient Israel

The Amorites appear in the Bible as one of the peoples who occupy the land before the arrival of Israel or even of their ancestors in Genesis. In Deuteronomy 3, Sihon king of Heshbon is an Amorite, and Abraham (Abram) lives among an Amorite community with Mamre in Genesis 14. Like the name "Canaan," however, the Amorite category is well known from Bronze Age writing in the wider Near East. Unlike Canaan, which appears mainly in Late Bronze Age Egyptian texts and the Amarna letters with reference to some part of the Levant, the word "Amorite" comes from much earlier and far away, never applied to people from the southern Levant. As Akkadian *amurrû(m)* and Sumerian *mar-tu*, the Amorites are found in Mesopotamian texts from the third millennium as some sort of outsiders, eventually identified with land and people west of Sumer. In early historical work on the origins of Israel and their relationship to the biblical narrative in Genesis, the migration of Abraham's family from Mesopotamian Ur to north Syrian Harran and finally to Canaan was understood to belong to large movements at the end of the third millennium that brought down the last great kingdom of Sumer. Mesopotamia's Amorites could be linked to a transition found archaeologically in the southern Levant from the Early Bronze to the Middle Bronze Age (ca. 2000 B.C.E.), and these phenomena offered a historical starting point for examining ancient Israel.[1]

This application of the Amorite name to both textual and archaeological evidence across the Near East involved the conflation of several different partly related phenomena in a way that can be seriously misleading. Even the known application of the word *amurrû* in itself varies significantly, and I will address only one part of this material that relates to collaborative politics.

---

[1] See, e.g., the synthesis by Bright (1981), chapter 1, "The World of Israel's Origins." Speaking of evidence in Egyptian texts for new towns in the Levant, he concludes, "That these newcomers were 'Amorites,' of the same Northwest-Semitic stock as those whom we have met in Mesopotamia, seems highly probable." The connection is made especially based on the character of their West Semitic personal names (p. 55).

In southeastern Mesopotamia, where the category is first attested, the Sumerian *mar-tu* refers to mobile herding communities that were woven fully into the fabric of society – to borrow Porter's metaphor (2012). After the fall of the last Sumerian power at Ur around 2000 B.C.E., the full participation of such communities in eastern Mesopotamian society is visible in the rise at Babylon, Larsa, and other cities of new kings who display lineages from outside those sites and who bear West Semitic personal names. These new rulers are somehow related to the Amorite/Martu category, which some writers affiliated with Ur came to identify as enemy and other. When we encounter such people across the landscape of early second-millennium Mesopotamia and Syria, the Amorite term is inadequate to define them, yet the word did not entirely lose its association with herding communities. These groups appear to have developed tribal forms of organization as a way to maintain social ties over distance and with associated towns. Such forms are particularly accessible in written evidence from the palace archives of Mari, which date roughly to the eighteenth century B.C.E.

The political landscape of the Mari archives presents a prominent role for decentralized politics, with various associations, long-term alliances, tribal unions, and powerful collectives. I devoted a full-length study to this material (*Democracy's Ancient Ancestors*, 2004a), only a small part of which warrants further development here. Mari's evidence for collaborative politics is bound up with the aspects of the region's society that involved tribal organization and the maintenance of long-distance herding communities. Based on the old Mesopotamian category, and as a convenient type with a provocative usage in Near Eastern studies, I will call this cultural stream "Amorite."[2] The texts from Mari and elsewhere in Mesopotamia that exhibit Amorite social and political organization contribute an important Near Eastern reference for ancient Israel, a phenomenon that stands in some kind of historical continuity with the later society of the Levant. The mix of tribal and settlement-based identities, along with the mix of long-distance herding and settled farming, characterized all the lands along the margins of the great Arabian desert. The biblical tradition of Israel's tribal aspect belongs to a social pattern long established in the Near East. Archaeological evidence for the Late Bronze and early Iron Ages in the southern Levant must likewise be approached with such structures in mind. With focus on the Amorites, we move closer to the world of Israel and begin to formulate a historical context for the Israelite political practices reflected in the Bible.

A. Amorites in the Mari Evidence

In my description of the early second-millennium Mesopotamian pastoralists and peoples who are not defined by their city centers – that is, the "tribal"

---

[2] The current Mari publication team has often resorted to the same category, with all its pitfalls; see, e.g., the serial *Amurru* (3 volumes); Charpin and Ziegler (2003).

population – I have purposely chosen the fraught category of "Amorites," or *amurrû*. While the original point of reference for this identification is uncertain and debated, by the early second millennium it had come to be identified with West Semitic speakers and overlapped strongly with these tribal peoples. In the literature of southeastern Mesopotamia from the end of the third millennium and the beginning of the second, the Amorites were a foreign people identified with "the west." They were familiar to Sumer and Babylonia, yet they could be isolated as uncivilized, living in tents and lacking the refinements of proper urban existence.[3] Without accepting the pejorative associations of the term, historians have long looked for the original Amorites (or Sumerian *mar-tu*) in the west, somewhere in Syria.

From contrasting theoretical perspectives, Anne Porter (2007) and Walther Sallaberger (2007) have both recently concluded that the Mesopotamian label referred originally to pastoralist communities as such rather than to any particular people from the west.[4] For Porter (2012, end of chapter 4), the Amorites of Mesopotamian literature come to represent the ultimate enemy not "because they are outsiders, marauders from the fringe, but because they are the very opposite: direct, *internal* competition for control of the four river banks.

---

[3] In the Marriage of Martu, a Sumerian text known only from copies in the Old Babylonian period (ca. eighteenth century B.C.E.), the Amorites as a population are embodied in a single superhuman or divine figure set in hoary antiquity at a mythical city called Inab. Porter (2012) proposes that the critique of Amorites in this text in fact reflects a refutation of such prejudice, and the story itself offers a positive point of view. Martu desires to marry the divine Adgarkidug, and he offers as incentive a gift of enormous generosity, enough to impress and attract her father Numušda, special deity of Inab. The gift consists of livestock, confirming the pastoralist associations of Martu, who is portrayed as having great wealth. With such wealth, and the generosity behind it, the people of Inab would be foolish to refuse Martu, yet Adgarkidug has a friend who voices a bias that seems to be familiar to the audience. Martu "eats the abomination" that is somehow connected with Nanna, the moon god associated with Ur; he is "always roaming," as if mobility by itself is an objection; he wears leather, not wool, as if weaving were an urban luxury; he lives in the highlands rather than in the cities of the river valleys; he gathers wild plants, perhaps mushrooms, and eats raw meat – a true insult; he does not live in a house; and he has no burial. The initial complaint in terms of the religion of Nanna suggests a connection of the prejudice with Ur, yet Adgarkidug rejects the entire criticism and declares in the closing line that she nevertheless intends to accept Martu in marriage. Porter therefore appears to be correct that the text takes a positive point of view toward the Amorites, and it may associate the bias with Ur, evidently during the great kingdom at the end of the third millennium. The Marriage of Martu may then have been composed in the period following the fall of Ur to express an alternative to the attitude that persisted in the popular Sumerian literature that was the staple of scribal education in the first part of the second millennium. As expressed in the Marriage of Martu, the bias against Amorites may be a caricature of actual attitudes, or at least an exaggeration, given that it is set up as an idea to be rejected. Martu himself is fully connected to the city of Inab, joining its residents in its economic and religious life. The story reflects a social tension even as it represents the Amorites as full participants in the city and its practices.

[4] See also Porter (2012), chapter 4, "Tax and Tribulation, or, Who Were the Amorrites?" These new approaches are more convincing than the old interpretations based on the established work of Michael Rowton (e.g., 1973a, b, 1974). Rowton's work represented an important conceptual breakthrough at the time and is still the basis for recent studies such as that of Jahn (2007).

It is their status as part of the Mesopotamian heartlands that gave rise to this very particular juxtaposition of the production of a past with the creation of a literary 'other.'" As we approach the evidence from Mari, we must recognize this backdrop for use of the word *amurrû* in an earlier place and period. Before examining the particular peoples identified with the Amorite rubric, the category itself warrants a closer look.

1. The Range of Use for the Term in Mari Evidence

A number of Mari specialists have undertaken to explain the varied use of the word *amurrû* in this material. There is a polity called Amurrum, just as mid-third millennium Ebla knew a polity called Martu (or Mardu) near the Jebel Bishri, south of the Euphrates River. Amurrum in the Mari archives seems to have been further west, not where Martu has usually been located. Dominique Charpin links the whole origin of the Amorites to this land, which he considers to have extended from the mountains east of Ugarit all the way to the Jebel Bishri. Jean-Marie Durand (1993, 46–7; cf. Charpin 2004, 57–8) likewise associates the name itself with the far west, as derived from the root /mrr/, "to be bitter," with reference to the salt water of the Mediterranean. There is also the language, as emphasized in a review of the evidence by Jack Sasson, and we shall return to this intriguing category (1998, 121–3). Beyond both of these, the word "Amurrû" can identify people in the realm of Mari's own kings, in a sweeping generalization that somehow indicates a population type that crosses the lines of kingdoms or tribes.

For my own discussion, I will combine the language and the population type, so that we are left with two main categories: the western polity and the use not defined by this. One letter associates the Binu Yamina people with three western realms, each defined by the term *mātum*, which is reserved for polities ruled by one or more kings (*šarrum*). These are the lands of Yamhad, Qatna, and Amurrum, the first two dominating the lowlands that flank the inland slopes of the Lebanese and western Syrian mountains.[5] In a new reading for an early second-millennium (Old Babylonian) extract of the Gilgamesh Epic, Andrew George identifies the home of Huwawa as "where the Amurrû lives," west of Ebla.[6] Other evidence confirms the far-western location of this realm. One brief missive confirms the writer has accounted for "messengers from Hazor and messengers from four Amurrû kings." This group is to join the king of Qatna's own messenger, who will escort them to that city.[7] Another letter reports that various men have arrived at Mari from points far west: two from

---

[5] For the text and discussion of A.2730, see Chapter 9, on the Binu Yamina and Benjamin.

[6] Schøyen-2, line 56. The Schøyen-2 tablet of Gilgamesh was originally published by George (2003, 1.232–40), and a revised edition then appears in George (2009, 32–3). Compare the reading in Fleming and Milstein (2010, 155).

[7] See Bonechi (1992, 10); the letter A.2760 is from king Samsi-Addu of the large upper-Mesopotamian realm to his younger son Yasmah-Addu, designated to rule the western dominions from Mari.

Hazor, two from Qatna, and three "Amurrû singers."[8] Such terminology may indicate their language, yet the geography matches the previous example.

The most obvious location for the land of Amurrum is that known for Amurru in the Late Bronze Age. According to evidence from el-Amarna, Ugarit, and Hatti, Amurru was based in the mountains between the Mediterranean coast and the Orontes River valley.[9] In the Amarna letters dispatched by Rib-Hadda, ruler of Gubla (or Byblos), the ruler of the Amurru peoples alternately importunes and assaults the coastal cities one by one until Gubla itself is in play. This attack on the coast presumes a highland center for Amurru as such. When Amurru passes from the domination of Abdi-Aširta to Aziru, this later leader writes repeatedly about the opposite frontier, to the north and east. Amurru faces threats from Hatti through the Orontes realm of Nuhašše. Later, after Aziru definitively abandons Egypt for alliance with Hatti, Amurru makes a treaty with Ugarit, as a separate coastal power to its northwest. Under Abdi-Aširta and then his plural sons, before the emergence of Aziru, Amurru seems to have consisted of allied peoples without any single settled center, recalling the "four Amurrû kings" who sent messengers to earlier Qatna.[10] Some portion of the Mari texts that have been associated with generic or ethnic Amorites may in fact pertain to the specific land of Amurrum. When Nur-Sin writes to his master Zimri-Lim about "Amurrû figs" in a delivery from the region of Yamhad, these may come from the western mountain land.[11] Such labels are also applied, however, to wool, to livestock, and even to a woman included in a delivery to the Mari palace, and we must be prepared for different points of reference in different contexts.

The existence of an individual western polity called Amurru recalls the question of Benjamin's relationship to the Binu Yamina. Late Bronze Age Amurru likewise stands at a considerable chronological and geographical distance from principal evidence for the label, and there is no reason to imagine that it was used with any awareness of what it once designated generically. Grounded in peoples with the same broad way of life and social organization, Amurru and Benjamin would both represent linguistic relics that preserve hints of the societies from which they survived.

As a whole, the Amurrû identity is not common in texts from Mari. The land of Amurrum was far away and contacts were rare. The word could be applied with more local considerations, but this did not occur often. This pattern in itself means something. So far as the word "Amurrû" defined some category of interest to the circle of Zimri-Lim and his people, it was not relevant to the

---

[8] *FM* III 143 was sent by a palace official of Zimri-Lim, king of Mari; see Ozan (1997, 296–7).

[9] For extended historical discussion, see Singer (1991). The Amarna evidence is most readily accessible through the translations of William Moran (1992).

[10] On Amurru as an alliance in the Amarna evidence, see the extended discussion of Brendon Benz (2012).

[11] *FM* VII 26, esp. lines 49 and 52; in Durand (2002, 99–102).

everyday experience of the supporters and servants who constantly reported back to the palace. What then is the basis for Amurrû identity?

2. Akkadian and Amorite

Very few texts are at stake. First of all, Mari scribes are known to distinguish an Amurrû language. One remarkable text boasts a scribe who is said to understand Akkadian and Subarian – evidently Hurrian – along with Amorite.[12] In another letter, Samsi-Addu, king of upper Mesopotamia, complains that his son Yasmah-Addu has requested a capable Sumerian scribe who can speak Amorite.[13] Such exists but is a valuable commodity, not available for posting to Mari at the drop of a hat. These references to language involve a self-conscious classification that does not follow simple political lines, and the speaking populations cannot be assumed isolated to fully separate living groups. By this date, and in this context, Sumerian was essential to scribal practice, and while it may still have been associated with the region downstream from Babylon, it reflected no particular political body. Šubarû evokes the allied kings of Šubartum, probably east of the Tigris, but the separate language must be distinct from the other broad types, perhaps as Hurrian, another category that crosses political lines. This leaves two clearly Semitic types, Akkadû and Amurrû. From a scribal point of view, these need not have represented comparable categories, in that Amorite seems not to have been written with cuneiform. Nevertheless, Akkadian and Amorite are identified as distinguishable types, each with a coherent, if overlapping, speaking community.

Across both Babylonia and the Mari region, where both Semitic language groups would have been in use, Akkadian and Amorite also labeled masses of people in broad terms that transcended political bounds. One Mari letter reports a treaty between several groups in the Jebel Sinjar and eastern Habur regions and an Akkadian power, which the sender admits could be either Ešnunna, a major power east of the Tigris River, or Babylon.[14] In his treaty with the king of Ešnunna, a copy of which was found at Mari, Zimri-Lim guarantees the loyalty to Ešnunna of any force he sends in support, whether it is identified with Mari, with its Hana people, with the Suhûm land long

---

[12] A.109, cited in isolation in Durand (1992, 125).

[13] M.7930+ is another letter from king Samsi-Addu to his son Yasmah-Addu; in Charpin (1992, 24–5). Sasson translates (1998, 121–2): "You have written me about sending you a man competent in Sumerian, 'Take for me [...] a man competent in Sumerian but speaks Amorite.' Who is the person competent in Sumerian and lives here? Please, am I to send you Šu-Ea who is competent in Sumerian? Šu-Ea and [...]; Iškur-zikalama is competent in Sumerian; but he holds an administrative post. Must he leave his post and run to you? Nanna-palil is competent in Sumerian; but I have to send him to Qabra. You have written me, '[My father] should send me a man from Rapiqum who is competent in Sumerian. There is no one here competent in Sumerian in [...]!'"

[14] ARM XXVII 135, letter to Zimri-Lim of Mari from Zimri-Addu, governor of the Qaṭṭunân district.

disputed between the two kingdoms, with any individual leader, or with any Amorite or Akkadian group.[15] We know from a badly damaged Mari letter that Zimri-Lim is once said to be "king of the Akkadian and the Amorite" equally.[16] Similarly, the Edict of Ammi-ṣaduqa, a slightly later ruler of Babylon, assumes the same breakdown of population types within his domain, as defining the full range of citizens who merit equal treatment under the king's declaration of debt cancellation.[17]

3. Amorites and Hana

What does this distinction then represent? It is applied to an indigenous naming of language types, yet this is only one dimension of the terminology. Regardless of geographical origin or associations, the third-millennium equivalent Martu are persistently identified with mobile pastoralism, or subsistence by herding flocks over distance. In the archives of early Old Babylonian Mari, such pastoralism is commonplace, and Zimri-Lim's own rule is even defined by this way of life. The standard word in the Mari archives for herdsmen who live at a distance from settlements is "Hana," perhaps derived from the act of "camping" in tents, and Zimri-Lim is "king of Mari and the Hana people (*māt* Hana)."[18] Most of the ubiquitous uses of the word "Hana" in the Mari correspondence take for granted that these are Zimri-Lim's own tribespeople, the Binu Sim'al, who are thus identified by their mobile herding component.

One oft-discussed letter to Zimri-Lim from the district governor of Mari sets up a duality that resembles the Akkadian/Amorite pair. Bahdi-Lim exhorts the king to respond carefully after consolidation of his rule over a part of his realm that includes an "Akkadian" population:

[My lord] must honor the head of his kingship. [Just as] you are the king of the Hana, [so] you are secondly the king of the Akkadian. [My lord] must not (therefore) ride a horse. My lord must (rather) ride [on] a litter and mules, if he is to honor the head of his kingship.[19]

In spite of efforts to isolate which of these modes of transportation is specifically "Akkadian" or "Hana," the main point seems to be that the horse is not an appropriate royal mount for ceremonial occasions. What is striking for

---

[15] A.361, in Charpin (1991, 141–5). The key list appears in two places, II 2′–4′ and III 13′–15′, more complete in the latter.

[16] A.489, in Charpin and Durand (1985, 323 n. 131); the letter is from an official named Rip'i-Dagan to Zimri-Lim and addresses the defeat of Išme-Dagan and Yasmah-Addu, the two sons of Samsi-Addu. Rip'i-Dagan reproaches some group that has not been adequately enthusiastic in its support for Zimri-Lim in the past. The reference to the population ruled by the Mari king seems to occur after this main preserved section, in the last visible lines, cited in Durand (1992, 113 n. 137).

[17] Kraus (1958), e.g., p. 30 paras. 2′:9′; 4′:24; 6′:1.

[18] Durand (1992, 13–14); with extended discussion of Zimri-Lim's Hana kingdom in Fleming (2004a, 147–69); reinterpreted in Fleming (2009).

[19] ARM VI 76, letter to Zimri-Lim from Bahdi-Lim, governor of the Mari district; discussed in Fleming (2004a, 156–9).

this discussion is the definition of Zimri-Lim as king of two broad populations, identified by "Akkadian" and a second term. In both this text and the reference to the "king of the Akkadian and the Amorite" (above), Zimri-Lim is characterized as ruling two broad groups, one of which is Akkadian. This is the only such identification of what Zimri-Lim rules by Akkadian and Hana. Based on the occurrence of the Akkadian/Amorite combination in the Ešnunna treaty and the Babylonian royal edict, the Amorite element appears to be standard to such pairing. Bahdi-Lim's use of "Hana" seems then to take the place of "Amorite" for Zimri-Lim's particular kingdom based at Mari.

If the pairing of Akkadian and Hana does indeed match that of Akkadian and Amorite, this may strengthen the association of the word *amurrû* with mobile pastoralists. As Hana, these are not isolated from the core settled population, whether as a distinct "ethnic" group or as separate "nomads." Most often, Zimri-Lim's Hana are his tribal kinsmen of the Binu Sim'al, fully integrated into the leadership of the kingdom, and the primary military force on which he relies. The Binu Sim'al occupy many towns and villages in the Mari kingdom, and it is impossible to disentangle the nomadic population from the social fabric of the settled tribespeople. While the Hana of Bahdi-Lim's schema represent Zimri-Lim's own people by name, the Amorites ruled as "Akkadian and Amorite" and in the Ešnunna treaty would identify the same pastoralist type by a category in wider use. As with Zimri-Lim's Hana, the Amurrû need not be restricted to mobile herdsmen only, for they could equally include whole populations that incorporate a significant mobile herding component.

As a language designation, then, the Amurrû category is particularly intriguing. In the eyes of certain scribes, at least, groups with such a mobile component are characterized by use of a language or set of dialects that could be considered separate from Akkadian. In the kingdom of Zimri-Lim, not only was Akkadian the language of formal correspondence, but the name could also identify distinct communities that could supply a coherent fighting force. Both these and the "Amorite" groups somehow represented definable speaking groups, if the treaty labels align with the language types.

As I understand the evidence, the identification of certain speakers with an "Amorite" language is bound up with the distinction of an "Amorite" component to the population, both set against what is "Akkadian." I prefer not to treat this distinction as "ethnic," a term laden with overtones of separation amidst inequalities of power that will only confuse our interpretation of early Mesopotamia. By my approach, both Ebla's Martu-land and the later land of Amurrum take their names from the identification of Amurrû population, and neither provides a geographical origin for "the Amorites," as if these were a single group migrating from the west. If the Amorite category in Old Babylonian evidence indicates peoples with a mobile pastoralist component, this use may preserve the original intent of the word "Martu" from the third millennium, before the distractions of Ur and its famous collapse.

In calling the tribal peoples of the Mari archives "Amorite," therefore, we adopt a usage that was still in use at Mari but seems to have been largely supplanted by the term "Hana." In this early second-millennium setting, "Amorite" would have been an archaic term, perhaps carrying with it a sense of antiquity and continuity that the contemporary word may have lacked. While the historical question of Israel's origins will continue to be debated, and the role of mobile pastoralists remains part of that debate, Israelite tradition in the Bible repeatedly envisions a background among herdsmen. The Amorites were not nomads; they were a population that integrated large-scale and long-distance herding with complex social organization, settlement, and cities. It appears that both Israel and the Aramean polities shared a heritage in such groups, and the tendency toward collaborative arrangements has a precedent in the pastoralist and tribal peoples known at Mari.

B. Specific Political Configurations in the Mari Evidence

Two different types of association receive considerable attention in the Mari archives and can be examined in detail. First, as discussed already with reference to Benjamin in Chapter 9, a large portion of the peoples who might be called Amorite in ancient Syria divided themselves as Sons of the Left Hand (Binu Sim'al) and Sons of the Right Hand (Binu Yamina). Because the Binu Sim'al association of peoples was identified with the royal family of Zimri-Lim and represented its primary power base, the Sim'al/Yamina duality was of essential importance to the kingdom. Second, there are three multiple-member polities mentioned often in the Mari archives that function as a single "land," or *mātum*. Ordinarily, the term *mātum* is reserved for entities ruled by individual kings, but the "lands" of Ida-Maraṣ, Zalmaqum, and Šubartum are made up of separate centers, each with its own king, so that they operate politically as collectives. The best known of these is Ida-Maraṣ, because of its close alliance with the Binu Sim'al and Zimri-Lim of Mari.[20]

1. The Binu Sim'al

The Binu Sim'al and the Binu Yamina were organized along strikingly different lines, and both systems offer points of reference for biblical patterns and a caution against assuming the ubiquity of a single political form for distributed power and collaborative governance. We know that the Binu Sim'al were once organized by constituent peoples because their *gayum*s remain the primary categories for identifying individuals from this association.[21] By the time of Zimri-Lim, however, all of the Binu Sim'al were ruled by the Mari-based king, and one reference to a diplomatic exchange even has Hammurabi of Babylon speak of Zimri-Lim as "the king of the Sim'alites," identified by this people

---

[20] On the use of *mātum* in the Mari evidence, see Fleming (2004a, 116–32, "The Basic Unit of Regional Politics in the Early Second Millennium").

[21] See Fleming (2004a, 43–63, "The Primary Constituents of the Confederacies: Sim'alite *gayum* and Yaminite *li'mum*," esp. pp. 50–8).

rather than by the central city of Mari.²² In Zimri-Lim's own titulary, he names his people as the Hana or "Tent-dwellers," as seems to be the norm for the Binu Sim'al, who thus understand themselves to embody a whole pastoralist way of life.²³ Although there were many Sim'alite leaders, and there was a vigorous tradition of assembly and popular participation, Zimri-Lim acknowledges no notion of confederacy or association, and there are no representative leaders for member groups in the Binu Sim'al.²⁴

It is difficult to be sure how stable this configuration was, with all member peoples accepting a single leader as king. The first king of a unified "Hana" people may have been Yahdun-Lim, whom Zimri-Lim claims as his father. In his Šamaš temple dedication inscription, Yahdun-Lim claims to have defeated a coalition of Hana peoples, after defeating a coalition of Binu Yamina centers.²⁵ His disc inscription then proclaims: "Seven kings, fathers of the Hana who fought together against me – I defeated them and restored their land to my side."²⁶ If these Hana have the same point of reference as they have under Zimri-Lim, the texts recall the forced submission of all Binu Sim'al to one ruler (Fleming 2004a, 152–3). Yahdun-Lim's son Sumu-yamam survived only two years before his father's longtime rival Samsi-Addu took the whole kingdom from his eastern base of power. Samsi-Addu set up his younger son Yasmah-Addu to rule this western addition, and while the son fared well enough as long as the father held regional power, the Binu Sim'al took back Mari and its dominions in the time of Zimri-Lim.

---

²² ARM XXVI 385:3′–8′: "Rim-Sîn (king of Larsa) sent out these hostile words. Except for the great gods who [came] to my aid, it was Zimri-Lim, the king of the Sim'alites, who put his life on the line with me again and again – there was no one else." See Fleming (2004a, 160) for discussion of this text and this identification of Zimri-Lim.

²³ Many texts display this identification. In one of the most explicit, an officer opens and closes his battle report with a chiastic affirmation of the well-being of the king's troops: "The Hana are well. The armies of my lord are well" (line 4); "The armies are well. The Sim'alites are well" (line 5′). The key insight into the identity of the Hana came from Charpin and Durand (1986, 153–5), who discovered that Zimri-Lim himself was a Sim'alite. Durand then proposed that the name derives from the verb "to camp" (ḫny) (1992, 113 and n. 138; 1998, 418). For extended discussion of the Hana terminology at Mari and further bibliography, see Fleming (2004a, 85–92).

²⁴ The custom of assembly among the peoples not defined by settled territory is associated with the word riḫṣum, which refers to "talks" held in large meetings, especially as internal to groups of Binu Yamina or Binu Sim'al (Fleming 2004a, 208–10). Among Zimri-Lim's Sim'alite people, the independence of participants can be impressive. Zimri-Lim's trusted aide Asqudum writes to his lord that he anticipates criticism of a major Binu Sim'al leader: "I am afraid that at the time of the talks, Ibal-pi-el may come under criticism by the (Sim'alite) Hana. . . . Now, my lord wrote to me about Itilim before the talks, and I will send Itilim either to (the town of) Ṭabatum or to Haya-sumu (king of Ilan-ṣurâ), so he will not be present at the talks. I will keep (here) the others who might stand up and complain about Ibal-pi-el in the talks" (ARM XXVI 45:4–6, 18–27).

²⁵ "He tore down the town of Haman, of(?) the tribal confederacy(?) of the Hana, which all the fathers of the Hana had built, and made it a mound and a ruin. Thus he defeated Kaṣuri-hala, its king" (lines iii 28–32). For the full text and bibliography, see Frayne (1990, 604–8), E4.6.8.2.

²⁶ Frayne (1990), E4.6.8.1:15–20.

After Hammurabi of Babylon forced Zimri-Lim's departure from Mari, the Binu Sim'al disappeared from view and cannot be traced in any surviving texts. There is certainly no long and stable line, based at a single capital, to compare with the house of David at Jerusalem. The situation resembles something more like the Israel portrayed for the early monarchy, when neither the royal house nor the capital is stable. Sumu-yamam's two-year reign recalls the repeated biblical references to sons of Israelite kings who survived into a second year only after their accession: Eshbaal/Ishbosheth of Saul, Nadab of Jeroboam, and Elah of Baasha. One wonders whether Sumu-yamam was also somehow a target for internal removal of support once he was through the year of his enthronement (see Chapter 18). Even with a unifying ruler, there was still diversity of leadership among the Binu Sim'al, especially in the traditional role of the *mer'ûm* or chief-of-pasture. The chiefs-of-pasture, whether or not more than one could exist at a time, are never identified as leaders of an individual *gayum* people or any other subset of the Binu Sim'al association (Fleming 2004a, 76–85).[27]

Under Yahdun-Lim and Zimri-Lim, there is no evidence that the *gayum*s of the Binu Sim'al remained politically viable. This situation resembles Israel as portrayed in the biblical stories about life under kings, where one speaks only of "Israel," even where there is indication of collective political power, as with David and Omri. If the comparison is valid, it may be that we cannot discount any political dimension to these group identities for either setting. Jacob's sayings in Genesis 49 admit the reality of kings in a text that attends to the special character of each people. The royal focus of the Mari archives also may ignore any decision-making role for the *gayum* unit. Mari's massive correspondence allows much more opportunity for inadvertent references to practices outside the palace interest, yet the similar biblical uncertainty gives pause.

2. The Binu Yamina

Neither the Binu Sim'al nor the Binu Yamina were identified by a settled land and urban capital, though they conquered cities and lands and took up residence there. With Yahdun-Lim and Zimri-Lim successful enough to hold Mari and lay claim to its Euphrates-based domain, the Binu Sim'al could be linked strongly to one kingdom, even as their identity was never subordinated to that center. It seems that both the Binu Sim'al and the Binu Yamina competed for farmland and political control along the Euphrates valley of Syria, so that when the Binu Sim'al took Mari, they were in a position to subdue a large population of settled Yaminites.[28]

---

[27] During the reign of Zimri-Lim, two *mer'ûm*s make frequent appearance, though never together and never with reference to the other. Durand concludes that in general, two *mer'ûm*s served at any given time (1997, 630–1 n. d, commenting on A.2741; cf. 1998, 471).

[28] There is considerable uncertainty about the nature of relations between Zimri-Lim's Binu Sim'al and the Binu Yamina at the start of his reign. By the end of his first year in power, Zimri-Lim

Unlike the Binu Sim'al, the Binu Yamina during the reign of Zimri-Lim had no unifying king. According to records and letters from the time of Zimri-Lim, five allied peoples, none defined by central towns, acknowledged five separate leaders, and the Sim'alite Mari king dealt with the Binu Yamina through these leaders. Two administrative lists name the five Yaminite peoples and their individual heads, not called "kings": the Yahrurû, the Yarihû, the Amnanû, the Rabbû, and the Uprapû.[29] In general, individuals would not call themselves "Yaminite" (Binu Yamina), a category usually applied from outside, as by Zimri-Lim's officials to the mass of Binu Yamina who occupied their own towns in the kingdom.[30] The Binu Yamina themselves would take the name of their own peoples, according to the five specific groups.[31] As far as the Mari texts allow us to see, the only occasion for unified action by the Binu Yamina peoples seems to have been war.[32]

To some extent, the consistent structure of this association may be artificial, as seen through the administrative lens of the Mari-based kingdom. There is no

seems to have initiated hostilities with the Binu Yamina in the traditional Euphrates domain of the Mari-based kingdom (Charpin, in Charpin and Ziegler 2003, 190). Relations were friendly before this period, although it is not clear to what extent the Binu Yamina were involved in the fall of Yasmah-Addu. In the same volume, Ziegler observes that Samsi-Addu's whole upper Mesopotamian kingdom came apart after his death under assault from multiple directions, only one of which was the Hana (p. 144). She does not include the Binu Yamina among the known attackers. The Terqa district of the Mari kingdom, upstream from the royal capital, had a longstanding Yaminite population, or at least a population that preceded Zimri-Lim's reign, and this was bound to produce tension with the Binu Sim'al, who now offered themselves as their overlords, by inheriting the Mari-based realm of the Euphrates valley (see the letters of ARM III; also Millet-Albà 2004). Samsi-Addu encouraged his son Yasmah-Addu to treat the Binu Yamina with sensitivity to their need for independence, and if Yasmah-Addu kept up such a policy, it is hard to imagine their joining the Binu Sim'al against him. The father writes: "You wrote to me about taking a census of the Yaminites. It is not a good idea to take a census of the Yaminites. If you take their census, their kin, the Rabbû who live across the river in the land of Yamhad, will hear (about it) and become provoked at them, so that they cannot return to their land. You must not take their census at all" (ARM I 6:6–13; translated in LAPO 17, no. 641, p. 342).

[29] Yaminite soldiers are recorded by numbers promised and then either present or undelivered for an expedition to help the Babylonians against Elam (ARM XXIII 428 and 429). These lists identify *all* of the Yaminites who could be accounted for by association with settlements in Zimri-Lim's districts of Mari, Terqa, and Saggaratum, who are supposed to serve with the king's armies. Although Zimri-Lim's administration never acknowledges the Binu Yamina leaders as kings (*šarrum*), the Yaminites could claim the title for their own leaders (see Durand 2004, 158).

[30] See, e.g., ARM III 6, 16, 21, etc; and Fleming (2004a, 92–103).

[31] In A.981, the elders of the town of Dabiš request alliance on tribal terms with the Sim'alites as identified with the Nihadû *gayum*; they call themselves Yahrurû, one of the five Binu Yamina peoples. For the original edition, see Durand (1992, 117–18). On this important text, see Fleming (2004a, 97–103); Miglio (2010, 45–58).

[32] The third year of Zimri-Lim's reign envisions engagement with the whole confederation, in the name, "Year in which Zimri-Lim defeated the Binu Yamina" (see Charpin and Ziegler 2003, 258). A specific example of the Binu Yamina gathered for war is found in ARM XXVI 24, below.

indication that the leaders of the Binu Yamina peoples are the sons of the previous leaders. At least, none is identified as part of a family or dynastic line, for Mari interest.[33] Even the title of "king" constitutes a claim of social parity only with those who rule from town capitals and *mātum* lands, the essential possessions of early second-millennium monarchy, as seen in texts (Fleming 2004a, 119–21). Individual rulers could have particular affiliations with town centers, although the relationships with these centers could be negotiable. One letter found at Mari offers an unexpected view of one Yaminite king in correspondence with another. The sender casts himself as a nomad-warrior, toughened by life in the backcountry, while the recipient is a supposed to be a ladies' man, weak and sheltered in a town base (A.1146, in Marello 1992). In fact, both rulers are understood to operate from a principal town, but their relationships to the town are different, both in fact and in portrayal.[34]

According to Hammi-ištamar, king of the Uprapû, his counterpart among the Yarihû is lazy and foolish. He is enlisting Yasmah-Addu and the Yarihû to join Zimri-Lim for war, and he fears that they will not cooperate:

Before I left, [I said,] "You (sg.) should go with me.... Zimri-Lim, to go.... " You [intend] to eat, to drink, and to go to bed, but you do not intend to go with me. Staying put and lolling in bed will not brown (your skin). As for me, if I sit around inside just one day before I go out into the back country to breathe free, my throat is choking.

You put your trust elsewhere, thinking, "I have given silver to my tribe." What is this silver of yours that you gave? All of your silver that you gave – I know about it. Yesterday, all your tribe assembled at Hen, and the one who loves you was saying, "Write to him so he will go," while the one who rejects ("hates") you was saying, "He should not bother coming." Now if I did not make a habit of turning up in person, they would never manage to act as one.

How then can you be taking this as slander? Neither hot wind nor cold ever struck your face. You bear a (*lipištum*=??) not your own, and the moment father and mother set eyes on your face, you having dropped from the vagina, here was a vagina waiting to receive you. You don't know the first thing about anything.[35]

At this point, Hammi-ištamar contrasts all this to his own daring life on the move, including repeated escape from uprisings against him at the town of Ahunâ. Regardless of whether the Yarihean ruler actually leaves his town base, it appears that the two men are pursuing different strategies in relation to these

---

[33] Charpin and Ziegler (2003, 264) gather the names and dates for the known rulers of the five Binu Yamina peoples. There appears to have been a general turnover after the war with Zimri-Lim, and only Dadi-hadun of the Rabbûm survived, perhaps because of his more western base in Abattum and Imar. I am not aware of evidence for identification by patronym or dynasty, although this may reflect the lack of Yaminite royal documents.

[34] Note that while each leader operates from a town base, the people or tribe is not named by that town.

[35] The context suggests a meaning for *lipištum* that is lewd and insulting, to suit the translation offered for the term in von Soden's dictionary: cf. *AHw* s.v. *lipištu(m)*, *lipiltu*, "scrotum"; vs. *CAD* s.v. *lipištu* 1 "(an abnormal fleshy or membranous substance)." Marello (1992) translates, "*Tu portes une race qui n'est pas la tienne*," following Durand (1990a, 282–3). Durand argues that at Mari, the term always has to do with "*progéniture, parenté très proche.*"

settled centers. Yasmah-Addu of the Yarihû operates more like Zimri-Lim, with reliance on a fixed capital, and his counterpart with the Uprapû is afraid that the Sim'alite king will consider this a threat, especially if the Yarihû do not contribute adequate men and supplies to the campaign of their ostensible overlord.[36]

The Binu Yamina compare in part to what Israel may have looked like as an association of peoples without a unifying king. Even in crisis, as with the war against Zimri-Lim, it is not evident that any one person came to the fore to lead the whole group. The Bible, and especially the book of Judges, shows no interest in describing early Israelite political structure in systematic terms. Or rather, the hero stories, even if rooted in early times, preserve no general knowledge of such structure. It is likely that each people did acknowledge one leader of its own, as found with the Binu Yamina of the Mari archives. At the same time, the Mari evidence sometimes depicts the Yaminites as acting collectively:

Asdi-takim and the kings of Zalmaqum, along with the leaders and the elders of the Yaminites, have slain the ass in the moon-god temple of Harran. The kings of the land of Zalmaqum kept advancing the following proposal: "We should go to war against Der, so we may take a stand as kings."[37]

We cannot tell how these leaders and elders relate to the five individual peoples of the Binu Yamina, and there is no reason to limit the group to their five kings. As viewed from outside, both the association of peoples and their leadership form an undifferentiated mass, somewhat like the elders of Israel who gather to anoint David king in 2 Sam. 5:1–3.

The Binu Yamina of the Mari archives offer some of the clearest evidence for an association of peoples that operate as individual political agents. In the influential analysis of de Geus, Israel's tribes were vague territories without political function (1976, 164). Against this view, the book of Judges, and the Song of Deborah in particular, depict the individual peoples of Israel making the choice of whether or not to go to war. The Mari material shows that decisions about waging war and making peace were the most significant political acts undertaken by distinct peoples, especially in collective mode through the process of muster.

3. The Mātum Alliances

In both the Mari archives and other contemporary usage, the primary political unit of the Mesopotamian landscape was the *mātum*, or "land." This is the common category that identifies each kingdom that contributes to the web of polities that crossed Mesopotamia with varying concentrations of population

---

[36] This analysis of Yasmah-Addu's reliance on his settled center was developed especially by Darya Zuravicky in my honors seminar in spring 2008 at New York University.

[37] ARM XXVI 24:10–15; the last line of the war declaration is uncertain. The "leaders" are the *sugāgum*, a common category of upper Mesopotamian political structure in the Mari archives.

and capacity to project power. It is best to avoid thinking in terms of states with boundaries, when even apparent frontiers are defined more by the affiliations of people and the ability to dominate travel routes than by control of space in its own right.[38] Likewise, the *mātum* designates a "land" in terms of its people, not a territory as such, and the word is not tied to kingship, in contrast to the biblical *mamlākâ* ("kingdom, realm"). Nevertheless, the *mātum* is consistently associated with kings, most often as the people who accept the leadership of a king. Generally, to warrant classification as a *mātum*, a polity would have had the combination of a ruler who could be ranked as a proper "king" (*šarrum*) and a fixed capital with palace, whether or not with a significant residential population distinct from these. By this terminology, Judah and Israel would have been acknowledged as the "lands" ruled from Jerusalem and Samaria, and the titulary of their rulers would have called them "king of Jerusalem and the land of Judah" and "king of Samaria and the land of Israel."[39]

The Mari evidence presents an unexpected variation on this pattern, still linked to kings yet not as a simple kingdom. Three "lands" in the upper Mesopotamian region were constituted as standing alliances of smaller city-based realms: Zalmaqum in the west, defined by four towns in the upper Balih River region; Šubartum, probably east of the Tigris, not well known to Mari and without distinction of its members; and Ida-Maraṣ between them in the Habur River drainage system, with a fluid constituency of at least ten smaller entities.[40] It was not necessary to name all members for every act, and membership seems to have been defined for the purposes of writing by the practical involvement of the groups directly affected.[41] Because the Ida-Maraṣ alliance was aligned closely with the Binu Sim'al peoples, and Zimri-Lim's kingdom extended north to include a district in the Habur River valley based at Qaṭṭunân, the Mari archives display this association in greater detail than the other two. One series of letters follows the negotiation of a treaty between Ida-Maraṣ and the Hana, as overseen by Ibal-el, one of the important Sim'alite chiefs-of-pasture (*mer'ûm*) under Zimri-Lim (see the previous note). Although Zimri-Lim is king of the Hana, and Ibal-el is his subordinate as their

---

[38] See the important article by Joannès (1996); Adam Smith makes a similar point in his discussion of geopolitical space (2003, 127). Against the popular interpretation of settlement patterns by "central-place analysis," he asks whether straight-line measures of distance are appropriate, rather than actual routes of transportation and communication.

[39] Cf. Zimri-Lim, as "king of Mari and the land of the Hana" (see Charpin and Durand, 1986, 151–2); and Fleming (2009).

[40] For the three alliances, see Fleming (2004a, 124–8).

[41] One example comes from a set of letters to be discussed next, related to the negotiation of a treaty between Ida-Maraṣ and Zimri-Lim's Hana (Binu Sim'al) people, as led by the chief-of-pasture Ibal-el (Charpin 1993, texts 2–3, 7–9). The alliance itself is reported in texts 7 and 8. In the first letter, the negotiation is led by the king of Ašnakkum along with "the elders of the land of Ida-Maraṣ" (A.2226:3–4), followed by mention of two specific representatives from Šuduhum and from Ašnakkum (no. 7; A.2226:8–9). Once the treaty has been ratified, Ibal-el speaks of having gone to Ašlakkâ to slay the ceremonial donkey to seal the treaty (no. 8; = ARM II 37:5–7).

chief-of-pasture, the treaty is defined by the Binu Sim'al as Hana, not by their king or by the capital at Mari. The *mātum*s of Ida-Maraṣ and Zalmaqum consisted of town-based centers, each of which could claim status as a kingdom in its own right, yet which related to Zimri-Lim and the Binu Sim'al mainly as a unit. They had "kings" individually but one "land" together.[42]

Although these *mātum* associations have membership in town-based polities, they share much with the Binu Yamina group. Ida-Maraṣ is never ruled by any single king, so that it faces the outside world as a collaborative team of leaders, each with influence suitable to the power of his own polity. No town or palace serves as capital for the whole *mātum*, nor is there any administration for the association as such. Two of the *mātum* alliances had strong affiliations with the peoples not defined by settlement: the Binu Yamina were specially bound to Zalmaqum, and the Binu Sim'al to Ida-Maraṣ. Thus, these political entities did not exclude "tribal" populations or connections. Rather, they took their identities from the forms of kingdoms and towns. Only the collaborative aspect betrays another background and social logic.

Early Israel, before or after the first "kings," may have incorporated polities beyond those eventually identified by the term *šēbeṭ*, or "tribe."[43] The Song of Deborah names Gilead and Machir, along with the mysterious Meroz, cursed for failing to come fight on Yahweh's behalf (Judg. 5:23).[44] The peoples loyal to Eshbaal (Ishbosheth) are defined to include Jezreel, which is otherwise known as a city, along with Gilead and the unknown "Ashurite" (2 Sam. 2:9). Judges 9 treats Shechem as one prominent town in a larger and unnamed kingdom of Abimelech, so that if Shechem was allied with early Israel, it may not have chosen this alignment by any "tribal" identification. Because the biblical tradition of separate peoples joined under the name "Israel" comes to be fixed in a scheme of twelve tribes, it is easy to treat this system as the essence of Israelite political association, as did Noth with his Greek-inspired "amphictyony." The variety of associations attested in the Mari archives for early second-millennium Mesopotamia displays the fluidity and variety of actual practice, and these few biblical texts preserve hints of the same traits in the formulation of Israel as an association of distinct peoples.

[42] In spite of the alliance between Ida-Maraṣ and the Hana, two of the years in Zimri-Lim's reign are named for victories over Ašlakkâ alone, perhaps the most powerful Ida-Maraṣ center. For years 4 and 13, see Charpin and Ziegler (2003, 258).

[43] We must keep in mind that the Bible's identification of "kings" does not come from writing that is contemporary with the figures in question, and even in the Mari archives, where chronology is not an issue, the application of titles is a matter of dispute and negotiation. Nevertheless, the repeated discussion of Saul as "the anointed of Yahweh" and David as his cautious and deferential successor suggests a particular sensitivity to the competing roles of these two early figures – evidently in the circle of David's house. If there were "kings" before Saul and David, the Bible has forgotten their importance.

[44] This verse is sometimes removed as secondary because of the reference to Yahweh and the peculiarity of Meroz (Neef 2002, 55–9, 66). Rather, the inexplicable character of Meroz more likely confirms its originality, as opposed to addition by any attempt to adjust the text toward other biblical writing.

Given that both the Binu Yamina and the Ida-Maraṣ *mātum* alliance share traits that are relevant to early Israel, it is worth isolating their differences. Although both have separate rulers over individual constituents and neither has a single ruler for the whole, Ida-Maraṣ and the *mātum* associations seem to have a geographical or territorial basis that is foreign to the Binu Yamina, who consist of peoples not defined by settlement. Binu Yamina and Binu Sim'al groups did live in towns, and their leaders generally adopted a town as principal base of operations, yet the constituent peoples are not identified by those central towns, in contrast to Ida-Maraṣ and Zalmaqum.[45] All the constituents of the *mātum* alliances appear to be named for central towns, or the towns named for the peoples.[46] The choice of names not taken from towns may reflect a priority for mobile herding components of the Binu Yamina and Binu Sim'al peoples, compared with the allied "lands." There is no reason to imagine that lands such as Ida-Maraṣ lacked herds or herding communities that traveled distances from settlement. Nevertheless, these polities identified themselves in a mode more like standard kingdoms with central capitals, which also would have supported herds and their communities in this period.

The text that defines the Binu Yamina and the Sima'lite Hana by their broad ranges of movement identifies the Hana specifically with Ida-Maraṣ, in this case not defined as a *mātum*.[47] The Binu Yamina are explicitly said to overlap three major "lands": Yamhad, Qatna, and Amurrum. Interestingly, Mari and its "land of the Hana" are left unnamed, perhaps assuming that all are familiar with the presence of both groups in this intermediate territory. This kind of geographical drawing outside the lines is somehow characteristic of the Binu Yamina and Binu Sim'al. By taking the name "Hana," "Tent-dweller," to identify the entire Binu Sim'al association, the people of Zimri-Lim stamped themselves as pastoralist by nature (Fleming 2009). This character is taken for granted in a letter to Zimri-Lim from the chief-of-pasture named Bannum, who appears to have played a leading military role in the conquest of Mari:

And if the Hana press you to appoint another chief-of-pasture, saying, "Now that Bannum, our chief-of-pasture, lives in the Banks of the Euphrates, we should appoint another chief-of-pasture"; you – answer them this way: "Previously, he lived in the steppe, and he maintained the status of the Binu Sim'al, the Numhâ, and the Yamutbal. Then, he left for the Banks of the Euphrates, where he forced open the fortified towns and so has secured your status in the Banks of the Euphrates. Now, because I myself have come here, I have left this man in the Banks of the Euphrates in order to hold the fortified

[45] The lack of detail regarding the makeup of Šubartum probably reflects the writers' ignorance.

[46] In the land of Ida-Maraṣ, the member kingdom of Qâ-and-Isqâ is composed of two towns that seem to be named for a "Qâ-ite" people. In ARM II 75, the town is rendered with both Qâ and Isqâ in first position. The name "Isqâ" appears to derive in some way from the Qâ element that both town names have in common, evidently through the prefixed *is-*. It seems simplest to imagine that Isqâ meant "belonging to (the) Qâ (people)," with *is-* corresponding to the Phoenician form of the determinative pronoun (*'eš*), as opposed to Akkadian *ša*, both meaning "the one of."

[47] See A.2730, cited above with the Binu Yamina in Chapter 9, on Benjamin.

towns. Now, as soon as I reach (Mari), I will send you back your chief-of-pasture." Answer them this way![48]

The "Banks of the Euphrates," or Ah Purattim, represents the core kingdom associated with the city of Mari, which changed hands from Yahdun-Lim to Samsi-Addu and his son Yasmah-Addu before Bannum and Zimri-Lim returned it to Sim'alite control. The Numhâ and the Yamutbal are other "tribal" peoples who are not defined by their settlements, though like the Binu Sim'al, their population comes to dominate other kingdoms. In the neighborhood of Mari, the Numhâ are the primary people of the kingdom centered at the town of Kurdâ, as are the Yamutbal at the town of Andarig,[49] though these groups are also linked to Hammurabi of Babylon and Kudur-mabuk's family at Larsa.[50] For Bannum in his role as chief-of-pasture, all three groups are significant for their status in the steppe, away from "fortified towns."

An earlier generation of biblical scholars and historians of ancient Israel resorted to Mari for evidence of a patriarchal world, to illuminate the setting portrayed in Genesis.[51] Evidence from Mari for men and women who speak on behalf of gods still offers a useful framework for the study of prophets and prophecy in the Bible.[52] The real riches of the Mari archives for biblical research, however, lie in the portrait of society – not for Genesis and the ancestor stories in particular but for a people understood to combine a background in tribes and local elements with eventual development into two kingdoms. The complex political fabric into which was woven the kingdom of Zimri-Lim offers a range of possible comparisons for political forms and practices from the later southern Levant, as useful for the study of Iron Age Jordan as for ancient Israel. Where inland regions preserved traditions of collaborative politics in the Iron Age, these may be evaluated profitably against the backdrop of "Amorite" society in the early second millennium.

---

[48] A.1098:6'–15', in Villard (1994, 297 and n. 33). For the new interpretation of line 12' as a reference to Bannum's conquest of Mari, see Charpin, in Charpin and Ziegler (2003, 176).

[49] Miglio (2010) adds considerably to our understanding of Zimri-Lim's relationships with these two tribal groups, and how their condition affected the survival of his kingdom. For the Numhâ, see esp. his section 4.3, "Pastoralist Numhâ and the Authoritative Resource of Tribal Territoriality" (pp. 80–96); and for the Yamutbal, see section 6.2, "The *Hipšum*-Alliance and Tribal Foreign Politics" (pp. 133–45).

[50] For Hammurabi, see Charpin and Durand (1986), the last section. On Kudur-mabuk, Warad-Sîn, and Rim-Sîn at Larsa, see the inscriptions for these kings in Frayne (1990, 440–66). The tribal affiliations of the Uruk dynasty can still be seen in the later letter of king Dingiram to Sîn-muballiṭ of Babylon near the beginning of Rim-Sîn's reign at Larsa, where the "troops of Uruk" are joined to the "troops of Amnan-Yahrur" and the "troops of Yamutbalum" (of Rim-Sîn?) (Falkenstein 1963, 56–9, lines i 28–30; cf. ii 27; iii 39).

[51] Thompson's volume on *Historicity* (1974) had as one goal to discredit Mari's place in such reconstructions, and this remains a source for earlier bibliography.

[52] See, e.g., the collected volume edited by Köckert and Nissinen (2003); and a recent individual study by Nissinen (2010).

14

Israel's Aramean Contemporaries

As seen in the variety of evidence for collaborative patterns outside the Near East, and equally distant from Greece and Rome, this dimension of political life is a factor in many settings. Within the Near East, Israel's decentralized political tradition and the more particular framework of associated groups are far from rare, and they are illuminated instead by the contrast visible in the distinct structures of Israel and Judah. To build a context for Israel, I began with the phenomenon of collaborative politics, pointing out its widespread expression by examples from historically unrelated situations. The Mari evidence then provides a starting point for understanding how such political patterns could take form in the Near East, though northward and centuries before the appearance of Israel. For one more contextual aid, I turn to the Arameans, a population first distinct in the late twelfth century in the region roughly corresponding to that occupied by the Binu Sim'al and the Binu Yamina, roughly covering modern Syria. These people and their political habits stand in even more direct continuity with the Amorites of the early second millennium than might those of Israel, yet the Arameans are Israel's contemporaries and offer an ideal final comparison before turning to matters of history.

A. Aram and the Arameans: Neither Polity nor Ethnicity

Thanks to incorporation into biblical geography with its continuous audience across two millennia, Aram has never been entirely forgotten. In the Bible, the name applies both to the kingdom centered at Damascus (e.g., 1 Kings 15:18; 20:1; etc.) and to a territory that overlaps that kingdom and stands in uncertain relation to it, as with the identification of Laban as an Aramean (*'ărammî*) who speaks Aramaic in Genesis 31.[1] The books of Daniel and Ezra include substantial sections in Aramaic, and this language never dropped out of Jewish

---

[1] See "Laban the Aramean" in Gen. 31:20 and 24, followed by his naming of a treaty cairn as Yegar-Sahadutha, which Jacob translates as the Hebrew Gal'ed, both meaning "(rock-)pile of

use in various dialects.[2] Although these facts have little to do with modern study of the Arameans, they shape the basic definitions that still inform such study. In a way, the Aramaic language offers clearer boundaries for identifying Arameans than any other evidence – or at least it is allowed to do so.

Archaeology offers much more raw material for investigation of the Aramean world than does writing, yet this material cannot often be defined as simply "Aramean." Each excavated site belongs to a certain period and place, and only a small proportion of these have produced Aramaic texts. Even for those that have done so, definition of identity by the language of elite writing could be simplistic or mistaken, and specialists handle the evidence from excavation with laudable caution. The local may be distinguishable from the foreign, as with spreading Assyrian presence in the ninth and eighth centuries,[3] but in early first-millennium Syria, local identities are complex and variable.[4]

It may be imprudent to suppose that every use of the Aramaic language demonstrates self-designation as Aramean, though the pattern of language usage is historically significant. The ultimate control for Aramean identity must be the name itself. Hélène Sader (2010, 275–6) observes that the name "Aram" first appears in Aramaic texts with reference to a geographical area in the eighth century. The treaty texts from Sefire (KAI 222–4) refer to "all Aram" and "upper" versus "lower" Aram, while texts from Breidj (KAI 201) and Afis (KAI 202) refer to the Damascus kingdom as Aram, like 1 Kings 15:19 and other biblical texts.[5] The most provocative occurrences are those from Sefire, because they suggest an Aramean identity that does not align with a single polity like Damascus. In the treaty from Sefire between the king of Arpad (Sefire) and the king of the otherwise unknown K-t-k, the participants in the arrangement are listed so as to ripple through time. These begin with the two kings, their sons, grandsons, and generations to follow (I A 1–3). Then the

---

witness" (v. 47). Gen. 29:4 links Laban to Harran (Hebrew Haran) in far northern Syria, though this site is not identified with Aram, which appears with Laban only in chapter 31.

[2] Dan. 2:4b – 7:28; Ezra 4:8–6:18.

[3] See the set of articles assembled by Kepinski and Tenu (2009a), introduced by their own piece (2009b). Anacleto D'Agostino (2009, 33–6) observes no change in material culture at Tell Barri in the upper Ḥabur through the period of Assyrian arrival. In Bīt Zammāni of the upper Tigris, Jeffrey Szuchman (2009, 63–4) observes a new predominance of local ceramics and small-scale architecture that "may represent a deliberate realignment of the cultural boundary of the inhabitants of the region that corresponds to a changing social boundary," rejecting Assyrian influence. This is a negative conclusion, however, and the local identity remains unnamed.

[4] It is possible that certain features of material culture may be defined as definitively Aramean, as observed by Hartmut Kühne (2009, 54) for the representational style of the stele of Tell Ashara and the reliefs from Tell Halaf, which he contrasts with both the Assyrian and the Luwian or Late Hittite. Without a clearer sense of naming and what it signifies, however, such categorization may be a convenience for grouping styles more than an accurate account of cultural or political identities.

[5] In 2 Sam. 10:6, the Ammonites enlist the help of "Aram Beth-Rehob" and "Aram Zobah" to fight David. On the Damascus kingdom, see the overview by Galil (2000); cf. Pitard (1987).

focus shifts to the peoples involved: K-t-k and Arpad; the leadership of each land (lines 3–4);[6] (broken); followed by a widening circle of further interested parties, including all Aram, Muṣr, future sons (of Arpad's king?), all upper and lower Aram, all who have dealings with the palace, and those who set up this monument (lines 5–6). Sader (2010, 276–7) concludes that the whole implied by "all Aram" is not defined by Aramaic language or Aramean ethnicity but rather by participation across most of Syria, regardless of language or affinity.[7]

By the eighth century, therefore, the term "Aram" could be conceived in broadly geographical terms (Sefire) or attached to a specific polity (Damascus). This later usage, however, does not solve the problems of what Aram originally identified and how that usage evolved to the point where the Sefire treaty could place a swath of Syria under its rubric without ethnic intent. Different interpretations of Aramean identity are constructed from the broad features of the societies linked by Aramaic language use, read through the lens of individual social-political frameworks. The groups and their Northwest Semitic language are new to the Iron Age, like Israel and its neighbors further south. Also like Israel in certain biblical traditions, they show a strong collaborative political dimension, which in some cases involves associations that could be called tribal. Unlike the south, these phenomena occur throughout a region that overlaps significantly with the range of evidence found in the Mari archives for a period several centuries earlier, and the possibility of historical continuity must be addressed. Aram and Aramaic are not central to my own research, and I rely on the work of others for what I propose here. As with other interpretations, mine reflects above all a certain sense of ancient society first developed with my study of the Mari archives and then pursued further with this probe of Israel and the Bible.[8]

B. Aramean Origins and Second-Millennium Syria

In broad historical terms, the most important feature of the Arameans is their influence on the Near East as a whole, especially as expressed in the spread of the Aramaic language across Mesopotamia in the early to mid-first millennium B.C.E, as the basis for becoming the administrative language of the Achaemenid Persian empire. Like the Amorites, therefore, a search for their origins – and thereby their significance – in some ancient local expression of

---

[6] The phrase is *b'ly ktk/'rpd*, matching the *ba'ălê šĕkem* as the leadership of Shechem throughout Judges 9 (v. 2 and *passim*). This collective term may be as broad as "all householders" or something more limited yet still treated as representing the whole population.

[7] See also the discussion of particular geographical implications for upper and lower Aram in Talshir (2003, 274–5). The conclusion of Nili Wazana (2008, 731) that "all Aram" is a religious-geographical-social entity, as in Amos 1:5, seems to go beyond what the treaty evidence will bear.

[8] For my review of specific Aramean peoples, I rely primarily on the syntheses of Paul-Eugène Dion (1997) and Edward Lipiński (2000).

the name "Aram" is not the key to their relevance.[9] Before the rise of a coherent social phenomenon in the late second millennium, such references to places or people called "Aram" may in some cases be unrelated even to each other, based on varied forms of rough homonyms. Even if some did reflect a consistent point of reference, then like the western land of Amurru, the names would more likely be derived from a social category than from a polity, even one defined as a "tribal" group.[10] It is more productive to examine the social and political traits of the first Arameans to appear in clear connection with the first-millennium phenomenon.

The first definite occurrence of "Arameans" is in the royal annals of the Assyrian king Tiglath-pileser I (1114–1076 B.C.E), who reports repeated conflicts with the "Aramean Ahlamû" along the whole length of the Syrian Euphrates River, from the Sūḫu of western Iraq as far as Carchemish in modern Turkey.[11] While these people must be pursued and engaged repeatedly, as opposed to besieging them in a fortified town or fighting a massed army with chariots, they do have settled towns, which Tiglath-pileser I counts as vaunted spoils of victory.[12] In spite of these self-proclaimed Assyrian successes, Aramean armies had penetrated the Assyrian homeland by the end of Tiglath-pileser I's reign, from which they had to be pushed back by concentrated effort.[13] During the reign of Aššur-bēl-kala (1073–1056), there are references to a "land of the Arameans" (KUR *A-ra-me*, and varied spellings).[14] This "land" does not seem to have been a unified kingdom with any known capital, although it is possible that the Assyrians attributed such to the Arameans, without knowing where they might be. The chronicle from late in Tiglath-pileser I's reign mentions "the houses of the Arameans" in broken context, somehow

---

[9] It is not particularly important, then, that the toponym *A-ra-mu*[ki] may occur at third-millennium Ebla and other early documents, a phenomenon reviewed in Lipiński (2000, 26–31); for Ebla, see Biggs (1980, 84–5). Lipiński combs through possible references to places called Aram, without confidence that town names have any "ethnic" connection to what he considers the "half-nomadic tribesmen of the Ǧazira and of the Syrian steppe" (p. 28). See also the discussion of these issues in Younger (2007a). With Ran Zadok (1991), Younger concludes, "The fact that the Arameans were nomadic pastoralists and were associated with the *Aḫlamû* seems to indicate that the Mount Bishri region was the particular area from which the Arameans originate" (p. 137). It is striking that this is the very region often proposed for the first Amorites, in what is likewise a misdirected attempt to explain a broadly Mesopotamian and Syrian phenomenon by a narrow point of origin.

[10] This derivative character is clearly true for the designation of the Damascus kingdom as Aram, and it may apply in a different way to the all-inclusive appellation for something like Syria in the Sefire inscriptions and references in the Bible such as Genesis 31.

[11] See Grayson (RIMA 2; 1991, 23), text A.o.87.1:46–47; p. 34, text A.o.87.2:28 (restored); p. 37, text A.o.87.3:29–30; p. 43, text A.o.87.4:34). See the basic treatments of Dion and Lipiński, as well as McLellan (1989); Sader (1987, 1989); and Schwartz (1989, 277).

[12] According to A.o.87.1:43–63 and A.o.87.2:28–29, there are six, in the vicinity of Jebel Bishri, south of the western Euphrates; A.o.87.12:4′-8′ mentions 17 captured settlements. Dion (p. 17) remarks the lack of fortifications or chariotry.

[13] See Grayson (1975, 189); Tadmor (1979, 1–14); and the discussion in Lipiński, pp. 35–6.

[14] RIMA II A.o.89.3:6′; A.o.89.6:7′; A.o.89.7:iii 1, 2, 8, 10, 13, etc.; A.o.89.9:4′.

acknowledging plural groups that were involved in attacks on Assyria's own countryside (lines 3′, 11′). The absence of information for the next century and beyond has more to do with the retreat of Assyrian power than with the situation of Aramean peoples, who appear to have thrived during this period, judging by their prominence in the ninth century, when written evidence is more robust.

Almost everyone who considers the question associates the early Arameans with Syrian pastoralism and organization by tribes. In their 1989 exchange, Sader and McLellan agree on the role of herding and a new social order, and McLellan disputes only Sader's interpretation of a "palace economy" that collapses at the end of the Late Bronze Age in inland Syria.[15] Both Dion and Lipiński envision some combination of the same factors.[16] Dion observes that the region across which Tiglath-pileser I first engaged Aramean enemies spans the same territory that had been inhabited by Amorite herdsmen and villagers since the late third millennium (pp. 17–18). The question then is what we expect from such a population, which has often been set in opposition to cities and the power of agriculturally driven states. In this regard, the approach of Glenn Schwartz (1989, 275) is particularly fruitful: "Although these groups are conceptualized as outsiders by the urban scribes, a closer examination of the evidence often reveals a complex symbiotic relationship between the urban states and the 'alien' groups. . . . "[17] At this date, Schwartz is working with the notion of interrelated but separate social groups proposed by Michael Rowton (see Chapter 13), and this is problematic for the ancient Near East generally. Nevertheless, he must be correct in concluding that "the term Aramaean was simply a new ethnic designation for sheep/goat nomadic pastoralists operating in the Euphrates and Habur regions in patterns comparable to the nomadic

[15] Against Sader's conclusion that there was a significant depopulation of Syrian settlements in the twelfth century, McLellan (170) observes a slight increase in settlements, probably related to similar population shifts with new settlements elsewhere in the Near East, including the southern Levant. For similar analysis, see also Sader (2000).

[16] Dion is the more cautious: in discussion of the "House of X" definition of Aramean polities, he concludes, "*Dans ces conditions, on peut supposer que les formules Maison d'Untel et Fils d'Until remontent au-delà de la plus ancienne documentation écrite sur les états araméens, et que cette phraséologie visait primitivement des societies tribales*" (p. 230). Lipiński sets his whole discussion of Aramean kingship into a nomadic matrix: "The ancestors of the Aramaeans, and the Aramaeans themselves at the time of their proto-history, were nomads or semi-nomads. Tribes in Babylonia continued that way of live [sic] down to the mid-first millennium B.C., and even later, and traces of nomadic customs subsisted also among the tribes which had settled down towards the end of the second millennium or in the beginning of the first millennium B.C. Any study of the Aramaean institutions, social, civil, political, military, and economic, should therefore take that nomadic or seminomadic background into account" (p. 491).

[17] See also Matthew Suriano (2007, 173–4): "Whoever the Arameans were (or better, included), scholars must focus on them as dynamic entities involving both urban and pastoralist components rather than as a group poised at a specific developmental stage along an evolutionary trajectory. Thus while Arameans are designated as a nomadic group (*aḫlamū aramāya*) as early as the twelfth-century in the records of Tiglath-pileser I, they continue to appear as such in incursions reported within the Assyrian Empire during the eighth century."

pastoralists of preceding centuries" (p. 283). Likewise, the process of Aramean state formation (his term) should have "an approximate analogue" in the process for the Amorites of the early second millennium (p. 285). This approach returns us to the Mari evidence and the social structures reflected there, as well as to Anne Porter's sweeping reconstruction of third- and early second-millennium society.

It is striking that the first clear definition of Arameans as a distinguishable population treats them as a single mass and fails to identify them with any focused political domain.[18] No leadership, royal or otherwise, is mentioned in connection with these sweeping western campaigns, as opposed to the "houses" that come into view when Aramean groups attack the Tigris River region of Assyria itself. Tiglath-pileser I claims not to have defeated a kingdom or a coalition but rather to have pushed back a population of a certain type. Based only on this evidence, it would be presumptuous to interpret "Aramean" as a "tribal" label, as if any single group identified itself that way as "the Arameans," and equally incautious to declare the term "ethnic," any more than Amorites, Hana, or Sutû could be called this.

Returning to the initial geography of Tiglath-pileser I's encounter, the broad range and undifferentiated characterization of these first Arameans indeed recalls the Amorites, who most likely took their name from a population type that was identified with mobile herding communities. The Assyrian king understands the Arameans to have occupied the Euphrates valley across all of modern Syria, with interests that reached south and west to Palmyra in the desert and to the base of the Lebanon mountains. In spatial terms alone, this was the core domain of long-distance mobile herding, an area associated for millennia with peoples that organized themselves in ways that maintained social bonds beyond the limits of easy face-to-face contact, as possible in concentrated areas of settlement. As part of her redefinition of entities usually distinguished as tribe and state, Anne Porter (2012, chapter 3) proposes that the mobility of such groups fosters an application of kinship concepts that work at both public and domestic levels. This is true "[n]ot because pastoralists are tribal, but because the practices of kinship, amongst other things, facilitate the extension of both time and space so that those who are physically apart may remain conceptually together." As evident from the social landscape of the Mari archives, which reflect much of the same space, this interplay of herding, mobility, and kinship is not to be explained as "nomadism" and relegated to the "periphery" of land dominated by city-centered states. Under king Zimri-Lim, Mari itself was the center of a "nomad" (Hana/tent-dweller) kingdom, a multifaceted society with all the attributes of urban and agricultural life interwoven with kinship structures that could maintain bonds between people who lived in towns

---

[18] At the same time, the late second-millennium Assyrian usage does not suggest a fixed territory called Aram, and it is no more likely that the term originates in a single locale than did the term Amurrû. Schniedewind (2002) identifies the first Aram as geographical, probably naming tribal groups in the upper and central Euphrates.

hundreds of miles apart and with herding communities on the move over equal distances. To borrow a term from the debate over state formation, this is the kind of "complex society" that we should keep in mind when trying to imagine what was meant by "Arameans" in the royal Assyrian inscriptions of the late second millennium. The evidence is too limited to permit an immediate solution, but it would be easy to consider the first Aramû to constitute a population and a designation much like the Amurrû and the Hana, West Semitic-speaking communities with substantial pastoralist elements and with traditions for maintaining bonds over distance.

If this is true, the language aspect is noteworthy. After the fall of Mari, a smaller kingdom came to occupy the Middle Euphrates valley upstream, documented in part by texts found at Terqa. This "Hana" kingdom took the very name that Zimri-Lim had associated with his Binu Sim'al people, and it would appear to have originated with West Semitic speakers like those of the Binu Sim'al and Binu Yamina populations (Podany 2002). The region of the Middle Euphrates continued to be called the land of Hana under outside rule, even under the Assyrians of the thirteenth to early eleventh centuries (Podany, 73–4). Further up the Euphrates, the town of Emar in the thirteenth century was likewise dominated by West Semitic language speakers, judging by both personal names and a range of West Semitic terms that underlie the Akkadian of the texts (Pentiuc 2001; Pruzsinszky 2003).[19] These regions of persistent Semitic language use stand in relation to the major phenomenon of Hurrian language intrusion into Syria, beginning in the third millennium.[20] Through the middle of the second millennium, filling much of the gap between Amorites in the Mari texts and the first Assyrian evidence for Arameans, a major Hurrian-associated kingdom called Mittani arose from a base in northeastern Syria, from which it came to dominate this same larger Syrian herding domain.[21] Emar shows that in spite of Mittani's power and the movement of Hurrian speakers westward across Syria all the way to the Mediterranean, some regions maintained overwhelmingly Semitic-speaking populations.

Comparing Emar at the great bend of the river with the appearance of "Arameans" less than a hundred years after Emar's fall, across a region that included Emar, it appears that these belong to the same phenomenon of longstanding Syrian populations that experienced minimal Hurrian influence. Tiglath-pileser I's sense of the Arameans put them along the Euphrates and to its south and west, in regions that seem to include both Semitic language dominance and long traditions of social ties over distance. During the late second millennium, these Aramean peoples need not be envisioned to speak "Aramaic"

[19] McLellan (1989, 170) cites evidence from the Emar archives for contact between the Euphrates region and Palmyra, in the southern desert, as a model for pastoralist movement and connections in the thirteenth/twelfth centuries.

[20] For background on the emergence of the Hurrian language and Hurrian language-speaking populations, see Wilhelm (1989).

[21] Eva von Dassow (2008) examines the social and political worlds of Mittani from the vantage of Alalakh, on the Orontes River in western Syria.

as known to the first millennium, itself a more diverse language family in the earlier attested evidence (Huehnergard 1995; Tropper 2001). So far as Aramaic developed from groups that spoke West Semitic dialects, however, it places the Arameans in continuity with the Amorite peoples who ranged across Syria and Mesopotamia several centuries earlier.

The potential implication of this comparison is striking and contrasts with common conceptions. It is increasingly plausible that the Amorites did not invade eastern Mesopotamia, in spite of the characterization of Amorites as western outsiders in writing from the land of Sumer. They were always there, involved with their herds and flocks in the steppe regions across Mesopotamia and Syria together. Whether by a West Semitic "Amorite" language family, which remains a delicate construction in any case, or by use of Akkadian in contrast to Sumerian, these peoples mingled and merged with the peoples of the southeastern river valleys. What then of the Arameans? As specific imped-iments to Assyrian expansion, groups by this name are linked to the whole pastoralist range of Syria. By the early first millennium, their non-Akkadian, West Semitic language exerted a powerful influence on populations in the east.[22] Like the Amorites, it is generally imagined that the Arameans migrated eastward. Could it be instead that such people were always nearby? Just as there were constant shifts in power and movements of people in earlier times, the same could apply later, yet in neither case would it be necessary to cast this as east against west, urban civilization against marauding nomads. The people whom the Assyrians finally identified as Aramean belonged to, and may even have been understood by name to represent, an old heritage of peoples with strong ties to the backcountry, who tended to organize themselves by lines of kinship that yielded associations that we naturally call "tribal." If such is the case, then the juxtaposition of Aramaic evidence with material from Mari is historically appropriate, even across several centuries.[23] Both represent a per-sisting population across a swath of Syria and Mesopotamia, the influence of which derives not from a habit of marauding, followed by sedentarization, but rather from the inability of city-based eastern Mesopotamians to define a world that excluded them.

C. Aramean Politics

As proposed above, the Aramean peoples represent a later manifestation of social patterns found earlier with the Amorites. Together, these show how

---

[22] See Beaulieu (2007, esp. p. 192) on the spread of Aramaic. Görke (2004) isolates specific Aramaic language influences on eighth-century Assyrian writing.

[23] This conclusion would confirm the approach proposed by Schwartz within a somewhat different social framework. Based on a more standard notion of "nomadic pastoralism," Younger (2007a, 140) compares the Arameans to the Amorites, adding more intriguingly that "vocabulary terms such as *ummatum*, *ḫibrum* ('clan, community') and *kaprum* ('village') may suggest affinities between the ancestors of the Arameans and the nonurban societies reflected in the 18th-century cuneiform texts from Mari." See also Rouault (2009).

decentralized political organization with a tribal component remained a consistent part of Syrian life for centuries through the late second millennium B.C.E. The early Arameans and the early Israelites were roughly contemporary and derived from roughly similar populations. It is unnecessary to conclude that Israel literally began as "Aramean," as if by way of migration or invasion. Nevertheless, we benefit by thinking of these groups as sprouting from the same kind of social soil, then shaped by the unique circumstances and choices of their individual settings.

When placed side by side with documentation from earlier periods, the written evidence for early Arameans raises provocative questions about social structures and their political expressions. If the Amorites offer a worthwhile comparison, the first visible "Aramean" polities may represent one more – and perhaps last – adjustment toward the local independence of peoples whose social structures linked settlement and steppe, before the Assyrians made empire the political rule. This may not have been the sedentarization of nomads so much as the realignment of power toward peoples with this composite culture. Once reestablished in regions closer to their longstanding presence, especially in the Euphrates valley and southwest, individual groups and leaders could expand their power into new areas.[24] The establishment of new polities dominated by what seem to be Aramean or Aramaic-speaking populations is visible in any case as the first millennium begins. Much of the earlier evidence comes from the outside looking in, through the eyes of a hostile Assyrian court.

Both of the recent syntheses on the Arameans do take on political life, especially as available in the first-millennium evidence. Dion (1997) addresses directly the political landscape in a chapter on the nature of the Aramean states (chapter 9), which he examines through the categories of "tribal entities," "urban principalities," "territorial states," and "coalitions." He contrasts the kingdoms of the Syrian Arameans with the Arameans of eastern Mesopotamia, whom he understands to have been marginal to urban societies (p. 233). The Aramean kingdoms may be defined as territorial states, not city-states, and without prominent ethnic sentiment (p. 239). Lipiński (2000) assembles the evidence for Aramean peoples by names and places, in a historical framework that seems to assume origins for all of them as invading nomads. As discussed earlier, however, the supposed movements of Aramean peoples must be approached cautiously. Generally, the notion of arrival from outside is based on the absence of evidence for these peoples before their first appearance in the sources. There are gaps in the distribution of sources for the earlier periods, especially, and the occurrence of names is not consistent enough to allow certainty about who is where before each people finally appears.[25]

---

[24] In discussion of "Aramaeans and Substratum Populations," Dion (1995a, 2.1284) observes the survival of non-Aramean language and culture at sites taken over by Aramean groups. He has in mind various northern sites: Hamath in the west, with a previous Hurrian presence; Zinjirli in the northwest; Harran and Tell Halaf on the upper Balih and upper Habur.

[25] For example, Lipiński explains the Arameans in Babylonia by the following process (p. 409): They begin as raiders in the north, while the Chaldeans settle in the south, in the eleventh/tenth

As a whole, the evidence for Aramean groups seems to be based on less familiarity with the people than the evidence from the Mari letters. At least, the nature of the documents seems to involve less detail. Nevertheless, the following represent apparent examples of polity by association.

1. *Laqē*

Lipiński counts twelve "places" with separate local rulers as belonging to early ninth-century Laqē,[26] which he considers to represent a tribal league based on the same tradition as biblical Israel.[27] Most local rulers are identified by individual towns or settlements, with no unifying king named. Assyria receives tribute from the "land of Laqē," which indicates a political unity. In Mari evidence, the association of Ida-Maraṣ may function in similar terms, and both Laqē and Ida-Maraṣ would compare to the terminology of "Israel" alone, without distinguishing any constituent tribes. A governor of Assyria's Sūḫu province, in the Euphrates valley upstream from Babylon, speaks of "the elders of his land and the elders of the land of Laqē," which Lipiński warns not to treat as more than "old men" with memory of the past (p. 492).[28] Defined as a group with reference to each polity, it seems more likely that these are indeed the collective leadership of Sūḫu and Laqē. Of all the Aramean entities, the Laqē association is most like what the Bible portrays for Israel. These elders probably represent individual peoples within the larger association, whether individually or in other combinations.[29]

2. *The House of X*

One of the particular features of Aramean polities is the definition of some by the phrase, "house of X,"[30] with cognate Akkadian and Aramaic nouns *bītu* and *bēt* for the first element. By their very connection to the Arameans, these

---

centuries. In the ninth century, Babylonians, Chaldeans, and Arameans join to fight Assyria. Aramean and north Arabian tribes settle Babylonia in the early eighth century, so that by the later eighth century, they fight together against Assyria, usually as allies of Chaldeans and Elamites.

[26] Lipiński (Chapter 3, pp. 77–108). Sader (2010, 282) categorizes the Laqē with other short-lived groups that never display significant urbanization.

[27] See pp. 77–8 for discussion of the twelve-tribe tradition, and pp. 100–1 for Lipiński's reconstructed list. Given that the biblical count of twelve appears to be a later and Judahite convention, not securely attested for Israel itself, the effort to reach twelve Laqē peoples is suspect. No single Assyrian list includes all twelve, and one list records two rulers under the one rubric of Šūr. Another text only separates each bank of the Euphrates as having a different ruler.

[28] See Frame (1995, RIMB 2, the inscriptions of Ninurta-kudurri-uṣur; texts S.O. 1002.1:47; S.O. 1002.2:34; S.O. 1002.8:19′–[20′]).

[29] This conclusion is based on analogy from the language of A.2226:3–7 in a Mari letter about treaty negotiations between Ida-Maraṣ and the Mari king's Hana people: "Išme-Addu the Ašnakkumite, the elders of Ida-Maraṣ, the elders of Urgiš, of Šinah, of Hurrâ, and the elders of Yapṭur came to Malahatum..." (in Charpin 1993, 182–4).

[30] For a resumé of this naming pattern in the southern Levant, see Couturier (2001, 2.74–5); Schwartz also discusses this category briefly (1989, 278–80).

names have been considered to be somehow tribal, and Dion proposes that the older examples of this type confirm this interpretation.[31] The immediate objection might be that a significant number of House-of-X polities are defined by a founding king, as with Israel's House of Omri and Judah's House of David, and as identified by outsiders. Based on the biblical narrative, both David and Omri can be identified not only as kings but also as the founders of royal houses. There is evidence for the same pattern in Aramean kingdoms, though some reconstruction may be involved.

Perhaps the best example is the kingdom of Arpad, which is also called Bēt-Gūš.[32] A "Gūš of Yahan" is mentioned as chieftain of an Aramean tribe in the annals of the Assyrian king Aššur-Dan II (934–12), in connection with paying tribute.[33] A "son of Gūš" already reigns by 858, and Assyrian texts designate all rulers of Arpad by this title.[34] Eventually, the Assyrians call the kingdom Bīt-Agusi (Parpola 1970, 76). In the case of Bēt-Bagyān of the tenth century, identified as Gozan by the early ninth century, Bagyān can only be reconstructed as the founder.[35] Lipiński imagines that Bēt-Zammāni reflects the same pattern, without evidence beyond the fact that Zammāni could have the form of a personal name.[36] In Assyrian inscriptions, Damascus is often called the "Land of His Donkeys" (*māt imērīšu*), but it can also be the Bīt-Haza'ili, which Dion considers not to reflect any indigenous usage (pp. 227, 231). Sader (1987) concludes from the prevalence of such examples that none of these names refers to tribes or ancestors, but Dion counters that at least Bīt-Ammana for the Ammonites (Hebrew *běnê 'ammôn*) cannot refer to a founding king (p. 229). If anything, Ammon would be a tribal name, not a royal ancestor. Dion likewise doubts that Bīt-Adini ever indicated a king or even that this people had a true hereditary monarchy.[37] In Syria–Palestine as a whole, the House-of-X phraseology is attached only to the Aramean kingdoms, along with Israel and Judah, and not to the Neo-Hittite polities or to city-states such as Sidon or Ashkelon (Dion, p. 232). If the formula really arose in Aramean circles, one wonders whether the House of David name copied the Aramean pattern. The Bēt Dāwîd is first attested in the Tel Dan inscription of the late ninth century,

---

[31] "*Dans ces conditions, on peut supposer que les formules Maison d'Untel et Fils d'Untel remontent au-delà de la plus ancienne documentation écrite sur les états araméens, et que cette phraséologie visait primitivement des societes tribales*" (p. 230); cf. Postgate (1974, 234).

[32] See Lipiński (chapter 8, pp. 195–219); Dion (pp. 225–7). For a detailed discussion of evidence related to the Bīt-Adīni and the Bīt-Agusi during the ninth century, see Yamada (2000).

[33] RIMA 2, texts A.0.98.1:23–32; A.0.98.2:6'-16'.

[34] Lipiński (p. 196 and n. 11, with the variants DUMU-Gusi and DUMU-Agusi). The Aramaic Zakkur inscription uses the phrase *br gš* (KAI 202 A:5), and the Sefire treaty texts name "the House of Gūš" (KAI 222 A:16; B:3, 11; KAI 223 B:10; see Dion, pp. 225–6).

[35] See Lipiński (chapter 5, pp. 119–33). As with Bīt-Agusi/Arpad, the Assyrians call the ruler of Gozan "the son of Bagyān"; see Sader (1987, 5–18).

[36] Lipiński (chapter 6, pp. 135–61).

[37] This would make the site interesting, as a monarchy that might face considerable resistance from a corporate political tradition. Lipiński considers that Bīt-Adini probably had no "centralized power" before Ashurnasirpal's campaign from 876 to 868 (p. 187).

contemporary with early evidence for the Aramean examples.[38] In contrast, the House of Omri in Assyrian texts may have no basis in the local region, as suggested by the fact that the Tel Dan text pairs "Israel" with the "House of David" (lines 8–9).

For Dion, the naming of kingdoms as the House of X goes back not to royal founders but to tribal ancestors.[39] The Bēt-X form reflects what he considers an ethnic sentiment, which contrasts with the territorial basis of the largest Syrian kingdoms: Sam'al, Arpad, Hamath, and Damascus. These larger kingdoms were centralized around a capital, tended to lack the House-of-X name, and incorporated a significant non-Aramean population. One exception is Arpad, which is also called Bīt-Agusi (p. 239). Bīt-Agusi absorbed part of Neo-Hittite Patina and pre-Aramean Aleppo, just as Hamath had been a Neo-Hittite state, and it annexed principalities that were more Phoenician than Aramean.

According to this analysis, Israel would compare more closely to the Aramean territorial kingdoms, without the House-of-X names, although the role of a central city was much less than for these Aramean entities. Sam'al, Arpad, and Hamath all absorbed large portions of other peoples or polities with different linguistic and cultural traditions. During the period of the monarchy, it is not clear how Israel ever accomplished this successfully. The one obvious effort may have come from Omri, who expanded Israelite presence in Jordan, according to the ninth-century Mesha inscription.[40] Linguistic and cultural differences between the Moabite and inland Israelite peoples, however, do not appear to have been overwhelming.

3. Specific Examples of Association

For some Aramean tribes in Babylonia, there seems to be more detail than is usually available for political structures and strategies. Unlike Mari, a relatively small proportion of the evidence for Aramean peoples comes from letters, and material from Nippur now adds to Babylonian examples of this type (Cole 1996). One letter suggests that the Puqūdu tribe could have several leaders at one time,[41] while a Nippur text shows these plural Puqūdu leaders making

---

[38] If identification of the Jerusalem-based kingdom as the House of David first occurred in the ninth century, perhaps by analogy to the Aramean pattern, then we must expect the first realm ruled by Rehoboam to have borne a different name. Only speculation is possible, but in Chapter 18 I suggest that the most likely alternative is "Israel" – the name successfully maintained by the dominant rival to the north.

[39] See also Sader (2010, 279–81).

[40] The Bible attributes such efforts to David in his defeats of the Philistines, Moab, Hadadezer of Zobah, and perhaps Damascus (2 Sam. 8:1–8), as well as the Ammonites (2 Samuel 10). These victories are not confirmed by external evidence, and there is little or no evidence for later periods that Israel or Judah incorporated the peoples of Philistia, Ammon, or elsewhere into their kingdoms. When read with this question in mind, the David texts emphasize glorious victory without claim of incorporation. David takes one site from the Philistines (Metheg-ammah, 8:1), no more. Moab pays tribute (v. 2). Even so far as these accounts reflect later situations, it does not occur to the writer that such peoples would become part of Israel itself.

[41] ABL 622+1279 r.4, in Lipiński (p. 431).

alliances with two other groups, the Bīt-Amukkāni and the Ḥamdān.[42] This kind of short-term association for war is more like the joining of Israel with Damascus against Shalmaneser III, which involved no long-term commitment or shared name, than the uniting of peoples under a common name such as Israel or Laqē.[43] The plurality of Puqūdu leaders by itself may indicate an association on a smaller scale, but the simple collectivity cannot be penetrated for further detail. This kind of language recalls the portrayal of representative leadership that ratifies the selection of kings: the "men of Judah" in 2 Sam. 2:4, and "all the elders of Israel" in 2 Sam. 5:3.[44] Also, the Song of Deborah in Judges 5 presents a series of leadership pluralities that appear to describe representatives rather than full assemblies for war: the mysterious *pĕrā'ôt* in Israel (v. 2),[45] the *ḥôqĕqê yiśrā'ēl* (v. 9),[46] the *mĕḥōqĕqîm* ("commanders"?) from Machir (v. 14), "those who lead by staff" from Zebulun (v. 14), and *śārîm* ("leaders") in Issachar (v. 15). It seems, then, that only the individual peoples are described in terms of leadership, while the introductory hymn emphasizes the unity of the whole people of Israel, in their muster.

Other than the Laqē in western Syria, we do not generally find long-term associations of distinct Aramean peoples under a single name, as the Bible

---

[42] Nippur IV no. 14; a short time later, the Puqūdu and the Bīt-Amukkāni were rivals again (ABL 275 = SLA 78).

[43] In the inscription of Shalmaneser III that recounts the Damascus–Israel alliance, language used for this one-time collaboration is different from that for an all-Aramean alliance described earlier in the text. In the case of Damascus, after the famous list of participants, we are told that its king "had taken these twelve kings as his allies" (12 MAN.MEŠ-*ni an-nu-ti a-na* ERIN.TAH-*ti-šú il-qa-a*). Previously, Haiiānu, the Sam'alite, Sapalulme, the Patinean, Ahunu, the man of Bīt Adini, and Sangara, the Carchemishite, put their trust in each other and prepared for war (*a-na re-ṣu-ti a-ha-miš i-tak-lu-ma ik-ṣu-ru*). The texts are RIMA 3 (Grayson 1996), A.o.102:i 42–44 (all Arameans); ii 89–95 (Damascus and Israel).

[44] Contrast the full assembly pictured in 1 Kings 12:1–3, etc., with the ad hoc audience of people present at the Jerusalem temple for the anointing of Joash (2 Kings 11) and the "people of the land" in 2 Kings 21:24 and 23:30.

[45] The translation of *pr'* is obscure and would be crucial for understanding the purpose of the text as a whole. It is tempting to imagine mustered groups rather than "leaders" (so, the dictionaries). The second half of Judg. 5:2 offers the complement, also a temporal infinitival phrase, "at the volunteering of the people," where the action is performed by the collective, not by its leadership. The best attested use of a verb *pr'* is "to let loose," and the feminine plural on the cognate noun would easily belong to a marked feminine noun (root *pr', pir'â?*), rather than the assumed masculine "leader." This meaning could also work for Deut. 32:42, wherein occurs the one other instance of the noun, again a feminine plural: "I will make my arrows drunk with the blood, and my sword will consume flesh – with the blood of the slain and the captives, with the (mustered) division commanders of the enemy."

[46] Again, modern readers have assumed the priority of leadership over the larger mass, even when grammar and poetic structure suggest otherwise. "The volunteers among the people" complement the phrase in question, and we should expect the group itself before its leaders. If the *po'el* of the verb *ḥqq* means "commander" in verse 14 (cf. Deut. 33:21; Isa. 33:22), as "one who prescribes," then the simple *qal* is most easily left as "those who inscribe," evidently a mark of commitment to fight. The concrete act would help us sketch a better social setting, but we have too little controlling evidence.

indicates for Israel. Tiglath-pileser III boasts in an early text that he defeated 35 Aramean peoples in the Babylonian region (Tadmor 1994, 272). Most of these peoples are not known before their occurrence in this list, except for one group of four.[47] The occasional affiliation of Aramean peoples for military purposes raises the question of whether groups that came to be part of Israel may likewise have joined in an earlier period for mutual defense without sharing the name.

If the two war stories in the Song of Deborah were in fact combined by a separate hand that added the introductory hymn (see Chapter 4), then we cannot assume the peoples listed in Judges 5:14–18 were associated under the name "Israel." The notion that certain peoples were called to fight and declined could give the false impression of an implicit Israel – unity under a name that is unknown to us. In fact, one could say that Reuben, Gilead, Dan, and Asher do no more than any groups might do when invited to join a battle not thrust upon them by urgent need. Modern readers may too easily assume the obligation of membership in Israel, because the opening hymn confirms our expectations that these are Israelite groups. Certainly, the writer of the hymn understood them as such. If "the people of Yahweh" in verse 13 introduce the battle list, then a different name is offered in the earlier text, one defined by the god who leads the fight. Such a religious basis for military association is impossible to measure in the similar alliances found with the Aramean peoples.

Dion observes that some of the more successful Aramean polities grew by annexation of nearby peoples. The Laqē federation extended northward to take over Dur-Katlimmu; Bīt-Adini annexed the Neo-Hittite kingdom of Masuwari (Til Barsip); Bīt-Agusi dominated the old kingdom of Aleppo and part of Patina; and the king Zakkur reunited the Lu'ush under him, along with the former Neo-Hittite realm of Hamath (p. 237). One of the Sefire treaty texts describes coalitions in terms of Upper and Lower Aram (A:5–6), and there is a broad unification around Arpad and Damascus (p. 238).[48] In the early stages of Israel's formation as a polity, we must consider the possibility of association on less than permanent terms. Although the name "Israel" is known from Merenptah in the late thirteenth century, we do not know that this consisted of separate associated peoples as described in the Bible. It is possible that the name "Israel" only became attached to a permanent political association at or near the time when this association was led by kings.

The Aramean evidence reminds us that peoples who shared a larger identity against an external enemy could unite on a temporary basis without defining themselves by a lasting name. At the same time, the Aramean peoples challenge ideas about Israelite "ethnicity" as a quality that can be separated from the

---

47 These are listed in RIMA III text A.0.104.210:10–11 as the 'Utu', the Rupu', the Haṭallu, and the Lab(a)dudu; also RIMB 2 text S.0.1002.2:17; S.0.1002.3:8'; see Lipiński, p. 486. See also Tadmor (1994, 158, 160, lines 5–10); cf. p. 272 line 10.

48 For Arpad, see Zakkur, KAI 202 A:4–9; for Damascus, RIMA 3, p. 23, A.0.102.2:ii 90–95, as twelve units.

political association of the peoples who came to be joined as the kingdom of Israel. Shared language did not require the political unification of Israel and Judah, and we cannot assume that these two peoples understood themselves to have a common language that excluded the easterners of Moab. After all, a minor phonological variation between the dialects of the eastern Gilead people and the western Ephraimites is recalled as adequate basis for identifying the enemy to slaughter in the shibboleth story of Judges 12. With the prominence of the god El east of the Jordan River, it is possible that the peoples who came to constitute Moab and the easterners who were aligned with Israel did not see themselves as worshiping different deities.[49] The basis for Israelite or "Hebrew" ethnicity before the clear definition of an Israelite polity is not substantial.

The linguistic contrast between Aramaic and other languages remains a complex problem. Aramaic would certainly have represented a substantially different language from Akkadian in eastern Mesopotamia, though it is not certain which groups spoke non-Akkadian or West Semitic dialects in which locations. To the west, Arameans would have encountered other Semitic speakers with distinct languages, especially Phoenician near the Mediterranean, and to the north, the contrasts would have been sharper still, especially with Luwian from Anatolia. Even where Aramaic speakers could have seen themselves to share a common language, in contrast to their neighbors or to subdued peoples, this does not prove that they understood themselves to represent a single ethnicity, to be defined against an oppressive external power. With the spread of Aramean peoples across Mesopotamia, there would have been no one antagonist before the Assyrian empire, and even then, individual Aramean groups were often an aggressive and expansive force, not seeking refuge in a shared name.[50] Lipiński speaks of an "Aramaean commonwealth" that comprised the mass of these peoples, "perceived by the Aramaeans themselves and by their neighbors, viz. the Assyrians, the Babylonians, the Israelites, and the Judaeans, as a relatively uniform social reality" (p. 497). This commonwealth would then explain references to the "king of Aram" in an inscription of Shalmaneser III,[51] and claimed for themselves separately by the kings of Arpad and Damascus.[52] It is more likely that the claims of Arpad and Damascus were intended to vaunt each ruler and realm as greatest among Arameans, thus representing them to the wider world. These kingdoms included only a tiny fraction of Aramaic speakers, and they had only local political power among Aramean peoples. Israel and Judah

---

[49] On the place of El among Israelites east of the Jordan, see Levine (2000, 217–30). Routledge (2004, 152–3) proposes that the late ninth-century Mesha inscription presents a novel view of Moab as a politically unified territory. Mesha represents an individual case in the larger retreat of Aramean and Israelite power, so that he converts dominance within Dibon into dominance over a whole land of Moab, in a kind of "ethnogenesis." If Routledge is correct, then the eastern territory before the late ninth century may not have been characterized by any local unity to set against the power or identity of "Israel."

[50] Ethnicity remains a difficult and disputed category; for further discussion, see Chapter 15.

[51] RIMA 3, text A.0.102.2:38.

[52] KAI 201:1, 3; KAI 202 A:4.

appear to be bound into something more limited, with Judah's sense of unity with Israel based on the origin of the house of David in rule over Judah's rival to the north.

With this conclusion of the Aramean evidence for collaborative politics, we turn to questions of history. In my discussion of biblical texts, I argue that the Bible's portrayal of Israel as consisting of tribes reflects a particularly Israelite tradition that recalls social and political organization as associated peoples. The process by which the name "Israel" came to be identified with this association is impossible to know with the evidence currently available. Whatever the specific history, the idea of Israel is intrinsically collective, derived from no individual city or ruler. Both for interpretation of the Bible's diverse accounts of Israel and for historical questions in themselves, this political character is essential to understand, and it is understood best in the context of similar phenomena in the Near East and in societies across time and space.

PART IV

ISRAEL IN HISTORY

15

The Power of a Name

Ethnicity and Political Identity

One primary purpose of this project is to suggest new directions for putting the Bible and history in dialogue. If we take seriously the particular character and heritage of Israel that are now embedded in a biblical framework dominated by Judah and its heirs, we may see different historical assumptions and possibilities in the Bible's Israelite material. At the same time, Israel's distinct political nature with its collaborative aspect raises its own historical questions about the place of this people in the Near East through time. With my own contribution, I leave to historians the systematic analysis of this region through each period of interest. Likewise, I leave to archaeologists the construction of frameworks for identifying and interpreting past societies through the review of all their material remains. I work primarily with texts, both biblical and inscriptional, including the cuneiform contribution to understanding the Bronze Age, and my historical offerings will be most useful and original when derived from this evidence.

With this reality in mind, the final section of this study is built around three chapters that move through blocks of time long relevant to Israel's history. To suit the Bible's primary narrative that represents my point of departure, these chapters span the period of Israel's antecedents through that of the two kingdoms. In the latter case, the books of Samuel and Kings can be mined for historical detail regarding structures and political trends (Chapter 18). The earlier parts of the narrative stand at greater distance from the times they treat, and their relationship to history requires a different approach in every case. For the region before Israel and after Israel's first emergence on the scene, I turn to issues that involve the intersection of naming and politics: the old problem of the 'apiru as this relates to the image in Genesis and Exodus of a pastoralist people (Chapter 16), and identity of Canaan in relation to Israel at a time when both coexisted (Chapter 17). All of these problems permit reflection on the biblical portrait without intention to evaluate any body of evidence in systematic terms: the Bible's treatment of the past, material finds through space and time, or a combination regarded as grist for writing history. Instead, each problem

tests different ramifications of the social and political pattern that I have understood to emerge from the biblical traditions regarding Israel. I therefore frame
the individual cases with discussions of naming (Chapter 15) and what I call
"genuine tradition" (Chapter 19), in order to define the contribution of texts
to history and of the Bible in particular.

A. The Power of a Name: "Israel"

Definitions for space and time are socially constructed, both for the objects
of study and for those who examine them, and it is impossible to establish
them without some entanglement in conventional usage from some community
or another. Space takes on the more meaningful character of place when it is
named. Naming allows reference and may involve overlapping intentions. Parts
of the country north and south of Jerusalem came to be named "the Ephraim
highlands" (*har 'eprayim*, e.g., Josh. 17:15) and "the Judah highlands" (*har
yĕhûdâ*, e.g., Josh. 11:21), with some perhaps irretrievable entanglement of
place and people. It is possible to identify space for purely geographical purposes, as landmarks or territory to traverse in travel, but ancient place names
are often attached to people, whether in single settlements or larger groups.
Where a place must be addressed as a body capable of action – a town, a
city, or a land – the name is political. Other social identification on a larger
scale is conceivable, such as ethnic or kinship naming that does not align
directly with organization for political decision-making. Geographical names
may have complex histories, where political and topographical aspects overlap
or exchange dominance, and full reconstruction of these histories tends to be
futile.

In current study of early Israel, if this entity is understood to have had a
stable existence before the kingdom by that name, it is frequently defined by the
category of ethnicity. The name "Israel" itself appears in one remarkably early
reference from late thirteenth-century Egypt, in the text of a monument set up
for the pharaoh Merenptah, as one of the enemies he defeated in the Levant.
In this context, there is no reason to regard "Israel" as an ethnic category, any
more than the names of Egypt's other conquered foes. As a specific enemy that
fought Egypt under this tag, Israel was a political identifier, and we do best to
begin with this basic character of the name. In the Bible, Israel is the name for
the larger Hebrew-speaking kingdom, where it indicates the people as a body
in their power to act, and it encompasses the same people in their unity during
the period before kings, whether or not this identity is integrated into texts that
portray an association of separate peoples as with the introductory hymn in
the Song of Deborah (Judges 5). These are likewise political uses.

The problem of names is central to understanding the social and political
history of the region through the Iron Age, especially during the long earlier
period lacking written evidence. In strictly historical terms, we do not know
who took the name "Israel" before the kingdom of the ninth century. I will
observe in Chapter 18 that the house of David cannot be assumed to have

relinquished the name when it separated from the people of Israel to launch a separate southern kingdom. We do not know what body was defeated by Merenptah under that name. And we do not know how the peoples that came to be associated with the Israelite kingdom were named. Our ignorance of how these people were named is emblematic of what we do not understand about the social and political landscape of the period. Rather than bypass the problem through the unification of broad types as Philistine, Canaanite, and Israelite, we should probe the names that are available and acknowledge the barriers represented by their larger absence.

To avoid circular reasoning about the Bible's historical relevance, even the basic assignment of a name to any polity or people in the Iron Age Levant depends on nonbiblical writing. There is not much available, but the small body of evidence provides an adequate framework for beginning. We have the Egyptian Merenptah stele, Assyrian references that begin with Shalmaneser III, the Moabite Mesha inscription, and the Aramaic Tel Dan inscription. Among the last three, Mesha and Tel Dan refer to a kingdom named Israel, and only one Assyrian royal inscription does likewise, the oldest mention of the kingdom in this evidence. It is crucial to consider the references to Israel in all four of these texts, because these will serve as a control for the evaluation of both biblical usage and material finds.

1. *Merenptah*

Famously, the earliest reference to Israel or to any political or social entity associated with Israel in the Bible occurs in the late thirteenth century in an Egyptian royal inscription from the reign of Merneptah.[1] If the first settlements of the Iron Age expansion in the highlands north and south of Jerusalem date to the twelfth century, as seems increasingly likely, then the Merenptah reference belongs to the social landscape of the Late Bronze Age, even if the group was new to the late thirteenth century.[2] Merenptah's Israel appears to be earlier than the new concentrations of Iron I villages in the highlands west of the Jordan

---

[1] There is a large bibliography that I will not cite in full here. The important overviews of early Israel and its neighborhood by Killebrew (2005, 154–5) and Faust (2006, 163–6) include basic references. For other recent work, see Kitchen (2004), in response to Dever (2009); Goedicke (2004); Hasel (2004); Hjelm and Thompson (2002); and Morenz (2008). There have been challenges to the identification of the name as "Israel," but these have been rejected by a wide range of specialists and historians on both phonological/linguistic and historical grounds. Especially in the company of named cities from the particular region of what would become the kingdom of Israel, alternative readings have the feel of logical contortions. For one careful discussion of the reading, see Görg (2001), who raises the possibility that a broken place-name list in a text from Amenhotep II of the early eighteenth Dynasty, centuries before Merenptah, could mention Israel in a cluster that includes Ashkelon and Canaan (see also van der Veen, Theis, and Görg 2010). Especially given the absence of Israel from the Amarna evidence, this seems intrinsically unlikely, given the early date and lacking a full reading. There is no historical context for a reading without secure link to the people known to the Iron Age.

[2] For further discussion of chronology, see Chapter 17 on naming in the thirteenth to tenth centuries.

rift valley. This fact is more important than the location of Israel, which most place in the Ephraim hills (e.g., Dever 2003, 206).[3]

Too little is said about Israel in the Merenptah text to give a firm sense of its character, and the details have been carefully and repeatedly mined. Against Ahlström and Edelman, the name is probably not a regional term, the highland counterpart to "Canaan."[4] Aside from arguments about the structure of the text, the sheer novelty of the name in Egyptian writing would make it a strange geographical reference point, and if the name appeared just in the late thirteenth century, this in turn must have a source. Israel is the last in a set of four specific enemies whom Merenptah claims to have defeated, in an odd addendum to a long text focused mainly on conflict with Libya.[5] In contrast to the cities of Ashkelon, Gezer, and Yenoam, Israel is marked as a people, a deliberate distinction from the others as a group not defined by a settled center.[6] Israel and the three cities share, however, their identification as individual enemies of Egypt, fought and defeated under these names. By defining the four peoples by a capacity to engage in war, the Merenptah stele treats all of them as polities, regardless of their particular social characters.[7] The one further detail regarding Israel is embedded in the manner of its defeat: "his seed is not," a detail that has been understood most often to refer to descendants.[8] Michael Hasel argues carefully that seed is most naturally understood as grain, destroyed by fire after battle, according to standard Egyptian tactics (Hasel 1994, 52–4; 2008, 53–4). He therefore concludes that Israel must be an "agricultural society," a category with dubious meaning, in spite of the evident distinction from the

[3] For recent discussion of the alternatives, see Hasel (2008, 50–3).

[4] See Ahlström and Edelman (1985); cf. Hjelm and Thompson (2002).

[5] Goedicke (2004, 54) argues that while the closing section may be distinct, it is not an extraneous piece of court poetry attached to the text; it is addressed to the king, as if derived from the "overthrown chiefs."

[6] The determinative comes up repeatedly in discussion of the text. It is clear that Israel is marked differently from all the entities surrounding it, with a marker that generally signifies people as opposed to territory; for a useful detailed description, see Hoffmeier (1996, 29–30). Niccacci (1997, 91) argues that while the distinction does identify a "people" as opposed to a territory, the determinative is used with enough variety such that we cannot use it to demonstrate that Israel is not sedentary. This caution makes sense in light of the fact that social organization and subsistence patterns often do not align by polar dualities, as nomad/pastoralist/tribal versus settled/farmer/town-identified.

[7] The name that follows Israel is Kharu, which appears to define Egyptian holdings in Asia more broadly rather than a specific enemy. Hasel (1994, 51) calls Israel "a socio-ethnic entity within the region of Canaan," like the three "city-states," and Faust uses the same term (2006, 164). It is unclear why an "ethnic" dimension must be included, when the distinction from Egypt is indeed shared by the city-based polities as well. Definition by population without a city center does not demonstrate ethnic character for Israel any more than for the Binu Yamina or the Binu Sim'al in the Mari archives. Morenz (2008, 10) concludes that the Egyptian author understood "Israel" as a self-designation, in contrast to broader population categories such as 'Apiru.

[8] Niccacci (1997) offers a balanced review of the problem, concluding that the text probably refers to descendants rather than grain, though a sharp distinction is unnecessary (p. 93).

"pastoral nomadic" *shosu.*[9] The Mari text cited with discussion of Benjamin (Chapter 9) for the delineation of ranges for the Binu Yamina and the Binu Sim'al Hana specifies each by the lands where the people "have their fill of barley and pasture their flocks."

A number of interpreters stress the limits of the Merenptah evidence for Israel. We can know that Israel existed, but we cannot know what it was.[10] Nevertheless, one important implication of the Egyptian text must be that there was an entity called Israel in the Iron Age I, between Merenptah and the ninth-century references. It would not have disappeared, only to reemerge centuries later under the same name, in the same general location, also as a polity. Merenptah's Israel may well have been transformed – indeed it was, when we find it as a kingdom. The populations represented and their internal relationships may likewise have changed; yet the name meant something that survives the intervening centuries. Israel of Merenptah and the early Iron Age would have stood in some kind of political continuity with what emerged as "Israel" in the Iron II period, when it was opposed to Judah. The strongest confirmation that something called "Israel" preceded the Iron II kingdom is the Merenptah stele, even though its application to the larger unity of regions or peoples could have arrived only with the emergence of the monarchy. The name "Israel" itself, and its choice for that kingdom, did not originate with monarchy. It evoked a people without kings and a past not defined by kings, even if Israel was just one group that gave its name to a larger association.

2. The Ninth Century

In the middle of the ninth century, the name "Israel" occurs in three different settings, each independent of the others. The royal annals of Assyria mention this kingdom several times over the course of a century and more, with the first two instances from the reign of Shalmaneser III.[11] His Kurkh Monolith speaks of "Ahab the Israelite" (853 B.C.E.), and the later Black Obelisk refers to "Jehu son of Omri" (841 B.C.E.).[12] By the time of Adad-nirari III, the Assyrians consider the kingdom "the land of Omri" (797 B.C.E.) and identify its ruler as "Joash the Samarian" (796). Through later contacts, both the Samaria and

---

[9] Rainey (2001) considers both the text and associated reliefs from Karnak to identify Israel with *shosu* pastoralists; Hasel (2003) then responds at length to Rainey's reasoning. The original link between the stele and the reliefs was proposed by Yurco (1986).

[10] See, e.g., Davies (1992, 57), who distinguishes Merenptah's Israel from the later kingdom; also Grabbe (2007a, 70). Whitelam (2000, 15) emphasizes the need to dissociate Merenptah's Israel from settlement in the Iron Age I highlands.

[11] On Shalmaneser III generally, see Fuchs (2008). For treatments of historical issues related to Shalmaneser III and the Levant, see Dion (1995b), Kelle (2002), and Younger (2008).

[12] On the Black Obelisk and the combination of images and text, see Uehlinger (2007, esp. 201–9). Two particular kings are represented pictorially, Jehu and Sua of Gilzanu, and this reflects a privileged position, submitting for reward. In the same volume, see further discussions by Younger (2007b, 270), on Jehu's relationship to Assyria; and Geller (2007), with consideration of Shalmaneser III's wider political situation.

the Omri names persist, while Israel appears only in the earliest text, from the mid-ninth century.[13] This unique occurrence suggests that the name "Israel" is indigenous to the people and follows its own tradition, whereas both Samaria and the House or Land of Omri depend on a monarchic framework familiar to and preferred by the imperial power.[14]

Closer to home, the evidence is even more sparse. In spite of the gradual increase in written sources through time, no alphabetic inscription from the southern Levant has been found that makes reference to Israel or Judah under any names during the eighth century. The only texts that do mention the two kingdoms are royal inscriptions from competing neighbors in the ninth century. The Moabite Mesha monument celebrates the king's victory over individual towns that had previously belonged to Israel, and Israel is named repeatedly throughout the text.[15] In the context of royal interest, both Moab and Israel are named first of all by their kings and are treated as populations unified under this rule. Mesha himself is "king of Moab," from Dibon; his father is said to have ruled Moab likewise, for thirty years; and Moab is what Omri and his unnamed son are said to have oppressed (lines 1–6).[16] Moab's chief enemy is defined immediately as Omri, "king of Israel" (lines 4–5), and it is the "king of Israel" that is said to have built (or renovated) Aṭarot and Yahaṣ (lines 10–11, 18–19). One more town was captured "from Israel" (Nebo, line 14), and Mesha reports that he used "the prisoners of Israel" for heavy labor in construction at his capital (lines 25–6). Before the text recounts Mesha's military successes and consequent building projects, it presents the entire scenario of onetime subordination and current liberation by the same combination of king and people. "I looked (victoriously) upon him and upon his house, and Israel was

---

[13] All of the references to the kingdom are gathered by Tappy (2001) in Appendix D, 601–11. Tappy (p. 564) follows Bob Becking (1992, 109) in concluding that Bīt Humri was the Assyrian name for the province, with "Samaria" a shorthand, although the royal capital is the more common designation. A complete collection is also now available in Cogan (2008), with Shalmaneser III treated in pp. 12–31.

[14] Kelle (2002, 645) wonders whether the indigenous name is used because the battle at Qarqar represented the first recorded contact of Israel with Assyria. Given that Judah, Moab, Edom, Tyre, and Sidon are left unnamed in the account of forces that oppose Assyria at Qarqar, Kelle considers that the Assyrians may have incorporated some unknown number of these under the name "Israel" as its vassals.

[15] The articles assembled in Dearman (1989) remain an essential reference. In his archaeologically based historical study, Routledge (2004, 133–53) devotes chapter 7 to "Mesha and the Naming of Names," with more recent bibliography. In Grabbe (2007c), see the contributions of Grabbe, Lemaire, Na'aman, and Thompson. Among the other material from the past twenty years, see especially Emerton (2002), Irsigler (1993), J. M. Miller (1992), Müller (1994), Na'aman (1997a), Niccacci (1994), and Thompson (2007b). For the slaughter tradition in particular, see Monroe (2007). Most recently, see the descriptive monograph by Erasmus Gass (2009), in chapter 1 on texts from Moab.

[16] Although Routledge (2004, 150) argues that Mesha's Moab was in fact something fundamentally new, Mesha himself portrays Moab as an enduring people, with a substantial history of monarchy, even through the years of outside intrusion. Van der Steen and Smelik (2007) propose that Dibon represents Mesha's tribe, rather than a town.

irrevocably ruined forever" (line 7).[17] In spite of this hyperbole, no part of the Mesha text claims defeat of the entire kingdom of Israel, which remains a larger entity. In contrast to most of the Assyrian texts, the Mesha inscription makes no reference to Samaria.

Within the land controlled by Israel and taken over for Moab, Mesha recognizes a people identified as "the men of Gad," who had lived in "the land of Atarot for ages" (line 10), a past time defined by the same noun as Israel's ruin into the future "forever." From Mesha's vantage, actual history aside, the Gadites had never lived anywhere else, and their settlement predated the oppression of Omri and son. Gad is not called a "tribe," but it is defined as more than the town that Israel's king had built (or rebuilt), and not defined by any town. Interestingly, the Mesha text mentions Gad more by way of commentary than as an object of royal ire. Israel's fortified city of Atarot is the target, identified by its longstanding location among the Gad people, and only the townspeople are slaughtered *ḥērem*-style with no further reference to Gad. It is as if they were not even considered part of Israel, and one could conclude that with Atarot now in Mesha's hands, the Gad population was his as well, not by forced submission but simply as a transfer from one outside royal power to another. In the Mari evidence, a comparable experience could be attributed to the river-valley population of the Banks-of-the-Euphrates (Ah Purattim) under the successive reigns of Yahdun-Lim, Yasmah-Addu, and Zimri-Lim.

Like the Mesha text, the Aramaic inscription from Tel Dan refers to "the king of Israel" (fragment A, line 8; cf. lines 11–12), in parallel with "the House of David" (line 9). An Aramean king of Damascus claims defeat of both peoples during what seems to be the late ninth century.[18] André Lemaire (1994) proposes that the "House of David" should be restored at the end of the Mesha text as well, where the Moabite ruler turns to his southern successes. Both the Mesha and the Tel Dan royal inscriptions claim victories over Israel at the kingdom's frontiers – the explicit east in Mesha, and implied by the find at Dan in the far north. Both would likewise assume a center in the western highlands, as expected for the capital at Samaria that is named repeatedly in the Bible and confirmed by Assyrian usage.

The most striking feature of this evidence, when combined with the Merenptah stele, is the continuity of the name "Israel." During the eighth century, the book of Hosea lets the highland region of Ephraim stand for the

---

[17] With my translation I seek to express the piling up of infinitive absolute with temporal noun.

[18] Two fragments of a much larger stele were published by the excavator and a colleague: Avraham Biran and Joseph Naveh (1993, 1995). The text, with its apparent reference to the House of David, attracted a flurry of attention that has produced an enormous bibliography. For a general sense of what has been written, see the unwieldy but thoughtful monograph by George Athas (2003); reviewed positively by Pardee (2006). The bibliography has multiplied rapidly and shows no sign of abating. After the book by Athas, see Athas (2006), Fosdal (2009), Kottsieper (2007), Staszak (2009), and Suriano (2007). Athas argues that the two fragments cannot be joined or placed side by side, and I cite fragment A separately.

whole kingdom,[19] and the book of Amos offers Samaria as the capital of self-indulgence.[20] As we have seen, Assyrian rulers could cast the land as "the House of Omri," named for what they perceived as its founding king. The pattern of Assyrian usage shows "Israel" as a name that is already passing from active use, at least on the international stage, while the two alphabetic texts confirm its primacy in the ninth century. If anything, the entity called "Israel" seems to reach back from the ninth century toward a foundation that has nothing to do with kings and their capitals, unlike the alternatives that become prominent in the eighth century. Based on the ninth-century material alone, we could imagine that the two kingdoms of the southern Levantine highlands were generally called Israel and the House of David, as in the fragmentary Tel Dan text. Israel could also be called the House of Omri, like its southern neighbor, whether or not the name had local use, and the outsider usage for the south in the Tel Dan inscription represents a parallel application of this form. It remains to be considered what the kingdom at Jerusalem may have been called at home during the ninth century. We cannot tell from this ninth-century evidence when the later designations began to apply: Ephraim and Samaria for Israel, and Judah for the House of David. All three of these names could be new to the eighth century; Judah first appears in an Assyrian text from Tiglath-pileser III.[21]

B. Archaeology and Naming in the Iron Age I

Through the past decade, the period between the withdrawal of Egypt from the Levant and the emergence of Israel and Judah as separate kingdoms has been the focus of intensive debate over the absolute chronology of the ceramic sequence (see Chapter 17). While the precise dating of the ceramic complexes through the first centuries of the Iron Age has important historical implications, the period between Merenptah and Shalmaneser III can be fixed at least roughly by Egyptian and Assyrian chronologies that are not tied to ceramics. Regardless of how the archaeological evidence is aligned, we are dealing with approximately 350 years during which something called "Israel" existed somewhere in the southern Levant before emerging on the international stage as a kingdom of significant size and power.[22] Perhaps the most interesting implication of a lower chronology for the early Iron Age, from the perspective of basic identities, would be the deeper identification of Merenptah's Israel with the Late Bronze Age. As the opening date for the Iron Age drifts lower – or plummets, depending on the scenario – it becomes harder to define Israel by the new settlement landscape of the Iron Age I, in terms of both timing and social character.

---

[19] See Hos. 4:17; 5:3, 5, 9, 11–14; 6:4, 10; 7:1, 8, 11; 8:9, 11; 9:3, 8, 11, 13, 16; 10:6, 11; 11:3, 8–9, 12; 12:1–2, 9, 15; 13:1, 12; 14:9.

[20] See Amos 3:9, 12; 4:1; 6:1; 8:14; cf. Hos. 7:1; 8:5–6; 10:5, 7; 14:1.

[21] A list of tribute bearers in 734 mentions Jehoahaz of Judah (Iauhazi Iaudāya); see Cogan (2008, 56), no. 11. The name is standard in later royal Assyrian inscriptions.

[22] By this characterization, I refer to the kingdom of Omri, Ahab, and Jehu, which was involved in military struggles and diplomatic engagement with distant Assyria.

Whatever the exact dates for the ceramic chronology, the problem of naming the inhabitants of the region through this period remains. While biblical scholars can claim historical agnosticism and declare that the evidence allows no possibility of conclusion, archaeologists are caretakers of a vast and growing body of material and settlement evidence for the period between Egyptian and Assyrian contact, evidence that demands historical interpretation. Much can be said without resorting to names. Nevertheless, with written evidence for the periods before and after, and the Bible's accounts begging for adjudication, it is difficult to avoid some effort at naming the peoples of the early Iron Age Levant.

1. Israel by Default

Given the Merenptah reference to Israel, it is natural and appropriate to look for Israel in the archaeological evidence for the period after Egyptian withdrawal from the Levant. In his earlier work, Israel Finkelstein (1988, 27–9) defined the Iron Age I highlands as primarily Israelite by extrapolating from anyone whose eleventh- or tenth-century descendants considered themselves Israelite. When he lost confidence in our ability to identify Israelites in the eleventh to tenth centuries, this solution became less attractive.[23] A more recent approach to naming Israel from material finds alone is based on the notions of ethnicity and ethnogenesis, still working from Finkelstein's observations on geographical association and material continuity with later periods – where he himself may now hesitate. This method allows caution and flexibility regarding the exact nature and bounds of "Israel" in its earliest emergence, yet its application remains problematic.

The earliest substantial contribution to definition of earliest Israel by ethnicity was published as an article by Elizabeth Bloch-Smith (2003), for whom the "quest for early Israel is a study of ethnogenesis" (p. 403). Bloch-Smith undertakes a thoughtful, careful exploration of Israelite ethnicity through the definition of a "meaningful boundaries" approach (p. 401), inspired by Fredrik Barth's (1969) notion of fluid social identities. She begins with the need for a myth of origin: "To define and legitimate itself, the resulting group asserts a (fabricated) common ancestry and adopts a culture legitimating the group's past, both real and alleged, spanning the distant to recent history" (p. 403). For this mythic foundation for group identity, Bloch-Smith appears to have in mind the Bible's own narrative, and perhaps the genealogical account of Genesis. For the adopted culture, she goes once again to the Bible to isolate features that may be historically significant: "Over the centuries, Israel supplied, redefined, reinterpreted and perhaps expunged or forgot primordial as well as circumstantial traits and features in crafting its 'collective memory'" (p. 405). Four specific cultural traits embody this group identity, especially for the purpose of creating a social boundary with the Philistines: circumcision,

---

[23] Several years later (1996b), Finkelstein declines to identify populations as "Israelite" based on archaeological evidence until the Iron II period.

short beards, abstinence from eating pork, and the lack of a professional warrior class (pp. 415–16). Throughout, Bloch-Smith appears to assume rather
than prove that ethnicity is the right category for defining early Israel. Much
later conceptions and texts from the Bible must be invoked to undergird this
hypothesis, and it is not clear how these traits must be attached to the name
"Israel."[24]

Ann Killebrew (2005, 149) offers Exod. 12:38 as a biblical hook for her
argument that the "group identity" of Israel emerged gradually from a "mixed
multitude" in the highlands of the southern Levant. This mixed population
characterizes the twelfth and eleventh centuries and generally shares origins
in Canaan, so that it would seem that the name "Israel" applies only to the
following period, although Killebrew acknowledges the Merenptah evidence
and considers Exodus 15 and Judges 5 to be very early, perhaps from Iron
Age I (pp. 13–14, 150, 154). If the group identity of Israel is still inchoate
during the twelfth and eleventh centuries, when the region is inhabited by a
mosaic of separate peoples, then Israel would seem to be just one of these.
Killebrew does not explain where Israel belongs as a named entity during the
period that she offers as formative. Geographically, she locates "what was later
to become the people identified as Israel" entirely in the western highlands,
saying that a boundary is indicated by striking differences of ceramic forms
between small agrarian settlements of the highland and lowland sites (p. 13).
This suggests a continuity of environment and material cultural expression that
may not easily be aligned with political organization and social identity. East
of the Jordan, would the people of Gad be traceable through the Iron Age, as
they attached themselves to Israel and then Moab in the ninth century, with
uncertain affiliations in earlier periods? It is not even clear that we gain greatly
by settling whether to call them "Israelite" or not.

Killebrew's conception of ethnogenesis is based on the work of Herwig
Wolfram, whose definition requires reference to texts that would make this
approach particularly useless for archaeologists.[25] Exodus 15 and Judges 5
do not provide a secure textual basis for establishing a sense of Israelite identity in Iron Age I – setting aside the fact that we are looking for nonbiblical
controls. The Song of the Sea never uses the name "Israel," and the Song of
Deborah invokes it only in the opening hymn. "The people of Yahweh" in the
battle account of Judg. 5:11 and 13 compare to "your people, Yahweh" in

---

[24] In his review of recent work on ethnicity and early Israel, James C. Miller (2008, 185) comes
to a similar conclusion that "in turning to biblical materials for help, one wonders how she can
be so confident that texts she dates in the exilic period contain reliable data regarding Israelite
identity from such an earlier time."

[25] Based on Wolfram (1990), Killebrew (2005, 149) lists three factors in ethnogenesis: a story or
stories of a primordial deed, a group that undergoes a religious experience, and the existence of
an ancestral enemy to cement group identity. With the possible exception of Egypt as an ancestral
enemy, which could apply to almost anyone in the southern Levant during this period, all of
these traits require entirely biblical evidence, the very thing that archaeologists must somehow
work around.

Exod. 15:16. We are left with little sense of how to identify Israel from archaeological evidence in the early Iron Age.

In contrast to Killebrew, Avraham Faust (2006, 7–8) consciously eschews dependence on texts to identify Israel, while he shares Finkelstein's earlier method of extrapolation back from a later period, which he defines simply as "Iron II," without addressing the problem of the tenth century. Faust creates a list of Iron II traits that he considers specifically Israelite, as distinguishable from other "ethnic" groups, and visible in the material remains recovered by archaeology (pp. 35–91). These include avoidance of eating pig, minimally decorated pottery, the absence of imported ceramics, a limited pottery repertoire that reflects simple village life (more Iron Age I than II); the four-room house, and circumcision (not recoverable by archaeology!). As a whole, these cultural features suggest an "egalitarian ethos" that is confirmed by other features lacking from the region: burials before the ninth/eighth centuries, Iron Age temples, and royal inscriptions (pp. 92–4). For Faust, the egalitarian character of Iron II Israel must be based on origin in "tribal" or "totemic" society from the preceding Iron Age I. When these groups were forged into "Israel," this ethos became a self-conscious point of separation from a highly stratified "other," whether Philistine or the earlier "Egyptio-Canaanite city-state system" (pp. 104–5). The primary definition of an Israelite ethnicity would have arisen with differentiation from the powerful Philistines, especially during the eleventh century (p. 137).[26] Finally, Faust does weigh the pattern of highland finds against the existence of the named people Israel in the Merenptah stele. His solution is somewhat unexpected: Merenptah's Israel is more ethnic, in distinguishing itself from the dominant Egyptian "other," but then during the Iron Age I, with reduced Egyptian threat, Israel becomes more "totemic" in its identity. In effect, the social category represented by the name "Israel" can be treated as more ethnic during the times when it appears in texts, while it is less ethnic during periods when it is invisible. The proposed pattern should give pause; we have little historical control for even the most basic delimitation of Israelite population at the time of Merenptah.

While Faust's analysis is sophisticated and provocative, and he embraces explicitly an archaeologist's need to evaluate ethnicity without texts, the effort is still plagued by the absence of names. Both Faust and Killebrew focus entirely on the ethnicity and ethnogenesis of "Israel" and thus rely on the Bible's final combination of Israel and Judah into one people under that name. Faust cites southern locations without questioning whether Iron Age II Judah must be joined into one ethnicity with Iron Age II Israel.[27] So far as features of the

---

[26] Unlike Killebrew, Faust defines ethnicity and "ethnogenesis" without direct dependence on writing. He cites a dictionary on the "construction of group identity" (Seymour-Smith 1986) and approves of Geoffrey Emberling's emphasis on the creation of new ethnic identities when a state conquers independent groups, so that "ethnicity can be seen as a form of resistance" (Faust, 2006, 19; Emberling 1997, 308).

[27] For example, on the avoidance of pig, he includes the far southern sites of Arad, Beersheba, and Tel Masos, along with Beth-Shemesh in the Shephelah (p. 35). Finkelstein makes a much

simple life characterize highland or inland peoples from Dan to Beersheba, it is not clear why only those who identify themselves with Israel would share them. Whether the outside opponent was Egypt or the Philistines, the groups that faced them need not have understood themselves to have in common a single identity, even in broad "ethnic" terms. If they did, this could as easily have been "Canaanite" as Israelite.[28]

To answer the question, we need texts, and even large quantities of written evidence may not solve the problem, if the identities they provide have no ethnic interest. In the Mari evidence from early second-millennium Mesopotamia, the thousands of letters, with all their detail, do little to account for ethnic sensibilities among the dozens of peoples described. Faced with attack from a true outsider, the powerful southern Iranian kingdom of Elam, the Yaminite leader Hammi-ištamar tells the Sim'alite Zimri-Lim that the enemy will not stop to distinguish between Binu Yamina and Binu Sim'al villages, as if it mattered what color these insects were before being swept away.[29] The text acknowledges the kinship of Syrian peoples before a foreigner, yet without any argument for an explicitly shared identity. It is not likely that the analytical category of ethnicity helps to unravel the ancient notions of relationship that underlie this confrontation and collaboration.[30]

For my own project, the uncritical use of the term "Israel" for discussion of the background to both Israel and Judah is the most striking feature of these studies.[31] The inland likewise presents a problem. Killebrew directly acknowledges the "close material-cultural connections" between what she calls the central hill country and the Transjordan during Iron Age I (pp. 165–6). She defines Israel, however, by the central hill country alone (p. 13). Faust also

---

sharper distinction between the background populations of Israel and Judah in the Late Bronze and early Iron Ages. "At the most general level, the population of Israel was heterogeneous: 'Israelites' in the highlands, 'Canaanites' in the lowlands, Phoenicians along the northern coast and Aramaeans on the eastern and northern frontiers. In contrast, the population of Judah was homogeneous, made up of sedentary local groups with roots in a pastoral past" (1999, 44).

[28] One illustration of the problem is provided by Finkelstein in his early discussion of Iron Age I Benjamin. Based on the Bible, he concludes that the Israelites occupied the east, while the western slopes belonged to the Hivites of Gibeon (1988, 65). No contrast in material culture distinguishes the two regions. Without names, as Finkelstein would probably now assert, there is no way to identify the population of this territory generally. It remains intriguing, however, to recognize that such a division could well have existed without material expression.

[29] The text is A.3080, in Durand (1990b); in his translation for LAPO 17 (1998), no. 722, pp. 488–90, Durand prefers "butterflies" to "ants," but in any case, the writer asks whether the Elamites will be looking at the color of bugs before disposing of them.

[30] Miglio (2010, 174–8) argues convincingly that the Elamite attack and Mesopotamian responses had nothing to do with the existence or establishment of an "Amorite" ethnic identity.

[31] Robert D. Miller (2005) follows Finkelstein's earlier notion of "proto-Israel" (p. 2) and acknowledges that discussion of archaeology for the relevant highland region must include areas outside "proto-Israel" (p. 15). The region south of Jerusalem was sparsely inhabited (p. 16), but Miller does discuss evidence for the hills north of the Beersheba Valley. In his brief treatment of ethnicity, Grabbe (2007a, 21) hesitates appropriately, observing that Judah is not identified as "Israel" by outsiders in non-Jewish writing until Roman times.

develops his evidence for Israelite ethnic markers entirely from western sites and brings up the Transjordan only at the very end of the book (pp. 221–4). The Bible and the Mesha inscription lead us to expect Israelites in the east, and for Faust, four-room houses in this region prove their presence (p. 223). He wonders whether with the Philistines farther away, ethnic boundaries may be less striking. For me, the distance of Philistia from both eastern and northern regions that attest to some of his material traits raises doubts about their value as a universal oppressor that can explain a sweeping ethnic identification as "Israel."

Ultimately, the problem with this search for Israelite ethnicity in the archaeological remains of the early Iron Age is that it depends on a name that occurs once in a late thirteenth-century Egyptian text. Israel in the Merenptah stele is a people that Egypt claims to have fought and defeated under that name. This is a political identity, without specific geographical location, and almost certainly not coterminous with the later kingdom of the Iron Age II. Even without evidence for names during the twelfth to tenth centuries, it is useful to realize that a polity named Israel, not defined by any city center, almost certainly existed through that time. Its material remains may not have differed noticeably from those of its highland neighbors, however they were named, and at whatever point some of these may have aligned themselves with this polity.

The Bible itself offers little direct help, even with focus on Israelite writing. In the book of Judges, "Israel" as a uniting identity seems to accompany later phases of Israelite compilation, as exhibited in the opening hymn for the Song of Deborah (chapter 5) and the recasting of Gideon as a spectator to Yahweh's military achievement (chapter 7). In tales of early military struggle, Ai and Benjamin take the field against a people named as Israel (Joshua 8; Judges 20). The people of Yahweh and El in the Balaam poems are named Jacob and Israel (Numbers 23–4). None of the biblical uses of "Israel" in reference to origins and early life can be pushed back definitively before the monarchy. The claim in 2 Samuel that David ruled Israel may be as early as any biblical text, if parts of this material date to soon after his reign (cf. Hutton 2009).

In the end, Merenptah's Israel is a surprise. Without it, the Bible itself would leave open-ended the question of Israel's existence by this name before the binding force of kingship. With it, we are compelled to consider that the name "Israel" already carried political weight long before the appearance of the monarchy, even as dated by reference to the biblical narrative. The Bible does offer a detailed political sense of what Israel was: an association of peoples or a powerful collective body that could act together, whether to fight or to choose leadership. In this latter sense, the early David accounts of rebellions under Absalom and Sheba may reflect the old character of "Israel" as an identity distinct from kings, an entity to be wooed and won. The old Israel of Merenptah at least gave its name to this association, whether as a coalition itself or as a dominant early member, around which the larger group took form. No proper answer will be possible without more texts.

2. Political Identity versus Ethnicity

I am not persuaded that the analytical category of "ethnicity" is finally of significant help in disentangling the historical problems of Israelite origins and early existence. On one side, it is not clear that the peoples of the southern Levant during the Late Bronze and early Iron Ages identified themselves in what can be considered "ethnic" terms. Even with all the names we could wish for, as in the Mari documentation, we would not have properly ethnic identities. On the other side, it is not clear that the Bible's Israel, with its constituent peoples, portrays an ethnic identity before the fall of the kingdoms and the dispersal of their populations. Especially in the time before empires, which arrived with the Assyrian invasion, I do not see that groups understood themselves in these terms. Even the desert Sutû, the pastoralist Amorites, the free-agent 'Apiru, and the later pastoralist Arameans strike me as social types without the kind of group cohesion and sense of belonging-by-name that accompanies ethnicity.

Modern study of ethnicity is shaped by the conclusion that ethnic boundaries result from interactions between groups in an opposition between "us" and "them." Ethnic definitions asserted by people in day-to-day life often cannot be identified on the basis of objective contrasts in language, material and expressive culture, polity, and territory (Jones 2008, 326). Effectively, ethnicity is situational and unstable, in a process of definition that involves both the self and others.[32] With such an ever-shifting target, it would seem that ethnicity is entirely in the minds of those who wield it, for or against, and its identification in the past is increasingly problematic. In her recent overview, Jones comments that since the 1990s, some have begun to challenge "the very existence of ethnic groups in the form of bounded, monolithic, territorially based entities" (p. 327). It is not possible, in these terms, to establish a one-to-one relationship between materially defined cultures and ethnic groups; to assert the existence of discrete, homogeneous cultures; and to understand group identities as related to distinct, territorially based social entities (p. 328).

Siân Jones' preoccupation with territory responds to the archaeologist's need to name people by their pots, as Andrew Jones puts it. For Andrew Jones, material objects do allow insight into the minds of their users, but they need to be approached with more nuance. In particular, he suggests the idea of "artefact biography," from the fact that "objects are utilised to express differing modes of identity at different points in their own lives, while various objects may themselves be used to express varied kinds of identity over the course of the lives of human beings" (2002, 84).[33] Andrew Jones cites with approval the sensitivity

---

[32] Working along this line of thought, Ronald Cohen (1978, 387–8) defines ethnicity as a "*series of nesting dichotomizations of inclusiveness and exclusiveness*," so, "a set of descent-based cultural identifiers used to assign persons to groupings that expand and contract in inverse relation to the scale of inclusiveness and exclusiveness of the membership."

[33] A. Jones emphasizes the need to examine the way pots are produced, used, and deposited *by* people. Identities are then created through "practice," the performance of social acts, a

to change in Julian Thomas' approach to objects: "For Thomas, artefacts are used as active components in the process of constructing different identities, and identities are constructed through the juxtaposition and manipulation of sets of artefacts" (p. 84). Thomas in turn was likewise trying to break the identifying link between "people and things": "The existence of a community as a bounded and self-contained entity is a form of self-interpretation on the part of a number of persons," and for most such "entities," relations extend outside of what we see as the "society" (1996, 75). In a focused study based on excavation in Africa, Scott Maceachern (1998, 109–12) acknowledges the real connection between shared artifacts and social relations but doubts that this is best explained by ethnic groups. "There is an active debate within anthropology concerning the status of ethnicity as a valid structuring mechanism for premodern societies."[34]

To bring this sense of caution back to the studies by Killebrew and Faust, it is not clear that the patterns observed by archaeologists can be identified with any one named entity, be it Israel or otherwise, and it is not clear that the patterns themselves are best understood as reflections of ethnicity, as opposed to other social and environmental trends.[35] In a study titled *Ethnic Identity in Greek Antiquity*, Jonathan Hall (1997) turns the discussion toward the active intentions of the people who make and use artifacts. "The problem that remains is how to distinguish active praxis from passive behaviour in the archaeological record." To determine intent with respect to matters of identity, we need to find "active signaling," which reflects "a deliberate emphasis on cultural distinctiveness, in circumstances where such distinctiveness is not otherwise immediately apparent, or on cultural conformity in situations where such conformity is not necessarily universally accepted" (p. 136). Perhaps such conscious expression of cultural contrast or conformity existed in specific settings where contact with Egyptian or Philistine power was direct and pressing, but even there, the mass of material habits reflected in the artifacts of the southern Levant cannot readily be explained by attempted self-distinction from those neighbors, and attributed to a single alternative "ethnic" identification as "Israel." Hall himself concludes that "[i]t is ... hopeless to believe that archaeological evidence can *identify* ethnic groups in the past" (p. 142). Artifacts can, however, be taken as "emblematic indicia of ethnic boundaries," such as language and religion. This is possible when the examples have already been identified as "discursively

---

perspective that "allows us to move away from an equation that simply relates specific forms of material culture with specific kinds of identity, and towards an examination of the way in which identities are instantiated by the contextual relationship of artefacts associated with different practices" (2002, 106).

34 The whole volume is characterized by similar caution.

35 Before any of the initiatives elaborated above, Diana Edelman (1996a, 55) already voiced a similar objection: "Modern ethnographic studies have indicated the complexity of the formation and maintenance of ethnic identification and the inability to predict markers on the basis of practices of various living groups or cultures."

constructed."[36] We are not in a position to do this for Israel in the thirteenth to tenth centuries B.C.E.

With these constraints in mind, we return to the evidence as we have it. If we set aside the Bible for now as under evaluation and recall the minimal written evidence for the twelfth to tenth centuries, archaeologists are forced to ask the simplest of questions: Can anyone from this region be distinguished as Israelite, and if so, as opposed to what? Ethnicity offers a category that could be analyzed on material grounds alone, without writing, or only keeping in mind the target of ninth-century names. This is an attractive proposition that would allow focus on the mass of evidence that does exist, rather than being eternally preoccupied by a biblical story that serves later audiences and by impossible questions from inscriptional tidbits.

Nevertheless, the entire discussion of ethnicity for the southern Levant before the ninth century is fraught with assumptions about identity that the evidence cannot sustain. In the end, ethnicity is a matter of identity, of self-identification in relation to others, and this involves naming. Without adequate written evidence, we know far too little about how the populations of the region actually named themselves throughout this period. It is almost certain that far more names were involved than just "Israel" for the twelfth to tenth centuries, aside from the Philistines, and that we have no idea what these were. There is far too little evidence to conclude that an Israelite name bound all the other named groups under one "ethnic" identity or that some other category such as "Hebrew" served such a purpose. Equally, it is unlikely that all these peoples understood themselves to be "Canaanite" in the way that Egypt identified the peoples of the Levant who submitted to their rule (cf. Killebrew 2005, 32, 51). In the early Iron Age, the region was indeed inhabited by a "motley crew," but this was not simply the raw material for eventual Israelite ethnicity. As indicated by the early reference in the Merenptah text, Israel must have coexisted with various peoples and polities in various relationships.

In spite of the frustrations inherent in giving up the ethnicity search, historians of the region are better off returning to the names provided by texts and to questions posed by those texts and names as applicable to polities and peoples, groups that name themselves or others for purposes of action and identification. Lacking names, as we so often do, archaeologists may guide us with regional and social distinctions, framed by the nature of evidence without writing. Much of the practical discussion by archaeological specialists involves just this kind of identification, and it is only when they are drawn into sweeping historical and popular debate about the nature of Canaan and the emergence of Israel that they resort to names that do not derive from their own evidence.

---

[36] Raz Kletter (2006) comes to a similar conclusion that archaeology alone cannot find ethnicity, in part by reflection on the work of Emberling and Siân Jones. My conclusions with regard to Merenptah are likewise much like Kletter's: Merenptah shows us that there is an Israel somewhere in the area for the Iron Age I, even if we cannot locate it.

Israel and the House of David, soon to be Judah, appear in the ninth century as polities, both as kingdoms that interact with other such polities on a regional stage. The first challenge, then, is to understand the nature of each polity at that date, and if possible, to consider its background. Answers must depend on weighing material evidence without oversimplifying the landscape of identities that must have been attached to it. The Bible offers at least a broader written perspective on these identities, with a conscious awareness of a past before the ninth century. The writers' knowledge of Israel and Judah before that time must be evaluated carefully, but there is at least material to consider. If the biblical writing can be sifted in a way that renders some of its contents more relevant to historical enquiry, then this could enlarge the textual base for the types of knowledge that writing can provide.

16

Before Israel

According to the finished primary narrative of Genesis through Kings, Israel's origins can be told in a sequence of differentiated stages. In Genesis, the place of Israel in the larger world is defined by blood relationship to Abraham, or the lack of any such immediate genealogical connection, and the peoples of Israel are explained as tribes with common ancestry under one father, Jacob. By the invitation of Joseph, the entire family moves to Egypt during a severe famine, and this change of venue sets the stage for the second main phase of Israel's origins, a miraculous extraction from slavery to Egypt recounted in the book of Exodus. Although Yahweh offers direct entry into a Promised Land, the people are petrified by their spies' report of giants in the land (Numbers 13–14), and this faithless generation is condemned to wander in the wilderness for forty years until they are replaced by their more willing offspring. The final phase of Israel's origins involves the invasion itself, begun by a sort of accidental conquest east of the Jordan River (Numbers 21; Deuteronomy 2–3), the prelude to the real thing described in the book of Joshua. After a pair of victories at Jericho and Ai, Israel defeats the assembled kings of southern and northern centers in open field battle (Joshua 10–11), and this is the basis for apportionment of the land along tribal lines.

I have argued that the primary elements of this sequential narrative derive from Israelite stories. These were not, however, placed in such a sequence, and their logic generally did not require reliance on other stories from the collection. The genealogical scheme of Jacob's family indeed assumes a time before Israel's various peoples shared the land, though entry and establishment in it comes with Jacob's return from life with Laban associated with Haran and Aram. Without envisioning prior residence in the land, the exodus from Egypt presents a stark existence as pastoralist outsiders who must find a new base of operations in the east. The various battle accounts are more difficult to cast in terms of origins. They portray Israel winning local dominance in various settings: in the eastern realms of Sihon and Og (Numbers 21; Deuteronomy 2–3), at Ai near Bethel in the western highlands (Joshua 8), over Canaan in the Jezreel Valley (Judges 4–5), over Midian in the Jordan Valley (Judg. 7:23–5), and against Benjamin at Gibeah (Judges 20). In the eastern assault on Sihon and Og, the people come from the southern inland wilderness, where they had lived among the sons of Esau (Deut. 2:2–4), but otherwise they are already present. The one account of what might be considered life before Israel's establishment in the land is found in Judges 9, where a local ruler named Abimelech destroys Shechem and is then killed himself in an assault on another town. The affiliations of all the participants in this story, including Shechem, are left ambiguous, as perhaps are those of Penuel and Succoth in Gideon's pursuit of two Midianite rulers into the inland east (Judges 8).

The specifics of these conflicts do little to explain the origins of Israel or to help identify the earliest Israelites in excavation. If a Late Bronze Age town were found destroyed at Ai, which seems not to have existed in that period, we would learn little more than we know by seeing that Israelite storytellers understood Ai to have been an early target.[1] In historical terms, it is the larger picture assumed by these stories that is capable of investigation in concert with archaeological and other textual evidence. We confront a landscape of independent towns that may be compelled to offer some kind of allegiance to outside leaders who are not defined by obvious territorial kingdoms or larger city centers (Gideon, Abimelech). Such towns may become the targets of groups looking to establish new bases of power, as envisioned for Ai, Heshbon, and perhaps originally Gibeah. In a political landscape that lacks any fixed major power – including Egypt – larger conflicts are possible only when the smaller local entities join. The first reference to Ephraim's alienation from its allies associates it with Naphtali, Asher, and Manasseh against two Midianite leaders named Oreb and Zeeb (Judg. 7:23–5). At the center of the Song of Deborah stands a battle between an alliance of Ephraim, Benjamin, Machir, Zebulun, Issachar, and Naphtali against "the kings of Canaan" (Judg. 5:14–19). Participants in these conflicts may be both independent towns and peoples not defined by individual settlement.

Evaluation of this collage of images from a political scene without the kingdoms of Israel and Judah may be pursued profitably along various lines, especially from archaeological evidence. For a specialist in cuneiform writing of the second millennium B.C.E., it draws the eye to the mid-fourteenth century archive from the Egyptian capital at el-Amarna (Akhetaten). This archive includes a body of letters sent by local rulers within a network not so different from what is on view in these Israelite traditions of time before kings.[2] One key

---

[1] So far as Ai can be identified with et-Tell near Bethel (Beitin), it displays an Early Bronze town that was left unoccupied for centuries before the establishment of an Iron Age I village (Callaway 1992; Rainey 2006a, 125).

[2] For the past generation, Nadav Na'aman has set a high standard by his careful historical evaluations of the Amarna evidence, including their value for understanding the background to earliest Israel. Much of his work in English is accessible in the second volume of his collected essays, *Ancient Israel and Its Neighbors: Canaan in the Second Millennium B.C.E.* (2005). Building in part on Na'aman's prodigious efforts, Brendon Benz now emphasizes the political variety

element from the society portrayed in the Amarna letters recalls a focus of intense discussion that once involved the background for the Bible's Israel: a population known as *'apiru*. Although the geographical range of the Amarna letters overlaps considerably with the lands of Israel and Judah, nothing in the texts indicates the presence of Israel or any of its peoples by name. Only towns such as Shechem and Jerusalem align with the biblical landscape. Amarna thus displays the southern Levant before Israel, over a century before the reference in Merenptah's stele. For my own reflection on how to read the Bible's accounts of earliest Israel against history of a time before Israel, the Amarna evidence makes a useful point of entry, and the *'apiru* offer a test for my interpretation of the politics and society out of which Israel emerged.

A. The *'apiru* in the Pre-Israelite Landscape

Egyptian texts for the Late Bronze Age name two classes of people in the southern Levant that are neither regional labels nor specific polities: the *shosu* and the *'apiru*. The former are associated more narrowly with the southeastern steppes that border the Arabian desert, while the latter are a class encountered more widely across the whole Levant and inland Syria. By the geography alone, it is not surprising that the *shosu* are linked to pastoralism and nomadic life, though Egyptian texts do occasionally mention the existence of towns in "*shosu*-land" (Routledge 2004, 77–8). The *'apiru* are more widespread and more difficult. They cannot be defined by cities and kingdoms in the standard fashion; indeed, they are regarded as the antithesis of these in some statements, and the category somehow identifies a nonstandard relationship to settlements and their polities. Many of the Amarna letters, especially those sent to the Egyptian court by their vassals in Canaan, mention the *'apiru*, often with the assumption that they stand outside the web of loyalty to the empire.[3] With the setting in the mid-fourteenth century, this image of outsiders to the Egyptian system has offered a tantalizing background to the emergence of Israel, even if there is no relation to the word "Hebrew" (*'ibrî*).[4] While the *'apiru* provide

assumed in the Amarna texts, with town-based domains balanced by coalitions not defined by a single center (2012).

[3] Na'aman (2005, 277) cautions that in contrast to Egypt's wars against the *shosu*, Egyptian scribes rarely treat the *'apiru* as enemies ("The Town of Ibirta and the Relations of the 'Apiru and the Shasu"). The writers of the Amarna letters thus reflected their own use of the term, with their own attempts to get the Egyptians to consider such people a danger. I use the category "Canaan" with reference to Egypt's power in the Levant, imitating the usage found in the Amarna letters themselves: EA 8:15, 17, 25; 9:19; 14 ii:26; 30:1; 109:46; 110:49; 131:61; 137:76; 145:46; 151:50; 162:41; 367:8.

[4] On this well-worn problem, with bibliography and a new proposal, see my recent work (forthcoming b). The biblical word "Hebrew" does not derive from the old West Semitic term *'apiru*, though it may come from the same root and be indirectly related. George Mendenhall (1962) first proposed that Israel began as *'apiru* who rejected the dominance of their Egyptian-affiliated city rulers. The hypothesis has been much-criticized, even as it opened the door to more durable interpretations that did not depend on bringing the Israelites in as outsiders by migration.

no direct link to Israel, as either vocabulary or a social entity, interpretation of the category demands a vision of the entire social landscape that defines the world into which Israel arose. Much changed in Egypt's Canaanite situation between the reigns of Akhenaten and Merenptah.[5] Nevertheless, such people must be accounted for, as Egypt worked to maintain power over their lowland centers.[6]

The following reinterpretation of the *'apiru* lays a foundation for understanding early Israel that complements the context already proposed with the Amorites and the Arameans. The numerous Amarna references to the *'apiru* have greatly influenced definitions of the type as renegade outsiders.[7] Dever calls them "landless" and among the impoverished and socially marginalized, the "social bandits" (2003, 179, 181).[8] Liverani argues that to become an *'apiru* meant to abandon the king and become a rebel.[9] More neutrally, they may be seen as refugees or migrants, populations that could represent a threat to the longstanding locals.[10]

Above all, the problem with the standard interpretation of the *'apiru* is the conclusion that they were not fully integrated into the society of town-dwellers. In the Amarna letters, the *'apiru* generally appear as powerful groups with effective political leadership on a scale that could be seen to threaten every city-based vassal in the Egyptian Levant. Peoples identified as *'apiru* defeated or won

---

[5] Singer (1988); cf Higginbotham (2000). The expansion of Egyptian authority under Ramses II through the earlier thirteenth century shifted the political landscape. Weinstein (1981) observes that the thirteenth and early twelfth centuries produced a period of increased military occupation, with more Egyptian construction and negative impact on local population.

[6] Redford (1992, 269) observes, "The sparsely populated hill country of central Palestine, already partly stripped of its inhabitants under the eighteenth Dynasty, held little attraction for the Egyptians who felt basically disinclined to police it." Even if they felt little attraction to the highlands, they surely intended to control them as much as possible, and the Amarna letters do not suggest a willingness to let the highland towns do as they wished.

[7] It is now generally agreed that the term represents a category rather than a proper noun, but this was once considered possible for some examples, at least; e.g., de Vaux (1968, 226–7); Pohl (1957, 159). An early (Marxist) argument that this is truly a social and not an ethnic group is offered by Ivanov (1974). Note that three Amarna letters use the KI-determinative for localities (EA 215:15; 289:24; 298:27), but this seems to reflects the scribes' attempt to treat these as comparable to political entities (see Astour 1999, 33).

[8] Dever aligns himself not far from Mendenhall, emphasizing the lowland urban origin of the new highland population and accepting a peasant revolt in some form, which he would call "agrarian reform" (p. 189). Gottwald considered them outlaws to the established order (1979, 401, 404).

[9] Liverani (1979); with the objection of Astour (1999, 32).

[10] Ahlström (1986, 12) compares them to the resident aliens described by the Hebrew term *gēr*. Na'aman defines them first of all as "migrants" and then discusses at length how the term took on a derogatory aspect in the Amarna letters. Buccellati (1977) likewise accepts the notion of displaced persons but distinguishes the *munnabtūtu* as "politically displaced" from the *'apirū* as "socially uprooted"; see also Diakonoff (1982, 96): "They were persons who, fleeing from their communities because of impoverishment, had lost their civil rights and roamed about the neighboring countries, settling in the difficult accessible maquis and living by robbery, hired labour or as hired warriors."

the support of major towns and would have incorporated large populations that were indistinguishable from those of the kingdoms they overwhelmed. The 'apiru peoples were never identified by a city center, however, and some of Egypt's vassals regarded them as intrinsically resistant to Egyptian authority. In the end, they have something in common with the Hana of Zimri-Lim and the Binu Sim'al, a population named by its mobile potential and yet carrying the identity of a whole city-based kingdom. Both the Binu Sim'al and the Binu Yamina represent modes of political and social identity not defined by towns, somehow like the 'apiru, a similarity to which we will return.

1. *Amarna's* 'apiru *Powers*

The 'apiru category appears in over fifty of the 350-plus letters found at el-Amarna in Egypt. Among Egypt's Asian vassals, 'apiru people were a constant presence and concern. In fact, however, a majority of these attestations refer not to unnamed bands of ne'er-do-wells but to particular political threats associated with two impressive leaders. To the north, the land of Amurru, a highland polity never defined by a city center, was led by Abdi-Aširta, the scourge of Rib-Hadda, the ruler of Byblos who lived with the persistent terror of being overrun by this powerful inland neighbor. Rib-Hadda repeatedly identifies Abdi-Aširta with the 'apiru in his missives to the Egyptian king, and he spits out the term as a pejorative epithet that proves at least an inclination to escape Pharaoh's authority. Further south, also in the highlands, Lab'ayu governed a people also linked strongly to the 'apiru. Brendon Benz (2012) proposes that Lab'ayu's domain included the city of Shechem but was not defined by this or any single center.

In large part because the Amarna letters reflect such concern about conflict with Abdi-Aširta and Lab'ayu, the majority of references to the 'apiru treat them as a military opponent – not from the Egyptians' own point of view, but from the view of individual city-based rulers in the Levant. Rib-Hadda of Byblos and others speak of "the war of the 'apiru" (EA 68, 71, 75, 185, 243, 313, 366), and there is repeated nervousness about who may "join" the 'apiru, not as individuals enlisting in banditry but as whole populations who could switch allegiance in favor of Abdi-Aširta or Lab'ayu, if not others. Such populations are often identified by their towns, either generically (EA 74, 116, 117, 144, 189) or with specific names, as Ṣumur (EA 76), Byblos (Gubla, EA 104), and Hazor (EA 148). Whole "lands" (*mātu*) are sometimes at stake (EA 77, 79, 85, 88, 272, 273, 290), and Rib-Hadda, never one to hold back for fear of overplaying his hand, once declares that *all* the lands of the Pharaoh, as far as Egypt, may become part of Abdi-Aširta's 'apiru (EA 88). Other letters describe more than just conflict and concern; actual 'apiru successes are characterized by incorporation of towns and lands (EA 83, 85, 90, 118, 286, 288).

This majority of Amarna references has generally been explained as derived from the primary identity of the 'apiru as a class of people who have lost all affiliation with the settled "towns" and "lands" that define ordered society under Egypt's empire and its vassal domains. Whether or not this can be maintained on some other basis, the mass of Amarna usage does not serve this interpretation. Most often, the *'apiru* are linked to major political powers in the Levantine highlands that seem to challenge the stable configuration of city-based dominions under Egyptian rule. Occasionally, these *'apiru* are distinguished from the individuals who lead them, so that they represent a separate social force, capable of acting in support of or against other groups or leaders. Abdi-Aširta's army is said to be strong "through the *'apiru*," who will enable him to take over two cities if he can assemble them for the purpose (EA 71; cf. 76, 85, 91). Later in his career, Rib-Hadda writes that Aziru, the son of Abdi-Aširta, has assembled the *'apiru* and addressed them with plans to assault Byblos (EA 132). The *'apiru* are viewed as a body that can gather to make decisions in distinction from an individual leader, even for the choice of such a leader.

In this respect, the *'apiru* of Abdi-Aširta and his son resemble the Hana of king Zimri-Lim at Mari, who counts on these kinsmen as his primary base of power and yet has to negotiate their support in any given undertaking. Also like the *'apiru*, the term *hana* defines a social category, in this case the people who live outside settlements with flocks on the move. In the peculiar Mari usage, Zimri-Lim's entire Sim'alite people is identified by this mobile pastoralist element, even though many of the Sim'alites are settled in towns. The Mari Hana do not explain the particular meaning of the word *'apiru*, but the parallel adds to the impression that the *'apiru* cannot easily be understood as marginal to the social and political landscape to which they contribute. In both cases, a category that derives from notions of mobility and separation from towns is linked to the core constituency of kings who have a base of power outside any one city center, yet still rule from urban capitals.

One of the rare letters from Lab'ayu himself offers a closer view of the *'apiru* that should not be pejorative. In EA 254, Lab'ayu responds to Pharaoh's request that he hand over his son for a visit to Egypt, an invitation that forced submission to the suzerain. Lab'ayu insists that he would give anything the king requests, including his own wife if so ordered. Unfortunately, his son has been frustratingly out of contact. Moran translates the excuse: "I did not know that my son was consorting with the Apiru. I herewith hand him over to Addaya." Without the assumption that the *'apiru* category is necessarily negative in this case, the key lines may be rendered differently: "I did not know that my son was going around with the *'apiru*, and I hereby entrust him to Addaya."[11] For Lab'ayu, if his son is not currently with him, he is naturally with the *'apiru*, who are understood to live or move at a distance from their king, rather like the Hana of Zimri-Lim. As addressed by Lab'ayu, the *'apiru* are a coherent population with an established relationship to himself, yet whose movements cannot be managed by the ruler they acknowledge.

[11] The verb translated by Moran as "consorting" is in the Gtn iterative stem of the verb *alāku* ("to go"), which I render by its common meaning for habitual movement, as "go around."

Such independence may reflect a life in more remote areas, especially in highlands and inland regions that were less accessible to Egyptian power. The realms of Abdi-Aširta and Lab'ayu appear to have been more difficult for Egypt to control than the city-centered polities of the lowlands, and we also find one rare positive reference to the *'apiru* in a letter from Biryawaza of Damascus, also inland. In proclaiming his loyalty and availability, Biryawaza lists his military resources:

Indeed I myself, along with my troops and my chariots, along with my kin, along with my *'apiru*, and along with my *sutû*, am at the service of the archer-troops, wherever my lord the king may command. (EA 195:24–32)

In this account, the ruler at Damascus seems to define his own people by the different categories of their relationship to himself, none of which need be considered outside the normal social order. By their combination, the opening troops and chariots appear to reflect Damascus itself, so that the other three groups all stand at a physical distance and must be associated with Biryawaza by commitments appropriate to their ways of life. First, his kin, or "brothers," would represent a following that is constituted as his own clan or tribe, a bond not dependent on residence in the same town or settlement. The Sutû are widely known as nomads.[12] In the Mari evidence, where large groups are defined by connections that bridge settlement and steppe, farming and flocks, in what are often called "tribal" peoples, the Sutû are a much smaller group, never identified with settled life and distinct from the well-attested Binu Sim'al and Binu Yamina populations.[13] In the Damascus letter as well, these may be nomads, entirely separate from towns. This leaves the *'apiru*, who are neither direct kin nor true nomads. However we define them, the *'apiru* are equally committed to Biryawaza as his own, with no greater sense of social or political distance. In another Amarna letter (EA 318), perhaps from somewhere in Syria, the term *'apiru* is followed by *habbātu*, perhaps even as a gloss on the common writing of *'apiru* as SA.GAZ: "Save me from powerful enemies, from the hand of the *'apiru*, the *habbātu*, and the Sutû – so save me, O great king, my lord!" The word *habbātu* in this use may be derived from a verb of movement, crossing from one domain to another, rather than "to rob," so that we cannot identify the *'apiru* here with "bandits."[14] We are left with the same combination of *'apiru* and Sutû.

---

[12] The one extended study is still that of Heltzer (1981).

[13] To my knowledge, there is no systematic treatment of the Sutû in the Mari evidence; for sporadic references, see Fleming (2004a, 99, 209); others can be found by browsing the published volumes of Mari letters.

[14] See *CAD* s.v. *habātu* A v. (1) to rob, take away by force; (2) to commit a robbery; *habātu* D v. (1) to move across, make an incursion, a razzia into enemy territory. Both verbs are common in the Old Babylonian period (early second millennium), with continued use in Babylonian dialects, as discussed in the dictionary articles. Na'aman (1994, 398–9) calls these "outlaw refugees." Von Soden (1984, 166) observes that the term SA.GAZ (for *habbātu*, the related noun) is usually read as "bandit," including in his own *AHw*, from the verb "to rob," but that there is

If we understand the *'apiru* as runaways, detached from the social bonds of settled society and gathered in bands of renegades on the fringes of regular civilization, one answer would be to consider such military support as grounded purely in financial and practical motives. When associated with Abdi-Aširta, Lab'ayu, and Biryawaza, the *'apiru* would then be understood as mercenaries.[15] Support for such an interpretation could then be found in EA 246, a letter to Pharaoh from Biridiya, ruler of Megiddo, who complains of payments to the *'apiru* in what might be taken as a scheme to buy military muscle. Biridiya concludes, "My lord the king should know: the two sons of Lab'ayu have indeed given their silver to the *'apiru* and to the Sutû," evidently in connection with war against Megiddo. Before we conclude that this describes an obvious mercenary arrangement, we must keep in mind that the Amarna evidence does not generally characterize the *'apiru* as professional soldiers for hire, and this is not the only way to account for such exchange. In a Mari letter published under the tantalizing title "Vie nomade," Hammi-ištamar, leader of the Yaminite Uprapû people, scoffs at the attempts of his counterpart to guarantee the support of his fighters by paying them silver:

You put your trust elsewhere, thinking, "I have given silver to my tribe." What is this silver of yours that you gave? All of your silver that you gave – I know about it. Yesterday, all your tribe assembled at Hen, and the one who loves you was saying, "Write to him so he will go," while the one who rejects ("hates") you was saying, "He should not bother coming." Now if I did not make a habit of turning up in person, they would never manage to act as one.[16]

Yasmah-Addu offers silver to his own *li'mum*, or "tribe," the term that defines his Yarihû people as a whole. This has nothing to do with the employment of foreigners and instead involves a leader's strategy for persuading his own people to join him in a dangerous military undertaking. Biridiya's opponents may well be the people of Lab'ayu and sons, classified by *'apiru* and Sutû groups, as in the list of Biryawaza's fighters at Damascus. In the Amarna correspondence, the *'apiru* represent the category more feared and loathed than the Sutû, and

a homonym meaning "to wander." The two verbs may have the same foundational meaning, so that the *'apiru* cannot be interpreted as outside the law based on this comparison. Bottéro (1972, 23–4) likewise emphasizes the importance of the SA.GAZ connection: if this truly means "bandit," then it would provide a firm starting point for a negative meaning – except that the root may not be universally pejorative. The basis for seeing the *'apiru* as unstable and dangerous really comes from Amarna.

[15] Ahlström (1986, 12) considers the lists of *'apiru* fighters in texts from Alalakh to be mercenaries (AT 180–4), and Grabbe (2007a, 48) mentions together the notions of mercenaries and thieves in connection with EA 68, 185, and 186. Bottéro (1972, 25) mentions the basis for considering them a military force; they are found in enlistment accounts already at Mari. This is also the entire purpose of their listing in the mid-second millennium text published by Mirjo Salvini (1996). Military enlistment does not mean "mercenary" service, as will be discussed further below. In fact, it is not entirely clear that the category of "mercenary" is appropriate to any military service in this pre-imperial period.

[16] The text is A.1146, in Marello (1992).

it is their name that embodies potential rebellion in the mind of Rib-Hadda at Byblos. It seems that in Amurru of the north, at least, the *'apiru* were most central to defining the political role of populations not identified by their settled abode.

2. *'apiru in Stable Relationships*

In all of the evidence for the *'apiru*, which has been gathered above all by Bottéro, it is clear that they are not defined by cities and settlements, even if they may inhabit these.[17] In this respect, we must keep in mind the ubiquitous Hana of the Mari archives, whom Zimri-Lim rules as his core Sim'alite population, towns and all, even though the word means something like "tent-dweller," the antithesis of settled life. Zimri-Lim's own people were identified by a way of life in which many of them did not participate. While the *'apiru* may be difficult to lay one's hands on, as with Lab'ayu's son in EA 254, the purely nomadic existence seems to be claimed already by the Sutû category. The explanation for such groups may remain elusive as well, but perhaps we do best to begin by looking back at the early phenomenon.

Several texts from the early second millennium, before the term *'apiru* became a fixed type, attest a verb that appears to be cognate with the noun, without being simply denominative.[18] Whatever the original meaning of the root, in common usage, the verb always has to do with departure from one's home to take up residence in a different place, especially a different political entity. Repeatedly, the verb accompanies a claim of legitimate absence and assumes a recognized standing, not just in the new location but in the home left behind.

In one Mari letter, the governor of Qaṭṭunān, the northernmost district of the kingdom, writes to the king to anticipate the possibility that men who came through Qaṭṭunān will file a false complaint. They may charge the governor with holding two diplomats in custody, when these prisoners are nothing of the sort: "One Numhean was resident in Saggaratum and moved away to Kurdâ; and one man is in the service of (a man named) Sagaran."[19] In this mix, Saggaratum is the city center of another district in Zimri-Lim's Mari-based kingdom; Numhâ is the name of a people identified specially with the

---

[17] The most systematic work on the cuneiform evidence has been that of Jean Bottéro, first in his 1954 volume, and updated in *RlA* 4 (1972), and finally in a 1981 article. See also Greenberg (1955). Other reviews of the evidence have largely been based on the primary evidence gathered by Bottéro.

[18] For listed examples, see the two long treatments by Bottéro, with Mari examples gathered in my "Mari's *'iBrum*." The verb is written in cuneiform with HA/IH, etc., and the labial B/P may be read either way. By comparison with the *'ayin* preserved at Ugarit and in Egyptian, the first consonant is surely this one, and the middle radical remains to interpret (see Borger 1958). Whichever consonant is to be found in the early second-millennium texts, the verb is almost certainly cognate with the noun.

[19] 1 *ⁱᵘNu-ma-ha-yu ù i-na Sa-ga-ra-tim*ᵏⁱ *wa-ši-ib ù a-na Kur-da* ³² *ih-bu-ra-am ù* 1 LÚ *wa-ar-ki Sa-ga-ra-an i-la-ak* (ARM XXVII 116:31–2).

city center of Kurdâ, so that this man "moved away" (verb *habārum/'apārum*) from a town where he was a relative foreigner back into the kingdom defined by his own Numhâ people. Although he is moving into something that looks like home terrain, it is still a departure from Zimri-Lim's authority. This is far from transformation into a person of outcast status. So far as one could still question whether the verb is in fact cognate with the noun, the Mari texts include references to the *'apiru* status itself that involve the same movement from one political domain to another. One letter from Terru, sometime ruler of Urkesh, defines the status by departure (verb *waṣûm*): "I make constant blessing on [my lord's] behalf. Now, I have had to abandon the comfort of my house, and so I have left to live as an outsider at (the town of) Šinah. My lord must not be neglectful regarding this."[20] Terru's town has forced him out of power, and he has fled to a neighboring polity.

The question, then, is how such displaced people came to be identified by large groups. The notion of their gathering in "bands" does not explain the scale and integration of the Amarna evidence and is not required by the *'apiru* evidence as a whole. In evidence slightly later than that of Mari, the so-called *habiru*-prism of Tunip-Teššup, from roughly the late seventeenth century, counts by name three groups of *'apiru* fighters joined under three leaders, in a total of 438 men available to the ruler of this upper Tigris kingdom (Salvini 1996). Neither the men nor their leaders receive any further title, and they are counted simply as *'apiru*, a category evidently sufficient to record their commitment to Tunip-Teššup. It would seem that this mass of men lives within Tunip-Teššup's domain but will not fight with town and village units, which are based on long-term solidarity and serve together. Wherever and however they live, they are joined for military service under a separate census category, and this is what unites them for classification purposes. In actual combat, such groups would probably have moved and camped and fought together, as they were organized under this heading.[21]

If the identification of *'apiru* groups in later texts does reflect a social reality with links to this terminology and experience, then it is possible that they initially consisted particularly of men who were gathered to fight as units and then maintained such communities over longer periods, beyond their commitments to the kings who identified them this way. Although the Tunip-Teššup text shows a kind of catch-all *'apiru* census, it may be that by declining to assimilate into other defined communities, they committed themselves to leaders without accepting the framework of census by settlements. In this respect they resemble Mari's Hana people, who also fought by independent agreement. Such independence from accounting by royal census would have been anathema to imperial rulers like the Egyptian pharaohs, even as large polities such

---

[20] "I have left to live as an outsider" is *a-na ha-pí-ru-tim at-ta-ṣí* (see ARM XXVIII 46:2'-8'); the translation depends on the meaning of the term under discussion, of course.

[21] Many of the earlier *'apiru* references from the early second millennium have to do with soldiers; see Bottéro 1954 for the texts.

as those of Abdi-Aširta with Amurru and of Lab'ayu in the southern highlands could be founded on such an alternative social order.

Most simply, it appears that the 'apiru of the later second millennium, including the usage associated with the Amarna letters, represent a social approximation of the Hana in the Mari letters. At Mari, that term may refer to Zimri-Lim's Binu Sim'al people but is ultimately a social category defining those not identified by town of residence. The 'apiru are rooted in a terminology as old as the Hana, though with a slightly different meaning. If the word *hana* derives from the root /ḫny/, "to camp," then the category focuses on the mode of residence, which depends on movable tents rather than fixed houses.[22] In contrast, the verb 'ab/pāru has to do with the movement itself, leaving one residence to take up another. Only the word Hana envisions life with movement as a habit, whereas the 'apiru category is rooted in the notion of a single disruption. They share, however, the picture of people who continue to be defined by the fact that they cannot be identified by a town of current and permanent residence. The question is who such people can be when they represent a large social class, and here again, Mari offers a useful point of reference, because this archive gives us an unusually detailed view of the world away from settlements.

In the social landscape offered by the Mari archives, there are no appreciable numbers of migrant bandits or gangs of dislocated people who live outside urban boundaries. Equally, there is no special concern to define "resident aliens," a class of permanent outsiders who may reside in a town long-term and yet who are always foreign.[23] Where groups of significant scale are considered as peoples identified by names, these are of the sort commonly called "tribal": the Binu Sim'al and the Binu Yamina, the Numhâ, the Yamutbal, and others. The question is what such groups may be when identified as a class by those who have no interest in their named associations. By the time of the Amarna letters, the answer may be 'apiru. The earliest treatment of 'apiru as massed groups appears to have been for military enlistment, when such people lived in the domain served and yet could not be said to originate there. We know neither the backgrounds of these people nor their current affiliations – only that the government did not know how to count them by towns. In the Amarna correspondence, however, the 'apiru are coherent, connected, and the primary political base for the kingdoms of Amurru and Lab'ayu, as seen from outside. If we set aside the assumption that the backcountry of the southern Levant was populated by disaffiliated bands with no durable identity, it is more likely that the population not defined by towns would have maintained identities that could transcend settled space. Such identities would look like those of the

---

[22] For this proposed etymology, which suits the actual usage of the noun, see Durand (1992, 113–14); cf. Fleming (2004a, 47).

[23] This is what is envisioned for the biblical *gēr*, a category that is compared to the 'apiru by Ahlström (1986, 12). In the Bible, this class is of interest for the individual legal standing of its members, not because any large communities of *gērîm* are recognized and feared or courted.

Binu Sim'al and the Binu Yamina at Mari, where they are called "tribal." One Mari text identifies a fighting force of *'apiru* as explicitly belonging to one such group, the Yamutbal, serving under a Yamutbal leader who has offered to help Mari capture a recalcitrant city.[24] These are not people who are displaced from their proper places in a social system; they are merely classed as a group traveling from what they might consider a fixed home base, or without one – yet identified adequately as Yamutbal on the move.[25]

The *'apiru* of Amarna would not be "tribes" in any direct sense, especially as viewed from inside. Rather, they would include so-called tribal peoples as viewed from outside by the rulers of towns not invested in this social framework, undifferentiated from others who lack town-based identity. This would explain why the Egyptians did not fight against the *'apiru* or consider them enemies; the *'apiru* who fought for Egypt were simply people from such tribelike groups – not nomads, not necessarily herdsmen, but listed this way as the most convenient way to take their census for military purposes. Viewed this way, the *'apiru* need not be detached from the social order, and we need not even assume that they had cut ties to settled homes and kin. They were identified as lacking a fixed town of residence, like Mari's Hana, but this may often have reflected an integrated society of farmers and herdsmen.

3. The 'apiru *in the Landscape of the Late Bronze Age Southern Levant*
The political landscape of the southern Levant during the Late Bronze Age remains something of a conundrum, worth further study (so, Benz 2012). In spite of the fact that archaeologists and historians alike know about the *'apiru*

---

[24] 30 [lú.meš]*Ya-mu-ut-ba-la-yu ha-bi-ru i-na qa-ti-šu i-la-ku*, "Thirty Yamutbalite *'apiru* are under his command" (A.2939:13–14, in Charpin 1993, 188); cf. Bottéro (1954, no. 19); Pohl (1957, 159).

[25] Although his sense of the ancient social landscape reflected earlier conceptions, Michael Astour offers an interpretation of the *'apiru* that anticipates mine and likewise works especially from the Amarna evidence. He observes that "the perfectly sane view of the Ḫapiru as seminomadic tribal intruders of the tilled land, for all its textual and historical support, was all but drummed out in the nineteen twenties and thirties" (p. 36). The idea of the *'apiru* as "aliens, i.e. immigrants, fugitives, refugees, people of most diverse geographical or ethnic origin, who had nothing in common with each other but their homelessness, who were kept apart from the indigenous population by special discriminatory laws" was a retrojection of post–World War I European experience onto the past by the likes of Benno Landsberger and Julius Lewy (pp. 36–7). Likewise, Michael Rowton followed Landsberger in denying the *'apiru* any tribal identity, even though there was no basis to know they lacked such organization: "If the Ḫapiru 'bands' were externally similar to tribal units, the right thing is to admit that they were indeed tribal units.... History shows that wherever one finds independent armed bands, these were always ethnically homogeneous" (p. 40). This is a remarkably independent and insightful line of reasoning, in response to the basic nature of the evidence. Note that Rowton (1976, 14) considered the *'apiru* to reflect the "continuous seepage from the tribe" that occurs when "nomadic" tribes are in close contact with sedentary populations – a reconstruction that displays his understanding of Near Eastern society as ultimately polarized between sedentary and nomad as fully separate groups.

and attempt to account for them, their supposed character as displaced persons places them outside the normal classifications of study based solely on excavation and survey. In search of identities for the inhabitants of any setting – urban, rural, or hinterland – the primary occupants are rarely considered not to belong. Instead, one speaks of townspeople and villagers, farmers and herdsmen, agricultural and pastoralist ways of life, degrees of craft specialization in urban situations, and so on. Where are the 'apiru in the excavated and surveyed landscape of the Late Bronze Age southern Levant?

Certain basic facts are available. In the early to mid-second millennium, the Middle Bronze Age IIB marked a high point in local life, as measured by large population in numerous sites. This thriving period overlapped with the so-called Hyksos rule in the Egyptian north, when links between Egypt and Asia were strong.[26] The end of the Middle Bronze came with Egyptian invasion of the Levant as one expression of a major political transition, and many of the great walled cities suffered destruction or damage. Egypt ruled the Mediterranean Levant as "Canaan" through the Late Bronze Age, from the later sixteenth century through the early part of the twelfth. Viewed from the Egyptian side, the earlier phases of conquest and consolidation were followed by the establishment of military strongholds and administrative centers in a system that resulted in the relatively stable rule of the more southern lands, at least through the Amarna period and the fourteenth century (Weinstein 1981).[27] The Egyptians faced more difficulty with the local regimes in the thirteenth century and responded with more intrusive policies, reflected in further construction.

There is considerable discussion over how Egyptian rule was expressed in actual local conditions as encountered in archaeological research. Gonen tracks the numbers of settlements across southern Palestine throughout the Late Bronze. The numbers for the Middle Bronze II are roughly matched by the thirteenth century, with gradual recovery after the vast drop-off in the sixteenth century.[28] Many more of the later sites are small, and where the Middle Bronze towns survive, it is often on a much smaller scale. The result would have been a vastly smaller population, concentrated near the coast and in the lowlands.[29] Although there is some question about the possible reuse of the great Middle Bronze ramparts at some sites, Late Bronze towns seem to have

---

[26] See Frankel et al. (2001, 129); cf. Broshi and Gophna (1986).

[27] Higginbotham (2000, 1) emphasizes the significant rebound of the region after the initial wave of Egyptian destructions in the sixteenth century. More recently, see Morris (2005).

[28] Gonen (1984, 63): MB II (54); sixteenth century (24); fifteenth century (28); fourteenth century (48); thirteenth century (56). These numbers are based only on excavated sites; survey sharpens the pattern (p. 66, table 2). Frankel et al. (2001, 128–30) observe a similar pattern for the Upper Galilee, which they compare with the Benjamin region, where the reduction is even sharper.

[29] Herzog (2003, 93), based on the Hebrew dissertation of Shlomo Bunimovitz (1989, 152). Bunimovitz estimated a change from 137,000 to 27,600 between MB II and LB I, with the early impact of the Egyptian takeover.

been generally unfortified. Reinforced palaces formed the central strongholds of these sites, reflecting their modest scale.[30] Bunimovitz (1995, 323) considers that while in the Middle Bronze, the concentration of large sites in the southern coastal plain suggests a unified polity – which he does not name – the Late Bronze shows little such political integration. This is the landscape of "semi-autonomous states" visible in the Amarna correspondence. In spite of Gonen's count of small settlements, Bunimovitz emphasizes the essentially urban nature of the Late Bronze population (p. 324).[31] For him, there was no true circle of "peasants" dependent on the urban centers that would provide the basis for a "revolt" in Mendenhall's terms. Instead, the conflict at the end of the Late Bronze must have been between sedentary and nonsedentary groups.

In general, this leaves us with a countryside occupied by few fixed settlements, without large populations of farming villages dependent on urban centers. People either live in towns or they do not, and if they do not, the first conclusion is that they are pastoralists. Yet the *shosu* herdsmen known to Egypt are identified with lands to the south and east of the highlands that came to be occupied by Israel and that are visible in the Amarna correspondence. Given the frequent association of the *'apiru* with the regions outside town centers, in highland strongholds such as Amurru to the north and the region surrounding Shechem to the south, we may wonder whether these peoples could also be involved with what Anne Porter (2012, chapter 1) calls "broad range" herding, beyond the limits of daily travel from towns. Mari shows us that such groups developed forms of social organization that allowed them to maintain bonds across space, with members resident both in settlements and in herding camps, thus distributing labor according to need. The actual names of groups not defined by town centers seem to have been beyond the interest of the vassals who reported to Egypt. Mari's insight into this world is rare in the ancient Near East, a reflection of the unusual identity and circumstances of Zimri-Lim.

If something like this scenario is conceivable, then the southern Levant in the thirteenth century would have been occupied by a mosaic of political forms with diverse characters. Some would have been constituted by central towns with limited scope, as commonly imagined. Especially in the highlands and further inland, however, society may not have been divided between socially separate urbanites and country pastoralists. The peoples of the steppe may have been linked by social bonds that formed the basis for polities incorporating urban populations as well. A model may be the kingdom of Lab'ayu in the Amarna evidence, where town centers such as Shechem did not define his people, and his son could conveniently be found far from town with the *'apiru* when his Egyptian overlords called.

---

[30] Herzog (2003, 89–92); cf. Gonen (1984, 69–70).

[31] Killebrew (2005, 97) contrasts the continuity between Middle and Late Bronze material culture patterns in Canaan with the breakdown into distinct regional material cultures in the early Iron Age.

B. The Beginnings of Israel in Biblical Terms

Against the backdrop of the *'apiru* in the Amarna letters, we return to the Bible. Israelite material treating the people's origins offers a collage of distinct images, not all from the same setting or date:

- Israel's ancestry is viewed in kinship or tribal terms, with the peoples of Israel descended from individuals bearing each name and defined as sons of one father (Genesis 29–30).
- This tribal family is kin to peoples outside the land, especially inland to the east and north (Genesis 29–31).
- As a body, Israel moved into and departed from Egypt, all the time maintaining their identity as herdsmen (Genesis 37, 39–47; Exodus 2–12).
- Before life in the land, the Israelites were associated with the wilderness, and their settlement involved movement from outside locations (Hosea 13:5–6; cf. 9:10; 12:10).
- Establishment in the territory of Sihon and Og is depicted entirely as a movement in the east, evidently out of the southern interior, and consciously avoiding the lands of other eastern peoples (Deuteronomy 2–3).
- Accounts of foundational victories in the west are cast as won by Israelites already living in the area (Joshua 8; Judges 5, 20). There is no systematic conquest and no unified move from east into west, crossing the Jordan River, considering the west to be a "Promised Land."
- Successful establishment in land held by rivals generally required the extermination of all previous inhabitants, by a sacred slaughter known as *ḥērem* (Deuteronomy 2–3; Joshua 8; cf. Judges 20).

Historical evaluation of these distinct images of Israel's past cannot proceed according to a single interpretive scheme, as with the "conquest" generally treated as the biblical view. There are both multiple peoples and a single Israel. There is movement involving regions outside Israel, including the northeastern interior of Syria and Jordan, the southern interior toward Arabia, and Egypt. There is military conflict, each time focused on a specific target, without the framework of a systematic campaign. Because the different conflict narratives assumed details that did not fit easily into the later conquest scheme, which selected Joshua as leader, they were incorporated into diverse literary settings, so that their commonalities are now obscured. Herding plays a prominent role, and the ancestors of Israel are consistently associated with subsistence by grazing herds and flocks at distances from settled camps and home villages.

What then is "the" biblical view of origins, when writing from Israel is separated from Judahite overlays? As I have presented the evidence, of course there is none. From one point of view, it is genealogical, revolving around an ancestral figure who already lived in the land that would become Israel. We cannot know how widely this idea was shared, though the core Jacob narrative has geographical links both to Bethel in the west and to various sites in the east

(Genesis 31). The tradition of family ties to Syria is attached to the genealogical explanation of origins, though this may be secondhand, not inherent in the birth narrative of Genesis 29–30 when read alone. The stories surrounding earliest Israel can be divided between those treating the ancestral family, which form the basis for the book of Genesis, and those assuming Israel as a people, whether settled or moving, whether or not by this name. One strand links these two eras through the Joseph and the exodus stories, both of which give Israel a settled base in Egypt for their shepherding life. These tales both show signs of currency in the central highlands of Ephraim, yet they are quite distinct as narratives, and one may even have been created to complement the other – more likely the Joseph story second. At some time in this region of Israel, the idea of a long association with Egypt seems to have taken root, evidently as a way of connecting the ancestral and the nonancestral lore. Without a clear account of what followed Egypt, however, this combination still does not constitute a coherent explanation of Israel's origins. If we piece together these Israelite narrative elements, allowing for diversity of ancient opinion, we do find Israel as a group coming out of Egypt, Israel as a group in the wilderness, and Israel as a group fighting battles against peoples in the land that will be theirs – all without reference to the association of independent peoples. None of this material invokes the separate tribes, so far as it goes back to an Israelite setting. Where they appear, as in the lists of Numbers or the tribal allotments of Joshua, the hand is visibly Judahite.

Throughout this variety of Israelite origins lore in the Bible, the assumption of early life as mobile herdsmen is striking. We first meet Jacob and Esau in the general region to be inhabited by these peoples, and there is no reason to consider a nomadic life the only way to get the ancestors to the land of their descendants. Moreover, the pastoralist life of the ancestral family, the people coming out of Egypt, and perhaps the eastern people who attack Sihon and Og contrasts with the economy of Israel and Judah in the first millennium, especially in the west. The Israelite writers imagine their forebears to have lived differently from themselves. This picture of early herdsmen is one of the most intriguing features of the biblical lore from Israel, when considered in relation to history.

C. Pastoralism and the Origins of Israel

Archaeological evidence and inquiry will always provide the framework for investigating what happened in the southern Levant in the Late Bronze and early Iron Ages. Without new texts, we will get little further by tracing the particular polity called "Israel." Setting aside the search for Israel by name, then, there remains the question of how to explain the changes of settlement patterns with transition to the Iron Age. It is not my purpose to resolve problems that will continue to occupy specialists for decades to come, as evidence builds and interpretive models change. The prominence of pastoralism in the Bible's Israelite traditions, however, at least offers an occasion for reconsidering our assumptions about the roles of herding and of movement in the ancient southern Levant.

In my study of politics and society as viewed from the Mari archives, in conversation with Anne Porter and her evolving interpretation of Bronze Age society in Syria and Mesopotamia, I found a complete integration of mobile herdsmen with settled farmers, even when the herdsmen lived in separate communities and moved seasonally over long distances.[32] The social structure that provides the concrete vehicle for this integration is what has commonly been called the "tribe"; the point is that these groups are constituted by bonds that are maintained across both distance and the conventional political boundaries of kingdoms. In the Mari landscape, communities of mobile herdsmen and settled farmers overlap and merge in various expressions, most clearly in the domain of Zimri-Lim himself. As already observed, Zimri-Lim was the leader of the Binu Sim'al, a group not defined by a settled center and yet marked by a large population with great geographical range. Individuals within the Binu Sim'al identified themselves by *gayum*, a word that could be translated as "tribe," in comparison with the Bible's *šēbeṭ*, as one unit in a larger association. The Hebrew cognate is *gōy*, as a "people" or polity. Zimri-Lim called himself "the king of Mari and the land of the Hana," where the Hana were particularly associated with his Binu Sim'al people, the "tribal" association defined neither by settled center nor by territory.[33] In naming his people the "Hana," he treated them all as mobile herdsmen, so that even the many settled Sim'alites in his kingdom were identified by those who tended flocks in seasonal movement. The kingdom as a whole was an amalgam of peoples, with the Hana given pride of place as the foundation of Zimri-Lim's power. Tribe and state cannot be disentangled in this political construction.

This blend of social and political structures at Mari must not be attributed to the conquest of a settled and agricultural land by marauding tribesmen. At the time of Zimri-Lim, the whole region of the Euphrates and Habur Rivers, and perhaps much of Mesopotamia as well, was characterized by an integration of settled and mobile peoples, with subsistence by both farming and long-range grazing of flocks in seasonal movement. The "tribal" structures of the Binu Sim'al and the Binu Yamina, among others, allowed the maintenance of social bonds across distance, so that communities in towns and communities living in the steppe could consider themselves one people.

It remains uncertain to what extent this northern landscape may cast light on the southern Levant, either in the Middle Bronze Age or later. Many conclusions on the question have taken for granted the dated analytical model of Michael Rowton, who distinguishes the transhumant nomadism of the Mari

---

[32] My own work is published mainly in *Democracy's Ancient Ancestors* (2004a), with a further developed sense of the monarchy at Mari in "Kingship of City and Tribe Conjoined: Zimri-Lim at Mari" (2009). Porter's ideas about early society are first expressed in her dissertation (2000); followed by articles in 2002, 2007, and 2009, all leading to the major 2012 volume.

[33] See Charpin and Durand (1986, 152–5). The title comes from Zimri-Lim's predecessor, Yahdun-Lim, who applied it to himself in the Šamaš temple dedication inscription (i:17–19).

archives as "enclosed" and "dimorphic." It was enclosed by its situation in the interstices of a heavily settled region and dimorphic by its direct participation in that sedentary society, with tribal peoples settled in towns ruled by their own chiefs.[34] While this notion of mutual dependence represented important progress in understanding the relationship between apparently separate groups, it still took for granted the essentially separate character of each, which Mari evidence alone confounds. With Rowton as point of reference, Thomas Thompson (1978b) argues that Mari nomadism must have taken a form different from the Palestinian, because it occupied a broad steppe unlike the mountain terrain of the south. The drier conditions and smaller population of the southern Levant would exclude a dimorphic society of Rowton's type. Thompson observes that tribal groups settle not by their own initiative, but only when forced by a socially and politically separate Mari administration for purposes of taxation and control (1978a, 9, 15).[35]

Thompson's work is useful in that it shows how past responses to the Bible's depiction of ancestral herdsmen depended on a now-dated understanding of evidence for Mesopotamian pastoralism.[36] A fresh approach to the archaeological evidence for the southern Levant is undertaken by Bruce Routledge in his study of Moab (2004). Routledge complains that Syro-Palestinian archaeology has been trapped in the use of static categories such as peasants, pastoralists, and tribesmen (p. 91). Evidence for the Late Bronze/Iron Age transition in the Transjordan underscores the need to break out of these rigid categories. Unlike what is usually imagined for the earliest Iron Age, the first Iron I settlements in the Transjordan are sometimes larger than what they replaced, which were not "urban" centers in any case. According to Routledge, "there is no necessary reason to presume that pastoralism and agriculture correlated with politically or socially bifurcated populations in Late Bronze Age Transjordan" (2004, 92). "[N]one of the dichotomies ... used to create collective actors (and to imply their prior unity) in the now-familiar syntheses from Palestine have a necessary, or even obvious, relevance to Transjordan": lowland/highland, urban/rural, agriculture/pastoral nomadism, cosmopolitan/traditional. Pastoralism does have increasing importance as one moves further south, as displayed in the association of this region with the *shosu* in Egyptian texts.[37]

Although the Transjordan is drier and far less populated than the upper Mesopotamia of the Mari period, Routledge argues for principles of social

---

[34] See Rowton (1967, 114–16; 1973b, 201–4).

[35] Niels-Peter Lemche reaches similar conclusions based on patterns among modern Middle Eastern nomads (1985, 125, 139–470).

[36] Killebrew (2005, 99 and n. 7) observes an increase in "seminomads" and "marginalized individuals" in the Late Bronze, compared with the Middle Bronze. She then comments that one must keep in mind the interdependence of urban and nomadic populations, citing Rowton for her interpretive framework.

[37] Redford (1992, 271–3) observes that the *shosu* of fifteenth- through thirteenth-century Egyptian texts are associated especially with the southern Transjordan regions of Moab, Edom, and the Arabah.

integration not so different from what I envision. The problem is the location. With an expectation that pastoralism is associated with less settled regions, joined to the assumption that mobile herding communities are socially separate from settled towns, interpreters of the western highlands have not generally looked for such integration. It is only imaginable where the steppe looms close. Especially in the Late Bronze and early Iron Ages, before population growth and shifts in subsistence habits may have pushed it into the eastern backcountry, I would look for a similar integration west of the Jordan River. In earlier Syria and Mesopotamia, such blended social systems may have been the norm, even where major cities and extensive irrigation agriculture were involved.[38] The tribal geography of the Bible, if taken as a whole, suggests links between peoples east and west, as does the repeated connection between these domains for the ninth/eighth-century kingdom. Because even the Israelite materials in the Bible take for granted a first-millennium framework, the stricter relationship between people and geography cannot automatically be applied to the earlier period, equivalent to the Iron Age I and before.[39] This interpretation is not a proven conclusion but rather a hypothesis for testing.

In his critique of Syro-Palestinian archaeology, Routledge comments that for all the valuable work in the field, most writers still end up talking about social masses, such as tribes and lineages, and the process of becoming, or "ethnogenesis": "we start out talking about identity but end up talking about groups" (p. 92). In the transition from the Late Bronze to the Iron Age in the region that included Israel, surely the social landscape need not be reduced to lowland urbanites and villagers, *shosu*-type mobile herdsmen, and renegade *'apiru* (see below). Rather, the townsmen, the herders, and the *'apiru* are likely to have had overlapping ways of life, so that identities cannot be determined just by moving people from one mode to another. An identity such as "Israel," which was defined in the Merenptah stele neither by the old Egyptian zone of domination as "Canaan" nor by any individual city center, must belong to the category of naming on other terms, either tribal or otherwise associative. Merenptah's Israel is either a single people not defined by settlement or an association of peoples that could incorporate any sort of political body. In Mari terms, it would either resemble the Binu Yamina or Ida-Maraṣ. In either case, it probably included a component that moved seasonally over distance with herds and flocks.

For this discussion, I do not intend to evaluate the "historicity" of the Bible's accounts, Israelite or otherwise. The issue is rather whether the Bible's stories from Israel provide any useful historical information about early Israel. Naturally, they tell us something about Israel in the early first millennium, when

---

[38] Anne Porter now argues this for all of Mesopotamia up to the Mari period, even behind the administrative centralization presented by the urban archives of Ebla and Ur (2012, chapter 1).

[39] Both aspects may be visible in the portrayal of associated peoples in the muster list of the Song of Deborah (Judg. 5:14–18). There, the people of Reuben are associated with herding (v. 16), which naturally takes place east of the Jordan, although we cannot tell whether the list assumes geographically defined groups with strict regional bounds. The more regional the perspective, the more the text would seem to reflect a first-millennium setting.

the core written material should probably be dated. For earlier periods, and for the nagging questions about how Israel came into existence, the Bible offers phenomena to test. Stripped of later schemas, the Israelite material in the Bible begs more serious consideration. What was the role of pastoralism in Israel's background? How did Egypt come to represent Israel's essential antagonist in a moment of liberation, when Egypt had become a less urgent presence by the last century of the second millennium?[40] What was Israel's status in the region east of the Jordan River, which has a significant role in Israelite narrative?[41] Was Merenptah's Israel already an association of peoples, and at what point was this essential to the definition of Israel?

Throughout, the Israelite narrators supply no idea at all of the chronological distance they envision between themselves and what they portray. We must imagine a scale of centuries. Even writing that is contemporary with the setting pictured is not simply "historical"; it must be turned inside-out to discover its assumptions. With lore that stands at such distance from its point of reference, we cannot even take for granted basic identities for people and places. Nevertheless, just as archaeologists can look for details in the Bible that would not have been invented in seventh-century Judah and later, the biblical text itself offers features that do not reflect the society in which it was composed.[42] Where Israelite writing can be separated from Judahite, and the contents still present a contrast with the ninth and eighth centuries, all such details are of particular historical interest. They suggest perspectives that reach back before the kingdom centered at Samaria, however far they may go.

[40] This is a key interest of Stephen Russell's Egypt study (2009).

[41] Anson Rainey (2001) argues for a primary location of Israel in the east, beginning with the Merenptah reference. Since then, he proposed that Hebrew is more closely related to Aramaic than to Phoenician (2007a, b); my appreciation to the author for providing me a pre-publication copy and for his generosity to me through his life. Reclassification of Hebrew as part of an Aramaic family or genealogical line, as opposed to Phoenician, may not be warranted, but I am interested in Rainey's observation that certain features of Hebrew and Moabite align with the dialects of Zakkur (Aramaic) and Deir 'Alla (debated). So far as the Zakkur and Deir 'Alla texts share usage, as with the waw-consecutive verbal form and clause structure, I wonder whether they reflect a southern inland influence that may not be shared in Phoenician dialects. I appreciate the help of John Huehnergard, who maintains the standard language divisions for the Northwest Semitic group, in thinking through these technical problems (personal communication, January 2009).

[42] While both Israel Finkelstein and Amihai Mazar express similar points of view on the dominance of late monarchic Judahite perspectives in biblical historiography, Mazar is interested in identifying biblical traditions that do not come from the seventh century and later, as suggested by archaeological evidence (Mazar 2003, 85–98). Elsewhere, Mazar characterizes "the bulk of the biblical historiographic texts" as "literary works biased by late Judean theology and ideology" (2007, 144), while Finkelstein observes of the conquest tradition that this is "the ideological world of late Monarchic Judah" (2003a, 75). Such statements are standard in archaeological evaluation of biblical writing; see also Killebrew's introductory comment that the historical books of the Bible were "written from the perspective of the last two centuries of the kingdom of Judah and later" (p. 1).

17

Israel and Canaan in the Thirteenth to Tenth Centuries

Individually, the Bible's Israelite tales of time before kings can be difficult to separate between those set before and those set after the first appearance of Israel under this name as a population in the land. The clarity of this temporal divide derives from the finished literary work, with its drama of escape, wandering in the wilderness, and concerted invasion. History itself may be as muddy as the individual stories, but Merenptah gives us Israel at the end of the thirteenth century, and we must deal with the block of time between that date and the clear evidence for an Israelite kingdom in the ninth century. A trove of archaeological evidence provides data to mine, with little notion of naming and considerable room for debate over chronology and conceptions of society. One way or another, in the thirteenth through the tenth centuries, Israel should be on the scene, yet our comprehension of it is limited, even where the material finds are rich. We do not know what belongs to Israel and what does not.[1]

In the Bible, this period is addressed in terms of two radically different settings: first, in the book of Judges as a time of decentralized organization without kings, and then as the arrival of monarchy with Saul, David, and Solomon in the books of Samuel and 1 Kings 1–11. In both literary and historical terms, the biblical narrative for the establishment of kingship depends on the house of David, which I will address in Chapter 18 – leaving to others the relentlessly debated achievements of its two biblical founders. Here, we will consider instead the foundational identities offered by the Bible for the first phase of life as a people in the land: Israel as the people of interest, and Canaan as their ultimate enemy, defined by prior possession and the necessity of replacing them.

---

[1] In his article on the coastal plain before and after the arrival of the Philistines, Yuval Gadot (2008, 55–6) chooses the same interval from the thirteenth through the tenth centuries and emphasizes the material continuity that underlies any changes reflecting Egyptian or Philistine presence.

A. Early Israel and the Bible

The pattern of Israelite material in the Bible suggests that the whole idea of a time without kings is associated with Israel and its peoples, a notion that did not include Judah. This nonmonarchic tradition is likewise linked to the notions that the name "Israel" defined an association for mutual defense and that the unity of the groups in this association could be explained by the bonds of a tribal family.[2] The geography of early Israel in the Bible's core accounts is focused on the highlands north and south of the Jezreel Valley, along with a persistent notion that its peoples could also be found to the east, in modern Jordan.[3] From Benjamin southward, Israel is shown to have some interest, but it is not clear what peoples from this region were associated with Israel. It is possible that the later split of David's house from Israel could have obscured a natural southern range, not defined by Judah. David and Absalom are said to launch their claims to rule Israel from the southern highland town of Hebron (2 Samuel 5 and 15).

Identification of populations in the region also demands consideration of who may be present that is not aligned with Israel. As portrayed in the Israelite material of Judges, the peoples of Israel are faced with potential enemies both around and amidst them. Without any systematic conquest, there is just survival against a variety of local foes. Close at hand, there was repeated conflict in the region of Benjamin, as depicted at Ai and Gibeah – even if the Ai conflict was a legend (Joshua 8; Judges 20). Another recurrent domain for conflict lay east of the Jordan River. Eastern opposition could involve competition for the same land from enduring rivals, as reflected in the tales of Ehud and Moab, Gideon and Midian, and both Jephthah and Saul against Ammon. Inland strife could also be understood as attempts to displace these rivals entirely, as with Sihon and Og, along with the Benjamin region battles. Old stories of displacement

---

[2] Collaboration for mutual defense recurs in several Judges stories. Naphtali and Zebulun fight Sisera in Judges 4. Naphtali, Asher, and Manasseh join Ephraim against Oreb and Zeeb of Midian in Judges 7. Above all, the Song of Deborah combines Ephraim, Benjamin, Machir, Zebulun, Issachar, and Naphtali. The participants are fairly consistent: entirely western, but both north and south of the Jezreel Valley.

[3] More surprisingly, the Song of Deborah names Dan and Asher as two groups that could have been expected to join battle from the Mediterranean coast (Judg. 5:17), the former identified with "ships" in a way that suggests an urban affiliation. Stager (1988, 228–32) renders the statement about Dan as, "why did he serve as a client on ships?" Based on the notion of the *gēr* as a "client" dependent on employment outside his own kinship unit for financial support, Stager compares this statement about Dan to the tradition of Levi as a tribe without land. Dan would have begun as a "client tribe, not in control of its tribal territory" and associated indirectly with the coast also in Judg. 1:34. I find the evidence insufficient to propose that the entire identity of Dan can be detached from a geographical base, which does seem to be coastal. It could be plausible, however, that "we might speculate that at least enough of the Danites had been hired or pressed into duty by the shipowners or shipping companies on the coast in the Jaffa region to inspire this saying about them." Asher is likewise located on the coast in Judg. 1:31–2, where this people is said to live "in the midst of the Canaanite."

are linked to the theme of *ḥērem*, the annihilation of a prior population, and these are confined to the central highlands and the east. Given this division of types, it is striking that the one Israelite story of battle with the Canaanites, as told in the Song of Deborah, treats them as a fixed competitor like Moab and Ammon. They are defeated as an army, not slaughtered as a population.

None of these clashes is imagined to involve either the southern coastal plain or the western foothills (Shephelah). The Philistines do not appear until the Saul–David narratives of 1 and 2 Samuel and other tales of the early monarchy, such as with Omri. In Judges 1:27–33, the Canaanites are the catch-all for lowland opposition, whether in northern valleys (e.g., Beth-shean and Taanach), on the coast (e.g., Dor), or in the western foothills (Gezer).[4] The Song of Deborah repeats the association of Canaanites with Taanach in the north (Judg. 5:19). Between Benjamin and the Jezreel Valley, Israel is not portrayed as fighting for space, unless this goes back to stories linked to Shechem and Jacob (Genesis 34; 48:22); in the northern highlands, Gideon wages war with Midianites at Tabor (Judg. 8:18).

One of the most striking and strange components of the Israelite writing about time before kings is Judges 9, where the city of Shechem suffers from the abusive rule of an outsider king named Abimelech, who is finally killed in a military adventure. In the original Abimelech narrative, neither Israel nor the regional people of Ephraim have any interest, and the central tension pits the ambitious ruler over an old city center against a tradition of collective political power that is defined by the city of Shechem alone.[5] In 1 Kings 12, Shechem is the rallying place for Israel in its resistance to Rehoboam, and Jeroboam I makes it his capital (vv. 1, 25). Taken on its own terms, however, Abimelech's Shechem is part of an independent kingdom with no evident relationship to Israel. Moreover, we cannot assume that an early Israelite association was purely "tribal," without constituents defined in other terms. Shechem alone, or a polity that included it without tribal identification, could have participated in early Israel as a coalition partner. In the biblical schema, another solution may have been to recast a town-based member of the association as a tribe. The people of Dan, as identified with the northern inland city, may have represented a polity defined essentially by its settled center. No other tribe in the biblical system thus shares its name with a primary settlement.

All of this biblical material suggests how complicated the definition of Israel, its affiliates, and its neighbors may have been in a period before stronger unification under kings. Peoples that came to be identified with Israel may

---

[4] The geography of the opposition to Naphtali in Judg. 1:33 is difficult, with the common name "Beth-Shemesh" well known for the western foothills but out of place for this people, and "Beth-Anath" impossible to locate with confidence.

[5] This kind of town-based collective tradition is also common to the wider ancient Near East; in upper Mesopotamia of the early second millennium, such collective governance is particularly noticeable in the long-established cities of Imar and Tuttul on the Euphrates River in Syria and in the old Hurrian town of Urkesh at the northern extreme of the Habur drainage (Fleming 2004a, 211–17).

have had concentrated populations in particular areas, especially in the various highlands, not marked by a strong association between them. The people of Gad make an interesting case. Their existence is confirmed for the ninth century in the Mesha inscription, yet with the notion that they were there before Omri – if not before "Israel" itself. The Song of Deborah does not identify them as part of the military alliance, and the east is represented by Gilead and Reuben. In all the Israelite material, Israel by name either engages a local enemy (Ai with Joshua; Benjamin against Gibeah; the Ammonites with Saul) or unites an association of participating peoples (Judges 5; 7:23; 2 Sam. 2:9). Neither usage appears to require a fixed definition of members or a fixed institutional framework. As found in the Bible's collected narrative for the time before David, Israel is a malleable identity, most often attached to alliance for war. Perhaps this description suits reasonably the parameters for Israel as found in the Merenptah text, where it represents one of Egypt's military foes.

B. Israel in the Late Bronze Age

I have nothing to add to the identification of Israel in the Merenptah stele, and discussion of the Iron Age I Levant must proceed without a clear sense of where to place Israel. One emerging fact, however, warrants fresh deliberation in light of the transition from Late Bronze to Iron Age. Merenptah's Israel does not align chronologically with the upsurge in settlements that marks the material beginning of the Iron Age. Rather, this still belongs to the world of the Late Bronze Age. The implications of this are considerable. According to a common scheme for placing archaeological evidence into a historical narrative, Israel's social roots are seen in the shift from the landscape of town-based polities of the Late Bronze to the swell of village population in the highlands in the early Iron Age. This explains Israel's decentralized society, often considered relatively egalitarian, in contrast to the urban dwellers of the preceding era. It does not matter whether the Iron Age population is to be called "Israel," whether it had lowland Canaanite or inland pastoralist/*shosu* background, and by what process it began and grew. Israel belongs to the new social landscape of the Iron Age. Against the backdrop of Iron Age I settlement, the occurrence of Israel in Merenptah comes as a surprise. One could argue from this that the reading itself must be incorrect, except that the continuity of time and space is still perfectly intelligible for Israel to exist in some form in 1207 or so B.C.E. The problem is the assumption that Israel's origin must be explained by the settlement changes of the Iron Age I.

One of the most interesting developments in the study of Israelite history in the past generation has been the proposal, advocated above all by Israel Finkelstein, that the beginning of the Iron Age be moved several decades later (1995, 1996a). The initial idea was argued especially from pottery use as it relates to space and time, with the one relatively fixed anchor the Egyptian dynastic chronology. The first appearance of Philistine pottery and presence along the southern Mediterranean coast has most often been dated to the early twelfth century (ca. 1175) by reference to a conflict during the eighth year of Ramses III, who claims to have defeated an alliance of Sea Peoples that included the Peleset, who are then imagined to have settled the nearby coast.[6] Meanwhile at Lachish, in the foothills above Philistia, the new Philistine pottery does not turn up until after the withdrawal of Egypt several decades later, about 1140. With a more secure Egyptian chronological correlation for Lachish, Finkelstein proposes that the first Philistines must be dated by the appearance of their pottery at this non-Philistine site, sometime in the last decades of the twelfth century.[7] The shift in dates for the earliest Philistine pottery then suggests a large-scale and involved realignment of ceramic sequences for all of the southern Levant, pushing the Iron Age chronology later by several decades. Amihai Mazar (1997) countered quickly that pottery need not be involved with trade or contact across such population boundaries and that the chronological realignment did not work well for the larger region, creating as many problems or more than it resolved.[8]

Appropriately, the debate then entered the domain of the specialists, who have argued at length the question of how a new chronology would work out for the larger region, aside from the specific issue of Philistine origins. Meanwhile, however, ongoing work with carbon dating has offered hope of reasoning on other grounds that might provide at least a sense of whether the chronology should be moved later, if not an exact amount. The results are still not clear, but in recent studies, Mazar moves the boundary between Iron I and II to ca. 960 or 950, forty or fifty years later than its once-conventional date of 1000, cutting in half the gap with the date proposed by proponents of the "low chronology" in the same volume.[9] Mazar's adjustments (2007) reflect a response to the ^{14}C evidence for the middle parts of the Iron Age, and he has given no ground on the logic of relating Philistine pottery to the inland, so that his Iron Age I is stretched to cover the greater span, with an Iron IA defined to precede the departure of the Egyptians (1200–1150/1140). It is difficult to avoid the impression, however, that carbon dates are pushing early Iron Age chronology more solidly into the twelfth century.[10]

---

[6] See, e.g., Mazar (1985); Singer (1985); Stager (1995).

[7] David Ussishkin, the excavator at Lachish, dates the withdrawal of Egypt from Canaan at the end of the Twentieth Dynasty to about 1130, especially with reference to a statue base for Ramses VI (1141–1133) found in the destruction layer for Late Bronze Megiddo (2007, 135–6).

[8] Bunimovitz and Faust (2001) add a more theoretically based argument along similar lines, that some parts of a "cultural assemblage" reflect interaction between groups while others reflect the retention of group separateness and identity.

[9] Mazar (2008, 112) proposes 950; this moves the endpoint of Mazar's Iron Age I period down by thirty years from his earlier date of 980 (2007). Mazar and Ramsey settle on 960 (2010). Compare also Sharon et al. (2008, 188); their final date of ca. 910 is based on the span of 925–885, which they also say could be 925–895, or ca. 915.

[10] The debate continues apace in recent literature, but deep differences in historical conception seem to separate even the interpretations of excavated strata. Finkelstein and Piasetzky (2010; 2011) maintain confidently a transition between Bronze and Iron Age ceramics near 1100 and between Iron Age I and IIA near 900 B.C.E. In spite of their optimism that the debate is

In light of this chronological debate, the Merenptah reference to Israel may become ever more deeply embedded in the Late Bronze Age, before Egypt's departure from Canaan, before Philistine arrival, and especially before the vast expansion of highland settlements. If this is true, then the archaeological context for Israel's first formation as a polity – capable of opposing Egypt in battle – is not the formation of rural highland peoples into "chiefdoms" or the like, which would belong to early phases of Israel's existence and coexistence with similar groups undergoing similar social change. Rather, Israel took political form out of the Late Bronze II landscape of established Egyptian power, in a time when there was relatively little highland village settlement and the population straddled somewhat shriveled towns and a more open countryside. The landscape that I described with reference to the *'apiru* would still apply to earliest Israel, as suddenly displayed in the Merenptah text. If the *'apiru* were people organized without identification by their city of origin, like the Binu Sim'al and the Binu Yamina of the Mari archives, then Israel's population could have overlapped with what polities like Ashkelon, Gezer, and Yenoam would have identified with this class.[11] This possibility would have little to do with past and present reconstructions by which Israel emerged in part from downtrodden *'apiru* peasants or displaced persons. The interpretive benefit of this association derives from recognition that alongside the city-based polities like Merenptah's other victims in the famous stele, other groups may have developed that need not be defined by a city base. There are hints of this in the kingdom of Lab'ayu during the Amarna age, when Shechem may have represented Egypt's natural focus of attention, but it served as only one urban center for a local ruler with a more broadly based population and power.[12]

If Merenptah's Israel belonged to the world of Egyptian power over Canaanite subordinates, before arrival of the Philistines and the boom of new highland settlement, there is no reason to separate its material expression absolutely from that of "Canaanites." Naturally, all of these categories are of different types: Canaan referred especially to what Egypt controlled, which was more focused in the lowlands; the *'apiru* were a way of defining people without

shifting their way, Mazar (2011) maintains the divide where it currently stands. In a refreshing contribution from material outside Israel, from Khirbet en-Nahas in central Jordan, Levy et al. (2010, 843) object that Finkelstein's chronology depends on the impossibility of complex polities in the southern Levant during the first three quarters of the tenth century, and en-Nahas presents just that. Finkelstein says that copper mining took place under Assyrian aegis only in the late eighth and seventh centuries, but in Jordan, "there is no question that the peak in Iron Age metal production occurred much earlier, during the tenth and ninth centuries BC." They are nevertheless prepared to accept some lowering of the chronology, with Mazar (2011, 840). For a similar view of the tenth century in the east, see Barako (2009).

[11] On the last and least known of these cities, see Na'aman (1977), who argues a location in Jordan rather than in the west. Rainey adopts the eastern location, with added argument from the related Karnak relief (Rainey 2006a, 100).

[12] Again, see Brendon Benz (2012) on Lab'ayu, against his common identification as king of a city-state based at Shechem (e.g., Na'aman, 1997b, 604).

reference to their own social organization, because this did not fit the city-centered basis for Egyptian diplomatic relations; and Israel was an individual name for the kind of political entity that Egypt had managed to ignore or redefine until this late period of its empire. To my mind, there is nothing gained by saying that the Israelites were "Canaanite" except to recognize that they appeared on Egypt's Levantine horizon as part of this complex world that the empire did not fully understand. In material terms, archaeologists use the name to emphasize the cultural continuity between the Iron Age I inhabitants of the region and those who came before, in contrast to the material novelties that accompany the arrival of the Philistines.[13]

Indeed, it makes sense to distinguish Merenptah's Israel from the Philistines; this Israel is homegrown, though by that we cannot determine the relationship within it of west and east, of town and backcountry, of farmer and herdsman, and we cannot tell whether any component of inland Levantine migration played a role. The name itself is a theophoric sentence name, a personal name attributed to a whole people. This alone suggests a kinship-oriented social context for the group, a natural continuity with the Bible's kinship organization as a tribal family.[14] As observed with discussion of the 'apiru, such organization would have been common to the Late Bronze Age, especially for peoples that maintained links with backcountry regions – probably integrated with urban populations.[15] Merenptah's association with Late Bronze strata in the Levant, as opposed to the Iron Age I settlement shift, only makes the material continuity more logical, even as it is an obstacle to identifying the material simplicity of the Iron I with Israel's very existence rather than highland life more generally in this period after Egyptian withdrawal.[16]

[13] This treatment as "Canaanite" was intended to counter the supposition that Israel arrived on the scene as complete cultural outsiders, especially with regard to religion. See the discussion of Israel's religious relationship to Canaan in Smith (1990, xx–xxiv).

[14] Divine names are standard to theophoric personal names, and the incorporation of the god El in the name "Yisra-El/el" does not indicate any religious component to the first definition of the group (contra Bloch-Smith and Alpert Nakhai 1999, 68). This is not to exclude a religious dimension to earliest Israelite identity; religion would always have played an essential role – for Israel as for every people in the region.

[15] By this interpretation of Late Bronze society as integrating farmer and herdsman, city and mobile pastoralist, the continuities of material culture between lowland towns and new highland sites in the succeeding periods would reflect a longstanding history of contact and shared culture, rather than seeing the highlands as taking their culture from western and lowland sites with the migration of population up from those areas (cf. Bloch-Smith and Alpert Nakhai 1999, 103).

[16] This debate plays out in recent discussion of highland burials in the Iron Age I, where Faust (2004, 183) proposes an "ideology of simplicity" that would contrast with the Late Bronze; cf. Kletter (2002), who emphasizes the relative poverty reflected in this pattern. This approach reflects Faust's overall explanation for "Israel's ethnogenesis." Bloch-Smith (2004) objects to Kletter's assumption that Late Bronze Age "Canaanite" sites display material culture different from Israelite Iron Age sites, a separation also reflected in Faust's approach. There is a continuity of burial style from the fourteenth/thirteenth to the twelfth/eleventh century, in spite of the small numbers, and she finds that the actual graves excavated show stratified groups, as opposed to the imagined simplicity of one-person graves (p. 87).

C. Canaan in the Early Iron Age

In Judges 1:27–33, the military failures of various Israelite peoples are contrasted to the early success of Joseph, which had managed to take Bethel as its central city (vv. 22–6). Manasseh, Ephraim, Zebulun, Asher, and Naphtali are then lamented for their inability to take specific cities from their own undefined regional homelands. Throughout verses 27–33, all such cities are identified as Canaanite, and the list as a whole could be taken as part of a blanket identification of Israel's conquered land as previously called Canaan. Without the larger biblical narrative, however, including the promises to Israel's ancestors and the notion of a systematic conquest after migration, it is less certain why these cities are considered Canaanite. In its current location at the start of Judges, this whole situation is regarded as part of Israel's experience in the land, where the major obstacle to territorial control takes the form of major urban centers. No timeline is given, and even before the outcomes listed for each people, Israel is shown to coexist as neighbors with a Canaanite city population. As observed earlier, these cities are concentrated at lower elevations, often outside the regions that one might assume to be primary to the Israelite group in question. For example, Ephraim only fails to take Gezer at the southwestern margin of the highlands that represent its heartland. The concentration of these cities in the vicinity of the Jezreel Valley in the north and in the lowlands along or near the Mediterranean coast adds to the sense that the whole land occupied by Israel is not being called "Canaan." Rather, particular sets of lowland cities are identified with this name, then perhaps generalized to apply to any towns that could not be taken over by Israelite peoples. The name could be applied from the later generalization to the whole land, but in this Israelite material, it is worth considering the alternative, that a more specific understanding of Canaan survives here. If so, this would be a Canaan of the early Iron Age, still present after the departure of the Egyptians. The very idea is not current in historical discussion, though new developments in archaeology would suit the possibility.[17]

1. *Identity Issues at Beth-Shemesh*

In a recent interpretation of their excavations at Beth-Shemesh, an important foothill town between Jerusalem and the Philistine city of Ekron, Bunimovitz and Lederman (2008) introduce the ubiquitous concept of ethnicity to a discussion not involving Israel. Before their work at the site, Iron Age I Beth-Shemesh was thought to have been dominated by the Philistines. According to new analysis, the Philistine presence seems less marked. The Iron I settlement has three

---

[17] Gadot (2008, 62–3) considers there to have been a "no man's land" in the coastal plain during Egypt's Twentieth Dynasty, after effective withdrawal from the region. The last datable finds from Egypt's centers at Jaffa, Aphek, and perhaps Gerisa come from the reign of Ramses II, in the late thirteenth century before Merenptah. Even with the arrival of the Philistines, the more northern coast is left untouched in the first decades of their settlement (p. 64).

phases between what Bunimovitz and Lederman date from the mid-twelfth to the early tenth centuries, with no evidence for a defensive wall. In the earliest phase, there are already two contiguous houses, including one "Patrician House" with two long halls and massive stone walls in a style that fits construction from the Late Bronze Age. Both the architecture and the pottery show affinity with lowland and Shephelah sites, as opposed to the highlands. Almost no evidence for the collared-rim store jar was found. Pottery included no Philistine Monochrome and only 5 percent Philistine Bichrome, an amount that indicates only small-scale contact, without a population of resident Philistines. Similar proportions occur at Gezer and Aphek (pp. 23–4).[18] Another line of evidence comes from dietary habits. Generally, the Late Bronze sites of the Shephelah and coastal plain show little use of pork, which changed radically with the arrival of the Philistines. Iron I Beth-Shemesh, however, continues to lack pig bones and in this way resembles contemporary highland sites (p. 25).

Having reviewed this material evidence, Bunimovitz and Lederman raise the issue of ethnicity. Does the lack of pig suggest self-differentiation from Philistines and therefore Israelite ethnic identification? Otherwise, the town shows strong continuity from a Late Bronze "Canaanite" past. They observe that insecure conditions lead groups to stress "belonging together" and that the number of occupied sites in the Shephelah dropped by half between the Late Bronze and Iron Age I. It appears that a Canaanite rural population was displaced from its own territory by newly arrived Philistines (p. 27). In contrast, the highlands above Beth-Shemesh, in what would become the lands of Judah and Benjamin, enjoyed a massive increase in settlement. Bunimovitz and Lederman conclude that the inhabitants of Beth-Shemesh faced a Philistine expansion at their doorsteps and had to define themselves against it, with the refusal to eat pork one possible expression of this. They do not identify Iron I Beth-Shemesh as Israelite, though they seem to understand the struggle in terms of Israel and Philistia.[19]

One way or another, it seems that the people of Iron Age I Beth-Shemesh distinguished themselves from their Philistine neighbors and yet show no particular sign of belonging to Israel. Without writing, of course we cannot identify them or determine whether they took any name beyond that of their own town. Nevertheless, the scenario of cultural contrast without Israelite

---

[18] It is interesting that both Gezer and Aphek belong to the list of Canaanite cities that resisted capture by Ephraim (Judg. 1:29) and Asher (v. 31).

[19] In a separate article, Bunimovitz and Lederman (2006) discuss the situation at Beth-Shemesh during the tenth and ninth centuries, when there are alternating periods with increased and decreased quantities of Philistine Bichrome pottery. The authors conclude that the periods with less Philistine material probably reflect identification with Israel during its early monarchy (p. 422). The lack of pig bones throughout the Iron I shows that the city was never Philistine, and they conclude rather that Philistine pressure "forced Canaanite Beth-Shemesh to redefine its identity" and affiliate with Israel. It is not clear from this account whether Bunimovitz and Lederman envision a self-conscious non-Philistine, non-Israelite identity for Beth-Shemesh for the period before the tenth century.

involvement suggests that if "ethnic" questions need to be asked for the Iron I period, then other identities must be considered.

2. Political Identities in the Iron Age I Southern Levant

This situation at Beth-Shemesh provokes a more general rethinking of which names might have been in play in the Iron I southern Levant, along with Philistia and Israel. The large division between Israelites and Philistines ultimately derives from the Bible's portrayal of the land at the time of Saul and David, adapted to the archaeological reality of new material finds along the coast in the Iron Age I.[20] Missing from this discussion of early Iron Age identity is "Canaan," which the Egyptians understood to represent the main body of their Levantine Asian vassals and which the later Bible identifies with the main body of peoples replaced by an emergent Israel.[21] Can we be certain, however, that our Egyptian and biblical informants have the final word on Canaanite identity? In textual terms, we have no evidence for Israelites, Philistines, or Canaanites by name in the Iron Age I, with or without the Low Chronology. A substantial circumstantial case can be made for the presence of Israel and some culture that became the Bible's Philistia. These names and associated groups, however, may not be adequate to describe the inhabitants of the southern Levant through the early Iron Age. Acknowledging our ignorance of the many local labels that people would have taken, one obvious candidate remains to place: Canaan, of the Late Bronze and Egyptian connections. Is it possible that the name "Canaan" could have survived as a self-attributed identity during the Iron Age I, thus explaining more adequately how it could have found its way into biblical writing of the first millennium? I will explore here a possible scenario, which naturally awaits further evidence and discussion.

According to the Bible, the peoples of the southern coast represented more than a cultural or ethnic type; the Philistine name defines an association of city-based domains that join for concerted action against their neighbors. In this respect, the Philistines were like Israel itself. If such political confederacies did exist outside Israel, we may wonder whether there were others. This brings us back to the situation described by Bunimovitz and Lederman for Iron I Beth-Shemesh, where a local population seems to have resisted assimilation with its Philistine neighbors. Without a geographical or material basis for arguing an identification with Israel, and based on the material continuity with earlier periods, Iron I Beth-Shemesh seems Canaanite. If this people maintained a

---

[20] In Killebrew's account of the period from 1300 to 1100, Egypt and Canaan define the region in the Late Bronze Age (2005, chapters 2 and 3), and the Israel and the Philistines represent the broad divisions for the early Iron Age (chapters 4 and 5).

[21] In spite of the debate over how exactly Canaan was defined in the Late Bronze period, the monograph by Lemche (1991) remains very useful for both its conceptual questions and collection of evidence, especially outside the Bible. For "Canaan" as the whole of what Egypt controlled in Asia, see Na'aman (1994, 120). This need not be considered an official or administrative name, as objected to by Lemche (p. 40), but nevertheless represents a general identification (see also Killebrew 2005, 32, 51).

conscious distinction of identity between themselves and a contrasting "Philistine" group nearby, we must take seriously the need for an actual name that
"identity" language implies. Regardless of what such a larger identity could
have been at Beth-Shemesh, the situation described by the excavators raises the
question of whether a truly "Canaanite" identity could have survived in the
Iron Age I.

3. Canaan in the Iron Age I

Although Israel and Philistia would represent new names for newly defined
associations in the Iron Age Levant, it is also possible that people who maintained continuity with their Late Bronze Age past took or kept names that
would preserve their old identities. The "Canaanite" name could have offered
just this result, in that even under Egyptian rule it remained an indigenous
term, applied only to the peoples of the Levant. If the Shephelah preserved
a non-Philistine population that was still not part of Israel, Judah, or any
highland-centered group, it could simply have been "Canaanite." Although
Egyptian references to Canaan generally reflect the New Kingdom power in
Asia and do not occur later than the twelfth century,[22] a solitary text from the
early first millennium names a messenger of "[the] Canaan and Philistia" as
two separate entities.[23] Both of these names would provide crucial reference
points for the political geography of the early Iron Age if defined with confidence, but we face a frustrating lack of detail and context. Taken literally, a
messenger sent to named places implies that specific polities are in view, rather
than vague regional names without reference to the man's working destination.
According to Ahituv, it is uncertain whether the brief inscription was added
during the Twenty-second or the Twenty-sixth Dynasty (late tenth/ninth or
seventh century), a choice with real significance for historical reconstruction.[24]
If the latter, it is hard to see "Canaan" as more than a generality, without
imaginable political meaning. If the former, we cannot rule out a historical
reference. Ahituv wonders whether the text envisions the Phoenician coast;
Lemche reads instead, "the envoy to Canaan in Palestine," as in Philistia, and
considers this the real political entity (p. 54). In the end, the text can take us
only so far, and we cannot be sure whether Egyptians were aware of any group
that called itself "Canaan" after the New Kingdom.

At this point in our investigation of names and identities, it is worth returning
to the tangled evidence of the Bible. Beyond the stereotyped notion that Israel
would take over "the land of Canaan" as a whole, and the list in Judg. 1:27–
33 that introduced my discussion here, two archaic poems present Canaan

---

[22] For a systematic listing, see Ahituv (1984, 83–5). The earliest example comes from the reign of
Amenhotep II and the last from the reign of Ramses III in the early twelfth century.

[23] For full bibliography, see Weippert (1974, 429). This translation comes from Weinstein (2001),
following Ahituv (1984, 43). This is the latest pharaonic period reference, on a Middle Kingdom
statuette reinscribed in the Third Intermediate Period (early eleventh to early seventh centuries)
for Pediese, son of a Near Easterner named 'Apy, who was evidently this messenger.

[24] Ahituv (1984, 84 n. 24), with reference to Bezalel Porten, *BA* 44 (1981) 43.

differently, as one association in a world of competing alliances: the Israelites, the Philistines, and the Canaanites, among others.[25] In the Song of the Sea, which I regard as an early Jerusalem composition, Yahweh's people parade to his highland sanctuary in the presence of petrified neighbors.[26] These include "the inhabitants of Philistia," "the chiefs of Edom," "the leaders of Moab," and "the inhabitants of Canaan" (Exod. 15:14–15).[27] From the vantage of Jerusalem, Edom and Moab would occupy the entire eastern margin, and Philistia would lie directly to the west.[28] In this company, there is no sense that Canaan occupies the same space as Yahweh and his people. As a neighbor, therefore, Canaan is left the space to the north and west, close enough to be adjacent. The Phoenician cities of Tyre and Sidon are too far north to be relevant.

In the Song of Deborah, the people of Yahweh face "the kings of Canaan" at Taanach, just south of Megiddo (Judg. 5:19). This text is definitely Israelite, belonging to the sphere of the later kingdom by that name, and the geographical focus is more northern, with the participating peoples straddling

---

[25] Canaan and Canaanites are embedded in other biblical texts that may have Israelite or earlier Judahite origins. "Canaanites and Perizzites" are combined in the nonpriestly account of the quarrel between the herdsmen of Abram and Lot (Gen. 13:7), and the same pair reappears in the Dinah story (Gen. 34:30), although Shechem itself was supposed to be inhabited by Hivites. It is hard to tell whether these texts reflect later listing traditions or feed them. In the Joseph story, the famine is in "the land of Canaan" (42:5, 7, 13, 28, 32; 44:8; 45:17, 25; 47:1–4), which suits the identification of the land from an Egyptian perspective. This language never appears in Israelite material related to military conflicts in the early occupation of the land. The camp at Shiloh is in "the land of Canaan" in Judg. 21:12, part of what Sara Milstein (2010) identifies as a later Judahite reworking of the episode for providing wives in 21:15–24. Genesis 50:11 mentions Canaanites living nearby who saw the mourning for Jacob at Atad. This defines a population of the Palestine region for the ancestor period, not as a target. Only the king of Arad is described as Canaanite, in sequence of Numbers and Joshua (Num. 21:1, 3). In general, a sweeping description of a Canaanite land in the Torah and afterward signals a non-Israelite and relatively later perspective. For example, "the land of the Canaanite" in Exod. 3:17 and 13:5, 11 probably reflects deuteronomistic writing; Joshua is filled with this language.

[26] The issue of the Song's date and provenance is much debated (see Russell 2009, 133–48). Without considering the Song of the Sea a late text, I am inclined to locate it at Jerusalem based on the considerable overlap of vocabulary and phrasing in Isaiah 11–12 and a number of Psalms. Brian Russell (2007, 97–130) argues that all of the closest comparisons between Exodus 15 and these Jerusalem texts display dependence of Isaiah and the Psalms on the Song of the Sea, not the reverse. With such connections between the Song and these Jerusalem texts, it is simplest to imagine that the Song was also composed in Jerusalem, rather than imagining an earlier creation that brought it only to Jerusalem, without impact on other Israelite writing.

[27] All the groups should represent each people as a whole, in the stance of a potential antagonist to Yahweh's own. Mark Smith (1997, 210 n. 21) considers the possibility that the last group could be "the enthroned" as rulers of Canaan, although this would apply equally to Philistia. Whether the description emphasizes leadership or populace, all four groups are presented in collective terms.

[28] As a set, the collection of names could be quite early. Both Edom and Moab occur in Egyptian texts from roughly the thirteenth century, at the time of Ramses II (Moab) and Seti II (Edom); see Ahituv (1984, 90, 143). Edom is the regional origin of *shosu* clans, and Moab is a land in which the Egyptians campaigned against the specific city of Botirat.

the Esdraelon/Jezreel plain. As in the Song of the Sea, Canaan is depicted in collective terms, except that the capacity to fight as a unit is put into action. Given that the Song of Deborah is the one Israelite text that opposes the people of Yahweh (5:13) to the assembled rulers of Canaan in a time before Israel's monarchy, it is striking that this was not considered part of a conquest. Perhaps the enumeration of distinct peoples who follow their individual interests could not fit the framework of unified invasion that characterizes the book of Joshua. Without reference to a larger conquest, there is no reason to distinguish this war against the Canaanites from the other local conflicts assembled in the book of Judges. In Judges 5, as in Exodus 15, Canaan is envisioned as a competing neighbor, to be defeated and driven back to its home territory. The distinct section devoted to Jael pictures Sisera's mother waiting with his household for a safe return, laden with plunder. It is clear who invades whom, and Sisera is the aggressor.

Together, these two texts portray Canaan with a political aspect similar to that of Israel, as an association of groups that could act together, especially in war. In the list of peoples from the Song of the Sea, Philistia, Edom, and Moab are all names that could be taken by the people themselves and are not simply labels applied to foreigners. Could the same be true of Canaan? That is, could some population in the southern Levant during the early Iron Age have called itself "Canaan" and even joined under that name to fight, as depicted of the enemy in the Song of Deborah? In light of these questions, it is intriguing that Israel Finkelstein has coined the term "New Canaan" to describe the persistence of Bronze Age material culture through the twelfth and eleventh centuries at Megiddo (level VIA) and in the northern valleys (2003a). While Finkelstein refers only to the continuity of population, the usage in Exodus 15 and Judges 5 raises the possibility that the name itself could have survived in a self-given identity, in one or more bastions of older traditions.[29] I do not endorse an "ethnic" interpretation of the name "Canaan," but it seems to me that in the Iron Age I, there is at least as strong an argument to be made for Canaanite ethnicity as for Israelite.

It is likely that with the arrival and establishment of the Philistines on the southeastern Mediterranean coast, and the withdrawal of Egypt from their Levantine holdings generally, some inhabitants of the region called themselves "Canaanites." This means that during the Iron Age I, Canaan was probably a neighbor to Israel, rather than simply a population to displace.[30] As such,

---

[29] Mazar (2008, 86) observes the same pattern for Canaanite material culture: it continues through the twelfth century at sites such as Megiddo, Dor, Tel Reḥov, and Lachish; and into the eleventh century in the Jezreel and Beth-shean Valleys, as well as in the coastal plain from Dor northward. These would reflect the earlier chronology, against Finkelstein. Mazar objects that Finkelstein's New Canaan envisions a "Canaanite renaissance" after a gap that does not in fact exist (p. 88) – a secondary issue.

[30] Finkelstein concludes that this New Canaan would have collapsed with the violent destructions at Megiddo, Kinneret, Dor, and Tel Hadar in the tenth century (2003a, 78). The highlands would not yet have held enough power to manage this, which leaves Sheshonq I, for whom the

the name may have held political significance, like the names "Israelite" and "Philistine," and perhaps the discussion of ethnic differentiation that is often attached to Israel applies at least as appropriately to Canaan. In turn, the hypothesis that some of Israel's immediate neighbors in the Iron I period may have called themselves Canaanite would help to explain how the Bible ends up treating Canaan as Israel's direct competitor for the same land in the southern Levant. We could even wonder whether the allied kings of Canaan in the northern valleys would have maintained this identity in the face of a threatening external power – not Philistia, but Israel.

destruction of wealth makes little sense. While Finkelstein obviously avoids the possibility of David, even the stories about him remind us that military power need not require large bases of wealth in its early stages.

18

Israel and Its Kings

The books of Samuel and Kings bring the Bible's primary narrative to a close with a more obvious perspective from the kingdom of Judah. Judah's final collapse brings the narrative to an end in 2 Kings 24–5, and the possibility that David's house could be restored is kept open by Jehoiachin's place at the Babylonian royal table in the last lines (25:27–30). Throughout the books of Kings, attention bounces back and forth between Israel and Judah, but Israel's kings are burdened with the constant reminder of Jeroboam's religious failure with the calves at Dan and Bethel (1 Kings 14:28; etc.), and only Judah's rulers have the capacity to please Yahweh fully, like David (1 Kings 14:11; etc.). The books of Samuel provide a background for this account of kings by introducing David as heroic founder. Although the David narrative is constructed from material that identifies him entirely by rule over Israel, its combination with the books of Kings makes clear the ultimate preoccupation of the writers with the royal house of Judah, which kept authority through all the centuries of this kingdom.

As we move to the first millennium, the relationship of the Bible to history may at first seem more straightforward than with the earlier narrative. At least these books present Israel as a kingdom, a name and form familiar to the ninth-century texts outside the Bible. Archaeologists and historians debate the utility of Samuel and Kings for historical study, with particular energy surrounding the possible extent of a realm for David and Solomon.[1] My immediate interest is rather the way in which the political structures of the biblical narrative shape historical interpretation, whether more or less is believed of the Bible's content. Faced with direct knowledge only of the two kingdoms in their later forms, the compilers produced a scheme for monarchy as a whole that resolved all

[1] For a recent introduction to this intense discussion and voluminous literature, see Kratz and Spieckermann (2010); especially the articles by Blum, Finkelstein, and Mazar. Blum emphasizes that neither "history" nor "literature" existed by our contemporary definitions, with the latter meaning fictional narrative with no claim to depict the real world (p. 61).

tensions by two names, Israel and Judah. The writers' own realm in the south was named Judah, and they portrayed the kingdom as maintaining this identity from the first moment of division at the time of Rehoboam. While the other kingdom may have borne more than one name, including the regional label Ephraim (Isa. 7:17; Hos. 4:17; etc.), the writers chose the broader designation as Israel to provide a stable identity in parallel to Judah. This solution may have served in part to establish a claim to onetime dominance by the house of David over both domains, based on traditions for David's rule over Israel. Tied to the separate tradition of Israel as an association of tribes, Judah could then be accounted for as one tribe within the larger entity (1 Kings 11:36; 12:20). By this arrangement, Israel becomes the only body to be ruled before the division at the time of Jeroboam and Rehoboam.

Both the names "Israel" and "Judah" are grounded in history, as confirmed by their use in nonbiblical texts. Nevertheless, both reflect particular choices and perspectives. Judah certainly names the kingdom that survived after Assyria engulfed the north, and scribes from the late monarchy would have known it by this identity. Israel, in contrast, seems to have been an ancient name that continued to apply in some uses to the other kingdom (Hos. 4:1, 15–16; etc.). Where the southern name is contemporary or close to it in use by one of Judah's own, the northern name evokes antiquity in use that is in some sense foreign to the Judahite writers who selected it. Just as the names of the two kingdoms appear to be rooted in historical usage, other structuring features of the biblical narrative are assumed as context and may prove historically useful. These include the names of kings and how long they ruled, as well as accounts of their capitals. In what follows, I propose an interpretation of Israel and its monarchy that responds to the political portrait that I have painted over the course of this volume. My intention is to offer an alternative structure for understanding Israel in relation to kingship, both by nature and through time, taking the Bible seriously as a source. The structure that I propose can then be tested against all available evidence and applied to a larger historical discussion.

A. United and Divided, North and South

Decades ago, Albrecht Alt explained the "northern" kingdom as having a "charismatic" aspect, whereby leadership could be more quickly deposed or raised, based on individual capacities.[2] He read this directly from the biblical narratives of Samuel and Kings, perceptively but without hesitation. Saul arose like the judges, chosen by the principle of "charismatic leadership." David and Solomon followed, charting their own political paths with a centralizing spirit. Only after Solomon's death, "the original and distinctive features of the monarchy in the kingdom of Israel, which had lain more or less hidden for two generations, completely reasserted themselves" (p. 246). Like Saul, Jeroboam I and Baasha were designated by Yahweh, and Israel's kingship began to change

---

[2] See Alt (1968, 241–59, on "The Monarchy in the Kingdoms of Israel and Judah").

only with Omri and then Jehu, who established a lasting capital at Samaria and the beginnings of dynastic succession.[3] The structural differences between Israel and Judah as separate kingdoms were shaped by this split into two. With its city-state of Jerusalem at center, Judah became more unified and rigid, especially as seen in David's enduring royal house (pp. 243, 251).[4]

Alt's essential recognition of the contrast between the political patterns of Israel and Judah remains profound, though it needs to be embedded in a clearer sense of Israel's political nature and history. In common usage, Israel is the universal identifier for the Hebrew-speaking peoples of the southern Levant during the Iron Age. Taking at face value the Bible's finished genealogical scheme and the ideal of abiding Davidic rule, Judah is a subset of Israel. Within this framework, the Iron Age kingdoms of these peoples have been defined by two phases: a "united monarchy" under Saul, David, and Solomon, and a "divided monarchy" after Solomon, when Rehoboam could not maintain his father's rule over Israel as a whole. This schema taken from Kings is increasingly challenged for historical usage, but the underlying logic of a deeper unity persists in other terminologies.[5] In particular, the two realms are often called the "northern kingdom" and the "southern kingdom," treating them as the divided parts of one Israel.[6] The "northern kingdom" seems to take the name "Israel" because this name was left available with the separation of Judah and the larger number of tribes now on their own.

---

[3] Jaruzelska (2004) more recently defends the historical plausibility of the Bible's notion that prophetic support contributed to the legitimation of kings who would establish new royal houses in Israel.

[4] In the tradition of Alt, in the best sense, Tomoo Ishida has written extensively and insightfully on the politics of monarchy in Israel and Judah, working entirely from the Bible, without questioning its capacity to portray the situations it describes. In *The Royal Dynasties in Ancient Israel* (1977), Ishida devotes chapter 5 to "The Royal-Dynastic Ideology of the House of David" (pp. 81–117), with no comparable chapter for Israel after Jeroboam I. Instead, he discusses "The Problems at the Passing of the Royal Throne" in chapter 7 (pp. 151–82), merging the details of both Israel and Judah. He observes that normal succession is father to son, with only two exceptions, caused by Egyptian and Babylonian interference (Jehoiakim in 2 Kings 23:34; and Zedekiah in 24:17; cf. Jehoram in 2 Kings 1:17, "because Athaliah had no son"). One later article delineates two types of seizure of the throne in the "northern kingdom": by the people in helping a war-leader to the throne (Saul, Jeroboam I, and Omri), and by usurpers in conspiracy (Baasha, Zimri, Shallum, Pekah, and Hoshea); "The People under Arms in the Struggles for the Throne" (Ishida 1999, 68–80).

[5] In spite of questions about the viability of the category as history, the united monarchy remains widely used as a category of analysis: see the articles by Finkelstein, Mazar, and Blum in Kratz and Spieckermann (2010). The problem of historical application is explored in Knoppers (1997); cf. Albertz (2010). The German *Grossreich* focuses on scope rather than unity, as in Michael Huber's *Gab es ein davidisch-salomonisches Grossreich?* (2010). The phrase "divided monarchy" remains common in discussions based on the books of Kings: e.g., Auld (2007); Barnes (1991).

[6] In the excellent history by Miller and Hayes (1986), this less biblically charged terminology replaces the notion of Israel united or divided. See, e.g., Köckert (2010); Finkelstein and Na'aman (2005).

Throughout this work, I have occasionally shared the convenience of the north/south pairing, when the point is the situation of one kingdom with respect to the other. Current historical study, however, has moved increasingly toward recognition of Israel and Judah as distinct entities with links that need to be defined more carefully. This chapter, like the project as a whole, both depends on this fresh sense of separate identities and develops it by examining their contrasting political traditions. Rather than set the finished biblical scheme against history as an ideological imposition, I explore details in the Bible's narrative that may be historically useful by suggesting new directions for understanding the character and evolution of the two kingdoms.

B. The Israelite Monarchy

Although our approaches to the earlier periods diverge, I find much to endorse in Philip Davies' critique of this common usage of terminology. Davies observes the Bible's twin applications of the name "Israel," one for the particular kingdom and the other for Israel and Judah together. "In fact," he concludes, "the historian must in the end be driven back to the only workable definition, namely the political: a *political* entity in the strict sense, a kingdom occupying the northern Palestinian highlands" (1992, 54). The difference between us lies above all in the fact that I understand Merenptah's Israel to be most likely political as well. Whether or not this Israel had a king or allied kings, Egyptian identification of a people without city center parallels the Bible's notion in Judges of a period when individual leaders arose according to need and Yahweh's provision, in the context of loose collaboration between regional groups. Only Judahite authors, in their efforts to create a systematic history of Israel, felt the need to define a particular moment when the people wanted a king, and the entire political order switched to a monarchy (1 Samuel 8). It is not clear that Israelite writers ever envisioned a "transition to monarchy" or pre- and postmonarchic ages – at least as a literary or narrative construction. The old Saul story that culminates in 1 Samuel 11 may not even have seen him as a king; at least, it is not preoccupied with the title. The strongest evidence that Saul himself took the title *melek* may be the effort made by David's partisans to argue his legitimate succession to a prior royal house.

Israel's stories of divinely inspired deliverers, including Saul, were preserved for their own sake, without intent to divide Israel's past into ages. We do not have a literature of Israelite kings from Israel itself, with the exception of Omri's brief narrative and in some sense the older David narrative, stripped of its effort to include Judah. If we recognize the dominant Judahite voice in the Bible's whole scheme of monarchic history, however, we must doubt that Israelites understood there to have been either any division of "Israel" in two parts or any essential transformation of its kingship. The possibility of a perspective not partial to David produces an alternative historical scenario in neutral terms. We should avoid the concept of a "united monarchy" as creating the false impression of a separate political phase. Politically, the periods before and after

Jeroboam I were generally the same. The only difference was the retrospective participation of Judah in the Israelite association under the leadership of David and Solomon as portrayed in Samuel and Kings. Historically, this raises the question of whether the kingdom based at Jerusalem was once related to Israel through a period when its founders ruled the other kingdom. We will take up this question shortly.

If we return to the possibility that Judah's place in the David narrative may have been added for a later southern audience, the picture becomes even sharper. The history of Israel would develop as follows.

(a) As reflected in the book of Judges, various Israelite writers developed a tradition of political life without kings. Accounts of dramatic crises that involved local groups within the eventual Israelite community tended to agglomerate, by the very fact that kings and the kingdom were irrelevant to them. Without the theme of kingship as a clear organizing principle, the basis for preservation seems to have been the local interest, often as memory of threats from peoples outside Israel. None of these older stories involves Judah, which seems not to have been included in this tradition. In contrast, Judah is defined politically by its attachment to the house of David, and maintenance of the David lore is Judah's preeminent contribution to the Bible's narrative for early Israel. This Israelite preservation of tales about local crises addressed under local leadership appears to confirm that Israel once existed as a polity without kings. The larger biblical notion that monarchy was a novelty would then be grounded in Israel's history.

(b) Instead of a "united monarchy," we should speak of an "Israelite monarchy," which began at least with David and is attributed to Saul. The Israelite monarchy balanced royal power and the possibility of filial succession against the collective power distributed across Israel, most visible when mustered as a fighting force. Simple identification as "Israelite" distinguishes it from the kingdom that maintained a separate capital at Jerusalem and that was finally named Judah.

(c) The balance of royal and collective Israelite power meant that the heirs to kings who launched new houses were understood to be vulnerable and could be easily deposed if they failed to gain the support of the wider political body of Israel, in whatever form. Israel's monarchy was not "unstable" but rather constrained by a decentralizing political tradition that allowed turnover of royal houses. The recollection of famous local events in the book of Judges represents the political complement to the Bible's supposition that Israel's royal houses could survive only with broad-based support.

(d) The "Israelite monarchy" continued without essential change until Omri established a permanent capital at Samaria, and then Jehu began a royal house that lasted four generations. The dispute involving Rehoboam and Jeroboam I, if we can imagine such an event, would not have altered the character of Israel's kingship.

(e) A second kingdom was created by the successful retreat of a king from the house of David (so, Rehoboam) to his southern capital after he failed to win support to rule. Rehoboam's avoidance of assassination and successful defense of Jerusalem and the south are proof of striking political strength. Jerusalem became the capital of a polity that owed its very existence to the decision of a king, unlike Israel. In spite of the impressive power displayed in this act of resistance, any reference to "secession" must apply to the house of David, not to Israel, as the entity that withdrew from the existing order.[7] Outside the Bible, this polity is first attested as the House of David and may only secondarily have been identified as Judah.

As conceived according to this interpretive framework, the kingdoms of Israel and Judah develop along quite different lines.

C. Monarchy under Constraint: The Kingdom of Israel

Within this construction of an Israelite monarchy, various patterns emerge from the biblical narrative. One can follow the progression of royal houses through that of Jehu, with repeated turnover that seems to follow a coherent logic. Up to and including the house of Jehu, the first king of a royal line is never assassinated: Saul, David, Jeroboam I, Baasha, Omri, and Jehu.[8] David's repeated refusal to kill Saul seems to play off of this Israelite ideal. In what may be a later recasting of his reluctance, this refusal is motivated by the impossibility of laying hands on "the anointed of Yahweh," perhaps not just the current legitimate king but the divinely designated founder of a new royal house.[9] The founder of a royal house appears to have bequeathed to a son the first right of consideration, but his confirmation as king depended on approval from a wider range of powers in Israel. Among these first six royal houses,

---

[7] See, e.g., "The Secession of the North" in Miller and Hayes (1986, 231). Wesley Toews (1993, 2) introduces the distinct religious practice of Jeroboam's kingdom with the comment that "after its secession from the Davidic-Solomonic kingdoms, the Israelite state developed its own institutions."

[8] The seven-day reign of Zimri, if this literary interval represents any historical reality, is ended by Omri's intervention on behalf of mustered Israel (1 Kings 16). Even in this case, no one kills Zimri; rather, he burns the citadel on top of himself (v. 18).

[9] 1 Sam. 24:6, 10; 26:9, 11, 16. We cannot know whether every Israelite king was anointed. Solomon is said to have been anointed as David's successor, perhaps claiming treatment as a new founder and the immunity from assassination that went with it (1 Kings 1:34, 39). While the stories of David having a chance to slay Saul may have a place in early David narrative, the joining of these by the motif of "Yahweh's anointed" is widely understood as part of a revision: see Conrad (2005); Dietrich (2004); Fischer (2004, 269–91). The combined Saul–David narrative represents a later stage in the composition of an extended David story, probably at a greater distance from the Israel-oriented starting point for recalling David's reign. We cannot tell therefore whether the particular addition of "Yahweh's anointed" would have come directly from any Israelite monarchic tradition. If it keeps any echo of Israel's royal practice, it would be carried with the David lore itself, in conscious reference to Saul as the previous king of Israel, with the assumption that the founder of the standing royal house must not be deposed.

the first sons of David, Omri, and Jehu maintained power: Solomon, Ahab, and Jehoahaz. Ishbosheth son of Saul, Nadab son of Jeroboam, and Elah son of Baasha are all said to have ruled just two years, as if this represented a stereotyped definition for rejected reigns, after the accession year as trial (2 Sam. 2:10; 1 Kings 15:25; 16:8). Men from his own Benjamin people murder Ishbosheth (2 Samuel 4); Baasha kills Nadab during battle against the Philistines (1 Kings 15:27); and Elah is struck down in the home of one official by Zimri, another member of the leadership circle (16:9–10).[10]

Along with the pattern of survival and assassination between founding rulers and their heirs, the accounts of the failed successors indicate the role of the larger Israelite community in each transition. As told from David's side, Ishbosheth (Eshbaal) rules after his father Saul only by the backing of Abner, who soon leans toward support of David. After Joab murders Abner, the narrator has David curry the favor of Israel by mourning this leader and denying any part in his death (2 Sam. 3:28–37).[11] David treats Ishbosheth's murderers more harshly than Joab; he has them executed and their bodies displayed publicly (4:11–12). Immediately thereafter, the collective leadership of Israel comes to David at Hebron to make him their king (5:1–3). Baasha kills Nadab in public, with the mustered people of Israel laying siege to the Philistine town of Gibbethon. As presented in the narrative, Baasha takes for granted the support of the people, once the former king is out of the way. On the surface, Zimri seems to replace Elah in the same way, proclaimed the new king after disposing of his predecessor. Omri's accession, however, is depicted as the result of general dissatisfaction with Zimri's act, which is rejected as illegitimate (1 Kings 16:16). As observed already, the collective Israel is essential to Omri's ability to take and hold office as king. Israel was ready to replace Elah, but not by Zimri – as recalled in a text that came from Omri's circle.

One indirect testimony to the decentralized character of Israel's monarchy is the varied geography of its royal houses, which are identified with significantly different regions:

- Saul comes from Benjamin, with further links to Shiloh and perhaps Ephraim.
- David has a raft of southern associations: Bethlehem as birthplace, in the highlands south of Jerusalem; circulation in the desert along the Dead Sea; contacts with the Philistine south; and Hebron as his initial base.

---

[10] It is interesting that no king is shown to have been assassinated by his own son, whether in Israel or in Judah. With this pattern in mind, the tale of Absalom becomes all the more striking. There appears to be a tradition against patricide as a route to power, and as a corollary, patricide would seem to undermine claims to legitimacy. Absalom's revolt is thus unique in portrayal of succession in Israel and Judah, presented as a complete anomaly; the premise of the narrative is an act understood to be a political impossibility in both realms.

[11] This behavior is one example of the literary pattern that leads Baruch Halpern (2001) to treat much of the David narrative as a defense of the king from a period very close to his reign.

- Jeroboam is linked to Ephraim (1 Kings 11:26).
- Baasha is identified with the "House of Issachar" (1 Kings 15:27), north of the Jezreel Valley.
- Omri is a military commander without clear geographical or tribal associations.
- Jehu launches his coup from Ramoth-gilead, east of the Jordan (2 Kings 9:4), and, like Omri, he has military credentials.

Likewise, the royal capital of Israel shifts numerous times, though not as a direct match to royal origins:

- Saul rules at Gibeah, within the territory of the tribe of Benjamin (1 Sam. 11:4; etc.). Because Gibeah is in Benjamin, Saul is assumed to be from that people, although hints in the text indicate origin in Ephraim.[12] The finished text treats Gibeah as Saul's hometown (1 Sam. 10:26).
- After Israel sends representatives to Hebron to accept David as king, his first act is presented as establishing a new base by conquering the Jebusite citadel of Jerusalem (2 Samuel 5). Jerusalem is neither a hometown nor a tribal center, reflecting the very different character of David's power.[13]
- Jeroboam begins his reign by rebuilding Shechem (verb *bnh*). He is then said to move on and rebuild Penuel, but this could mean the creation of an eastern base to go with the western center (1 Kings 12:25).[14]
- It appears to be Baasha, not Jeroboam, who makes Tirzah his base of power (1 Kings 15:33, cf. v. 21).[15] After Zimri assassinates Baasha's son Elah at Tirzah, Zimri is trapped in the citadel and burns it down on top of himself (16:9, 18).
- Omri once again establishes his new royal house by acquiring the site of Samaria as a new stronghold (1 Kings 16:24).[16]

---

[12] See Sara Milstein's argument for the link between Judges 21 and 1 Samuel 1 by reference to the feast at Shiloh (2010, chapter 4). The latter text has long been recognized to display a folk etymology for Saul rather than Samuel, and this would place the king in Ephraim.

[13] Here, as always, we have to acknowledge that what we know absolutely is only what the narrative offers us. David is remembered or portrayed as having a strikingly different power base. It is nevertheless difficult to account for the notion that David was an outsider to both Israel and Judah by any later political circumstances. David's base at Hebron may also have nothing to do with Judah (Chapter 6).

[14] In 1 Kings 14:17, Jeroboam's wife is said to go back to their home at Tirzah. Nothing before this verse located Jeroboam at this site, which appears to be read back from the narratives that follow. In Jeroboam's case, Jerusalem was not available, and he was thus compelled to find other options.

[15] In the report of Ahijah's prophecy against Jeroboam, the king's wife is said to go home to Tirzah to see her sick son, after having visited the prophet at Shiloh (1 Kings 14:17).

[16] The note on the length of Omri's reign in 1 Kings 16:23 divides its twelve years equally between Tirzah and Samaria. This comment may extrapolate from the larger narrative, because the immediate Omri report does not indicate any further association with the ruined citadel of Baasha's house.

Until Jehu, every royal house is portrayed as selecting a new base of power, a pattern that suggests a change in Israelite kingship during the ninth century. The geographical spread of capitals is most striking for the earlier period, and it is noteworthy that the range narrows to the Ephraim highlands even while new founding kings still choose new royal cities. Overall, this geographical pattern suggests a distribution of power and resistance to centralized authority – not political instability.

The interplay of political influence between kings and an Israelite tradition of noncentralized power may be understood by the model of coexisting network and corporate strategies (Blanton et al. 1996, as discussed in Chapter 11). Throughout Israel's monarchy, both political modes exist side by side, in constant competition, yet lacking a single moment of transition from one type to the other. Judged by the duration of would-be dynasties, the centralized authority of kings gains some ground by the time Samaria is established as capital. The houses of Omri and Jehu last longer than their predecessors, and Jehu keeps Samaria rather than building a new central city. Within Israelite political tradition, it is Judah that offers the anomaly through the centralization and permanence of power at Jerusalem. This is made possible only outside the framework of Israel.

D. The Jerusalem Offshoot: David's House and Judah

In political terms, Judah came into existence only through a royal act: Rehoboam's refusal to disappear after the selection of Jeroboam I as his replacement. This act constituted a kingdom with Jerusalem as symbolic center and strategic bastion, defined by the persistence of the "house of David." The contrasting political tradition of Judah, with its centralization of palace and temple at Jerusalem, appears to be rooted in these origins. Although Israel is rightly characterized as geographically diverse, Judah likewise incorporated regions at some distance from Jerusalem and the nearby highlands. Before Sennacherib's invasion in 701, the western foothills represented a prominent subsidiary region with an old urban tradition and its own political force;[17] after Sennacherib, the kingdom reached its greatest extent, in part based on expanding population in the inland south and east.[18] Benjamin became part of Judah during the seventh century as well. Nevertheless, Jerusalem remained the dominant center of

---

[17] Herzog and Singer-Avitz (2004, 222) observe that the Iron Age IIA, which they date from the mid-tenth to the late ninth or mid-eighth centuries, is "a time of great prosperity in the foothills."

[18] An earlier concentration of population in the Beersheba Valley appears to reflect a polity unrelated to the house of David and Jerusalem, perhaps centered at Tel Masos (Finkelstein 2002). Only after the Iron IIA do we find a set of fortified settlements in the Shephelah foothills (e.g., Lachish IV) and the southern lowlands (e.g., Arad XI and Beersheba VI-IV) that indicate an emerging central government (Herzog and Singer-Avitz 2004, 228). The dates for these settlements are caught up in the debate over chronology and may vary by several decades. For the seventh century as the period of greatest population in Judah, see Faust (2008).

Judah, and in the eighth century, it displayed this in fantastic numerical growth. Geography alone does not account for the political differences between Israel and Judah.

The central fact in the biblical narrative about Judah is its commitment to the single royal house of David and its capital at Jerusalem. Identification of a realm south of Israel by "the House of David" (*byt dwd*) in the late ninth-century text from Tel Dan appears to reflect the same tradition, which is developed by a careful royal genealogy in the books of Kings. As the oldest nonbiblical reference to the realm, designation as the House of David challenges any assumption that it could always have been considered the kingdom of Judah. One could conclude that Rehoboam and his successors embraced such a monarchic identity, given the royal establishment of the polity. Identification as the Bet Dawid comes from the Arameans at Damascus, however, not from the people or leadership themselves. The same may be said for the Bit Humri (Bet 'Omri) in the Assyrian royal annals, during roughly the same period. In both cases, naming the polity by its king emphasizes individual authority and excludes whatever collective identity and political capacity may underlie such names – in contrast to "Israel," "Judah," and "Ephraim."

The Bible's chronology for the two kingdoms is based on a record of royal reigns that begins with Jeroboam and Rehoboam, in contrast to the forty years each attributed to David and Solomon.[19] It is therefore likely that the Jerusalem-based kingdom can be traced back to the late tenth century as an entity separate from Israel. If it was called the House of David by others, or at least for contact with outside powers, what would it have been called at home? For now, there can be no certain answer, but my interpretation of the David lore as originally defined by Israel offers one logical possibility. Rehoboam's realm could have claimed the name "Israel," in competition with the kingdom from which it withdrew. A modern comparison may be found in the Republic of China, which is now confined to the island of Taiwan but which carried its name with the leadership that fled there when the Communist Party gained power in 1949. Early identification as Israel would have created a need for alternative designations on both sides, especially for contact with the outside world, which could distinguish them by what they perceived as their founding royal houses. Also, this hypothesis would explain the Judahite notion in Isa. 8:14 that there are "two houses of Israel," acknowledging the reality of the other kingdom while maintaining a Davidic claim to the name. After the larger kingdom was dismantled by the Assyrians, Judah could take over the name "Israel" with a sense of proprietorship, finally receiving back what had once been lost to the line of David – as recalled in 1 Kings 12.

---

[19] Jeroboam is said to have ruled for twenty-two years (1 Kings 14:20), while Rehoboam reigned for seventeen years "in Jerusalem" (v. 21). In the chronological record, there is no account of any reign for Rehoboam over Israel. Contrast the forty years attributed to David in 2 Sam. 5:4–5 and 1 Kings 2:11 and to Solomon in 1 Kings 11:42.

As already observed with discussion of David (Chapter 6), the regional identity of Judah may be quite old, whether as a purely geographical label for the southern highlands or as a people identified with that land. Only with the first attestation of Judah in Assyrian sources of the late eighth century do we find clear evidence that the kingdom bore this name. By taking such a regional identity, the Davidic kingdom may have imitated Israel, or perhaps even Ephraim, names unrelated to rulers or their capitals. Like Israel, the kingdom based at Jerusalem would also have had a collective aspect, which may have varied in character and influence over the centuries of its separate existence. Its particular origin as the refuge of David's house, however, marked it from beginning to end, and this accounts for the centralizing traditions linked to Jerusalem.

E. Continuity between the Kingdoms: The Question of Writing and Language

When viewed in light of the political distinction between Israel and Judah, various specific historical issues can be framed in different terms. Not all aspects of culture need reflect such contrast, and it is important to recognize both categories. In general, houses with a four-room style and the family structures accommodated by these houses would be largely the same across Israel and Judah, as would ceramic styles. Especially where material or intellectual culture is determined by the local patterns of households and families, or even of village-scale communities, there is no reason to expect differences between Israel and Judah that are rooted in the distinct natures of each polity. Only what is tied to the political formations of Israel and Judah will be expected to show substantial contrast.

In this context, the question of language and scribal practice is worth particular note. In general, I do not treat these as following the political lines of Israel and Judah. Northern and southern dialects are often distinguished, though the differences are not large.[20] Moreover, it is not clear that we have adequate evidence to align these dialectal differences along political lines, to match the actual kingdoms.[21] For instance, it is not known whether diphthongs

---

[20] Gary Rendsburg proposes a list of dialect features drawn from biblical texts (1990). His method assumes that stories about northern judges and northern kings can be read as northern Hebrew, which is not obvious. Most would accept a more limited distinction derived from inscriptional evidence (next note).

[21] W. Randall Garr (1985) is cautious about what the evidence can tell us. After a long list of features that distinguish Hebrew from other Northwest Semitic languages and dialects, he comments: "The extent to which this analysis pertains to northern Hebrew as well as the southern dialect, however, is uncertain. Most direct linguistic evidence came from texts of southern provenience, supplemented by BH data. Where direct evidence for the northern dialect was available, it did not necessarily conform to the southern speech pattern. For example, the northern dialect exhibited complete monophthongization (2:8) and a formation of 'year' derived from *šan-t (3:6c); the southern dialect had uncontracted diphthongs and formed 'year' from *šan-at" (p. 227). These two northern features align with Phoenician and Moabite, indicating

and triphthongs were contracted in Benjamin or throughout the territory ruled as part of Israel in the ninth and eighth centuries. Rough regional variation in language is no different from the same for pottery or other material features, not attributable to any "cultural" contrast between Israel and Judah. Some of these questions remain unanswered or unanswerable without considerable new evidence. Garr explores the possibility that the "degree of political unification" could affect dialectal variety. Whereas the Aramean states exhibit a number of local dialects, Judah was "a single linguistic entity."[22] Further, "This linguistic unity may be accounted for, in some degree, by the political and religious centralization of the southern kingdom" (p. 234), a situation that would have been atypical in regional terms.

In contrast to language, scripts can be judged in regional terms even with texts of limited length. Christopher Rollston (2006, 59) concludes that by the time of the earliest definite Old Hebrew inscriptions, with dates that span the eighth century, a unified "independent national script" was shared across both Israel and Judah.[23] Working from Rollston's argument for "synchronic consistency," Seth Sanders (2009) then seeks to explain how scribal education could be effectively uniform through both kingdoms.[24] Since evidence indicates a range of settings for Hebrew writing, generally outside large institutions, the explanation must be the continuity of artisanal norms, independent of royal demands. "It is precisely in the Iron Age, when the people of Israel and Judah were autonomous in their land, that a local literature created a kind of politics beyond the state" (p. 155).

While the separation of writing from the constraints of royal power makes sense in the settings that produced the Bible, Rollston's foundational analysis of a unified development across Israel and Judah is based on the same assumption of a single identity that burdens the ethnicity studies for earlier periods. Even his language of a "national script" appears to envision a unity of Israel and Judah as found in the Bible's narrative rather than as proved by epigraphic and excavated evidence. In fact, there may still be too little epigraphic evidence to answer the stimulating questions pursued by both Rollston and Sanders, and this domain may prove significant for the exploration of how the political

---

that they spread into Israel but "stopped at the Judean border" (p. 233). Other northern Hebrew features can be inferred where they occur in both Phoenician and Ammonite, because Israel lay between these two places geographically. These include the relative particle *'š* and certain vowel patterns.

[22] According to Garr (1985, 234; cf. Kaufman 1974, 9), "no two Syrian Aramaic-speaking communities spoke the identical dialect in this period.... The texts from Jerusalem, Arad, Yavneh-Yam, and Lachish (somewhat later) showed identical phonology, morphology, and syntax."

[23] See also the systematic collection of early Hebrew inscriptions in Renz (1997). I have not been able to obtain Rollston's new book-length study (2010) in time for the final revisions to this book.

[24] See, esp. chapter 4: "Decentralized training could not plausibly have produced the paleographic and orthographic consistency of the Hebrew inscriptions, or the extensive use of the complicated hieratic numeral system. The epigraphic evidence implies coherent training: Hebrew writing was not just a style, it was an institution" (p. 131).

distinction of Israel and Judah manifested itself in daily life. The inscriptions from Kuntillet 'Ajrud in the southern desert demonstrate the activity of Israelites in a region far from their main population, recalling my inquiry regarding the Genesis traditions for Abraham and Isaac.[25] Beyond this unique site, which lies outside particularly Judahite territory as well, the rest of the eighth-century evidence cited by Rollston appears to belong either to Israel before its fall in 720 or to Judah after the end of Israel.[26] That is, epigraphy does not in fact offer a synchronic picture of both Israelite and Judahite writing for the period when both kingdoms were active. Instead, we appear to have a collection of Israelite writing, with the practices of Judah visible only once it was the only realm standing. Palaeographic and orthographic features of the earliest Judah material may therefore reflect developments that were not shared by Israel, even if there is substantial connection between them. For example, Rollston proposes an orthographic development across both Israel and Judah by which internal vowel markers (*matres lectionis*) first appear at the very end of the eighth century – the moment when Judah first becomes the setting for inscriptional evidence (p. 64). In the end, there is probably too little basis for drawing sweeping conclusions about the relationship of scribal education and practice to the political division between Israel and Judah in the ninth and eighth centuries.

The distinction between Israel and Judah is above all political, defined by the existence of each as a kingdom and by the different structures of their political lives. Before the emergence of a second kingdom based at Jerusalem, the relationship of the southern region to Israel remains uncertain. Given their geographical juxtaposition in the highlands, a connection should not be surprising, and Israelite evidence indicates an interest in the south beyond the eventual realm of Judah. The inscriptions from Kuntillet 'Ajrud refer to both Yahweh of Samaria and Yahweh of Teman, the latter site in the inland southern

---

[25] Rollston (2006) considers this the earliest Old Hebrew inscription of substantial length and certain date, at the very start of the eighth century (pp. 51–2); see also Emerton (1999); Hadley (1987b). One text invokes "Yahweh of Samaria," a clear Israelite interest, though not necessarily identifying the writer.

[26] Rollston gathers the evidence systematically (pp. 51–2) and presents the following list of secure texts, which he judges to include both "north" and "south": Kuntillet 'Ajrud (very early eighth century); Samaria ostraca (early eighth century); Khirbet el-Qom (eighth century); Beth-shean ostraca (eighth century); Samaria Joint Expedition cursive inscriptions (late eighth century); Royal Steward inscription (late eighth or early seventh century). The Samaria texts are directly affiliated with the Israelite capital, and Beth Shean is solidly in the north. The date of the Khirbet el-Qom texts is important, because the site is west of Hebron in what should be solidly Judahite territory. Hadley (1987a) begins with a date in the mid-eighth century but qualifies this with Frank Cross's preference for ca. 700. In terms of political geography and regional history, the difference is substantial, and Cross's later date would match the pattern of Judahite writing visible only after the fall of Samaria and Israel. Finally, the Royal Steward text comes from the vicinity of Jerusalem at Siloam but is dated by Rollston himself to the period after Israel's demise (see Avigad 1953).

land of Edom.[27] Judah cannot therefore be equated with all things "southern" and rather must be defined by Jerusalem and its institutions. Contrasts between Israel and Judah will then involve at least two major categories. The monarchy itself is central, and everything touching kings and kingship, including the kingship of Yahweh, will not look the same through Israelite and Judahite lenses. Then, with the preeminent temple of Yahweh located at Jerusalem, right beside the royal palace, religion and its authorities are bound to be affected by the political frameworks in which they are embedded.[28]

[27] In Habakkuk 3:3, part of an archaic poem picked up in this Judahite prophetic book, Yahweh goes to war from Teman. This tradition of an Edomite location for Yahweh's sacred mountain appears in several poetic texts that include probable Israelite material, and it may be an Israelite rather than a Jerusalem-based idea (see Deut. 33:2, Sinai, Seir, and Mount Paran; Judg. 5:4–5, Seir, Edom, and Sinai [perhaps added]; and Hab. 3:3, Teman and Mount Paran).

[28] One important domain is that of religion. In the preparation of this study, I explored aspects of biblical writing that could reflect religious divergence between Israel and Judah or origin in Israel, including El and Yahweh as Israel's traditional deities and the particular nature of Jerusalem literature, which may not always share Israelite religious perspectives. The problems in this material are so complex, however, and the secondary literature so extensive, that I have chosen to omit such discussion from this volume.

19

Genuine (versus Invented) Tradition in the Bible

For any study of the Bible as an ancient body of writing, whether that antiquity is understood as Iron Age or Hellenistic, literary history becomes a methodological necessity. Even if the ultimate interest lies elsewhere – in interpretation of ideas, in religion, in society, in history – the need to know whose world we are examining drives us to probe the settings of biblical writing and revision. The problem is that the Bible remains to some degree a black box, impossible to penetrate and therefore requiring analysis entirely by external means, because the earliest manuscripts and translations already date to the period after its completion.[1] By the time of these earliest textual versions, Israel and Judah have passed from the scene, and the descendants who maintain the Bible have constituted themselves as Jews – under various names – in a social and political landscape radically different from those of the probable writers. If we insist on reading the early manuscripts as the literature of Roman-period Judaism and beyond, it is obvious that we are far from the society and intellectual world of the Bible's creation.[2]

Along with the chronological distance between the settings of writing and revision and those of our first copies, it is clear that the Bible was not composed at one time and place. Most parts of the Bible present themselves as clear compilations, and more than two centuries of modern scholarship have been occupied with untangling the evolution of each finished text. Generations of specialists have tried to date the layers of textual transformation, often to specific events and actors. With such a complex product and manuscripts from

---

[1] By the Roman period, the earliest textual evidence for the Bible exhibits considerable fluidity, and study of literary history can already involve comparison of known manuscripts; see Emmanuel Tov (2001, chapter 7). Nevertheless, the larger part of composition and revision had taken place by this time.

[2] This situation contrasts with what Assyriologists face with cuneiform texts. Mesopotamian literature may also date from periods long after the settings portrayed, especially when those settings are cast back in time to a legendary past, yet the copies come from the world of living composition and revision, as if biblical scholars had copies from the eighth to fifth centuries.

long after its completion, however, the more precise the chronological solution, the more fragile may be its persuasive power. In order to read the Bible for its intellectual world, its society, its religion, and for history, I seek more lasting solutions that are less dependent on narrow definitions of time and place.

For this purpose, the most important chronological units are defined by elements of continuity. In a constantly changing world, there is no simple scheme of absolute stasis broken by moments of transformation. We can nevertheless observe continuity and change in specific institutions and conditions that shape human experience. Looking back from Judah of the seventh century, we see a kingdom that had existed at least since the ninth century, when we find it called the "House of David" in the Aramean text found at Tel Dan. The palace and temple in the royal capital at Jerusalem represent a longstanding combination. As the Bible would have it, both the Jerusalem capital and these monumental buildings go back to the founding of the house of David as rulers over a distinct kingdom called "Israel," several generations earlier. The house of David split from Israel in the late tenth century under a king named Rehoboam, who was able to retreat to Jerusalem and resist eviction by Israel from his reduced domain. Meanwhile, the larger kingdom called "Israel" is known to have been dismantled by the Assyrians in the late eighth century, after at least 150 years in existence, going back to a figure named Omri. Again, the Bible proposes a scenario whereby this kingdom had an earlier history that spanned another century and more, but it also envisions a period of loose confederation before kings, of uncertain duration. For Israel, Omri's establishment of Samaria as a stable political center represents a key transition, though the Israelite monarchy never duplicated the centralization of Judah at Jerusalem.

For both kingdoms, the Assyrian invasions brought radical disruption on a new scale: Israel was dismantled into multiple dependent provinces, without its own ruler, while Judah survived and thrived with a completely reordered population. Judah faced its own demise with the Babylonian defeats of the early sixth century, and its people were divided between those exiled to Babylonia, those who fled to Egypt or elsewhere, and those who remained in the land. Continuation as one group involved self-identification in truly "ethnic" terms, against the sequence of great external powers that dominated the Middle East and Mediterranean through the next centuries.

These are the major transitions for Israel and Judah as polities, yet for specific questions about these peoples or the Bible, individual continuities and disjunctures may be more important. In spite of the transformations of the eighth century, Jerusalem and its core institutions remained remarkably constant for the whole period of the kingdom: the one royal house of David, Jerusalem as capital, and the palace and temple combined there. Israelite institutions such as the sanctuary at Bethel likewise may have remained active through political changes. At northern sites such as the city of Dan and eastern sites contested by the Moabites, ninth-century conflicts with the Arameans, the Ammonites, and the Moabites in some cases ended Israelite control. Other such regional disruptions affected individual groups at various times.

For biblical composition and revision, questions of continuity and change are perhaps the most relevant to understanding the contents. Communal habit and communal memory are based on continuity with practices rooted in the past. Much of the Bible is concerned with establishing links to the past, and we are left to work out how far these links are organic and how much they reflect the fresh effort of writers to address moments of crisis and transition. My entire distinction between writing from Israel and from Judah is an attempt to establish one primary boundary for answering these questions. Incorporation of biblical texts into discussions of history depends in part on how we judge the continuity of these texts with practices and perspectives that predate composition. As a rule, writing about Israel by people from Israel will have greater continuity with its subject than writing about Israel by people from Judah. This section is devoted to exploring these issues, recognizing here, as throughout this book, that only a sampling of relevant material can be addressed.

A. Genuine and Invented Tradition

With its obvious chronological gaps between actual copies and composition, and between composition and the settings portrayed, the Bible offers a natural application for the ideas published in a book of anthropological studies edited by Eric Hobsbawm and Terence Renger (1983). The contributors discuss the phenomenon of "invented" tradition through documented cases from the last two hundred years. In his introductory chapter, Hobsbawm attempts to avoid the sloppy application of this idea that may in fact be all too common. He defines "invented tradition" as a precise idea: "It includes both 'traditions' actually invented, constructed and formally instituted and those emerging in a less easily traceable manner within a brief and datable period – a matter of a few years perhaps – and establishing themselves with great rapidity" (1983, 4). Application of Hobsbawm's model also may be affected by his definition of tradition, which is different from common usage among biblical scholars. For Hobsbawm, traditions are "practices" with a ritualized aspect. They are not stories or lore and are not defined primarily by texts. He distinguishes traditions from "customs," with tradition fossilized by the authority of the past, invented or not, and custom capable of modification, as long as this is compatible with precedent. This process generally belongs to what I characterized earlier as "continuity." Hobsbawm imagines that the invention of tradition has taken place in all historical settings, but he expects it "to occur more frequently when a rapid transformation of society weakens or destroys the social patterns for which 'old' traditions had been designed, producing new ones to which they were not applicable" (1983, 4). These conditions apply especially to the nineteenth and twentieth centuries of our era.

Hobsbawm is careful not to overstuff the proposed concept, and we should share his sensitivity to nuance. Old forms can often be used for new purposes, and sometimes a break in continuity can be perceived "even in traditional *topoi* of genuine antiquity." Not all tradition fits this category by any definition.

"On the other hand the strength and adaptability of genuine traditions is not to be confused with the 'invention of tradition.' Where the old ways are alive, traditions need be neither revived nor invented" (pp. 7–8). This last statement is crucial. Continuity of living patterns and practices means that tradition maintains a "genuine" connection to the past.

In the Bible, the traditions that directly relate to Hobsbawm's concept are especially ritual. The best application is perhaps the torah of Moses, which assembles diverse traditions of practice (Hobsbawm's word) and gives them the authority of the past in Moses' name. Even if the convention of Moses' mediation is "invented," it is not at all clear that the adjective applies to any given practice. The answer will vary according to the practice and text in question. Where the practice is rooted in "the old ways" before the Babylonian defeat, the ritual/legal "tradition" itself should not be considered "invented," at least not for that disruption.

It is less certain whether the work of Hobsbawm and his colleagues is appropriate for questions of narrative. The connected narrative of Israel's origins and experience, leading to the prominence of Judah, serves to build an identity from the authority of the past. The reader faces issues similar to those found with tradition-based practice, in part because the practices studied by Hobsbawm and the others are rationalized by narratives.[3] It is perhaps the very language of "invented tradition" that so easily invites applications to traditions of biblical narrative, once these are considered to derive from settings long after those portrayed. What attracts me is the range of possible origins for tradition that is presented as rooted in time gone by. Hobsbawm recognizes both "invented" and "genuine" tradition, where the genuine quality of the latter comes not from any supposed "historicity" – to borrow a hallowed term from the Bible field. Genuine tradition is practice that stands in continuity with a web of living institutions that reach back in time without any major disruption. Between the two are reused traditions that may still show their old forms but that have been reshaped for a new generation.

These possibilities are equally apt for biblical narrative. If a story or a component of it is attributed to hoary antiquity but is demonstrably later, by whatever proof, it can well be called "invented." Westermann (1985, 33–4) argues for Genesis that the book is composed entirely of what Hobsbawm would call genuine tradition, because the literary sources are consistently "bearers of tradition." In the debate over how to characterize biblical tradition, Hobsbawm offers not just a useful terminology but, more important, a model for understanding the social conditions of each possibility. As a whole, the elements

---

[3] The first case study offered in the book is that of the Scottish systems of tartans and clans. As Hugh Trevor-Roper (1983, 17) tells it, the crucial narrative effort was undertaken in the 1760s by James Macpherson and John Macpherson: "by two distinct acts of bold forgery, they created an indigenous literature for Celtic Scotland and, as a necessary support to it, a new history." Naturally, these writers had older sources, which Trevor-Roper identifies as Irish – where they exist at all.

of the biblical story of Israel that derive entirely from Judah, with no organic connection to the people and institutions that belonged to Israel, may be called "invented tradition." The transfer of the name "Israel" to Judah after the fall of the "northern kingdom" represents an example of an old tradition reused.

I have begun my analysis with the idea that all Israelite narrative, the material that serves Israelite identity in the social and political matrix of corporate "Israel," may be considered "genuine tradition" – if its bearers still belong to that world. Israelite tradition comes from settings where continuity with the past has not been lost, where "the old ways are alive," and "traditions need be neither revived nor invented." None of this means that Israelite traditions represent "history," but it does mean that they are not the products of social meltdown. We can expect them to reflect some smoother progress of social change in more stable settings. They point backward in time, even where we cannot evaluate adequately their relationship to the settings they describe. By this analysis, the great challenge for both method and result is the fall of Israel in 720 and its uncertain aftermath. Large swaths of the Bible are given shape by the fall of Judah in the early sixth century, and this calamity inspired both the preservation and the reinterpretation of a past that was torn away from its community. In the process, biblical writers both maintained "genuine" tradition and invented it – in relative quantities that are debated intensely. It is equally possible that the longest Israelite collections still discernible in the Bible, such as the Jacob cycle and the final hero collection in Judges 3–9, along with the prophetic books of Hosea and Amos, are the work of an Israelite "exile" community, one fresh from a similar catastrophe and determined to preserve an identity defined by the past. If so, we face the same questions regarding the handling of tradition, with similar expectation of a mixed result. Israelite material will hold a possibility of genuine tradition that is inconceivable for writing about Israel composed from scratch in Judah, yet it becomes crucial to judge the degree of its continuity with Israelite life. Can we tell whether the "old ways are still alive"? We will return to the question.

Evaluation of biblical narrative for social continuity depends on considering how texts were created and preserved in specific social settings that fostered the activity of scribes. For example, Van der Toorn identifies biblical writing and revision entirely with temples, especially the one in Jerusalem.[4] To my mind, this conception of scribal work is unnecessarily narrow, but the emphasis on the social realities of writing is essential. For cuneiform writing, the palace and royal administration provide common settings for writing, though very little in the Bible suggests a palace venue. While the collections of Samuel and

---

[4] "Scribes in Israel were attached to the palace or the temple" (2007, 82). Van der Toorn then sets about to demonstrate that the Jerusalem temple "was the more likely center of production of the traditional literature that came to constitute the Bible" (p. 86). His focus on the temple is based on first ruling out the significant contribution of palace scribes to writing in the Hebrew Bible, a conclusion with which I agree.

Kings are preoccupied with the monarchies of Israel and Judah, their contents display a mindset too independent to work as palace propaganda. From the perspective of cuneiform archives found in large population centers, the institutions of kings and gods are the principal locations of writing, especially writing that serves communal interests. Jerusalem offers a combination of these dominant forces, yet even for Judahite writing in the Bible the influences of palace and temple are more often indirect rather than the immediate points of origin.

In Israel, where power was not centralized, the possible settings for transmission of texts and traditions appear to be more varied and are even harder to identify. As with writing from Judah, there is little evidence for products of the palace, so Samaria is not a likely focus, unlike Jerusalem.[5] The relative absence of Samaria in biblical writing about Israel reflects the separation of Israelite material from the center of royal power. Sacred sites such as Bethel remain likely alternatives, although the Bible's content only rarely shows explicit interest.[6] With most Israelite material, such as the exodus from Egypt or the saviors in Judges, no obvious geographical setting suggests itself, at least in particular terms. It is possible to guess eastern or western origins, and sometimes more specific regional affinities for individual stories, yet named sites for preservation generally elude us.

In the preceding discussion, I envision actual writing in Israel of material that came to be part of the Bible, although the specific settings escape me. Many narratives assume Israelite social and political frameworks, and these show considerable variety and length: Rather than look for a way to fit this material into the expected milieu of the palace and its dependents, I prefer to explore the possibilities of a noncentralized society. Very little nonbiblical writing from the ninth and eighth centuries survives from either Israel or Judah – too little to allow a clear sense of where writing most thrived. I do not share William Schniedewind's confidence that even by the eighth century, "writing was still closely tied to the palace" as "an activity of royal scribes" (2004, 85).[7] Based in large part on this conclusion, Schniedewind attributes the first significant period of biblical writing to the court of Hezekiah, where the palace fostered the collection of oral lore from both Judah and the refugees of fallen Israel (p. 63 and chapter 5). We lack concrete inscriptional evidence to demonstrate the production of such diverse texts in the Jerusalem court, and the contents of the Bible themselves do not indicate this setting for Israelite material. I find more

---

[5] The one notable exception may be the Omri narrative in 1 Kings 16.

[6] Knauf (2006, 291) begins his argument for Bethel as the primary point of entry for Israelite tradition into Judah's Bible with the statement that Bethel is the most frequently mentioned place in the Bible, after Jerusalem. Bethel warrants further discussion in a later part of this chapter.

[7] Even Na'aman's reading of the situation strikes me as presumptuous, assuming a centralization of power and technology that is unproven (1996b, 173). In his view, writing in the tenth to ninth centuries must be confined to a small group of scribes in the Jerusalem court, mainly for administration or diplomacy.

productive the line of analysis by Seth Sanders that writing in Israel and Judah was embedded in a wider range of social settings and entirely decentralized. The best evidence for learning to write is represented by the abecedaries, and these appear in "just those places least suitable to be schools: tombs, desert shrines or way stations, palace steps, and caves" (2009, 131; cf. Haran 1988). "Hebrew, then, was engineered and spread but not monopolized by a geographically wide-ranging group of skilled artisans" (p. 133). The Israelite material in the Bible by itself confirms the likelihood that during the later stages of Israel's life as a kingdom, narrative texts of modest length could be written and transmitted outside royal circles.

This discussion of palace domination of writing leaves open the issue of composition by Israelites after the kingdom fell. Even if an Israelite "exile" community in Jerusalem was involved in creating a body of Israelite written tradition, there is no evidence to locate such activity in the palace or court of Judah. It is more fruitful to think in terms of Israelite settings, even if they lie behind refugee populations who moved away. In spite of the obstacles, it remains useful and important to consider the basis for continuity in the Israelite contexts that could provide the frameworks for transmitting "genuine traditions" about early Israel. Two main categories must be considered: first, archaeological evidence for the presence of Israelite sites through the Iron Age, and second, particular lines of tradition that could be affected by capacity for continuity.

B. Iron Age Continuity

To envision continuity of tradition expressed in the continuity of what scribes produce, one expects a continuity of settlement. For the maintenance of scribal work in stable conditions, specific towns must be occupied without significant break, if their institutions are to offer possible settings for the transmission of texts. Without clear identification of Israelite sites for the composition and collection of biblical material, this problem remains more theoretical than concrete, yet it is important to grapple with the issue of possible text production outside Jerusalem and Samaria. Even if the narrative versions that entered the Bible were written in the eighth century, near the end of Israel or after it, grounded in the institutions and communities that existed in the last days of the kingdom, what is the basis for continuity with the past? Along with the social locations that could have sustained scribal practice beyond the rudimentary production of documents, is there any basis for continuity of communal sharing of Israelite lore? Interpretation of earlier biblical content as oral must likewise depend on such settings for repetition and reproduction. We may consider events such as the muster to battle, when it reached across regions and peoples, and perhaps the festivals that gathered people from larger regions to sacred centers.

One example of the latter could be the feast at Shiloh that brings Hannah's family once a year from their home in Ramathaim, a town mentioned only in

1 Samuel 1.[8] The Shiloh tradition indicates the problem of transmission: excavation confirms the abandonment or destruction of Shiloh during the middle or later part of the Iron Age I, and its interest for the Bible must be attached to other sites (Finkelstein et al. 1993, 371–93). David's transfer of the ark to Jerusalem begins with its supervision by the priest Eli in Shiloh, but the story belongs to Jerusalem and its interests. The story of Saul's birth, as it lies behind the name now changed to Samuel, would also depend on the idea that Eli was the priest at Shiloh, and the ark narrative may depend on this prior Saul tradition, which Sara Milstein (2010) considers to lie at the core of the earliest Saul complex, independent of David and joined to 1 Sam. 11:1–11 (see Chapter 9, on Benjamin). Shiloh also appears in the explanation for how the Benjamin people was saved from annihilation (Judg. 21:15–24), which Milstein links to Saul's birth account in 1 Samuel 1. The starting point for preservation of stories about Shiloh thus appears to be the land of Benjamin, among partisans of Saul. We may then wonder where in Benjamin the tradition of Saul would have survived, especially after the fall of his royal house.

Archaeological evidence more generally provides a framework for evaluating possible settings for the sharing of communal lore and the transmission of specific stories by scribes. In light of Judah's first major narrative contribution with David, it is noteworthy that the population of the Judean highlands was small during the early Iron Age, regardless of the precise chronology.[9] Setting aside the controversy over the reigns of David and Solomon, which the Bible vaunts as powerful and glorious – though not based on their Judahite component – it is not surprising that Judah otherwise contributes little to the biblical narrative before the establishment of the Jerusalem-based kingdom.[10]

Israelite settlement raises one major problem with regard to continuity across the Iron Age before arrival of the Assyrians. Avraham Faust (2006, 124) proposes that all highland villages were abandoned either during the last decades of the twelfth century (Giloh, the Bull Site, and Mount Ebal) or in the middle of the eleventh century (Raddana, Ai, Shiloh, and Tell el-Ful/Gibeah).[11] Most excavated sites in other regions were abandoned slightly later, close to 1000 (Izbet Ṣartah, Tel Masos, Ras Ali, Avot, and Harashim). Faust imagines that external pressure on the highlands drove the population from smaller

---

[8] Anson Rainey argues that this is an alternative name for Ramah in Benjamin, but the conclusion appears to be based on the identification of Saul with Benjamin in 1 Samuel 9 (Rainey 2006a, 143).

[9] See Lehmann (2003, 157). The population of the inland valleys and the coastal plain was much larger and denser during this period.

[10] Based on the small population of highland Judah during the Iron I and IIA periods, Lehmann (p. 157) objects to the argument by Na'aman (1996a, 23) that a population increase in Iron IIA provided the manpower to supply David's effective army. The Bible itself portrays David as building his power base from an independent population of followers, derived from neither Judah nor Israel, and his kingdom is celebrated as Israel, not Judah.

[11] Faust already developed the argument in a 2003 article; for extended discussion of Faust's proposal, see "Forum" (2007).

settlements into several large centers, including Tell en-Naṣbeh (Mizpah) and Tell el-Farʿa North (Tirzah). In effect, there would be no rural village population during a period of about a hundred years. Interestingly, Routledge observes a similar pattern east of the Jordan River, with significant abandonment of Iron I sites before a new landscape of settlements is established in the late ninth century (2004, 200, cf. 137; 2008, 171). If this vast shift of population did take place near the time when kingship emerged in Israel, then the political character of Israel would also have been significantly affected, as would the continuity of tradition. Ideas about life before kings would have to be transmitted in settings severed from the communities of that earlier landscape. Traditions such as the muster of soldiers from towns and villages through local authorities, even under kings such as Omri, could then emerge from a new landscape of settlements, not founded on ancestral patterns that go back to peoples that preceded kings – or not directly so, at least.

In a direct rebuttal, Israel Finkelstein argues that Faust's conclusions are not viable (2005a). Faust (2003, 154–5) links the concentration of population in larger centers to the emergence of a substantial monarchy, which may have responded to a Philistine threat by forced resettlement for purposes of security. According to Finkelstein (2005a), however, Faust too quickly combines groups of sites that are in fact diverse: excavated Iron I sites in the highlands, supposed new foundations in the tenth century, and rural settlements established in the ninth to seventh centuries. Nothing proves that all the new towns of Faust's tenth century belonged to the same territorial polity, and even the group of later sites cannot be said to belong to one process. One key difference between the two is Faust's proposal that conclusions must be based on excavated sites only, leaving aside survey evidence that provides inadequate basis for interpretation (pp. 149–51). Excavation allows the identification of whole pottery assemblages rather than dates by the peak use of individual forms, and this can lead surveys to find "Iron II" occupation without distinguishing early and later ceramics. Finkelstein considers that along with an unconvincing categorization of sites into broad groups by date and type, the very idea of a century without rural life is without parallel in the ancient Near East (p. 206).

However this argument develops, it is evident that highland settlements did not in general remain inhabited throughout the Iron Age without interruption.[12] Finkelstein points out that the abandonment of different Iron I sites could have different explanations and need not result from a single Philistine threat and response under kings (p. 202). This is likely enough, yet whatever polities and causes were involved, the discontinuity itself remains. Finkelstein accepts only Megiddo and Hazor as substantial centers throughout the Iron IIA, placing the growth of en-Naṣbeh, Lachish, and Beersheba to slightly later periods. For our interest in the continuity of Israelite tradition,

---

[12] Faust's notion that there was a period without significant rural village life has gained the least ground (see "Forum" 2007). Nonetheless, the core observation remains important: many Iron I sites were abandoned near the time of transition to Iron II.

both of these cities are treated as outside Israel's control in the period before kings (Judges 4–5). Finkelstein himself says that the transition between Iron I and late Iron II can be established only site by site with excavation (p. 204), and the degree and alignment of settlement disruptions in the early Iron Age II will remain a focus of archaeological interpretation.

Most of the Israelite sacred sites that have important narrative roles in the Bible are in the western highlands south of the Jezreel Valley, to suit the prominence of Joseph, Ephraim, and Bethel in various traditions for Israelite origins. Gibeah and Tirzah are portrayed as early royal centers without sacred associations; Shechem is a meeting point for Israel with significance mainly in earlier periods; Shiloh, Mizpah, and Bethel are explicit sacred sites. Among these, Shiloh is abandoned, as observed. Mizpah (Tell en-Naṣbeh) existed through the Iron Age II, whether or not it had developed into an urban center in the early Iron II.[13] Faust considers Bethel to be another Iron I village that developed into a city during Iron IIA, but in a recent reevaluation based on fresh review of the material now stored at the Pittsburgh Theological Seminary, Finkelstein and Singer-Avitz express doubt about Bethel's occupation during just that period.[14]

One immediate impression from the archaeological situation is that direct continuity of scribes working in Israelite towns can be maintained only for roughly the period when Israel is known to outside sources, during the ninth and eighth centuries. This may not be surprising, given that written Hebrew emerges as a distinct script only in the ninth century, and the social environment for writing in Israel would probably have looked very different before the time of Omri. Aside from the continuity of institutions or town centers that could sustain scribal transmission, there is the issue of how people assembled for public occasions that would have helped to preserve shared lore. Public performance and spectacle have been reconsidered recently as a domain for cultivating a collaborative political life, beyond the mere manipulation by elite power.[15] We know far too little about how public spectacle functioned in Israel. Excavation does not reveal the plazas of Mesoamerica or the ball courts of the American Southwest, yet simpler spaces must have existed.

One scenario is suggested by the prophecy of Micaiah to kings Ahab of Israel and Jehoshaphat of Judah, addressed to them on their thrones at the "threshing

---

[13] Finkelstein says that en-Naṣbeh became an urban center only in the Iron IIB, while Faust makes this town a centerpiece of his analysis for the Iron IIA.

[14] Finkelstein and Singer-Avitz (2009) conclude that the principal activity at Bethel occurred during the Late Bronze II and early to middle Iron I periods, followed by an interval of uncertain occupation, until the town revived vigorously in the eighth and early seventh centuries (pp. 42–3). There is then little activity at Bethel until the Hellenistic period, during the third century.

[15] See especially the studies gathered in Inomata and Cohen (2006). In their introduction, the editors observe that "[t]he inherent multivocality of theatrical signs make [*sic*] the propagation of dominant ideologies difficult if not impossible" (p. 26). Performance can express resistance, even if the "public transcript" is a tool of the elite. Moreover, the elite themselves may consider themselves bound by values shared more broadly in such spectacle.

floor" (*gōren*) outside the city gate of Samaria (1 Kings 22:10). It is a public occasion, dominated by the spectacle of massed prophets promising victory over the Arameans, including one Zedekiah, who dances about with iron horns to gore the enemy (v. 11). Clearly, the whole royal entourage is gathered, but we can imagine a much larger audience at this public site outside the city walls, on the occasion of muster for battle. As observed in connection with the Mari evidence, the assembly of fighters before battle was a normal occasion for open discussion that could spill beyond the rulers and their officials. In Israel, where warfare could involve people from more than one region and subgroup, military muster may have been one occasion for contacts across greater distances – more so than religious festivals, which would not require the wider participation at a single site and so could be observed more locally by smaller gatherings. Moreover, this kind of assembly would not have been confined to a single location. After the establishment of a fixed capital at Samaria, this could have provided a natural meeting point – though here, also, a Judahite writer may assume muster at the capital when this need not have been the logical site in Israel. In general, muster would depend on the geographical demands of the threat and need not be restricted to one place. When considering the long-term shifts in town sites and settlement patterns in Israel, the military setting offers one social location for maintaining continuity of tradition. A remarkable number of the Israelite stories preserved in the Bible have to do with confrontations with enemies, the most notable exceptions being the ancestor stories of Genesis and their kinship concerns.

In general, where there is continuity of population and institutions, there is at least the capacity to maintain practices that carry with them ideas about identity and the past. This does not mean that such practices and ideas will persist without change, but they are likely to go through a process of transmission that builds on what exists already, rather than to abandon tradition absolutely in favor of the new. In Hobsbawm's language, "genuine" tradition survives in environments of continuity. In particular, ideas about identity that are tied to accounts of the past present themselves as having roots in time gone by, as stories to remember from the ages. Where such stories appear to be Israelite and about Israel, it is important to know the social and settlement history of the people who would have recounted them. This is first of all the work of archaeology, and there is much more to consider regarding the links between lore from Israel itself and the settlement landscape.

C. Bethel

One testing ground for the continuity of tradition in the Bible's Israelite material is the town of Bethel,[16] which both Knauf and Davies identify as an essential conduit for Israelite tradition into Judah circles – whether before or after the

---

[16] Note the two monographs by Gomes (2006) and Köhlmoos (2006), both of which review the biblical material related to Bethel.

Babylonian victories of the early sixth century.[17] In the Bible, the key point of reference for identifying the town within Israel is Judg. 1:22–6, in which Bethel counts as the center of a "Joseph" people, distinct from Ephraim and Manasseh (cf. Amos 5:6, 15; 6:6).[18] In Genesis 48, these two groups are rendered Joseph's sons, with Ephraim given preference over his brother. The land allotments in the book of Joshua then attempt to accommodate the Genesis scheme by treating the Joseph–Bethel unit as a defining center for the larger pairing of Manasseh and Ephraim (16:1–4). Bethel itself is not attributed to Ephraim but rather turns up as part of the northern boundary of Benjamin (18:13), then counted as a Benjaminite town (18:22). Given that the Joshua land allotments as a whole give Judah pride of place and belong to the Judahite sphere, this inclusion of Bethel as part of Benjamin likewise incorporates the town into the southern kingdom of the seventh century, like the lists of regions in Jeremiah (see Chapter 3).[19] This placement with Benjamin is surely secondary to the notion of a distinct Joseph people that requires no reference to Benjamin – as evident in the birth narrative of Genesis 30 and the opening scene of the Joseph story, in which he is the favored youngest son (Genesis 37). Joseph is solidly part of Israel and its biblical traditions, therefore, and is originally identified with neither Benjamin nor Judah.

The same applies to Bethel. It is a decidedly Israelite town, perhaps the southernmost center when Benjamin is left distinct. In the Bible's Israelite narrative, Bethel's absence can be as significant as its appearance. Although 1 Kings 12:25–33 proclaims Bethel the southern location for one of Jeroboam I's calf shrines (cf. 2 Kings 10:29), the accounts of Israel's kings through the rest of these books pay no heed at all to the site.[20] Based on the Kings narratives alone, we could not conclude easily that Bethel had strong ties to the Israelite monarchy and its Samaria capital. Stepping back in the narrative sequence, the reigns of David and Solomon are recounted without a single mention of Bethel,

[17] These interpretations return us to the state of scholarship discussed in my introduction (Chapter 1): Davies (2007b) and Knauf (2006). Although Davies focuses on Benjamin as a people, he sees the Bethel traditions as the key body of lore transmitted from Israel into Judah through Benjamin (p. 110).

[18] De Geus understands Ephraim and Manasseh to be the original tribes, only combined artificially into a single Joseph descendance (1976, 78–9). He treats Joseph in Judg. 1:22 as part of a deuteronomistic composition and Amos 5–6 as disparaging references to the whole kingdom, in place of the name "Ephraim" (pp. 85, 92). These conclusions miss the particular association of these texts with Bethel. The combination of Ephraim and Manasseh into one Joseph family is indeed probably late, forgetting the connection of the name to Bethel.

[19] Koenen (2003, 13) comments that Alt's Josianic date for the land lists in Joshua would work particularly well for the Benjamin list, as reflecting its incorporation into Judah, based especially on its handling of Bethel.

[20] Bethel plays a role in the prophet stories of 1 Kings 13 (the "man of God") and 2 Kings 2 (Elijah/Elisha), which reflect different authorship and settings but which share a removal from any interest in kings and courts. Interest in the town reappears in 2 Kings 17:28, in which the Assyrians are said to encourage the continuation of Israelite religious practices at Bethel, and then Josiah is credited with desecrating the sanctuary there (2 Kings 23:15; cf. vv. 4, 17, 19).

even in their final forms (2 Samuel 2–1 Kings 11).[21] Again, this is a site that derives no status from association with kings. If we can imagine the preservation of tales about Israel as distinct peoples even during the monarchy, Bethel could offer a location for such an alternative perspective. Finally, when considering such evidence from silence, the absence of Joseph from the Song of Deborah is as noteworthy as the absence of Judah. Benjamin appears as Ephraim's kin, and Ephraim itself is the first listed participant. Without Joseph, Bethel is not likely to be the location for composition or transmission of the Song of Deborah. Further, Bethel is largely missing from the core set of hero-dominated stories in Judges 2–16, appearing only as a geographical note to Deborah's function as judge in 4:5, suggesting at most a copyist's interest at a late stage in pre-Judah reproduction of this material. Bethel appears only as a center for Israel's collaborative tradition, first setting the standard for success in conquest of Canaanite cities (chapter 1), then in the landscape of the Benjamin war (chapters 20–1), especially as the site for Israel's assembly to ask divine guidance (20:18, 26). Once again, Bethel has no traditional standing as a center of power wielded by individual leaders, even in time before kings. As we undertake to weigh the site's importance to the preservation of Israelite material in the Bible, we must begin by acknowledging its absence from enormous swaths of the narrative that recounts Israel's existence in its own land. Whether we consider Judges, Samuel, or Kings, Bethel appears only occasionally, almost always with a religious role as sacred site and not essential to the main flow of narrative about Israel.

What then does Bethel contribute to the Israelite content in the biblical narrative from Genesis through Kings? First, it is central to the Jacob material in Genesis. The classic etiology for the Bethel sacred site is embedded in the Jacob story as the place where he meets God on the outward journey to Laban in Syria (Gen. 28:10–22; cf. 31:13; 35:7). Jacob goes back to Bethel only in Genesis 35, in a composite text that could be secondary to the earlier story even from its origins, as the anticipated counterpart to the vow and hope of return.[22] Genesis 31–3 are instead occupied with various eastern sites, ending with Succoth, where Jacob makes his initial settlement (33:17). The two sacred sites that provide bookends to Jacob's sojourn, each one visited in transit, are Bethel and Peniel (Penuel), both names explained with etiologies that describe encounters with God (Elohim; 28:17,19; 32:31). Both west and east are encompassed in the account of how Jacob acquired the family of Israel, and there is no way to assign Bethel the essential role. Nevertheless, with Joseph the awaited son of Rachel in Gen. 30:23–4, and the association of Bethel with Joseph in Judg. 1:22 and Amos 5:6, one could consider this a plausible setting for preserving

---

[21] David is said to have some dealings with Bethel and other listed sites during the period of his residence at Ziklag in Philistine territory (1 Sam. 30:27). Saul likewise has no reference to Bethel, except at the moment of his selection, when Bethel is said to be a pilgrimage site for three travelers (1 Sam. 10:3).

[22] David Carr still maintains the Israelite date and setting for the main Jacob cycle, including this material (2011, chapter 16).

at least one form of the Jacob narrative.[23] In contrast to Bethel's absence from stories about kings and earlier leaders, the Jacob tradition indicates a vigorous interest at this site in the explanation of Israel's peoples as a family.

Bethel does not play a direct part in other Israelite narratives about early times, but there are other possible associations that would suit transmission at this site. By its continued interest in Rachel's son, the original Joseph story suggests the same possible connection carried by the birth narrative for Jacob's children. Joshua 8 recounts the conquest of Ai under the inspired leadership of Joshua, and the decisive ambush is set up between Bethel and Ai (v. 12). If this is the principal Israelite story of Joshua and perhaps the starting point for the elaborate Joshua tradition focused in the biblical book, then the notion of Joshua as heroic warrior would be part of this body of lore. Joshua would be the sole individual hero associated at all with Bethel, and his victory is isolated from those in the book of Judges, instead forming the core of a separate literary work with a completely different rationale.

Of the principal Israelite materials surrounding the early existence and background of the people, the one other story that shows signs of association with the western highlands is the exodus from Egypt under Moses as prophet. By itself, the biblical version of this story in the book of Exodus offers no geographical clues, and Moses himself is a Levite with no special connection to Joseph or Ephraim. The language of escape, however, is consistent with a wider western tradition in the Bible, and Hos. 12:14 links this escape specifically to a prophet.[24] The book of Hosea speaks of Beth Aven as a sacred site rather than Bethel (4:15; 5:8; 10:5), and Bethel is only named as a city to be destroyed (10:15) and as the place of Jacob's meeting God (12:5).[25] This last reference is important, because it indicates that the Hosea writer knows a version of the Jacob story that includes the divine encounter at Bethel, and this is the one sacred site mentioned in the Jacob allusions in Hos. 12:4–5 and 13. In fact,

[23] De Pury (2001, 238) places the current version of the Jacob cycle at Bethel in the period after the kingdom fell in 720. Harran in Gen. 27:43 and 29:4 would reflect its prominence in the Assyrian empire, and the survivors at Bethel would still be invested in Israelite tradition and identity. The role of Bethel in the story and Jacob's association with Bethel may well be older, as reflected in Hos. 12:5 and 7 (p. 240). We should also note that Bethel ends up linked to Abraham in Gen. 12:8 and 13:3–4, providing a northern point of reference that contrasts with his Hebron/Beersheba connections. This interest suggests that some part of the Abraham tradition was drawn into the Bethel circle and transmitted there, especially the Lot–Abraham combination. It is not clear when this would have taken place, but it does offer one scenario for Israelite (or post-Israelite Bethel-based) possession of Abraham lore.

[24] Stephen Russell (2009, 48–50, 104–13) distinguishes the western Israelite notion of departure "up" from Egypt (verb *'lh*) from the image of "deliverance" (verb *yṣ'*), where the first indicates travel toward a destination and the second assumes no movement, in spite of the verb's base meaning of "to depart." The idea of escape by "going up" occurs in Hos. 2:17 and 12:14, as well as in Amos 2:10; 3:1; and 9:7.

[25] The reading of "Bethel" is widely considered unlikely in Hos. 10:15, and Wolff replaces it with "house of Israel," mainly because the book otherwise refers only to Beth-aven (1974, 181). He leaves the reading in 12:5, where it is clearly essential and at home, noting that the Greek has Beth Aven, and it is not obvious which text corrected which (p. 206).

the conflict with God in verses 4–5 could evoke the other sacred location of the Genesis Jacob journey, at Peniel, yet no place is named. Where Genesis straddles the sacred interests of east and west, Hosea comes down solidly in the west, with Bethel the only name offered. This detail suggests that the Jacob tradition known to the Hosea writer came through Bethel, and whatever the relationship of Bethel to the writing and transmission of the whole book, some connection is thus likely.[26] The indirect reference to Moses as prophet in Hos. 12:14 is attached to the cluster of Jacob allusions, then, and continued association with Bethel is plausible. If the Hosea references to Jacob as ancestor and the escape from Egypt reflect Bethel transmission, this means that something like the narrative in the book of Exodus was probably known and reproduced in this setting, wherever the specific version in Exodus was written. All the major components of Israel's narrative for the ancestors and Egypt that show signs of preservation in the western highlands show signs of transmission at Bethel.

This hypothesis of Bethel transmission does not exclude other locations, and it does not imply the origin of the individual narratives at Bethel. Furthermore, I do not envision any attempt at Bethel to turn all of these materials into a single text. Most of the texts in question show primary interest in other sites or regions, even if Bethel has become integrated somehow into their geographical scope. It appears that Bethel was a point of collection, probably at a late phase of Israelite textual transmission and formulation. Narratives were known and reproduced individually, like the stories known to cuneiform scribes in Mesopotamia. Possibly, some shorter combinations were first carried out at Bethel, as perhaps the Jacob cycle of Genesis, though this need not be the case.

This impression that Bethel was a center for the transmission of Israelite literature before it reached Judah, yet after its initial composition, works adequately with the site's settlement history. According to the careful review of the evidence by Finkelstein and Singer-Avitz (2009), Bethel had its main activity in the Late Bronze II to Iron I periods and then in the Iron IIB, with relatively little there between these periods. More precisely, they align the dates of abandonment or destruction at Bethel and Shiloh, with the latter placed ca. 1050–1000 by ^{14}C dating. There are signs of renewed activity in the later Iron IIA, which they place in the mid- to late ninth century, before the significant revival of the city at the beginning of the eighth century. The most important finding by Finkelstein and Singer-Avitz is that Bethel was a very minor site during the Babylonian and Persian periods of the sixth to fourth centuries. The pottery dated by the excavators to the sixth century is identical to their "Iron II" material, and comparison with the late seventh and early sixth centuries at Lachish (Stratum II) indicates very little to match this period and later at Bethel. If they are correct, then any interpretation of Bethel that involves a significant

---

[26] Knauf considers Hosea 4–11 to have been composed at Bethel after 720, as one of the main Bethel contributions to the Bible (2006, 320). Before the Assyrian invasion, Bethel was addressed as Beth Aven, then restored to Bethel in Hos. 10:15 and 12:5 only after the fall of Israel.

population and influence for the exilic and Persian postexilic periods is cast in doubt.

Many new interpretations of biblical transmission are based on just this conception of Bethel. Knauf's entire approach is based on the notion of Bethel continuity for centuries after the fall of Samaria in 720. He rejects the idea that Jerusalem grew during the late eighth century in part from a population of refugees from Israel (2006, 293) and concludes that the identity-building process took place concurrently in both Israel and Judah during the Persian period, fortified by the collection and ordering of traditions from both realms. Bethel was the crucial site in the Neo-Babylonian (exilic) period, before Jerusalem regained its leading role under Achaemenid rule.[27] Northern literary traditions reached Judah by way of Bethel, first in the late seventh and early sixth centuries, when Judah incorporated Benjamin into its kingdom. Knauf proposes that key elements of the Bible's form, including the prominence of Israel in it, reflect an ongoing competition between Jerusalem and Bethel that produced waves of literary effects (pp. 318–19). After the initial arrival of Bethel's Israelite tradition into Judah ca. 650–586, Bethel's stories of Jacob and the exodus took precedence over Jerusalem's David lore. Jerusalem's temple and scribal classes were put out of commission during Babylonian rule (586–ca. 520), so that its traditions had to be preserved either in Babylonia or at Bethel. Jerusalem was initially restored as a city without political status, before Nehemiah (ca. 520–445), and this remained a time of competition between the two sites. Bethel traditions were fully integrated into the Torah as a constitution for the people of Yehud only during the later period of Persian rule (ca. 450–300).

The reevaluation of ceramics by Finkelstein and Singer-Avitz offers a caution against too quickly attributing such important activity to Bethel centuries after the fall of Israel. At the same time, Knauf's hypothesis raises a question that is crucial to my own investigation of Israelite tradition. How long would the survivors of the Israelite kingdom retain a coherent sense of its political character as distinct from that of Judah? Can this be imagined to have continued for centuries, through the Persian-period competition with Jerusalem envisioned in his analysis? It is generally acknowledged that Bethel was incorporated into Judah at some point in the seventh century, along with Benjamin.[28] Whatever Bethel's experience under direct Assyrian rule, this change would have thrown the town into Judah's centralized political world. In particular, the kinship-based argument in the Jacob story for the unity of separate Israelite peoples is attuned to a political tradition that would have exploded immediately with the

---

[27] Blenkinsopp (2003, 95) concludes likewise from Kelso's original excavation report: "There is therefore no reason to doubt that Bethel continued to function down to the Neo-Babylonian period."

[28] Na'aman (2010, 17–20) considers this to have occurred during the time of Josiah, rather than earlier, because he sees no reason for the Assyrians to have ceded such territory to Judah; contra Davies (2007b). He imagines that Josiah may even have "plundered scrolls deposited in the temple of Bethel," including the Jacob cycle, the Book of Saviors, Amos and Hosea, and some prophetic stories (p. 20).

fall of the kingdom and imperial domination. A community of survivors could maintain traditions from the time when Israel was a living political entity, but after this had disappeared, only the stories themselves could bear such memory, and this memory would tend to drift with the assumptions of newer political circumstances. I have no precise answer to this question, but I am disinclined to date Israelite material in the Bible to a period long after the demise of the kingdom.

If we return to the fresh archaeological analysis by Finkelstein and Singer-Avitz, the logical period for Bethel's influence on the formation and transmission of Israelite biblical tradition would be the eighth and early seventh centuries, straddling the last generations of Israel's monarchy and the first generation or so after its end. This period matches perfectly the settings and reception of Hosea and Amos, and it suits well the sense that Bethel was a destination for Israelite lore that may have originated elsewhere. Bethel's evident standing as a sacred center, reflected most directly for this time in Hosea and Amos, would be reflected in the claim that Jacob founded the site and in the concentration of prophetic interest. The picture of Moses himself as prophet in Hos. 12:14 and implied in the exodus exchanges with Pharaoh is at home in this setting. As a pilgrimage site for major festivals, as envisioned in the book of Amos, Bethel may have had a particular interest in the unity of Israel in terms not defined by the monarchy. The birth narrative for the family of Jacob, with Joseph the favorite, implies a special role for Bethel in Israel's identity as an association of distinct peoples. With such institutional distance from Samaria and its court, in spite of the misperception inflicted on us by a Judah scribe in Amos 7:12–13, there is no reason to push this literature entirely into the period after Israel's end. Equally, we must take seriously the large blocks of Israelite writing with little or no concern for Bethel. Bethel played one important part in the gathering of Israelite material into the Bible – but only one. For the rest, we must look elsewhere – a project for further study.

This review of Bethel and its role in biblical formation calls up a larger set of questions about how Israelite tradition was preserved before incorporation into Judah's Bible and its world of assumptions. The recent hypotheses of Knauf and Davies, among others, envision an impetus toward passing down old Israelite lore in the Benjamin/Bethel region that bridged Israel and Judah geographically. Before it could be taken into the Judahite/Jewish heritage, such literature had to emerge from an Israelite milieu. It would be useful to pursue further what exactly would have been intended by the Israelite writers who undertook this task. As readers of Judah's Bible, we can jump quickly to the Jewish reception of Israelite tradition, without considering carefully how the survivors of Israel may have hoped to establish by these efforts a basis for identity and durable community. Did they succeed at all on their own terms, apart from being drawn into Judah's sphere? This would be the work of an Israelite "exile" community, anticipating and perhaps even offering a model for Judah's exile literature that became the framework for the Bible as we have it. For example, the Jacob story in its current form is framed by a forced departure linked to promise of return in a way that could be assumed "exilic" in the Babylonian sense except that the contents are so overwhelmingly Israelite. Unless this is just an expression of a universal and powerful theme of loss and hope, one explanation would be that the narrative is indeed "exilic," but the exile is Israelite and the emotion that of an older calamity, brought about by Assyria in the late eighth century.[29]

D. Genuine Tradition and Israelite History

Any use of the Bible for reconstruction of Israelite history must be evaluated on its merits, not based on a particular notion of compositional date. By sifting content that originated in Israel from the matrix of Judah's literature, I highlight the profound difference in political assumptions that can accompany such material when compared with that of Judah. The distinct political organization and tradition of Israel then have implications for other dimensions of religion and society. Further, the collaborative stream in this political tradition belongs to a pattern of Near Eastern life that is displayed elaborately in the early second-millennium Mari archives and suggested in both written and archaeological evidence across centuries before the emergence of Israel in the southern Levant. Judah likewise emerged against the same social backdrop, but its specific origin derived from a royal act, the separation of the house of David from Israel in order to maintain a political life for itself based in Jerusalem. This origin in monarchy shaped its institutions and politics with enduring effect, producing a noticeable contrast with those of Israel.

Increasingly, biblical scholars have emphasized the dominance of the late seventh century and beyond in production of the Bible. Often, it is the Persian period that gives shape to interpretations of narrative and other biblical literature. Confidence about earlier sources and composition is difficult to find. Archaeologists have long demanded freedom for their evidence to set its own interpretive agenda, and it is easy to let the Bible recede into a framing or confirming role. At the same time, however, the Bible's rich narrative and literature may likewise demand a hearing, when it is not easily explained as the work of imaginative authors completely detached from the settings and situations portrayed. When relatively late compositional dates are envisioned, these may belong to Judah and its survivors, both before and after the kingdom's end. The perspectives of a Judahite world may be as essential to the ideas conveyed as the view from before or after Babylonian defeat. By separating Israelite content from this material, fresh historical perspectives can emerge, and these can provide a basis for reconsidering the value of biblical writing for historical questions.

The logic of this application of biblical writing depends on the nature of the tradition in question. Value judgment aside, if it is "invented," cut off from any

---

[29] The notion of Israelite "exilic" literature first came up in conversation with Sara Milstein. In a graduate seminar paper, the specific idea that the Jacob narrative in Genesis may be formed by an exilic sensibility was conceived and developed by Clémence Boulouque.

strand of social experience that would connect it to earlier times, the tradition will have little to say about any time before the moment of its creation. There is, however, a world of "genuine" tradition – still just the reflection of customary practice and thought with an age of mutable history behind them. Yet such genuine tradition offers a way back into the past, the possibility of connection to habits and ideas that are the shared property of some community across time. Woven into the literature of Judah are threads from a distinct community that we do well to acknowledge for itself, that of Israel. In recovering its legacy, we have hope of understanding better why Judah's history begins with the story of Israel. That biblical story of Israel may then shed new light on the people of the Iron Age southern Levant who are still sometimes called "ancient Israel."

Bibliography

Achenbach, Reinhard. 2003. "Die Erzählung von der gescheiterten Landnahme von Kadesch Barnea (Numeri 13–14) als Schlüsseltext der Redaktionsgeschichte des Pentateuchs." *ZABR* 9: 56–123.

Ackroyd, Peter R. 1991. *The Chronicler in His Age*. Sheffield: JSOT.

Ahituv, Shmuel. 1984. *Canaanite Toponyms in Ancient Egyptian Documents*. Jerusalem: Magnes.

Ahlström, Gösta W. 1986. *Who Were the Israelites?* Winona Lake, Ind.: Eisenbrauns.

———. 1993. *The History of Ancient Palestine*. Minneapolis, Minn.: Fortress.

Ahlström, Gösta W., and Diana Edelman. 1985. "Merneptah's Israel." *JNES* 44: 59–61.

Albertz, Rainer. 2010. "Secondary Sources also Deserve to Be Historically Evaluated: The Case of the United Monarchy." Pp. 31–45 in Philip R. Davies and Diana V. Edelman (eds.), *The Historian and the Bible: Essays in Honour of Lester L. Grabbe*. London: T. and T. Clark.

Albright, William F. 1922. "The Earliest Forms of Hebrew Verse." *Journal of the Palestine Oriental Society* 2: 69–86.

———. 1957. *From the Stone Age to Christianity: Monotheism and the Historical Process*. Garden City, N.Y.: Doubleday.

d'Alfonso, Lorenzo, Yoram Cohen, and Dietrich Sürenhagen (eds.). 2008. *The City of Emar among the Late Bronze Age Empires: History, Landscape, and Society*. Münster: Ugarit-Verlag.

Alt, Albrecht. 1953. *Kleine Schriften zur Geschichte des Volkes Israel*. Munich: C. H. Beck.

———. 1968. *Essays on Old Testament History and Religion*. Garden City, N.Y.: Anchor Books.

Amit, Yairah. 2006. "The Saul Polemic in the Persian Period." Pp. 647–61 in Oded Lipschits and Manfred Oeming (eds.), *Judah and the Judeans in the Persian Period*. Winona Lake, Ind.: Eisenbrauns.

Andersen, Francis I., and David Noel Freedman. 1980. *Hosea*. New York: Doubleday.

———. 2000. *Micah*. New York: Doubleday.

Astour, Michael C. 1999. "The Hapiru in the Amarna Texts: Basic Points of Controversy." *UF* 31: 31–50.

Athas, George. 2003. *The Tel Dan Inscription: A Reappraisal and a New Interpretation.* London: T. and T. Clark.

———. 2006. "Setting the Record Straight: What Are We Making of the Tel Dan Inscription?" *JSS* 51: 241–55.

Auld, A. Graeme. 1999. "What Was the Main Source of the Books of Chronicles?" Pp. 91–9 in Graham M. Patrick (ed.), *The Chronicler as Author.* Sheffield: Sheffield Academic Press.

———. 2000. "The Deuteronomists between History and Theology." Pp. 53–67, 358–9 in A. Lemaire and M. Saebo (eds.), *Congress Volume, Oslo 1998.* Leiden: Brill.

———. 2007. "Reading Kings on the Divided Monarchy: What Sort of Narrative?" Pp. 337–43 in H. G. M. Williamson (ed.), *Understanding the History of Ancient Israel.* Oxford: Oxford University Press.

Aurelius, Erik. 2003. *Zukunft jenseits des Gerichts: Eine redaktionsgeschichtliche Studie zum Enneateuch.* Berlin: de Gruyter.

Avigad, Nahman. 1953. "The Epitaph of a Royal Steward from Siloam Village." *IEJ* 3: 137–52.

Barako, Tristan J. 2009. "Solomon's Patrimonial Kingdom: A View from the Land of Gilead." Pp. 5–15 in J. David Schloen (ed.), *Exploring the Longue Durée: Essays in Honor of Laurence E. Stager.* Winona Lake, Ind.: Eisenbrauns.

Barnes, William H. 1991. *Studies in the Chronology of the Divided Monarchy of Israel.* Atlanta, Ga.: Scholars Press.

Barrick, Boyd. 1974. "On the Removal of the High Places in I and II Kings." *Bib* 55: 257–9.

Barth, Fredrik. 1969. "Introduction." Pp. 9–38 in Fredrik Barth (ed.), *Ethnic Groups and Boundaries.* Boston: Little, Brown.

Bartlett, John R. 1989. *Edom and the Edomites.* Sheffield: Sheffield Academic Press.

Beaulieu, Paul-Alain. 2007. "Official and Vernacular Languages: The Shifting Sands of Imperial and Cultural Identities in First-Millennium B.C. Mesopotamia." Pp. 191–220 in Seth L. Sanders (ed.), *Margins of Writing, Origins of Cultures.* Chicago, Ill.: Oriental Institute.

Becker, Uwe. 1990. *Richterzeit und Königtum: Redaktionsgeschichtliche Studien zum Richterbuch.* Berlin: de Gruyter.

———. 1997. *Jesaja – Von der Botschaft zum Buch.* Göttingen: Vandenhoeck & Ruprecht.

———. 2000. "Die Reichstellung nach I Reg 12." *ZAW* 112: 210–29.

———. 2009. "Jakob in Bet-El und Sichem." Pp. 159–85 in Anselm C. Hagedorn and Henrik Pfeiffer (eds.), *Die Erzväter in der biblischen Tradition: Festschrift für Matthias Köckert.* Berlin: de Gruyter.

Becking, Bob. 1992. *The Fall of Samaria: An Historical and Archaeological Summary.* Leiden: Brill.

Ben Zvi, Ehud. 1991. *A Historical-Critical Study of the Book of Zephaniah.* Berlin: de Gruyter.

———. 2005. *History, Literature and Theology in the Book of Chronicles.* London: Equinox.

———. 2007. "Who Knew What? The Construction of the Monarchic Past in Chronicles and Implications for the Intellectual Setting of Chronicles." Pp. 349–60 in Oded Lipschits, Gary N. Knoppers, and Rainer Albertz (eds.), *Judah and the Judeans in the Fourth Century B.C.E.* Winona Lake, Ind.: Eisenbrauns.

Benz, Brendon C. 2012. "The Varieties of Sociopolitical Experience in the Amarna Age Levant and the Rise of Early Israel." Ph.D. dissertation, New York University.

Berlin, Adele. 1994. *Zephaniah.* New York: Doubleday.

Beyerle, Stefan. 1997. *Mosesegen in Deuternomium: Eine text-, kompositions-, und formkritische Studie zu Deuteronomium 33.* Berlin: de Gruyter.

Biggs, Robert D. 1980. "The Ebla Tablets: An Interim Perspective." *BA* 43: 76–87.

Biran, Avraham, and Joseph Naveh. 1993. "An Aramaic Stele Fragment from Tel Dan." *IEJ* 43: 81–98.

———. 1995. "The Tel Dan Inscription: A New Fragment." *IEJ* 45: 1–18.

Blanton, Richard E., and Lane Fargher. 2008. *Collective Action in the Formation of Pre-Modern States.* New York: Springer.

Blanton, Richard E., Gary M. Feinman, Stephen A. Kowalewski, and Peter S. Perigrine. 1996. "A Dual-Processual Theory for the Evolution of Mesoamerican Civilization." *Current Anthropology* 37: 1–14.

Blenkinsopp, Joseph. 1997. "Structure and Meaning in the Sinai-Horeb Narrative (Exodus 19–34)." Pp. 109–25 in Eugene E. Carpenter (ed.), *A Biblical Itinerary: In Search of Method, Form and Content – Essays in Honor of George W. Coats.* Sheffield: Sheffield Academic Press.

———. 2000. *Isaiah 1–39.* New York: Doubleday.

———. 2003. "Bethel in the Neo-Babylonian Period." Pp. 93–107 in Oded Lipschits and Joseph Blenkinsopp (eds.), *Judah and the Judeans in the Neo-Babylonian Period.* Winona Lake, Ind.: Eisenbrauns.

———. 2006. "Benjamin Traditions Read in the Early Persian Period." Pp. 629–45 in Oded Lipschits and Manfred Oeming (eds.), *Judah and the Judeans in the Persian Period.* Winona Lake, Ind.: Eisenbrauns.

———. 2009. *Judaism: The First Phase. The Place of Ezra and Nehemiah in the Origins of Judaism.* Grand Rapids, Mich.: Eerdmans.

Bloch-Smith, Elizabeth. 2003. "Israelite Ethnicity in Iron I: Archaeology Preserves What Is Remembered and What Is Forgotten in Israel's History." *JBL* 122: 401–25.

———. 2004. "Resurrecting the Iron I Dead." *IEJ* 54: 77–91.

Bloch-Smith, Elizabeth, and Beth Alpert Nakhai. 1999. "A Landscape Comes to Life: The Iron Age I." *NEA* 62: 62–127.

Blum, Erhard. 1984. *Die Komposition der Vätergeschichte.* Neukirchen-Vluyn: Neukirchener.

———. 2009. "Hosea 12 und die Pentateuchüberlieferungen." Pp. 291–321 in Anselm C. Hagedorn and Henrik Pfeiffer (eds.), *Der Erzväter in der biblischen Tradition: Festschrift für Matthias Köchert.* Berlin: de Gruyter.

———. 2010. "Solomon and the United Monarchy: Some Textual Evidence." Pp. 59–78 in Reinhard G. Kratz and Hermann Spieckermann (eds.), *One God – One Cult – One Nation: Archaeological and Biblical Perspectives.* Berlin: de Gruyter.

Bonechi, Marco. 1992. "Relations amicales syro-palestiniennes: Mari et Haṣor au XVIIIe siècle av. J.C." *FM* 1: 9–22.

Booij, Th. 1984. "Mountain and Theophany in the Sinai Narrative." *Bib* 65: 1–26.

Borger, Riekele. 1958. "Das Problem der *'apiru* ['Ḫabiru']." *ZDPV* 74: 121–32.

Bottéro, Jean. 1954. *Le problème des Ḫabiru à la 4e Rencontre Assyriologique Internationale.* Paris: Imprimerie Nationale.

———. 1972. "Ḫabiru," *RlA* 4: 14–27.

———. 1981. "Les Ḫabiru, les nomades et les sédentaires." Pp. 89–107 in J. Silva Castillo (ed.), *Nomads and Sedentary Peoples.* Mexico City: Collegio de Mexico.

Brettler, Marc. 2002. *The Book of Judges*. London: Routledge.

———. 2007. "The Poet as Historian: The Plague Tradition in Psalm 105." Pp. 19–28 in Kathryn F. Kravitz and Diane M. Sharon (eds.), *Bringing the Hidden to Light: The Process of Interpretation. Studies in Honor of Stephen A. Geller*. Winona Lake, Ind.: Eisenbrauns.

Bright, John. 1981. *History of Israel*, 3rd edition. Philadelphia: Westminster.

Broshi, Magen, and Israel Finkelstein. 1992. "The Population of Palestine in Iron Age II." *BASOR* 287: 47–60.

Broshi, Magen, and Ram Gophna. 1986. "Middle Bronze Age II Palestine: Its Settlements and Population." *BASOR* 261: 73–90.

Brumfiel, Elizabeth M. 1994. "Factional Competition and Political Development in the New World: An Introduction." Pp. 3–13 in Elizabeth M. Brumfiel and John W. Fox (eds.), *Factional Competition and Political Development in the New World*. Cambridge: Cambridge University Press.

Buccellati, Giorgio. 1977. "'Apirū and Munnabtūtu: The Stateless of the First Cosmopolitan Age." *JNES* 36: 145–7.

Bunimovitz, Shlomo. 1989. "The Land of Israel in the Late Bronze Age: A Case Study of Socio-cultural Change in a Complex Society." Ph.D. dissertation, Tel Aviv University (Hebrew).

———. 1995. "On the Edge of Empires: Late Bronze Age (1500–1200 BCE)." Pp. 320–31 in Thomas E. Levy (ed.), *The Archaeology of Society in the Holy Land*. New York: Facts on File.

Bunimovitz, Shlomo, and Avraham Faust. 2001. "Chronological Separation, Geographical Segregation, or Ethnic Demarcation? Ethnography and the Iron Age Low Chronology." *BASOR* 322: 1–10.

Bunimovitz, Shlomo, and Zvi Lederman. 2006. "The Early Israelite Monarchy in the Sorek Valley: Tel Beth-Shemesh and Tel Batash [Timnah] in the 10th and 9th Centuries BCE." Vol. 2, pp. 407–27 in Aren M. Maier and Pierre de Miroschedji (eds.), *"I Will Speak the Riddles of Ancient Times": Archaeological and Historical Studies in Honor of Amihai Mazar on the Occasion of His Sixtieth Birthday*. Winona Lake, Ind.: Eisenbrauns.

———. 2008. "A Border Case: Beth-Shemesh and the Rise of Ancient Israel." Pp. 21–31 in Lester L. Grabbe (ed.), *Israel in Transition: From Late Bronze II to Iron IIa (c. 1250–850 B.C.E.)*, Vol. 1: *The Archaeology*. London: T. & T. Clark.

Cahill, Jane M. 2003. "Jerusalem at the Time of the United Monarchy: The Archaeological Evidence." Pp. 13–80 in Andrew G. Vaughn and Ann E. Killebrew (eds.), *Jerusalem in Bible and Archaeology: The First Temple Period*. Leiden: Brill.

Callaway, Joseph. 1992. "Ai." Vol. 1, pp. 125–30 in David Noel Freedman (ed.), *ABD*. New York: Doubleday.

Campbell, Anthony F. 1986. *Of Prophets and Kings: A Late Ninth-Century Document (1 Samuel 1–2 Kings 10)*. Washington, D.C.: CBA of America.

Campbell, Edward F. 1991. *Shechem II: Portrait of a Hill Country Vale. The Shechem Regional Survey*. Atlanta, Ga.: Scholars Press.

Caquot, André, and André Lemaire. 1977. "Les textes araméens de Deir `Alla." *Syria* 54: 189–208.

Carr, David M. 1996. *Reading the Fractures of Genesis: Historical and Literary Approaches*. Louisville, Ky.: Westminster John Knox.

———. 2001. "Genesis in Relation to the Moses Story: Diachronic and Synchronic Perspectives." Pp. 273–95 in André Wénin (ed.), *Studies in the Book of Genesis*. Leuven: Peeters.

———. 2005. *Writing on the Tablet of the Heart: Origins of Scripture and Literature*. Oxford: Oxford University Press.

——— 2011. *The Formation of the Hebrew Bible: A New Reconstruction*. Oxford: Oxford University Press.

Carroll, Robert P. 1986. *Jeremiah: A Commentary*. Philadelphia: Westminster.

de Castelbajac, Isabelle. 2001. "Histoire de la rédaction de Juges XI: Une Solution." *VT* 51: 166–85.

Caton, Steven C. 1990. *"Peaks of Yemen I Summon": Poetry as Cultural Practice in a North Yemeni Tribe*. Berkeley: University of California Press.

Charpin, Dominique. 1991. "Un traité entre Zimri-Lim de Mari et Ibâl-pî-El II d'Ešnunna." Pp. 139–66 in Dominique Charpin and Francis Joannès (eds.), *Marchands, diplomats et empéreurs: Études sur la civilization mésopotamienne offertes à Paul Garelli*. Paris: Éditions Recherche sur les Civilisations.

———. 1992. "Les malheurs d'un scribe ou de l'inutilité du sumérien loin de Nippur." Pp. 7–27 in Maria de Jong Ellis (ed.), *Nippur at the Centennial*. CRRAI 35; Philadelphia: University Museum.

———. 1993. "Un souverain éphémère en Ida-Maraṣ: Išme-Addu d'Ašnakkum." *M.A.R.I.* 7: 165–91.

———. 2004. "Histoire politique du Proche-Orient amorrite (2002–1595)." Pp. 25–480 in *Mesopotamien: Die altbabylonische Zeit*. Göttingen: Vandenhoeck & Ruprecht.

Charpin, Dominique, and Jean-Marie Durand. 1985. "La prise du pouvoir par Zimri-Lim." *M.A.R.I.* 4: 293–343.

———. 1986. "'Fils de Sim'al': Les origines tribales des rois de Mari." *RA* 80: 141–81.

Charpin, Dominique, and Nele Ziegler. 2003. *Mari et le Proche-Orient à l'époque amorrite: Essai d'histoire politique*. FM VI; Paris: SEPOA.

Coats, George W. 1987. "The Book of Joshua: Heroic Saga or Conquest Theme?" *JSOT* 38: 15–32.

Cogan, Mordechai. 2008. *The Raging Torrent: Historical Inscriptions from Assyria and Babylonia Relating to Ancient Israel*. Jerusalem: Carta.

Cohen, Ronald. 1978. "Ethnicity: Problem and Focus in Anthropology." *Annual Review of Anthropology* 7: 379–403.

Cole, Steven W. 1996. *Nippur IV: The Early Neo-Babylonian Governor's Archive from Nippur*. Chicago, Ill.: Oriental Institute.

Conrad, Joachim. 2005. "Die Unschuld des Tollkühnen: Überlegungen zu 1 Sam 24." Pp. 23–42 in Rüdiger Lux (ed.), *Ideales Königtum: Studien zu David und Salomo*. Leipzig: Evangelische Verlagsanstalt.

Conroy, Charles. 1978. *Absalom Absalom! Narrative and Language in 2 Sam 13–20*. Rome: Biblical Institute Press.

Coote, Robert B. 1991. *In Defense of Revolution: The Elohist History*. Minneapolis, Minn.: Fortress.

Couturier, Guy. 2001. "Quelques observations sur le *bytdwd* de la stele araméenne de Tel Dan." Vol. 2, pp. 72–98 in P. M. Michèle Daviau, John W. Wevers and Michael Weigl (eds.), *The World of the Aramaeans: Studies in History and Archaeology in Honour of Paul-Eugène Dion*. Sheffield: Sheffield Academic Press.

Cross, Frank M. 1950. "Studies in Ancient Yahwistic Poetry." Ph.D. dissertation, Johns Hopkins University.

———. 1988. "Reuben, the Firstborn of Jacob: Sacral Traditions and Early Israelite History." *ZAW* 100: 46–66.

Cross, Frank M., and David Noel Freedman. 1975. *Studies in Ancient Yahwistic Poetry.* Missoula, Mont.: Scholars Press.

Crumley, Carole L. 1995. "Heterarchy and the Analysis of Complex Societies." Pp. 1–5 in Robert Ehrenreich, Carole L. Crumley, and Janet E. Levy (eds.), *Heterarchy and the Analysis of Complex Societies.* Arlington, Va.: American Anthropological Association.

———. 2003. "Alternative Forms of Social Order." Pp. 136–45 in Vernon L. Scarborough, Fred Valdez, and Nicholas Dunning (eds.), *Heterarchy, Political Economy, and the Ancient Maya: The Three Rivers Region of the East-Central Yucatán Peninsula.* Tucson: University of Arizona Press.

D'Agostino, Anacleto. 2009. "The Assyrian-Aramean Interaction in the Upper Khabur: The Archaeological Evidence from Tell Barri Iron Age Layers." Pp. 17–41 in Christine Kepinski and Aline Tenu (eds.), *"Dossier: Interaction entre Assyriens et Araméens."* Syria 86.

von Dassow, Eva. 2008. *State and Society in the Late Bronze Age: Alalaḫ under the Mittani Empire.* Bethesda, Md.: CDL.

Davies, Philip R. 1992. *In Search of "Ancient Israel".* Sheffield: Sheffield Academic Press.

———. 2007a. *The Origins of Biblical Israel.* London: T. & T. Clark.

———. 2007b. "The Trouble with Benjamin." Pp. 93–111 in Robert Rezetko, Timothy H. Lim, and W. Brian Aucker (eds.), *Reflection and Refraction: Studies in Biblical Historiography in Honour of A. Graeme Auld.* Leiden: Brill.

Dearman, J. Andrew. 1989. *Studies in the Mesha Inscription and Moab.* Atlanta, Ga.: Scholars Press.

Delnero, Paul. 2010. "Sumerian Extract Tablets and Scribal Education." *JCS* 62:53–69.

Dever, William G. 2003. *Who Were the Early Israelites and Where Did They Come from?* Grand Rapids, Mich.: Eerdmans.

———. 2009. "Merenptah's 'Israel,' the Bible's, and Ours." Pp. 89–96 in J. David Schloen (ed.), *Exploring the Longue Durée: Essays in Honor of Laurence E. Stager.* Winona Lake, Ind.: Eisenbrauns.

Diakonoff, Igor M. 1982. "The Structure of Near Eastern Society before the Middle of the 2nd Millennium B.C." *Oikumene* 3: 7–100.

Dietrich, Walter. 2000. "Prophetie im deuteronomistischen Geschichtswerk." Pp. 47–65 in Thomas Römer (ed.), *The Future of the Deuteronomistic History.* Leuven: Peeters.

———. 2001. "Jakobs Kampf am Jabbok (Gen 32, 23–33)." Pp. 197–210 in Jean-Daniel Macchi and Thomas Römer (eds.), *Jacob: Commentaire à plusieurs voix de Gen 25–36.* Geneva: Labor et Fides.

———. 2004. "Die zweifache Verschonung Sauls (I Sam 24 und 26): Zur 'diachronen Synchronisierung' zweier Erzählungen." Pp. 232–53 in Walter Dietrich (ed.), *David und Saul im Widerstreit – Diachronie und Synchronie im Wettstreit: Beiträge zur Auslegung des ersten Samuelbuches.* Göttingen: Vandenhoeck & Ruprecht.

———. 2007. *The Early Monarchy in Israel: The Tenth Century B.C.E.* Leiden: Brill.

Dijkstra, Meindert. 1995. "The Geography of the Story of Balaam: Synchronic Reading as a Help to Date a Biblical Text." Pp. 72–97 in Johannes C. de Moor (ed.),

Synchronic or Diachronic? A Debate on Method in Old Testament Exegesis. Leiden: Brill.

Dion, Paul-Eugène. 1995a. "Aramaean Tribes and Nations of First-Millennium Western Asia." Vol. 2, pp. 1281–94 in Jack M. Sasson (ed.), *CANE*.

———. 1995b. "Syro-Palestinian Resistance to Shalmaneser III in the Light of New Documents." *ZAW* 107: 482–9.

———. 1997. *Les Araméens à l'âge du fer: Histoire politique et structures sociales.* Paris: J. Gabalda.

Dossin, Georges. 1939. "Benjaminites dans les textes de Mari." Pp. 981–96 in *Mélanges syriens offerts à M. René Dussaud.* Paris: Paul Geuthner.

Dozeman, Thomas B. 2000. "Hosea and the Wilderness Wandering Tradition." Pp. 55–70 in Steven McKenzie and Thomas Römer (eds.), *Rethinking the Foundations: Historiography in the Ancient World and in the Bible. Essays in Honour of John Van Seters.* Berlin: de Gruyter.

———. 2002. "Geography and Ideology in the Wilderness Journey from Kadesh through the Transjordan." Pp. 173–89 in Jan Christian Gertz, Konrad Schmid, and Markus Witte (eds.), *Abschied vom Jahwisten: Die Komposition des Hexateuch in der jüngsten Diskussion.* Berlin: de Gruyter.

Durand, Jean-Marie. 1990a. "Documents pour l'histoire du royaume de Haute-Mésopotamie II." *M.A.R.I.* 6: 271–301.

———. 1990b. "Fourmis blanches et fourmis noires." Pp. 101–8 in François Vallat (ed.), *Mélanges Jean Perrot: Contribution à l'histoire de l'Iran.* Paris: Éditions Recherche sur les Civilisations.

———. 1992. "Unité et diversités au Proche-Orient à l'époque amorrite." Pp. 97–128 in Dominique Charpin and Francis Joannès (eds.), *La circulation des biens, des personnes et des idées dans le Proche-Orient ancien.* CRRAI 38. Paris: Éditions Recherche sur les Civilisations.

———. 1993. "Le mythologème du combat entre le dieu de l'Orage et la Mer en Mésopotamie," *M.A.R.I.* 7: 41–61.

———. 1997, 1998, 2000. *Documents épistolaires du palais de Mari, Tomes I, II, III.* LAPO 16–18. Paris: du Cerf.

———. 2002. *Le culte d'Addu d'Alep et l'affaire d'Alahtum.* FM VII. Paris: SEPOA.

———. 2004. "Peuplement et société à l'époque amorrite (I): Les clans Bensim'alites." Pp. 111–97 in Christophe Nicolle (ed.), *Amurru 3: Nomades et sédentaires dans le Proche-Orient ancien.* CRRAI 46. Paris: Éditions Recherche sur les Civilisations.

Dus, Jan. 1968. "Die Geburtslegende Samuels I. Sam 1 (Eine traditionsgeschichtliche Untersuchung von I. Sam 1–3)." *RSO* 43: 163–94.

Dutcher-Walls, Patricia. 1996. *Narrative Art, Political Rhetoric: The Case of Athaliah and Joash.* Sheffield: JSOT.

Dyck, Jonathan E. 1998. *The Theocratic Ideology of the Chronicler.* Leiden: Brill.

Echols, Charles L. 2008. *"Tell Me, O Muse": The Song of Deborah.* New York: T. & T. Clark.

Edelman, Diana V. 1984. "Saul's Rescue of Jabesh-Gilead (I Sam 11;1–11): Sorting Story from History." *ZAW* 96: 195–209.

———. 1996a. "Ethnicity and Early Israel." Pp. 25–55 in Mark G. Brett (ed.), *Ethnicity and the Bible.* Leiden: Brill.

———. 1996b. "Saul ben Kish in History and Tradition." Pp. 142–59 in Volkmar Fritz and Philip R. Davies (eds.), *The Origins of the Ancient Israelite States.* Sheffield: Sheffield Academic Press.

———. 2001. "Did Saulide-Davidic Rivalry Resurface in Early Persian Yehud?" Pp. 69–91 in J. Andrew Dearman and M. Patrick Graham (eds.), *The Land That I Will Show You: Essays on the History and Archaeology of the Ancient Near East in Honor of J. Maxwell Miller*. Sheffield: Sheffield Academic Press.

———. 2003. "Gibeon and the Gibeonites Revisited." Pp. 153–67 in Oded Lipschits and Joseph Blenkinsopp (eds.), *Judah and the Judeans in the Neo-Babylonian Period*. Winona Lake, Ind.: Eisenbrauns.

Emberling, Geoffrey. 1997. "Ethnicity in Complex Societies: Archaeological Perspectives." *JAR* 5: 295–344.

Emerton, J. A. 1999. "'Yahweh and His Asherah': The Goddess or Her Symbol?" *VT* 49: 315–37.

———. 2002. "The Value of the Moabite Stone as an Historical Source." *VT* 52: 483–92.

———. 2004. "The Date of the Yahwist." Pp. 107–29 in John Day (ed.), *In Search of Pre-exilic Israel*. London: T. & T. Clark.

Evans-Pritchard, E. E. 1940. *The Nuer*. Oxford: Clarendon.

Falkenstein, Adam. 1963. "Zu den Inschriftenfunden der Grabung in Uruk-Warka 1960–1961." *BaM* 2: 1–82.

Faust, Avraham. 2000. "The Rural Community in Ancient Israel during Iron Age II." *BASOR* 317: 17–39.

———. 2003. "Abandonment, Urbanization, Resettlement and the Formation of the Israelite State." *NEA* 66: 147–61.

———. 2004. "'Mortuary Practices, Society and Ideology': The Lack of Iron Age I Burials in the Highlands in Context." *IEJ* 54: 174–90.

———. 2006. *Israel's Ethnogenesis: Settlement, Interaction, Expansion and Resistance*. London: Equinox.

———. 2008. "Settlement and Demography in Seventh-Century Judah and the Extent and Intensity of Sennacherib's Campaign." *PEQ* 140: 168–94.

Fechter, Friedrich. 1998. *Die Familie in der Nachexilszeit: Untersuchungen zur Bedeutung der Verwandtschaft in ausgewählten Texten de Alten Testaments*. Berlin: de Gruyter.

Feinman, Gary M. 2000. "Dual-Processual Theory and Social Formations in the Southwest." Pp. 207–24 in Barbara J. Mills (ed.), *Alternative Leadership Strategies in the Prehispanic Southwest*. Tuscon: University of Arizona Press.

Feinman, Gary M., and Joyce Marcus (eds.). 1998. *Archaic States*. Santa Fe, N.M.: School of American Research.

Feinman, Gary M., Kent G. Lightfoot, and Stendman Upham. 2000. "Political Hierarchies and Organizational Strategies in the Pueblan Southwest." *American Antiquity* 65: 453–54.

Finkelstein, Israel. 1988. *The Archaeology of the Israelite Settlement*. Jerusalem: Israel Exploration Society.

———. 1995. "The Date of the Settlement of the Philistines in Canaan," *TA* 22: 213–39.

———. 1996a. "The Archaeology of the United Monarchy: An Alternative View." *Levant* 28: 177–87.

———. 1996b. "Ethnicity and the Origin of the Iron I Settlers in the Highlands of Canaan: Can the Real Israel Stand Up?" *BA* 59: 198–212.

———. 1999. "State Formation in Israel and Judah: A Contrast in Context, a Contrast in Trajectory." *NEA* 62: 35–52.

———. 2002. "The Campaign of Shoshenq I to Palestine: A Guide to the 10th Century BCE Polity." *ZDPV* 118: 109–35.

———. 2003a. "City-States to States: Polity Dynamics in the 10th–9th Centuries B.C.E." Pp. 75–83 in William G. Dever and Seymour Gitin (eds.), *Symbiosis, Symbolism, and the Power of the Past: Canaan, Ancient Israel, and Their Neighbors from the Late Bronze Age through Roman Palaestina*. Winona Lake, Ind.: Eisenbrauns.

———. 2003b. "The Rise of Jerusalem and Judah: The Missing Link." Pp. 81–101 in Andrew G. Vaughn and Ann E. Killebrew (eds.), *Jerusalem in Bible and Archaeology: The First Temple Period*. Leiden: Brill.

———. 2005a. "[De]formation of the Israelite State: A Rejoinder on Methodology." *NEA* 68: 202–8.

———. 2005b. "Shechem of the Amarna Period and the Rise of the Northern Kingdom of Israel." *IEJ* 55: 172–93.

———. 2008. "The Settlement History of Jerusalem in the Eighth and Seventh Centuries BC." *RB* 115: 499–515.

———. 2010. "A Great Monarchy? Archaeological and Historical Perspectives." Pp. 3–28 in Reinhard G. Kratz and Hermann Spieckermann (eds.), *One God – One Cult – One Nation: Archaeological and Biblical Perspectives*. Berlin: de Gruyter.

Finkelstein, Israel, and Oded Lipschits. 2010. "Omride Architecture in Moab: Jahaz and Ataroth," *ZDPV* 126: 29–42.

Finkelstein, Israel, and Nadav Na'aman. 2005. "Shechem of the Amarna Period and the Rise of the Northern Kingdom of Israel." *IEJ* 55: 172–93.

Finkelstein, Israel, and Eli Piasetzky. 2010. "Radiocarbon Dating the Iron Age in the Levant: A Bayesian Model for Six Ceramic Phases and Six Transitions." *Antiquity* 84: 374–85.

———. 2011. "The Iron Age Chronology Debate: Is the Gap Narrowing?" *NEA* 74: 50–4.

Finkelstein, Israel, and Lily Singer-Avitz. 2009. "Reevaluating Bethel." *ZDPV* 125: 33–48.

Finkelstein, Israel, Shlomo Bunimovitz, and Zvi Lederman. 1993. *Shiloh: The Archaeology of a Biblical Site*. Tel Aviv: Tel Aviv University.

Fischer, Alexander A. 2004. *Von Hebron nach Jerusalem: Eine redaktionsgeschichtliche Studie zur Erzählung von König David in II Sam 1–5*. Berlin: de Gruyter.

Fischer, Georg. 2001. "Die Josefsgeschichte als Modell für Versöhnung." Pp. 243–71 in André Wénin (ed.), *Studies in the Book of Genesis*. Leuven: Peeters.

Fish, Suzanne K., and Paul R. Fish. 2000. "The Institutional Contexts of Hohokam Complexity and Inequality." Pp. 154–67 in Barbara J. Mills (ed.), *Alternative Leadership Strategies in the Prehispanic Southwest*. Tuscon: University of Arizona Press.

Fleming, Daniel E. 1992a. "A Limited Kingship: Late Bronze Emar in Ancient Syria." *UF* 24: 59–71.

———. 1992b. *The Installation of Baal's High Priestess at Emar: A Window on Ancient Syrian Religion*. Atlanta, Ga.: Scholars Press.

———. 1998. "Mari and the Possibilities of Biblical Memory." *RA* 92: 41–78.

———. 1999. "The Seven-Day Siege of Jericho in Holy War." Pp. 211–28 in Robert Chazan, William W. Hallo, and Lawrence H. Schiffman (eds.), *Ki Baruch Hu: Ancient Near Eastern, Biblical, and Judaic Studies in Honor of Baruch A. Levine*. Winona Lake, Ind.: Eisenbrauns.

———. 2000. *Time at Emar: The Cultic Calendar and the Rituals from the Diviner's Archive*. Winona Lake, Ind.: Eisenbrauns.

————. 2004a. *Democracy's Ancient Ancestors: Mari and Early Collective Governance.* Cambridge: Cambridge University Press.

————. 2004b. "Genesis in History and Tradition: The Syrian Background of Israel's Ancestors, Reprise." Pp. 193–232 in James K. Hoffmeier and Alan Millard (eds.), *The Future of Biblical Archaeology: Reassessing Methodologies and Assumptions.* Grand Rapids, Mich.: Eerdmans.

————. 2008. "From Joseph to David: Mari and Israelite Pastoral Traditions." Pp. 78–96 in Daniel I. Block (ed.), *Israel: Ancient Kingdom or Late Invention?* Nashville, Tenn.: B & H Academic.

————. 2009. "Kingship of City and Tribe Conjoined: Zimri-Lim at Mari." Pp. 227–40 in Jeffrey Szuchman (ed.), *Nomads, Tribes, and the State in the Ancient Near East: Cross-Disciplinary Perspectives.* Chicago: Oriental Institute.

————. Forthcoming a. "David and the Ark: A Jerusalem Festival Reflected in Royal Narrative." In David Vanderhooft (ed.), volume on biblical and Near Eastern Studies in honor of Peter Machinist.

————. Forthcoming b. "Mari's *'iBrum* and the Bible's *'ibrî*: An Alternative Origin for 'Hebrew'," *CBQ.*

Fleming, Daniel E., and Sara J. Milstein. 2010. *The Buried Foundation of the Gilgamesh Epic: The Akkadian Huwawa Narrative.* Leiden: Brill.

"Forum." 2007. *NEA* 70:4–26.

Fosdal, Lisa. 2009. "Was the Tel Dan Inscription Referring to 'BYT DWD' as a Fundamentalistic Faction?" *SJOT* 23: 85–102.

Frakel, David. 2002. *The Murmuring Stories of the Priestly School: A Retrieval of Ancient Sacerdotal Lore.* Leiden: Brill.

Frame, Grant. 1995. *Rulers of Babylonia: From the Second Dynasty of Isin to the End of Assyrian Domination: 1157–612 BC.* RIMB 2. Toronto: University of Toronto Press.

Frankel, Rafael, et al. 2001. *Settlement Dynamics and Regional Diversity in Ancient Upper Galilee: Archaeological Survey of Upper Galilee.* Jerusalem: Israel Antiquities Authority.

Frayne, Douglas R. 1990. *Old Babylonian Period (2003–1595 BC).* RIME 4; Toronto: University of Toronto.

Freedman, David Noel, and Brian E. Kelly. 2004. "Who Redacted the Primary History?" Pp. 39–47 in Chaim Cohen et al. (eds.), *Sefer Moshe: The Moshe Weinfeld Jubilee Volume.* Winona Lake, Ind.: Eisenbrauns.

Freedman, David Noel, and Sara Mandell. 1993. *The Relationship between Herodotus' History and Primary History.* Atlanta, Ga.: Scholars Press.

Friedman, Richard E. 1987. *Who Wrote the Bible?* New York: Summit Books.

————. 2005. *The Bible with Sources Revealed: A New View into the Five Books of Moses.* San Francisco, Calif.: Harper.

Fritz, Volkmar. 1977. *Tempel und Zelt: Studien zum Tempelbau in Israel und zu dem Zeltheiligtum der Priesterschaft.* Neukirchen-Vluyn: Neukirchener.

————. 2003. *1 and 2 Kings: A Continental Commentary.* Minneapolis, Minn.: Fortress.

————. 2006. "The Complex of Traditions in Judges 4 and 5 and the Religion of Pre-state Israel." Vol. 2, pp. 689–98 in Aren M. Maier and Pierre de Miroschedji (eds.), *"I Will Speak the Riddles of Ancient Times": Archaeological and Historical Studies in Honor of Amihai Mazar on the Occasion of His Sixtieth Birthday.* Winona Lake, Ind.: Eisenbrauns.

Fuchs, Andreas. 2008. "Über den Wert Befestigungslagen." *ZA* 98: 45–99.

Gadot, Yuval. 2008. "Continuity and Change in the Late Bronze to Iron Age Transition in Israel's Coastal Plain: A Long Term Perspective." Pp. 55–73 in Alexander Fantalkin and Assaf Yasur-Landau (eds.), *Bene Israel: Studies in the Archaeology of Israel and the Levant during the Bronze and Iron Ages in Honour of Israel Finkelstein.* Leiden: Brill.

Galil, Gershon. 2000. "The Boundaries of Aram-Damascus in the 9th–8th Centuries BCE." Pp. 35–41 in Gershon Galil and Moshe Weinfeld (eds.), *Studies in Historical Geography and Biblical Historiography Presented to Zecharia Kallai.* Leiden: Brill.

Garcia Lopez, Felix. 1994. "Deuteronomy 34, Deuteronomistic History, and the Pentateuch." Pp. 47–61 in F. Garcia Martinez et al. (eds.), *Studies in Deuteronomy: In Honour of C. J. Labuschagne on the Occasion of His 65th Birthday.* Leiden: Brill.

Gardner, Andrew. 2008. "Agency." Pp. 95–108 in R. Alexander Bentley, Herbert D. G. Maschner, and Christopher Chippindale (eds.), *Handbook of Archaeological Theories.* Plymouth, U.K.: Altamira.

Garr, W. Randall. 1985. *The Dialect Geography of Syria-Palestine, 1000–586 B.C.E.* Philadelphia: University of Pennsylvania Press.

Gass, Erasmus. 2009. *Die Moabiter: Geschichte und Kultur eines ostjordanischen Volkes im 1. Jahrtausend v. Chr.* Wiesbaden: Harrassowitz.

Geller, Markham J. 2007. "Akkadian Sources of the Ninth Century." Pp. 229–41 in H. G. M. Williamson (ed.), *Understanding the History of Ancient Israel.* Oxford: Oxford University Press.

George, Andrew R. 2003. *The Babylonian Gilgamesh Epic: Introduction, Critical Edition and Cuneiform Texts.* Oxford: Oxford University Press.

———. 2009. *Babylonian Literary Texts in the Schøyen Collection.* Bethesda, Md.: CDL.

Geraty, Lawrence T. 1997. "Hesban," *OEANE* 3: 19–22.

Gertz, Jan Christian. 2006. "Kompositorische Funktion und literarhistorischer Ort von Deuteronomium 1–3." Pp. 103–23 in Markus Witte et al. (eds.), *Die deuteronomistischen Geschichtswerke: Redaktions- und religionsgeschichtliche Perspektiven zur "Deuteronomismus" – Diskussion in Tora und Vorderen Propheten.* Berlin: de Gruyter.

de Geus, C. H. J. 1976. *The Tribes of Israel: An Investigation into Some of the Presuppositions of Martin Noth's Amphictyony Hypothesis.* Assen: van Gorcum.

Gillingham, Susan E. 2010. "The Levitical Singers and the Editing of the Hebrew Psalter." Pp. 91–123 in Erich Zenger (ed.), *The Composition of the Book of Psalms.* Leuven: Peeters.

Ginsburg, H. L. 1982. *The Israelian Heritage of Judaism.* New York: Jewish Theological Seminary of America.

Goedicke, Hans. 2004. "Remarks on the 'Israel Stela.'" *Wiener Zeitschrift für die Kunde des Morgenlandes* 94: 53–72.

Gomes, Jules F. 2006. *The Sanctuary of Bethel and the Configuration of Israelite Identity.* Berlin: de Gruyter.

Gonen, Rivka. 1984. "Urban Canaan in the Late Bronze Period." *BASOR* 253: 61–73.

Görg, Manfred. 2001. "Israel in Hieroglyphen." *BN* 106: 21–4.

Görke, Susanne. 2004. "Aramäischer Einfluss in Assyrien." Pp. 325–33 in Mirko Novak, Friedhelm Prayon, and Anne-Maria Wittke (eds.), *Die Aussenwirkung des späthethitischen Kulturraumes: Güteraustausch – Kulturkontakt – Kulturtransfer.* Münster: Ugarit-Verlag.

Gottwald, Norman K. 1979. *The Tribes of Yahweh: A Sociology of the Religion of Liberated Israel, 1250–1050*. Maryknoll, N.Y.: Orbis.

Grabbe, Lester L. 2003. "The Priests in Leviticus: Is the Medium the Message?" Pp. 207–24 in Rolf Rendtorff and Robert A. Kugler (eds.), *The Book of Leviticus: Composition and Reception*. Leiden: Brill.

———. 2007a. *Ancient Israel: What Do We Know and How Do We Know It?* London: T. & T. Clark.

———. 2007b. "The Kingdom of Israel from Omri to the Fall of Samaria: If We Had Only the Bible ... " Pp. 54–99 in Lester L. Grabbe (ed.), *Ahab Agonistes: The Rise and Fall of the Omri Dynasty*. London: T. & T. Clark.

Grabbe, Lester L. (ed.). 2007c. *Ahab Agonistes: The Rise and Fall of the Omri Dynasty*. London: T. & T. Clark.

Graupner, Axel. 2002. *Der Elohist: Gegenwart und Wirksamkeit des transcendenten Gottes in der Geschichte*. Neukirchen-Vluyn: Neukirchener.

Gray, George Buchanan. 1903. *A Critical and Exegetical Commentary on Numbers*. New York: Charles Scribner's Sons.

Grayson, Albert Kirk. 1975. *Assyrian and Babylonian Chronicles*. Locust Valley, N.Y.: Augustin.

———. 1991. *Assyrian Rulers of the Early First Millennium BC*, vol. 1: *1114–859 BC*. RIMA 2. Toronto: University of Toronto Press.

———. 1996. *Assyrian Rulers of the Early First Millennium BC II (858–745 BC)*. RIMA 3. Toronto: University of Toronto Press.

Greenberg, Moshe. 1955. *The Ḫab/piru*. New Haven: American Oriental Society.

Grønbaek, Jakob H. 1971. *Die Geschichte vom Aufstieg Davids (1. Sam 15–2. Sam 5)*. Copenhagen, Munksgaard.

Gross, Walter. 2009. *Richter*. Freiburg: Herder.

Guillaume, Philippe. 2004. *Waiting for Josiah: The Judges*. London: T. & T. Clark.

———. 2008. "Jerusalem 720–705 BCE: No Flood of Israelite Refugees." *SJOT* 22: 195–211.

Hackett, Jo Ann. 1980. *The Balaam Text from Deir 'Alla*. Chico, Calif.: Scholars Press.

Hadley, Judith M. 1987a. "The Khirbet el-Qom Inscription." *VT* 37: 50–62.

———. 1987b. "Some Drawings and Inscriptions on Two Pithoi from Kuntillet 'Ajrud." *VT* 37: 180–211.

Hall, Jonathan M. 1997. *Ethnic Identity in Greek Antiquity*. Cambridge: Cambridge University Press.

Halpern, Baruch. 1991. "Jerusalem and the Lineages in the Seventh Century BCE: Kinship and the Rise of Individual Moral Liability." Pp. 11–107 in Baruch Halpern and Deborah W. Hobson (eds.), *Law and Ideology in Monarchic Israel*. Sheffield: Sheffield Academic Press.

———. 2001. *David's Secret Demons: Messiah, Murderer, Traitor, King*. Grand Rapids, Mich.: Eerdmans.

Haran, Menahem. 1978. *Temples and Temple Service in Ancient Israel*. Oxford: Clarendon.

———. 1988. "On the Diffusion of Literacy and Schools in Ancient Israel." Pp. 81–95 in J. A. Emerton (ed.), *Congress Volume: Jerusalem, 1986*. Leiden: Brill.

Hasel, Michael. G. 1994. "Israel in the Merneptah Stela." *BASOR* 296: 45–61.

———. 2003. "Merneptah's Inscription and Reliefs and the Origin of Israel." Pp. 19–44 in Beth Alpert Nakhai (ed.), *The Near East in the Southwest: Essays in Honor of William G. Dever*. Boston: ASOR.

———. 2004. "The Structure of the Final Hymnic-Poetic Unit on the Merneptah Stela." *ZAW* 116: 75–81.

———. 2008. "Merneptah's Reference to Israel: Critical Issues for the Origin of Israel." Pp. 47–59 in Richard Hess, Gerald Klingbeil, and Paul J. Ray (eds.), *Critical Issues in Early Israelite History*. Winona Lake, Ind.: Eisenbrauns.

Hawk, Daniel. 2008. "Conquest Reconfigured: Recasting Warfare in the Redaction of Joshua." Pp. 145–60 in Brad E. Kelle and Frank R. Ames (eds.), *Writing and Reading War: Rhetoric, Gender, and Ethics in Biblical and Modern Contexts*. Atlanta, Ga.: Society of Biblical Literature.

Heltzer, Michael. 1981. *The Suteans*. Naples: Istituto Universitario Orientale.

Hendel, Ronald S. 2005. *Remembering Abraham: Culture, Memory, and History in the Hebrew Bible*. Oxford: Oxford University Press.

Hentschel, Georg, and Christina Niessen. 2008. "Der Bruderkrieg zwischen Israel und Benjamin (Ri 20)." *Bib* 89: 17–38.

Herzog, Ze'ev. 2003. "The Canaanite City between Ideology and Archaeological Reality." Pp. 85–96 in Cornelis G. den Hertog, Ulrich Hübner, and Stefan Münger (eds.), *Saxa Loquentur: Studien zur Archäologie Palästinas/Israels (Festschrift Volkmar Fritz)*. Münster: Ugarit Verlag.

Herzog, Ze'ev, and Lily Singer-Avitz. 2004. "Redefining the Centre: The Emergence of State in Judah." *TA* 31: 209–44.

Hiebert, Theodore. 1986. *God of My Victory: The Ancient Hymn in Habakkuk 3*. Atlanta, Ga.: Scholars Press.

Higginbotham, Carolyn R. 2000. *Egyptianization and Elite Emulation in Ramesside Palestine: Governance and Accommodation on the Imperial Periphery*. Leiden: Brill.

Hillers, Delbert R. 1984. *Micah*. Philadelphia: Fortress.

Hjelm, Ingrid, and Thomas L. Thompson. 2002. "The Victory Song of Merneptah, Israel and the People of Palestine." *JSOT* 27: 3–18.

Hobsbawm, Eric. 1983. "Introduction: Inventing Traditions." Pp. 1–14 in Eric J. Hobsbawm and Terence O. Renger (eds.), *The Invention of Tradition*. Cambridge: Cambridge University Press.

Hobsbawm, Eric J., and Terence O. Renger (eds.). 1983. *The Invention of Tradition*. Cambridge: Cambridge University Press.

Hoffman, Yair. 1989. "A North Israelite Typological Myth and a Judaean Historical Tradition: The Exodus in Hosea and Amos." *VT* 39: 170–81.

———. 1999. "The Deuteronomistic Concept of the Herem." *ZAW* 111: 196–210.

Hoffmeier, James K. 1996. *Israel in Egypt: The Evidence for the Authenticity of the Exodus Tradition*. Oxford: Oxford University Press.

Hoftijzer, Jean, and G. van der Kooij (eds.). 1991. *The Balaam Text from Deir 'Alla Reevaluated*. Leiden: Brill.

Holladay, William L. 1986. *Jeremiah 1: A Commentary on the Book of the Prophet Jeremiah, Chapters 1–25*. Minneapolis, Minn.: Fortress.

———. 1989. *Jeremiah 2: A Commentary on the Book of the Prophet Jeremiah, Chapters 26–52*. Minneapolis, Minn.: Fortress.

de Hoop, Raymond. 1999. *Genesis 49 in Its Literary and Historical Context*. Leiden: Brill.

Hossfeld, Frank-Lothar, and Erich Zenger. 2005. *Psalms 2: A Commentary on Psalms 51–100*. Minneapolis, Minn.: Fortress.

Houk, Brett A. 2003. "The Ties that Bind: Site Planning in the Three Rivers Region." Pp. 52–63 in Vernon L. Scarborough, Fred Valdez, and Nicholas Dunning (eds.),

Heterarchy, Political Economy, and the Ancient Maya: The Three Rivers Region of the East-Central Yucatán Peninsula. Tucson: University of Arizona Press.

Huber, Michael. 2010. *Gab es ein davidisch-salomonisches Grossreich? Forschungs-geschichte und neuere Argumentationen aus der Sicht der Archäologie.* Stuttgart: Katholisches Bibelwerk.

Huehnergard, John. 1995. "What Is Aramaic?" *ARAM* 7: 261–82.

Hutton, Jeremy M. 2009. *The Transjordanian Palimpsest: The Overwritten Texts of Personal Exile and Transformation in the Deuteronomistic History.* Berlin: de Gruyter.

Hylander, Ivan. 1932. *Der literarische Samuel-Saul Komplex (I Sam 1–15): Traditions-geschichtlich untersucht.* Uppsala: Almqvist & Wiksell.

Inomata, Takeshi, and Lawrence S. Cohen (eds.). 2006. *Archaeology of Performance: Theaters of Power, Community, and Politics.* Lanham, Md.: Alta Mira.

Irsigler, Hubert. 1993. "Grossatzformen in Althebräischen und die Syntaktische Struktur der Inschrift des Konigs Mescha von Moab." Pp. 81–121 in Hubert Irsigler (ed.), *Syntax und Text.* St. Ottilien: EOS.

Ishida, Tomoo. 1977. *The Royal Dynasties in Ancient Israel.* Berlin: de Gruyter.

———. 1999. *History and Historical Writing in Ancient Israel: Studies in Biblical Historiography.* Leiden: Brill.

Ivanov, V. V. 1974. "Ḫabiru in Cuneiform Hittite and Luwian Texts." Pp. 39–40 in *Internationale Tagung der Keilschriftforscher der sozialistischen Länder.* Budapest: Komoroczy Géza.

Jahn, Brit. 2007. "The Migration and Sedentarization of the Amorites from the Point of View of the Settled Babylonian Population." Pp. 193–209 in Marlies Heinz and Marion H. Feldman (eds.), *Representations of Political Power: Case Histories from Times of Change and Dissolving Order in the Ancient Near East.* Winona Lake, Ind.: Eisenbrauns.

Jans, Edgar. 2001. *Abimelekh und sein Königtum: Diachrone und synchrone Unter-suchungen zu Ri 9.* St. Ottilien: EOS.

Japhet, Sara. 1989. *The Ideology of the Book of Chronicles and Its Place in Biblical Thought.* Frankfurt am Main: Peter Lang.

———. 2006. "The Wall of Jerusalem from a Double Perspective: Kings versus Chronicles." Pp. 205–19 in Yairah Amit et al. (eds.), *Essays on Ancient Israel in Its Near Eastern Context: A Tribute to Nadav Na'aman.* Winona Lake, Ind.: Eisenbrauns.

Jaroš, Karl. 1977. *Studien zur Sichem-Area.* Göttingen: Vandenhoeck & Ruprecht.

———. 1982. *Die Stellung des Elohisten zur kanaanäischen Religion.* Göttingen: Vandenhoeck & Ruprecht.

Jaruzelska, Izabela. 2004. "Les prophètes face aux usurpations dans le royaume du nord." *VT* 54: 165–87.

Jenks, Alan W. 1977. *The Elohist and North Israelite Traditions.* Missoula, Mont.: Scholars Press.

Jeremias, Jörg. 1998. *The Book of Amos.* Louisville Ky.: Westminster John Knox.

Joannès, Francis. 1996. "Routes et voies de communication dans les archives de Mari." *Amurru* 1: 323–61.

Johnson, Gregory A. 1989. "Dynamics of Southwestern Prehistory: Far Outside, Looking In." Pp. 371–89 in Linda S. Cordell and George J. Gumerman (eds.), *Dynamics of Southwestern Prehistory.* Washington, D.C.: Smithsonian Institution Press.

Jones, Andrew. 2002. *Archaeological Theory and Scientific Practice.* Cambridge: Cambridge University Press.

Jones, Siân. 2008. "Ethnicity: Theoretical Approaches, Methodological Implications." Pp. 321–34 in R. Alexander Bentley, Herbert D. G. Maschner, and Christopher Chippindale (eds.), *Handbook of Archaeological Theories*. Plymouth, U.K.: Altamira.

Kaiser, Otto. 1972. *Isaiah 1–12: A Commentary*. Philadelphia: Westminster.

Kalimi, Isaac. 2005. *The Reshaping of Ancient Israelite History in Chronicles*. Winona Lake, Ind.: Eisenbrauns.

———. 2009. "Placing the Chronicler in His Own Historical Context: A Closer Examination." *JNES* 68: 179–92.

Katz, Dina. 1987. "Gilgamesh and Akka: Was Uruk Ruled by Two Assemblies?" *RA* 81: 105–14.

Kaufman, Stephen A. 1974. *The Akkadian Influences on Aramaic*. Chicago, Ill.: University of Chicago Press.

Kelle, Brad E. 2002. "What's in a Name? Neo-Assyrian Designations for the Northern Kingdom and Their Implications for Israelite History and Biblical Interpretation." *JBL* 121: 639–66.

Kepinski, Christine, and Aline Tenu (eds.). 2009a. "Dossier: Interaction entre Assyriens et Araméens." *Syria* 86.

———. 2009b. "Interaction entre Assyriens et Araméens: Avant-propos." Pp. 7–15 in Christine Kepinski and Aline Tenu (eds.), "Dossier: Interaction entre Assyriens et Araméens." *Syria* 86.

Khoury, Philip S., and Joseph Kostiner. 1990. "Introduction: Tribes and the Complexities of State Formation in the Middle East." Pp. 1–22 in Khoury and Kostiner (eds.), *Tribes and State Formation in the Middle East*. Berkeley: University of California Press.

Killebrew, Ann E. 2003. "Biblical Jerusalem: An Archaeological Assessment." Pp. 329–45 in Andrew G. Vaughn and Ann E. Killebrew (eds.), *Jerusalem in Bible and Archaeology: The First Temple Period*. Leiden: Brill.

———. 2005. *Biblical Peoples and Ethnicity: An Archaeological Study of Egyptians, Canaanites, Philistines, and Early Israel, 1300–1100 B.C.E.* Atlanta, Ga.: Scholars Press.

King, Eleanor M., and Leslie C. Shaw. 2003. "A Heterarchical Approach to Site Variability: The Maax Na Archaeology Project." Pp. 64–76 in Vernon L. Scarborough, Fred Valdez, and Nicholas Dunning (eds.), *Heterarchy, Political Economy, and the Ancient Maya: The Three Rivers Region of the East-Central Yucatán Peninsula*. Tucson: University of Arizona Press.

Kitchen, Kenneth. 2004. "The Victories of Merenptah, and the Nature of Their Record." *JSOT* 28: 259–72.

Klein, Johannes. 2002. *David versus Saul: Ein Beitrag zum Erzählsystem der Samuelbücher*. Stuttgart: Kohlhammer.

Klein, Ralph W. 2006. *1 Chronicles: A Commentary*. Minneapolis, Minn.: Fortress.

Kletter, Raz. 2002. "People without Burials? The Lack of Iron I Burials in the Central Highlands of Palestine." *IEJ* 52: 28–48.

———. 2006. "Can a Proto-Israelite Please Stand Up? Notes on the Ethnicity of Iron Age Israel and Judah." Vol. 2, pp. 573–86 in Aren M. Maeir and Pierre de Miroschedji (eds.), *"I Will Speak the Riddles of Ancient Times": Archaeological and Historical Studies in Honor of Amihai Mazar on the Occasion of His Sixtieth Birthday*. Winona Lake, Ind.: Eisenbrauns.

Knauf, Ernst Axel. 1990. "Hesbon, Sihons Stadt." *ZDPV* 106: 135–44.

————. 1991. "King Solomon's Copper Supply." Pp. 167–83 in Eduard Lipiński (ed.), *Phoenicia and the Bible*. Leuven: Peeters.

————. 1997. "Le roi est mort, vive le roi! A Biblical Argument for the Historicity of Solomon." Pp. 81–95 in Lowell K. Handy (ed.), *The Age of Solomon: Scholarship at the Turn of the Millennium*. Leiden: Brill.

————. 2005a. "Auf der Suche nach dem geschichtliche Salomo." Pp. 91–105 in Rüdiger Lux (ed.), *Ideales Königtum: Studien zu David und Salomo*. Leipzig: Evangelische Verlagsanstalt.

————. 2005b. "Deborah's Language: Judges Chapter 5 in Its Hebrew and Semitic Context." Pp. 167–82 in B. Burrea and H. Younansardaroud (eds.), *Studia Semitica et Semitohamitica. Fs. R. Voigt*. Münster: Ugarit Verlag.

————. 2006. "Bethel: The Israelite Impact on Judean Language and Literature." Pp. 291–349 in Oded Lipschits and Manfred Oeming (eds.), *Judah and the Judeans in the Persian Period*. Winona Lake, Ind.: Eisenbrauns.

————. 2008. *Josua*. Zürich: Theologischer Verlag.

Knohl, Israel. 1995. *The Sanctuary of Silence: The Priestly Torah and the Holiness School*. Minneapolis, Minn.: Fortress.

Knoppers, Gary N. 1997. "The Vanishing Solomon: The Disappearance of the United Monarchy from Recent Histories of Ancient Israel." *JBL* 116: 19–44.

————. 2003a. *1 Chronicles 1–9*. New York: Doubleday.

————. 2003b. "Greek History and the Chronicler's History: A Reexamination." *JBL* 122: 627–50.

Köckert, Matthias. 2010. "YHWH in the Northern and Southern Kingdom." Pp. 357–94 in Reinhard G. Kratz and Hermann Spieckermann (eds.), *One God – One Cult – One Nation: Archaeological and Biblical Perspectives*. Berlin: de Gruyter.

Köckert, Matthias, and Martti Nissinen (eds.). 2003. *Propheten in Mari, Assyrien und Israel*. Göttingen: Vandenhoeck & Ruprecht.

Koenen, Klaus. 2003. *Bethel: Geschichte, Kult und Theologie*. Göttingen: Vandenhoeck & Ruprecht.

Köhlmoos, Melanie. 2006. *Bet-El – Erinnerungen an eine Stadt: Perspektiven der ältesten Bet-El-Überlieferung*. Tübingen: Mohr Siebeck.

Kottsieper, Ingo. 2007. "The Tel Dan Inscription (KAI 310) and the Political Relations between Aram-Damascus and Israel in the First Half of the First Millennium BCE." Pp. 104–34 in Lester L. Grabbe (ed.), *Ahab Agonistes: The Rise and Fall of the Omri Dynasty*. London: T. & T. Clark.

Kowalewski, Stephen A. 1994. "Internal Subdivisions of Communities in the Prehispanic Valley of Oaxaca." Pp. 127–37 in Elizabeth M. Brumfiel and John W. Fox (eds.), *Factional Competition and Political Development in the New World*. Cambridge: Cambridge University Press.

Kratz, Reinhard G. 2000. "Israel als Staat und als Volk." *ZTK* 97: 1–17.

————. 2002. "Der vor- und der nachpriesterschriftliche Hexateuch." Pp. 295–323 in Jan Chr. Gertz (ed.), *Abschied vom Jahwisten*. Berlin: de Gruyter.

————. 2005. *The Composition of the Narrative Books of the Old Testament*. London: T. & T. Clark.

————. 2006. "Israel in the Book of Isaiah," *JSOT* 31: 103–28.

Kratz, Reinhard G., and Hermann Spieckermann (eds.). 2010. *One God – One Cult – One Nation: Archaeological and Biblical Perspectives*. Berlin: de Gruyter.

Kraus, F. R. 1958. *Ein Edikt des Königs Ammi-ṣaduqa von Babylon*. Leiden: Brill.

Kuan, Jeffrey K. 1993. "Was Omri a Phoenician?" Pp. 231–44 in M. Patrick Graham, William P. Brown, and Jeffrey K. Kuan (eds.), *History and Interpretation: Essays in Honour of John J. Hayes*. Sheffield: Sheffield Academic Press.

Kühne, Hartmut. 2009. "Interaction of Aramaeans and Assyrians on the Lower Khabur." Pp. 43–54 in Christine Kepinski and Aline Tenu (eds.), "Dossier: Interaction entre Assyriens et Araméens." *Syria* 86.

Lang, Bernhard. 2002. *The Hebrew God: Portrait of an Ancient Deity*. New Haven, Conn.: Yale University Press.

Lehmann, Gunnar. 2003. "The United Monarchy in the Countryside: Jerusalem, Judah, and the Shephelah during the Tenth Century B.C.E." Pp. 117–62 in Andrew G. Vaughn and Ann E. Killebrew (eds.), *Jerusalem in Bible and Archaeology: The First Temple Period*. Leiden: Brill.

Lemaire, André. 1986. "Vers l'histoire de la rédaction des livres des Rois." *ZAW* 98: 221–36.

———. 1994. "'House of David' Restored in Moabite Inscription." *BARev* 20/3: 30–7.

———. 2007. "The Mesha Stele and the Omri Dynasty." Pp. 135–44 in Lester L. Grabbe (ed.), *Ahab Agonistes: The Rise and Fall of the Omri Dynasty*. London: T. & T. Clark.

Lemche, Niels-Peter. 1985. *Early Israel: Anthropological and Historical Studies on the Israelite Society before the Monarchy*. Leiden: E. J. Brill.

———. 1991. *The Canaanites and Their Land: The Tradition of the Canaanites*. Sheffield: Sheffield Academic Press.

Leonard-Fleckman, Mahri. 2011. "The Centrality of Israel in the David Story." Society of Biblical Literature Annual Meeting.

Levin, Christoph. 1982. *Der Sturz der Königin Atalja: Ein Kapitel zur Geschichte Judas im 9. Jahrhundert v. Chr.* Stuttgart: Katholisches Bibelwerk.

———. 1995. "Das System der zwölf Stämme Israels." Pp. 163–78 in J. A. Emerton (ed.), *Congress Volume: Paris 1992*. Leiden: Brill.

———. 2000. "Das vorstaatliche Israel." *ZTK* 97: 385–403.

Levine, Baruch A. 1993. *Numbers 1–20*. New York: Doubleday.

———. 2000. *Numbers 21–36*. New York: Doubleday.

Levinson, Bernard M. 1997. *Deuteronomy and the Hermeneutics of Legal Innovation*. Oxford: Oxford University Press.

Levy, Thomas E., Levy, Mohammad Najjar, and Thomas Higham. 2010. "Ancient Texts and Archaeology Revisited – Radiocarbon and Biblical Dating in the Southern Levant." *Antiquity* 84: 834–47.

Lindars, Barnabus. 1995. *Judges 1–5: A New Translation and Commentary*. Edinburgh: T. & T. Clark.

Lipiński, Edward. 1973. "L'étymologie de Juda." *VT* 23: 380–1.

———. 2000. *The Aramaeans: Their Ancient History, Culture, Religion*. Leuven: Peeters.

Lipschits, Oded. 2005. *The Fall and Rise of Jerusalem: Judah under Babylonian Rule*. Winona Lake, Ind.: Eisenbrauns.

Liu, Li, and Xingcan Chen. 2003. *State Formation in Early China*. London: Duckworth.

Liverani, Mario. 1974. "L'histoire de Joas." *VT* 24: 438–53.

———. 1979. "Farsi Habiru." *Vicino Oriente* 1–2: 65–77.

Long, Burke O. 1991. *2 Kings*. Grand Rapids, Mich.: Eerdmans.

Loretz, Oswald. 1984. *Habiru-Hebräer: Eine sozio-linguistische Studie über die Herkunft des Gentiliziums 'ibrî vom Appellativum habiru*. Berlin: de Gruyter.

Lundbom, Jack R. 1999. *Jeremiah 1–20*. New York: Doubleday.

———. 2004. *Jeremiah 21–36*. New York: Doubleday.

Macchi, Jean-Daniel. 1999. *Israël et ses tribus selon Genèse 49*. Göttingen: Vandenhoeck & Ruprecht.

———. 2001. "Genèse 31,24–42. La dernière rencontre de Jacob et de Laban." Pp. 144–62 in Jean-Daniel Macchi and Thomas Römer (eds.), *Jacob: Commentaire à plusieurs voix de Gen 25–36*. Geneva: Labor et Fides, 2001.

Maceachern, Scott. 1998. "Scale, Style, and Cultural Variation: Technological Traditions in the Northern Mandara Mountains." Pp. 107–31 in Miriam T. Stark (ed.), *The Archaeology of Social Boundaries*. Washington, D.C.: Smithsonian Institution.

Machinist, Peter. 2005. "Hosea and the Ambiguity of Kingship in Ancient Israel." Pp. 153–81 in John T. Strong and Steven S. Tuell (eds.), *Constituting the Community: Studies on the Polity of Ancient Israel in Honor of S. Dean McBride Jr*. Winona Lake, Ind.: Eisenbrauns.

Magen, Yitzhak. 2004. "The Land of Benjamin in the Second Temple Period." Pp. 1–28 in Yitzhak Magen et al., *The Land of Benjamin*. Jerusalem: Israel Antiquities Authority.

Malamat, Abraham. 1950. "The Last Wars of the Kingdom of Judah." *JNES* 9: 218–27.

———. 2004. "The Punishment of Succoth and Penuel by Gideon in the Light of Ancient Near Eastern Treaties." Pp. 69–71 in Chaim Cohen, Avi Hurvitz, and Shalom Paul (eds.), *Sefer Moshe: The Moshe Weinfeld Jubilee Volume. Studies in the Bible and the Ancient Near East, Qumran, and Post-Biblical Judaism*. Winona Lake, Ind.: Eisenbrauns.

Mann, Michael. 1986. *The Sources of Social Power*, vol. 1: *A History of Power from the Beginning to A.D. 1760*. Cambridge: Cambridge University Press.

Marcus, Joyce. 1986. "Ancient Maya Political Organization." Pp. 111–83 in Jeremy Sabloff and John S. Henderson (eds.), *Lowland Maya Civilization in the Eighth Century A.D.* Washington, D.C.: Dumbarton Oaks Research Library and Collection.

Marello, Pierre. 1992. "Vie nomade." *FM* I: 115–25.

Mastin, B. A. 2009. "The Inscriptions Written on Plaster at Kuntillet 'Ajrud," *VT* 59: 99–115.

Mayes, A. D. H. 1974. *Israel in the Period of the Judges*. Naperville, Ill.: A. R. Allenson.

———. 1979. *Deuteronomy*. London: Oliphants.

———. 1983. *The Story of Israel between Settlement and Exile: A Redactional History of the Deuteronomistic History*. London: SCM.

———. 1997. "Kuntillet 'Ajrud and the History of Israelite Religion." Pp. 51–66 in John R. Bartlett (ed.), *Archaeology and Biblical Interpretation*. London: Routledge.

Mazar, Amihai. 1985. "The Emergence of Philistine Culture." *IEJ* 35: 95–107.

———. 1997. "Iron Age Chronology: A Reply to I. Finkelstein." *Levant* 29: 157–67.

———. 2003. "Remarks on Biblical Traditions and Archaeological Evidence concerning Early Israel." Pp. 85–98 in W.G. Dever and S. Gitin eds., *Symbiosis, Symbolism and the Power of the Past: Canaan, Ancient Israel, and Their Neighbors from the Late Bronze Age through Roman Palaestina*. Winona Lake, Ind.: Eisenbrauns.

———. 2007. "The Spade and the Text: The Interaction between Archaeology and Israelite History Relating to the Tenth–Ninth Centuries BCE." Pp. 143–72 in H.G.M. Williamson (ed.), *Understanding the History of Ancient Israel*. Oxford: Oxford University Press.

———. 2008. "From 1200 to 850 B.C.E.: Remarks on Some Selected Archaeological Issues." Pp. 86–120 in Lester L. Grabbe (ed.), *Israel in Transition: From Late Bronze II to Iron IIa (c. 1250 – 850 B.C.E.)*, vol. 1: *The Archaeology*. London: T. & T. Clark.

———. 2010. "Archaeology and the Biblical Narrative: The Case of the United Monarchy." Pp. 29–58 in Reinhard G. Kratz and Hermann Spieckermann (eds.), *One God – One Cult – One Nation: Archaeological and Biblical Perspectives*. Berlin: de Gruyter.

———. 2011. "The Iron Age Chronology Debate: Is the Gap Narrowing? Another Viewpoint." *NEA* 74: 105–11.

Mazar, Amihai, and Bronk Ramsey. 2010. "A Response to Finkelstein and Piasetzky's Criticism and 'New Perspective.'" *Radiocarbon* 52: 1681–88.

McAnany, Patricia A. 1995. *Living with the Ancestors: Kinship and Kingship in Ancient Maya Society*. Austin: University of Texas Press.

McCarter, P. Kyle. 1980. *I Samuel*. New York: Doubleday.

———. 1984. *II Samuel*. New York: Doubleday.

McCulloch, Warren S. 1945. "A Heterarchy of Values Determined by the Typology of Nervous Nets." *Bulletin of Mathematical Biophysics* 7: 89–93.

McIntosh, Roderick J. 1998. *The Peoples of the Middle Niger: The Island of Gold*. Oxford: Blackwell.

McIntosh, Susan Keech. 1999. "Modeling Political Organization in Large-Scale Settlement Clusters: A Case Study from the Inland Niger Delta." Pp. 66–79 in Susan Keech McIntosh (ed.), *Beyond Chiefdoms: Pathways to Complexity in Africa*. Cambridge: Cambridge University Press.

McKane, William. 1970. *Proverbs: A New Approach*. Philadelphia: Westminster.

McKenzie, Steven L. 1991. *The Trouble with Kings: The Composition of the Book of Kings in the Deuteronomistic History*. Leiden: Brill.

———. 1998. "Mizpah of Benjamin and the Date of the Deuteronomistic History." Pp. 149–55 in Klaus-Dietrich Schunck and Matthias Augustin (eds.), *"Lasset uns Brücken bauen": Collected Communications to the XVth Congress of the International Organization for the Study of the Old Testament, Cambridge 1995*. Bern: Peter Lang.

———. 2000. "The Trouble with Kingship." Pp. 286–314 in Thomas Römer and Albert de Pury (eds.), *Israel Constructs its History*. Sheffield: Sheffield Academic Press, 2000.

McLellan, Thomas L. 1989. "Twelfth Century B.C. Syria: Comments on H. Sader's Paper." Pp. 164–73 in William A. Ward and Martha Sharp Joukowsky (eds.), *The Crisis Years: The Twelfth Century B.C. from Beyond the Danube to the Tigris*. Dubuque, Iowa: Kendall/Hunt.

van der Meer, Michael. 2004. *Formation and Reformulation: The Redaction of the Book of Joshua in the Light of the Oldest Textual Witnesses*. Leiden: Brill.

Mendenhall, George. 1962. "The Hebrew Conquest of Palestine." *BA* 25: 66–87.

Mettinger, Tryggve N. D. 1971. *Solomonic State Officials: A Study of the Civil Government Officials of the Israelite Monarchy*. Lund: C.W.K. Gleerup.

———. 1976. *King and Messiah: The Civil and Sacral Legitimation of the Israelite Kings*. Lund: C.W.K. Gleerup.

Miglio, Adam E. 2010. "Solidarity and Political Authority during the Reign of Zimrī-Līm (c. 1775–1762 B.C.)." Ph.D. dissertation, University of Chicago.

Milgrom, Jacob. 1991. *Leviticus 1–16*. New York: Doubleday.

Miller, Daniel, and Christopher Tilley. 1984. "Ideology, Power and Prehistory: An Introduction." Pp. 1–15 in Daniel Miller and Christopher Tilley (eds.), *Ideology, Power and Prehistory*. Cambridge: Cambridge University Press.

Miller, J. Maxwell. 1974. "Saul's Rise to Power: Some Observations Concerning 1 Sam 9:1–10:16; 10:26–11:15 and 13:2–14:46." *CBQ* 36: 157–74.

———. 1989. "The Israelite Journey through (around) Moab and Moabite Toponymy." *JBL* 108: 577–95.

———. 1992. "Early Monarchy in Moab?" Pp. 77–91 in Piotr Bienkowski (ed.), *Early Edom and Moab: The Beginning of the Iron Age in Southern Jordan*. Sheffield: J. R. Collis.

Miller, J. Maxwell, and John H. Hayes. 1986. *A History of Ancient Israel and Judah*. Philadelphia: Westminster.

Miller, James C. 2008. "Ethnicity and the Hebrew Bible: Problems and Prospects." *Currents in Biblical Research* 6: 170–213.

Miller, Robert D. 2005. *Chieftains of the Highland Clans: A History of Israel in the Twelfth and Eleventh Centuries B.C.* Grand Rapids, Mich.: Eerdmans.

Millet-Albà, Adélina. 2004. "La localization des terroirs benjaminites du royaume de Mari." Pp. 225–34 in Christophe Nicolle (ed.), *Nomades et sédentaires dans le Proche-Orient ancient*. CRRAI 46; Paris: Éditions Recherche sur les Civilisations.

Mills, Barbara J. (ed.). 2000. *Alternative Leadership Strategies in the Prehispanic Southwest*. Tuscon: University of Arizona Press.

Milson, David. 1987. "The Design of Temples and Gates at Shechem." *PEQ* 119: 97–105.

Milstein, Sara J. 2010. "Expanding Ancient Narratives: Revision through Introduction in Biblical and Mesopotamian Texts." Ph.D. dissertation, New York University.

Monroe, Lauren A. S. 2007. "Israelite, Moabite and Sabaean War-herem Traditions and the Forging of National Identity: Reconsidering the Sabaean Text RES 3945 in Light of Biblical and Moabite Evidence." *VT* 57: 318–41.

———. 2011. *Josiah's Reform and the Dynamics of Defilement: Israelite Rites of Violence and the Making of a Biblical Text*. Oxford: Oxford University Press.

Moran, William L. 1992. *The Amarna Letters*. Baltimore, Md.: Johns Hopkins University Press.

Morenz, Ludwig D. 1997. "Kanaanäisches Lokalkolorit in der Sinuhe-Erzählung und die Vereinfachung des Urtextes." *ZDPV* 113: 1–18.

———. 2008. "Wortwitz – Ideologie – Geschichte: 'Israel' im Horizont Mer-en-ptahs." *ZAW* 120: 1–13.

Morris, Ellen F. 2005. *Architecture of Imperialism: Military Bases and the Evolution of Foreign Policy in Egypt's New Kingdom*. Leiden: Brill.

Morschauser, Scott. 2000. "What Made Sinuhe Run: Sinuhe's Reasoned Flight." *JARCE* 37: 187–98.

Müller, Hans-Peter. 1992. "Kolloquialsprache und Volksreligion in den Inschriften von Kuntillet Aǧrud und Hirbet el-Qom," *Zeitschrift für Althebraistik* 5: 15–51.

———. 1994. "König Mêšaʿ von Moab und der Gott der Geschichte." *UF* 26: 373–95.

Naʾaman, Nadav. 1977. "Yenoʾam." *TA* 4: 168–77.

———. 1986. "Habiru and Hebrews: The Transfer of a Social Term to the Literary Sphere." *JNES* 45: 271–86.

———. 1991. "The Kingdom of Judah under Josiah." *TA* 18: 3–71.

———. 1994. "The Canaanites and Their Land." *UF* 26: 397–418.

———. 1996a. "The Contribution of the Amarna Letters to the Debate on Jerusalem's Political Position in the Tenth Century B.C.E." *BASOR* 304: 17–27.

———. 1996b. "Sources and Composition in the History of David." Pp. 170–86 in Volkmar Fritz and Philip R. Davies (eds.), *The Origins of the Ancient Israelite States.* Sheffield: Sheffield Academic Press.

———. 1997a. "King Mesha and the Foundation of the Moabite Monarchy." *IEJ* 47: 83–92.

———. 1997b. "The Network of Canaanite Late Bronze Kingdoms and the City of Ashdod." *UF* 29: 599–626.

———. 1997c. "Prophetic Stories as Sources for the Histories of Jehoshaphat and the Omrides." *Bib* 78: 153–73.

———. 1999. "The Contribution of Royal Inscriptions for a Re-evaluation of the Book of Kings as a Historical Source." *JSOT* 82: 3–17.

———. 2005. *Ancient Israel and Its Neighbors: Canaan in the Second Millennium B.C.E..* Winona Lake, Ind.: Eisenbrauns.

———. 2007a. "Royal Inscription versus Prophetic Story: Mesha's Rebellion According to Biblical and Moabite Historiography." Pp. 145–83 in Lester L. Grabbe (ed.), *Ahab Agonistes: The Rise and Fall of the Omri Dynasty.* London: T. & T. Clark.

———. 2007b. "When and How Did Jerusalem Become a Great City? The Rise of Jerusalem as Judah's Premier City in the Eighth-Seventh Centuries B.C.E." *BASOR* 347: 21–56.

———. 2009a. "The Growth and Development of Judah and Jerusalem in the Eighth Century BCE: A Rejoinder." *RB* 116: 321–35.

———. 2009b. "Saul, Benjamin and the Emergence of 'Biblical Israel' (Part 1)." *ZAW* 121: 211–24; Part 2, 121: 335–49.

———. 2010. "The Israelite–Judahite Struggle for the Patrimony of Ancient Israel." *Bib* 91: 1–23.

Neef, Heinz-Dieter. 2002. *Deboraerzählung und Deboralied: Studien zu Jdc 4,1–5,31.* Neukirchen-Vluyn: Neukirchener.

Nelson, Richard D. 1981. "Josiah in the Book of Joshua." *JBL* 100: 531–40.

———. 1997. *Joshua.* Louisville, Ky.: Westminster John Knox.

———. 2002. *Deuteronomy: A Commentary.* Louisville, Ky.: Westminster John Knox.

Niccacci, Alviero. 1994. "The Stele of Mesha and the Bible: Verbal System and Narrativity." *Or* 63: 226–48.

———. 1997. "La stele d'Israël: Grammaire et stratégie de communication." Pp. 43–107 in Marcel Sigrist (ed.), *Études égyptologiques et bibliques à la mémoire du Père B. Couroyer.* Paris: J. Gabalda.

Nicholson, Ernest W. 1965. "The Meaning of the Expression *'am hā'āreṣ* in the Old Testament." *JSS* 10: 59–66.

Niemann, Hermann M. 1997. "The Socio-Political Shadow Cast by the Biblical Solomon." Pp. 252–99 in Lowell K. Handy (ed.), *The Age of Solomon: Scholarship at the Turn of the Millennium.* Leiden: Brill.

Nissinen, Martti. 2010. "Biblical Prophecy from a Near Eastern Perspective: The Cases of Kingship and Divine Possession." Pp. 441–68 in André Lemaire (ed.), *Congress Volume: Ljubljana 2007.* Leiden: Brill.

Noth, Martin. 1943. *Überlieferungsgeschichtliche Studien: Die sammelnden und bearbeitenden Geschichtswerke im Alten Testament.* Darmstadt: Max Niemeyer.

———. 1960. *The History of Israel,* 2nd edition. London: A. & C. Black.

———. 1966a. *The Laws in the Pentateuch and Other Studies.* London: SCM.

———. 1966b. *Das System der zwölf Stämme Israels*. Darmstadt: Wissenschaftliche Buchgesellschaft.

———. 1971. *Das Buch Josua*. Tübingen: Mohr-Siebeck.

———. 1972. *A History of Pentateuchal Traditions*. Englewood Cliffs, N.J.: Prentice-Hall.

———. 1981. *The Deuteronomistic History*. Sheffield: JSOT.

Obsomer, Claude. 1999. "Sinouhé l'Égyptien et les raisons de son exil." *Le Muséon* 112: 207–71.

Oswald, Wolfgang. 2009. *Staatstheorie im Alten Israel: Der politische Diskurs im Pentateuch und in den Geschichtsbüchern des Alten Testaments*. Stuttgart: Kohlhammer.

Otto, Eckart. 2000. *Das Deuteronomium in Pentateuch und Hexateuch: Studien zur Literaturgeschichte von Pentateuch und Hexateuch im Lichte des Deuteronomiumsrahmen*. Tübingen: Mohr-Siebeck.

———. 2002. "Forschungen zum nachpriesterschriftlichen Pentateuch." *Theologische Rundschau* 67: 125–55.

Ozan, Grégoire. 1997. "Les letters de Manatân." *FM* III: 291–305.

Pakkala, Juha. 2009. "The Date of the Oldest Edition of Deuteronomy." *ZAW* 121: 388–401.

Pardee, Dennis. 2006. "Review of George Athas (2003), *The Tel Dan Inscription: A Reappraisal and a New Interpretation*." *JNES* 65: 289–91.

Parker, Simon B. 2006. "Ancient Northwest Semitic Epigraphy and the 'Deuteronomistic' Tradition in Kings." Pp. 213–27 in Markus Witte et al. (eds.), *Die deuteronomistischen Geschichtswerke: Redaktions- und religionsgeschichtliche Perspektiven zur "Deuteronomismus" – Diskussion in Tora und Vorderen Propheten*. Berlin: de Gruyter.

Parkinson, W. (ed.). 2002. *The Archaeology of Tribal Societies*. Ann Arbor, Mich.: International Monographs in Prehistory.

Parpola, Simo. 1970. *Neo-Assyrian Toponyms*. Neukirchen-Vluyn: Neukirchener.

Parrot, André. 1950. "Les tablettes de Mari et l'Ancien Testament." *RHPR* 30: 1–11.

Pentiuc, Eugen. 2001. *West Semitic Vocabulary in the Akkadian Texts from Emar*. Winona Lake, Ind.: Eisenbrauns.

Perlitt, Lothar. 1969. *Bundestheologie im Alten Testament*. Neukirchen-Vluyn: Neukirchener.

———. 1985. "Deuteronomium 1–3 im Streit der exegetischen Methoden." Pp. 149–63 in Norbert Lohfink (ed.), *Das Deuteronomium: Enstehung, Gestalt und Botschaft*. Leuven: Peeters.

Pitard, Wayne T. 1987. *Ancient Damascus: A Historical Study of the Syrian City-State from Earliest Times until Its Fall to the Assyrians in 732 B.C.E.*. Winona Lake, Ind.: Eisenbrauns.

Podany, Amanda H. 2002. *The Land of Hana: Kings, Chronology, and Scribal Tradition*. Bethesda, Md.: CDL.

Pohl, Alfred. 1957. "Einige Gedanken zur Ḫabiru-Frage." *WZKM* 54: 157–60.

Porter, Anne. 2000. "Mortality, Monuments and Mobility: Ancestor Traditions and the Transcendence of Space." Ph.D. dissertation, University of Chicago.

———. 2002. "The Dynamics of Death: Ancestors, Pastoralism and the Origins of a Third Millennium City in Syria." *BASOR* 325: 1–36.

———. 2007. "You Say Potato, I Say … Typology, Chronology and the Origin of the Amorites." Pp. 69–115 in Catherine Marro and Catherine Kuzucuoglu (eds.), *Sociétés humaines et changement climatique à la fin du Troisième Millénaire: Une crise a-t-elle eu lieu en Haute-Mésopotamie?* Istanbul: Institut Français d'Études Anatolienne Georges-Dume'zil.

———. 2009. "Beyond Dimorphism: Ideologies and Materialities of Kingship as Time–Space Distanciation." Pp. 201–25 in Jeffrey Szuchman (ed.), *Nomads, Tribes, and the State in the Ancient Near East: Cross-Disciplinary Perspectives.* Chicago: Oriental Institute.

———. 2010. "From Kin to Class – And Back Again! Changing Paradigms of the Early Polity." Pp. 72–8 in L. MacGuire and D. Bolger (eds.), *The Development of Prestate Communities in the Ancient Near East: Studies in Honour of Edgar Peltenburg.* Oxford: Oxbow.

———. 2012. *Mobile Pastoralism and the Formation of Near Eastern Civilizations: Weaving Together Society.* Cambridge: Cambridge University Press.

Postgate, Nicholas. 1974. "Some Remarks on Conditions in the Assyrian Countryside." *JESHO* 17: 225–43.

Preuss, Horst D. 1982. *Deuteronomium.* Darmstadt: Wissenschaftliche Buchgesellschaft.

Propp, William H. 1999. *Exodus 1–18.* New York: Doubleday.

Provan, Iain. 1988. *Hezekiah and the Book of Kings: A Contribution to the Debate about the Deuteronomistic History.* Berlin: de Gruyter.

Pruzsinszky, Regine. 2003. *Die Personennamen der Texte aus Emar.* Bethesda, Md.: CDL.

de Pury, Albert. 1975. *Promesse divine et legende cultuelle dans le cycle de Jacob: Genèse 28 et les traditions patriarcales.* Paris: Gabalda.

———. 2001. "Situer le cycle de Jacob: Quelques réflexions vingt-cinq ans plus tard." Pp. 213–41 in André Wénin (ed.), *Studies in the Book of Genesis.* Leuven: Peeters.

von Rad, Gerhard. 1962 and 1965. *Old Testament Theology,* 2 vols. New York: Harper & Row.

———. 1966. *The Problem of the Hexateuch and Other Essays.* Edinburgh: Oliver & Boyd.

Rainey, Anson F. 2001. "Israel in Merenptah's Inscription and Reliefs." *IEJ* 51: 57–75.

———. 2006a. Chapters 1–16, pp. 9–296, in Rainey, Anson F., and Steven R. Notley, *The Sacred Bridge: Carta's Atlas of the Biblical World.* Jerusalem: Carta.

———. 2006b. "Sinuhe's World." Pp. 277–99 in Aren Maeir and Pierre de Miroschedji (eds.), *"I Will Speak the Riddles of Ancient Times,"* vol. 1: *Archeological and Historical Studies in Honor of Amihai Mazar on the Occasion of His Sixtieth Birthday.* Winona Lake, Ind.: Eisenbrauns.

———. 2007a. "Redefining Ancient Hebrew." *Maarav* 14: 67–81.

———. 2007b. "Whence Came the Israelites and Their Language?" *IEJ* 57: 41–64.

Redford, Donald B. 1970. *A Study of the Biblical Story of Joseph (Genesis 37–50).* Leiden: Brill.

———. 1992. *Egypt, Canaan, and Israel in Ancient Times.* Princeton, N.J.: Princeton University Press.

Reich, Ronny, and Eli Shukron. 2003. "The Urban Development of Jerusalem in the Late Eighth Century B.C.E." Pp. 209–18 in Andrew G. Vaughn and Ann E. Killebrew (eds.), *Jerusalem in Bible and Archaeology: The First Temple Period.* Leiden: Brill.

Reich, Ronny, Eli Shukron, and Omri Lernau. 2008. "The Iron Age II Finds from the Rock-Cut 'Pool' Near the Spring in Jerusalem: A Preliminary Report." Pp. 138–43 in Lester L. Grabbe (ed.), *Israel in Transition: From Late Bronze II to Iron IIa (c. 1250–850 B.C.E.)*, vol. 1: *The Archaeology*. London: T. & T. Clark.

Reichert, Andreas. 1986. "The Song of Moses (Deuteronomy 32) and the Quest for Early Deuteronomic Psalmody." Pp. 33–60 in *Proceedings of the Ninth World Congress of Jewish Studies*. Jerusalem: World Union of Jewish Studies.

Rendsburg, Gary A. 1990. *Linguistic Evidence for the Northern Origin of Selected Psalms*. Atlanta, Ga.: Scholars Press.

Rendtorff, Rolf. 1990 (1977). *The Problem of the Process of Transmission in the Pentateuch*. Sheffield: JSOT.

———. 1995. "Sihon, Og und das israelitische 'Credo.'" Pp. 198–203 in Manfred Weippert and Stefan Timm (eds.), *Meilenstein: Festgabe für Herbert Donner zum 16. Februar 1995*. Wiesbaden: Harrassowitz.

Renz, Johannes. 1997. *Schrift und Schreibertradition: Ein paläographische Studie zum kulturgeschichtlichen Verhältnis von israelitischem Nordreich und Südreich*. Wiesbaden: Harrassowitz.

Richter, Wolfgang. 1964. *Die Bearbeitung des "Retterbuches" in der deuteronomistischen Epoche*. Bonn: Peter Hanstein.

———. 1966. *Traditionsgeschichtliche Untersuchungen zum Richterbuch*, 2nd edition. Bonn: Peter Hanstein.

Roberts, J. J. M. 2005. "Bearers of the Polity: Isaiah of Jerusalem's View of the Eighth-Century Judean Society." Pp. 145–52 in John T. Strong and Steven S. Tuell (eds.), *Constituting the Community: Studies on the Polity of Ancient Israel in Honor of S. Dean McBride Jr*. Winona Lake, Ind.: Eisenbrauns.

Robertson, David A. 1972. *Linguistic Evidence in Dating Early Hebrew Poetry*. Missoula, Mont.: Scholars Press.

Rollston, Christopher A. 2006. "Scribal Education in Ancient Israel: The Old Hebrew Epigraphic Evidence." *BASOR* 344: 47–74.

———. 2010. *Writing and Literacy in the World of Ancient Israel: Epigraphic Evidence from the Iron Age*. Atlanta, Ga.: Society of Biblical Literature.

Römer, Thomas. 2005. *The So-Called Deuteronomistic History: A Sociological, Historical and Literary Introduction*. London: T. & T. Clark.

———. 2006a. "The Elusive Yahwist: A Short History of Research." Pp. 9–27 in Thomas B. Dozeman and Konrad Schmid (eds.), *A Farewell to the Yahwist? The Composition of the Pentateuch in Recent European Interpretation*. Leiden: Brill.

———. 2006b. "Entstehungsphasen des 'deuteronomistischen Geschichtswerkes'." Pp. 45–70 in Markus Witte et al. (eds.), *Die deuteronomistischen Geschichtswerke: Redaktions- und religionsgeschichtliche Perspektiven zur "Deuteronomismus" – Diskussion in Tora und Vorderen Propheten*. Berlin: de Gruyter.

———. 2007. "Israel's Sojourn in the Wilderness and the Construction of the Book of Numbers." Pp. 419–45 in Robert Rezetko, Timothy H. Lim, and W. Brian Aucker (eds.), *Reflection and Refraction: Studies in Biblical Historiography in Honour of A. Graeme Auld*. Leiden: Brill.

Römer, Thomas, and Albert de Pury (eds.). 2000a. "Deuteronomistic Historiography (DH): History of Research and Debated Issues." Pp. 24–141 in Thomas Römer and Albert de Pury (eds.), *Israel Constructs its History*. Sheffield: Sheffield Academic Press, 2000.

———. 2000b. *Die sogenannte Thronfolgegeschichte Davids: Neue Einsichten und Anfragen*. Göttingen: Vandenhoeck & Ruprecht.

Römer, Thomas, and Konrad Schmid (eds.). 2007. *Les dernières rédactions du Pentateuque, de l'Hexateuque et de l'Ennéateuque*. Leuven: Peeters.

Rose, Martin. 1981. *Deuteronomist und Jahwist: Untersuchungen zu den Berührungspunkten beider Literaturwerke.* Zürich: Theologischer Verlag.

———. 1989. "Empoigner le Pentateuque par sa fin! L'investiture de Josué et la mort de Moïse." Pp. 129–47 in Albert de Pury (ed.), *Le Pentateuque en question.* Geneva: Labor et Fides.

Rost, Leonhard. 1926. *Die Überlieferung von der Thronnachfolge Davids.* Stuttgart: Kohlhammer.

Rouault, Olivier. 2009. "Assyrians, Aramaeans and Babylonians: The Syrian Lower Middle Euphrates Valley at the End of the Bronze Age." Pp. 133–39 in Christine Kepinski and Aline Tenu (eds.), "Dossier: Interaction entre Assyriens et Araméens." *Syria* 86.

Routledge, Bruce. 2004. *Moab in the Iron Age: Hegemony, Polity, Archaeology.* Philadelphia: University of Pennsylvania Press.

———. 2008. "Thinking 'Globally' and Analysing 'Locally': South-Central Jordan in Transition." Pp. 144–76 in Lester L. Grabbe (ed.), *Israel in Transition: From Late Bronze II to Iron IIa (c. 1250–850 B.C.E.),* vol. 1: *The Archaeology.* London: T. & T. Clark.

Rowton, Michael B. 1967. "The Physical Environment and the Problem of Nomads." Pp. 109–21 in André Finet (ed.), *Actes de la 15e Rencontre Assyriologique Internationale.* Liège: Les Belles Lettres.

———. 1973a. "Autonomy and Nomadism in Western Asia." *Or* 42: 247–58.

———. 1973b. "Urban Autonomy in a Nomadic Environment." *JNES* 32: 201–15.

———. 1974. "Enclosed Nomadism." *JESHO* 17: 1–30.

———. 1976. "Dimorphic Structure and the Problem of the 'apirû-'ibrîm." *JNES* 35: 13–20.

Rudnig, Thilo Alexander. 2006. *Davids Thron: Redaktionskritische Studien zur Geschichte von der Thronnachfolge Davids.* Berlin: de Gruyter.

Russell, Brian D. 2007. *The Song of the Sea: The Date of Composition and Influence of Exodus 15:1–21.* New York: Peter Lang.

Russell, Stephen C. 2009. *Images of Egypt in Early Biblical Literature: Cisjordan-Israelite, Transjordan-Israelite, and Judahite Portrayals.* Berlin: de Gruyter.

Sachsse, Eduard. 1910. *Bedeutung des Namens Israel: Eine quellenkritische Untersuchung.* Bonn: C. Georgi.

———. 1922. *Bedeutung des Namens Israel: Eine geographisch-geschichtliche Untersuchung.* Gütersloh: C. Bertelsmann.

Sader, Hélène S. 1987. *Les états araméens de Syrie: Depuis leur fondation jusqu'à leur transformation en provinces assyriennes.* Wiesbaden: Franz Steiner.

———. 1989. "The Twelfth Century B.C. in Syria: The Problem of the Rise of the Aramaeans." Pp. 157–63 in William A. Ward and Martha Sharp Joukowsky (eds.), *The Crisis Years: The Twelfth Century B.C. from Beyond the Danube to the Tigris.* Dubuque, Iowa: Kendall/Hunt.

———. 2000. "The Aramaean Kingdoms of Syria: Origin and Formation Processes." Pp. 61–76 in Guy Bunnens (ed.), *Essays on Syria in the Iron Age.* Leuven: Peeters.

———. 2010. "The Aramaeans of Syria: Some Considerations on Their Origin and Material Culture." Pp. 273–300 in André Lemaire and Baruch Halpern (eds.), *The Books of Kings: Sources, Composition, Historiography and Reception.* Leiden: Brill.

Sahlins, Marshall. 1968. *Tribesmen.* Englewood Cliffs, N.J.: Prentice-Hall.

Sallaberger, Walther. 2007. "From Urban Culture to Nomadism: A History." Pp. 417–56 in Catherine Marro and Catherine Kuzucuoglu (eds.), *Sociétés humaines et changement climatique à la fin du Troisième Millénaire: Une crise a-t-elle eu lieu en Haute-Mésopotamie?* Istanbul: Institut Français d'Études Anatolienne Georges-Dumézil.

Sals, Ulrike. 2008. "The Hybrid Story of Balaam (Numbers 22–24): Theology for the Diaspora in the Torah." *Biblical Interpretation* 16: 315–35.

Salvini, Mirjo. 1996. *The Ḥabiru Prism of King Tunip-Teššup of Tikunani.* Rome: Istituti editoriali e poligrafici internazionali.

Sanders, Paul. 1996. *The Provenance of Deuteronomy 32.* Leiden: Brill.

Sanders, Seth L. 2009. *The Invention of Hebrew.* Urbana: University of Illinois Press.

Santis, David V. 2004. "The Land of Transjordan Israel in the Iron Age and Its Religious Traditions." Ph.D. dissertation, New York University.

Sasson, Jack M. 1998. "About Mari and the Bible." *RA* 92: 97–123.

Sauer, James A. 1994. "The Pottery at Hesban and Its Relationships to the History of Jordan: An Interim Hesban Pottery Report, 1993." Pp. 225–81 in David Merling (ed.), *Hesban: After 25 Years.* Berrien Springs: Institute of Archaeology, Andrews University.

Scarborough, Vernon L., and Fred Valdez. 2003. "The Engineered Environment and Political Economy of the Three Rivers Region." Pp. 3–13 in Vernon L. Scarborough, Fred Valdez, and Nicholas Dunning (eds.), *Heterarchy, Political Economy, and the Ancient Maya: The Three Rivers Region of the East-Central Yucatán Peninsula.* Tucson: University of Arizona Press.

Scarborough, Vernon L., Fred Valdez, and Nicholas Dunning (eds.). 2003. *Heterarchy, Political Economy, and the Ancient Maya: The Three Rivers Region of the East-Central Yucatán Peninsula.* Tucson: University of Arizona Press.

Schloen, J. David. 1993. "Caravans, Kenites, and Casus Belli: Enmity and Alliance in the Song of Deborah." *CBQ* 55: 18–38.

Schmid, Hans H. 1976. *Der sogenannte Jahwist: Beobachtungen und Fragen zur Pentateuchforshung.* Zürich: Theologischer Verlag.

Schmid, Konrad. 2006. "Buchtechnische und sachliche Prolegomena zur Enneateuchfrage." Pp. 1–14 in Martin Beck and Ulrike Schorn (eds.), *Auf dem Weg zur Endgestalt von Genesis bis II Regum.* Berlin: de Gruyter.

———. 2010. *Genesis and the Moses Story: Israel's Dual Origins in the Hebrew Bible.* Winona Lake, Ind.: Eisenbrauns.

Schmidt, Ludwig. 1970. *Menschlicher Erfolg und Jahwes Initiative: Studien zu Tradition, Interpretation und Historie in den Überlieferungen von Gideon, Saul und David.* Neukirchen-Vluyn: Neukirchener.

Schmitt, Hans-Christoph. 1988. "Das Hesbonlied Num. 21,27aβb-30 und die Geschichte der Stadt Hesbon." *ZDPV* 104: 26–43.

Schmökel, Hartmut. 1950. "Alttestamentliches aus dem Briefarchiv von Mari." *TLZ* 75: 690.

Schneider, Kitty. 2004. "The Omrids: Too Much Theology, Too Little Context?" *Old Testament Essays* 17: 267–81.

Schniedewind, William M. 2002. "The Rise of the Aramean States." Pp. 276–87 in Mark W. Chavalas and K. Lawson Younger (eds.), *Mesopotamia and the Bible: Comparative Explorations.* Sheffield: Sheffield Academic Press.

———. 2003. "Jerusalem, the Late Judahite Monarchy, and the Composition of the Biblical Texts." Pp. 375–93 in Andrew G. Vaughn and Ann E. Killebrew (eds.), *Jerusalem in Bible and Archaeology: The First Temple Period.* Leiden: Brill.

————. 2004. *How the Bible Became a Book: The Textualization of Ancient Israel.* Cambridge: Cambridge University Press.

Schöpflin, Karen. 2004. "Jotham's Speech and Fable as Prophetic Comment on Abimelekh's Story: The Genesis of Judges 9." *SJOT* 18: 3–22.

Schorn, Ulrike. 1997. *Ruben und das System der zwölf Stämme Israels: Redaktions-geschichtliche Untersuchungen zur Bedeutung des Erstgeborenen Jakobs.* Berlin: de Gruyter.

Schüle, Andreas. 2001. *Israels Sohn – Jahwes Prophet: Ein Versuch zum Verhältnis von kanonischer Theologie und Religionsgeschichte anhand der Bileam-Perikope (Num 22–24).* Münster: LIT Verlag.

Schunck, Klaus-Dietrich. 1963. *Benjamin: Untersuchungen zur Entstehung und Geschichte eines israelitischen Stammes.* Berlin: Alfred Töpelmann.

Schwartz, Glenn M. 1989. "The Origins of the Aramaeans in Syria and Northern Mesopotamia: Research Problems and Potential Strategies." Pp. 275–91 in O. M. C. Haex, H. H. Curvers, and P. M. M. G. Akkermans (eds.), *To the Euphrates and Beyond: Archaeological Studies in Honour of Maurits N. van Loon.* Rotterdam: A. A. Balkema.

Schweitzer, Steven. 2007. *Reading Utopia in Chronicles.* London: T. & T. Clark.

Schwienhorst, Ludwig. 1986. *Die Eroberung Jerichos: Exegetische Untersuchung zu Josua 6.* Stuttgart: Katholisches Bibelwerk.

Seiler, Stefan. 1998. *Die Geschichte von der Thronfolge Davids (2 Sam 9–20; 1 Kön 1–2): Untersuchungen zur Literarkritik und Tendenz.* Berlin: de Gruyter.

Seitz, Christopher R. 1989. *Theology in Conflict: Reactions to the Exile in the Book of Jeremiah.* Berlin: de Gruyter.

Service, Elman R. 1975. *Origins of the State and Civilization: The Process of Cultural Evolution.* New York: W. W. Norton.

Seymour-Smith, Charlotte. 1986. "Ethnogenesis." P. 97 in *Macmillan Dictionary of Anthropology.* London: Macmillan.

Sharon, Ilan, Ayelet Gilboa, and Elisabetta Boaretto. 2008. "The Iron Age Chronology of the Levant: The State-of-Research at the 14C Dating Project, Spring 2006." Pp. 177–92 in Lester L. Grabbe (ed.), *Israel in Transition: From Late Bronze II to Iron IIa (c. 1250–850 B.C.E.),* vol. 1: *The Archaeology.* London: T. & T. Clark.

Short, J. Randall. 2010. *The Surprising Election and Confirmation of King David.* Cambridge, Mass.: Harvard Theological Studies.

Shryock, Andrew. 1997. *Nationalism and the Genealogical Imagination: Oral History and Textual Authority in Tribal Jordan.* Berkeley: University of California Press.

Singer, Itamar. 1985. "The Beginning of Philistine Settlement in Canaan and the Northern Boundary of Philistia." *TA* 12: 109–22.

————. 1988. "Merneptah's Campaign to Canaan and the Egyptian Occupation of the Southern Coastal Plain of Palestine in the Ramesside Period." *BASOR* 269: 1–10.

————. 1991. "A Concise History of Amurru." Pp. 135–95 in Shlomo Izre'el, *Amurru Akkadian: A Linguistic Study.* Atlanta, Ga.: Scholars Press.

Ska, Jean-Louis. 2006. *Introduction to Reading the Pentateuch.* Winona Lake, Ind.: Eisenbrauns.

Smith, Adam T. 2003. *The Political Landscape: Constellations of Authority in Early Complex Polities.* Berkeley: University of California Press.

Smith, Mark S. 1990. *The Early History of God: Yahweh and the Other Deities in Ancient Israel.* San Francisco, Calif.: Harper and Row.

————. 1997. *The Pilgrimage Pattern in Exodus.* Sheffield: Sheffield Academic Press.

———. 2001. *The Origins of Biblical Monotheism: Israel's Polytheistic Background and the Ugaritic Texts*. Oxford: Oxford University Press.

———. 2004. *The Memoirs of God: History, Memory, and the Experience of the Divine in Ancient Israel*. Minneapolis, Minn.: Fortress.

———. 2009. "What is Prologue is Past: Composing Israelite Identity in Judges 5." Pp. 43–58 in John J. Ahn and Stephen L. Cook (eds.), *Thus Says the Lord: Essays on the Former and Latter Prophets in Honor of Robert R. Wilson*. New York: T. & T. Clark.

———. 2010. *The Priestly Vision of Genesis*. Minneapolis, Minn.: Fortress.

von Soden, Wolfram. 1948. "Das altbabylonische Briefarchiv von Mari." *WO* 1: 197–8.

———. 1984. "Review of Oswald Loretz (1984), *Ḫabiru-Hebräer: Eine sozio-linguistische Studie über die Herkunft des Gentiliziums 'ibrî vom Appellativum ḫabiru*." *UF* 16: 364–8.

Soggin, J. Alberto. 1981. *Judges: A Commentary*. Philadephia: Westminster.

Sourouzian, Hourig. 2001. "Merenptah." Vol. 2, pp. 379–81 in Donald B. Redford (ed.), *Oxford Encyclopedia of Ancient Egypt*. Oxford: Oxford University Press.

Sparks, Kenton L. 2003. "Genesis 49 and the Tribal List Tradition in Ancient Israel." *ZAW* 115: 327–47.

Stager, Lawrence E. 1988. "Archaeology, Ecology, and Social History: Background Themes to the Song of Deborah." Pp. 221–34 in J. A. Emerton (ed.), *Congress Volume: Jerusalem, 1986*. Leiden: Brill.

———. 1995. "The Impact of the Sea Peoples in Canaan (1185–1050 BCE)." Pp. 332–48 in Thomas E. Levy (ed.), *The Archaeology of Society in the Holy Land*. New York: Facts on File.

———. 1999. "The Fortress-Temple at Shechem and the 'House of El, Lord of the Covenant.'" Pp. 228–49 in Prescott. H. Williams and Theodore Hiebert (eds.), *Realia Dei: Essays in Archaeology and Biblical Interpretation in Honor of Edward F. Campbell, Jr. at His Retirement*. Atlanta, Ga.: Scholars Press.

Stahl, Ann Brower. 2004. "Political Economic Mosaics: Archaeology of the Last Two Millennia in Tropical Sub-Saharan Africa." *Annual Review of Anthropology* 33: 145–72.

Staszak, Martin. 2009. "Zur einer Lesart und dem historischen Hintergrund des Fragments B der Stele von Tel Dan." *BN* 142: 67–77.

Steadman, S., and J. Ross (eds.). 2010. *Agency and Identity in the Ancient Near East: New Paths Forward*. London: Equinox.

van der Steen, Eveline, and Klaas A. D. Smelik. 2007. "King Mesha and the Tribe of Dibon." *JSOT* 32: 139–62.

Steiner, Margreet. 2003. "The Evidence from Kenyon's Excavations in Jerusalem: A Response Essay." Pp. 347–63 in Andrew G. Vaughn and Ann E. Killebrew (eds.), *Jerusalem in Bible and Archaeology: The First Temple Period*. Leiden: Brill.

Stern, Philip D. 1991. *The Biblical ḥerem: A Window on Israel's Religious Experience*. Atlanta, Ga.: Scholars Press.

Steuernagel, Carl. 1901. *Einwanderung der israelitischen Stämme in Kanaan: Historisch-kritische Untersuchungen*. Berlin: C. A. Schwetschke.

Stoellger, Philipp. 1993. "Deuteronomium 34 ohne Priesterschrift." *ZAW* 105: 31–5.

Suriano, Matthew J. 2007. "The Apology of Hazael: A Literary and Historical Analysis of the Tel Dan Inscription." *JNES* 66: 163–76.

Sweeney, Marvin A. 2007. *I and II Kings: A Commentary*. Louisville, Ky.: Westminster John Knox.

Szuchman, Jeffrey. 2009. "Bit Zamani and Assyria." Pp. 55–65 in Christine Kepinski and Aline Tenu (eds.), "Dossier: Interaction entre Assyriens et Araméens." *Syria* 86.

Tadmor, Hayim. 1958. "Historical Implications of the Correct Rendering of Akkadian *dâku.*" *JNES* 17: 129–41.

———. 1979. "The Decline of Empires in Western Asia ca. 1200 B.C.E." In Frank M. Cross (ed.), *Symposia Celebrating the Seventy-fifth Anniversary of the Founding of the American School of Oriental Research (1900–1975)*. Cambridge, Mass.: ASOR.

———. 1994. *The Inscriptions of Tiglath-Pileser III, King of Assyria: Critical Edition with Introductions*. Jerusalem: Israel Academy of Science and Humanities.

Talmon, Shemaryahu. 1967. "The Judaean *'am ha'areṣ* in Historical Perspective." Pp. 171–6 in *Fourth World Congress of Jewish Studies, Papers*. Jerusalem: World Union of Jewish Studies.

Talshir, David. 2003. "The Relativity of Geographic Terms: A Re-investigation of the Problem of Upper and Lower Aram." *JSS* 48:259–85.

Tappy, Ron E. 1992. *The Archaeology of Israelite Samaria*. Atlanta, Ga.: Scholars Press.

———. 2001. *The Archaeology of Israelite Samaria*, vol. 2: *The Eighth Century BCE*. Atlanta, Ga.: Scholars Press.

———. 2008. "Tel Zayit and the Tel Zayit Abecedary in Their Regional Context." Pp. 1–44 in Ron E. Tappy and P. Kyle McCarter (eds.), *Literate Culture and Tenth-Century Canaan: The Tel Zayit Abecedary in Context*. Winona Lake, Ind.: Eisenbrauns.

Thames, John. 2011. "A New Discussion of the Meaning of the Phrase *'am hā'āreṣ* in the Hebrew Bible." *JBL* 130: 109–25.

Thomas, Julian. 1996. *Time, Culture and Identity: An Interpretive Archaeology*. London: Routledge.

Thompson, Thomas L. 1974. *The Historicity of the Patriarchal Narratives: The Quest for the Historical Abraham*. Berlin: de Gruyter.

———. 1978a. "The Background of the Patriarchs: A Reply to William Dever and Malcolm Clark." *JSOT* 9: 2–43.

———. 1978b. "Historical Notes on 'Israel's Conquest of Palestine: A Peasants' Rebellion.'" *JSOT* 7: 20–7.

———. 2007a. "A Testimony of the Good King: Reading the Mesha Stele." Pp. 236–92 in Lester L. Grabbe (ed.), *Ahab Agonistes: The Rise and Fall of the Omri Dynasty*. London: T. & T. Clark.

———. 2007b. "Mesha and Questions of Historicity." *SJOT* 21: 241–60.

Thurston, Tina L. 2001. *Landscapes of Power, Landscapes of Conflict: State Formation in the South Scandinavian Iron Age*. New York: Kluwer Academic.

Timm, Stefan. 1982. *Die Dynastie Omri: Quellen und Untersuchungen zur Geschichte Israels im 9. Jahrhundert vor Christus*. Göttingen: Vandenhoeck & Ruprecht.

Toews, Wesley. 1993. *Monarchy and Religious Institutions in Israel under Jeroboam I*. Atlanta, Ga.: Scholars Press.

van der Toorn, Karel. 1996. *Family Religion in Babylonia, Syria, and Israel: Continuity and Change in the Forms of Religious Life*. Leiden: Brill.

———. 2007. *Scribal Culture and the Making of the Hebrew Bible*. Cambridge, Mass.: Harvard University Press.

Tourtellot, Gair, Francisco Estrada Belli, John J. Rose, and Norman Hammond. 2003. "Late Classic Maya Heterarchy, Hierarchy, and Landscape at La Milpa, Belize." Pp. 37–51 in Vernon L. Scarborough, Fred Valdez, and Nicholas Dunning (eds.),

Heterarchy, Political Economy, and the Ancient Maya: The Three Rivers Region of the East-Central Yucatán Peninsula. Tucson: University of Arizona Press.

Tov, Emmanuel. 2001. *Textual Criticism of the Hebrew Bible,* 2nd revised edition. Minneapolis, Minn.: Fortress.

Trevor-Roper, Hugh. 1983. "The Invention of Tradition: The Highland Tradition of Scotland." Pp. 15–42 in Eric J. Hobsbawm and Terence O. Renger (eds.), *The Invention of Tradition.* Cambridge: Cambridge University Press.

Tropper, Josef. 2001. "Dialektvielfalt und Sprachwandel im frühen Aramäischen Soziolinguistische Überlegung." Vol. 3, pp. 213–22 in P. M. Michèle Daviau, John W. Wevers, and Michael Weigl (eds.), *The World of the Aramaeans: Studies in Language and Literature in Honour of Paul-Eugène Dion.* Sheffield: Sheffield Academic Press.

Uehlinger, Christoph. 2007. "Neither Eyewitnesses nor Windows to the Past, but Valuable Testimony in Its Own Right: Remarks on Iconography, Source Criticism and Ancient Data Processing." Pp. 173–228 in H.G.M. Williamson (ed.), *Understanding the History of Ancient Israel.* Oxford: Oxford University Press.

Uriel, Joe, and Itzhaq Shai. 2007. "Iron Age Jerusalem: Temple-Palace, Capital City." *JAOS* 127: 161–70.

Ussishkin, David. 2003. "Solomon's Jerusalem: The Text and the Facts on the Ground." Pp.103–15 in Andrew G. Vaughn and Ann E. Killebrew (eds.), *Jerusalem in Bible and Archaeology: The First Temple Period.* Leiden: Brill.

———. 2007. "Archaeology of the Biblical Period: On Some Questions of Methodology and Chronology of the Iron Age." Pp. 131–41 in H.G.M. Williamson (ed.), *Understanding the History of Ancient Israel.* Oxford: Oxford University Press.

Vaughn, Andrew G., and Ann E. Killebrew (eds.). 2003. *Jerusalem in Bible and Archaeology: The First Temple Period.* Leiden: Brill.

van der Veen, Peter, Christoffer Theis, and Manfred Görg. 2010. "Israel in Canaan [Long] before Pharaoh Merenptah? A Fresh Look at Berlin Statue Pedestal Relief 21687." *Journal of Ancient Egyptian Interconnections* 2/4: 15–25.

Van Seters, John. 1972. "The Conquest of Sihon's Kingdom: A Literary Examination." *JBL* 91: 182–97.

———. 1975. *Abraham in History and Tradition.* New Haven, Conn.: Yale University Press.

———. 1980. "Once Again – The Conquest of Sihon's Kingdom." *JBL* 99: 117–19.

———. 1983. *In Search of History: Historiography in the Ancient World and the Origins of Biblical History.* New Haven, Conn.: Yale University Press.

———. 1992. *Prologue to History: The Yahwist as Historian in Genesis.* Louisville, Ky.: Westminster John Knox.

———. 1994. *The Life of Moses: The Yahwist as Historian in Exodus – Numbers.* Louisville, Ky.: Westminster John Knox.

de Vaux, Roland. 1968. "Le problème des Ḫapiru après quinze années." *JNES* 27: 221–8.

Vermeylen, Jacques. 2000. *La loi du plus fort: Histoire de la rédaction des récits davidiques de 1 Samuel 8 à 1 Rois 2.* Leuven: Peeters.

———. 2010. "La révolte d'Absalom comme événement historique." Pp. 327–45 in A. Graeme Auld and Erik Eynikel (eds.), *For and Against David: Story and History in the Books of Samuel.* Leuven: Peeters.

Villard, Pierre. 1994. "Nomination d'un scheich." *FM* II: 291–7.

Vorländer, Hermann. 1978. *Die Entstehungszeit des jehowistischen Geschichtswerkes.* Bern: Peter Lang.

Wächter, Ludwig. 1987. "Zur Lokalisierung des Sichemitischen Baumheiligtums." *ZDPV* 103: 1–12.

Wahl, Harald-Martin. 1997. *Die Jakoberzälungen*. Berlin: de Gruyter.

Wazana, Nili. 2008. "From Biqʻat to KTK: 'All Aram' in the Sefire Inscription in the Light of Amos 1:5." Pp. 713–32 in Chaim Cohen et al. (eds.), *Birkat Shalom: Studies in the Bible, Ancient Near Eastern Literature, and Postbiblical Judaism Presented to Shalom M. Paul on the Occasion of His Seventieth Birthday*. Winona Lake, Ind.: Eisenbrauns.

Weimar, Peter. 2006. "Gen 37 – Eine vielschichtige literarische Komposition." *ZAW* 118: 485–512.

Weinstein, James M. 1981. "The Egyptian Empire in Palestine: A Reassessment." *BASOR* 241: 1–28.

———. 2001. "Canaan." Vol. 1, p. 228 in Donald B. Redford (ed.), *Oxford Encyclopedia of Ancient Egypt*. Oxford: Oxford University Press.

Weippert, Helga. 1972. "Die 'deuteronomistischen' Beurteilungen der Könige von Israel und Juda und das Problem der Redaktion der Königsbucher." *Bib* 53: 301–39.

Weippert, Manfred. 1971. *The Settlement of the Israelite Tribes in Palestine*. Naperville, Ill.: Allenson.

———. 1973. "Fragen des israelitischen Geschichtsbewusstseins." *VT* 23: 415–42.

———. 1974. "Semitische Nomaden des zweiten Jahrtausends: Über die š3św der ägyptischen Quellen." *Bib* 55: 265–80.

———. 1979. "The Israelite 'Conquest' and the Evidence from Transjordan." Pp. 15–34 in *Symposia Celebrating the Seventy-fifth Anniversary of the Founding of the American Schools of Oriental Research (1900–1975)*. Cambridge, Mass.: ASOR.

Wellhausen, Julius. 1885. *Prolegomena to the History of Israel*. Edinburgh: A. & C. Black.

Westermann, Claus. 1985. *Genesis 12–36: A Commentary*. Minneapolis, Minn.: Augsburg.

Whalen, Michael E., and Paul E. Minnis. 2000. "Leadership at Casas Grandes, Chihuahua, Mexico." Pp. 168–79 in Barbara J. Mills (ed.), *Alternative Leadership Strategies in the Prehispanic Southwest*. Tuscon: University of Arizona Press.

White, Marsha C. 1997. *The Elijah Legends and Jehu's Coup*. Atlanta, Ga.: Scholars Press.

Whitelam, Keith W. 2000. "'Israel is laid waste; his seed is no more': What If Merneptah's Scribes Were Telling the Truth?" *Biblical Interpretation* 8: 8–22.

Wildberger, Hans. 1981. *Isaiah 1–12: A Commentary*. Minneapolis, Minn.: Fortress.

Wilhelm, Gernot. 1989. *The Hurrians*. Warminster: Aris and Phillips.

Williamson, H.G.M. 1977. *Israel in the Books of Chronicles*. Cambridge: Cambridge University Press.

———. 2011. "Judah as Israel in Eighth-Century Prophecy." Pp. 81–95 in Jamie A. Grant, Alison Lo, and Gordon J. Wenham (eds.), *A God of Faithfulness: Essays in Honour of J. Gordon McConville on His 60th Birthday*. London: T. & T. Clark.

Willis, Timothy M. 2001. *The Elders of the City: A Study of the Elders-Laws in Deuteronomy*. Atlanta, Ga.: Society of Biblical Literature.

Wilson, Robert R. 1977. *Genealogy and History in the Biblical World*. New Haven, Conn.: Yale University Press.

Witte, Markus. 2002. "Der Segen Bileams: Eine redaktionsgeschichtliche Problemanzeige zum 'Jahwisten' in Num 22–24." Pp. 191–213 in Jan Christian Gertz,

Konrad Schmid, and Markus Witte (eds.), *Abschied vom Jahwisten: Die Komposition des Hexateuch in der jüngsten Diskussion*. Berlin: de Gruyter.

Wolff, Hans Walter. 1974. *Hosea*. Philadelphia: Fortress.

———. 1977. *Joel and Amos*. Philadelphia: Fortress.

———. 1990. *Micah: A Commentary*. Minneapolis, Minn.: Augsburg.

Wolfram, Herwig. 1990. "Einleitung oder Überlegungen zur Origo Gentis." Vol. 1, pp. 19–34 in Herwig Wolfram and Walter Pohl (eds.), *Typen der Ethnogenese unter besonderer Berücksichtigung der Bayern: Berichte des Symposions der Kommission für Frühmittelalterforschung, 27. bis 30.Oktober, 1986, Stift Zwettl, Niederösterreich*. Vienna: Verlag Österreichischen Akademie der Wissenschaften.

Wong, Gregory. 2006. *Compositional Strategy of the Book of Judges*. Leiden: Brill.

Wright, David P. 2009. *Inventing God's Law: How the Covenant Code of the Bible Used and Revised the Laws of Hammurabi*. Oxford: Oxford University Press.

Wright, Jacob L. 2011. "War Commemoration and the Interpretation of Judges 5:15b-17." *VT* 61: 505–21.

———. Forthcoming. "Deborah's War Memorial: The Composition of Judges 4–5 and the Politics of War Commemoration." *ZAW*.

Würthwein, Ernst. 2008. "Die Revolution Jehus: Die Jehu-Erzählung in altisraelitischer und deuteronomistischer Sicht." *ZAW* 120: 28–48.

Yamada, Shigeo. 2000. *The Construction of the Assyrian Empire: A Historical Study of the Inscriptions of Shalmaneser III (859–824 B.C.) Relating to His Campaigns to the West*. Leiden: Brill.

Yoffee, Norman. 2005. *Myths of the Archaic State: Evolution of the Earliest Cities, States, and Civilizations*. Cambridge: Cambridge University Press.

Younger, K. Lawson. 1990. *Ancient Conquest Accounts: A Study of Ancient Near Eastern and Biblical History Writing*. Sheffield: Sheffield Academic Press.

———. 2007a. "The Late Bronze Age/Iron Age Transition and the Origins of the Arameans." Pp. 131–74 in K. Lawson Younger (ed.), *Ugarit at Seventy-five*. Winona Lake, Ind.: Eisenbrauns.

———. 2007b. "Neo-Assyrian and Israelite History in the Ninth Century: The Role of Shalmaneser III." Pp. 243–77 in H.G.M. Williamson (ed.), *Understanding the History of Ancient Israel*. Oxford: Oxford University Press.

———. 2008. "Shalmaneser III and Israel." Pp. 225–56 in Daniel I. Block (ed.), *Israel: Ancient Kingdom or Late Invention?* Nashville, Tenn.: B. & H. Academic.

Yurco, Frank J. 1986. "Merenptah's Canaanite Campaign." *JARCE* 23: 189–215.

Zadok, Ran. 1991. "Elements of Aramean Pre-History." Pp. 104–17 in Mordechai Cogan and Israel Eph'al (eds.), *Ah, Assyria . . . : Studies in Assyrian History and Ancient Near Eastern Historiography Presented to Hayim Tadmor*. Jerusalem: Magnes.

Zenger, Erich. 1996. "Wie und wozu die Tora zum Sinai kam: Literarische und theologische Beobachtungen zu Exodus 19–34." Pp. 265–88 in Marc Vervenne (ed.), *Studies in the Book of Exodus: Redaction – Reception – Interpretation*. Leuven: Peeters.

———. 1999. "Der Psalter als Heiligtum." Pp. 115–30 in Beate Ego, Armin Lange, and Peter Pilhofer (eds.), *Gemeinde ohne Tempel = Community without Temple: zur Substituierung und Transformation des Jerusalemer Tempels und seines Kults im Alten Testament, antiken Judentum und frühen Christentum*. Tübingen: Mohr Siebeck.

Zevit, Ziony. 2001. *The Religions of Ancient Israel: A Synthesis of Parallactic Approaches*. London: Continuum.

Zobel, Hans-Jürgen. 1965. *Stammespruch und Geschichte*. Berlin: Alfred Töpelmann.

Zorn, Jeffrey R. 2003. "Tell en-Naṣbeh and the Problem of the Material Culture of the Sixth Century." Pp. 413–47 in Oded Lipschits and Joseph Blenkinsopp (eds.), *Judah and the Judeans in the Neo-Babylonian Period*. Winona Lake, Ind.: Eisenbrauns.

Index of Biblical Texts

Index of Near Eastern Texts

Subject Index